The Complete Guide to National Symbols and Emblems

The Complete Guide to National Symbols and Emblems

Volume 2

James Minahan

GREENWOOD PRESS
An Imprint of ABC-CLIO, LLC

A B C ☰ C L I O

Santa Barbara, California • Denver, Colorado • Oxford, England

Library of Congress Cataloging-in-Publication Data

Minahan, James.
   The complete guide to national symbols and emblems / James Minahan.
      p. cm.
   Includes bibliographical references and index.
   ISBN 978-0-313-34496-1 (set : alk. paper) — ISBN 978-0-313-34497-8 (set ebook) —
ISBN 978-0-313-34498-5 (vol. 1 : alk. paper) — ISBN 978-0-313-34499-2 (vol. 1 ebook) —
ISBN 978-0-313-34500-5 (vol. 2 : alk. paper) — ISBN 978-0-313-34501-2 (vol. 2 ebook)
   1. Emblems, National—Encyclopedias.   2. National characteristics—Encyclopedias.   I. Title.
   CR191.M56   2010
   929.903—dc22   2009036963

14   13   12   11   10   1   2   3   4   5

This book is also available on the World Wide Web as an eBook.
Visit www.abc-clio.com for details.

Greenwood Press
An Imprint of ABC-CLIO, LLC

ABC-CLIO, LLC
130 Cremona Drive, P.O. Box 1911
Santa Barbara, California 93116–1911

This book is printed on acid-free paper ∞

Manufactured in the United States of America

For Emili Roig Navarra
¡Gracies!

Contents

Alphabetical List of Entries

Guide to Related Topics

Preface

This volume was compiled to give a detailed guide to the symbols we see every day, the waving flags that adorn the entrances to hotels and auditoriums, the colorful uniforms at international sports events, the exotic national dishes increasingly available to everyone, the anthems that accompany official visits or event winners at the Olympic Games, national airlines seen at world airports, and the many other national symbols we encounter on a daily basis on the Internet. This guide is presented as a unique reference source to the symbols that are daily becoming more visible around the world.

The world's nations and territories represent a perplexing diversity of symbols chosen to represent them and their cultures. Containing over 200 entries, this guide highlights the many national symbols that represent each of the world's independent nations and many of the dependent nations and territories that increasingly function as autonomous political entities. The worth of this volume in part derives from its up-to-date information on national symbols and other aspects of each country and territory.

Each national entry is divided into several parts or headings: the name and alternative name or names of the country or territory, including the English-language version; the latest population estimate; the name and nickname of the inhabitants; the national or official language and other spoken languages; the religions represented; the national flag; the national coat of arms or seal; the national motto; the capital city; the type of government; the national emblems or symbols; the national colors; the national anthem, generally in English translation; the patron saint or saints (where applicable); the national currency; the national Internet identifier; the vehicle identification plate or sticker code; the national passport; the national airlines (the flag carrier or carriers, if any, and other important airlines); national flora and fauna and national resources; national foods and dishes; national sports teams; national heroes or personifications; the national holiday or independence day; important festivals and fairs; and significant events in the formation of each national identity.

The national population figures are the author's estimates for the year 2009. These figures are designated by "(2009e)" alongside the appropriate statistics. The population figures represent information gleaned from a large number of sources representing the latest census results, official estimates, and figures published by international bodies, such as the United Nations. Information on spoken languages and religious affiliation are mostly derived from official government publications or other recognized reference material.

Information on the national flags, coats of arms, seals, and national mottos are mostly taken from official publications or specialized reference volumes and Web sites. Although flag enthusiasts are very interested in official measurements and sizes, the information included here is more concerned with the colors and symbolism of flags and the other official symbols of each nation.

Few of the world's countries developed in isolation; rather, they were and are shaped by their relations with neighboring governments and peoples. In our ever-increasingly globalized world, influences often come from countries and cultures geographically distant. To facilitate the reader's identification of countries mentioned in the text, the name of each country appears with an asterisk (*) on first reference within a section. An extensive subject index at the end of the volume provides a convenient way to access desired information.

This volume was compiled to provide a precise guide to the national symbols that represent all nations, but that to most of us present a colorful but incomprehensible chaos. In order to make the book as comprehensive as possible not only independent nations are included but also dependent states and territories and many other territories that actively seek greater autonomy, including recognition of their own national symbols.

A special thank-you to all the national governments, tourist offices, information offices, embassies, and consulates that so kindly forwarded information. And my forgiveness to those governments or other national representatives that ignored my requests and pleas.

Introduction

The world's population quadrupled during the 20th century, and the number of independent states grew from about 35 in 1900 to around 200 in 2000. Each of these countries, along with many still-dependent territories, has adopted symbols to represent its people and culture. National symbols are outward displays of each country or territory's national characteristics. These symbols developed as part of each national group's culture, reflecting the historical, ethnic, religious, and territorial influences that became part of it.

National symbols are not exclusive to the world's independent states. Many national groups and dependent territories also employ national symbols that characterize their particular histories and aspirations. Included are a representative sample of the many nonindependent territories that are seeking greater visibility as separate political entities, most importantly through their use of national symbols that represent their aspirations and distinct histories. The nonindependent territories included in this study are those that are attempting, with the support of a sizable portion of their respective populations, to attain more independence and greater recognition as distinct national entities. National symbols are an important political statement, embodying the history, geography, and aspirations of each culture. These symbols are so important that one of the first acts of a conqueror or dictator is to suppress the legitimate or traditional national symbols as a means of subjugation.

The most widely recognized symbols are national flags, but as the number of countries proliferated, so did the number of different, often unique, symbols that were adopted to represent them. With the dawn of the information age, these national symbols and many others took on even more importance. Government departments, diplomatic missions, tourist boards or departments, trade delegations, and tens of thousands of Web sites now use national symbols to represent the focus country or territory.

In these volumes, the world's countries and territories are presented with useful background material and detailed information on their national symbols. Included in each national survey are the official name; the national population; the inhabitants' name or names, including nicknames; languages and religions; the national flag; the national coat of arms or seal; the capital city; the type of government; and the significant events that shaped each national identity. Other national information, where applicable, includes the national motto; the national emblem or symbol; the national colors; the national anthem; the patron saint or saints; the national currency; the Internet identifier; the vehicle identification initials; the national passport; the national airline; the national flower, tree, plant, animal, bird, and fish;

national resources; national foods and dishes; national sports teams; national heroes or personifications; the national holiday or holidays; and annual festivals and fairs.

Each national survey begins with the short name of the country and the official name in all official languages, with translation into English when necessary. The country or territory's population is given with author's estimates for 2009 (2009e) based on official census figures or calculations. The demonym, the name used to describe the inhabitants, is given, along with alternatives and any nicknames. The languages and religions of the inhabitants are listed, with any official status indicated. The capital cities and types of government of the various countries and territories are also included.

Each country or territory's national symbols begin with the national flag, the most visible and widely known of all international symbols. The coat of arms or seal at times reflects the design of the national flag but is usually an amalgam of symbols representing economic activities, geographic features, flora and fauna, and other additions, such as a national motto.

The national emblems or symbols are included, but, as with many national symbols, the category is not applicable to every country or territory. Examples of well-known national emblems or symbols are such landmarks as the Eiffel Tower in France, the Hagia Sofia in Turkey, and the Statue of Liberty in the United States; the trident symbol that represents Ukraine; and the zebra that represents Botswana. National colors are also very popular symbols, used in correspondence, on airplanes and ships, and in the uniforms or kits worn by national sports teams.

The national anthem is another very important national symbol. English translations are included for nearly all of the anthems, mostly gathered from specialized publications or Web sites. The translations have been edited to clarify meaning or to conform to American grammar and spelling. A few of the anthems are presented in the original language when an English translation was not available.

Lesser-known symbols, such as patron saints, national currencies, and national Internet identifiers, all of which are considered important national representations, are included as well. Initials from vehicle identification plates or stickers, usually one to three letters that identify a vehicle's origin, are becoming more important as national barriers to cross-border travel disappear.

The national symbols most identified with modern international travel are passports and airlines. Information on the front cover of national passports is included with each national entry. The colors of the national passports have been omitted, because they change much more often than the actual cover presentation. National airlines, sometimes referred to as a country's roving ambassadors, are often called flag carriers—the national airline designated as the official airline by the addition of the national flag as part of the paint job or airline livery. Following a spate of bankruptcies, many national airlines have disappeared, but others have emerged as replacement national carriers. Many countries now have more than one national airline carrying the national colors and the national flag as part of the airline's livery.

Symbols of a country's flora and fauna are also very important representations. The national flower, tree, plant, animal, bird, fish or sea creature, fruit, insect, and stone are presented when applicable. Many of these symbols are popularly accepted but have not been officially adopted, which is indicated by a notation of *unofficial* in parentheses. Many countries have no national symbols that represent their national flora and fauna.

A country's national resources also represent the country or territory, as its economic well-being, or lack thereof, is often all too visible, whether in the evident poverty of some resource-poor countries or the showy opulence of countries rich in natural resources. National resources may be the visible signs of a country's history, geography, and culture as seen by tourists and visitors. National dishes and national foods are also symbolic of a country's culture and history.

One of the most obvious representations of national pride are each country's national sports teams. International sports venues, such as regional games, international sports meetings, and the Olympic Games, are characterized by the colorful and distinctive national flags of the participating nations, which are usually reflected in the kits or uniforms worn by the participants. National sports federations are represented by logos decorated with national symbols and colors, while national uniforms or kits carry national color combinations and usually other representations of the country or territory they represent. The international sports teams of each country or territory are listed in each entry.

A country's national personification and national heroes are icons that loom large in most cultures. Our own Uncle Sam is used or alluded to in magazines, newspapers, cartoons, film, and television. Many other countries have equivalent characterizations that represent their cultures. Most countries have a national holiday, often the date of independence or a date that recalls other events in the national history; some even have more than one, which are noted in each national entry. Festivals and fairs are also representative of the nation's culture, history, or present circumstances. Most of the festivals and fairs are annual or semiannual, although some are celebrated at greater intervals.

The last part of each national survey is made up of the significant events that formed each national culture or identity. The dates and events are presented in chronological order to give a timeline of each national history, from its inception to the present day.

4

Middle East and North Africa

The symbols of this predominately Muslim region are often based on the symbols of the Muslim religion. The crescent moon and star, originally adopted by the Turkish Ottoman Empire, which once ruled much of the region, are still evident in many flags, coats of arms, and other symbols. The color green, the color of Islam, is also widely used, as is the color red, originally the color of the Ottomans. The colors of the Arab Revolt against Ottoman rule during World War I, red, white, green, and black, are also widely used. Traditional color schemes and symbols are also used, particularly among the countries of the Persian Gulf region. In Israel, the predominant symbol is the Star of David, which appears on the blue and white national flag and on many other national symbols.

Kurdistan, Palestine, and Sahrawi are included in this section although they are not generally considered independent nations, in spite of official recognition of Palestine and Sahrawi by dozens of national governments. These nations are attempting, often violently, to establish their independence under their own national symbols. Palestine's national symbols are among the most recognized in the world.

ALGERIA

OFFICIAL NAME

Al-Jumhūrīyah al-Jazā'irīyahad-Dīmuqrāṭīyah ash-Sha'bīyah (transliteration from Arabic); People's Democratic Republic of Algeria (English)

POPULATION

33,716,000 (2009e)

INHABITANTS' NAME/NICKNAME

Algerian(s)

LANGUAGE/LANGUAGES

Arabic (official); French, Kabyle (co-official in Kabylia), other Berber languages (in Berber-inhabited regions)

RELIGION/RELIGIONS

Sunni Muslim, 98 percent; Roman Catholic, other or no religion

NATIONAL FLAG

The Algerian national flag is divided vertically into equal rectangles of green and white, with a centered red crescent and five-pointed red star. The white represents peace; the green, the beauty of nature and Islam; and the red, the blood of the martyrs who fought in the war of independence from 1954 to 1962. The crescent and star represent Islam.

COAT OF ARMS/SEAL

The coat of arms is a circle based on a well-known national symbol, the Hand of Fatima, above the crescent and star of Islam, The emblem also includes symbols reflecting modern Algerian farming and industry and the name of the country in Arabic script around the edge of the circle.

MOTTO

From the people and for the people

CAPITAL CITY

Algiers

TYPE OF GOVERNMENT

Semipresidential republic

NATIONAL EMBLEM

Hand of Fatima

NATIONAL COLORS

Green, white, and red

NATIONAL ANTHEM

The poem *"Qassaman"* or *"Kassaman"* was originally written by Moufdi Zakaria while imprisoned by the French colonial authorities in 1956. The poem's anti-French lyrics were eliminated when it was set to music and adopted as the national anthem in 1962.

KASSAMAN (TRANSLITERATION FROM ARABIC); WE PLEDGE (ENGLISH)

We swear by the lightning that destroys,
By the streams of generous blood being shed,
By the bright flags that wave,
Flying proudly on the high mountains,
That we have risen up, and whether we live
    or die,
We are resolved that Algeria shall live
So be our witness—be our witness—be our
    witness!

We are soldiers in revolt for truth
And we have fought for our independence.
When we spoke, none listened to us,
So we have taken the noise of gunpowder as
    our rhythm
And the sound of machine guns as our
    melody,
We are resolved that Algeria shall live
So be our witness—be our witness—be our
    witness!

From our heroes we shall make an army come
    to being,
From our dead we shall build up a glory,
Our spirits shall ascend to immortality

And on our shoulders we shall raise the
    standard.
To the nation's Liberation Front we have
    sworn an oath,
We are resolved that Algeria shall live
So be our witness—be our witness—be our
    witness!

The cry of the Fatherland sounds from the
    battlefields.
Listen to it and answer the call!
Let it be written with the blood of martyrs
And be read to future generations.
Oh, Glory, we have held out our hand to
    you,
We are resolved that Algeria shall live
So be our witness—be our witness—be our
    witness!

PATRON SAINT

Cyprian of Carthage; Our Lady of Africa

CURRENCY

Algerian dinar

INTERNET IDENTIFIER

.dz

VEHICLE IDENTIFICATION PLATES/ STICKERS

DZ

PASSPORT

The passport cover has the name of the country in Arabic, English, and French; the coat of arms; and the word *passport* in the same three languages.

AIRLINE

Air Algérie

NATIONAL FLOWER

Red poppy (unofficial)

NATIONAL TREE

Date palm (unofficial)

NATIONAL BIRD

Black-shouldered kite (unofficial)

NATIONAL RESOURCES

Natural resources include petroleum, natural gas, iron, uranium, lead, zinc, and phosphates. Ancient cities and monuments, combined with Algeria's many sandy beaches and pleasant climate, hold the potential for tourism and development that has been unfulfilled because of decades of violence and instability.

FOODS

Couscous, a dish of semolina pasta served with a variety of vegetables or meat, is the national dish. The dish can be traced back to ancient Carthage, where it was introduced to the indigenous Berber peoples of North Africa. *Pastilla,* a layered, flaky pastry filled with shredded chicken or squab, is also considered a national dish. Other dishes include *shorba,* a chicken soup with vegetables; *bourek,* pastry rolls stuffed with minced meat; *shorba bil hout,* a fish soup with tomato and potato; *chlada fakya,* a salad of fresh fruits; and *el ham lahlou,* a slightly sweet lamb dish normally served for Ramadan.

SPORTS/SPORTS TEAMS

The most popular sport in Algeria is football (soccer). Other sports, such as basketball and athletics, are also popular. Algeria national teams participate in many sports at an international level.

TEAM SPORTS

Badminton

Algeria Badminton Team

Basketball

Algeria Basketball Team; Algeria Women's Basketball Team; Algeria Wheelchair Basketball Team

Football

Algeria Football Team, nickname Les Fennecs or Renards du Désert (the Desert Foxes) or Les Verts (the Greens); Algeria Women's Football Team, nickname the Greens; Algeria Futsal Team; Algeria Rugby Union Team

Handball

Algeria Handball Team; Algeria Women's Handball Team

Hockey

Algeria Ice Hockey Team; Algeria Field Hockey Team

Racing

Algeria Speedway Team

Table Tennis

Algeria Table Tennis Team

Tennis

Algeria Davis Cup Team; Algeria Fed Cup Team

Volleyball

Algeria Men's Volleyball Team; Algeria Women's Volleyball Team

INDIVIDUAL SPORTS

Algeria Amateur Boxing Team; Algeria Athletics Team; Algeria Biathlon Team; Algeria Canoeing Team; Algeria Chess Team; Algeria Cycling Team; Algeria Equestrian Team; Algeria Fencing Team; Algeria Gymnastics Team; Algeria Judo Team; Algeria Modern Pentathlon Team; Algeria Rowing Team; Algeria Sailing Team; Algeria Shooting Team; Algeria Swim Team; Algeria Tae Kwon Do Team; Algeria Weight Lifting Team; Algeria Wrestling Team

NATIONAL HEROES OR PERSONIFICATIONS

Emir Abd al-Qadir, Algeria's national hero, an Islamic scholar and military leader who led the struggle against the French invasion of North Africa in the mid-19th century; Messali Hadj, a leader of the independence movement; Ahmed Ben Bella, a nationalist leader and the first premier of independent Algeria

NATIONAL HOLIDAY/INDEPENDENCE DAY

Revolution Day, November 1

FESTIVALS/FAIRS

National Theater Festival, June; Jijel Music Festival, August

SIGNIFICANT EVENTS IN FORMATION OF NATIONAL IDENTITY

1200 B.C.E.   Ancient Berber kingdoms flourish, influenced by Carthage and later under Roman rule.

Fifth century–eighth century C.E.   The Roman decline in North Africa allows the creation of independent states. Roman cities and towns are overrun, and the Berbers, who had been pushed back to the edges of the Roman Empire, return to the more fertile lands along the Mediterranean.

8th century–11th century   Arab invaders introduce Islam as the major religion and spread their Arabic language.

700–1200   Various Berber dynasties spread Islam across North Africa and into Europe.

1500s   Beginning in 1518 and lasting through 1830, Algeria is a territory of the Ottoman Turkish Empire. During this period, it is one of the centers of the Barbary pirates. Between 1530 and 1539, Algeria and Tunisia* are united by Khayr Ad-Din, known in Europe as Barbarossa, the most famous of the Barbary pirates.

18th century–19th century   Barbary pirates prey on European and American shipping in the Mediterranean. To put an end to Barbary attacks, the United States* declares war on Algiers in 1815.

1830   France seizes the coastal region and gradually expands its rule inland against Algerian resistance and repeated rebellions.

19th century–early 20th century   During the years of French domination, the struggle to sur-

vive, to co-exist, to gain equality, and finally to achieve independence shape a large part of the Algerian national identity.

1945–1962   After World War II, Algerian nationalism increases, and French efforts to retain control result in a bitter civil war. In 1958, Algeria becomes an integral part of the French Republic. This effort to maintain the territory's association with France fails, and in 1962, the defeated French withdraw and Algeria becomes independent.

1991   The first democratic elections in Algerian history produce a victory for Islamic fundamentalists, and the military nullifies the electoral results. This provokes a bloody terrorist campaign by the fundamentalists. Political and religious violence is estimated to have claimed some 100,000 lives since Algerian independence in 1962.

2001   Scores of demonstrators are killed in clashes between security forces and Berber protesters in the mainly Berber region of Kabylia. The major Berber political party withdraws from the government in protest against government handling of the widening Berber protests.

2002   The Berber language is recognized as a national language, and the government promises greater investment in Kabylia and greater recognition of the Berber culture and language as an integral part of Algerian culture.

2006   Under a government amnesty, many Islamic militants, jailed during the violence of the 1990s, are freed.

2007–2008   Bombings around the country mark an upsurge in violence by Islamic fundamentalist groups. Some groups claim affiliation with the Al-Qaeda terrorist groups.

2009   Many Berbers continue to protest discrimination and a lack of opportunities. Berbers continue to leave for Europe in search of work and security.

BAHRAIN

OFFICIAL NAME

Mamlakat al-Bahrayn (transliteration from Arabic); Kingdom of Bahrain (English)

POPULATION
1,147,100 (2009e)

INHABITANTS' NAME/NICKNAME
Bahraini(s)

LANGUAGE/LANGUAGES
Arabic (official); English, Farsi, Urdu, others

RELIGION/RELIGIONS
Muslim, 80 percent (approximately 60–70% Shia, 30–40% Sunni); Christian, 9 percent; Hindu, other or no religion

NATIONAL FLAG
The flag has a red field with a white stripe at the hoist, limited by a serration of five white triangles representing the five pillars of Islam. Red is the traditional color for the flags of the Persian Gulf states.

COAT OF ARMS/SEAL
The coat of arms has the same design as that found on the national flag located on a shield in the center. A red and white mantling surrounds the shield.

CAPITAL CITY
Manama

TYPE OF GOVERNMENT
Constitutional monarchy

NATIONAL EMBLEM
Al-Fatih Mosque in Manama

NATIONAL COLORS
Red and white

NATIONAL ANTHEM
The anthem was adopted upon Bahrain's independence in 1971. The original words were changed in 2002, when Bahrain became a kingdom and the ruler became a king rather than an emir.

Bahrainona (Our Bahrain)

Our Bahrain
Our King
A symbol of the harmony
Its constitution is high in the place and the position
Its charter is the way of (method of) Sharia, Arabism and the values
Long live the kingdom of Bahrain
Country of nobles
Cradle of peace
Its constitution is high in the place and the position
Its charter is the way of (method of) Sharia, Arabism and the values
Long live the kingdom of Bahrain

CURRENCY
Bahraini dinar

INTERNET IDENTIFIER
.bh

VEHICLE IDENTIFICATION PLATES/STICKERS
BRN

PASSPORT
The passport cover has the name of the country in Arabic and English, the coat of arms, and the word *passport* in Arabic and English.

AIRLINES
Gulf Air; Bahrain Air

NATIONAL TREE
Thorn tree (unofficial)

NATIONAL ANIMAL
Jerboa (unofficial)

NATIONAL BIRD
White-cheeked bulbul

NATIONAL RESOURCES
Natural resources include oil, natural gas, fish, and pearls. The islands have a fascinating

culture, thousands of years of history, and a pro-Western attitude, making Bahrain one of the most popular tourist destinations in the Middle East. Other resources include a strategic position between East and West, fertile lands, freshwater, and the Middle East's most important financial center.

FOODS

Machboo, a rice dish with either meat or fish, is considered the national dish. Other national dishes include *kapsa,* a dish of chicken, tomatoes, onions, raisins, and spices, served with rice; *kofta bel baqdoonis,* ground beef or lamb mixed with onions and parsley and then baked; *roz bel jamberry,* a dish of shrimp and rice; *sidreyat al dajaj,* chicken prepared with rice flour, cardamom, milk, sugar, and rose water; *salata khadra,* a mixture of cucumber, tomatoes, and parsley.

SPORTS/SPORTS TEAMS

Association football (soccer) is the most popular sport. Racing is also very popular, and Bahrain hosts the annual Bahrain Grand Prix. Bahrain national teams participate in many sports at an international level.

TEAM SPORTS

Badminton

Bahrain Badminton Team

Basketball

Bahrain Wheelchair Basketball Team

Cricket

Bahrain Cricket Team

Football

Bahrain Football Team, nickname the Reds; Bahrain Women's Football Team, nickname the Reds; Bahrain Beach Soccer Team; Arabian Gulf Rugby Union Team; Arabian Gulf Rugby Union Team (Sevens), nickname Arabian Gulf Sevens or Arabian Gulf 7s; Arabian Gulf Women's Rugby Union Team (Sevens), nickname Arabian Gulf Sevens or Arabian Gulf 7s (Arabian Gulf teams represent a number of Persian Gulf countries)

Handball

Bahrain National Handball Team; Bahrain National Beach Handball Team

Racing

A1 Team Bahrain

Table Tennis

Bahrain Table Tennis Team

Tennis

Bahrain Davis Cup Team

Volleyball

Bahrain Men's Volleyball Team

INDIVIDUAL SPORTS

Bahrain Amateur Boxing Team; Bahrain Athletics Team; Bahrain Cycling Team; Bahrain Equestrian Team; Bahrain Fencing Team; Bahrain Modern Pentathlon Team; Bahrain Rowing Team; Bahrain Sailing Team; Bahrain Shooting Team; Bahrain Swim Team; Bahrain Tae Kwon Do Team; Bahrain Weight Lifting Team

NATIONAL HEROES OR PERSONIFICATIONS

Magrin ibn Zamil, ruler of eastern Arabia who was killed fighting a Portuguese invasion in 1521; Ahmed Al Fateh, the first Al Khalifa emir of Bahrain in the late 18th century; King Hamad ibn Isa Al Khalifah, who succeeded to the throne in 1999, instituted free elections for parliament, gave women the vote, and released all political prisoners.

NATIONAL HOLIDAY/INDEPENDENCE DAY

National Day, December 16

Festivals/Fairs

Ashura, celebrated by the Shia Muslims to commemorate the martyrdom of Husayn ibn Ali, February; Milad al-Nabi, the largest festival to commemorate the birthday of Muhammad, April; Independence Day, June

Significant Events in Formation of National Identity

2300 B.C.E.–2000 B.C.E. Archaeological evidence identifies Bahrain as the site of the ancient civilization of Dilmun, dating from the third millennium B.C.E.

600 B.C.E. The region is absorbed into the Babylonian Empire by about 600 B.C.E.

330 B.C.E. The army of Alexander the Great arrives, adding the region to his growing empire.

330 B.C.E.–629 C.E. From the time of the Greeks until the coming of Islam in the seventh century, Bahrain is known by the Greek name of Tylos, even though it is mostly under Persian rule for many centuries. Bahrain is one of the first territories outside mainland Arabia to accept the new religion called Islam in 629 C.E.

7th century–14th century Part of the Muslim caliphate, Bahrain again prospers as an important port on the trade routes between the Middle East and India.

1487–1602 The Omanis, from the eastern part of Arabia, conquer Bahrain in 1487, just two years after the first visit by a European expedition. The Portuguese, interested in the pearls that have made Bahrain famous, stay in the region until driven out by the Bahrainis themselves in 1602.

18th century The present ruling house, the Al-Khalifa, arrives in the islands in the mid-18th century from Kuwait*, where they helped their relatives, the Al-Sabah, to establish power. At first, the Al-Khalifa settle in present Qatar*, but in the early 1780s, they drive the Persians from Bahrain and occupy the principal islands.

1859–1861 In 1859, a British squadron is sent to protect the islands from Arabian incursions, and in 1861, the British impose a treaty making Bahrain a British protectorate.

1861–1932 The islands remain poor and isolated, known mainly for pearls, until the discovery of oil in 1932.

1935–1970 As the first in the region to exploit their oil reserves, the Bahrainis are the first to experience a marked improvement in their standard of living.

1971 Bahrain achieves full independence under the rule of the Al-Khalifa family as the State of Bahrain.

1979–1982 Influenced by the Islamic Revolution in Iran*, radicals in Bahrain attempt a coup against the Al-Khalifa dynasty. The coup ultimately fails but some of the more restrictive laws are rescinded.

1994–1999 In 1999, Hamad ibn isa Al-Khalifa succeeds as head of state and institutes much-needed reforms. A parliament is elected, women are given the right to vote, and all political prisoners are released. The creation of an indigenous middle class, unique in the Persian Gulf region, means that Bahrainis are generally more liberal than their neighbors. Part of the liberalization has meant democratic rights, even for fundamentalists and dissidents.

2002 The State of Bahrain officially becomes a kingdom.

2006 Elections in 2006 see big gains by Islamic groups, both Shia and Sunni. Bahraini moderates respond to the growing power of religious parties by organizing campaigns to defend basic personal freedoms from being legislated away.

2008 The Bahraini oil reserves prove quite small compared to those of neighboring countries. Today, Bahrain produces only a token quantity of oil. Without the resources for an oil boom, Bahrain has moved more slowly and thoughtfully into the modern world. The need to diversify the economy and a long tradition as an important trading nation have proved to be a fortunate set of circumstances for the modern kingdom.

2009 Neighboring Iran reiterates ancient territorial claims to Bahrain as its 14th province, raising tensions in the region and bringing other Arab nations to Bahrain's defense.

EGYPT

OFFICIAL NAME

Gumhūriyyet Maṣr el-Arabiyyah (transliteration from Arabic); Arab Republic of Egypt (English)

POPULATION

75,051,400 (2009e)

INHABITANTS' NAME/NICKNAME

Egyptian(s)

LANGUAGE/LANGUAGES

Arabic (official); Egyptian Arabic dialect; English, French, others

RELIGION/RELIGIONS

Muslim, 90 percent; Coptic Orthodox, 9 percent; other Christian, 1 percent; other or no religion

NATIONAL FLAG

The flag has three horizontal stripes of red, white, and black, bearing the national arms, the Eagle of Saladin in gold, centered on the white. The red symbolizes the period before the revolution, when a group of army officers came to power after deposing King Farouk as the country struggled against British occupation. The white symbolizes the advent of the 1952 revolution that ended the monarchy without bloodshed. The black symbolizes the end of oppression by the monarchy and British colonialism.

COAT OF ARMS/SEAL

The cost of arms is the Eagle of Saladin standing on a pedestal that carries the name of the country in Arabic script. The country's colors appear as a shield or breastplate, al-though in a vertical rather than a horizontal configuration.

CAPITAL CITY

Cairo

TYPE OF GOVERNMENT

Semipresidential republic

NATIONAL EMBLEM

Eagle of Saladin; pyramids of Giza

NATIONAL COLORS

Red, white, and black

NATIONAL ANTHEM

The anthem was originally written in 1956 and adopted as the official anthem in 1960, but following the 1979 peace accord with Israel*, new, more peace-oriented lyrics were adopted.

Bilady, Bilady, Bilady (transliteration from Arabic); My Country, My Country, My Country (English)

My country, my country, my country,
You have my love and my heart.
My homeland, my homeland, my homeland,
You have my love and my heart.

Egypt! O mother of all lands,
My hope and my ambition,
And on all people
Your Nile has countless benefits.

Chorus

My homeland, my homeland, my homeland,
My love and my heart are for thee.
My homeland, my homeland, my homeland,
My love and my heart are for thee.

Egypt! Most precious jewel,
Shining on the brow of eternity!
O my homeland, be for ever free,
Safe from every foe!

Chorus

My homeland, my homeland, my homeland,
My love and my heart are for thee.

My homeland, my homeland, my homeland,
My love and my heart are for thee.

Egypt! Noble are thy children,
Loyal, and guardians of thy soil.
In war and peace
We give our lives for thy sake.

Chorus

My homeland, my homeland, my homeland,
My love and my heart are for thee.

PATRON SAINT

Saint Mark the Evangelist

CURRENCY

Egyptian pound

INTERNET IDENTIFIER

.eg

VEHICLE IDENTIFICATION PLATES/ STICKERS

ET

PASSPORT

The passport cover has the name of the country in Arabic and English, the coat of arms, and the word *passport* in Arabic and English.

AIRLINES

Egyptair; Almasria Universal Airlines

NATIONAL FLOWER

Egyptian lotus

NATIONAL RESOURCES

Natural resources include petroleum, natural gas, iron ore, phosphates, manganese, limestone, gypsum, talc, and asbestos. A thriving tourist industry depends on Egypt's numerous antiquities. Egyptians living and working abroad, particularly in Saudi Arabia*, the Persian Gulf, and Europe, number over 3 million and are a source of valuable foreign currency and investment.

FOODS

Ful medames, a dish of partially mashed fava beans slow-cooked and served with olive oil, parsley, onion, garlic, and lemon, topped with sliced eggs and vegetables, is the national dish. *Khoushari,* a dish of rice, brown lentils, garbanzos, and macaroni topped with garlic, vinegar, and a spicy tomato sauce, is another national dish. Other specialties include *ful nahed,* a soup of beans and vegetables; *ta'mia,* ground garbanzo beans shaped into balls, deep-fried, and often served on pita bread; and *halawa tahiniya,* a sweet made of sesame seed paste and pistachios.

SPORTS/SPORTS TEAMS

Association football (soccer) is the de facto national sport. Tennis and handball are also very popular. Egypt national teams participate in many sports at an international level

TEAM SPORTS

Badminton

Egypt Badminton Team

Basketball

Egypt Basketball Team; Egypt Women's Basketball Team

Cricket

Egypt Cricket Team

Football

Egypt Football Team, nickname the Pharaohs; Egypt Women's Football Team, nickname the Cleopatras; Egypt Under-20 Football Team, nickname the Young Pharoahs; Egypt Futsal Team; Egypt Beach Soccer Team

Handball

Egypt Handball Team; Egypt Women's Handball Team; Egypt Beach Handball Team; Egypt Women's Beach Handball Team

Hockey
Egypt Field Hockey Team

Kabaddi
Egypt Kabaddi Team

Racing
Egypt Speedway Team

Table Tennis
Egypt Table Tennis Team

Tennis
Egypt Fed Cup Team; Egypt Davis Cup Team

Volleyball
Egypt Men's Volleyball Team; Egypt Women's Volleyball Team

Water Polo
Egypt Water Polo Team

INDIVIDUAL SPORTS
Egypt Amateur Boxing Team; Egypt Archery Team; Egypt Athletics Team; Egypt Bodybuilding Team; Egypt Canoeing Team; Egypt Cycling Team; Egypt Equestrian Team; Egypt Fencing Team; Egypt Gymnastics Team; Egypt Judo Team; Egypt Modern Pentathlon Team; Egypt Rowing Team; Egypt Sailing Team; Egypt Shooting Team; Egypt Swim Team; Egypt Tae Kwon Do Team; Egypt Triathlon Team; Egypt Weight Lifting Team; Egypt Wrestling Team

NATIONAL HEROES OR PERSONIFICATIONS
Muhammad 'Ali, founder of modern Egypt under Ottoman Turkish rule; Gamal Abdel Nasser, a leader of the Egyptian Revolution and second president of Egypt from 1956 to 1970; Anwar El Sadat, third president of Egypt and a hero of the October War in 1973; Hosni Mubarak, present president since 1981; Ahmed Faud Pasha (Faud I), the first king of modern Egypt and the founder of the University of Cairo; Ahmed Orabi, an early nationalist leader; Mustafa Kamel, a leading member of the anticolonial and prodemocratic political group in the early 20th century

NATIONAL HOLIDAY/INDEPENDENCE DAY
Revolution Day, July 23

FESTIVALS/FAIRS
Cairo International Film Festival, November; Sham en Nisim (Spring Festival), April; Prophet Mohammed Festival, May; Wafaa al Nil (Nile Festival), September; Art Festival, August

SIGNIFICANT EVENTS IN FORMATION OF NATIONAL IDENTITY
3150 B.C.E.   A united Egyptian kingdom is created, giving rise to a series of dynasties that rule for the next 3,000 years over a sophisticated and advanced culture.

332 B.C.E.   Alexander the Great conquers Egypt. The Ptolemaic dynasty, the successors to Alexander, rule from a new capital at Alexandria. The city is a center of Greek learning and culture, centered on the famous Library of Alexandria.

30 B.C.E.   Egypt becomes a province of Rome, becoming the granary of the empire. Christianity is introduced in the first century C.E.

395 C.E.–420 C.E.   The decline of Roman power and the separation of the empire into eastern and western successors bring Egypt under eastern, or Byzantine, control.

451   A distinct Egyptian Coptic Church is firmly established.

639   Muslim Arabs invade Egypt, bringing with them the new Muslim religion. The majority of the population is converted to Islam. Muslim rulers nominated by the Islamic Caliphate rule Egypt for the next six centuries.

1517–1998 The Ottoman Turks conquer the country. Egypt remains under the authority of semiautonomous local rulers and is regarded as a vassal state, not a province, of the Ottoman Empire.

1798 The French invade Egypt under Napoleon Bonaparte. The French have a great social impact on the country and its culture, as Egyptians are exposed to the principles of the French Revolution and are granted self-governance. A series of civil wars follow the evacuation of French troops. An Albanian mercenary, Muhammad 'Ali, becomes the Ottoman viceroy and establishes a dynasty.

1869 With the building of the Suez Canal that connects the Mediterranean to the Indian Ocean, Egypt becomes an important trading center and a center of world transportation.

1882 The country becomes heavily indebted to various European countries. The British seize control of Egypt's government to protect their financial interests, particularly those in the Suez Canal.

1882–1906 A local movement for independence, triggered by British actions, emerges.

1914–1919 At the outbreak of the First World War, the British declare Egypt a protectorate under an Egyptian monarch. At the end of the war, nationalists gain a majority in the local legislative assembly. When the British exile nationalist leaders, a revolt spreads across the country.

1922 Constant revolts impel the British to issue a unilateral declaration of Egypt's independence as an autonomous kingdom within the British Empire.

1936 The Anglo-Egyptian Treaty is concluded, formalizing British control of many aspects of the Egyptian government.

1952 Anti-British agitation results in the overthrow of the monarchy, which marks the beginning of the Egyptian Revolution.

1953–1956 The Egyptian Republic is declared. Gamal Abdel Nasser, the leader of the revolution, takes control of the government in 1954. Nasser becomes president and declares the full independence of Egypt from the United Kingdom*. His nationalization of the Suez Canal prompts an international crisis.

1967–1970 Egypt and other Muslim states invade Israel, setting off the Six Day War. Israeli victories end with the occupation of the Sinai. Nasser dies and is succeeded by Anwar Sadat.

1973 Egypt and Syria* launch an attack on Israel in the October War in an attempt to recapture the Sinai.

1977–1981 Sadat makes an historic visit to Israel, which leads to the 1979 peace treaty in exchange for a complete Israeli withdrawal from Sinai. Sadat is assassinated by a fundamentalist militant and is succeeded by Hosni Mubarak. Mubarak creates an authoritarian government.

2003 The Egyptian Movement for Change is launched to seek a return to democracy and greater civil liberties. Discrimination against women and religious minorities continues.

2007 President Mubarak introduces constitutional amendments that increase presidential powers and ban political parties based on religion, race, or ethnicity.

2008 An Egyptian court rules that members of faiths other than Islam may obtain identity cards without listing their faith, a ruling that is widely protested by the growing number of Islamic fundamentalist organizations.

2009 Dissidents continue to suffer harassment or imprisonment. Religious minorities, particularly the Christian Copts, also face discrimination. Attacks on the vital tourist industry by Islamic radicals continue to disrupt the nation.

IRAN

OFFICIAL NAME
Jomhūrī-ye Eslāmī-ye Īrān (transliteration from Farsi); Islamic Republic of Iran (English)

POPULATION
70,623,400 (2009e)

INHABITANTS' NAME/NICKNAME

Iranian(s)

LANGUAGE/LANGUAGES

Farsi (Iranian), Kurdish, Azeri, Luri, Arabic, Baluch, others

RELIGION/RELIGIONS

Shia Muslim, 90 percent; Sunni Muslim, 8 percent; Zoroastrian, Jewish, Christian, Baha'i, other or no religion

NATIONAL FLAG

The flag is a horizontal tricolor of green, white, and red, each color separated by a stylized version of the Kufic script used for the Qur'an; the phrase *Allahu Akbar* (God is great) is repeated 22 times. The coat of arms centered on the white is a geometric form of the word *Allah* in red. The green color symbolizes vigor, the white is for peace, and the red is for courage.

COAT OF ARMS/SEAL

The coat of arms consists of four black crescents and a sword. The four crescents stand for the word *Allah* and, at the same time, the phrase *La ilaha illa Allah* (There is no God but Allah). Above the sword is a *shadda,* or sign of emphasis, in the shape of a tulip, which was formerly a flower of memorials but in recent years has become a symbol of martyrdom.

CAPITAL CITY

Tehran

TYPE OF GOVERNMENT

Islamic republic

NATIONAL EMBLEM

Stylized name of Allah, the coat of arms

NATIONAL COLORS

Green, white, and red

NATIONAL ANTHEM

The anthem was adopted in 1990, following the death of Ayatollah Ruhollah Khomeini.

National Anthem of the Islamic Republic of Iran (English)

Upwards on the horizon rose the eastern sun
The light in the eyes of the believers in justice.
Bahman is the zenith of our faith.
Your message, O Imam, of sovereignty and
   freedom
Is imprinted on our souls.
O martyrs! Your clamors echo in the ears of
   time:
Be enduring, continuing, and eternal,
The Islamic Republic of Iran.

PATRON SAINT

Saint Maruthas

CURRENCY

Iranian rial

INTERNET IDENTIFIER

.ir

VEHICLE IDENTIFICATION PLATES/ STICKERS

IR

PASSPORT

The passport has the coat of arms, the name of the country in Farsi, the phrase *Allahu Akbar* (God is Great) in Kufic script, the full name Government of the Islamic Republic of Iran, and the word *passport* in English.

AIRLINE

Iran Air

NATIONAL FLOWER

Tulip

NATIONAL TREE

Tree of all seeds (mythical) (unofficial)

NATIONAL ANIMAL

Iranian cheetah (unofficial); lion (historical)

NATIONAL RESOURCES

Natural resources include petroleum, natural gas, coal, chromium, copper, iron ore, lead, manganese, zinc, and sulfur. The country's ancient ruins, historic monuments and cities, sandy beaches on the Persian Gulf, and unique culture could sustain a thriving tourist industry, but Iran's poor world image, unstable regional conditions, and an absence of effective planning hinder the growth of the industry. Iranians living outside the country are a source of remittances to families in Iran and could be a source of investment.

FOODS

The cuisine of Iran is diverse, with each province featuring traditional dishes, as well as culinary customs and styles, distinct to the region. National dishes include *chelo khoresh,* a rice dish with vegetables, meat, and a nut sauce; *polo chele,* rice pilaf with vegetables; *polo chirin,* sweet-and-sour saffron rice with raisins, almonds, and orange; *kofte,* minced meat formed into meatballs; *dolmeh,* stuffed eggplant, zucchini, or peppers; and *chelo kebab,* skewers of meat cooked over charcoal and served with rice, which is considered the national dish.

SPORTS/SPORTS TEAMS

Association football (soccer) is the most popular sport. Wrestling has traditionally been referred to as Iran's national sport. Iran national teams participate in many sports at international level.

TEAM SPORTS

Badminton

Iran Badminton Team

Baseball

Iran Baseball Team; Iran Softball Team

Basketball

Iran Basketball Team; Iran Women's Basketball Team; Iran Wheelchair Basketball Team

Cricket

Iran Cricket Team

Football

Iran Football Team, nickname Team Melli (the Team); Iran Women's Football Team, nickname Team Melli Zanan (the Ladies' Team); Iran Under-23 Football Team; Iran Under-20 Football Team; Iran Under-17 Football Team; Iran Rugby Union Team, nickname Team Melli (the Team); Iran Futsal Team; Iran Beach Soccer Team; Iran Women's Futsal Team

Handball

Iran Handball Team; Iran Women's Handball Team

Hockey

Iran Field Hockey Team; Iran Women's Field Hockey Team

Kabaddi

Iran Kabaddi Team

Racing

Iran Speedway Team

Table Tennis

Iran Table Tennis Team

Tennis

Iran Davis Cup Team

Volleyball

Iran Men's Volleyball Team; Iran Women's Volleyball Team; Iran Men's Under-21 Volleyball Team; Iran Men's Under-19 Volleyball Team

INDIVIDUAL SPORTS

Iran Amateur Boxing Team; Iran Archery Team; Iran Athletics Team; Iran Canoeing Team; Iran Cycling Team; Iran Equestrian Team; Iran Fencing Team; Iran Gymnastics Team; Iran Judo Team; Iran Karate Team: Iran Modern Pentathlon Team; Iran Rowing Team; Iran Shooting Team; Iran Swim Team; Iran Tae Kwon Do Team; Iran Triathlon Team; Iran Weight Lifting Team; Iran Wrestling Team

WINTER SPORTS

Iran Alpine Ski Team; Iran Biathlon Team

NATIONAL HEROES OR PERSONIFICATIONS

The image of a robed and turbaned ayatollah is the personification of the Islamic Republic of Iran.

National heroes include Cyrus the Great, founder of the unified Persian Empire in the sixth century B.C.E.; Muhmud of Ghazni, founder of the medieval Ghaznavid Empire; Ayatollah Ruhollah Khomeini, founder of the Islamic Republic of Iran; and Sattar Khan, a leader of the Iranian Constitutional Revolution in the early 20th century.

NATIONAL HOLIDAY/INDEPENDENCE DAY

Islamic Republic Day, April 1

FESTIVALS/FAIRS

International Festival of Peace Poetry, May; Shia Festival (the birth of Imam Mahdi), August; Sadeh Festival (Midwinter Festival), December; Mobarak Festival, August

SIGNIFICANT EVENTS IN FORMATION OF NATIONAL IDENTITY

10th century B.C.E.–7th century B.C.E. Zoroaster is born sometime between the 10th and seventh centuries B.C.E. His teachings spread across the region of ancient Persia.

550 B.C.E.–530 B.C.E. The Persian Empire is created. Cyrus the Great conquers neighboring regions and extends the empire's boundaries.

330 B.C.E.–312 B.C.E. Persia is conquered by Alexander the Great and forms part of the Macedonian (Greek) Empire.

246 B.C.E.–649 C.E. The Parthian Empire is established. The Persians are frequently at war with the Romans and, later, the Byzantines over control of the Middle East.

649 C.E. Invading Arabs conquer Persia, introducing the Muslim religion. Persian culture resists Arab influences, outside of religion.

902–1221 Persia fragments into numerous small states that fall to the Seljuk Turks in 1118, followed by another period of fragmentation and the Mongol invasion.

1501–1508 The Empire of Persia (literally called The God-Protected Realms of Iran) is reunited. Portuguese expeditions begin to visit the southern ports.

18th century Afghans invade and occupy Persia. Russia* and the Turkish Ottoman Empire take territories in the north and west.

1907–1921 Russia and the United Kingdom* partition Persia into spheres of influence. In 1917, the two powers occupy the country. From 1919, Persia is a de facto British protectorate.

1925–1935 Reza Khan overthrows the weakened kingdom and creates the Pahlavi Dynasty. The ancient—and, later, English—name Persia is officially discarded in favor of Iran.

1941–1946 During the Second World War, Iran is occupied by the United Kingdom and the Soviet Union to protect oil supplies. At the end of the war, the Soviets support autonomous states in Iranian Azerbaijan* and Kurdistan*.

1951–1953 A new government with Dr. Mohammad Mossadegh as prime minister nationalizes Iran's oil reserves, aggravating Cold War tensions. The United Kingdom and the United

States* orchestrate the overthrow of Mossadegh and the creation of a pro-Western government under Mohammad Reza Pahlavi as Shah of Iran.

1953–1979 The shah's government becomes increasingly authoritarian, while forcing modernization of the economy, railroads, and other infrastructure projects in the so-called White Revolution. The shah's policies alienate the conservative Shia hierarchy, led by Ayatollah Rutollah Khomeini from his exile in France*.

1979–1981 Khomeini returns to Iran to lead the overthrow of the imperial government and the establishment of the Islamic Republic of Iran. The invasion of the United States Embassy in Tehran initiates a grave diplomatic crisis. Embassy personnel are held hostage until early 1981. Iran wars with neighboring Iraq* under Saddam Hussein. Antigovernment movements in Kurdistan, Iranian Azerbaijan, and Baluchistan are brutally suppressed.

1981–1988 The new Islamic government disbands the Iranian military, imposes religious laws in place of civil law, and represses modernization, tolerance, and freedom of expression. The Iran-Iraq War ends inconclusively but leaves between 500,000 and 1 million dead.

1988–2005 More moderate, pragmatic leaders concentrate on improving the faltering economy without breaking with Islamic revolutionary ideals. In 2004, flawed elections are held, with many reformists prohibited from running.

2005–2008 Conservative populist Mahmoud Ahmadinejad, with the support of the ayatollahs, becomes Iran's head of state. Tensions mount with the West over Iran's development of a nuclear arsenal. The limited liberalizations of the period from 1988 to 2005 are eliminated or reversed. Iran's ongoing territorial claims to Bahrain* cause a growing rift between Iran and the Arab nations.

2009 Iran's 2009 elections, denounced as fraudulent and illegal by the more moderate groups in the country, lead to mass demonstrations and confrontations with police. The demonstrations spread across the country as other grievances surface. Arrests of opposition leaders, in September, again raised tensions and spur a new round of demonstrations and confrontations.

IRAQ

OFFICIAL NAME

Jumhūriyyat ul-Irāq (transliteration from Arabic); Komarâe Iraq (transliteration from Kurdish); Republic of Iraq (English)

POPULATION

34,831,600 (2009e)

INHABITANTS' NAME/NICKNAME

Iraqi(s)

LANGUAGE/LANGUAGES

Arabic (official); Kurdish (official in Kurdish regions); Turkoman, Assyrian, Armenian, others

RELIGION/RELIGIONS

Shia Muslim, 60–65 percent; Sunni Muslim, 32–37 percent; Christian, other or no religion

NATIONAL FLAG

The flag is a horizontal tricolor of red, white, and black, with *Allahu Akbar* (God Is Great) in green Kufic script on the white stripe. The colors are those of the Hashemite leaders of the Arab Revolt in the early 20th century. The red symbolizes the descendants of the Prophet, the green represents Islam, white symbolizes mourning for the lost Arab empire, and black represents the Prophet Mohammad. A new national flag, acceptable to the non-Arab peoples of the country, is to be selected later.

COAT OF ARMS/SEAL

The coat of arms consists of a centered shield of the Iraqi flag. Behind the shield is the golden Eagle of Saladin, which is associated with the 20th-century pan-Arab movement. Below the shield is a green scroll with the words *al-Jumhuriya al-'Iraqiya* (the Iraqi Republic). The coat of arms will be changed along with the national flag in the future.

Motto

Allahu akbar (transliteration from Arabic); God Is Great (English)

Capital City

Baghdad

Type of Government

Developing parliamentary democracy under U.S. military occupation

National Emblem

Eagle of Saladin

National Colors

Green and white

National Anthem

The anthem, a popular folk tune throughout the Arab world, was adopted in 2004. The government is considering the adoption of a new national anthem more acceptable to the non-Arab populations of the country.

Mawtini (Transliteration from Arabic); My Homeland (English)

My homeland, my homeland
Majesty and beauty, sublimity and
  splendor,
Are in your hills, are in your hills,
Life and deliverance, pleasure and hope
Are in your air, are in your air
Will I see you? Will I see you?
Safe and comforted, sound and honored
Will I see you in your eminence?
Reaching to the stars, reaching to the stars
My homeland, my homeland
My homeland, my homeland
The youth will not tire, 'till your
  independence
Or they die, or they die

We will drink from death
And we will not be to our enemies
Like slaves, like slaves
We do not want, we do not want
An eternal humiliation
Nor a miserable life,
We do not want
But we will bring back
Our great glory, our great glory
My homeland, my homeland
The sword and the pen
Not the talk nor the quarrel
Are our symbols, are our symbols
Our glory and our covenant
And a duty to be faithful
Arouse us, arouse us
Our glory, our glory
Is an honorable cause
And a waving standard
O, behold you
In your eminence
Victorious over your enemies
Victorious over your enemies
My homeland, my homeland

Currency

Iraqi dinar

Internet Identifier

.iq

Vehicle Identification Plates/ Stickers

IRQ

Passport

The passport cover has the name of the country in Arabic, the coat of arms, the name of the country in English, and the word *passport* in English and Arabic.

Airline

Iraqi Airways

National Flower

Rose

NATIONAL ANIMAL

Camel; lion (creature from Iraq's mythology) (unofficial)

NATIONAL BIRD

Falcon

NATIONAL RESOURCES

Natural resources include petroleum, natural gas, phosphates, and sulfur. The economy depends on the petroleum industry. The Iraqi Diaspora is a valuable resource as a source of foreign currency and investment.

FOODS

National dishes include *masgouf,* a dish of fresh fish baked with tamarind and served with onions and tomatoes; *biryani,* an Indian-influenced rice dish with vegetables and spices; kebab, skewered meat cooked over charcoal; and dolma, marinated grape leaves stuffed with rice and minced meat

SPORTS/SPORTS TEAMS

Association football (soccer) is the country's most popular sport. Basketball is also very popular. Iraq national teams participate in many sports at an international level.

TEAM SPORTS

Badminton

Iraq Badminton Team

Baseball

Iraq Softball Team

Basketball

Iraq Basketball Team; Iraq Women's Basketball Team; Iraq Wheelchair Basketball Team

Football

Iraq Football Team, nickname Asood Al Rafidain (Lions of Mesopotamia); Iraq Women's Football Team, nickname Asood Al Rafidain (Lionesses of Mesopotamia); Iraq Under-19 Football Team: Iraq Women's Under-19 Football Team; Iraq Futsal Team

Handball

Iraq Handball Team; Iraq Women's Handball Team

Hockey

Iraq Field Hockey Team

Table Tennis

Iraq Table Tennis Team

Tennis

Iraq Davis Cup Team; Iraq Fed Cup Team

Volleyball

Iraq Men's Volleyball Team; Iraq Women's Volleyball Team

INDIVIDUAL SPORTS

Iraq Amateur Boxing Team; Iraq Archery Team; Athletics Team; Iraq Canoeing Team; Iraq Cycling Team; Iraq Fencing Team; Iraq Gymnastics Team; Iraq Judo Team; Iraq Karate Team; Iraq Rowing Team; Iraq Shooting Team; Iraq Swim Team; Iraq Tae Kwon Do Team; Iraq Weight Lifting Team; Iraq Wrestling Team

NATIONAL HEROES OR PERSONIFICATIONS

Umar, the second caliph, who extended the Islamic Empire to include Egypt, Persia, and Jerusalem; Harun al-Rashid, caliph under whose rule Baghdad became the world's preeminent center of trade, culture and learning; King Faisal, the first Hashemite king of Iraq

NATIONAL HOLIDAY/INDEPENDENCE DAY

National Day, July 14

FESTIVALS/FAIRS

Babylon International Cultural Festival, September

SIGNIFICANT EVENTS IN FORMATION OF NATIONAL IDENTITY

3100 B.C.E.–539 B.C.E.   Sumerian, Akkadian, Assyrian, and Babylonian civilizations flourish in the region called the Cradle of Civilization.

539 B.C.E.   Cyrus the Great of Persia conquers Mesopotamia.

331 B.C.E.–312 B.C.E.   The Greeks under Alexander the Great conquer Mesopotamia. A new capital at Seleucia becomes a center of Hellenistic culture.

64 B.C.E.   The Persians conquer the region.

Fourth century–fifth century C.E.   The population is mostly converted to Nestorian Christianity, while the elite retains the ancient Zoroastrian religion.

627–680   Muslim Arabs conquer the weakened Persian Empire. The schism between the Sunni Muslims and the Shia Muslims becomes final.

762–892   A new capital for the Islamic Empire, the Caliphate, is built at Baghdad. Wars, usurpers and the rivalry between the Sunni and Shia Muslims greatly reduces the territory of the Caliphate to just the territory that approximates present Iraq.

1055–1258   Seljuk Turks overrun the Caliphate. They later erect a separate sultanate. The Arabs return to power, but Baghdad falls to the Mongols, who destroy the city and end the Caliphate. The economy is destroyed for centuries.

1533   Iraq comes under the rule of the Ottoman Empire. Peace allows agriculture and the economy to revive and flourish.

17th century   Portuguese, Dutch, and English sailors visit the port cities on the Gulf of Persia. Trading posts are established under European control.

1870s   The Ottoman authorities introduce modernization. Tramways are built in Baghdad, and a regular steamship service is begun.

1914–1919   At the outbreak of the First World War, British troops invade Iraq. The British and the French divide Western Asia in the Sykes-Picot Agreement. Iraq becomes a League of Nations mandate under the United Kingdom*.

1920–1932   Arabs in southern Iraq rebel against British rule. Prince Faisal of Hejaz, of the Hashemite line, becomes king of Iraq. The Shia majority in the south and the Kurds in the north fight for separation from Iraq and independence. King Faisal requests the British to stay to help maintain order.

1958   The monarchy is overthrown by army officers of the pan-Arab clique in a coup known as the July 14 Revolution. The royal family is executed. Iraq is declared a republic.

1960s–1970s   The Arab nationalist Baath Party overthrows the government in 1963. Saddam Hussein becomes president. War with Iran begins.

1988–1989   The Iraq government uses chemical weapons against the Kurdish city of Halabjah, leaving thousands dead. The Iran-Iraq War ends inconclusively. Massacres of dissident Shiites occur in the south of the country and in Baghdad.

1990–1991   The Iraqis invade Kuwait*, which is incorporated as a province in Iraq. The United States* leads a coalition of countries to oust the Iraqis from Kuwait. Iraq is bombed, but a cease-fire leaves Saddam Hussein in power in Baghdad. A United Nations safe haven is established in Iraqi Kurdistan*.

1995   Iraq is allowed to resume oil exports to buy food and medicine.

2003   The bombing of Baghdad and other cities marks the start of the Iraq War. American and British ground troops invade the country. Saddam Hussein disappears in the spreading chaos but is later captured. Kurdish troops aid the invasion and take control of the north.

2004   A spreading insurgency by Sunni supporters of Saddam Hussein includes suicide bombers targeting American soldiers, Kurds, and Shia Muslims, the largest population group in the country. Shia militias also target coalition troops as demands grow for majority control in the country.

2005   Shia political groups win national elections, with the Kurds winning in the north. Amid escalating violence, a new government is formed, with a Kurdish president and a Shia prime minister. Iraqi Kurdistan becomes a self-governing state within Iraq.

2006 In spite of an enlarged American military presence, the Sunni insurgency continues, and violence between Sunnis and Shiites leaves hundreds dead. Saddam Hussein is convicted of crimes against humanity and is executed.

2007 The security situation continues to deteriorate. U.S. President George W. Bush announces a dramatic increase in the number of troops to be sent to the country.

2008 By mid-2008, estimates of the causalities due to the Iraq War are over 1 million Iraqi deaths, thousands more injured, and 1.5 million refugees both inside and outside the country. About 4,500 military deaths have occurred between the American and coalition forces. Iraq remains a very unstable, divided country on the verge of disintegration.

2009 President Barack Obama of the United States announces plans to withdraw all American troops from Iraq by the end of 2011. Other coalition nations also announce the planned withdrawal of their troops.

ISRAEL

OFFICIAL NAME

Medīnat Yisrā'el (transliteration from Hebrew); Dawlat Isrā'īl (transliteration from Arabic); State of Israel (English)

POPULATION

7.283,600 (2009e)

INHABITANTS' NAME/NICKNAME

Israeli(s)

LANGUAGE/LANGUAGES

Hebrew, Arabic (official); English, Russian, others

RELIGION/RELIGIONS

Jewish, 76 percent; Muslim, 17 percent; Christian, 2 percent; Druze, 1.5 percent; other or no religion

NATIONAL FLAG

The flag depicts a blue Star of David on a white field between two horizontal blue stripes. The Zionist Movement first adopted the flag in 1891. The basic design symbolizes the *tallit,* the Jewish prayer shawl, which has blue and white stripes. The hexagram in the center is the *Magen David,* the Star or Shield of David.

COAT OF ARMS/SEAL

The coat of arms is a shield or crest showing a menorah surrounded by olive branches and the name of the country, Israel, in Hebrew letters beneath the menorah. The menorah has been a Jewish symbol for nearly 3,000 years, having been used in the Temple in Jerusalem. The olive branches symbolize peace.

CAPITAL CITY

Jerusalem; some embassies and administrative departments are in Tel Aviv

TYPE OF GOVERNMENT

Parliamentary democracy

NATIONAL EMBLEM

Magen David (Shield or Star of David); menorah

NATIONAL COLORS

White and blue

NATIONAL ANTHEM

The anthem was adopted at independence in 1948 and was probably originally a folk song based on a European folk song of unknown origin in the 19th century.

Hatikvah (Hebrew); The Hope (English)
As long as deep in the heart,
The soul of a Jew yearns,
And toward the east
An eye looks to Zion,
Our hope is not yet lost,

The hope of 2,000 years,
To be a free people in our land,
The land of Zion and Jerusalem.

CURRENCY

New Israeli sheqel

INTERNET IDENTIFIER

.il

VEHICLE IDENTIFICATION PLATES/STICKERS

IL

PASSPORT

The passport cover has the name of the country in Hebrew and English, the coat of arms, and the word *passport* in Hebrew and English

AIRLINES

El Al Israel Airlines; Arkia Israel Airlines

NATIONAL FLOWER

Rose of Sharon (unofficial)

NATIONAL ANIMAL

Allenby's gerbil (unofficial)

NATIONAL RESOURCES

Natural resources include timber, potash, copper ore, natural gas, phosphate rock, magnesium bromide, clays, and sand. Despite limited natural resources, intense development of agriculture and industry has made the country largely self-sufficient in food production. Tourism, particularly religious tourism, is a very important resource. The Jewish Diaspora is a source of foreign currency and investment.

FOODS

Falafel, the staple of Mizrahi Jews for centuries, is the national dish. It consists of deep-fried balls of mashed chickpeas served in pita bread with hummus (chickpea sauce) and *tahina* (sesame seed sauce); *shishlik,* grilled, skewered meats; *shwarma,* thin slices of grilled meat served in pita bread; *cholent,* a meat stew; and gefilte fish, a marinated white fish.

SPORTS/SPORTS TEAMS

Association football (soccer) and basketball are the two most popular sports in Israel. Israel national teams participate in many sports at an international level.

TEAM SPORTS

Badminton

Israel Badminton Team

Baseball

Israel Baseball Team; Israel Softball Team

Basketball

Israel Basketball Team; Israel Women's Basketball Team; Israel Wheelchair Basketball Team

Bowls

Israel Bowls Team

Cricket

Israel Cricket Team

Curling

Israel Curling Team

Football

Israel Football Team; Israel Women's Football Team; Israel Under-21 Football Team; Israel Rugby Union Team; Israel Rugby Union Team (Sevens), nickname Israel Sevens or Israel 7s; Israel Women's Rugby Union Team (Sevens), nickname Israel Sevens or Israel 7s; Israel American Football Team; Israel Beach Soccer Team; Israel Futsal Team

Handball

Israel Handball Team; Israel Women's Handball Team

Hockey

Israel Ice Hockey Team; Israel Junior Ice Hockey Team; Israel Field Hockey Team

Netball

Israel Netball Team

Racing

Israel Speedway Team

Table Tennis

Israel Table Tennis Team

Tennis

Israel Davis Cup Team; Israel Fed Cup Team

Volleyball

Israel Men's Volleyball Team; Israel Women's Volleyball Team; Israel Men's Beach Volleyball Team; Israel Women's Beach Volleyball Team

INDIVIDUAL SPORTS

Israel Amateur Boxing Team; Israel Archery Team; Israel Athletics Team; Israel Canoeing Team; Israel Cycling Team; Israel Equestrian Team; Israel Fencing Team; Israel Gymnastics Team; Israel Judo Team; Israel Karate Team: Israel Modern Pentathlon Team; Israel Rowing Team; Israel Sailing Team; Israel Shooting Team; Israel Swim Team; Israel Wrestling Team; Israel Tae Kwon Do Team; Israel Triathlon Team; Israel Weight Lifting Team; Israel Wrestling Team

WINTER SPORTS

Israel Alpine Ski Team; Israel Bandy Team; Israel Bobsled Team; Israel Curling Team; Israel Ice Hockey Team; Israel Junior Ice Hockey Team; Israel Luge Team; Israel Skating Team

NATIONAL HEROES OR PERSONIFICATIONS

Srulik, an illustrated character, symbolizes the Israeli culture and people. Srulik is the diminutive for the name Yisrael or Israel.

National heroes include Arthur Balfour, the British foreign secretary responsible for the Balfour Declaration of 1917, which supported the establishment of a Jewish homeland in Palestine*; David Ben-Gurion, the first prime minister of Israel; Theodor Herzl, the founder of modern Zionism; Moshe Dayan, military leader during the Six Day War; Yitzhak Rabin, military leader and prime minister until his assassination in 1995; and Golda Meier, prime minister during the Yom Kippur War.

NATIONAL HOLIDAY/INDEPENDENCE DAY

Yom Ha'Atzmaut (Israel Independence Day), date varies based on the Jewish calendar, usually late April or early May

FESTIVALS/FAIRS

Israel Festival, June; Red Sea Jazz Festival, August; Karmiel Dance Festival, July; Acco Fringe Theater Festival, October; Jerusalem International Film Festival, September

SIGNIFICANT EVENTS IN FORMATION OF NATIONAL IDENTITY

17th century B.C.E.   Israelites settle the Promised Land.

11th century B.C.E.–10th century B.C.E.   The first of a series of Jewish kingdoms is established. Jewish kingdoms and states rule the region intermittently for the next 1,000 years. In 960 B.C.E., King Solomon constructs the First Temple.

722 B.C.E.–720 B.C.E.   The Assyrians conquer Israel. Ten Jewish tribes are deported, becoming the 10 lost tribes.

586 B.C.E.–515 C.E.   The region is conquered by the Babylonians, and the First Temple is destroyed. Many Jews are taken to Babylonia as captives and slaves, the beginning of the Jewish

Diaspora. Many Jews return from Babylonia and the temple is rebuilt.

332 B.C.E.–160 B.C.E.   The Greeks of Alexander the Great conquers the region, and Greek culture is introduced. The Maccabean revolt begins against Greek restrictions on the practice of Judaism and desecration of the temple as part of an effort to impose Greek culture on the entire population of Judea.

129 B.C.E.–63 B.C.E.   Judea becomes an independent kingdom with expanded borders. Jewish cultural life flourishes. The Romans capture Jerusalem and impose Roman rule on Judea, which becomes a vassal kingdom.

66 C.E.–70 C.E.   The Jews revolt against Roman rule. The Romans destroy Jerusalem and the Second Temple. Many Jews are deported as slaves. A second revolt, the Bar Kokhba revolt, breaks out and is crushed. The majority of the Jews are driven from their homes by Roman soldiers and dispersed throughout the known world.

395–636   Israel is ruled by Greek Byzantines, the successors to the Roman Empire in the east. The region becomes a mainly Christian territory with a small Jewish minority that is barred from holding public office and is forbidden to enter Jerusalem except on one day each year, to mark the destruction of the temple.

636–1099   The Arab conquest introduces the Arabs' new religion, Islam. The majority of the Christians and pagans in the region adopt the religion of the conquerors. The Jews and Christians who retain their religions live under restrictions.

1099–1291   European Crusaders conquer the Holy Land. Massacres of non-Christians further devastate the Jewish population before Muslim rule is restored.

1517   The Holy Land comes under the rule of the Turkish Ottoman Empire. Jews who are persecuted or expelled from Europe are allowed to settle in Palestine.

1882–1917   Large-scale Jewish immigration from Russia* and Poland* begins as thousands flee the increasing persecutions and pogroms. The First Zionist Congress convenes under Theodor

Herzl in 1897, and the idea of a Jewish state in the ancestral homeland is adopted. Four centuries of Ottoman rule ends with Turkish defeat in the First World War. British Foreign Minister Arthur Balfour pledges support for the establishment of a Jewish national home in Palestine.

1918–1925   The British take over the region, later as a League of Nations mandate. Jewish immigration continues, mainly from Soviet Russia and Poland. Transjordan, later called Jordan*, is created on three-quarters of Palestine. Jewish nationalism becomes a potent political movement.

1933–1939   German Jews fleeing the rise of the Nazis and increasingly harsh restrictions flood into the region until the British place restrictions on immigration.

1939–1947   The Second World War breaks out in Europe, eventually leading to the Holocaust, the mass murder of over 6 million Jews. The United Nations proposes the establishment of an Arab state and a Jewish state in the remaining territory of the British mandate.

1948–1952   The British, unable to control the region, withdraw. Jewish leaders proclaim the independence of Israel, which is immediately invaded by armies from the surrounding Muslim states. Jordan takes control of the West Bank and East Jerusalem, and Egypt* takes over the Gaza Strip, but the Israelis hold the coast and most of present Israel until a cease-fire is imposed. Thousands of Arabs flee or are expelled from territory held by the Israelis. The Israeli victory begins a period of mass immigration of Jewish populations from Europe, the Middle East, and North Africa.

1967   War again breaks out in the Six Day War. The Israelis conquer the West Bank, reunite Jerusalem, overrun the Gaza Strip and Egypt's Sinai, and take the Golan Heights from Syria*.

1973   Egypt and Syria launch a surprise attack on Israel, beginning the Yom Kippur War.

1977–1982   Egypt and Israel sign a peace treaty and establish diplomatic relations. The Israelis return the Sinai to Egyptian control. Close diplomatic and military ties are maintained with the United States*.

1991–1994 A series of talks is held in an effort to establish a lasting peace in the region. The Palestinians under Israeli rule are granted limited self-government. Israel joins the ranks of the developed nations of the world.

2006–2008 Israel unilaterally withdraws from the Gaza Strip. Talks are undertaken between the Israeli government and the Palestinian Authority, the Palestinian autonomous government. Israel celebrates 60 years of independence. Peace talks begin between Israel and Syria. Israeli military forces enter the Gaza Strip after repeated rocket attacks from the strip targeting nearby Israeli cities and settlements.

2009 A cease-fire is arranged, and military forces leave the Gaza Strip. The launching of rockets into nearby Israeli settlements continues.

JORDAN

OFFICIAL NAME

Al-Mamlakahal-Urdunniyyahal-Hāšimiyyah (transliteration from Arabic); the Hashemite Kingdom of Jordan (English)

POPULATION

6,202,400 (2009e)

INHABITANTS' NAME/NICKNAME

Jordanian(s)

LANGUAGE/LANGUAGES

Arabic (official); English, others

RELIGION/RELIGIONS

Sunni Muslim, 90 percent; Christian, 7 percent; Shia Muslim, 2 percent; other or no religion

NATIONAL FLAG

The flag is a horizontal tricolor of black, white, and green with a red triangle at the hoist bearing a small, seven-pointed white star. The flag is based on the flag of the Arab Revolt against the Ottoman Empire during the First World War. The horizontal colors represent the Abbasid, Umayyad, and Fatimid caliphates (dynasties of the Arab Muslim Empire). The red triangle represents the Hashemite dynasty and the Arab revolt. The white star stands for the seven verses of the first sura in the Qur'an, and also for the unity of the Arab peoples.

COAT OF ARMS/SEAL

The coat of arms is a white field charged with a red sash and a crown. The crown symbolizes the monarchy. The sash symbolizes the Hashemite throne, and the scarlet color represents sacrifice, while the white background symbolizes purity. On the white is an eagle, symbolizing loftiness and might, perched on a blue globe, symbolizing the spread of Islam across the world. In front of the globe is a bronze shield, representing the defense of truth and right. Behind the eagle are two Arab Revolt flags. Traditional Arab weapons are arranged behind the shield, with three branches of wheat and a palm branch below. Stretching down from between the wheat and palm branches is the highest Jordanian medal, the decorative order of al-Nahda. Above the medal is a golden ribbon with the name of the country in Arabic.

CAPITAL CITY

Amman

TYPE OF GOVERNMENT

Constitutional monarchy

NATIONAL EMBLEM

Ancient city of Petra

NATIONAL COLORS

White and red

NATIONAL ANTHEM

The anthem has been in use since the country achieved independence in 1946. It was originally written as an anthem for a united country of all the Arabs.

As-salami Al-Malaki Al-Urdoni (transliteration from Arabic): Long Live the King (English)

Long live the King!
Long live the King!
His position is sublime,
His banners waving in glory supreme.

We achieved our goal,
On the day you gave us the mark,
A revolution gives us our motivation!
Flying over the shoulders of the highest
 comets

Oh! You king of Arabs,
From the best prophet you have.
The honor of dynasty,
Talked about in the depths of books!

All the youthful men
Are your armed armies
His determination never dies out!
(Literal translation) Getting from your mean-
 ing a symbol of well-being!/(Meaning) Get-
 ting from you the manners you have!

Oh! You king of Arabs
From the best prophet you have
The honor of dynasty,
Talked about in the depths of books!
May you stay the light and the guide,
A master in being away of all sins and
 wrongdoing,
Living your life happily and well-respected!
Under your flying flag rests the glory of all
 Arabs.

Oh! You king of Arabs,
From the best prophet you have.
The pleasure of dynasty,
Talked about in the depths of books!

CURRENCY

Jordanian dinar

INTERNET IDENTIFIER

.jo

VEHICLE IDENTIFICATION PLATES

HKJ

PASSPORT

The passport cover has the name of the country in Arabic and English, the coat of arms, and the word *passport* in Arabic and English.

AIRLINE

Royal Jordanian Airlines (ALIA)

NATIONAL RESOURCES

Natural resources include phosphates, potash, and shale oil. Jordan is a small country with limited natural resources. The country has traditionally relied on exports of phosphates and potash, overseas remittances, and foreign aid, but manufacturing and a more diversified economy are changing the traditional occupations.

FOODS

National dishes include *meze*, a variety of small dishes such as hummus, a dip made of chickpeas, and tabbouleh, a salad of bulgur, tomatoes, parsley, and lemon juice; kebab, skewered meat cooked over charcoal; *musakhan*, chicken roasted in olive oil and onion sauce on Arab bread; and *mensaf*, stewed lamb with yogurt served on a bed of rice.

SPORTS/SPORTS TEAMS

Association football (soccer) and basketball are the country's most popular sports. Jordan national teams participate in many sports at an international level.

TEAM SPORTS

Badminton

Jordan Badminton Team

Baseball

Jordan Softball Team

Basketball

Jordan Basketball Team; Jordan Wheelchair Basketball Team

Football

Jordan Football Team, nickname Nashama; Jordan Futsal Team

Table Tennis

Jordan Table Tennis Team

Tennis

Jordan Davis Cup Team; Jordan Fed Cup Team

Volleyball

Jordan Men's Volleyball Team; Jordan Women's Volleyball Team

INDIVIDUAL SPORTS

Jordan Amateur Boxing Team; Jordan Athletics Team; Jordan Cycling Team; Jordan Equestrian Team; Jordan Fencing Team; Jordan Gymnastics Team; Jordan Judo Team; Jordan Karate Team; Jordan Rowing Team; Jordan Shooting Team; Jordan Swim Team; Jordan Tae Kwon Do Team; Jordan Triathlon Team; Jordan Weight Lifting Team; Jordan Wrestling Team

NATIONAL HEROES OR PERSONIFICATIONS

The turbaned and robed Bedouin Arab is the personification of the Jordanian people.

National heroes include King Abdullah I, the first king of independent Jordan; and King Hussein, ruler of Jordan from 1952 to 1999.

NATIONAL HOLIDAY/INDEPENDENCE DAY

Independence Day, May 25

FESTIVALS/FAIRS

Jordan Festival, July; Jerash Festival of Culture and Arts, July

SIGNIFICANT EVENTS IN FORMATION OF NATIONAL IDENTITY

2000 B.C.E. Semetic Amorites settle around the Jordan River in the region called Canaan.

1950 B.C.E.–1550 B.C.E. Many of the large, fortified city-states are abandoned. Large and distinct communities seem to have arisen in northern and central Jordan, while the south was populated by a nomadic, Bedouin-type group of people.

334 B.C.E. Romans gain control over the Middle East.

632 C.E. Islam is introduced from Arabia to the south. The region becomes part of the Arab-Islamic empire under the Umayyads.

759–1258 The Abassids gradually lose control of the empire. Invasions by Mongols devastate much of the region and end the Arab Muslim Caliphate.

1512–1520 Ottoman Turks take control of the Arab lands. Palestine* becomes an Ottoman province.

1887–1888 The Turkish authorities divide Palestine into three districts—Jerusalem, Akka, and Nablus, which includes the east bank of the Jordan River, a region known as the Emirate of Transjordan.

1914 The Ottoman Empire joins Germany* and Austria-Hungary* when the First World War begins. The Arabs of the empire, encouraged by the British, begin a widespread revolt against Turkish rule.

1916–1918 The Arabs declare the independence of Arab provinces of the Ottoman Empire, but the British and French decide to divide the Arab region and retain the region as League of Nations mandates at the end of the war. The British occupy Palestine, including Transjordan.

1928 Transjordan, the region east of the Jordan, comprising about two-thirds of the Palestinian Mandate, is separated as a British client state under the rule of the Hashemite King Abdullah I.

1946–1949 The British relinquish their mandate at the end of the Second World War, and

Transjordan becomes independent. Jordan joins the other Arab states in attacking newly independent Israel*. When a cease-fire is signed, Jordan retains control of the region west of the Jordan River, known as the West Bank, and the eastern Arab section of the city of Jerusalem. Tens of thousands of Palestinian refugees remain in the kingdom.

1951 A Palestinian nationalist opposed to Jordanian control of the West Bank assassinates King Abdullah I. His successor, King Hussein, takes the throne and begins to modernize the kingdom.

1967 Jordan again joins the Arab states in war with Israel, resulting in the loss of East Jerusalem and the West Bank to Israeli control.

1970–1971 Palestinian militants, known as *fedeyeen,* become very powerful, threatening the sovereignty and security of the kingdom. Open fighting between the *fedeyeen* and the Jordanian military erupts. In 1971, the Jordanians drive the militants out of the country.

1994 Jordan concludes a peace treaty with Israel.

2000 Jordan offers to mediate when fighting breaks out between Israelis and Palestinians.

2003 Jordan remains carefully neutral when the United States* and its allies invade neighboring Iraq*.

2005 Three simultaneous bombs explode in luxury hotels in Amman, killing 57 people and leaving 115 wounded. The terrorist attacks, the worst in Jordan's history, are claimed by Al-Qaeda in Iraq.

2005–2009 The upheaval of the Iraqi War continues to disrupt the country. Several hundred thousand Iraqi refugees remain in the country, further straining resources.

KURDISTAN

OFFICIAL NAME

Herêma Kurdistan (Kurdish); Iraqi Kurdistan Region (English)

Kurdewari (Kurdish); Kürdistan (Kurdish); Kurdistan (English)

The name Kurdistan denotes a historical/ethnic/cultural/linguistic region divided between Turkey*, Iran*, Iraq*, Syria*, Azerbaijan*, and Armenia*. Herêma Kurdistan is the autonomous Kurdish state in northern Iraq.

POPULATION

5,930,800 (Iraqi Kurdistan, 2009e). The total Kurdish population of the Middle East is estimated at between 25 and 35 million.

INHABITANTS' NAME/NICKNAME

Kurd(s); Kurdistani(s)

LANGUAGE/LANGUAGES

Kurdish, Arabic, Assyrian (Syriac), Turkmen, others

RELIGION/RELIGIONS

Sunni Muslim, Shia Muslim, Christian, others

NATIONAL FLAG

The flag of Iraqi Kurdistan is the traditional Kurdish flag, recognized throughout the Kurdish regions of the Middle East. It consists of a horizontal tricolor of red, white, and green, with a golden sun with 21 rays in the center. Red symbolizes the blood of Kurdish martyrs and the continuing struggle for Kurdish freedom and dignity. Green symbolizes the beauty of the Kurdish landscape. White stands for peace and equality. The gold sun is an ancient Kurdish symbol, and the color stands for the source of life and the light of the people.

COAT OF ARMS/SEAL

The coat of arms has a central eagle holding the Kurdish sun above its head. The eagle is the symbol of the ancient Median Empire. The eagle has four wing feathers and four tail feathers, symbolizing the division of Kurdistan among four states, Turkey, Iraq, Iran, and Syria. The sun is also an ancient symbol representing the Kurds and Kurdistan. Below the eagle is a banner inscribed with the initials KRG, for the Kurdistan Regional Government.

CAPITAL CITY
Arbil

TYPE OF GOVERNMENT
Parliamentary democracy within United States*–occupied Iraq

NATIONAL EMBLEM
Golden sun

NATIONAL COLORS
Red, white, and green

NATIONAL ANTHEM
The anthem is based on a revolutionary poem written in 1938. It was adopted by Kurdish political parties and organizations across Kurdistan and became the official anthem of autonomous Kurdistan in Iraq.

Ey Reqîb (Kurdish); Hey Enemy! (English)

Oh enemy, the Kurdish nation is alive, its language is yet spoken
It shall not be defeated by the weapons of any age
Let no one say Kurds are dead
Kurds are living

Kurds are living, their flag will never fall
We, the youth, are the red color of the revolution
Watch our blood that we shed on this way
Let no one say Kurds are dead
Kurds are living

Kurds are living, their flag will never fall
We are the children of Medes and Cyaxares
Both our faith and religion are our homeland
Both our faith and religion are Kurd and Kurdistan
Let no one say Kurds are dead
Kurds are living

Kurds are living, their flag will never fall
The Kurdish youth have risen like lions
To adorn the crown of life with blood
Let no one say Kurds are dead
Kurds are living

Kurds are living, their flag will never fall
The Kurdish youth are ever-present and
Forever will be ready to sacrifice their lives
Sacrifice each life they have, each life they have!

CURRENCY
Iraqi dinar

VEHICLE IDENTIFICATION PLATES/STICKERS
IRQ Iraq (official); KDN Kurdistan (unofficial)

PASSPORT
Iraqi Kurds are Iraqi citizens and travel on Iraqi passports. Kurds living in other countries travel on the passports of those countries.

AIRLINE
Air Kurdistan

NATIONAL FLOWER
Yellow *nergis*

NATIONAL BIRD
Eagle

NATIONAL RESOURCES
Natural resources include coal, uranium, chrome, copper, iron, and hydropower. The Kurdish populations in neighboring countries and the Kurdish immigrant groups in Europe are a major source of foreign currency and investment. Petroleum, the region's major export, is shared with other parts of Iraq.

FOODS
National dishes vary from region to region. National specialties in Iraqi Kurdistan include

dokliw, a thick soup of meat and vegetables; *biryani,* a rice dish originally from India*; *kuki,* meat or vegetable pastries; *birinc,* white rice served with meat or vegetables; and *kofta* and *kubba,* dumplings stuffed with meat or vegetables.

Sports/Sports Teams

Association football (soccer) is the most popular game in Kurdistan. Traditional sports, such as wrestling and horse racing, are also very popular. Iraqi Kurdistan participates in football at an international level.

Team Sports

Football
Iraqi Kurdistan Football Team

National Heroes or Personifications

Al-Dinawari, Kurdish writer of the first book about the Kurds; Saladin, Muslim leader of 12th-century resistance to the European Crusaders; Prince Sharaf al-Din Biltisi, Kurdish noble who wrote a history of the Kurds in 1597; Abdal Khan, leader of a widespread Kurdish revolt against Ottoman rule in 1655; Muhammad Pasha of Rawanduz, leader of a Kurdish rebellion around Mosul and Erbil in the 1830s

National Holiday/Independence Day

Newroz, Kurdish national day, usually between March 18 and 23

Festivals/Fairs

Newroz, Kurdish New Year, usually between March 18 and 23

Significant Events in Formation of National Identity

612 B.C.E.   The ancestors of the Kurds capture Nineveh. The event is now celebrated as Newroz, the most important Kurdish holiday.

Second century B.C.E.   Tribal peoples occupy the region around the Zagros Mountains. The region often changes hands, although Persian influence is the most important.

Seventh century C.E.   Invading Arabs overrun the region, which becomes part of the Muslim Empire, the Caliphate. The Arabs' new religion, Islam, spreads across Kurdistan.

11th century   Seljuk Turks conquer most of Kurdistan, ending Arab domination.

12th century   During a brief period of independence, the Kurdish leader, Saladin, leads the Muslims against the incursion of the European armies during the Crusades.

1514–1800   The Ottoman Turks defeat the Persians and take control of western Kurdistan. Ruled as a separate principality, the Kurds are allowed considerable autonomy as the guardians of the Ottomans' eastern frontier.

19th century   The government of the Ottoman Empire centralizes all administration, ending the Kurds' autonomy, which triggers Kurdish uprisings in 1826, 1834, 1853–55, and 1880. The rebellions consolidate the Kurdish national movement. Kurds participate in massacres of the empire's minority Christians.

1914–1919   When the First World War begins, the Kurds are promised independence in return for fighting the Turks as allies of the British and French. Encouraged by the Turkish defeat and U.S. President Woodrow Wilson's project for independence for the non-Turkish peoples of the Ottoman Empire, the Kurds organize their independent state.

1920–1923   The Allies include provisions for an independent Kurdish state in the 1920 Treaty of Sèvres, a treaty the resurgent Turks reject. A second treaty, the Treaty of Lausanne, signed by the Allies and Turkey in 1923, omits the Kurds. Turkey, Iran, and the French and British occupation governments of Syria and Iraq partition historic Kurdistan over the opposition and pleas of the Kurdish people.

1922–1932 Betrayed by the West, the Kurds of northern Iraq rebel, provoking harsh reprisals by the British military. Sporadic revolts continue to disrupt British Iraq, revolts that continue following Iraqi independence in 1932. The Barzani clan becomes the leaders of the movement for Kurdish rights in Iraq.

1958–1968 The overthrow of the Iraqi monarchy allows the Kurds to organize politically. The Barzani clan leads a revolt against Iraqi rule, with support from neighboring Iran. A peace plan including Kurdish autonomy is adopted but is never implemented, following the overthrow of the Iraqi government by the radical Arab Baath Party. Iraqi Kurdistan is granted autonomy, but the terms of the agreement are never carried out.

1975–1979 An agreement between Iran and Iraq leads to the end of the Kurdish rebellion. The government initiates a program of forced Arabization. After renewed clashes between Iraqis and Kurd guerillas in 1977, the government destroys 600 Kurdish villages and deports 200,000 Kurds to other parts of Iraq. Saddam Hussein becomes president of Iraq.

1980–1988 The outbreak of the Iraq-Iran war initiates another Kurdish uprising. Saddam Hussein's government begins a systematic repression of the Kurdish region of northern Iraq, including a chemical attack on the city of Halabja, killing up to 5,000 civilians and leaving up to 10,000 injured. Ethnic Arabs are moved into depopulated Kurdish districts,

1991–2003 Saddam Hussein's invasion of Kuwait* provokes the West to begin the First Persian Gulf War. The Allies set up a no-fly zone over Iraqi Kurdistan. The Iraqi government withdraws from the region, allowing Iraqi Kurdistan to become a de facto independent state. The Iraqi government imposes an economic blockade on the region.

2003 The Second Persian Gulf War ends with the invasion of Iraq and the overthrow of Saddam Hussein. The Kurds are given autonomy in return for their participation in a United States*–backed Iraqi government.

2003–2008 The Iraqi Kurdistan region is a self-governing state within occupied Iraq. Oil production brings prosperity and a period of peace, a first for the Iraqi Kurds.

2009 The announcement of the planned withdrawal of American troops from Iraq by the end of 2011 raises new fears among the Kurdish population of renewed conflict and discrimination by the Arab majority in Iraq.

See also Iraq

KUWAIT

OFFICIAL NAME
Dawlat al-Kuwayt (transliteration from Arabic); State of Kuwait (English)

POPULATION
3,921,800 (2009e)

INHABITANTS' NAME/NICKNAME
Kuwaiti(s)

LANGUAGE/LANGUAGES
Arabic (official); English, others

RELIGION/RELIGIONS
Muslim, 85 percent (Sunni 70%, Shia 30%); Christian, Hindu, Parsi, other or no religion

NATIONAL FLAG
The flag has three equal horizontal stripes of green, white, and red, with a black trapezoid at the hoist. The flag carries the pan-Arab colors, the colors of the Arab Revolution in the early 20th century. Black symbolizes the defeat of Kuwait's enemies, green symbolizes the fertile land, white stands for purity, and red is the color of blood on Kuwaiti swords.

COAT OF ARMS/SEAL
The coat of arms consists of a small shield of the national flag superimposed on a falcon

with spread wings supporting a disk depicting an Arab dhow on blue and white water with a blue and white sky above and the name of the country in Arabic.

CAPITAL CITY

Kuwait City

TYPE OF GOVERNMENT

Constitutional monarchy

NATIONAL EMBLEM

Arab dhow; Kuwait Towers

NATIONAL COLORS

Blue and white

NATIONAL ANTHEM

The anthem was adopted in 1978 and is played only on special occasions, so that it is rarely heard in Kuwait itself.

Al-Nasheed Al-Watani (transliteration from Arabic); National Anthem (English)

Kuwait, Kuwait, Kuwait,
My country,
In peace live, in dignity,
Your face bright,
Your face bright,
Your face bright with majesty,
Kuwait, Kuwait, Kuwait,
My country.

O cradle of ancestry,
Who put down its memory,
With everlasting symmetry,
Showing all eternity,
Those Arabs were heavenly,
Kuwait, Kuwait, Kuwait,
My country.

Blessed be
My country,
A homeland for harmony,
Warded by true sentry,
Giving their souls aptly,
Building high its history,
Kuwait, Kuwait, Kuwait,
My country.

We're for you, my country,
Led by faith and loyalty,
With its Prince equally,
Fencing us all fairly,
With warm love and verity,
Kuwait, Kuwait, Kuwait,
My country,
In peace live, in dignity.

CURRENCY

Kuwaiti dinar

INTERNET IDENTIFIER

.kw

VEHICLE IDENTIFICATION PLATES/STICKERS

KWT

PASSPORT

The passport cover has the name of the country in Arabic and English, the coat of arms, and the word *passport* in Arabic and English.

AIRLINE

Kuwait Airways

NATIONAL FLOWER

Arfaj

NATIONAL TREE

Royal palm (unofficial)

NATIONAL BIRD

Falcon (unofficial)

NATIONAL RESOURCES

Natural resources, other than petroleum, natural gas, fish, and shrimp, are negligible. Kuwait's oil reserves, among the largest in the world, support an affluent lifestyle for the Kuwaitis.

FOODS

Hummus, a spread or dip made of chickpeas, sesame, and olive oil; falafel, fried patties of mashed chickpea; *foul,* a slow-cooked mash of brown beans and red lentils; *marag,* meat or fish fried or boiled and then combined with other ingredients and spices and steamed together in a large pot; and *aish,* Arab flatbread, are considered national dishes.

SPORTS/SPORTS TEAMS

Association football (soccer) is the country's most popular sport. Rugby football is also very popular. Kuwait national teams participate in many sports at an international level.

TEAM SPORTS

Badminton

Kuwait Badminton Team

Basketball

Kuwait Women's Basketball Team; Kuwait Wheelchair Basketball Team

Cricket

Kuwait Cricket Team

Football

Kuwait Football Team, nickname Al Azraq; Kuwait Women's Football Team; Kuwait Futsal Team; Arabian Gulf Rugby Union Team (Sevens), nickname Arabian Gulf Sevens or Arabian Gulf 7s; Arabian Gulf Women's Rugby Union Team (Sevens), nickname Arabian Gulf Sevens or Arabian Gulf 7s; Arabian Gulf Rugby Union Team (Arabian Gulf teams represent several Arab countries in the Persian Gulf region)

Handball

Kuwait Handball Team; Kuwait Women's Handball Team; Kuwait Beach Handball Team; Kuwait Women's Beach Handball Team

Hockey

Kuwait Ice Hockey Team; Kuwait Field Hockey Team

Table Tennis

Kuwait Table Tennis Team

Tennis

Kuwait Davis Cup Team

Volleyball

Kuwait Men's Volleyball Team; Kuwait Women's Volleyball Team

INDIVIDUAL SPORTS

Kuwait Amateur Boxing Team; Kuwait Archery Team; Kuwait Athletics Team; Kuwait Cycling Team; Kuwait Equestrian Team; Kuwait Fencing Team; Kuwait Judo Team; Kuwait Karate Team; Kuwait Modern Pentathlon Team; Kuwait Rowing Team; Kuwait Sailing Team; Kuwait Shooting Team; Kuwait Swim Team; Kuwait Tae Kwon Do Team; Kuwait Weight Lifting Team

WINTER SPORTS

Kuwait Ice Hockey Team

NATIONAL HEROES OR PERSONIFICATIONS

Sabah bin Jaber, the first emir in the mid-18th century; Abdullah III al-Salim al-Sabah, the emir who ended the British protectorate and gave Kuwait its independence in 1961

NATIONAL HOLIDAY/INDEPENDENCE DAY

National Day, February 25; Liberation Day, February 26

FESTIVALS/FAIRS

National Day celebrations, February; Liberation Festival, February; Ramadan, dates vary; Gift Exhibition, biannual in January

SIGNIFICANT EVENTS IN FORMATION OF NATIONAL IDENTITY

Third century B.C.E.   Greeks colonize Falaka Island on the coast of present Kuwait.

127 B.C.E.–**325** C.E.   The Greek-speaking state of Characene is founded around the large Bay of

Kuwait. The region comes under Roman rule but continues as an important trading center between the Mediterranean and Europe.

Seventh century Arab Muslims from southern Arabia conquer the region, which comes under the Bani Khaled rulers of eastern Arabia.

1612–1750 Tribal groups from central Arabia settle the region around Kuwait Bay and accept Bani Khaled authority. The name *Kuwait* comes from the small *kout,* or castle, of a prince of the Bani Khaled. Kuwait becomes a major center of the spice trade between India* and Europe, attracting traders from across the Arab world and beyond.

1756–1897 Bani Khaled power wanes, and the Kuwaitis become more independent. They elect Sabah bin Jaber as the first emir. The power of the Ottoman Empire expands to include Kuwait, which becomes a vassal state under the al-Sabah emirs.

1897–1922 The Ottoman authorities recognize Kuwait as autonomous emirate. In 1899, the emir signs a protectorate agreement with the British. The British and Ottoman empires diplomatically recognize the autonomy of Kuwait City and its hinterlands in 1913. A treaty with Saudi Arabia* sets the boundaries between the two countries in 1922.

1961–1980 Kuwait becomes fully independent as the British protectorate ends. Oil turns the small country into a major exporter and one of the world's most affluent countries.

1980–1990 Kuwait heavily finances neighboring Iraq* during its eight-war with the Islamic Republic of Iran*. At the end of the war, Iraqi leader Saddam Hussein asks Kuwait to forgive a U.S. $65 billion debt, but the Kuwaiti government refuses. Tensions between the two countries mount, and several border skirmishes occur.

1990–1994 Saddam Hussein's Iraqi military invades Kuwait, which is annexed to Iraq as a province. After diplomatic efforts fail, the United States* leads a coalition of nations in the liberation of Kuwait. The Iraqis retreat, but damage hundreds of oil wells, sack museums and private homes, and steal hundreds of luxury cars. Many Kuwaitis disappear during the Iraqi occupation. Iraq accepts the demarcation of the Kuwait-Iraqi border.

2000–2009 In the aftermath of the Iraqi invasion, politics are more liberalized and more Kuwaitis are given the vote. Some new restrictions on newspapers and other media are implemented in 2005. Women vote for the first time in 2006. Kuwait becomes the most cosmopolitan country in the Persian Gulf region, with a population drawn from the Middle East, India, Europe, and other areas.

LEBANON

OFFICIAL NAME

Al-Jumhūriyyah al-Lubnāniyyah (transliteration from Arabic); La République Libanaise (French); Lebanese Republic (English)

POPULATION

4,199,300 (2009e)

INHABITANTS' NAME/NICKNAME

Lebanese

LANGUAGE/LANGUAGES

Arabic (official); French (de facto official); English, Armenian, others

RELIGION/RELIGIONS

Seventeen religious sects (named in parentheses) are recognized by the Lebanese government: Muslim, 50 percent (Shia, Sunni, Druze, Isma'ilite, Alawite); Christian, 38 percent (Maronite Catholic, Greek Orthodox, Melkite Catholic, Armenian Orthodox, Syrian Catholic, Armenian Catholic, Syrian Orthodox, Roman Catholic, Chaldean, Assyrian, Copt, Protestant); other or no religion

NATIONAL FLAG

The flag has three horizontal stripes of red, white, and red, the white twice the width of the red stripes. A centered green cedar tree on the white touches the red stripes. The red represents the Lebanese people's struggle for independence, and white stands for peace and purity and the white snow that covers Lebanon's mountains. The cedar represents happiness and prosperity.

COAT OF ARMS/SEAL

The coat of arms is a red shield with a diagonal white stripe charged with a centered green cedar tree. The symbolism of the colors and tree are the same as on the national flag.

MOTTO

All for country, for glory, and the flag! (English translation)

CAPITAL CITY

Beirut

TYPE OF GOVERNMENT

Parliamentary republic

NATIONAL EMBLEM

Cedar tree (the cedars of Lebanon)

NATIONAL COLORS

Red and white

NATIONAL ANTHEM

The anthem was adopted as the Lebanese anthem in 1927, before the country achieved independence from France.

Koullouna Lilouataan Lil Oula Lil Alam (transliteration from Arabic); National Anthem of Lebanon (English)

We are all for our nation, for our emblem and glory!
Our valor and our writings are the envy of the ages.
Our mountains and our valleys, they bring forth stalwart men.
And to Perfection all our efforts we devote.

We are all for our Nation, for our emblem and glory!

Our Elders and our children, they await our Country's call,
And on the Day of Crisis they are as Lions of the Jungle.
The heart of our East is forever Lebanon,
May God preserve Him until the end of time?
We are all for our Nation, for our emblem and glory!

The Gems of the East are his land and sea.
Throughout the world his good deeds flow from pole to pole.
And his name is his glory since time began.
The Cedar Symbol—His symbol for Eternity—is His Pride.
We are all for our Nation, for our emblem and glory!

PATRON SAINT

Saint Maron

CURRENCY

Lebanese lira

INTERNET IDENTIFIER

.lb

VEHICLE IDENTIFICATION PLATES/ STICKERS

RL

PASSPORT

The passport cover has the name of the country and the word *passport* in Arabic, an outline map of Lebanon behind a cedar tree, and the name of the country and the word for passport in French.

AIRLINE

Middle East Airlines MEA

NATIONAL FLOWER

Cyclamen (unofficial)

NATIONAL TREE
Lebanon cedar

NATIONAL RESOURCES
Natural resources include limestone, iron ore, salt, a surplus of water in a water-poor region, and arable land. The well-educated population has the highest proportion of skilled labor in the Arab world, a level comparable to most European countries. Tourism has been damaged by political upheavals but has the potential to become a major industry.

FOODS
Meze, variety of small dishes or appetizers; *kebbeh,* lamb pounded to a fine paste and mixed with bulgur, served raw or baked in flat patties or rolled into balls and fried; *lahm mishwi,* a dish of lamb or mutton, tomatoes, peppers, and onions; hummus, a sauce or dip of chickpeas; and tabbouleh, a salad of bulgur, tomatoes, parsley, and mint, are considered national dishes.

SPORTS/SPORTS TEAMS
Basketball and football are the most popular sports. Lebanon national teams participate in many sports at an international level.

TEAM SPORTS
Badminton
Lebanon Badminton Team

Basketball
Lebanon Basketball Team; Lebanon Women's Basketball Team; Lebanon Wheelchair Basketball Team

Football
Lebanon Football Team, nickname the Cedars; Lebanon Women's Football Team; Lebanon Rugby Union Team, nickname the Cedars; Lebanon Futsal Team; Lebanon Touch Football Team; Lebanon Women's Touch Football Team; Lebanon Rugby League Team, nickname the Cedars

Handball
Lebanon Handball Team; Lebanon Women's Handball Team

Hockey
Lebanon Field Hockey Team

Racing
A1 Team Lebanon

Table Tennis
Lebanon Table Tennis Team

Tennis
Lebanon Davis Cup Team; Lebanon Fed Cup Team

Volleyball
Lebanon Men's Volleyball Team; Lebanon Women's Volleyball Team

INDIVIDUAL SPORTS
Lebanon Aikido Team; Lebanon Amateur Boxing Team; Lebanon Archery Team; Lebanon Athletics Team; Lebanon Canoeing Team; Lebanon Cycling Team; Lebanon Equestrian Team; Lebanon Fencing Team; Latvia Judo Team; Lebanon Karate Team; Lebanon Modern Pentathlon Team; Lebanon Rowing Team; Lebanon Sailing Team; Lebanon Shooting Team; Lebanon Swim Team; Lebanon Tae Kwon Do Team; Lebanon Weight Lifting Team; Lebanon Wrestling Team

WINTER SPORTS
Lebanon Alpine Ski Team; Lebanon Biathlon Team

NATIONAL HEROES OR PERSONIFICATIONS
Émile Eddé, prime minister under French rule and a leader of the independence move-

ment; Bechara El Khoury, first president of independent Lebanon; Rafik Hariri, the former prime minister assassinated, possibly by Syrian agents, in 2005. His death set off the Cedar Revolution, leading to the withdrawal of all Syrian military troops from the country.

NATIONAL HOLIDAY/INDEPENDENCE DAY
Independence Day, November 22

FESTIVALS/FAIRS
Baalbeck Festival, July–August; Beiteddine Festival, July; Byblos Festival, July; Tyre Festival, July

SIGNIFICANT EVENTS IN FORMATION OF NATIONAL IDENTITY
2700 B.C.E.–450 B.C.E. The Phoenician civilization flourishes as a Mediterranean maritime culture.

333 B.C.E. The Greeks of Alexander the Great overrun the region. At Alexander's death, his general creates the Seleucid Empire in Mesopotamia and the eastern Mediterranean.

64 B.C.E. Syria* and Lebanon become part of the Roman Empire.

395 C.E. The Roman Empire is divided into a western empire and an eastern, or Byzantine, empire that takes control of Lebanon.

Sixth century A series of powerful earthquakes destroys many cities and kills over 30,000 people, adding to the disorder and chaos prevailing in the Byzantine Empire. The turbulence weakens the Byzantine Empire just as the Muslims surge out of Arabia.

635 Arabian Muslims overrun the region, with many Byzantine Christians taking refuge in the mountains.

Ninth century–11th century Shia Muslims move into the area, followed by the Druze in the eleventh century. Each ethnic and religious group maintains control of a specific geographical area.

1516 The Turks conquer Lebanon and add it to their expanding Ottoman Empire.

19th century The large Christian groups, particularly the Maronites, adopt French culture and styles. In 1861, following persecution of the Christians of the region, the French establish a protectorate, a small, mostly Christian enclave on the coast.

1918–1926 At the end of the First World War, France* establishes a League of Nations mandate over Syria and Lebanon. Districts bordering the Christian enclave are added to the area the French call Greater Lebanon.

1941 Lebanon is declared an independent republic by the Free French during the Second World War. Lebanon's unwritten national pact dictates a Christian president and a Muslim prime minister. Called the Switzerland of the Middle East, multicultural and multireligious Lebanon flourishes as banking and recreation center for the Arab world.

1948 Lebanon, pressured by Arab neighbors, joins the Arabian attack on the new state of Israel*. With the Arab defeat, over 100,000 Palestinians flee to Lebanon.

1950–1975 The high birthrate of the Muslims residents of Lebanon, particularly the Shia portion of the population, reduces the former Christian majority to a minority, creating serious religious tensions. Interference by neighboring countries adds to the growing chaos. Fighting breaks out between Christians and Muslims, leading to the 15-year Lebanese civil war.

1990–1995 The strife is ended by the occupation of Lebanon by Syrian forces. The country's militias disarm, except for the Shia Hezbollah, and the country begins to recover.

2005 Mass demonstrations demand the withdrawal of Syrian troops, the so-called Cedar Revolution.

2006–2008 In south Lebanon, a Hezbollah attack on an Israeli patrol begins the July War. Israel responds with intense air strikes and incursions by Israeli ground forces. The July War greatly harms Lebanon's economy, which was just beginning to flourish again after the Lebanese Civil War, and exacerbates tensions between the many religious sects in the country. All major Lebanese parties sign an accord in an effort to bring peace to the country. Lebanon establishes diplomatic relations with Syria for the first time since the two countries gained independence in the 1940s.

2009 The largely Shia Muslim south bordering on Israel* remains tense, amid calls from religious leaders for the continued militarization of the region. Beirut and areas in the north continue to recover as economic activity expands.

LIBYA

Official Name

al-jamāhīriyyatu l-'arabiyyatu l-lībiyyatu š-ša'biyyatu l-ištirākiyyatu l-'uZmà (transliteration from Arabic); Great Socialist People's Libyan Arab Jamahiriya (English)

Population

6,174,600 (2009e)

Inhabitants' Name/Nickname

Libyan(s)

Language/Languages

Arabic (official); Italian, English, Berber dialects, others

Religion/Religions

Sunni Muslim, 97 percent; others or no religion

National Flag

The flag is a solid green field, the only national flag in the world with just one color and with no design, insignia, or other symbols. The green reflects the people's devotion to Islam and is the national color of Libya.

Coat of Arms/Seal

The coat of arms has a central solid green shield, representing the green cloak of the prophet Muhammad, as well as Muammar al-Gaddafi's Green Revolution. Behind the shield is the Hawk of Quraysh, the emblem of the tribe of the prophet Muhammad. A banner below the hawk is inscribed, in Arab script, "Federation of Arab Republics."

Capital City

Tripoli

Type of Government

Military dictatorship

National Emblem

Muammar al-Gaddafi's Green Book

National Colors

Green

National Anthem

The anthem is based on the Muslim call to prayer and was originally an Egyptian military marching song.

Allahu Akbar (transliteration from Arabic); God Is Great! (English)
God is great, God is great
God is above any attacker's tricks,
And God is the best helper for the oppressed,
God is above any attacker's tricks,
And God is the best helper for the oppressed,
With certainty and with weapons I shall defend
My nation, truth's light shining in my hand;
Say it with me, say it with me:
God is greatest, God is greatest, God is greatest!

God is great over the attacker's tricks!
O this world, watch and listen:
The enemy came coveting my position,
O this world, watch and listen:
The enemy came coveting my position,
I shall fight with weapons and defenses
And if I die, I'll take him with me!
Say it with me, say it with me:
God is greatest, God is greatest, God is greatest!
God is above any attacker's tricks!

CURRENCY

Libyan dinar

INTERNET IDENTIFIER

.ly

VEHICLE IDENTIFICATION PLATES/ STICKERS

LAR (unofficial)

PASSPORT

The passport cover has the name of the country in Arabic, the coat of arms, and the word *passport* in Arabic.

AIRLINES

Libyan Airlines; Afriqiyah Airlines

NATIONAL BIRD

Peregrine falcon

NATIONAL RESOURCES

Natural resources include petroleum, natural gas, and gypsum. The Libyan economy depends primarily upon revenues from the oil sector, which contribute about 95 percent of export earnings, Substantial revenues from the energy sector coupled with a small population give Libya one of the highest per capita gross domestic products in Africa, but little of this income flows down to the lower orders of society.

FOODS

Usban, entrails of sheep or camels stuffed with rice and meat is the national dish. Couscous, cracked wheat or semolina pasta, is a national dish, often prepared with a spicy sauce of hot peppers, tomatoes, chickpeas, and vegetables. Other national specialties include macaroni, a legacy of Italian colonization; *ruuz,* a rice dish with a variety of spices, meat, and vegetables; *sharba libiya,* a spiced lamb and tomato soup; *baxin,* barley pasta; *tajeen dajad,* chicken cooked in a special ceramic pot called a *tagine; tabikha bil houmous,* chicken prepared with chickpeas; *tabikha bil karate,* beef and leek soup; and *haraymi,* a chicken dish with okra, tomato, and spices.

SPORTS/SPORTS TEAMS

Association football (soccer) is the country's most popular sport. Basketball is also widely played. Libya national teams participate in many sports at an international level.

TEAM SPORTS

Basketball

Libya Basketball Team; Libya Women's Basketball Team; Libya Wheelchair Basketball Team

Football

Libya Football Team, nickname the Greens; Libya Women's Football Team, nickname the Greens; Libya Futsal Team

Handball

Libya Handball Team; Libya Beach Handball Team; Libya Handball Team; Libya Women's Handball Team

Hockey

Libya Field Hockey Team

Table Tennis

Libya Table Tennis Team

Tennis

Libya Davis Cup Team

Volleyball

Libya Men's Volleyball Team

INDIVIDUAL SPORTS

Libya Archery Team; Libya Athletics Team; Libya Cycling Team; Libya Equestrian Team;

Libya Gymnastics Team: Libya Judo Team; Libya Rowing Team; Libya Sailing Team; Libya Shooting Team; Libya Swim Team; Libya Tae Kwon Do Team; Libya Weight Lifting Team

NATIONAL HEROES OR PERSONIFICATIONS

Abdullah ibn Saad, the leader of the Arab conquerors of the region in the seventh century; Sulaiman al-Barouni, the leader of the anti-Italian movement in Tripolitania from 1911; Omar Mukhtar, leader of the Libyan uprising against Italian rule; Muammar al-Gadaffi, leader and guide of the Green Revolution

NATIONAL HOLIDAY/INDEPENDENCE DAY

Revolution Day, September 1

FESTIVALS/FAIRS

National Day celebrations, September; Nalut Spring Festival, March

SIGNIFICANT EVENTS IN FORMATION OF NATIONAL IDENTITY

Fourth century B.C.E.–fifth century B.C.E. Phoenicians establish posts for trade with the indigenous Berber tribes. Carthage, the greatest of the Phoenician colonies, extends its authority across North Africa.

630 B.C.E. Greeks establish the city of Cyrene and other colonies in eastern Libya.

96 B.C.E.–45 B.C.E. The Romans take control of the region, creating the provinces of Tripolitania and Cyrenaica.

300 B.C.E.–435 C.E. Christianity is introduced and becomes the major religion. Vandals crossing from Europe devastate the region in 435. Tripolitania, Cyrenaica, and the interior region of Fezzan later comes under Byzantine rule.

643–645 Invading Arabs conquer Tripolitania and Cyrenaica, absorbing or displacing the earlier population. Islam replaces Christianity as the predominant religion.

1517–1553 The Turks of the Ottoman Empire conquer the region, keeping the traditional regions as *vilayets,* or provinces.

1911–1934 Italians occupy Tripolitania, Cyrenaica, and Fezzan during the Italo-Turkish War. The three colonies are merged into the Italian colony of Libya.

1943–1947 During the Second World War, the British occupy Tripolitania and Cyrenaica and the French take control of Fezzan. Italy* relinquishes all claims in Libya.

1951–1969 Libya becomes independent as the United Kingdom of Libya under King Idris I. King Idris maintains close relations with the United Kingdom* and the United States*. Libya prospers from its extensive oil reserves.

1969 A coup led by Colonel Muammar al-Gadaffi overthrows the monarchy. Revolutionaries proclaim the Libyan Arab Republic. Colonel Gadaffi closes American and British bases and nationalizes many industries.

1980s Libya is accused of sponsoring terrorist groups in Europe, Asia and Africa, including masterminding the 1988 bombing of Pan Am flight 103 over Scotland*. Western demands for Libya to extradite the culprits begin a decade of negotiations and economic sanctions.

1999 The Libyan government turns over the bombing suspects and makes other policy changes designed to lessen tensions with the Western powers.

2003 The Gadaffi government announces its decision to abandon its weapons of mass destruction programs and pay almost U.S. $3 billion to the victims of the 1988 Pan Am bombing.

2006–2008 The United States restores diplomatic relations with Libya after decades of tensions. In September 2008, the Italian government apologizes for colonial damage to Libya and agrees to pay U.S. $5 billion in compensation.

2009 Gaddafi is elected chairman of the African Union, formally ending Libya's long political isolation.

MAURITANIA

OFFICIAL NAME

Al-Jumhūriyyah al-Islāmiyyah al-Mūrītāniyyah (transliteration from Arabic); Islamic Republic of Mauritania (English)

POPULATION

3,112,500 (2009e)

INHABITANTS' NAME/NICKNAME

Mauritanian(s)

LANGUAGE/LANGUAGES

Arabic (official); French, Pulaar, Soninke, Hassaniya, Wolof, others

RELIGION/RELIGIONS

Sunni Muslim, 99 percent; traditional beliefs, other or no religion

NATIONAL FLAG

The flag is a green field with a large gold crescent moon, points to the top, and a gold five-pointed star. The colors are considered pan-African colors, although the green symbolizes Islam and the gold stands for the sands of the Sahara Desert. The crescent moon and star are traditional symbols of Islam, the country's primary religion.

COAT OF ARMS/SEAL

The coat of arms is a circle bearing the same green background and gold crescent and star as the national flag, with the addition of a white palm tree and desert plants. The white border around the circle is inscribed with the name of the country in Arabic and French.

MOTTO

Honneur, fraternité, justice (French); Honor, Fraternity, Justice (English)

CAPITAL CITY

Nouakchott

TYPE OF GOVERNMENT

Parliamentary republic

NATIONAL COLORS

Green and gold

NATIONAL ANTHEM

The anthem is based on an old poem and has a unique rhythm known as *fatchou* that makes it difficult to sing, so the anthem is often listed erroneously as instrumental only.

Anthem of Mauritania

Be a helper for God, and censure what is
  forbidden,
And turn with the law which, which he wants
  you to follow,
Hold no one to be useful or harmful, except
  for him,
And walk the path of the chosen one, and die
  while you are on it!
For what was sufficient for the first of us, is
  sufficient for the last one, too.
And leave those people who do evil things
  with respect to God.
They misrepresented him by making him similar, and made all kinds of excuses.
They made bold claims, and blackened
  notebooks.
They let the nomads and the sedentary people, both make bitter experiences,
And the great sins of their [doctrinal] innova-
  tions bequeathed small.
And just in case a disputant calls you to dispute about their claims,
Do not, then, dispute on them, except by way
  of an external dispute.

CURRENCY

Mauritanian ouguiya

INTERNET IDENTIFIER

.mr

VEHICLE IDENTIFICATION PLATES/ STICKERS

RIM

PASSPORT

The passport cover has the name of the country in Arabic and French, the coat of arms, and the word for passport in Arabic and French.

AIRLINE

Mauritania Airways

NATIONAL TREE

Palm (unofficial)

NATIONAL RESOURCES

Natural resources include iron ore, gypsum, copper, phosphate, diamonds, gold, oil, and fish. The national waters in the Atlantic are among the richest fishing grounds in the world, but overexploitation by foreign fishing boats threatens this key resource. Exports of iron ore, gold, and copper have increased in recent years.

FOODS

National dishes include *mechoui,* whole roast lamb; couscous, a tiny pasta made of semolina and flour, steamed and served with fish or lamb and vegetables in the Mauritanian version of this popular North African dish; *chakchouka,* a salad of greens and vegetables in tomato sauce with poached eggs; and *chubbagin lélé et raabie,* fish prepared with eggplant, carrots, cabbage, sweet potatoes, onions, and hot peppers.

SPORTS/SPORTS TEAMS

Association football (soccer) is the country's most popular sport. Mauritania national teams participate in many sports at an international level.

TEAM SPORTS

Basketball

Mauritania Basketball Team; Mauritania Women's Basketball Team

Football

Mauritania Football Team, nickname Mourabitounes; Mauritania Women's Football Team, nickname Mourabitounes; Mauritania Rugby Union Team

Handball

Mauritania Handball Team

Table Tennis

Mauritania Table Tennis Team

Volleyball

Mauritania Men's Volleyball Team

INDIVIDUAL SPORTS

Mauritania Athletics Team; Mauritania Fencing Team; Mauritania Judo Team; Mauritania Swim Team; Mauritania Wrestling Team;

NATIONAL HEROES OR PERSONIFICATIONS

Nasr ad-Din, a Berber leader who led the resistance to the Arab invasion in the 17th century; Ma al'Aynayn, a religious and political leader who fought European colonization in the 19th century; Ahmed al-Hiba, leader of the anti-French resistance at the end of the 19th century

NATIONAL HOLIDAY/INDEPENDENCE DAY

Independence Day, November 28

FESTIVALS/FAIRS

Korite Festival, variable dates; Tabaski Festival, variable dates

SIGNIFICANT EVENTS IN FORMATION OF NATIONAL IDENTITY

Third century C.E.–seventh century C.E. Berber migrations from North Africa displace the earlier African tribal people. Traders introduce Islam, but most Berbers maintain their tribal religion.

9th century–10th century The African Empire of Ghana has its capital in present southwestern

Mauritania. In 1076, Islamic warriors known as Almoravid attack and conquer the Ghana Empire.

15th century–16th century Arab invaders and migrants overcome most resistance from the local Berbers. European sailors and traders establish settlements.

1644–1674 The Berbers, led by Nasr ad-Din, fight the invading Maqil Arabs, led by the Beni Hassan tribe. The war is known as the Char Bouba war or the Mauritanian Thirty Years' War. The defeated Berbers become a subordinate class under the domination of the Arabs.

1850s–1860s French colonial forces move north from Senegal* to take control of southern Mauritania.

1898–1904 The French win the allegiance of the Moors, the predominate group in Mauritania. The French extend their rule over the Mauritanian emirates in the north of the country and create a colonial administration in 1904.

1912–1920 The last emirate, Adrar, falls to French forces. Mauritania becomes part of French West Africa. The French bring an end to legal slavery and the endemic tribal wars.

1946–1960 Mauritania becomes an overseas territory of the French Republic. In 1958, the country is given autonomous status within the French Union and becomes independent in 1960.

1976 Mauritania and Morocco* divide the territory of the abandoned Spanish colony of Western Sahara (Sahrawi*) over the objections of its inhabitants, who fight for independence. In 1979, Mauritania withdraws from Western Sahara and Morocco annexes the whole region.

1989 Riots break out in Mauritania and Senegal over a border dispute. Tens of thousands of black Mauritanians are driven from their homes and forced across the border into Senegal. Others are attacked by the Arab Mauritanians, who seize lands and properties. Hundreds die in the violence.

2002–2005 The political party Action for Change, which campaigns for greater rights for blacks and descendants of slaves, is banned. Several coup plots are uncovered or fail. Locusts obliterate crops, with food aid coming from the United Nations and other countries. A military coup overthrows the government.

2006–2008 Offshore oil production begins. The parliament outlaws slavery, which is still widespread. A military coup overthrows the new president, the country's first democratically elected leader.

2009 Mauritania joins the ranks of the world's oil producers. Sanctions by the African Union remain in place following the 2008 military coup.

MOROCCO

OFFICIAL NAME
Al-Mamlaka al-Maghribiyya (transliteration from Arabic); Kingdom of Morocco (English)

POPULATION
33,854,900 (2009e)

INHABITANTS' NAME/NICKNAME
Moroccan(s)

LANGUAGE/LANGUAGES
Arabic (official); French, Amazigh (Berber), others

RELIGION/RELIGIONS
Muslim, 98 percent; Christian, 1 percent; Jewish, other or no religion

NATIONAL FLAG
The flag is a red field charged with a black-bordered green interwoven star or pentagram. Red represents Morocco's royal family's descent from Muhammad through Fatima, the wife of Ali, the fourth caliph of the Muslim Empire. The flag of Morocco before 1915 was a plain red field.

COAT OF ARMS/SEAL
The coat of arms has a central crest showing a green interwoven star on a red background

before a representation of the Atlas Mountains and a rising star. Above the crest is a royal crown, and the crest is supported by two golden lions. Below the crest is a banner inscribed in Arabic with a verse from the Qur'an that translates as "If you assist God, he will assist you."

MOTTO

Allāh, al waṭan, al malik (transliteration from Arabic); God, Nation, King (English)

CAPITAL CITY

Rabat

TYPE OF GOVERNMENT

Constitutional monarchy

NATIONAL EMBLEM

Star of Morocco (green interwoven star or pentagram)

NATIONAL COLORS

Red and green

NATIONAL ANTHEM

The anthem, a tune popular in Morocco during the French protectorate, was adopted in 1956, and a new set of lyrics was added in 1970.

Hymne Chérifien (Arabic); Hymn of the Sharif (English)

Fountain of freedom, source of light
Where sovereignty and safety meet,
Safety and sovereignty may you ever combine!
You have lived among nations with title
    sublime,
Filling each heart, sung by each tongue,
Your champion has risen and answered your
    call.
For your soul and your body,
The victory they have conquered,
In my mouth and in my blood
Your breezes have stirred both light and fire.
Up! my brethren, strive for the highest.
We call to the world that we are here ready.

We salute as our emblem
God, homeland, and king.

CURRENCY

Moroccan dirham

INTERNET IDENTIFIER

.ma

VEHICLE IDENTIFICATION PLATES/ STICKERS

MA

PASSPORT

The passport cover has the name of the country in Arabic and French, the coat of arms, and the word *passport* in Arabic and French.

AIRLINE

Royal Air Maroc RAM; Jet4You

NATIONAL FLOWER

Almond blossom (unofficial)

NATIONAL TREE

Argan tree (unofficial)

NATIONAL ANIMAL

Lion

NATIONAL RESOURCES

Natural resources include phosphates, iron ore, manganese, lead, zinc, fish, salt, sandy beaches, a pleasant climate, and arable land. The mining of phosphates is the primary source of income, followed by remittances from Moroccans living in Europe. Tourism, supported by a range of scenery, ancient cities, a unique culture, and sandy beaches, is the third-largest source of income.

FOODS

Couscous, considered the national dish, is a fine pasta of semolina wheat coated in finely ground flour. It is normally served with lamb and vegetables. Other specialties include *pastilla,* a dish of thin dough layered with shredded chicken and spices under a crisp layer of ground almonds, cinnamon, and sugar; *tajine,* slow-cooked stews of meat, fish, or vegetables prepared in a special ceramic dish; *harira,* a thick soup of tomatoes, lentils, chickpeas, onions, eggs, and spices; *hout,* a hearty fish soup; and *djaja mahamara,* chicken stuffed with almonds, semolina, and raisins.

SPORTS/SPORTS TEAMS

Association football (soccer) is the most popular sport. Traditional sports, such as athletics, are also popular. Morocco national teams participate in many sports at an international level.

TEAM SPORTS

Badminton
Morocco Badminton Team

Baseball
Morocco Baseball Team

Basketball
Morocco Basketball Team; Morocco Women's Basketball Team: Morocco Wheelchair Basketball Team

Cricket
Morocco Cricket Team

Football
Morocco Football Team, nickname Lions de l'Atlas (the Lions of the Atlas); Morocco Women's Football Team, nickname Lions de l'Atlas (the Lionesses of the Atlas); Morocco Under-23 Football Team, nickname Les Lions Espoir; Morocco Under-20 Football Team, nickname Junior Lions; Morocco Under-17 Football Team, nickname Les Li-onceaux (the Atlas Cubs); Morocco Women's Under-19 Football Team; Morocco Rugby Union Team; Morocco Rugby League Team; Morocco Futsal Team; Morocco American Football Team; Morocco Rugby Union Team (Sevens), nickname Morocco Sevens or Morocco 7s

Handball
Morocco Handball Team

Hockey
Morocco Ice Hockey Team; Morocco Field Hockey Team

Racing
Morocco Speedway Team

Table Tennis
Morocco Table Tennis Team

Tennis
Morocco Davis Cup Team; Morocco Fed Cup Team

Volleyball
Morocco Men's Volleyball Team

INDIVIDUAL SPORTS

Morocco Amateur Boxing Team; Morocco Aikido Team; Morocco Archery Team; Morocco Athletics Team; Morocco Canoeing Team; Morocco Cycling Team; Morocco Equestrian Team; Morocco Fencing Team; Morocco National Gymnastics Team; Morocco Modern Pentathlon Team; Morocco Rowing Team; Morocco Sailing Team; Morocco Shooting Team; Morocco Swim Team; Morocco Tae Kwon Do Team; Morocco Triathlon Team; Morocco Weight Lifting Team; Morocco Wrestling Team

WINTER SPORTS

Morocco National Biathlon Team; Morocco National Ice Hockey Team

NATIONAL HEROES OR PERSONIFICATIONS

Mohammed V, the sultan of Morocco who negotiated independence in 1956; Moulay Idriss, the founder of the first Muslim state in Morocco; Tarik Ibn Ziad, the leader of the invasion of Spain* in the eighth century; Mehdi Ben Barka, who actively opposed Hassan II and his authoritarian government and disappeared in 1965.

NATIONAL HOLIDAY/INDEPENDENCE DAY

Throne Day (accession of King Mohamed VI to the throne), July 30

FESTIVALS/FAIRS

Traditional Handicrafts Fair, May; Rose Festival, mid-May; Cherry Festival, June; Olive Festival, December; Date Festival, October; Fantasia Festival, September; Porcelain Festival, September; Gnawa Festival, June; Marrakesh Festival of Popular Arts, July

SIGNIFICANT EVENTS IN FORMATION OF NATIONAL IDENTITY

8000 B.C.E. Berber peoples related to the early peoples of Europe occupy the region.

Sixth century B.C.E.–fifth century B.C.E. Phoenician colonies are founded on the coast and major rivers. Carthage, the most important Phoenician colony, becomes the supreme power in North Africa.

40 C.E.–fourth century C.E. After the defeat of Carthage, the Roman Empire takes control of North Africa. Christianity is introduced in the second century C.E., and by the fourth century, the majority of the population is Christian.

680–788 Muslim Arab invaders defeat the Berbers to conquer Morocco. After about a century of Arab rule, successive Moorish dynasties begin to rule the country, which breaks away from the rule of the Muslim Caliphate in distant Baghdad. Idriss I founds the Idrisid Dynasty and becomes the first ruler. In 711, the Arabs invade Europe, bringing much of Spain and Portugal* under Muslim rule. Many Berbers adopt the new religion, often shaping it to their own folk religions.

10th century–12th century A succession of dynasties and religious movements takes control of Morocco. Several Berber dynasties are founded, led by religious reformers and tribal confederations that control North Africa and Muslim Spain for over two centuries.

1559–1659 Successive Arab tribes claiming descent from the Prophet Muhammad conquer the region. The last, the Alaouites, create a dynasty that remains in power into the 21st century.

1777 Morocco becomes one of the first nations to recognize the new United States*.

1860 A dispute over the Spanish colony of Ceuta on Morocco's north coast leads to war. Spain gains another enclave at Melilla.

1884–1912 Spain and France* carve out zones of influence that remain nominally part of the Sultanate of Morocco.

1921–1926 The Riffian Berbers of northern Morocco declare the independence of the Republic of the Rif, which fights off Spanish and French troops until final defeat in 1926.

1934–1943 Nationalists demand reforms, including the admission of Moroccans to government positions and the establishment of representative councils.

1956 Morocco gains independence from France and Spain. The Spanish cede all of northern Morocco, except the important port enclaves of Ceuta and Meliaa.

1961–1971 King Hassan II, who succeeds to the throne in 1961, initiates an oppressive government. Widespread disturbances break out, and the king declares a state of emergency following a failed coup attempt.

1973–1975 The Polisario movement is formed in the Spanish Sahara colony. The Spanish abandon the colony in 1974 without leaving behind an effective government. Amid the chaos, the Polisario leaders declare Sahrawi* independent. King Hassan orders 350,000 civilians to march across the border in the so-called Green March to enforce Moroccan claims to Western Sahara.

1975–1976 Morocco and Mauritania* divide the former Spanish territory. Heavy fighting ensues with Polisario fighters, a considerable financial drain on the country. Mauritania withdraws, and Morocco occupies the southern sector as well.

1982–1985 The war in Western Sahara continues, with thousands of soldiers dying. The king cancels elections amid growing unrest and economic crisis. Morocco leaves the Organization of African Unity to protest the admission of Western Sahara.

1991 A United Nations cease-fire begins in Western Sahara, but the territory's status remains unresolved.

1999 Hassan II dies and is succeeded by Mohammed VI.

2003 A bomb set off by Islamic radicals kills 45 people in Casablanca.

2005 A truth commission investigates the excesses committed during the reign of Hassan II, including the deaths of hundreds of people while in official custody.

2006 The Spanish prime minister visits the Spanish territories of Ceuta and Melilla in northern Morocco, a move denounced by the Moroccan government, which continues to claim sovereignty over the enclaves.

2007–2008 The Moroccan government proposes another autonomy plan for Western Sahara, which is rejected by the Polisario. The Spanish king visits the enclaves, further angering the Moroccan government, which demands the return of the enclaves to Moroccan sovereignty.

2009 Morocco breaks off diplomatic relations with Iran* after a senior Iranian official reiterates Iranian territorial claims to Bahrain*.

OMAN

OFFICIAL NAME
Sulṭanat ʿUmān (transliteration from Arabic); Sultanate of Oman (English)

POPULATION
3,428,900 (2009e)

INHABITANTS' NAME/NICKNAME
Omani(s)

LANGUAGE/LANGUAGES
Arabic (official); English, Baluchi, Urdu, several Indian languages, others

RELIGION/RELIGIONS
Ibadi Muslim, 75 percent; Sunni Muslim and Shia Muslim, 12 percent; Hindu, 5 percent; Christian, Buddhist, other or no religion

NATIONAL FLAG
The flag consists of three equal horizontal stripes of white, red, and green, with a vertical red stripe at the hoist containing the national emblem of Oman. The white symbolizes peace and prosperity, the green symbolizes fertility and the Green Mountains, and the red stands for battles against foreign invaders.

COAT OF ARMS/SEAL
The national emblem, the badge of the Albusaidi Dynasty, consists of a traditional *jambiya,* a curved dagger in a sheath; two crossed *khanjars;* and an ornate horse bit that links the weapons. The *khanjar* is a traditional long dagger that all Omani men wore until recently and still wear on formal occasions.

CAPITAL CITY
Muscat

TYPE OF GOVERNMENT
Absolute monarchy

NATIONAL EMBLEM
Khanjar, the traditional long dagger

NATIONAL COLORS
Red and white

NATIONAL ANTHEM
The bandmaster of a visiting British ship wrote the anthem for the sultan in 1932 as a salutation.

Nashid As-Salaam As-Sultani (transliteration from Arabic); The Sultan's Anthem (English)

O Lord, protect for us our Majesty the Sultan
And the people in our land,
With honor and peace.
May he live long, strong and supported,
Glorified be his leadership.
For him we shall lay down our lives.
May he live long, strong and supported,
Glorified be his leadership.
For him we shall lay down our lives.
O Oman, since the time of the Prophet
We are a dedicated people among the noblest
　Arabs.
Be happy! Qaboos has come
With the blessing of heaven.
Be cheerful and commend him to the protec-
　tion of our prayers.

CURRENCY

Omani rial

INTERNET IDENTIFIER

.om

VEHICLE IDENTIFICATION PLATES/ STICKERS

OM

PASSPORT

The passport cover has the name of the country in Arabic and English, the national emblem, and the word *passport* in Arabic and English.

AIRLINE

Oman Air

NATIONAL RESOURCES

Natural resources include petroleum, copper, asbestos, some marble, limestone, chromium, gypsum, and natural gas. Oman is heavily dependent on dwindling oil resources, but sustained high oil prices in recent years have helped build Oman's budget and trade surpluses and foreign reserves. As a result of its dwindling oil resources, the government is trying to diversify the economy and is attempting to Omanize the labor force by replacing foreign expatriate workers with local workers.

FOODS

Shuwa, meat with herbs and spices cooked very slowly in underground clay ovens, is considered the national dish. Other specialties include *mashuai,* spit-roasted kingfish often served with lemon rice; *maqbous,* a rice dish with saffron and chunks of spicy meat; *halwa,* a sticky dessert made of brown sugar, eggs, honey, and spices; and *laban,* a salted buttermilk yogurt, the favored drink.

SPORTS/SPORTS TEAMS

Association football (soccer) and rugby are the most popular sports. Oman national teams participate in many sports at an international level.

TEAM SPORTS

Basketball

Oman Basketball Team; Oman Wheelchair Basketball Team

Cricket

Oman Cricket Team

Football

Oman Football Team, nickname Al Ahmar (the Reds); Oman Women's Football Team, nickname Al Ahmar (the Reds); Oman Futsal Team; Arabian Gulf Rugby Union Team (Sevens), nickname Arabian Gulf Sevens or Arabian Gulf 7s; Arabian Gulf Women's Rugby Union Team (Sevens), nickname Arabian Gulf Sevens or Arabian Gulf 7s (Arabian Gulf teams represent a number of Persian Gulf countries)

Handball

Oman Handball Team; Oman Beach Handball Team

Hockey
Oman Field Hockey Team

Table Tennis
Oman Table Tennis Team

Tennis
Oman Davis Cup Team

Volleyball
Oman Volleyball Team

INDIVIDUAL SPORTS

Oman Amateur Boxing Team; Oman Athletics Team; Oman Cycling Team; Oman Equestrian Team; Oman Sailing Team; Oman Shooting Team; Oman Swim Team; Oman Triathlon Team; Oman Wrestling Team

NATIONAL HEROES OR PERSONIFICATIONS

Nasr ibn Murshid, the leader who unified the interior tribes to drive the Portuguese from Oman in the 17th century; Ahmad ibn Sa'id, who drove the Persians from Oman in 1749; Qaboos bin Said al-Said, the present sultan, who overthrew his eccentric and reclusive father in 1970 and led Oman into the modern world

NATIONAL HOLIDAY/INDEPENDENCE DAY

Birthday of Sultan Qaboos, November 18

FESTIVALS/FAIRS

Muscat Festival, January; Khareef Festival, July–August

SIGNIFICANT EVENTS IN FORMATION
OF NATIONAL IDENTITY

Sixth century B.C.E.–fourth century B.C.E. Ancient Iranian dynasties control or influence the Oman Peninsula, the gateway to the Gulf of Persia.

Third century B.C.E.–third century C.E. The Parthians, later called Persians, garrison Oman to control shipping in the Gulf of Persia.

Seventh century Arab invaders overrun the region and convert the population to Islam during the lifetime of the Prophet.

Ninth century The Ibadi sect of Islam begins ruling the interior through a succession of elected and hereditary imams.

1507–1650 The Portuguese take control of the coastal ports as part of their trade routes between Europe and India*. The Europeans are finally expelled in 1650.

17th century–18th century The Omanis extend their rule to the east coast of Africa, controlling the slave ports of Mombasa and Zanzibar*. The Omani Empire, built on slavery and the maritime trade of the region, grows rich and powerful.

1737–1749 The Persians invade the sultanate but are driven out in 1749. The Al Bu Said dynasty comes to power and rules into the 21st century.

1832–1856 Sultan Zaid transfers the capital of the empire from Muscat to the economically more important Zanzibar. At his death in 1856, one of his sons inherits Zanzibar and the East Africa territory; the other inherits Muscat and Oman.

1913–1920 The sultan loses control of the interior to the Ibadi imams. Under an agreement brokered by the British in 1920, the sultan recognizes the autonomy of the interior provinces.

1954 War breaks out between the forces of the imam, seeking a separate independent state in the interior, and the sultan's military. Sultan Said ibn Taimur regains control of the interior, but eccentric behavior and a feudal and isolationist outlook characterize his rule.

1964 Oil reserves are discovered. Extraction begins in 1967.

1965–1975 The southern Dhofar region, ethnically and geographically distinct, rebels against the old sultan. Qaboos bin Said al-Said overthrows his father and becomes sultan in 1970. The Dhofar rebellion in the south is finally defeated.

1997–2002 Sultan Qaboos decrees that woman can stand for elections and vote. Voting rights are extended to all citizens over the age of 21. Tribal leaders, businessmen and government functionaries previously chose voters.

2007–2008   Oman maintains close ties to U.S. antiterrorist organizations after discovering cells of Islamic fundamentalists in the country.

2009   An official sanctuary for the nearly extinct Arabian oryx is deleted from the UNESCO World Heritage list after being opened to oil prospectors.

PALESTINE

OFFICIAL NAME
As-Sulta Al-Wataniyya Al-Filastīniyya (transliteration from Arabic); Palestinian National Authority (English)

POPULATION
4,235,600 (2009e). The Palestinian population in the Palestinian Authority area and neighboring countries is estimated to number up to 11 million.

INHABITANTS' NAME/NICKNAME
Palestinian(s)

LANGUAGE/LANGUAGES
Arabic, English (official); Hebrew, others

RELIGION/RELIGIONS
Gaza Strip: Muslim, 98 percent; Christian, other or no religion
West Bank: Muslim, 75 percent; Jewish, 17 percent; Christian and other, 8 percent

NATIONAL FLAG
The flag is a horizontal tricolor of black, white, and green with a red triangle at the hoist. The flag is modeled on that of the first widespread Arab revolt in history, the Arab Revolt against the Ottoman Empire in 1916–1918.

COAT OF ARMS/SEAL
The coat of arms has a central shield showing the colors of the national flag featuring the pan-Arab colors. A gray and black eagle, the Eagle of Saladin, supports the flag. Below the eagle is a scroll inscribed with *The Palestinian Authority* in Arabic.

CAPITAL CITY
Ramallah (de facto); Gaza City (seat of the legislature); East Jerusalem (declared capital of Palestine, under direct Israeli control)

TYPE OF GOVERNMENT
Republic

NATIONAL EMBLEM
Eagle of Saladin

NATIONAL COLORS
Green and white

NATIONAL ANTHEM
The anthem is from the 1970s and is also known as "Anthem of the Intifada" and "Anthem of the Palestinian Revolution."

> **Biladi (transliteration from Arabic); My Country (English)**
> My country, my land, land of my ancestors
> My country, my country, my country
> My people, people of perpetuity
> With my determination, my fire, and the volcano of my revenge
> With the longing in my blood for my land and my home
> I have climbed the mountains and fought the wars
> I have conquered the impossible and crossed the frontiers
> My country, my country, my country
> My people, people of perpetuity
> With the resolve of the winds and the fire of the guns
> And the determination of my nation in the land of struggle

Palestine is my home, Palestine is my fire,
  Palestine is my revenge and the land of
  endurance
My country, my country, my country

My people, people of perpetuity
By the oath under the shade of the flag
By my land and nation and the fire of pain
I will live as a *fida'i,* I will remain a *fida'i,*
  I will end as a *fida'i*—until my country
  returns
My country, people of perpetuity.

PATRON SAINT

Mary, Queen of Palestine; Saint George (patron saint of Palestinian Christians)

CURRENCY

Israeli new shekel; Jordanian dinar (West Bank only)

INTERNET IDENTIFIER

.ps

VEHICLE IDENTIFICATION PLATES/STICKERS

PS

PASSPORT

The passport cover has the name of the Palestinian Authority in Arabic and English, the coat of arms, and the word *passport* in Arabic and English. Although Palestine is not an independent state, the passport has been acknowledged by nearly 100 national governments.

AIRLINE

Palestinian Airlines

NATIONAL BIRD

Eagle of Saladin

NATIONAL RESOURCES

Natural resources include arable land, natural gas, and limestone. Remittances from Palestinians living outside the territories of the Gaza Strip and the West Bank are a very important source of foreign currency and investment. International financial aid is also a very important resource.

FOODS

The Palestinian cuisine varies from region to region, but some dishes are shared by the regional cuisines, including *meze,* a variety of small dishes, such as olives, hummus, a dip of chickpeas, and tabbouleh, a chilled salad of bulgur wheat with tomatoes, parsley, mint, and lemon juice; *kibbe,* minced meat with onions, often cooked on a skewer; and baklava, a dessert pastry filled with nuts and honey.

SPORTS/SPORTS TEAMS

Association football (soccer) is the most popular sport. Boxing and martial sports are also very popular. Palestine national teams participate in many sports at an international level.

TEAM SPORTS

Badminton
Palestine Badminton Team

Basketball
Palestine Basketball Team; Palestine Women's Basketball Team; Palestine Wheelchair Basketball Team

Football
Palestine Football Team; Palestine Women's Football Team; Palestine Futsal Team

Table Tennis
Palestine Table Tennis Team

Volleyball
Palestine Men's Volleyball Team

INDIVIDUAL SPORTS

Palestine Amateur Boxing Team; Palestine Athletics Team; Palestine Equestrian Team; Palestine Fencing Team; Palestine Judo Team; Palestine Karate Team: Palestine Rowing Team; Palestine Sailing Team; Palestine Tae Kwon Do Team; Palestine Wrestling Team

NATIONAL HEROES OR PERSONIFICATIONS

Handala, a cartoon boy, is the Palestinian symbol of defiance and has become the personification of the Palestinian people.

National heroes include Amin al-Husayni, Arab leader under the British mandate; Yasser Arafat, the leader of the Palestinian independence movement from the 1960s to the 1990s; Mahmoud Darwish, known as the poet of the revolution; Amal Amireh, the national hero for ordinary men and women; and Barwan Barghouti, a leader of the Palestinian movement.

NATIONAL HOLIDAY/INDEPENDENCE DAY

National Day, November 15

FESTIVALS/FAIRS

Palestine Film Festival, September; Ramadan Nights Festival, September

SIGNIFICANT EVENTS IN FORMATION OF NATIONAL IDENTITY

3000 B.C.E.–2500 B.C.E.   The Canaanites arrive and settle the region.

1250 B.C.E.   The Canaanites are conquered by Israel.

63 B.C.E.   Palestine becomes part of the Roman Empire.

132 C.E.–135 C.E.   The Bar Kokhba revolt leads to the mass deportation of the Jews. The original Canaanite population remains as the majority.

330–640   Palestine comes under Byzantine rule. Christianity spreads through the region.

638   Invading Arabs from the south overrun the region, driving the Byzantines from Palestine.

660–1250   Islam becomes the majority religion, with Christian and Jewish minorities tolerated under Muslim rule. Great Muslim monuments are constructed in Jerusalem, the Dome of the Rock and the al-Aqsa mosque.

1099–1291   European crusaders invade the region, intent on capturing the sites mentioned in the Bible and taking territory for personal gain. The Muslims are defeated, and the Latin Kingdom of Jerusalem is established. Kurdish military leader Saladin defeats the crusaders and recaptures Jerusalem and other crusader strongholds.

1516   Palestine becomes part of the Turkish Ottoman Empire.

1876–1878   Elected Palestinian deputies attend the first Ottoman Parliament. The first modern Jewish agricultural colony is established.

1882–1903   Waves of Eastern European Jews, fleeing poverty and anti-Semitic pogroms, settle in the region.

1896–1897   Theodor Herzl publishes *Der Judenstaat,* the proposal for the establishment of a Jewish state in Palestine or elsewhere. The First Zionist Congress calls for the establishment of a home for the Jewish people in their ancient homeland in Palestine.

1900–1916   A second wave of Jewish immigrants arrives from Europe.

1916   The British side with the leaders of the Arab Revolt against the Ottomans during the First World War and agree that the Arab provinces of the Ottoman Empire will have British support for a united independence. A secret pact, the Sykes-Picot Agreement, divides the Arab provinces between France* and Britain. The independence of the Arab provinces in proclaimed.

1917–1918   The Balfour Declaration pledges British support for a Jewish national homeland in Palestine. Allied military forces occupy Palestine just before World War I ends.

1919–1923   A third wave of Jewish immigration increases the Jewish population of Palestine. The first Palestinian National Congress in Jerusalem sends a memorandum to the Paris Peace

Conference rejecting the Balfour Declaration and demanding the Arab independence promised by the United Kingdom* in 1916. Sectarian violence begins between Jews and Palestinian Arabs.

1922–1925 France and the United Kingdom are given League of Nations mandates over the former Arab territories of the Ottoman Empire.

1929–1939 Increasing anti-Semitism and economic upheavals in Europe lead to new waves of Jewish immigration to Palestine, numbering over 250,000 by 1939. Arabs demand an end to the mandate and plead for fellow Arabs to stop selling land to Jews. Violence between Arabs and Jews increases, including attacks on the British authorities by both sides.

1940–1945 The Second World War engulfs Europe, leading to the deaths of millions, including some six million Jews murdered in the Holocaust.

1945–1948 Jewish refugees from Europe enter Palestine illegally as the British stop legal immigration. Plans for the creation of two states in Palestine, one for the Jews and the other for the Arabs, are rejected. The region east of the Jordan River, Transjordan, is separated from Palestine to become the new Kingdom of Jordan* in 1946. The British give up and submit the Palestinian dilemma to the new United Nations, which proposes a new partition plan that the Arab countries reject. A United Nations vote approves the creation of the independent state of Israel.

1948–1949 The armies of seven Arab countries invade Palestine. Many Arabs flee the fighting at the urging of Arab leaders; others are forced out of their homes by Jewish or Arab militaries. The war ends with Israel victorious over the Arab armies. Tens of thousands of Palestinian Arabs are stranded in neighboring Arab countries.

1964–1967 The Palestine Liberation Organization (PLO) is founded, with the stated goals of the destruction of the Israeli state through armed struggle and its replacement with a Palestinian state from the Jordan River to the Mediterranean Sea. Israel again defeats the armies of neighboring countries in the Six Day War. Yasser Arafat becomes chairman of the PLO.

1970–1972 The PLO becomes a quasi government in areas with large Palestinian populations but is driven out of Jordan and Lebanon*, where it challenges the national governments. The PLO and other organizations turn to terrorism to press their cause, including massacres at large European airports and the Munich Massacre at the Olympics in 1972.

1982 Lebanese Christian militias massacre Palestinians in refugee camps near Beirut following Israeli incursions into Lebanon.

1988–1989 An independent State of Palestine is proclaimed. The first suicide attacks by religious fanatics begin.

1993 An agreement is signed on interim self-government and the creation of the Palestinian National Authority under Yasser Arafat, who is awarded the Nobel Peace Prize for his part in the peace accord.

2000–2004 Yasser Arafat rejects a final-solution plan that would lead to an independent Palestinian state in the Gaza Strip and the West Bank. The United Nations approves a two-state plan for a Palestinian state alongside Israel. Yasser Arafat, the undisputed leader of Palestine, dies.

2006–2007 The Israelis unilaterally disengage from the Gaza Strip, which comes under the rule of Hamas, a radical organization. Fighting erupts between Hamas and the forces of the Palestinian Authority.

2008–2009 The Gaza Strip, controlled by the fundamentalist Hamas organization, is invaded and bombed by Israeli military forces following a long series of rocket attacks on Israeli towns and cities. The Israeli forces withdraw following the agreement on a cease-fire.

See also Israel

QATAR

OFFICIAL NAME

Dawlat Al-Qatar (transliteration from Arabic); State of Qatar (English)

POPULATION
1,457,900 (2009e)

INHABITANTS' NAME/NICKNAME
Qatari(s)

LANGUAGE/LANGUAGES
Arabic (official); English, Hindi, Urdu, Farsi, Filipino, others

RELIGION/RELIGIONS
Muslim, 76 percent (90% Sunni, 10% Shia), Christian, 9 percent; Hindu, Baha'i, others

NATIONAL FLAG
The flag is a deep maroon field with a broad, serrated band of nine white points at the hoist. The maroon color represents the blood shed during the wars involving Qatar, especially in the late 19th century. White represents peace. The serrated line of nine points represents Qatar's position as the ninth member of the reconciled emirates of the Persian Gulf, following the Qatari-British treaty of 1916.

COAT OF ARMS/SEAL
The coat of arms is a circle with a central yellow disk with two crossed scimitars around a sailing dhow, blue waves, and an island with palm trees. The yellow is surrounded by a broad circle divided into the colors of the national flag. On the upper, white half, the name of the country is inscribed in Kufi script.

CAPITAL CITY
Doha

TYPE OF GOVERNMENT
Constitutional monarchy

NATIONAL EMBLEM
Oryx

NATIONAL COLORS
White and maroon

NATIONAL ANTHEM
The anthem, which begins with an oath, was adopted in 1996, upon the accession to the throne of Emir Sheikh Hamad Bin Kalifa al-Thani.

As Salam Al Amiri (transliteration of Arabic); National Anthem of Qatar (English)
Swearing by God who erected the sky
Swearing by God who spread the light
Qatar will always be free
Sublimed by the souls of the sincere
Proceed thou on the manners of the
    ascendants
And advance on Prophet's guidance
In my heart,
Qatar is an epic of glory and dignity
Qatar is land of the early men
Who protect us in time of distress,
Doves they can be at times of peace,
Warriors they are at times of sacrifice

CURRENCY
Qatari riyal

INTERNET IDENTIFIER
.qa

VEHICLE IDENTIFICATION PLATES/STICKERS
Q

PASSPORT
The passport cover has the name of the country in Arabic and English, the coat of arms, and the word passport in Arabic and English.

AIRLINE
Qatar Airways

NATIONAL ANIMAL
Arabian oryx

NATIONAL BIRD

Falcon (unofficial)

NATIONAL FISH

Hammour (grouper) (unofficial)

NATIONAL RESOURCES

Natural resources include petroleum, natural gas, and fish. Before the discovery of oil, Qataris depended on fishing and pearling. The discovery of oil in the 1940s completely transformed Qatar into modern state with a high standard of living and generous social services for its citizens.

FOODS

Majboos, a spiced lamb stew served with rice, is the national dish. Other typical dishes include *harees,* a dish of cracked wheat with lamb and seafood, served with seasoned rice; *umm Ali,* a type of bread pudding; *esh asaraya* (harem bread), a type of cheesecake; *mehalabiya,* a pudding of rosewater and pistachios; *thareed,* a vegetable curry served with flatbread; *warak inab,* vine leaves stuffed with minced meat, rice, and vegetables; and *kousa ablama,* stuffed eggplant.

SPORTS/SPORTS TEAMS

Association football (soccer) is the most popular sport. Qatar national teams participate in many sports at an international level.

TEAM SPORTS

Basketball

Qatar Basketball Team; Qatar Woman's Basketball Team; Qatar Wheelchair Basketball Team

Cricket

Qatar Cricket Team

Football

Qatar Football Team, nickname Annabi (the Maroon); Qatar Women's Football Team, nickname Annabi (the Maroon); Qatar Rugby Union Team; Qatar Futsal Team; Arabian Gulf Rugby Union Team (Sevens), nickname Arabian Gulf Sevens or Arabian Gulf 7s; Arabian Gulf Women's Rugby Union Team (Sevens), nickname Arabian Gulf Sevens or Arabian Gulf 7s; Arabian Gulf Rugby Union Team (Arabian Gulf teams represent a number of countries in the Persian Gulf)

Handball

Qatar Handball Team; Qatar Women's Handball Team

Hockey

Qatar Field Hockey Team

Netball

Qatar Netball Team

Racing

Qatar Speedway Team

Table Tennis

Qatar Table Tennis Team

Tennis

Qatar Davis Cup Team

Volleyball

Qatar Men's Volleyball Team; Qatar Women's Volleyball Team

INDIVIDUAL SPORTS

Qatar Amateur Boxing Team; Qatar Archery Team; Qatar Athletics Team; Qatar Canoeing Team; Qatar Cycling Team; Qatar Equestrian Team; Qatar Fencing Team; Qatar Gymnastics Team; Qatar Judo Team; Qatar Rowing Team; Qatar Sailing Team; Qatar Shooting Team; Qatar Swim Team; Qatar Tae Kwon Do Team; Qatar Triathlon Team; Qatar Weight Lifting Team; Qatar Wrestling Team

NATIONAL HEROES OR PERSONIFICATIONS

Rahman ibn Jabir Al Jalahima, a famous raider in the Persian Gulf region in the late 18th century; Muhammad ibn Thani, leader of the resistance to Ottoman domination in the 19th century; Abd Al Thani, the first ruler of Qatar after the withdrawal of the Ottomans in 1913

NATIONAL HOLIDAY/INDEPENDENCE DAY

Independence Day, September 3; National Day, December 18

FESTIVALS/FAIRS

Eid al-Fitr, variable dates; Eid al-Adha (Festival of the Sacrifice), variable dates; Ashurra, variable dates

SIGNIFICANT EVENTS IN FORMATION OF NATIONAL IDENTITY

2000 B.C.E.–600 C.E.   The region is often under the rule of nearby Persia. A Persian-influenced culture flourishes as a trading center.

Seventh century   Zealous Muslims occupy the region as part of the early Muslim expansion. Muslim influence quickly spreads.

7th century–15th century   Although often nominally independent, Qatar remains under Persian influence.

17th century   Migrants to the region establish pearling and trading settlements on the coast.

1867   A conflict with neighboring Bahrain* leads to war and the virtual destruction of Doha. A treaty between Bahrain and the United Kingdom* recognizes Qatar as a separate entity rather than a dependency of Bahrain.

1871–1813   Qatar comes under the rule of the Ottoman Empire. A Turkish garrison is established. The Ottoman authorities withdraw, leaving Qatar vulnerable to more powerful neighbors and nomadic raiders.

1916   The emir signs a treaty with the United Kingdom, giving the British responsibility for external affairs in return for guaranteeing security and British protection.

1939–1950   Oil reserves are discovered. Production is delayed due to the Second World War, but by the 1950s, oil has replaced pearling and fishing as the Qataris' major source of revenue. The modernization of Qatar begins.

1968–1971   The United Kingdom announces its intention to withdraw from the Persian Gulf. Qatar becomes fully independent.

1972   Infighting within the ruling family leads to a royal coup.

1990   Qatari troops take part in the liberation of Kuwait* during the First Gulf War.

1995   A royal coup replaces the eccentric emir with his son, Hamad, who supports the modernization and democratization of Qatar.

1996   Al-Jazeera satellite TV is launched and becomes one of the largest news sources in the Middle East.

2001–2003   Qatar settles long-running border disputes with Bahrain and Saudi Arabia*. The country's first constitution is written. Qatar serves as a military center during the U.S.-led invasion of Iraq*.

2005   The country's first constitution is adopted, allowing democratic reforms.

2007–2008   Qatar and Dubai become the two biggest shareholders of the London Stock Exchange, the world's third largest. Massive profits from high oil prices continue to flow into the country.

2009   Lower oil prices and a global economic slump curtail Qatar's rapid economic growth.

SAHRAWI

OFFICIAL NAME

Al-Jumhūrīyya al-'Arab īyya aṣ-Ṣahrāwīyya ad-Dīmuqrātīyya (transliteration from Arabic); Sahrawi Arab Democratic Republic (English) as-Ṣaḥrā' al-Gharbīyah (transliteration from Arabic); Sahara Occidental (Spanish); Western Sahara (English)

POPULATION
384,600 (2009e)

INHABITANTS' NAME/NICKNAME
Sahrawi(s)

LANGUAGE/LANGUAGES
Hassaniya Arabic (official); Moroccan Arabic, Spanish, other

RELIGION/RELIGIONS
Sunni Muslim, 99 percent; other or no religion

NATIONAL FLAG
The flag, originally the flag of the Polisario Front, consists of three equal horizontal stripes of black, white, and red with a red isosceles triangle at the hoist and a red crescent moon and star on the white. The colors are the pan-Arab colors, the original colors of the Arab Revolt in the early 20th century. The crescent moon and star represent the people's Islamic religion.

COAT OF ARMS/SEAL
The coat of arms has two crossed rifles, each with a national flag hanging from the muzzle. Centered above the guns are a red crescent and star, representing Islam. Surrounding the guns and crescent are two olive branches. At the bottom is a red banner with the national motto.

MOTTO
Liberty, Democracy, Unity (English translation)

CAPITAL CITY
El Aaiun (under Moroccan control); Bir Lehlou (temporary capital); Tindouf refugee camps in Algeria* (de facto capital)

TYPE OF GOVERNMENT
Nominal republic mostly under Moroccan military occupation

NATIONAL COLORS
Green, white, black, and red

NATIONAL ANTHEM
The anthem was adopted at independence in 1976 and is now used by the government-in-exile.

> **Yābaniy Es-Saharā (transliteration from Arabic); O Sons of the Sahara (English)**
> O sons of the Sahara! In the battlefield,
> you are torch holders in the long road
> Make revolution in our nation
> and follow this path for her sake.
> Cut off the head of the invader.
> Cut off the head of the invader.
>
> O revolutionaries, the homeland will be glorious.
> Cut off the estates in this region.
> Remove in war the causes for protest and abandon it;
> no submission, no yielding.
> No agent, no invader, no agent, no invader.
> You who ask about us: we are the ones who drive the transforming struggle.
> We are the ones who smash that idol,
> we are the ones who understand the beautiful lesson.
> We are the people of the path; we are the people of the path.
> We are the ones who revealed the path against the raid, the one that burns up the raiders.
> It is the war to erase the oppressor and establish the right of the laborers.
> We are the people of the path; We are the people of the path.
> The uprising is for the people and will advance in the Arab lands.
> It will produce unity forever in the hearts and will establish justice and democracy.
> Every century, every generation, every century, every generation.

CURRENCY
Moroccan dirham

INTERNET IDENTIFIER
.eh

VEHICLE IDENTIFICATION PLATES/ STICKERS

MA Morocco (official); WSA Sahrawi (unofficial)

PASSPORT

Sahrawis are Moroccan citizens and travel on Moroccan passports.

NATIONAL ANIMAL

Camel

NATIONAL RESOURCES

National resources include phosphates, iron ore, fisheries, and possible offshore oil and natural gas. Due the long conflict for control of the region, the natural resources have not been fully exploited. Tens of thousands of Sahrawis live outside the region, in refugee camps in Algeria or in other countries, so remittances are an important part of the economy. The region depends on nomadic pastoralists, fishing, and phosphate mining.

FOODS

Couscous, small semolina pasta, served with meat, vegetables, and chickpeas, is considered the national dish. Other specialties include *tagine*, a dish of meat and vegetables; *mechoui,* roast lamb or goat; *harira,* a type of soup; *kefta,* minced meat molded to a skewer and cooked over charcoal; and *mourouzia,* a dish of lamb with raisins, almonds, and honey.

SPORTS/SPORTS TEAMS

Association football (soccer) and basketball are the most popular sports. Sahrawi national teams participate in football and basketball at an international level.

TEAM SPORTS

Basketball

Western Sahara Basketball Team; Western Sahara Women's Basketball Team

Football

Western Sahara Football Team

NATIONAL HEROES OR PERSONIFICATIONS

Shaykh Ma al-Aynayn, the leader of a Sahrawi uprising in 1904; El-Ouali Mustapha Sayed, first leader of the Polisario Front; Mohammed Abdelaziz, independence leader and president of the government-in-exile; Abdelkader Taleb Oumar, the prime minister of Sahrawi

NATIONAL HOLIDAY/INDEPENDENCE DAY

Independence Day, February 27

FESTIVALS/FAIRS

International Film Festival, July

SIGNIFICANT EVENTS IN FORMATION OF NATIONAL IDENTITY

1000 B.C.E.   Berber tribes in the region have contact with Carthage on the coast of North Africa.

Eighth century   Invading Arabs introduce their language and culture and spread their new religion, Islam.

11th century   A tribal confederation founds the Almohad dynasty, which leads the conquest of much of present Morocco*, parts of Algeria, and Spain*.

17th century–18th century   As an important part of the trans-Saharan caravan trade, many merchants prosper. The slave trade becomes an important economic activity.

1884   During the European scramble for Africa, the Berlin Conference assigns the region, called Western Sahara, to Spain. The Spanish begin to establish military posts in the territories of Río de Oro and Saguia el-Hamra. Strong indigenous resistance is encountered.

1900–1915   Spain and France* delimit the boundaries of the territories they control in northwestern Africa. In 1904, a rebellion led by Shaykh

Ma al-Aynayn disrupts the region and is not ended until France sends reinforcements in 1910.

1924–1934 The two territories are combined to form Spanish Sahara. Successive uprisings continue to erupt periodically, preventing Spanish control of the interior until 1934.

1957 Moroccan insurgents and Sahrawi rebels invade the region in an attempt to drive out the Spanish, initiating the Ifni War. French military aid helps to end the invasion.

1965 The Spanish territory of Ifni, just north of Western Sahara, is ceded to Morocco*. Nationalists form the Polisario Front to fight for the liberation of Spanish Sahara.

1967–1970 Peaceful demonstrations demand the end of the Spanish occupation. A violent crackdown in 1970 leads to a more militant national movement.

1975–1976 Morocco and Mauritania* claim Western Sahara, culminating in the Green March, the invasion of some 350,000 unarmed Moroccan civilians into the colony. Spain withdraws its forces and settlers and abandons the region. Sahrawi leaders declare independence. The territory is divided between Morocco and Mauritania.

1978 Mauritania renounces its claim after Polisario attacks. The Moroccans occupy the entire region amid heavy fighting with Polisario forces. Tens of thousands flee across the border into Algeria.

1980–1990 The Moroccan government builds over a thousand miles of rock walls topped with sensors and explosives to protect Moroccan colonies and the important phosphate mines. The conflict is taken to the United Nations but remains without resolution after several attempts to organize a referendum.

1999 A scheduled vote on independence is postponed and then sidelined by the Moroccan government.

2000–2009 The United Nations considers the territory not yet decolonized and continues to insist on a referendum. Some 45 national governments and the African Union (AU) recognize the Sahrawi republic, but most of its population remains under Moroccan occupation or languishes in vast refugee camps in Algeria.

See also Morocco

SAUDI ARABIA

OFFICIAL NAME

al-Mamlaka al-'Arabiyya as-Su'ûdiyya (transliteration from Arabic); Kingdom of Saudi Arabia

NICKNAME

Land of the Two Holy Mosques

POPULATION

24,563,900 (2009e)

INHABITANTS' NAME/NICKNAME

Saudi(s); Saudi Arabian(s)

LANGUAGE/LANGUAGES

Arabic (official); English, others

RELIGION/RELIGIONS

Sunni Muslim; Shia Muslim, others

NATIONAL FLAG

The flag is a green field charged with the *shahadah*, the Islamic declaration of faith, in the Thuluth script, and a white scimitar. The color green is represents Islam. The *shahadah* translates as "There is no god but God (Allah), and Muhammad is his messenger." The sword, called the Sword of a Thousand Truths, symbolizes the victories of Ibn Saud, the unifier of Saudi Arabia.

COAT OF ARMS/SEAL

The coat of arms consists of two crossed Arabic swords, or scimitars with gold handles below a green date palm tree. The two swords represent the regions of Saudi Arabia united under the House of Saud in 1926, Nejd and Hejaz. The date palm represents the people of the kingdom that is protected by the monarchy.

Motto

La ilaha ill allah muhammadun rasul allah (transliteration from Arabic); There is no god but God (Allah), and Muhammad is his messenger (English)

Capital City

Riyadh

Type of Government

Absolute monarchy

National Emblem

Sword of a Thousand Truths (shown on the national flag)

National Colors

White and green

National Anthem

The anthem was officially adopted in 1950. It praises Allah and asks that he grant the King of Saudi Arabia long life.

> **Aash Al Maleek (transliteration from Arabic); Long Live Our Beloved King (English)**
>
> Hasten to glory and supremacy,
> Glorify the Creator of the heavens!
> And raise the green flag
> Carrying the emblem of Light,
> Repeating: God is the greatest,
> O my country!
> My country, you have lived the glory of Muslims!
> Long live the King for the flag and the country!

Currency

Saudi riyal

Internet Identifier

.sa

Vehicle Identification Plates/ Stickers

SA

Passport

The passport cover has the coat of arms, the *shahadah* as it appears on the national flag, the name of the country in English and Arabic, and the word *passport* in Arabic and English.

Airline

Saudi Arabian Airlines

National Tree

Phoenix palm

National Bird

Falcon

National Resources

Natural resources include petroleum, natural gas, iron ore, gold, and copper. Saudi Arabia has an oil-based economy, with strong government controls over all major economic activities. The country possesses more than 20 percent of the world's proven petroleum reserves, ranks as the world's largest exporter of petroleum, and plays a leading role in the Organization of Petroleum Exporting Countries (OPEC).

Foods

Islamic dietary laws forbid the eating of pork and the consumption of alcoholic beverages, laws strictly enforced throughout Saudi Arabia. *Kabsa,* a rice dish of meat, vegetables, and spices, is considered the national dish. Other typical dishes include *kultra,* skewered chicken or lamb cooked over charcoal; *meze,* an array of appetizers; *khobz* or *pitta,* a flat, unleavened bread that accompanies most meals; falafel, deep-fried balls of ground chickpeas; *shawarma,* sliced lamb cooked on a spit; *ful medames,* a paste of fava beans, garlic, and lemon juice served with *khobz;* hummus, a paste of chickpeas, garlic, and lemon; and *burghul,* a dish of cracked wheat.

SPORTS/SPORTS TEAMS

Association football (soccer), rugby, and basketball are the most popular sports. Saudi Arabia national teams participate in many sports at an international level.

TEAM SPORTS

Basketball

Saudi Arabia Basketball Team; Saudi Arabia Women's Basketball Team; Saudi Arabia Wheelchair Basketball Team

Cricket

Saudi Arabia Cricket Team

Football

Saudi Arabia Football Team, nickname Al Soqour Al Kothor (the Green Falcons) or Al Akhdar (the Greens) ; Saudi Arabia Futsal Team; Arabian Gulf Rugby Union Team (Sevens), nickname Arabian Gulf Sevens or Arabian Gulf 7s; Arabian Gulf Rugby Union Team (Arabian Gulf teams represent a number of Persian Gulf countries)

Handball

Saudi Arabia Handball Team

Racing

Saudi Arabia Speedway Team

Table Tennis

Saudi Arabia Table Tennis Team

Tennis

Saudi Arabia Davis Cup Team

Volleyball

Saudi Arabia Volleyball Team

INDIVIDUAL SPORTS

Saudi Arabia Amateur Boxing Team; Saudi Arabia Athletics Team; Saudi Arabia Archery Team; Saudi Arabia Cycling Team; Saudi Arabia Equestrian Team; Saudi Arabia Fencing Team; Saudi Arabia Gymnastics Team; Saudi Arabia Judo Team; Saudi Arabia Karate Team; Saudi Arabia Shooting Team; Saudi Arabia Swim Team; Saudi Arabia Tae Kwon Do Team; Saudi Arabia Weight Lifting Team; Saudi Arabia Wrestling Team

NATIONAL HEROES OR PERSONIFICATIONS

Abdul ibn Aziz Saud, the unifier and first king of Saudi Arabia; Faisal ibn Abdul Aziz-Al-Saud, the king in the 1960s and 1970s, who was instrumental in the social, educational and structural development of the country; the Prophet Muhammad, the founder of the Muslim religion; King Faisal, assassinated by a member of the royal family in 1975. He's honored for modernizing the kingdom.

NATIONAL HOLIDAY/INDEPENDENCE DAY

Unification of the Kingdom/National Day, September 23

FESTIVALS/FAIRS

Annual pilgrimage to Mecca, the hajj; Qurban Bayram (the Great Festival), December; National Festival, September; Al Jenadriyah Heritage and Cultural Festival, October

SIGNIFICANT EVENTS IN FORMATION OF NATIONAL IDENTITY

3000 B.C.E.–500 C.E. Various cultures inhabit the region, often separated by impenetrable deserts.

610 C.E.–632 C.E. Muhammad begins to teach at Mecca before moving to Medina. His teaching unites the tribes of Arabia into a religious theocracy. Muhammad's death in 632 opens a heated debate over his successor that led to the schism between Sunni and Sh'ia Muslims.

700–1500 The Arabian Peninsula becomes a marginal part of the Muslim world, which is centered on areas of Mesopotamia and Syria*. The harsh climate restricts settlements to the few fertile areas and oasis regions controlled by tribal chiefs.

1744–1887 The Saudi clan establishes a small state in central Arabia. Invasions by nomads twice threaten the state's existence. The Ottoman Empire takes control of part of the peninsula. Civil war breaks out, leading to conquest by the Al-Rashid clan.

1891–1902 The Saudis are exiled to Kuwait* by the ruling Al-Rashids. Led by Ibn Saud, the resurgent Saudis capture Riyadh, the Saudis' ancestral capital, from the Al-Rashids.

1912 The Ikhwan (Muslim Brotherhood) is founded, based on strict Muslim law called Wahabism. It grows quickly and provides support for Ibn Saud's conquests.

1912–1932 From Riyadh, Ibn Saud conquers most of the other regions and states of the peninsula and establishes the Kingdom of Saudi Arabia. The Ikhwan turns against Ibn Saud due to the modernization of the country and is defeated in battle

1938–1955 Oil is discovered, and production begins under the U.S.-controlled Arabian American Oil Company (ARAMCO). Strict Islamic law is applied in the kingdom, including severe restrictions on women.

1960–1973 Saudi Arabia becomes a founding member of OPEC. The Saudi government gains control of 20 percent of ARAMCO in 1972, lessening American control over Saudi Arabia's oil. The government leads an international oil boycott against the West, which is accused of supporting Israel* in the October War against Egypt* and Syria*. Oil prices quadruple.

1979 Saudi Arabia severs diplomatic relations with Egypt for making peace with Israel. Islamic extremists seize the Grand Mosque of Mecca.

1980 The Saudi government takes full control of ARAMCO from the United States*.

1986 The king adds "Custodian of the Two Holy Mosques" to his string of titles. The government resumes relations with Egypt.

1990–1991 Saudi Arabia supports the U.S.-led Gulf War to expel Iraqi invaders from neighboring Kuwait. Foreign troops are allowed in the country for the first time.

1992–1993 The king allows the creation of a consultative council.

1994 After involvement in terrorist activities, Islamic dissident Osama Bin Laden is stripped of his Saudi nationality.

1999 Twenty women are allowed to attend the consultative council for the first time.

2000 Human-rights groups criticize Saudi Arabia's treatment of women as "untenable" by any legal or moral standard.

2001 Islamic terrorists attack New York and Washington, D.C.; most are citizens of Saudi Arabia. The government calls for the eradication of Islamic terrorism as un-Islamic. Identity cards are finally issued to women.

2003 Hundreds of intellectuals, including women, sign a petition calling for much-needed political and social reforms. Unprecedented human-rights demonstrations in Riyadh lead to hundreds of arrests.

2003–2008 Government plans focus on diversification of the economy away from overdependence on oil. A project is launched to allow education and inclusion in society of women.

2009 Lower oil prices and the global economic crisis curtail Saudi Arabia's rapid growth and lead to the postponement of development plans.

SUDAN

OFFICIAL NAME

Jumhuriyat as-Sūdān (transliteration from Arabic); Democratic Republic of Sudan (English)

POPULATION

39,459,800 (2009e)

INHABITANTS' NAME/NICKNAME

Sudanese

LANGUAGE/LANGUAGES

Arabic, English (both official); Nubian, Ta Bedawie, Nilotic dialects, Nilo-Hamitic dialects, Sudanic dialects

RELIGION/RELIGIONS

Sunni Muslim, 70 percent; Christian, 5 percent; indigenous beliefs and others

NATIONAL FLAG

The flag is horizontal tricolor of red, white, and black with a green triangle at the hoist. The colors are the pan-Arab colors and are linked to the Arab peoples and the Islamic religion. The red represents the struggle for independence and the sacrifices of the country's martyrs, the white represents peace, light, and optimism, and the black represents Sudan, which in Arabic means black. The black stripe also represents those who fought colonial rule during the late 19th century Mahdi Revolution.

COAT OF ARMS/SEAL

The coat of arms features a secretary bird with a shield from the time of Muhammad ibn Abd Allah, the self-proclaimed Mahdi who briefly ruled Sudan in the 19th century. Two banners are placed above and below. The banner below the arms has the name of the country in Arabic; the banner between the bird's wings has the national motto in Arabic.

MOTTO

Al-nasr lana (transliteration from Arabic); Victory is Ours (English)

CAPITAL CITY

Khartoum

TYPE OF GOVERNMENT

Transitional government of national unity

NATIONAL COLORS

Red and white

NATIONAL ANTHEM

The anthem was originally the song of the Sudanese armed forces prior to independence in 1956. As independence was rushed, there was no time to write an anthem, so this military song was adopted.

> **Nahnu Djundulla Djundulwatan (transliteration from Arabic); We Are the Army of God and of Our Land (English)**
>
> We are the army of God and of our land,
> We shall never fail when called to sacrifice.
> Whether braving death, hardship or pain,
> We give our lives as the price of glory.
> May this our land, Sudan, live long,
> Showing all nations the way.
> Sons of the Sudan, summoned now to serve,
> Shoulder the task of preserving our country.

PATRON SAINT

Saint Josephine Bakhita

CURRENCY

Sudanese pound

INTERNET IDENTIFIER

.sd

VEHICLE IDENTIFICATION PLATES/STICKERS

SUD (unofficial)

PASSPORT

The passport cover has the name of the country in Arabic, the coat of arms, the name of the country in English, and the word *passport* in Arabic and English.

AIRLINE

Sudan Airways

NATIONAL TREE

Palm

NATIONAL ANIMAL

Rhinoceros (unofficial)

NATIONAL BIRD

Secretary bird

NATIONAL RESOURCES

Natural resources include petroleum, small reserves of iron ore, copper, cobalt, chromium ore, zinc, tungsten, mica, silver, gold, and hydropower. In 1999, Sudan began exporting oil, which has helped to revive light industry and greatly expanded exports. Sudan remains a very poor country, with abundant resources that have not been developed.

FOODS

Shahan ful, a coarse paste of fava beans served with green onions, tomatoes, chilies, yogurt, fresh cheese, olive oil, and spices, is the national dish. Other national dishes include *khoodra mafrooka,* a dish of sliced beef or chicken, onions, spinach, and garlic; *kissra be omregayga,* a dish of beef or chicken, onions, *wayk* (okra powder), and garlic; *shorbet ada,* a soup of lentils and vegetables; and *naeamia be dakwa,* a dish of yogurt, *dakwa* (peanut butter), and tomatoes.

SPORTS/SPORTS TEAMS

Association football (soccer) is the most popular sport. Sudan national teams participate in many sports at an international level.

TEAM SPORTS

Badminton

Sudan Badminton Team

Basketball

Sudan Basketball Team; Sudan Women's Basketball Team

Football

Sudan Football Team, nickname Sokoor al-Jediane (the Jediane Falcons) or the Nile Crocodiles); Sudan Women's Football Team nickname Sokoor Al-Jediane (the Jediane Falcons); Sudan Futsal Team

Hockey

Sudan National Field Hockey Team

Table Tennis

Sudan National Table Tennis Team

Tennis

Sudan Davis Cup Team

Volleyball

Sudan Men's Volleyball Team

INDIVIDUAL SPORTS

Sudan Amateur Boxing Team; Sudan Athletics Team; Sudan Canoeing Team; Sudan Cycling Team; Sudan Equestrian Team; Sudan Judo Team; Sudan Rowing Team; Sudan Shooting Team; Sudan Swim Team; Sudan Tae Kwon Do Team; Sudan Weight Lifting Team; Sudan Wrestling Team

NATIONAL HEROES OR PERSONIFICATIONS

Muhammad Ahmad ibn as Sayyid Abd Allah, the self-proclaimed Mahdi who led the resistance to colonialism and ruled the country briefly in the 19th century; Ahmed Urabi, the leader of a revolt against Egyptian and European influence in the region in the late 19th century; Abdallahi ibn Muhammad, the military leader of the siege of Khartoum in 1884–1885.

NATIONAL HOLIDAY/INDEPENDENCE DAY

Independence Day, January 1

FESTIVALS/FAIRS

Ramadan Bairam, dates vary based on the Islamic calendar; Kurban Bairam, dates vary; Moulid al Nabi, March; Sham al Nassim (Spring Festival), March–April

SIGNIFICANT EVENTS IN FORMATION OF NATIONAL IDENTITY

6000 B.C.E.–350 C.E. The Nubian civilization, called Kush by the Egyptians, develops along the upper Nile. Under successive dynasties, the kingdom lasts until the destruction of the capital, Meroe, around 350 B.C.E.

Sixth century Three kingdoms emerge in the region. Byzantine missionaries introduce Christianity, which becomes the major religion.

Seventh century Islam gradually spreads through the population through intermarriage and contact with Arab merchants and settlers.

16th century–1821 A powerful Muslim sultanate is established at Sinnar, known as the Blue Sultanate. The sultanate lasts until an invasion from Egypt* ends its independence. Sudan is untied with Egypt under nominal Ottoman Turkish rule.

1879 A rebellion against the Turkish-Egyptian government, called the Urabi Revolt for its leader, Ahmed Urabi, threatens Egyptian control. The Egyptians appeal to the British, who use the appeal as a pretext to occupy both Egypt and Sudan in 1882.

1883–1885 A religious leader, Muhammad Ahmad ibn as Sayyid Abd Allah, known as the Mahdi, the Guided One, leads a widespread revolt in northern Sudan culminating in the siege of Khartoum and the death of General Charles George Gordon (Gordon of Khartoum) in 1885.

1884–1898 The Mahdi creates a military state administered as a theocracy. The zealous Mahdist troops fight for expansion on all sides, finally invading British Egypt in 1889 and suffering a rare defeat that ends the legend of the Mahdi's invincibility.

1899–1956 Sudan is under a joint government administered by the United Kingdom* and Egypt. Sudan is rushed to independence in 1956, despite protests and delays from the non-Arab peoples of the south.

1962 Civil war breaks out between the African south and the Arab north, while coups and military intervention disrupt the government in Khartoum.

1972–1978 A peace agreement provides for an autonomous state in Southern Sudan*. Oil is dis-

covered in Southern Sudan, again raising tensions between the African tribal peoples and the Arab-dominated government.

1983 The government adopts Muslim Sharia law, which is also extended to the non-Muslim south.

1999 Oil exportation begins to alleviate the poor economic position of the country.

2002–2005 A peace agreement ends the civil war in the south. Southern Sudan becomes an autonomous state.

2006 Conflict in the western Darfur region becomes serious. The government is accused of financing militias that rampage through the region, looting, raping, and driving the population from their homes. The country has one of the highest rates of AIDS in the world, mostly due to a lack of information and government inaction.

2008–2009 The International Criminal Court calls for the arrest of the country's president on charges of crimes against humanity, genocide, and war crimes in Darfur, the first time the court requests the arrest of an acting head of state. Fighting breaks out along the border between north and south over the disputed territory of Abyei. A referendum on the independence of Southern Sudan is tentatively scheduled for January 2011, when the Nuba Mountain region and the Blue Nile region also will vote on whether to stay with Sudan or join the new republic to the south. A Sudanese woman is found guilty of wearing trousers, a practice deemed indecent by the Sudanese government. Journalists paid her fine but she could have been sentenced to 40 lashes.

SYRIA

OFFICIAL NAME

Al-Jumhūriyyah al-Arabiyyah as-Sūriyyah (transliteration from Arabic); Syrian Arab Republic (English)

POPULATION

19,578,600 (2009e)

INHABITANTS' NAME/NICKNAME

Syrian(s)

LANGUAGE/LANGUAGES

Arabic (official); Kurdish, French, English, others

RELIGION/RELIGIONS

Sunni Muslim, 74 percent; other Muslim (Alawite, Druze), 16 percent; Christian, 10 percent; other or no religion

NATIONAL FLAG

The flag is a horizontal tricolor of red, white, and black charged with two green five-pointed stars on the white stripe. The colors are the pan-Arab colors and are inspired by the flag of the Arab Revolt during World War I. The flag, based on the design of the flag used in 1958–61, was readopted in 1980.

COAT OF ARMS/SEAL

The coat of arms consists of a central shield with the tricolor and green stars of the national flag. Holding the shield is the Syrian hawk, or Hawk of Qureysh, with a green scroll in its claws, inscribed with the name of the country in Arabic.

CAPITAL CITY

Damascus

TYPE OF GOVERNMENT

Presidential republic

NATIONAL EMBLEM

The Syrian hawk, the emblem of Muhammad

NATIONAL COLORS

Red and white

NATIONAL ANTHEM

The anthem was adopted in 1936 as a local anthem while Syria was still under French rule.

Homat el Diyar (transliteration from Arabic); Guardians of the Homeland (English)

Defenders of our realm,
Peace be upon you;
The proud spirits will
Not be subdued.
The lion-abode of Arabism,
A hallowed sanctuary;
The seat of the stars,
An inviolable preserve.
Our hopes and our hearts,
Are entwined with the flag,
Which unites our country.

PATRON SAINT

Saint Barbara

CURRENCY

Syrian pound

INTERNET IDENTIFIER

.sy

VEHICLE IDENTIFICATION PLATES/ STICKERS

SYR

PASSPORT

The passport has the name of the country in Arabic, English, and French, the coat of arms, and the word *passport* in the three languages.

AIRLINE

Syrian Arab Airlines (Syrianair)

NATIONAL FLOWER

Jasmine

NATIONAL BIRD

Syrian hawk

NATIONAL RESOURCES

Natural resources include petroleum, phosphates, chrome and manganese ores, asphalt, iron ore, rock salt, marble, gypsum, and hydropower. Syria depends on agriculture, oil production, industry, and tourism; however, the oil reserves are small and declining, widespread corruption and official bureaucracy hinder industry, and instability and a poor international image have hampered the growth of tourism. Remittances from Syrians living outside the country, mainly in the Persian Gulf region, are an important source of foreign currency and investment.

FOODS

Tabbouleh, a cold dish of bulgur, parsley, mint, tomato, scallions, lemon juice, and olive oil, is considered the national dish. Other Syrian specialties include *yabra*, grape leaves stuffed with minced meat and onions; *shawarma*, thinly shaved meat, onions, tomato, and yogurt in a crepelike flatbread; *mahshe*, zucchini stuffed with minced meat; *kibbeh*, a mixture of bulgur, minced meat, and spices shaped into balls or other shapes and then fried; *majaddara*, a dish of lentils cooked with cracked wheat or rice and served garnished with sautéed onions; and *meze*, a very popular assortment of small dishes or appetizers.

SPORTS/SPORTS TEAMS

Association football (soccer) and volleyball are the most popular sports. Syria national teams participate in many sports at an international level.

TEAM SPORTS

Badminton

Syria National Badminton Team

Basketball

Syria National Basketball Team; Syria Women's National Basketball Team; Syria National Wheelchair Basketball Team

Football

Syria National Football Team; Syria Under-20 National Football Team. The football authority is the Syrian Football Federation.

Handball

Syria Handball Team

Table Tennis

Syria Table Tennis Team

Tennis

Syria Davis Cup Team; Syria Fed Cup Team

Volleyball

Syria Men's Volleyball Team; Syria Women's Volleyball Team

INDIVIDUAL SPORTS

Syria Amateur Boxing Team; Syria Archery Team; Syria Athletics Team; Syria Cycling Team; Syria Equestrian Team; Syria Gymnastics Team; Syria Judo Team; Syria Rowing Team; Syria Shooting Team; Syria Swim Team; Syria Tae Kwon Do Team; Syria Triathlon Team; Syria Weight Lifting Team; Syria Wrestling Team

NATIONAL HEROES OR PERSONIFICATIONS

Saladin (Salah al Din), medieval Muslim leader honored for his defeat of the European crusaders; Ibrahim Hanano, anti-French leader after World War I; Youssef Al Azmah, a leader of the independence movement; Mehemet Ali, the leader of the revolt that drove the Turks from Syria in 1831; Hafez al-Assad, dictator of Syria from 1971 to 2000 who brought stability but also repression; Muhammad Ali, the *wali* or governor of Egypt* who brought Syria under his rule after deposing the Ottoman authorities; Sultan Pasha al-Atrash, a leader of the Great Syrian Revolution against French rule in the mid-1920s; Yusuf al-Aznah, a military leader against Ottoman rule that led to Syrian independence in 1918

NATIONAL HOLIDAY/INDEPENDENCE DAY

Independence Day, April 17

Festivals/Fairs

International Flower Fair, April–May; Technical Palymyra Fair, May–June; Cotton Festival, July; Damascus International Fair, August; Passion and Joy Festival (Lattakia Festival), August; Desert Festival, September; Damascus Cinema Festival, November

Significant Events in Formation of National Identity

1750 B.C.E.–750 B.C.E.   The region becomes part of the Babylonian Empire. Over the next thousand years, Hittites, Assyrians, Chaldeans, and Persians conquer the territory.

333 B.C.E.   Alexander the Great conquers Persia and Syria.

301 B.C.E.   Seleucus, one of Alexander's generals, inherits the region at Alexander's death. He creates the Seleucid Empire, centered in present Syria.

64 B.C.E.   Syria becomes part of the Roman Empire.

Fourth century C.E.   Byzantine rule replaces that of Rome. Christianity becomes the dominant religion.

634–750   Zealot Muslims from Arabia conquer most of Syria. Damascus is the center of the Muslim Empire from 661 to 750, when the capital is moved to Baghdad.

1095–1187   The First Crusade establishes Latin (European) states on the Syrian coast. In 1187, Saladin (Salah al Din) leads the Muslims to overrun the Latin Kingdom of Jerusalem.

13th century   The Mongols invade, destroying cities and irrigation systems. The discovery of a sea route to the east ends the need for an overland route through Syria.

1516   Syria is incorporated into the Turkish Ottoman Empire.

1831–1840   Mehemet Ali leads a rebellion against Turkish rule and drives the Ottoman forces out of Syria, but Turkish rule is restored. Syria is opened to European trade.

1880–1914   French firms with contracts from the Ottoman authorities build roads, ports, and railways.

1916–1918   Despite promises of Arab independence and aid to the Arab Revolt against the Turks during World War I, France* and the United Kingdom* sign a secret agreement to partition the Ottoman Empire. Syria declares independence but is assigned to French control by the peace treaties.

1919–1926   The Syrians call for independence and resist the imposition of French rule. Syria is made a League of Nations mandate under French administration. A nationalist uprising spreads across Syria in 1925–26.

1936–1946   France promises independence within three years, but martial law is imposed in 1939. Liberated from the fascist Vichy French by a British expedition, the Syrians proclaim their independence in 1944. The French resist, but independence is finally realized in 1946.

1947–1974   Coups, instability, and political and ethnic conflicts continue to disrupt the country. Hafez al-Assad comes to power in 1971. Wars with Israel* end with heavy Syrian losses and Israeli control of Syria's Golan Heights.

1982–2000   Syrian troops intervene in neighboring Lebanon* and finally stay as an occupation force. Hafez al-Assad dies and is succeeded by his son, Basher.

2004–2005   The United States* imposes sanctions over what it calls support for terrorism and Syria's failure to prevent militants from entering U.S.-occupied Iraq*. Syrian troops leave Lebanon after mass demonstrations and international criticism.

2005–2008   Tens of thousands of Iraqis cross into Syria to escape the continued fighting. The government imposes tight visa restrictions to stem the flow. Human-rights activists and critics of the regime receive long jail sentences. Syria establishes diplomatic relations with Lebanon for the first time since the two countries gained independence in the 1940s.

2009 High-level contacts with Israel continue. Trading is launched on Syria's stock exchange, which is taken as a sign of the gradual liberalization of the state-controlled economy. In mid-2009, the law governing punishment for men charged with killing female relatives for sex outside marriage or for wearing revealing clothing is raised from one year to a maximum of two years. As many as 5,000 women may die each year in so-called honor killings.

TUNISIA

OFFICIAL NAME

Al-Jumhūriyyah at-Tūnisiyyah (transliteration from Arabic); Tunisian Republic (English)

POPULATION

10,325,700 (2009e)

INHABITANTS' NAME/NICKNAME

Tunisian(s)

LANGUAGE/LANGUAGES

Arabic (official); French, Berber dialects, others

RELIGION/RELIGIONS

Muslim, 98 percent; Christian, 1 percent; Jewish, other or no religion

NATIONAL FLAG

The flag is a red field with a centered white disk charged with a red crescent moon and a red five-pointed star. The crescent and star are traditional symbols of Islam and are considered to be symbols of good luck. The color red represents the blood of martyrs killed during the Turkish conquest in 1534. The white symbolizes peace, while the crescent moon and star represent the unity of all Muslims and the Five Pillars of Islam.

COAT OF ARMS/SEAL

The coat or arms is a white disk outlined in red charged with the red crescent moon and star above a pale gold shield with depictions of a sailing ship, a lion holding a sword, and a balance. Just below the ship is a gold banner inscribed with the national motto in Arabic.

MOTTO

Hurriya, nidham, 'adala (transliteration from Arabic); Liberty, Order, Justice (English)

CAPITAL CITY

Tunis

TYPE OF GOVERNMENT

Parliamentary republic

NATIONAL COLORS

Red and white

NATIONAL ANTHEM

The anthem was introduced in 1987 to replace the previous anthem that was closely tied to the government of Habib Bourguiba.

Humat Al Hima (transliteration from Arabic); Defenders of the Homeland (English)

O defenders of the homeland!
Rally around to the glory of our time!
The blood surges in our veins,
We will die for the sake of our land.

Let the heavens roar with thunder.
Let thunderbolts rain with fire.
Men and youth of Tunisia,
Rise up for her might and glory.

No place for traitors in Tunisia,
Only for those who defend her!
We live and die loyal to Tunisia,
A life of dignity and a death of glory.

PATRON SAINT

Immaculate Conception of Mary

CURRENCY

Tunisian Dinar

INTERNET IDENTIFIER

.tn

VEHICLE IDENTIFICATION PLATES/STICKERS

TN

PASSPORT

The passport cover has the name of the country in Arabic and French, the coat of arms, and the word *passport* in Arabic and French.

AIRLINE

Tunisair

NATIONAL FLOWER

Jasmine

NATIONAL ANIMAL

Camel (unofficial)

NATIONAL BIRD

Eagle (unofficial)

NATIONAL RESOURCES

Natural resources include petroleum, phosphates, iron ore, lead, zinc, and salt. Tourism, supported by sandy beaches, a pleasant climate, varied scenery, historical monuments, and a unique culture, is an important resource. Tunisia's association agreement with the European Union (EU) came into force in 1998, giving it access to duty-free trade. The agreement was the first such agreement between the EU and a Mediterranean country.

FOODS

Couscous, a fine pasta of semolina served with vegetables, chicken, or meat, is the national dish. Other national specialties include *brik*, a type of pie made of a thin dough filled with cheese, minced meat, potatoes, or other vegetables; *chorba*, a lamb and vegetable soup with tiny pasta; *kelaya zaara*, lamb prepared with saffron; *chakchouka*, a dish of eggs, green peppers, onions, and tomatoes; *tagine betinjal*, a dish of eggs and eggplant with onions, cloves, cheese, and spices traditionally cooked in a special crock; and *salata méchouia nablia*, a salad of grilled red pepper, chilies, and tomatoes.

SPORTS/SPORTS TEAMS

Association football (soccer) is the most popular sport and is considered the national sport. Tunisia national teams participate in many sports at an international level.

TEAM SPORTS

Baseball

Tunisia Baseball Team; Tunisia Softball Team

Basketball

Tunisia Basketball Team; Tunisia Women's Basketball Team

Football

Tunisia Football Team, nickname Les Aigles de Carthage (the Eagles of Carthage) or Onze (the Eleven); Tunisia Women's Football Team, nickname Les Aigles de Carthage (the Eagles of Carthage); Tunisia Rugby Union Team; Tunisia Futsal Team; Tunisia Rugby Union Team (Sevens), nickname Tunisia Sevens or Tunisia 7s; Tunisia Futsal Team

Handball

Tunisia Handball Team; Tunisia Women's Handball Team

Hockey

Tunisia Field Hockey Team

Racing

Tunisia Speedway Team

Table Tennis

Tunisia Table Tennis Team

Tennis

Tunisia Davis Cup Team; Tunisia Fed Cup Team

Volleyball

Tunisia Men's Volleyball Team; Tunisia Women's Volleyball Team

INDIVIDUAL SPORTS

Tunisia Amateur Boxing Team; Tunisia Athletics Team; Tunisia Canoeing Team; Tunisia Cycling Team; Tunisia Equestrian Team; Tunisia Fencing Team; Tunisia Gymnastics Team; Tunisia Judo Team; Tunisia Modern Pentathlon Team; Tunisia Rowing Team; Tunisia Sailing Team; Tunisia Shooting Team; Tunisia Swim Team; Tunisia Tae Kwon Do Team; Tunisia Weight Lifting Team; Tunisia Wrestling Team

NATIONAL HEROES OR PERSONIFICATIONS

Hannibal, the Carthaginian who led the resistance to Rome around 200 B.C.E.; Ali Bach Hamba, founder of the pro-independence Destour in 1920; Habib Bourguiba, the independence leader and president of the country from 1957 to 1987; Bahri Guiga, a leader of the independence movement in the 1940s

NATIONAL HOLIDAY/INDEPENDENCE DAY

Independence Day, March 20

FESTIVALS/FAIRS

Yasmine Hammamet Festival, July; International Festival of Jazz, July; Carthage Festival, August; Ulysse Festival, July; Symphonic Music Festival, August; Sahara Douz Festival, November; Oasis Festival, November; Medina Festival, variable dates

SIGNIFICANT EVENTS IN FORMATION OF NATIONAL IDENTITY

10th century B.C.E.–ninth century B.C.E. Phoenicians from the eastern Mediterranean establish settlements on the coast, coming into contact with the local Berber people.

Eighth century B.C.E.–fifth century B.C.E. The Phoenician colony of Carthage becomes the dominant civilization in the western Mediterranean.

Second century B.C.E. War begins between Carthage and Rome for domination of the Mediterranean. The Romans eventually conquer Carthage in 146 B.C.E., and the city is completely destroyed.

Second century B.C.E.–fifth century C.E. Latinized and Christian, the region becomes one of the granaries of the empire. As Roman power collapses, Vandals from Europe overrun the region, which is devastated, giving rise to the modern word *vandal*.

7th century–12th century Invading Arabs conquer the region and introduce their new Muslim religion. Successive Muslim dynasties rule from Kairouan, including a Berber dynasty from 909.

15th century The port towns become the centers of Barbary pirates preying on Christian shipping in the Mediterranean. The region comes under Turkish rule and is governed by a local bey.

1705 The Hussein dynasty is established, and the beys of the line govern until 1957.

1878–1881 Severe financial problems and a raid by a local tribe into French Algeria* give the French an excuse to invade in 1880, forcing the bey to accept a protectorate agreement.

1910–1930 Younger Tunisians organize to resist the colonial administration and to press for independence. In 1934, Habib Bourguiba and others join the organization.

1942–1943 Tunisia is the scene of major fighting during World War II.

1946–1956 Bourguiba leads the independence movement. Tunisia gains its independence from France*.

1957 Bourguiba becomes the first president. The constitutional role of the bey is abolished.

1981 The first multiparty parliamentary elections since independence are held.

1987 A bloodless coup deposes Bourguiba after 30 years in power.

1999 The first ever multiparty presidential elections are held.

2006–2009 The government launches a campaign against the headscarves worn by some Muslim women. Several incidents involving Islamic militants lead to greater security, especially for tourist locations.

UNITED ARAB EMIRATES

OFFICIAL NAME

Dowlat Al-Imārāt al-'Arabīya al-Muttaḥida (transliteration from Arabic); United Arab Emirates (English)

POPULATION

5,434,600 (2009e)

INHABITANTS' NAME/NICKNAME

Emirati(s)

LANGUAGE/LANGUAGES

Arabic (official); English, Farsi (Persian), Hindi, Urdu, Filipino, others

RELIGION/RELIGIONS

Muslim, 76 percent (Sunni 85%, Shia 15%); Hindu, 10 percent; Christian, 9 percent; Buddhist, 5 percent; other or no religion

NATIONAL FLAG

The flag is a horizontal tricolor of green, white, and black with a broad red vertical stripe at the hoist. The colors are the pan-Arab colors, the colors of the Arab Revolt in the early 20th century. Green stands for fertility, white for neutrality, black for the flag of the Prophet Muhammad, and red for unity.

COAT OF ARMS/SEAL

The coat of arms has a central circle with the colors of the national flag surrounded by a border with seven stars, representing the seven states of the federation. It is supported by a gold and white falcon holding a red parchment inscribed with the name of the federation in white Arabic script.

MOTTO

Ilah, balad, rais (transliteration from Arabic); God, Nation, President (English)

CAPITAL CITY

Abu Dhabi

TYPE OF GOVERNMENT

Federal constitutional monarchy

NATIONAL COLORS

Red and white

NATIONAL ANTHEM

The anthem was adopted in its instrumental form in 1971. Words were added in 1996.

Ishy Biladi (transliteration from Arabic); Long Live My Nation (English)

Live, my country; may the union of our emirates live.
May you live for a nation
Whose religion is Islam, and whose guide is the Qur'an.
You are stronger in the name of God, O homeland.
My country, my country, my country, O country.
God protect you from the evils of the time.
We have sworn to build and to work.
To work, to be loyal, to work, to be loyal.
As long as we may live, we will be loyal.
May safety endure, and the flag live, our Emirates,
The symbol of Arabism.
We would all make sacrifices for you, and with our blood saturate you.
We would give up our souls for you, O homeland.

CURRENCY

U.A.E. dirham

INTERNET IDENTIFIER

.ae

VEHICLE IDENTIFICATION PLATES/ STICKERS

UAE

PASSPORT

The passport cover has the name of the country in Arabic and English, the coat of arms, and the word *passport* in Arabic and English.

AIRLINES

Emirates Airlines (national airline of Dubai); Etihad Airways (national airline of Abu Dhabi); RAK Airways (national airline of Ras el Khaima); Air Arabia (national airline of Sharjah); Kang Pacific Airlines (national airline of Frujah)

NATIONAL TREE

Date palm

NATIONAL ANIMAL

Camel; Arabian horse

NATIONAL BIRD

Falcon

NATIONAL RESOURCES

Natural resources include petroleum and natural gas. Since the discovery of oil in the United Arab Emirates more than 30 years ago, the federation has undergone a profound transformation from an impoverished region of small desert principalities to a modern state with a high standard of living.

FOODS

Ghuzi, roast lamb with rice and nuts, is considered the national dish. Other national specialties include hummus, a chickpea and sesame paste served with pita or flat-bread; tabbouleh, a dish of bulgur wheat, tomatoes, onions, mint, parsley, and lemon juice; *warak enab,* vine leaves stuffed with minced meat and onions; *koussa mashi,* zucchini or small squash stuffed with meat or fish; *makbous,* a dish of spicy lamb with rice; *kapsa,* a dish of chicken with rice; and *kadee,* a sweet dessert bread usually served with sweet tea.

SPORTS/SPORTS TEAMS

Association football (soccer) and rugby are the most popular sports. United Arab Emirates national teams participate in many sports at an international level.

TEAM SPORTS

Bandy

United Arab Emirates Bandy Team

Basketball

United Arab Emirates Wheelchair Basketball Team

Cricket

United Arab Emirates Cricket Team; United Arab Emirates Women's Cricket Team

Football

United Arab Emirates Football Team, nickname Al Sukoor (the Falcons); United Arab Emirates Women's Football Team, nickname Al Sukoor (the Falcons); United Arab Emirates Under-21 Football Team: United Arab Emirates Women's Under-19 Football Team; United Arab Emirates Beach Soccer Team; Arabian Gulf Rugby Union Team (Sevens), nickname Arabian Gulf Sevens or Arabian Gulf 7s (Arabian Gulf teams represent a number of Persian Gulf countries)

Hockey

United Arab Emirates Ice Hockey Team; United Arab Emirates Field Hockey Team

Kabaddi

United Arab Emirates Kabaddi Team

Netball

Dubai Netball Team

Racing

United Arab Emirates Speedway Team

Table Tennis

United Arab Emirates Table Tennis Team

Tennis

United Arab Emirates Davis Cup Team

Volleyball

United Arab Emirates Men's Volleyball Team

INDIVIDUAL SPORTS

United Arab Emirates Amateur Boxing Team; United Arab Emirates Athletics Team; United Arab Emirates Canoeing Team; United Arab Emirates Cycling Team; United Arab Emirates Equestrian Team; United Arab Emirates Fencing Team; United Arab Emirates Judo Team; United Arab Emirates Modern Pentathlon Team; United Arab Emirates Rowing Team; United Arab Emirates Sailing Team; United Arab Emirates Shooting Team; United Arab Emirates Swim Team; United Arab Emirates Tae Kwon Do Team; United Arab Emirates Weight Lifting Team; United Arab Emirates Wrestling Team

WINTER SPORTS

United Arab Emirates Bandy Team; United Arab Emirates Ice Hockey Team

NATIONAL HEROES OR PERSONIFICATIONS

Sheikh Zayed bin Sultan an-Nahyan, the ruler of Abu Dhabi since 1966 and the first president of the United Arab Emirates in 1971; Sheikh Rashid Bin-Saeed Al Maktoum, the modernizer of Dubai

NATIONAL HOLIDAY/INDEPENDENCE DAY

Independence Day, December 2

FESTIVALS/FAIRS

Dubai Shopping Festival, January; Dubai International Jazz Festival, March; Nokia Abu Dhabi International Jazz Festival, May; National Day Festival, December; Eid al-Fitr, December

SIGNIFICANT EVENTS IN FORMATION OF NATIONAL IDENTITY

2300 B.C.E.–2000 B.C.E.   The region is site of the ancient civilization of Dilmun, dating from the third millennium B.C.E.

330 B.C.E.   The Greeks of Alexander the Great conquer the Persian Empire and the region of the gulf.

629 C.E.   The Persians remain the dominant power in the gulf region, which is one of the first territories outside central Arabia to accept the new religion called Islam in 629 C.E.

7th century–14th century   As part of the Muslim caliphate, the string of small states prospers on the trade routes between the Middle East and India.

1487   The Portuguese, interested in the pearls that have made the region famous, visit the ports.

18th century   The small ports are used by pirates preying on shipping by both local and European traders.

1819–1820   A British squadron is sent to end the pirate threat to British shipping between Europe and India*. The British sign individual treaties with the small emirates, known as the Trucial States.

1892   New agreements give the United Kingdom* control of each state's foreign affairs and defense, while the emirs retain control over internal affairs.

1952   The Trucial Council is formed by the seven states to promote cooperation in the region.

1960 Oil is discovered, and production begins in 1962.

1968 The British announce their complete withdrawal from the gulf by 1971. Talks begin on the formation of a federation of the small emirates.

1971 The British complete their withdrawal, and the federation becomes independent and joins the Arab League.

1981 The Gulf Cooperation Council, an alliance of the states on the Arab side of the Persian Gulf, is formed to control the influence of Iran*.

1990–1991 The Emirates support Kuwait* following the invasion by Iraq*.

1996–1999 A long-running dispute over three small islands, and their surrounding oil-rich waters, becomes more serious when Iran builds an airport on one of them.

2006–2008 A new law allows workers to form trade unions. A small number of handpicked voters chooses half the members of the advisory council. The Emirates and Qatar* become the major shareholders of the London Stock Exchange.

2009 Lower oil prices lead to liquidity problems and a slowing of the region's rapid economic expansion. Economic problems in free-spending Dubai makes financial support from more conservative Abu Dhabi an embarrassing necessity.

Western Sahara. *See* Sahrawi

YEMEN

OFFICIAL NAME

Al-Jumhūriyyah al-Yamaniyyah (transliteration from Arabic); Republic of Yemen (English)

POPULATION

23,022,800 (2009e)

INHABITANTS' NAME/NICKNAME

Yemeni(s)

LANGUAGE/LANGUAGES

Arabic (official); English, others

RELIGION/RELIGIONS

Muslim (Sunni, Zaydi, Isma'ili) 99 percent; Christian, Jewish, Hindu, other or no religion

NATIONAL FLAG

The flag is a horizontal tricolor of red, white, and black, the pan-Arab colors. Red symbolizes the bloodshed of the martyrs and unity, the white represents a bright future, and the black symbolizes the dark past.

COAT OF ARMS/SEAL

The coat of arms has a small central shield depicting a cotton plant, the Marib Dam, and wavy lines representing water. The shield is supported by a stylized, golden-winged grosbeak holding crossed national flags in its talons above a green banner inscribed with the name of the country in Arabic.

MOTTO

Allah, al-watan, al-thawra, al-wehda (transliteration from Arabic); God, nation, revolution, unity (English)

CAPITAL CITY

Sana (San'a')

TYPE OF GOVERNMENT

Presidential republic

NATIONAL EMBLEM

Curved Yemeni dagger, the *jambiyah*

NATIONAL COLORS

Red, white, and black

NATIONAL ANTHEM

The anthem was adopted as the instrumental anthem of South Yemen in 1979. Following unification in 1990, it was adopted as the official anthem of united Yemen with new lyrics.

United Republic

Repeat, O world, my song.
Echo it over and over again.
Remember, through my joy, each martyr.
Clothe him with the shining mantles.
Repeat, O world, my song.
Repeat, O world, my song.
O my country, we are sons and grandsons of your men.
We will guard all of your majesty in our hands.
Its light will be immortal on all ways
Every rock on your mountains, all atoms of your soils
All the moisture of your waters, are now mine.
There are for our greatest wishes, and our right
Came from your past's pretty glories.
Repeat, O world, my song.
Repeat, O world, my song.
My unity, O marvelous song, fill myself
You are promise in our response
My banner, O cloth nailed from every sun
Raise forever on every peak
My nation, give me strength, O source of strength
And save me for you, best nation
In faith and love I am part of mankind.
An Arab I am in all my life.
My heart beats in tune with Yemen.
No foreigner shall dominate Yemen.
Repeat, O world, my song.
Echo it over and over again.
Remember, through my joy, each martyr.
Clothe him with the shining mantles.
Repeat, O world, my song.
Repeat, O world, my song.

CURRENCY

Yemeni rial

INTERNET IDENTIFIER

.ye

VEHICLE IDENTIFICATION PLATES/ STICKERS

YEM

PASSPORT

The passport cover has the name of the country in Arabic and English, the coat of arms, and the word *passport* in Arabic and English.

AIRLINE

Yemenia

NATIONAL FLOWER

Coffee flower (*Coffea arabica*)

NATIONAL TREE

Coffee tree

NATIONAL BIRD

Golden-winged grosbeak

NATIONAL RESOURCES

Natural resources include petroleum, fish, rock salt, marble, and small deposits of coal, gold, lead, nickel, and copper, with fertile soil in the west. Yemen, one of the poorest countries in the Arab world, depends mostly on declining oil resources, but the country is trying to diversify its earnings. Tourism is a growing industry, but attacks on tourists in 2007–2008 gravely hurt the burgeoning industry.

FOODS

Saltah, a dish of meat or chicken, rice, scrambled eggs, potatoes, beans, and spices, served with *sahawqa,* a sauce of chilies, tomatoes, garlic, and herbs, is considered the national dish. Other specialties include *maraq,* a meat stew; *tharid,* a dish made of pieces of bread in vegetable or meat broth; *murtabak,* a dish of minced mutton, garlic, egg, and onion, served with a curry sauce; *haradha,* a dish of minced meat and peppers; *marag lahm,* a meat and vegetable soup; *hanid,* lamb cooked in a traditional ceramic oven; and *kabsa,* a rice dish with lamb.

Sports/Sports Teams

Association football (soccer) is the most popular game. Yemen national teams participate in many sports at an international level.

Team Sports

Basketball

Yemen Basketball Team; Yemen Women's Football Team

Football

Yemen Football Team; Yemen Women's Football Team; Yemen Under-20 Football Team; Yemen Under-17 Football Team

Table Tennis

Yemen Table Tennis Team

Volleyball

Yemen Men's Volleyball Team

Individual Sports

Yemen Amateur Boxing Team; Yemen Athletics Team; Yemen Cycling Team; Yemen Equestrian Team; Yemen Gymnastics Team; Yemen Fencing Team; Yemen Judo Team; Yemen Karate Team; Yemen Swim Team; Yemen Tae Kwon Do Team; Yemen Weight Lifting Team; Yemen Wrestling Team

National Heroes or Personifications

Iman Yahya ibn Muhammad Hamid ad-Din, the ruler during the independence struggle who was killed in an uprising in 1948; Ali Abdallah Saleh, the president of the republic who ended a period of upheaval in the late 1970s; 'Ali Nasir Muhammad al-Hasani, leader of the people's republic in southern Yemen in the 1980s

National Holiday/Independence Day

Unification Day, May 22

Festivals/Fairs

Sana Festival, variable dates; Mukalla Tourist Festival, July; Inshad Festival, October; Dialogue Festival, September; Taiz Festival, November; European Film Festival, October

Significant Events in Formation of National Identity

2300 B.C.E.–600 C.E.   The region, one of the oldest centers of civilization in the world, forms part of successive kingdoms and empires. The lucrative spice trade attracts many conquerors.

Sixth century–seventh century   Many migrants leave the region following the Persian conquest. Arabs from central Arabia conquer the region and introduce the Muslim religion.

7th century–11th century   Yemen forms part of the Muslim Caliphate and later comes under the rule of imams of the Zaydi Muslim sect.

16th century–19th century   Egyptians and Turks of the Ottoman Empire control the region at various times. North Yemen and south Yemen are often separated under different administrations.

1839   The British occupy the port of Aden, which becomes a British colony, and the small states in southern Yemen are made British protectorates.

1918   At the end of the First World War, the Ottoman Empire collapses, and northern Yemen becomes independent under Iman Yahya.

1962   A military coup creates the Yemen Arab Republic (North Yemen), sparking civil war between royalists supported by Saudi Arabia* and republicans aided by Egypt*.

1967–1975   Aden and the southern protectorates are joined as South Yemen. A people's republic is formed, and a socialist government takes power. Clashes between the two states begin along the common border.

1978   Ali Saleh becomes president of North Yemen and gradually restores security and calm. Efforts begin to unite the two Yemeni states.

1986   Thousands are killed in South Yemen as factional fighting breaks out.

1990–1993   The two states join in the United Republic of Yemen under Ali Saleh and a coalition government of the ruling parties of both regions.

1994   Relations between the two regions deteriorate, and fighting erupts. The southern leaders declare South Yemen independent, which ends when northern troops invade the south.

2000–2006   Islamic militants attack a U.S. warship, the British embassy, and other targets. A dissident Shia cleric leads an uprising in northern Yemen. A tribal rebellion begins in the north of the country but is quickly suppressed.

2008   Clashes are renewed in the north, and violent demonstrations in the south are prompted by job discrimination. A series of bomb attacks ensues on police, the government, foreign businesses, tourists, and other targets. Many foreign embassies evacuate nonessential personnel and other nationals.

2009   In spite of its cooperation with the United States* in its war on terror, the government announces the release of 176 Al-Qaeda suspects on condition of good behavior. The tribal rebellion in the north again erupts leaving many dead and wounded and at least 50,000 people displaced.

5

North America and the Caribbean

The symbols utilized in the United States greatly influenced those adopted by other countries that gained independence in the Americas during the 19th century. The U.S. colors of red, white, and blue are reflected in the colors adopted by Cuba, Puerto Rico, and the Dominican Republic. Canada's red and white came about through a compromise following the decision to replace the British-style flag and other symbols that represented the English-speaking provinces, but not the French-speaking populations of Quebec and New Brunswick. The wave of decolonization in the latter half of the 20th century led to a proliferation of national symbols in the Caribbean area. Many of these new symbols are based on political organizations formed during the colonial era or draw on earlier traditions or the region's flora and fauna. Colors such as blue, representing the Caribbean Sea; green for the verdant islands; and red for the people's suffering under slavery and colonialism are prominent colors in the region.

A number of the territories included in this section are not independent nations but are dependent territories with their own identity and symbols, the remnants of the former European empires. The other nonindependent nations that are included—Nevis, Quebec, and Puerto Rico—are actively seeking greater self-government or recognition of their distinct cultures, including their own national symbols. Referendums in Nevis and Quebec on the question of independence so far have been narrowly defeated, but future votes may lead to a change in their present status.

ANGUILLA

OFFICIAL NAME
British Overseas Territory of Anguilla

POPULATION
13,800 (2009e)

INHABITANTS' NAME/NICKNAME
Anguillan(s), Belonger(s)

LANGUAGE/LANGUAGES
English (official); Leeward Caribbean Creole English

RELIGION/RELIGIONS
Anglican 30 percent; Methodist 23 percent; other Protestant 30 percent; Roman Catholic 6 percent; other or no religion

NATIONAL FLAG
The official flag is a blue field bearing the island's coat of arms on the fly and the British Union Jack as a canton on the upper hoist. The unofficial flag, the Dolphin Flag, considered the national flag, used more frequently than the official flag, is a white field bearing three orange dolphins in a circle with a broad turquoise stripe at the bottom. The three orange dolphins represent endurance, unity, and strength, and they leap from the sea in a circle, representing continuity. The

white background stands for peace and tranquility, with the turquoise-blue base representing the surrounding sea and also faith, youth, and hope.

Coat of Arms/Seal

The coat of arms of Anguilla consists of the emblem found on the Flag of Anguilla, a traditional symbol of the nation, three dolphins leaping over the sea. This emblem is the basis of the Dolphin Flag.

Motto

Strength and Endurance

Capital City

The Valley

Type of Government

Parliamentary democracy as a self-governing overseas territory of the United Kingdom*

National Emblem

Dolphin

National Colors

White, pale blue, and orange

National Anthem

The anthem of the United Kingdom, "God Save the Queen," is the official anthem of all British territories. The local anthem is often heard after the official anthem.

God Bless Anguilla

God bless Anguilla
Nurture and keep her
Noble and beauteous
She stands midst the sea
Oh land of the happy
A haven we'll make thee
Our lives and love
We give unto thee

Chorus

With heart and soul
We'll build a nation

Proud, strong and free
We'll love her, hold her
Dear to our hearts for eternity
Let truth and right
Our banner be
We'll march ever on

Mighty we'll make her
Long may she prosper
God grant her leaders
Wisdom and grace
May glory and honor
Ever attend her
Firm shall she stand
Throughout every age

Currency

East Caribbean dollar

Internet Identifier

.ai

Vehicle Identification Plates

AXA (unofficial)

Passport

Anguillans are British citizens and travel on British passports.

National Flower

White cedar

National Tree

White cedar

National Animal

Bottlenose dolphin

National Bird

Mourning dove

National Fish

Eel (unofficial)

National Resources

Anguilla's thin, arid soil is largely unsuitable for agriculture. Anguilla has few natural resources other than salt, fish, and lobster; however, sandy beaches, a pleasant climate, and a unique Caribbean culture have made tourism the major industry. Its main industries are tourism, offshore incorporation and management, offshore banking, and fishing. Many insurance and financial businesses are headquartered in Anguilla.

FOODS

Spiny lobster, rice and peas, and johnnycakes are considered national dishes. Other specialties include baked eel; coconut red beans and rice; papaya and orange soup; saltfish salad; and *ducuna,* a dessert made of grated sweet potatoes, raisins, and spices.

SPORTS/SPORTS TEAMS

Sailing is the acknowledged national sport of Anguilla. This makes the island unique, as it is the only former British colony in the Caribbean whose national sport is not cricket, although cricket is also very popular and is the most widely played team sport. Anguilla national teams participate in many sports at an international level.

TEAM SPORTS

Baseball

Anguilla Baseball Team; Anguilla Softball Team

Basketball

Anguilla Basketball Team; Anguilla Women's Basketball Team

Cricket

Anguilla Cricket Team; Anguilla Under-13 Cricket Team; West Indies Cricket Team (both men and women), nickname the Windies (West Indies teams represent a number of English-speaking Caribbean countries)

Football

Anguilla Football Team; Anguilla Women's Football Team; Anguilla Women's Under-19 Football Team; West Indies Rugby League Team, nickname the Wahoos (West Indies teams represent a number of English-speaking Caribbean countries)

Kabaddi

West Indies Kabaddi Team (West Indies teams represent a number of English-speaking Caribbean countries)

Volleyball

Anguilla Men's Volleyball Team; Anguilla Women's Volleyball Team

INDIVIDUAL SPORTS

Anguilla Athletics Team; Anguilla Sailing Team

NATIONAL HEROES OR PERSONIFICATIONS

Ronald Webster, the political leader who championed Anguilla's separation from Saint Kitts

NATIONAL HOLIDAY/INDEPENDENCE DAY

Anguilla Day, May 30

FESTIVALS/FAIRS

Annual Art Festival, early December; Anguilla Regatta, July

SIGNIFICANT EVENTS IN FORMATION OF NATIONAL IDENTITY

2000 B.C.E. Anguilla is first settled in prehistory by Amerindian tribes migrating from South America.

1493–1565 The date of the first European visit is uncertain. Some claim Columbus sights the island in 1493, while others believe French ships first see Anguilla in 1564 or 1565. Anguilla is named for the sea eels, probably because of its long and narrow shape that looks like an eel when seen from the sea.

1650–1656 British colonists from Saint Kitts settle on the island in 1650. The colonists are massacred by a group of fierce Caribs, noted for their skill as warriors.

1700–1800 The English eventually return, but despite attempts at cultivation, Anguilla's thin soil prevents their farms from ever becoming profitable. By the early 1700s, the slave-plantation system is the dominant economic system on the island. Anguilla is administered from Antigua as part of the Leeward Islands. Anguilla has its own deputy governor, with a local council or assembly. Like the other Caribbean islands, it is caught in the power struggle between the English and the French. The French attack the island in 1745 and 1796 but are unsuccessful.

1825 The island sends a representative to sit in the Saint Kitts legislature, while a new local council, the Vestry, is established in Anguilla. Most of Anguilla's landowners protest the sending of a representative to Saint Kitts, which is, in effect, a legislative union with that island.

1871–1882 Anguilla and Saint Kitts are joined in a federation. The majority of the Anguillans, dissatisfied with their subordinate status and the enforced union, petition the colonial office in London for direct rule from Britain in 1875. In 1882, the island of Nevis* is added to the federation, further complicating Anguilla's situation.

1918–1960 The British install a telephone system after World War I, which consists of 14 hand-cranked telephones. In 1960, a hurricane knocks down or damages the cables and telephone poles. The government on Saint Kitts sends repairmen, but instead of repairing the tiny telephone network, they remove the damaged telephone exchange. Anguilla would wait another 25 years for telephone service. The island's infrastructure is badly neglected.

The neglect of Anguilla is reflected in the naming of the tripartite federation Saint Kitts-Nevis with no mention of Anguilla until the name is changed in 1951. The three-island federation enters the West Indies Federation in 1958 but reverts to separate status in 1962, with Anguillans still very unhappy with their forced union with Saint Kitts and Nevis.

The Anguillans petition Canada for aid in building a pier where seafaring ships could dock.

The Canadians send the money to the central government on Saint Kitts, and the pier is built, but on Saint Kitts, not Anguilla. Adding to the Anguillans' indignation, the new pier is christened Anguilla Pier.

1967 On February 27, 1967, Saint Kitts-Nevis-Anguilla is granted autonomy as a British associated state under the new West Indies Act. The Anguillans seize the opportunity, evict 17 Kittian policemen, and organize a referendum on secession from the three-island federation. On July 11, 1967, the referendum is held, with 1,813 voting in favor of secession and only five voting to retain the political ties. On the strength of the referendum vote, the Anguillans organize their own government through a local council. The Anguillan rebellion creates a political crisis in the region. The new Anguillan government states its grievances clearly.

Anguilla has no general electric connection, a one-room school for 350 children, less than half a mile of paved road, and very poor medical facilities. The islanders believe all their requests for improvements are downgraded in favor of projects on the other islands, with the funds siphoned off to Saint Kitts. Added to the neglect is also a geographic element, as Anguilla is situated some 70 miles from Saint Kitts and Nevis, with several Dutch and French islands in between.

1968 The political impasse is finally addressed, with a British adviser sent to help the Anguilla Council govern the island for a period of one year, January 1968 to January 1969. The Anguilla revolutionary leader, Ronald Webster, seeks a political solution, but toward the end of 1968, the Saint Kitts government and the Anguilla Council fail to agree on an extension of the agreement.

1969 The agreement ends on January 8, 1969, and with it all British aid. On February 6, a new referendum is organized to confirm the islanders' wish to remain apart from Saint Kitts-Nevis. The vote, 1,739 to four, is followed by the declaration of Anguilla as an independent republic.

The declaration pushes the British government to try to find a solution to the problem. A junior minister is sent from London with proposals for an interim British administration. The proposals are found unacceptable, and the junior minister leaves the island within a few hours.

Britain's reaction is immediate. Over 300 British paratroopers, supported by two frigates, invade Anguilla. Royal engineers and members of the London Metropolitan Police follow the paratroopers. The invasion is dubbed the Bay of Piglets.

1971–1980 An interim agreement in 1971 is followed by a new constitution for Anguilla in 1976. It is not until December 1980 that Anguilla is formally separated from Saint Kitts-Nevis to become a separate British territory.

1997 The Anguilla Trust opens an exhibit commemorating the 30th anniversary of the Anguilla Revolution. A permanent exhibition is created in the local museum.

2005–2007 The economy of Anguilla expands rapidly, especially the tourism sector, which is driving major new development in partnership with multinational companies. This boom, beginning gently during 2005–2006, accelerates through 2007 and is expected to continue for years.

2008 The oil and financial crisis of 2008 somewhat curtails the Anguilla boom. In an effort to prevent the economy from overheating, a moratorium is placed on nonbelongers (foreigners) buying land in Anguilla.

2009 Although the global economic slump is felt, Anguilla's reputation as an upmarket destination and a haven for the wealthy somewhat mitigates the effects of the crisis.

See also United Kingdom

ANTIGUA AND BARBUDA

OFFICIAL NAME
Antigua and Barbuda

POPULATION
84,600 (2009e)

INHABITANTS' NAME/NICKNAME
Antiguan(s), Barbudan(s)

LANGUAGE/LANGUAGES
English (official); Antiguan Creole

RELIGION/RELIGIONS
Anglican, 26 percent; Seventh-day Adventist, 12 percent; Pentecostal, 11 percent; Moravian, 11 percent; Roman Catholic, 10.5 percent; Methodist, 8 percent; Baptist, 5 percent; Church of God, 4.5 percent; other or no religion

NATIONAL FLAG
The flag is a red field divided by a large V from the upper fly and hoist to the bottom center of white, pale blue, and black stripes with a seven-pointed gold sun on the black. The sun symbolizes the dawning of a new era. The colors have different meanings: the black is for the African ancestry of the people, the blue for hope, the red for energy. The successive coloring of yellow, blue, and white (from the sun down) also stands for the sun, sea, and sand. The blue represents the Caribbean Sea, and the V-shape is the symbol of victory.

COAT OF ARMS/SEAL
At the top of the coat of arms is a pineapple, a fruit for which the islands are famous. There are several plants found around the shield, all abundant in the country: red hibiscus, sugarcane, and yucca plant. Supporting the shield is a pair of deer representing the wildlife of the islands. The design on the shield shows the sun, also found on the flag, rising from a blue and white sea. The sun symbolizes a new beginning, and the black background represents the African origins of many of the nation's citizens. At the bottom of the shield, in front of the sea, sits a stylized sugar mill. At the bottom is a scroll upon which is written the national motto.

MOTTO
Each endeavoring, all achieving

CAPITAL CITY
Saint John's

TYPE OF GOVERNMENT
Federal parliamentary democracy

NATIONAL COLORS
Red and yellow

NATIONAL ANTHEM
Upon achieving limited statehood within the British Commonwealth in 1967, Antigua adopted this anthem. When full independence was granted in 1981, Antigua, now in a federation with Barbuda, adopted new lyrics but retained the 1967 melody.

Fair Antigua, We Salute Thee

Fair Antigua and Barbuda!
We thy sons and daughters stand
Strong and firm in
Peace or danger
To safeguard our native land
We commit ourselves to building
A true nation brave and free;
Ever striving, ever seeking,
Dwell in love and unity

Raise the standard! Raise it boldly!
Answer now to duty's call
To the service of thy country,
Sparing nothing, giving all;
Gird your loins and join the battle
'Gainst fear, hate, and poverty,
Each endeavoring, all achieving,
Live in peace where man is free.

God of nations, let thy blessings
Fall upon this land of ours;
Rain and sunshine ever sending,
Fill her fields with crops and flowers;
We her children do implore thee,
Give us strength, faith, loyalty,
Never failing, all enduring
To defend her liberty.

PATRON SAINT
Saint John

CURRENCY
East Caribbean dollar

INTERNET IDENTIFIER
.ag

VEHICLE IDENTIFICATION PLATES/STICKERS
AG

PASSPORT
The passport cover has the initials CC for Caribbean Community, the name of the country, the coat of arms, and the word *passport*.

AIRLINE
Leeward Islands Air Transport (LIAT)

NATIONAL FLOWER
Agave (dagger log); red hibiscus

NATIONAL TREE
Whitewood

NATIONAL FRUIT
Black pineapple

NATIONAL STONE
Petrified wood

NATIONAL ANIMAL
Fallow deer

NATIONAL BIRD
Magnificent frigate bird

NATIONAL SEA CREATURE
Hawksbill turtle

NATIONAL FISH
Barracuda (unofficial)

NATIONAL RESOURCES
Natural resources are negligible; however, tourism dominates the economy and ac-

counts for more than half the country's annual income. Antigua's rugged 90 miles of coastline has many beautiful beaches and coves.

FOODS

Fungi, a dish similar to Italian polenta; pepperpot, a soup of fish and sweet potatoes; and *ducana,* a sweet grilled dumpling made from sweet potatoes, raisins, and cinnamon, are considered the national dishes. Other specialties include papaya pie, a dessert of fresh papayas; carrot and coconut bread; rice and pigeon peas; two-of-each soup, a mixture of onions, apples, celery, bananas, and sour cream; and *mauby,* a drink made of *mauby* bark.

SPORTS/SPORTS TEAMS

Cricket is the most popular sport and is considered the national sport. Antigua and Barbuda national teams participate in many sports at an international level.

TEAM SPORTS

Baseball

Antigua and Barbuda Softball Team

Basketball

Antigua and Barbuda Basketball Team

Cricket

Antigua and Barbuda Cricket Team; and West Indies Cricket Team (both men and women), nickname the Windies (West Indies teams represent a number of English-speaking Caribbean countries)

Football

Antigua and Barbuda Football Team; West Indies Rugby League Team, nickname the Wahoos (West Indies teams represent a number of English-speaking Caribbean countries)

Kabaddi

West Indies Kabaddi Team (West Indies teams represent a number of English-speaking Caribbean countries)

Netball

Antigua and Barbuda Netball Team

Tennis

Antigua and Barbuda Davis Cup Team; Antigua and Barbuda Fed Cup Team; Eastern Caribbean Davis Cup Team; Eastern Caribbean Fed Cup Team (Eastern Caribbean teams represent a number of English-speaking Caribbean countries)

Volleyball

Antigua and Barbuda Men's Volleyball Team

INDIVIDUAL SPORTS

Antigua and Barbuda Amateur Boxing Team; Antigua and Barbuda Athletics Team; Antigua and Barbuda Canoeing Team; Antigua and Barbuda Cycling Team; Antigua and Barbuda Equestrian Team; Antigua and Barbuda Judo Team; Antigua and Barbuda Sailing Team; Antigua and Barbuda Swim Team; Antigua and Barbuda Tae Kwon Do Team; Antigua and Barbuda Triathlon Team; Antigua and Barbuda Weight Lifting Team

NATIONAL HEROES OR PERSONIFICATIONS

Vere Cornwall Bird, Antigua and Barbuda's first prime minister, is credited with bringing Antigua and Barbuda and the Caribbean into a new era of independence.

NATIONAL HOLIDAY/INDEPENDENCE DAY

Independence Day/National Day, November 1

FESTIVALS/FAIRS

Annual Carnival, August

SIGNIFICANT EVENTS IN FORMATION OF NATIONAL IDENTITY

2400 B.C.E.–1500 C.E. The first settlers are prehistoric Amerindian tribes from South America. Later, Arawak and Carib tribes move north to populate the islands. The warlike Caribs dominate the islands for centuries until the arrival of the Europeans.

1493–1667 Christopher Columbus lands on Antigua on his second voyage in 1493. He names the island Santa Maria de la Antigua after a church in Seville, Spain*. Malnutrition, slavery, and poor treatment devastate the native population. English colonists replace the early Spanish settlements in 1632, with a brief period of French rule in 1666. The British colony of Antigua is established in 1667.

1667–1834 Roman Catholic Irish, captured during the frequent rebellions against English rule in Ireland*, are the first slaves to be sent to the islands. Later, as agricultural needs increase, particularly on the sugar plantations, slaves are imported from Africa and other parts of the Caribbean. The abolition of slavery in 1834 ends the sugar economy of the islands. The majority of the European planters leave the islands, leaving their former slaves to survive on subsistence farming and fishing.

1939–1951 Poor labor conditions persist until 1939, when the first labor union is formed. The Antigua Trades and Labor Union is the vehicle for Vere Cornwall Bird, who becomes the first president of the union in 1943. Bird and other trade unionists form the Antigua Labour Party (ALP), which runs candidates in the 1946 local elections and becomes the majority political party in 1951.

1967–1981 Antigua is granted associated state status within the British Commonwealth in 1967. The islands become an independent state within the Commonwealth of Nations on November 1, 1981, with Bird as the first prime minister.

1981–2000 Bird leads his political party to a string of victories and establishes a political dynasty in the federation. During the elections of 1994, power passes from Bird to his son, Lester

Bird, but their party, the ALP, remains in power, winning 11 of 17 parliamentary seats.

2004–2008 Elections in 2004 finally end the Bird government, the longest-serving elected government in the Caribbean. In 2007, Louise Lake-Tack becomes the first female to hold the position of governor-general, the Commonwealth's vice-regal representative in the federation.

2009 Rising oil prices and a falling U.S. dollar curtail the federation's growth in 2009.

ARUBA

OFFICIAL NAME
Aruba

POPULATION
112,200 (2009e)

INHABITANTS' NAME/NICKNAME
Aruban(s)

LANGUAGE/LANGUAGES
Dutch, Papiamento (official); Spanish, English, others

RELIGION/RELIGIONS
Roman Catholic, 82 percent; Protestant, 8 percent; Hindu, Muslim, Jewish, other or no religion

NATIONAL FLAG
The flag is a blue field with two narrow yellow stripes at the base and a red four-pointed star outlined in white on the upper hoist. The star represents the four cardinal directions, which in turn refer to the many countries of origin of the people of Aruba. The white border of the star represents purity and honesty. The two narrow stripes represent the movement toward self-government and the flow of people and ideas to the island. The yellow also represents the sun, Aruba's golden beaches, and abundance, as well as the yellow of the national flower, the *wanglo*.

COAT OF ARMS/SEAL

Aruba's coat of arms is a shield divided into four quadrants below a red lion and surrounded by laurel leaves. In the four quadrants are pictured aloe, which represents the first source of wealth for the island; the outline of Hooiberg Hill, which symbolizes Aruba arising out of the sea; the handshake, which represents the friendly ties Aruba maintains with other nations and peoples; and the cog, which symbolizes industry as the island's main source of progress. The cross in the center is the symbol of devotion and faith, while the lion atop the coat of arms represents power and generosity. The laurel leaves surrounding the shield are symbols of peace and friendship.

MOTTO

One Happy Island

CAPITAL CITY

Oranjestad

TYPE OF GOVERNMENT

Parliamentary democracy associated with the Netherlands*, a constitutional monarchy

NATIONAL EMBLEM

Hooiberg Hill

NATIONAL COLORS

Yellow and blue

NATIONAL ANTHEM

Aruba's anthem is unusual, as it is a waltz written in the national language, Papiamento.

Aruba Dushi Tera (Papiamento); Aruba Precious Country (English)

Aruba our beloved home
our venerated cradle
though small and simple you may be
but you are indeed esteemed.

Chorus

Aruba our dear country
our rock so well beloved
our love for you is so strong
that nothing can destroy it. (*repeat*)
Your beaches so much admired
with palm trees all adorned
your coat of arms and flag
is the pride of us all!

Chorus

The greatness of our people
is their great cordiality
and may God guide and preserve
his love for freedom!

PATRON SAINT

Saint Nicholas

CURRENCY

Aruban florin

INTERNET IDENTIFIER

.aw

VEHICLE IDENTIFICATION PLATES/ STICKERS

NL Netherlands (official); ARU Aruba (unofficial)

PASSPORT

Arubans are Dutch citizens and travel on Dutch passports.

AIRLINE

Tiara Air

NATIONAL FLOWER

Yellow *wanglo*

NATIONAL TREE

Divi-divi tree (unofficial)

NATIONAL ANIMAL

Aruba burro (unofficial)

NATIONAL BIRD

Aruba brown pelican (unofficial)

NATIONAL FISH

Blue parrotfish (unofficial)

NATIONAL RESOURCES

Natural resources are negligible, and the island's economy has historically been dominated by four main industries: gold mining, aloe export, petroleum, and tourism. The island's sandy beaches, unique culture, and impressive desert scenery make tourism the leading industry, responsible for giving the Arubans one of the highest standards of living in the Americas.

FOODS

Pan bati, Aruban corn bread; *funchi,* cornmeal mush; *calco tempura,* pickled conch; and goat stew are considered national dishes. Other specialties include *banana den forno,* baked bananas; *bitterbal,* meat croquettes; coconut shrimp; and Aruban iced coconut soup.

SPORTS/SPORTS TEAMS

Water sports are very popular, as are tennis, association football (soccer), and baseball. Aruba national teams participate in many sports at an international level.

TEAM SPORTS

Badminton

Aruba Badminton Team

Baseball

Aruba Baseball Team; Aruba Softball Team

Basketball

Aruba Basketball Team; Aruba Women's Basketball Team

Football

Aruba Football Team; Aruba Women's Football Team; Aruba Futsal Team

Korfball

Aruba Korfball Team

Table Tennis

Aruba Table Tennis Team

Tennis

Aruba Davis Cup Team

Volleyball

Aruba Men's Volleyball Team; Aruba Women's Volleyball Team; Aruba Men's Beach Volleyball Team; Aruba Women's Beach Volleyball Team

INDIVIDUAL SPORTS

Aruba Amateur Boxing Team; Aruba Athletics Team; Aruba Archery Team; Aruba Canoeing Team; Aruba Chess Team; Aruba Cycling Team; Aruba Fencing Team; Aruba Judo Team; Aruba Shooting Team; Aruba Swim Team; Aruba Tae Kwon Do Team; Aruba Triathlon Team; Aruba Weight Lifting Team

NATIONAL HEROES OR PERSONIFICATIONS

Betico Croes, leader of the movement for separation from the Netherlands Antilles* and for greater autonomy for Aruba in the 1980s and 1990s

NATIONAL HOLIDAY/INDEPENDENCE DAY

Flag Day/National Day, March 18; Saint Nicholas Day, December 5

FESTIVALS/FAIRS

Annual Carnival, February-March; Aruba Catamaran Regatta, November; Caribbean Marketplace, January

SIGNIFICANT EVENTS IN FORMATION OF NATIONAL IDENTITY

2000 B.C.E.–1000 B.C.E.   The island is populated by Arawak tribes from the South American mainland. They are a peaceful, agricultural people living in small villages as farmers or fishermen.

1499–1508 Europeans first learn of Aruba when the Spanish explorers Amerigo Vespucci and Alonso de Ojeda come across it in 1499. Vespucci describes the island as forested with brazilwood trees. In 1508, Ojeda is appointed Spain's first governor of the island, then called Nueva Andalucia.

1508–1636 Aruba remains a Spanish colony for over a century. In 1634 the Dutch take control of the island. Dutch authority is confirmed two years later as compensation for the cession of New Amsterdam (New York) to the English.

1636–1816 The Dutch import slaves from Africa to work on their plantations, as the Arawaks prove to be poor plantation workers. Other European and South American immigrants add to the racial mixture on the island. Aruba is under British occupation during the Napoleonic wars in Europe from 1799 to 1802, and again from 1805 to 1816.

1824–1914 Gold is discovered in 1824 and remains the mainstay of the Aruban economy until the early 20th century.

1940–1945 During World War II, Aruba becomes a British protectorate from 1940 to 1942 and a U.S. protectorate from 1942 to 1945. On February 16, 1942, a German submarine attacks Aruba's oil processing refinery, one of the largest in the region. Miraculously, the refinery is not seriously damaged, as the refinery is the main supplier of oil to the Allies at the time.

1946–1947 At the end of the war, a separate Aruban nationality begins to take hold. The Arubans feel increasingly distinct from the peoples of the other Dutch islands in the Caribbean. In 1947, Aruba presents its first petition for the status of independent state within the Kingdom of the Netherlands.

1972 At a conference in Surinam*, Betico Croes of the MEP (People's Electoral Movement)) proposes Aruba's independence, and the creation of a Dutch Commonwealth of four states: Aruba, the Netherlands, Surinam, and the Netherlands Antilles. Politicians propose a referendum to be held in Aruba for the people to determine the island's separate status or *status aparte* as a completely autonomous state under the authority of the Dutch crown.

1976 Preparing the people of Aruba to exercise Aruba's right to self-determination and independence, a national flag and national anthem are introduced by a special committee appointed by Betico Croes. The national flag symbolizes Aruba's *status aparte* as a self-governing state.

1977–1981 The first referendum for self-determination is held with the support of the United Nations. Although only 57 percent of the electorate participates, 82 percent vote for immediate independence. In 1981, the Arubans agree to postpone a referendum on independence until 1988, following a Dutch government agreement on separate status for the island within the Dutch kingdom.

1983–1985 In 1983, Aruba reaches a final official agreement with the Kingdom of the Netherlands, the State of the Netherlands Antilles, and the island governments to become a member state within the Kingdom of the Netherlands, with its own constitution. Aruba's constitution and independence are unanimously approved and proclaimed in August 1985, and an election is held for the people to elect Aruba's first national parliament and institute its first national government.

1986–1994 The first Aruban stamps are issued. Aruba's separation from the Netherlands Antilles on January 1, 1986, is considered an interim solution in preparation for full independence in 1996. However, the prosperity of the island, guaranteed by Dutch control of the island's defense and foreign affairs, leads many Arubans to question the need for full independence. In 1994, the Aruban government announces an indefinite postponement of the transition to independence until the people decide to hold another referendum.

1999 In 1999, the Arubans celebrate the 500th anniversary of the first encounter between Europeans and Arawaks on Aruba. The Arawaks remain an important part of the ethnic composition of the Aruban nation.

2000–2009 Deficit spending has been a staple of Aruba's recent history. Recent changes to Aruba's financial policies are correcting this, and the island state will have its first balanced budget in 2009. Aruba receives some financial aid from the Netherlands each year, but this aid ends in 2009, as part of a deal to ensure Aruba's financial independence.

See also Netherlands

BAHAMAS

OFFICIAL NAME
Commonwealth of the Bahamas

POPULATION
331,600 (2009e)

INHABITANTS' NAME/NICKNAME
Bahamian

LANGUAGE/LANGUAGES
English (official); Bahamian English, Creole (used by Haitian immigrants), Spanish, others

RELIGION/RELIGIONS
Baptist, 35 percent; Anglican, 15 percent; Roman Catholic, 14 percent; Pentecostal, 8 percent; Church of God, 5 percent; Methodist, 4 percent; other or no religion

NATIONAL FLAG
The flag is a horizontal tricolor of aquamarine, yellow, and aquamarine bearing a black triangle at the hoist. The black stands for the unity and determination of the people of the Bahamas, who are primarily of African descent. The triangle is oriented toward the three stripes, symbolizing the country's natural resources. The two aquamarine stripes represent the sea around the islands, and the yellow represents the sun that shines on the islands.

COAT OF ARMS/SEAL
The coat of arms is a composition of things indigenous to the Bahamas. The crest of the arms, a light pink conch shell, symbolizes the marine life of the Bahamas. Behind it are several wavy green palm fronds, symbolic of the natural vegetation. The Santa Maria, flagship of Christopher Columbus, appears on a shield at the center of the coat of arms. Wavy barrulets of blue symbolize the waters of the Bahamas. The shield is charged with a resplendent or radiant sun to signify the world-famous balmy resort climate, and it also connotes the bright future of these islands. A flamingo, the national bird, and a silvery blue marlin support the shield. The national motto is draped across the base of the coat of arms.

MOTTO
Forward, upward, onward together

CAPITAL CITY
Nassau

TYPE OF GOVERNMENT
Commonwealth

NATIONAL EMBLEM
Uniformed Bahamian police; pink government house in Nassau

NATIONAL COLORS
Aquamarine, yellow, and black

NATIONAL ANTHEM
The anthem was chosen from the entries submitted to a national competition and was adopted when the Bahamas achieved independence in 1973.

March On, Bahamaland

Lift up your head to the rising sun, Bahamaland;

March on to glory your bright banners waving high.
See how the world marks the manner of your bearing!
Pledge to excel through love and unity.
Pressing onward, march together to a common loftier goal;
Steady sunward, tho' the weather hide the wide and treacherous shoal.
Lift up your head to the rising sun, Bahamaland,
'Til the road you've trod lead unto your God, march on, Bahamaland.

PATRON SAINT(S)
Saint John; Saint Anne

CURRENCIES
Bahamian dollar; U.S. dollar

INTERNET IDENTIFIER
.bs

VEHICLE IDENTIFICATION PLATES/STICKERS
BS

PASSPORT
The passport cover has the initials CC for Caribbean Community, the coat of arms, the name of the country, and the word *passport*.

AIRLINE
Bahamasair

NATIONAL FLOWER
Yellow cedar (yellow elder)

NATIONAL TREE
Tree of life (lignum vitae)

NATIONAL ANIMAL
Conch

NATIONAL BIRD
Flamingo

NATIONAL FISH
Bonefish (unofficial)

NATIONAL RESOURCES
Natural resources include salt, aragonite, timber, and arable land. The islands' white sandy beaches, pleasant climate, friendly people, and island culture make tourism the primary economic activity.

FOODS
Cracked conch, conch sliced and pounded and then breaded and fried, is considered the national dish. Other specialties include rice and beans; lobster curry; baked snapper with coconut; cassava pone, a type of bread; pineapple coleslaw, a salad of cabbage, onions, and pineapple; bread pudding, a dessert of bread, raisins, and cinnamon; and *conkies*, a dessert dumpling made of sweet potatoes, coconut, corn flour, and spices steamed in a banana leaf.

SPORTS/SPORTS TEAMS
Cricket is considered the national sport. Association football (soccer) is also very popular. Sloop sailing was defined as the national sport by law in 1993. Bahamas national teams participate in many sports at an international level.

TEAM SPORTS

Baseball
Bahamas Baseball Team; Bahamas Softball Team

Basketball
Bahamas Basketball Team; Bahamas Women's Basketball Team

Cricket
Bahamas Cricket Team

Football

Bahamas Football Team, nickname Rake n' Scrape Boyz or the Batha Boyz; Bahamas Women's Football Team, nickname the Batha Girlz; Bahamas Rugby Union Team; Bahamas American Football Team; Bahamas Rugby Union Team (Sevens), nickname Bahamas Sevens or Bahamas 7s; Bahamas Women's Rugby Union Team (Sevens), nickname Bahamas Sevens or Bahamas 7s

Hockey

Bahamas Field Hockey Team

Tennis

Bahamas Fed Cup Team; Bahamas Davis Cup Team

Volleyball

Bahamas Men's Volleyball Team; Bahamas Women's Volleyball Team; Bahamas Men's Beach Volleyball Team, nickname the Platinum Tips; Bahamas Women's Beach Volleyball Team, nickname the Bullets

INDIVIDUAL SPORTS

Bahamas Amateur Boxing Team; Bahamas Athletics Team; Bahamas Cycling Team; Bahamas Gymnastics Team; Bahamas Judo Team; Bahamas Sailing Team; Bahamas Swim Team; Bahamas Tae Kwon Do Team; Bahamas Weight Lifting Team; Bahamas Wrestling Team

NATIONAL HEROES OR PERSONIFICATIONS

Lynden Pindling, the colony's first black premier in 1967; Sir Milo Butler, an early activist working to invoke pride consciousness among the black people of the Bahamas and governor-general of the islands from 1973 to 1979

NATIONAL HOLIDAY/INDEPENDENCE DAY

Independence Day, July 10

FESTIVALS/FAIRS

Junkanoo Summer Festival, June–August; Junkanoo Parade, Boxing Day, December 26

SIGNIFICANT EVENTS IN FORMATION OF NATIONAL IDENTITY

5000 B.C.E.–2000 B.C.E. Many historians and scientists believe the ancient people known as the Siboney inhabited the islands as early as 7,000 years ago. The first known inhabitants are the seafaring Taino or Arawak people, who move into the south Bahamas from Hispaniola and Cuba*. In the islands, they come to be known as Lucayans.

1492 The Lucayan population numbers an estimated 40,000 at the time of Columbus' first voyage of discovery. Christopher Columbus's first landfall in the New World is on San Salvador Island, also known as Watling's Island, in the southern part of the archipelago. Columbus makes contact with the Lucayans and exchanges gifts with them. The Lucayans provide the weary sailors with fresh water and food. After observing the shallow sea around the islands, Columbus calls them the islands of the *baja mar* (shallow sea), and effectively names the archipelago the Bahamas, the Islands of the Shallow Sea.

16th century–18th century Spanish slavers raid the Lucayan settlements for slaves. Many are sent to Hispaniola and Cuba as forced laborers. Within two decades of Columbus' first visit, disease, warfare, and slave raids have devastated the Lucayan population. The islands are virtually uninhabited until English settlers from Bermuda* arrive as settlers in 1647. The late 1600s and early 1700s are the golden age of pirates in the Caribbean region. Most of the famous pirates use the islands as their home ports at one time or another. The numerous islands, with their complex shoals and channels, provide excellent concealment for the plunderers of the seas.

1718–1780 The Bahamas become a British crown colony. Over 8,000 Empire loyalists and their slaves flee to the Bahamas when the British lose the American colonies. The majority of the loyalists come from New York, Virginia, and the

Carolinas between 1776 and 1780, many bringing their slaves with them.

1834 The emancipation of the slaves in the British Empire in 1834 frees the majority of the island population. Most former slaves settle on small plots as subsistence farmers. Black freedom in the Bahamas leads many escaped slaves from the southern United States* to brave the shark-infested waters for the promise of a better life in the islands.

1860–1865 During the American Civil War, the islands become a meeting point for Southern blockade-runners and British merchants seeking the cotton they have carried through the Union blockade of Southern ports. The blockade-runners exchange their cotton for British and European goods, which they sell in Charleston and other ports for huge profits. The end of the Civil War brings an end to the islands' brief prosperity. Most of the islanders remain subsistence farmers or laborers on estates owned by British landlords.

1898–1933 The Hotel and Steam Ship Service Act of 1898 provides British government support for the construction of hotels in the islands and subsidizes steamship service to and from the islands. This act is acknowledged as the birth of the tourism industry in the Bahamas. Nassau soon becomes a fashionable winter resort. Tourism again blossoms during the Prohibition era, when affluent Americans visit the islands. The influx of visitors increases the demand for lodging, food, and entertainment. Consequently, the banking industry also expands rapidly as new hotels are constructed, restaurants open, and resorts are planned and promoted.

When the United States passes the Fourteenth Amendment prohibiting the sale of alcohol in 1919, large-scale smuggling returns to the islands and, with it, a renewed prosperity. Scotch whiskey becomes the largest import to the islands, so much so that the colonial government greatly expands warehouse space and Prince George Wharf in Nassau is built especially to handle the huge flow of alcohol.

1934–1945 Prohibition ends in 1934, and with it the enormous profits pouring into the islands.

The tourism industry, too, goes into a slump with the end of Prohibition. A profitable sponge harvesting industry collapses a few years later. The economic hardships of the 1930s last until World War II, when the Bahamas become an air and sea way station in the Atlantic. Construction of the military facilities provides jobs to many Bahamians.

1961–1963 In 1961, the island of Cuba, with its glittering casinos, beautiful beaches, and world-class resorts, is closed to American tourists, shifting attention to the nearby Bahamas. Capitalizing on its close proximity to the United States, the Bahamas government begins a campaign to draw in ever-increasing numbers of tourists. New construction, the dredging of Nassau harbor for cruise ships, and other improvements turn the islands into one of the major tourist destinations in the Caribbean.

1964–1973 The United Kingdom* grants the islands limited self-government in 1964, paving the way for full independence in 1973. Independence ends 325 years of British rule, although the Bahamians decide to retain their ties to the United Kingdom and other former British territories through the Commonwealth of Nations.

2000 Tourism continues to expand, bringing the Bahamians much development and even affluence. By 2000, tourism provides 50 percent of the total economy and employs, directly or indirectly, about half the Bahamian population.

2008–2009 The Bahamians enjoy the third-highest per capita income in the Western Hemisphere, and the highest in the Caribbean. Despite the widespread prosperity in the islands, the country still faces significant challenges in areas such as education, health care, international drug trafficking, and illegal immigration.

BARBADOS

OFFICIAL NAME
Barbados

NICKNAME
Land of the Flying Fish; Little England

POPULATION

282,200 (2009e)

INHABITANTS' NAME/NICKNAME

Barbadian(s); Bajan(s)

LANGUAGE/LANGUAGES

English (official); Bajan (local dialect, a recognized regional language); others

RELIGION/RELIGIONS

Anglican, 40 percent; Pentecostal, 8 percent; Methodist, 7 percent; Roman Catholic, 4 percent; other or no religion

NATIONAL FLAG

The flag is a vertical tricolor of ultramarine, gold, and ultramarine bearing a trident, Neptune's Trident, in black centered on the gold. The broken trident is symbolic of Neptune, the mythical god of the sea. The head of the trident also symbolizes Barbados' independence from the United Kingdom*. The ultramarine stripes symbolize the ocean and sky, and the golden stripe symbolizes the golden sands of Barbados.

COAT OF ARMS/SEAL

The golden shield bears two pride of Barbados flowers and the bearded fig tree, after which Barbados is named. The shield is supported by a dolphin, symbolic of the fishing industry, and a pelican, for a small island called Pelican Island that existed off Barbados. Above the shield is a helmet and mantling, and above that is a hand of a Barbadian holding two crossed pieces of sugarcane, symbolic of the formerly predominant Barbados sugar industry. The cross formed by the cane is a reference to the cross on which Saint Andrew was crucified; Barbados' Independence Day is celebrated on November 30, Saint Andrews Day.

MOTTO

Pride and Industry

CAPITAL CITY

Bridgetown

TYPE OF GOVERNMENT

Parliamentary Democracy

NATIONAL EMBLEM

Neptune's Trident

NATIONAL COLORS

Ultramarine and Gold

NATIONAL ANTHEM

The anthem was adopted upon independence in 1966.

In Plenty and in Time of Need

In plenty and in time of need
When this fair land was young
Our brave forefathers sowed the seed
From which our pride was sprung
A pride that makes no wanton boast
Of what it has withstood
That binds our hearts from coast to coast
The pride of nationhood

Chorus

We loyal sons and daughters all
Do hereby make it known
These fields and hills beyond recall
Are now our very own
We write our names on history's page
With expectations great
Strict guardians of our heritage
Firm craftsmen of our fate
The Lord has been the people's guide
For past three hundred years.
With him still on the people's side
We have no doubts or fears.
Upward and onward we shall go,
Inspired, exalting, free,
And greater will our nation grow
In strength and unity.

PATRON SAINT
Saint Andrew

CURRENCY
Barbadian dollar

INTERNET IDENTIFIER
.bb

**VEHICLE IDENTIFICATION PLATES/
STICKERS**
BDS

PASSPORT
The passport cover has the initials CC for Caribbean Community; the name of the country, Barbados; the coat of arms; and the word *passport*.

NATIONAL FLOWER
Pride of Barbados

NATIONAL TREE
Bearded fig tree

NATIONAL ANIMAL
Dolphin

NATIONAL BIRD
Pelican

NATIONAL FISH
Flying fish

NATIONAL RESOURCES
Natural resources include petroleum, fish, and natural gas. The country's Caribbean culture, sandy beaches, pleasant climate, and stable government support an important tourist industry. Historically, the economy of Barbados was dependent on sugarcane cultivation and related activities, but in recent years, it has diversified into the tourism and manufacturing sectors. Offshore finance and

information services have become increasingly important sources of foreign exchange, and there is a healthy light-manufacturing sector.

FOODS
Flying fish with *cou-cou,* grilled flying fish with a cornmeal and okra dumpling, is considered a national dish. Other specialties include pepper pot, a spicy stew of beef, pork, and chicken cooked with spicy peppers; fried flying fish with hot pepper sauce; rice and peas; Bajan roast pork; Bajan sweet bread; Bajan plain cake, a dessert; Bajan beans and rice; buttered yucca; coconut sugar cakes; and coconut bread

SPORTS/SPORTS TEAMS
Cricket is considered the national sport. Football (soccer) and rugby are also very popular. Barbados national teams participate in many sports at an international level.

TEAM SPORTS

Badminton
Barbados Badminton Team

Baseball
Barbados Softball Team

Basketball
Barbados Basketball Team; Barbados Women's Basketball Team

Cricket
West Indies Cricket Team, nickname the Windies (West Indies teams represent a number of English-speaking Caribbean countries)

Football
Barbados Football Team, nickname the Bajans; Barbados Women's Football Team, nickname the Bajans or the Pride of Barbados; Barbados Under-23 Football Team,

nickname the Bajans; Barbados Rugby Union Team; West Indies Rugby League Team, nickname the Wahoos (West Indies teams represent a number of English-speaking Caribbean Countries)

Hockey

Barbados Field Hockey Team

Kabaddi

West Indies Kabaddi Team (West Indies teams represent a number of English-speaking Caribbean countries)

Netball

Barbados Netball Team

Table Tennis

Barbados Table Tennis Team

Tennis

Barbados Davis Cup Team; Barbados Fed Cup Team

Volleyball

Barbados Men's Volleyball Team; Barbados Women's Volleyball Team

INDIVIDUAL SPORTS

Barbados Amateur Boxing Team; Barbados Archery Team; Barbados Athletics Team; Barbados Chess Team; Barbados Cycling Team; Barbados Equestrian Team; Barbados Fencing Team; Barbados Gymnastics Team; Barbados Judo Team; Barbados Rowing Team; Barbados Sailing Team; Barbados Shooting Team; Barbados Swim Team; Barbados Tae Kwon Do Team; Barbados Triathlon Team; Barbados Weight Lifting Team

NATIONAL HEROES OR PERSONIFICATIONS

Horatio Nelson, the naval hero of the Napoleonic Wars, served in the Caribbean and is considered a national hero, with a statue in Bridgetown's National Heroes Square that predates Nelson's Column in London by 27 years. Another national hero is Sir Grantley Adams, the man who led Barbados to independence and the country's first premier.

NATIONAL HOLIDAY/INDEPENDENCE DAY

Independence Day/St. Andrew's Day, November 30

FESTIVALS/FAIRS

Crop Over Festival, June; Jazz Festival, January; Holders Season, March; Gospelfest, May; Celtic Festival, May; National Independence Festival, November–December

SIGNIFICANT EVENTS IN FORMATION OF NATIONAL IDENTITY

350 B.C.E.–13th century C.E. The first inhabitants of the island are seafaring Amerindians from the South American mainland. The tribal peoples arrive in three waves. The first wave arrives in approximately 350–400 B.C.E.; the second, the Arawaks, around 800 C.E.; and the warlike Caribs, who displace the earlier inhabitants, in the 13th century.

16th century The Portuguese are the first Europeans to visit the islands in the mid-16th century. Many Caribs are probably taken from the island by the Portuguese as slaves. Other Caribs escape by boat to neighboring islands. The Portuguese, apart from their possible role in the disappearance of the Carib population from the island, ignore the island in favor of their South American territories. By the early 17th century, the Portuguese had abandoned the island, leaving Barbados virtually uninhabited.

1625–1639 British sailors land on the island in 1625, finding only feral pigs descended from those left behind by the Portuguese. British settlers arrive two years later to validate the British claim to the island. From its earliest settlement, the island enjoys a large measure of local autonomy. Its House of Assembly first meets in 1639.

18th century Sugar production, introduced by Jews from Brazil*, quickly overtakes other crops to become the island's main export. Barbados is divided into large plantation estates that replace the smallholdings of the earliest settlers. The large landowners who dominate the island import large numbers of black slaves to work the sugar plantations. By the early 19th century, the population of the island is largely black, with a small ruling white minority.

1807–1834 The British abolish the slave trade in 1807, but slavery in the islands continues. In 1816, the continuing practice of slavery results in the largest slave rebellion in the island's history. Some 20 thousand slaves from over 70 plantations eventually join the rebellion. They drive the white families from the plantations, yet they carefully avoid mass killings. The rebellion ultimately fails, with 120 rebels killed in combat or immediately executed and many more brought to trial and later executed. Slavery in the islands, and the rest of the British Empire, is finally abolished in 1834. In the Caribbean islands, full emancipation from slavery is preceded by an apprenticeship period of four years. The majority of former slaves settle into a life of subsistence farming.

1835–1938 Plantation owners and a merchant class of British descent still dominate the life of the island. Owing to the high income qualifications required for voting, only a small minority are eligible to vote. Only in the 1930s do the descendants of emancipated slaves begin a movement for political rights. One of the leaders of the movement, Grantley Adams, founds the Barbados Labour Party, then known as the Barbados Progressive League, in 1938.

1939–1958 A loyal defender of the British monarchy, Adams and his party demand more rights for the poor and for the people of Barbados in general. Progress is finally made in 1942, when the exclusive income qualifications are finally lowered giving many more Barbadians the vote. Women are also enfranchised at the same time. By 1949, control of the government has been wrested from the former ruling class, and in 1958, Adams becomes the island's premier.

1958–1962 Barbados is a member state of the West Indies Federation from 1958 to 1962. The federation flounders on nationalist issues among its various members and on the fact that, as British colonies, the members have only limited legislative power. When the federation is dissolved, Barbados reverts to its former status as a self-governing British colony.

1964–1966 Adam's preference for continued ties to the British monarchy means that he loses support and finally retires from politics. In 1966, island leaders begin negotiations with the United Kingdom* on its future status. After years of peaceful, democratic progress, Barbados becomes an independent state within the Commonwealth of Nations on November 30, 1966.

1966–2009 Barbados settles into a democratic system with two major political parties. Peaceful elections become an expected part of the island's political life. Economically, the island is among the most prosperous in the Caribbean. A building boom that begins in 2003 continues through 2008 with the construction of several multimillion-dollar projects, although the global economic slump curtails growth in 2009.

BERMUDA

OFFICIAL NAME
Bermuda

POPULATION
65,500 (2009e)

INHABITANTS' NAME/NICKNAME
Bermudian(s)

LANGUAGE/LANGUAGES
English (official); Portuguese

RELIGION/RELIGIONS
Anglican, 23 percent; Roman Catholic, 15 percent; African Methodist Episcopal, 11 percent; other or no religion

NATIONAL FLAG
The national flag of Bermuda is composed of a red field with the Union Jack as a canton in the upper left and the Bermuda coat of arms

in the lower fly. From 1910, when Bermuda received its own coat of arms, unofficial versions of the union flag incorporating the arms appeared in Bermuda.

COAT OF ARMS/SEAL

The coat of arms shows a ship, the *Sea Venture*, foundering on rocks. The rocky coast is shown to the left of the shield, and the sea is to the right. The ship appears to be hitting the rocks. (The *Sea Venture* was wrecked on the coast of Bermuda in about 1609.) The shield is held from behind by a large red lion, in such a way that its paws appear at the edges of the shield and its head appears above it like a crest.

MOTTO

Quo fata ferunt (Latin); Whither the fates carry us (English)

CAPITAL CITY

Hamilton

TYPE OF GOVERNMENT

Self-governing parliamentary democracy as a British Overseas Territory. The United Kingdom* retains control of defense, internal security, and foreign affairs.

NATIONAL EMBLEM

Pink buildings in Hamilton

NATIONAL COLORS

Blue and white

NATIONAL ANTHEM

"God Save the Queen" is the official anthem of all British territories. An unofficial local anthem is used alongside the official anthem.

Hail to Bermuda

Hail to Bermuda
My island in the sun
Sing out in glory
To the nation we've become
We've grown from heart
To heart
And strength to strength
For loyalty is prime
So sing long live Bermuda
Because this island's mine
Hail to Bermuda
My homeland dear to me
This is my own land
Built on strength
And unity
We've grown from heart
To heart
And strength to strength
This privilege is mine
So sing long live Bermuda
Because this island's mine!

PATRON SAINT

Saint Therese of Lisieux is the patron saint of the Roman Catholic Diocese of Bermuda.

CURRENCY

Bermuda dollar

INTERNET IDENTIFIER

.bm

VEHICLE IDENTIFICATION PLATES/STICKERS

BM

PASSPORT

Bermudians are British citizens and travel on British passports.

NATIONAL FLOWER

Bermudiana (blue-eyed grass)

NATIONAL TREE

Bermuda cedar (unofficial)

NATIONAL ANIMAL

Dolphin (unofficial)

NATIONAL BIRD

White-tailed tropicbird (Bermuda long tail) (unofficial)

NATIONAL FISH

Wahoo (unofficial)

NATIONAL RESOURCES

Natural resources, other than limestone for building, are negligible. A pleasant climate, sandy beaches, and Bermuda's geographic location close to major population centers on the North American mainland foster a flourishing tourist industry. As the offshore domicile of many international companies, Bermuda has a highly developed business economy; it is a financial center for insurance and other financial services. Tourism is the second largest industry, with over half a million visitors annually.

FOODS

Bean soup, first introduced by Portuguese immigrants over 150 years ago, is now a national tradition. Cassava pie, which dates to at least 1612, is another traditional dish. Other specialties include codfish and bananas; Bermuda fish chowder; fish cakes; salt cod and potatoes; and sweet potato casserole.

SPORTS/SPORTS TEAMS

Cricket and sailing are the most popular sports, followed by golf, football (soccer), and rugby. Cricket is considered the de facto national sport. Bermuda national teams participate in many sports at an international level.

TEAM SPORTS

Badminton

Bermuda Badminton Team

Baseball

Bermuda Softball Team

Basketball

Bermuda Basketball Team; Bermuda Women's Basketball Team

Cricket

Bermuda Cricket Team; Bermuda Women's Cricket Team; Bermuda Under-18 Cricket Team

Football

Bermuda Football Team the Warriors; Bermuda Women's Football Team; Bermuda Under-20 Football Team; Bermuda Women's Under-19 Football Team; Bermuda Rugby Union Team

Hockey

Bermuda Field Hockey Team

Lacrosse

Bermuda Lacrosse Team; Bermuda Under-19 Lacrosse Team

Netball

Bermuda Netball Team

Table Tennis

Bermuda Table Tennis Team

Tennis

Bermuda Davis Cup Team; Bermuda Fed Cup Team

Volleyball

Bermuda Men's Volleyball Team; Bermuda Women's Volleyball Team; Bermuda Men's Beach Volleyball Team; Bermuda Women's Beach Volleyball Team

INDIVIDUAL SPORTS

Bermuda Amateur Boxing Team; Bermuda Athletics Team; Bermuda Archery Team; Bermuda Chess Team; Bermuda Cycling Team; Bermuda Equestrian Team; Bermuda Gymnastics Team; Bermuda Judo Team; Bermuda

Rowing Team; Bermuda Sailing Team; Bermuda Shooting Team; Bermuda Swim Team; Bermuda Tae Kwon Do Team; Bermuda Triathlon Team

WINTER SPORTS

Bermuda Luge Team

NATIONAL HEROES OR PERSONIFICATIONS

Dame Lois Browne-Evans, the first female opposition political leader in the Commonwealth, as well as Bermuda's first barrister and first black woman legislator; Sir Henry Tucker, the first premier of the autonomous Bermuda government

NATIONAL HOLIDAY/INDEPENDENCE DAY

Bermuda Day, May 24

FESTIVALS/FAIRS

Bermuda Day Festival, May; Queen's Birthday, June; The Bermuda Festival of the Performing Arts, January–February; Bermuda International Film Festival, March–April; Bermuda Music Festival, October

SIGNIFICANT EVENTS IN FORMATION OF NATIONAL IDENTITY

1503 According to early accounts, the islands are first sighted by Europeans in 1503 by Spaniard Juan Bermudez, for whom the islands are eventually named.

1609 Over the next century, the islands are sighted or visited frequently, but no permanent settlements are attempted. The first British colonies established in Virginia on the American mainland flounder, leading to a more determined effort to relieve the Jamestown colonists in 1609. A flotilla of ships leaves England under Admiral Sir George Somers, but when the flotilla is separated during a violent storm, the flagship, the *Sea Venture*, makes landfall on Bermuda, making the crew and passengers the first settlers.

1615 In 1615, the new colony passes to a new company, the Somers Isles Company. It bears the name originally given the islands, the Somers Isles, after the captain of the *Sea Venture*.

1620 The local legislature, the House of Assembly, which was created to implement self-government in 1620, is the fifth oldest in the world, behind only England, the Isle of Man*, Iceland*, and Poland*. The limited resources of the islands lead to the creation of what might be the earliest conservation laws in the Americas. In 1616 and 1620, legislation is passed banning the hunting of certain birds and young tortoises.

18th century Due to its limited land area, Bermuda relies on steady emigration to keep its population stable.

1790–1812 After the American Revolution, the Royal Navy improves Bermuda's harbors and builds a large dockyard as its principal naval base, which is used for the attack on Washington, D.C., in 1812.

1860–1865 During the American Civil War, the islands are regularly used by Confederate blockade-runners to evade Union naval vessels and deliver desperately needed war goods to the South.

1900–1919 The islands become a favorite destination for wealthy tourists. Prohibition, the banning of liquor sales in the United States from 1919, also aids the growth of Bermudian commerce, which thrives on the illegal liquor trade.

1970s The white majority that controls the government and commerce begins to lose some of its privileges during the turbulent 1970s. Black Bermudians, who normally hold menial jobs, mostly in the tourist industry, show their discontent with the existing situation with protests and strikes. Violence flares on several occasions, particular on March 10, 1973, when members of a black proindependence organization assassinate the British governor and his aide. The execution of the assassins on December 2, 1977, sets off a week of violence and riots.

1978–1982 A royal commission in 1978 recommends independence for Bermuda. The first black Bermudian elected to head the government, Sir John Swan, in 1982, initially opposes independence due to financial and administrative concerns.

1995 On August 15, 1995, Bermudians vote on the issue of independence. A boycott by the majority black opposition party, which calls for constitutional reform and a general election prior to the vote, helps the anti-independence group. The vote is 74 percent against independence, indicating that a majority prefers to retain ties to the United Kingdom.

2006–2009 The question of independence, which has proved divisive in the past, has been mostly removed from island politics for the time being. Bermudians, both black and white, are quite content with the present political situation, which helps support their affluent and buoyant economy and one of the highest standards of living in the Americas.

See also United Kingdom

BRITISH VIRGIN ISLANDS

OFFICIAL NAME
British Virgin Islands

POPULATION
23,300 (2009e)

INHABITANTS' NAME/NICKNAME
British Virgin Islander(s); BV Islander(s); Belonger(s)

LANGUAGE/LANGUAGES
English (official); English Creole, Spanish, others

RELIGION/RELIGIONS
Methodist, 33 percent; Anglican, 17 percent; Roman Catholic, 10 percent; Church of God, 9 percent; Seventh-day Adventist, 6 percent; Baptist, 4 percent; other or no religion

NATIONAL FLAG
The flag is a blue field bearing the Union Jack as a canton on the upper hoist and the coat of arms of the British Virgin Islands on the hoist. The coat of arms features Saint Ursula and the lamps of her virgin followers, which give the islands their name. When Christopher Columbus sighted the islands in 1493, the numerous islands were said to have reminded him of the story of the martyrdom of Saint Ursula and her virgins.

COAT OF ARMS/SEAL
The coat of arms or seal of the British Virgin Islands is a green shield showing Saint Ursula and 11 lamps, representing the 11,000 virgins martyred with her. The arms of the colony were chosen as a representation of the story of the saint.

MOTTO
Vigilate (Latin); Be Watchful (English)

CAPITAL CITY
Road Town

TYPE OF GOVERNMENT
Parliamentary democracy as a British Overseas Territory

NATIONAL EMBLEM
Saint Ursula framed by 11 oil lamps

NATIONAL COLORS
Green and gold

NATIONAL ANTHEM
"God Save the Queen," the official anthem of the United Kingdom* and its associated territories.

PATRON SAINT
Saint Ursula

CURRENCY
U.S. dollar

INTERNET IDENTIFIER
.vg

VEHICLE IDENTIFICATION PLATES/ STICKERS
BVI

PASSPORT
The people of the British Virgin Islands are British citizens and travel on British passports.

NATIONAL FLOWER
Yellow cedar

NATIONAL TREE
Guavaberry (unofficial)

NATIONAL BIRD
Mourning dove

NATIONAL FISH
Queen trigger (unofficial)

NATIONAL RESOURCES
Natural resources in the island are negligible; however, sandy beaches, a pleasant climate, underwater reefs, and a vibrant culture support a tourist industry that draws some half a million visitors a year. Tourism and financial services are the twin pillars of the local economy. Land, most of which is owned by the islanders, is the basis of the local sense of autonomy and independence.

FOODS
Fungi, cornmeal mixed with okra, is served as part of fish and *fungi,* the national dish. Johnnycakes, peas and rice, and fried fish are all considered national dishes. Other specialties include buttered yucca, cassava chips, coconut bread, grilled lobster with coconut, and shrimp stew.

SPORTS/SPORTS TEAMS
Cricket is the islands' most popular sport. Association football (soccer) is also very popular. British Virgin Islands national teams participate in many sports at an international level.

TEAM SPORTS
Baseball
British Virgin Islands Baseball Team; British Virgin Islands Softball Team

Basketball
British Virgin Islands Basketball Team; British Virgin Islands Women's Basketball Team

Cricket
Leeward Islands Cricket Team and West Indies Cricket Team (both Leeward Islands and West Indies teams represent a number of English-speaking Caribbean countries)

Football
British Virgin Islands Football Team; British Virgin Islands Women's Football Team; British Virgin Islands Rugby Union Team; British Virgin Islands Women's Under-19 Football Team; West Indies Rugby League Team, nickname the Wahoos (West Indies teams represent a number of English-speaking Caribbean countries)

Kabaddi
West Indies Kabaddi Team (West Indies teams represent a number of English-speaking Caribbean countries)

Volleyball
British Virgin Islands Men's Volleyball Team; British Virgin Islands Women's Volleyball Team

INDIVIDUAL SPORTS
British Virgin Islands Athletics Team; British Virgin Islands Canoeing Team; British Virgin Islands Judo Team; British Virgin Islands Sailing Team; British Virgin Islands Tae Kwon Do Team

National Heroes or Personifications

H. Lavity Stoutt was the first popularly elected chief minister following constitutional reforms in 1967. At the time of his death in office in 1995, he had served four terms and was the longest-serving chief executive in the Caribbean; Ralph T. O'Neal, the first premier of the British Virgin Islands under the reformed constitution of 2007.

National Holiday/Independence Day

Territory Day, July 1; Saint Ursula's Day, October 22

Festivals/Fairs

A festival celebrating emancipation of the slaves on August 1, 1834, is held annually for three days in July and August; Sweethearts of the Caribbean, February; BVI Music Festival, May; Highland Springs, June and July; Spring Regatta, March and April

Significant Events in Formation of National Identity

100 B.C.E.–15th century C.E.   The islands are first settled by Arawak people from South America around 100 B.C.E., although there is some evidence of Amerindian presence as far back as 1500 B.C.E. In the 15th century, the more warlike Caribs take control of the islands. The Caribs, a tribe moving north from the Lesser Antilles, would later give their name the Caribbean Sea.

1493–1648   Christopher Columbus, on his second voyage to the New World, sights and names the islands *Santa Ursula y las Once Mil Virgenes* (Saint Ursula and the Eleven-Thousand Virgins), later shortened to the Virgin Islands. European diseases, slavery in the copper mines of the Spanish in the early 16th century, and violent conflicts devastate the indigenous population, which disappears by 1648. The islands become a notorious haunt for pirates, while English, Dutch, French, Spanish, and Danish fleets attempt to gain and maintain control.

1648   The Dutch establish a permanent settlement on the island of Tortola. The English capture Tortola from the Dutch in 1672, and the annexation of the other islands follows in 1680. The Danes gain control of the nearby islands of Saint Thomas, Saint John, and Saint Croix.

18th century–19th century   The British consider the islands a strategic territory, but sugarcane production flourishes, and African slaves are imported to work the plantations. The islands' prosperity sags when sugar beet production begins in Europe and the United States*. Slavery is outlawed in the British Empire in 1837, ending the plantation system. Most former slaves settle on small plots as subsistence farmers or fishermen.

1917–1960   The United States purchases Saint John, Saint Thomas, and Saint Croix from Denmark, renaming them the United States Virgin Islands. Subsequently, the British rename the islands they control as the British Virgin Islands. The islands are variously administered as part of the British Leeward Islands Colony or united with Saint Kitts and Nevis*, with an administrator representing the government in the islands. The U.S. dollar is adopted as the official currency in 1959.

1960–2009   The islands gain separate-colony status in 1960 and become an autonomous state in 1967. Since the 1960s, the Islands have diversified away from their traditionally agriculture-based economy toward tourism and financial services, becoming one of the richest areas in the Caribbean. The per capita income of the British Virgin Islands is over $38,000, making the islands one of the most prosperous regions in the Americas.

See also United Kingdom

CANADA

Official Name

Canada

Population

33,447,200 (2009e)

Inhabitants' Name/Nickname

Canadian(s), Canuck(s)

LANGUAGE/LANGUAGES

English, French (official); Italian, indigenous languages, German, Ukrainian, others

RELIGION/RELIGIONS

Roman Catholic, 44 percent; United Church, 9.5 percent; Anglican, 7 percent; Baptist, 2.5 percent; Lutheran, 2 percent; Muslim, 2 percent; Jewish, other or no religion

NATIONAL FLAG

The Canadian Flag, colloquially known as the Maple Leaf Flag in English and *l'Unifolié* in French, is a red field with a large white square in the center bearing a single red, stylized, 11-pointed maple leaf. The maple leaf has served as a symbol celebrating the environment and nature of Canada since the 1700s. The color red comes from Britain's Saint George's Cross, and the white is from the French royal emblem.

COAT OF ARMS/SEAL

The coat of arms, also known as the Royal Arms of Canada, has been the official arms of the Canadian monarch and thus also of Canada since 1921. The shield is divided into five sections: the first division at the top left contains the three golden lions, symbolizing England; the second quarter bears the red lion of Scotland; the third shows the Irish harp; the fourth shows the golden fleur-de-lis of France on blue; and the lower division is white with three red and gold maple leaves. The ribbon around the shield bears the Latin inscription *desiderantes meliorem patriam* (desiring a better country). Above the shield is a royal helmet, draped in white and red, the Canadian colors, symbolizing Canada's sovereignty. The crest, a gold lion, is based on the Royal Crest of England but with the addition of a maple leaf. Above the crest is Saint Edward's Crown, the style preferred by the queen. Supporting the shield on either side are an English lion and a Scottish unicorn, which also support the coat of arms of the United Kingdom*. Below, on a blue banner, is written in gold the Latin motto of the country.

MOTTO

A mari usque ad mare (Latin); From sea to sea (English)

CAPITAL CITY

Ottawa

TYPE OF GOVERNMENT

Federal parliamentary democracy

NATIONAL EMBLEM

Maple leaf

NATIONAL COLORS

Red and white

NATIONAL ANTHEM

The anthem was written in 1880 and was sung later that year in Quebec City in French. The English version, translated from the French and created to fit the melody, was written later. The anthem was unofficial, used alongside the official anthem, "God Save the Queen," until it was adopted as the official anthem in 1980, one century after it was first sung.

O Canada

O Canada! Our home and native land!
True patriot love in all thy sons command.
With glowing hearts we see thee rise,
The true north strong and free!
From far and wide,
O Canada, we stand on guard for thee.
God keep our land glorious and free!
O Canada, we stand on guard for thee.
O Canada, we stand on guard for thee.

O Canada! Where pines and maples grow.
Great prairies spread and lordly rivers flow.
How dear to us thy broad domain,

From east to western sea,
Thou land of hope for all who toil!
Thou true north, strong and free!
God keep our land glorious and free!
O Canada, we stand on guard for thee.
O Canada, we stand on guard for thee.

O Canada! Beneath thy shining skies
May stalwart sons and gentle maidens rise,
To keep thee steadfast through the years
From east to western sea,
Our own beloved native land!
Our true north, strong and free!
God keep our land glorious and free!
O Canada, we stand on guard for thee.
O Canada, we stand on guard for thee.

Ruler supreme, who hearest humble prayer,
Hold our dominion within thy loving care;
Help us to find, O God, in thee
A lasting, rich reward,
As waiting for the better day,
We ever stand on guard.
God keep our land glorious and free!
O Canada, we stand on guard for thee.
O Canada, we stand on guard for thee.

PATRON SAINT

Saint Anne, mother of the Virgin Mary; Saint Joseph; the Martyrs of North America

CURRENCY

Canadian dollar

INTERNET IDENTIFIER

.ca

VEHICLE IDENTIFICATION PLATES

CDN

PASSPORT

The passport cover has the name *Canada,* the coat of arms, and the word *passport* in both English and French

AIRLINES

Air Canada; Air Transat; WestJet

NATIONAL FLOWER

Maple leaf (unofficial); each province has a separate official flower

NATIONAL TREE

Sugar maple

NATIONAL ANIMAL

Beaver; Canadian horse

NATIONAL BIRD

Common loon

NATIONAL FISH

Arctic cod (unofficial)

NATIONAL RESOURCES

Natural resources include iron ore, nickel, zinc, copper, gold, lead, molybdenum, potash, diamonds, silver, fish, timber, wildlife, coal, petroleum, natural gas, and hydropower. Canada is unusual for a developed nation as it is a net exporter of energy. Vast offshore reserves of natural gas off the east coast and the huge Athabasca Oil Sands in Alberta give Canada the largest oil reserves behind Saudi Arabia. In other parts of Canada, hydroelectricity is an inexpensive and clean source of renewable energy. Canada is also one of the world's most important suppliers of agricultural products. Tourism, based on Canada's natural attractions, friendly people, and historic cities, is a very important resource.

FOODS

Canadian food varies greatly from region to region. Generally, the traditional cuisine of English Canada resembles those of the United Kingdom and the United States*, while the food traditions of French Canada evolved from French cuisine and the winter provisions of early fur traders. Foods considered national dishes are haddock and chips in English Canada and *tourtière* and *pâte* *à la ràpure* (Quebec meat pies) in French Canada.

SPORTS/SPORTS TEAMS

Football (Canadian football, American football, Association football or soccer, and rugby), basketball, baseball, and hockey are all very popular. National sports, as defined by law, are lacrosse, the national summer sport, designated in 1859; and ice hockey, the national winter sport, designated in 1994. Canada national teams participate in many sports at the international level.

TEAM SPORTS

Badminton

Canada Badminton Team

Baseball

Canada Baseball Team; Canada Softball Team

Basketball

Canada Basketball Team, nickname Team Canada; Canada Women's Basketball Team, nickname Team Canada; Canada Wheelchair Basketball Team; Canada Women's Wheelchair Basketball Team; Canada Under-21 Basketball Team

Cricket

Canada Cricket Team; Canada Women's Cricket Team

Bowls

Canada Bowls Team

Curling

Canada Curling Team

Football

Canada Football Team (Men's Soccer Team), nickname the Canucks or Les Rouges (the Reds); Canada Women's Football Team (Women's Soccer Team), nickname Big Red;

Canada Rugby Union Team, nickname the Canucks; Canada Women's Rugby Union Team, nickname the Canucks; Canada Under-20 Men's Soccer Team, nickname the Canucks, the Maple Leaves, Les Rouges (the Reds); Canada Rugby League Team, nickname the Cougars; Canada Rugby Union Team (Sevens), nickname Canada Sevens or Canada 7s; Canada Women's Rugby Union Team (Sevens), nickname Canada Sevens or Canada 7s; Canada Australian-Rules Football Team, nickname the Northwind; Canada Women's Australian-Rules Football Team, nickname the Northwind; Canada Wheelchair Rugby Team; Canada American Football Team; Canada Beach Soccer Team; Canada Futsal Team; Canada Touch Football Team; Canada Women's Touch Football Team

Handball

Canada Handball Team; Canada Women's Handball Team; Canada Beach Handball Team; Canada Women's Beach Handball Team

Hockey

Canada Men's Ice Hockey Team, nickname Team Canada; Canada Women's Ice Hockey Team, nickname Team Canada; Canada Junior Ice Hockey Team, nickname Team Canada; Canada Under-17 Ice Hockey Team; Canada Under-18 Ice Hockey Team; Canada Under-20 Ice Hockey Team; Canada Under-18 Women's Ice Hockey Team; Canada Field Hockey Team; Canada Women's Field Hockey Team; Canada Bandy Team

Kabaddi

Canada Kabaddi Team

Korfball

Canada Korfball Team

Lacrosse

Canada Lacrosse Team; Canada Women's Lacrosse Team; Canada Under-19 Lacrosse

Team; Canada Women's Under-19 Lacrosse Team

Netball

Canada Netball Team

Polo

Canada Polo Team

Racing

A1 Team Canada; Canada Speedway Team

Table Tennis

Canada Table Tennis Team

Tennis

Canada Davis Cup Team; Canada Fed Cup Team

Volleyball

Canada Men's Volleyball Team; Canada Women's Volleyball Team; Canada Men's Beach Volleyball Team; Canada Women's Beach Volleyball Team

Water Polo

Canada Men's Water Polo Team; Canada Women's Water Polo Team

INDIVIDUAL SPORTS

Canada Amateur Boxing Team; Canada Archery Team; Canada Athletics Team; Canada Canoeing Team; Canada Cycling Team; Canada Equestrian Team; Canada Fencing Team; Canada Gymnastics Team; Canada Judo Team; Canada Karate Team; Canada Modern Pentathlon Team; Canada Sailing Team; Canada Shooting Team; Canada Swim Team; Canada Triathlon Team; Canada Weight Lifting Team; Canada Wrestling Team

WINTER SPORTS

Canada Alpine Ski Team; Canada Biathlon Team; Canada Bobsleigh and Tobogganing Team; Canada Curling Team; Canada Men's Ice Hockey Team, nickname Team Canada; Canada Women's Ice Hockey Team, nickname Team Canada; Canada Junior Ice Hockey Team, nickname Team Canada; Canada Under-17 Ice Hockey Team; Canada Under-18 Ice Hockey Team; Canada Under-20 Ice Hockey Team; Canada Under-18 Women's Ice Hockey Team; Canada Luge Team; Canada Skating Team

NATIONAL HEROES OR PERSONIFICATIONS

Johnny Canuck, Canada's national personification, began as a political cartoon and is often seen resisting the bullying of other nations. He is depicted as simple fellow in the garb of a farmer or lumberjack, and his influence on Canadian fashion can be seen even today. Other legends and heroes include the Royal Canadian Mounted Police (the Mounties); Canada, the Great Provider; Big Joe Mufferaw, a French Canadian folk hero equivalent to Paul Bunyan in the United States; Reginald Fessenden, one of the inventors of early radio devices; George Beurling, the most successful Canadian fighter pilot of the Second World War; Marilyn Bell, the first person to swim across Lake Ontario in 1954; Nellie McClung, a feminist, social activist, and politician in the early 1900s; and William Lyon Mackenzie King, the 10th prime minister of Canada, a lawyer, university professor, civil servant, journalist, and politician who led Canada during World War II

NATIONAL HOLIDAY/INDEPENDENCE DAY

Canada Day, July 1

FESTIVALS/FAIRS

Calgary Stampede, Canada's largest rodeo and exhibition, July; Quebec City Winter Carnival, the world's largest winter carnival, January–February; Canadian National Exhibition, August–September; Pacific

National Exhibition, August–September; Toronto International Film Festival, September; Canadian Music Week, March; Stratford Shakespeare Festival, Stratford, Ontario, April–November

SIGNIFICANT EVENTS IN FORMATION OF NATIONAL IDENTITY

24,500 B.C.E.–7,500 B.C.E. According to aboriginal tradition, the First Peoples have inhabited parts of Canada since the dawn of time.

1000 B.C.E.–1534 Europeans first appear when the Vikings cross the North Atlantic to briefly settle at L'Anse aux Meadows around 1000 C.E. Europeans begin to explore the Atlantic coast in the 15th century, among them John Cabot, sailing under the English flag, who visited the Atlantic coast in 1497, followed by Jacques Cartier of France in 1534.

1603–1689 Samuel de Champlain establishes the first permanent European settlement in Canada. French colonists settle the areas known as New France and Acadia. Fur trappers and traders explore the Great Lakes and Hudson Bay. Catholic missionaries make contact with many First Peoples from the Great Lakes down the Mississippi to Louisiana.

1610–1689 English fishing outposts are established in Newfoundland around 1610. English companies enter the fur trade, which becomes Canada's major industry.

1689–1774 A series of wars between France and England erupt between 1689 and 1763, which end with a complete French withdrawal from mainland North America. To avert conflict in Quebec, the Quebec Act of 1774 expands the province's boundaries and reestablishes the French language, the Catholic faith, and French civil law in Quebec.

1783–1790 Approximately 50,000 United Empire Loyalists flee the new United States to British territory in Canada. The Constitutional Act of 1791 divides the province into French-speaking Lower Canada and English-speaking Upper Canada.

1815–1858 Large-scale immigration to Canada begins in 1815, mostly from Britain and Ireland. The desire for responsible government results in an aborted rebellion in 1837. The signing of the Oregon Treaty between Britain and the United States in 1846 extends the border westward along the 49th parallel and paves the way for British colonies on Vancouver Island in 1849 and British Colombia in 1858.

1867 The British North America Act brings about a confederation under the name Dominion of Canada with four provinces: Quebec, Nova Scotia, Ontario, and New Brunswick.

1949 In 1949, Newfoundland joins the Confederation. Post-war prosperity and economic expansion ignite a baby boom and attract immigration from war-ravaged Europe.

1960–1980 The separatist Parti Québécois comes to power in Quebec in 1976. A majority rejects a referendum on separation from Canada in 1980.

1995–1997 A second referendum on Quebec independence, in 1995, is rejected by a very slim margin of just 50.6 percent to 49.5 percent. In 1997, the Canadian Supreme Court rules that unilateral secession by a province is unconstitutional.

1960s–2008 In 2008, Canada's government officially apologizes for abuses at residential schools created to culturally assimilate aboriginal peoples between World War I and the 1970s.

2009 Opposition parties unite to bring down the government, but a brief suspension of parliament and a later stimulus package ensure the survival of the government. The global economic crisis leads to slower economic growth in most of Canada's provinces.

See also Quebec

CAYMAN ISLANDS

OFFICIAL NAME
Cayman Islands

POPULATION
63,200 (2009e)

INHABITANTS' NAME/NICKNAME

Cayman Islander(s); Caymanian(s)

LANGUAGE/LANGUAGES

English (official); Spanish, others

RELIGION/RELIGIONS

Christian, 79 percent (mainly Presbyterian, with Anglican, Roman Catholic, others); Jewish, 1.5 percent; Baha'i, Hindu, other or no religion

NATIONAL FLAG

The flag is a blue field bearing the Union Jack as a canton on the upper hoist and the coat of arms centered on the fly.

COAT OF ARMS/SEAL

The coat of arms has a central crest or shield with wavy blue and white lines across the bottom representing the Caribbean Sea and three green, five-pointed stars edged in gold representing the three major islands. On the upper part of the shield is a rampant lion on a red background, symbolizing historic ties to England. Above the shield are a green turtle and a golden pineapple. Below the shield is a banner inscribed with the national motto.

MOTTO

He hath founded it upon the seas

CAPITAL CITY

George Town

TYPE OF GOVERNMENT

Parliamentary democracy as a British Overseas Territory

NATIONAL EMBLEM

Sea turtle; pirate

NATIONAL COLORS

Red and blue

NATIONAL ANTHEM

The official anthem, as in all British territories, is "God Save the Queen." The local anthem was written in 1930 and was sung for many years as an island song before being adopted as the islands' national song.

Beloved Isle Cayman

O land of soft, fresh breezes,
Of verdant trees so fair
With the Creator's glory reflected
  ev'rywhere.
O sea of palest em'rald,
Merging to darkest blue,
Whene'er my thoughts fly Godward,
I always think of you.

Chorus

Dear, verdant island, set
In blue Caribbean Sea,
I'm coming, coming very soon, O beauteous
  isle, to thee.
Although I've wandered far,
My heart enshrines thee yct.
Homeland! Fair Cayman Isle
I cannot thee forget

Away from noise of cities,
Their fret and carking care,
With moonbeams' soft caresses,
Unchecked by garish glare,
Thy fruit and rarest juices,
Abundant, rich and free,
When sweet church bells are chiming,
My fond heart yearns for thee.

Chorus

When tired of all excitement,
And glam'rous worldly care,
How sweet thy shores to reach,
And find a welcome there,
And when comes on the season,
Of peace, good will to man,
'Tis then I love thee best of all,
Beloved isle, Cayman!

PATRON SAINT

Saint Ignatius

CURRENCY
Cayman dollar

INTERNET IDENTIFIER
.ky

VEHICLE IDENTIFICATION PLATES/STICKERS
GB (official); KY or CI (unofficial)

PASSPORT
Cayman Islanders are British citizens and travel on British passports.

AIRLINES
Cayman Airways

NATIONAL FLOWER
Wild banana orchid

NATIONAL TREE
Silver thatch palm

NATIONAL ANIMAL
Sea turtle (unofficial)

NATIONAL BIRD
Grand Cayman parrot

NATIONAL FISH
Southern stingray (unofficial)

NATIONAL RESOURCES
Natural resources include are negligible, other than fish, a pleasant climate, and beaches that support the important tourist industry. The economy of the Cayman Islands was once centered on turtling. However, this industry began to disappear in the 20th century, and tourism and financial services became the economic mainstays during the 1970s. The United States* is the Cayman Islands' largest trading partner. With an average income of around $42,000, Caymanians enjoy the highest standard of living in the Caribbean and the eighth highest in the world.

FOODS
Turtle soup, a traditional dish in the islands, is considered the national dish. Conch is also very popular and is prepared in a number of ways. Other island specialties include iced coconut soup, seafood soup, peas and rice, buttered yucca, and coconut bread.

SPORTS/SPORTS TEAMS
Association football (soccer) is the most popular sport. Rugby union is gaining popularity, and cricket remains a favorite sport. Cayman Islands national teams participate in many sports at an international level.

TEAM SPORTS
Badminton
Cayman Islands Badminton Team

Baseball
Cayman Islands Softball Team

Basketball
Cayman Islands Basketball Team; Cayman Islands Women's Basketball Team

Football
Cayman Islands Football Team; Cayman Islands Women's Football Team; Cayman Islands Rugby Union Team; Cayman Islands Women's Rugby Union Team; Cayman Islands Rugby Union Sevens, nickname Cayman Sevens or 7s; Cayman Islands Beach Soccer Team. The football authority is the Cayman Islands Football Association.

Hockey
Cayman Islands Field Hockey Team

Netball

Cayman Islands Netball Team

Volleyball

Cayman Islands Men's Volleyball Team; Cayman Islands Women's Volleyball Team

INDIVIDUAL SPORTS

Cayman Islands Amateur Boxing Team; Cayman Islands Athletics Team; Cayman Islands Cycling Team; Cayman Islands Equestrian Team; Cayman Islands Judo Team; Cayman Islands Rowing Team; Cayman Islands Sailing Team; Cayman Islands Shooting Team; Cayman Islands Swim Team; Cayman Islands Tae Kwon Do Team; Cayman Islands Triathlon Team; Cayman Islands Weight Lifting Team

NATIONAL HEROES OR PERSONIFICATIONS

Pirates, due to the islands' history, are considered the personification of the national culture. Pirates Week, the national festival, celebrates the pirate heroes of the Cayman Islands; McKeeva Bush, the longest-serving member of the Cayman Islands legislature, affectionately known as the "Father of the House"

NATIONAL HOLIDAY/INDEPENDENCE DAY

Constitution Day, first Monday in July; Discovery Day, May 18

FESTIVALS/FAIRS

Batabano (Grand Cayman), annual carnival held near Easter; Brachanal (Cayman Brac), held a week after Batabano; Pirate's Week, 10-day national festival at the end of October or early November

SIGNIFICANT EVENTS IN FORMATION OF NATIONAL IDENTITY

1503–1586 The islands are uninhabited when Christopher Columbus sights the two smaller islands on his fourth trip to the New World in 1503.

He names them Las Tortugas after the numerous sea turtles. Sir Francis Drake is the first recorded English visitor, who lands in 1586. By the time of Drake's visit, the islands are known as the Caymanas, after a Carib word for crocodiles.

1586–1660 No effort is made to settle the islands, although ships of many nations stop for water and food, mostly turtles. The islands become the haunt of pirates preying on Spanish shipping in the Caribbean. The earliest inhabitants are a mixture of buccaneers, exiled debtors, and shipwrecked sailors.

1670–1734 Spain* claims the Caymans but mostly ignores them until pirate outrages spur action. The islands are ceded to England in 1670. The first English settlement is founded on Grand Cayman in 1734. The Cayman Islands are governed as part of the colony of Jamaica*. Slaves are imported, mostly from Africa, to work on the farms and plantations.

1831–1877 A legislative assembly is formed on Grand Cayman. Families from Grand Cayman settle Cayman Brac and Little Cayman in 1833. All slaves in the island are declared free in 1835. Sailing ships from many nations visit the islands, which remain generally quiet and tranquil, relying on fishing and farming.

1950s–1960s Divers discover the island's reefs and fascinating underwater gardens early in the 1950s. Tourism quickly becomes a leading industry, and the Caymanians organize a private banking system that attracts international attention.

1953–1959 The first airfield is opened near George Town. Upon the formation of the Federation of the West Indies, the islands' dependency status with Jamaica is ended 1959. A new constitution extends the vote to women.

1966–1972 Legislature is passed to enable and encourage the burgeoning banking industry in the islands. A new constitution gives the islands wide autonomy.

2004 The islands are hit by Hurricane Ivan, which causes mass devastation and flooding. The islands have the dubious honor of being hit by the most hurricanes in the history of the Caribbean.

2005 In 2005, the population is estimated to include over 100 nationalities, although the largest group, about 60 percent, is of mixed race, mostly African and European. Of the remaining 40 percent, about half are of European descent and half of African descent, many from Jamaica. The islands' standard of living is the highest in the Caribbean.

2008–2009 Home to 279 banks, the Cayman Islands are the fifth-largest banking center in the world. There is some criticism internationally of money laundering and ties to international narcotics. Support for full independence is gaining.

See also United Kingdom

CUBA

OFFICIAL NAME

República de Cuba (Spanish); Republic of Cuba (English)

POPULATION

11,239,400 (2009e)

INHABITANTS' NAME/NICKNAME

Cuban(s)

LANGUAGE/LANGUAGES

Spanish (official); English, others

RELIGION/RELIGIONS

Roman Catholic, Protestant, Jehovah's Witness, Jewish, Santeria, other or no religion

NATIONAL FLAG

The flag consists of five blue and white stripes and a red triangle at the hoist bearing a white five-pointed star. The blue stands for the sea that surrounds Cuba and the three historic divisions of the island, the white stands for the purity of the patriotic cause and the strength of the independent ideal, the red triangle symbolizes the blood shed in battle and also equality, fraternity, and freedom, and the white star represents independence and absolute freedom among the Cuban people.

COAT OF ARMS/SEAL

The coat of arms has a shield crowned by a Phrygian cap, all supported by an oak branch on one side and a laurel branch on the other. The shield, or escutcheon, is divided into three parts. At the top is a key on a blue sea between two rocks below an orange sun with many rays symbolizing Cuba's geographic position as the key to the Gulf of Mexico. The blue and white stripes in the second part, at lower left, stand for the situation of the island. The third part, at lower right, shows a country scene with a large royal palm tree, the symbol of the unbreakable character of the Cuban people. The oak support represents the strength of the nation, and the laurel represents honor and glory. The oak and laurel also symbolize the rights of man: equality, liberty, and fraternity. The Phrygian cap symbolizes liberty, and the single star on the cap represents independence.

MOTTO

Patria o muerte (Spanish); Homeland or Death (English)

CAPITAL CITY

Havana

TYPE OF GOVERNMENT

Socialist republic

NATIONAL EMBLEM

Fidel Castro; Cuban cigars

NATIONAL COLORS

Blue, white, and red

NATIONAL ANTHEM

The anthem was originally performed during the battle of Bayamo in 1868 as an anti-Spanish tract. Officially adopted as the national anthem in 1940, the anthem was retained even after the communist revolution in 1959.

La Bayamesa (Spanish); The Bayamo Song (English)

Hasten to battle, men of Bayamo,
For the homeland looks proudly to you.
You do not fear a glorious death
Because to die for the country is to live.

To live in chains
Is to live in dishonor and ignominy.
Hear the clarion call,
Hasten, brave ones, to battle!

PATRON SAINT

Our Lady of Charity of El Cobre; Virgin de Regla

CURRENCY

Cuban peso

INTERNET IDENTIFIER

.cu

VEHICLE IDENTIFICATION PLATES/STICKERS

C

PASSPORT

The passport cover has the name of the country in Spanish, the coat of arms, and the Spanish word for passport.

AIRLINE

Cubana (Cubana de Aviación)

NATIONAL FLOWER

Mariposa blanca (white butterfly jasmine)

NATIONAL TREE

Royal palm

NATIONAL ANIMAL

Cuban crocodile

NATIONAL BIRD

Tocororo (Cuban trogon)

NATIONAL RESOURCES

Natural resources include cobalt, nickel, iron ore, chromium, copper, salt, timber, silica, petroleum, arable land, sandy beaches, a pleasant climate, and potential petroleum. Sandy beaches, colonial cities, a unique culture, and a pleasant climate are the reasons Cuba is becoming a popular tourist destination. The Cuban Diaspora, particularly in the United States*, is a valuable source of hard currency.

FOODS

Cuban food is a fusion of Spanish and Caribbean influences. *Ropa vieja,* a dish of shredded beef, and *platillo Moros y Cristianos* (black beans and rice), served with plantains, are the staples of Cuban cuisine and are considered national dishes. Other specialties include *harina rellena,* a cornmeal pastry filled with minced meat; *frituras de carita,* black-eyed pea fritters; *aporreado de tasajo,* a stew of dried beef and vegetables; *papas con chorizo,* potatoes with spicy sausage; *potaje de pescado,* fish soup; and *huevos fritos a la Cubana,* fried eggs served with black beans, rice, and fried plantains.

SPORTS/SPORTS TEAMS

Baseball, introduced from the United States, is the island's most popular sport and the de facto national sport. Other popular sports are association football (soccer) and basketball. Cuba national teams participate in many sports at an international level.

TEAM SPORTS

Badminton

Cuba Badminton Team

Baseball

Cuba Baseball Team; Cuba Softball Team

Basketball

Cuba Basketball Team; Cuba Women's Basketball Team; Cuba Wheelchair Basketball Team; Cuba Women's Wheelchair Basketball Team

Cricket

Cuba Cricket Team

Football

Cuba Football Team, nickname Leones del Caribe (Lions of the Caribbean); Cuba Women's Football Team. Cuba Futsal Team

Hockey

Cuba Field Hockey Team

Racing

Cuba Speedway Team

Tennis

Cub Davis Cup Team; Cuba Fed Cup Team

Volleyball

Cuba Men's Volleyball Team; Cuba Women's Volleyball Team; Cuba Beach Volleyball Team; Cuba Women's Beach Volleyball Team; Cuba Men's Volleyball Team; Cuba Women's Volleyball Team

INDIVIDUAL SPORTS

Cuba Amateur Boxing Team; Cuba Archery Team; Cuba Athletics Team; Cuba Canoeing Team; Cuba Cycling Team; Cuba Equestrian Team; Cuba Fencing Team; Cuba Gymnastics Team; Cuba Judo Team; Cuba Modern Pentathlon Team; Cuba Rowing Team; Cuba Sailing Team; Cuba Shooting Team; Cuba Table Tennis Team; Cuba Tae Kwon Do Team; Cuba Triathlon Team; Cuba Weight Lifting Team; Cuba National Wrestling Team

NATIONAL HEROES OR PERSONIFICATIONS

Fidel Castro, the leader of the Cuban Revolution and the official head of state from 1960 until 2008, is considered the personification of Cuba. National heroes include Che Guevarra, an icon of the Cuban Revolution who attempted to spread the revolution to other Latin American countries; and José Marti, leader of the Cuban fight for independence in the 1890s.

NATIONAL HOLIDAY/INDEPENDENCE DAY

Triumph of the Revolution Day, January 1

FESTIVALS/FAIRS

Carnaval (Carnival) February–March; Mamarrachos (Summer Carnival), July; International Jazz Festival, February; International Book Fair, February–March; Fire Fiesta (Caribbean Festival), July; International Crafts Fair, December

SIGNIFICANT EVENTS IN FORMATION OF NATIONAL IDENTITY

5300 B.C.E.–1200 C.E. The Caribbean islands are initially settled by peoples moving north from South America. Two tribal groups form on the island, the Taino and the Ciboney.

1492 C.E. Christopher Columbus sights Cuba during his first voyage of discovery and claims the territory for Spain*.

1511–1515 The coast of Cuba is fully mapped, and the first Spanish settlement is founded at Baracoa. Other settlements, including Havana, soon follow.

16th century European diseases, slavery, and widespread violence used against the native peoples quickly reduce the Tainos and Ciboney to just a handful of survivors. A mixed population, the mestizos, becomes a large part of the island's population.

17th century The destruction of the aboriginal peoples leaves the island short of workers. The settlers begin to import African slaves, who soon become a significant portion of the inhabitants of Cuba.

17th century–19th century Cuba remains a Spanish possession for 388 years, ruled by a governor in Havana, with an economy based on plantation agriculture and the export of agricultural products such as sugar, coffee and tobacco, first to Europe and later to North America.

1820s When the other parts of Spain's huge empire in Latin America rebel and form independent states, the Cuban elite remains loyal..

1865 The idea of Cuban independence from Spain is revived, leading to a rebellion in 1868 that results in a prolonged conflict known as the Ten Years War.

1884–1895 Slavery is abolished in Cuba. Former slaves and other groups are granted formal civic equality in 1893. Spanish emigration to Cuba continues, with large numbers leaving the poorer regions of Spain.

1895 Spanish neglect, arbitrary government, and restrictions imposed on Cuban trade provoke a new war for independence led by José Marti.

1895–1896 The Spanish herd rural residents and their livestock into fortified camps later called concentration camps. Hundreds of thousands perish from hunger, disease, and violence in the camps.

1897–1898 The destruction of the U.S. battleship *Maine*, in the Spanish colony of the Philippines*, brings the United States into the war in Cuba in the Spanish-American War. The Spanish sue for peace.

1902 Cuba gains formal independence, with the United States retaining the right to intervene in Cuban affairs and a long lease on the military base at Guantánamo Bay.

1925–1935 Another coup and governmental confusion finally allow a former army sergeant, Fulgenio Batista, to take power. Batista is the head of state for various periods until 1959.

1948–1959 American investments and gambling money pour into the island, fueling a boom that raises the standard of living and promotes the creation of an urban middle class. The inequality between the privileged and the poor becomes wider.

1952–1959 Batista, facing sure defeat in presidential elections, seizes power. The Batista regime is notorious for corruption, violence, and links to international crime figures. Fidel Castro leads an attack on a barracks, beginning the Cuban Revolution. After years of fighting, Castro takes Havana on January 1, 1959, and Batista flees the island.

1959 Many Cubans flee abroad, mostly to Florida in the United States. Castro purges liberals and anticommunists from the new government. Many Cubans who initially supported the revolution also leave.

1960–1965 The first economic and political agreements are signed with the Soviet Union. The United States reacts with a trade embargo and a failed invasion of Cuban exiles called the Bay of Pigs. The decision to allow the Soviets to place missiles in Cuba brings the world to the brink of nuclear war. In 1965, Castro's political party is renamed the Communist Party of Cuba.

1970s–1980s Cuba is economically and politically dependent on the Soviet Union. Boat people, Cubans escaping the island by small boats, enlarge the growing Cuban exile community in the United States.

1991 The collapse of the Soviet Union ends decades of economic subsidies, leaving Cuba destitute and in crisis. While communist regimes in other parts of the world give way to democratic institutions, Fidel Castro maintains a tight hold on Cuba.

1990s The Castro government allows limited liberalization of the economy and finds new allies in Venezuela* and Bolivia*, major oil and gas producers under revolutionary governments.

2006 A gravely ill Fidel Castro delegates his duties to his brother, Raúl.

2007 Modest reforms allow Cubans to operate some small businesses. For the first time since 1958, Christmas Day is declared a holiday.

2008 Raúl Castro replaces his brother as chief of state, president of Cuba, and commander in chief of the armed forces in February. Fidel Castro announces his intention to return to power, but he becomes incapacitated. The first Russian warships visit Cuba since the end of the Cold War.

2009 Several senior officials from the Fidel Castro era resign after admitting "errors". The U.S. Congress votes to lift restrictions on Cuban-Americans visiting the island and sending money to relatives.

CURAÇAO

OFFICIAL NAME

Pais Kòrsou (Papiamento); Country of Curaçao (English)

POPULATION

140,800 (2009e)

INHABITANTS' NAME/NICKNAME

Curaçaoan(s); Curacaoan(s)

LANGUAGE/LANGUAGES

Dutch, Papiamento (both official); English, Spanish, Creole, others

RELIGION/RELIGIONS

Roman Catholic, 85 percent; Protestant, Muslim, Hindu, Jewish, other or no religion

NATIONAL FLAG

The flag is a blue field with a horizontal yellow stripe slightly below the midline and two white, five-pointed stars on the upper hoist. The upper blue portion represents the sky and the lower strip represents the sea. The yellow stripe stands for the bright sun that bathes the islands. The two stars stand for the islands of Curaçao and Klein Curaçao and also for love and happiness. The five points on each star represent the five continents from which the island people have come.

COAT OF ARMS/SEAL

The coat of arms is a shield or crest divided vertically beneath a golden crown. The two sides show a sailing ship on a blue sea and a green tree with golden fruit. A smaller crest, that of the Dutch city of Amsterdam, is centered on the vertical divide and represents the island's historic commercial and governmental ties to Amsterdam.

CAPITAL CITY

Willemstad

TYPE OF GOVERNMENT

Autonomous parliamentary state as part of the Kingdom of the Netherlands*

NATIONAL EMBLEM

Pastel facades of old buildings in Willemstad, a UNESCO World Heritage site

NATIONAL COLORS

Blue, yellow, and white

NATIONAL ANTHEM

The anthem was used as the anthem of the entire Netherlands Antilles* until it was replaced in 1964. The anthem was adopted as the official anthem of the new Curaçao state in 2008.

> **Himno di Kòrsou (Papiamento); Hymn of Curaçao (English)**
>
> Let us raise our voice to sing
> About the glory of Curaçao
> Curaçao, a small island
> Rock in the sea
> Curaçao, we love you
> Above all countries
> We sing about your honor
> Deep from our heart.
>
> And if we are far from home
> We do always think
> About the sun and the beaches of Curaçao
> The pride of us all
> Let us honor our Creator
> All times and without end
> That he has made us being worthy
> To be a child of Curaçao.

PATRON SAINT

Saint Nicholas

CURRENCY

Netherlands Antilles guilder; likely to be replaced with a new currency when Curaçao assumes its new autonomous status

INTERNET IDENTIFIER

.an (until the planned dissolution of the Netherlands Antilles)

VEHICLE IDENTIFICATION PLATES/ STICKERS

NA Netherlands Antilles (official until Curaçao assumes its new status as an autonomous country within the Kingdom of the Netherlands*); CUR Curaçao (unofficial)

PASSPORT

The Curaçaoans are Dutch citizens and travel on Dutch passports.

AIRLINE

Insel Air

NATIONAL FLOWER

Kibrahacha (hatchet-breaker)

NATIONAL TREE

Divi-divi

NATIONAL ANIMAL

Iguana (unofficial)

NATIONAL BIRD

Trupial (oriole)

NATIONAL RESOURCES

Natural resources are negligible, other than phosphates. The sandy beaches, pleasant climate, underwater reefs, colonial architecture, and unique culture support a vibrant tourist industry. Other main industries of the island are oil refining and financial services. Shipping and other activities related to Willemstad's port also make a considerable contribution to the economy. As in the Netherlands, prostitution is legal. A large, open-air brothel, called Le Mirage or Campo Alegre, has operated near the main Curaçao airport since the 1940s.

FOODS

Piské korá, red snapper with tomatoes, onion, peppers, and garlic, is considered the national dish. Popular dishes include *kabritu stobá*, a stew made with various ingredients, such as papaya and goat; *guiambo*. A soup made from okra and seafood; *kadushi*, cactus soup; *funchi*, a cornmeal porridge similar to polenta; *tutu*, a dish of cornmeal and black-eyed peas; *sòpi de piska*, a fish soup with green peppers, tomatoes, carrots, celery, potatoes, and spices; *sòpito*, a soup of fish and coconut milk; *bakiou*, salt cod prepared with onion, peppers, and tomatoes; and *bobl di pan*, bread pudding.

SPORTS/SPORTS TEAMS

Association football (soccer) is the most popular sport. Baseball, introduced from the United States*, is also very popular. Curaçao national teams participate in many sports at an international level.

TEAM SPORTS

Badminton

Curaçao Badminton Team

Baseball

Curaçao Baseball Team; Curaçao Softball Team

Basketball

Curaçao Basketball Team; Curaçao Women's Basketball Team

Football

Curaçao Football Team; Curaçao Women's Football Team; Curaçao Futsal Team

Hockey

Curaçao Field Hockey Team; Curaçao Women's Field Hockey Team

Korfball

Curaçao Korfball Team

Table Tennis

Curaçao Table Tennis Team

Tennis

Curaçao Davis Cup Team

Volleyball

Curaçao Men's Volleyball Team; Curaçao Women's Volleyball Team

INDIVIDUAL SPORTS

Curaçao Amateur Boxing Team; Curaçao Athletics Team; Curaçao Canoeing Team; Curaçao Cycling Team; Curaçao Equestrian Team; Curaçao Fencing Team; Curaçao Judo Team;

Curaçao Karate Team; Curaçao Sailing Team; Curaçao Shooting Team; Curaçao Swim Team; Curaçao Triathlon Team; Curaçao Weight Lifting Team

NATIONAL HEROES OR PERSONIFICATIONS

Tula, the leader of the island's most serious slave rebellion in 1795; Izaline Calister, internationally known singer mixing local Curaçao music with jazz; Jan Gerald Palm a 19th century musician known as the "Farther of Curaçao Music"; Moses Frumencio da Costa Gomez, a former permier of the Netherlands Antilles and the leader of the Curaçao autonomy movement; Joseph Sickman Corsen, early 20th century poet and musician

NATIONAL HOLIDAY/INDEPENDENCE DAY

Flag Day, July 2; Saint Nicholas Day, December 6

FESTIVALS/FAIRS

Saint Nicholas Day, December; Culture Week, September; Heineken Regatta, November; Carnival, February–March; Slave Uprising Commemoration, August; Curaçao Jazz Festival, May

SIGNIFICANT EVENTS IN FORMATION OF NATIONAL IDENTITY

2000 B.C.E.–1450 C.E. The Arawaks, an Amerindian group from the nearby mainland of South America, settle the island hundreds of years before the arrival of Europeans.

1499 A Spanish expedition claims the islands for Spain*. Spanish interest quickly wanes, as no gold is found and farming is difficult due to a lack of freshwater.

1634–1750 The Dutch West India Company claims Curaçao and begins the settlement of the islands. The salt ponds that prevent irrigation become an asset as salt develops as the major export. Plantation agriculture using slave labor flourishes. The port of Willemstad becomes a major trading port and a center of the Caribbean slave trade.

1795 The numerous slave population, mistreated and humiliated on the island's plantations, rebels in a mass movement that lasts two months.

1815 During the Napoleonic Wars, the island changes hands several times before returning to Dutch rule.

1828–1845 The three southern Dutch islands are governed from Dutch Suriname*. Curaçao, Bonaire, and Aruba* are joined with the Dutch Windward islands to form a single political unit ruled from Willemstad.

1863 Slavery is abolished in the islands. The end of the slave economy causes economic hardship, driving many people to leave the islands. The freed slaves mostly settle as small subsistence farmers on abandoned plantations.

1914–1915 Oil is discovered in nearby Venezuela*. Royal Dutch Shell and the Dutch government construct an oil refinery that quickly reverses the economic decline that had continued since the abolition of slavery.

1954 Curaçao gains self-government as an island territory of the Netherlands Antilles, which becomes an autonomous part of the Kingdom of the Netherlands.

1960s The tourist boom brings much-needed work and a modest prosperity. Willemstad becomes an important stop for Caribbean cruise ships.

1970s A labor conflict in 1969 leads to rioting and arson and calls by nationalists for independence for Curaçao. The rioting damages the tourist trade, which does not recover until the mid-1970s. The island develops an important banking center.

1970s–1980s The decolonization of the British islands in the Caribbean raises the question of independence, which is favored by the Dutch government.

1977–1988 Aruba* votes to separate from the Netherlands Antilles, and by 1978, all the islands have accepted the idea of self-determination. In 1980, preparatory talks begin. Independence referendums, to be held on each island in 1988, are postponed. The smaller islands prefer to remain under Dutch rule rather than in a federation dominated by Curaçao.

1993 The people of Curaçao vote against following Aruba in separating from the Netherlands Antilles.

2000 The inhabitants of Saint Maarten* vote to withdraw from the federation, beginning the process that will break up the federation into five separate countries.

2005 Curaçaoans vote to become an autonomous state within the Kingdom of the Netherlands.

2006–2007 Agreements with the Netherlands are at first rejected as inadequate but are finally accepted.

2008–2009 A referendum on the autonomy agreement, held on May 15, 2009, showed 52 percent in favor of autonomy as a separate country within the Dutch Kingdom with a large minority against, including the growing independence movement. Curaçao was scheduled to leave the Netherlands Antilles on December 15, 2008. The date is postponed until sometime in 2010 or 2011.

See also Netherlands; Netherlands Antilles

DOMINICA

OFFICIAL NAME
Commonwealth of Dominica

NICKNAME
Nature Isle of the Caribbean

POPULATION
71,800 (2009e)

INHABITANTS' NAME/NICKNAME
Dominican(s)

LANGUAGE/LANGUAGES
English (official); Antillean Creole French (mother tongue of about 80% of the population), others

RELIGION/RELIGIONS
Roman Catholic, 61 percent; Seventh-day Adventist, 6 percent; Pentecostal, 6 percent; Baptist, 4 percent; Methodist, 4 percent; Church of God, 1.5 percent; other or no religion

NATIONAL FLAG
A red centered disk on a green field features a Sisserou, or Imperial Amazon, parrot, Dominica's national bird, surrounded by 10 green stars, representing the country's ten parishes and also hope and equality. Behind the disk, stripes of three colors, yellow, black, and white, radiate horizontally and vertically from the center, forming a cross. The cross reflects the country's Christian faith, and each set of three lines individually represents the Trinity. The green color represents the

island's green landscape, the red stands for social justice, the yellow represents sunshine and agriculture, the black stands for the earth and the population's African heritage, and the white represents the clear waters around the island and purity.

COAT OF ARMS/SEAL

The coat of arms consists of a shield braced by two guardian Sisserou parrots, atop which is a raging lion. The quadrants of the shield depict a canoe, a banana tree, a palm, and a mountain frog. Below the crest is the national motto.

MOTTO

Après bondie, c'est la ter (Antillean Creole); After God is the Earth (English)

CAPITAL CITY

Roseau

TYPE OF GOVERNMENT

Parliamentary democracy

NATIONAL EMBLEM

Sisserou parrot

NATIONAL COLORS

Green, yellow, and black

NATIONAL ANTHEM

The anthem was composed and written when Dominica achieved associated state status in 1967. It was maintained as the national anthem at independence in 1978.

> **Isle of Beauty, Isle of Splendor**
>
> Isle of beauty, isle of splendor,
> Isle to all so sweet and fair,
> All must surely gaze in wonder
> At thy gifts so rich and rare.
> Rivers, valleys, hills and mountains,
> All these gifts we do extol.
> Healthy land, so like all fountains,
> Giving cheer that warms the soul.

> Dominica, God hath blest thee
> With a clime benign and bright,
> Pastures green and flowers of beauty
> Filling all with pure delight,
> And a people strong and healthy,
> Full of godly, rev'rent fear.
> May we ever seek to praise Thee
> For these gifts so rich and rare.
> Come ye forward, sons and daughters
> Of this gem beyond compare.
> Strive for honor, sons and daughters,
> Do the right, be firm, be fair.
> Toil with hearts and hands and voices.
> We must prosper! Sound the call,
> In which ev'ryone rejoices,
> "All for each and each for all."

PATRON SAINT

Our Lady of Fair Haven

CURRENCY

Eastern Caribbean dollar

INTERNET IDENTIFIER

.dm

VEHICLE IDENTIFICATION PLATES/STICKERS

WD

PASSPORT

The passport has the initials CC for Caribbean Community, the coat of arms, the name of the country, and the word *passport*.

NATIONAL FLOWER

Bwa Kwaib, or *bois Carib*

NATIONAL TREES

Banana; palm

NATIONAL ANIMAL

Mountain frog

NATIONAL BIRD

Sisserou (Imperial Amazon) parrot

NATIONAL FISH

Sperm whale (unofficial)

NATIONAL RESOURCES

Natural resources include timber, hydro-power, and arable land. Spectacular scenery, a pleasant climate, and island culture support a growing tourist industry. Ross University, an offshore-owned medical school, is an important asset with over 1,000 students, mostly from the United States* and Canada*. The lack of a large international airport and sandy beaches limits opportunities for standard tourism, but the island's rain forests and beautifully preserved environment are a lure for ecotourism. It is remarked that of all the islands of the Caribbean, Dominica is the only one Christopher Columbus might still recognize.

FOODS

Bakes, fritters stuffed with cod, tuna, or cheese, are considered the national dish. Callaloo and pumpkin soups are very popular. *Crapaud,* also known as mountain chicken or frog legs, is another national dish. *Buljow,* cod cooked with onions, hot peppers, spring onions, tomatoes, and plantains in coconut milk, is also very popular for special meals. Other specialties include *conconete,* coconut buns; black bean soup; saltfish cakes; corn pudding; and *sancocho,* a stew of meat and vegetables.

SPORTS/SPORTS TEAMS

Cricket is the most popular sport, along with association football (soccer). Dominica national teams participate in many sports at an international level.

TEAM SPORTS

Basketball

Dominica Basketball Team; Dominica Women's Basketball Team

Cricket

West Indies Cricket Team, nickname The Windies (West Indies teams represent a number of English-speaking Caribbean countries)

Football

Dominica Football Team; Dominica Women's Football Team; West Indies Rugby League Team, nickname the Wahoos (West Indies teams represent a number of English-speaking Caribbean countries)

Kabaddi

West Indies Kabaddi Team (West Indies teams represent a number of English-speaking Caribbean countries)

Netball

Dominica Netball Team

Table Tennis

Dominica Table Tennis Team

Tennis

Eastern Caribbean Fed Cup and Davis Cup teams (Eastern Caribbean teams represent a number of English-speaking Caribbean countries)

Volleyball

Dominica Men's Volleyball Team; Dominica Women's Volleyball Team

INDIVIDUAL SPORTS

Dominica Amateur Boxing Team; Dominica Archery Team; Dominica Athletics Team; Dominica Judo Team; Dominica Rowing Team; Dominica Swim Team; Dominica Tae Kwon Do Team

NATIONAL HEROES OR PERSONIFICATIONS

Edward Oliver LeBlanc, national leader during the transition to independence and one of the founders of the nation; Eugenia Charles, the first woman elected as head of state in North America and the prime minister from 1980 to 1995; Jean Rhys, a noted author and essayist on Dominican life

NATIONAL HOLIDAY/INDEPENDENCE DAY

Independence Day, November 3

FESTIVALS/FAIRS

Mas Domnik (Carnival), February–March; World Creole Music Festival, October–November; Independence Festival, October–November

SIGNIFICANT EVENTS IN FORMATION OF NATIONAL IDENTITY

14th century The island's indigenous Arawaks are expelled or exterminated by invading Caribs. The Caribs call the island Waitikubuli, which means "tall in her body."

1493 Christopher Columbus sights the island, calling it after the day of the week on which he first saw it, a Sunday (*Doménica* in Italian).

1635 The French lay claim to the island. French missionaries are the first Europeans to live on the island.

1660–1700 France* and England agree to leave the islands of Dominica and Saint Vincent* to the Caribs. European diseases devastate the Carib population.

1700–1763 The French establish a settlement on the island. African slaves are imported to work the forests and plantations. The British conquer the island, which officially becomes a British possession..

1831–1832 Three black islanders are elected to the legislative assembly. Following the abolition of slavery in 1838, Dominica becomes the first and only British Caribbean colony to have a black-controlled assembly in the 19th century.

1896 The island is made a crown colony, and all political rights for the nonwhite majority are curtailed.

1920–1958 A representative government association, supported by the island's majority, wins a third of the elected seats in the assembly in 1924 and half in 1936. Dominica joins the short-lived West Indies Federation.

1978 The Commonwealth of Dominica is granted independence, but independence does little to alleviate severe problems stemming from centuries of underdevelopment.

1979 Hurricane David devastates the island, leaving 42 dead and 75 percent of buildings destroyed or damaged.

1980–1995 Eugenia Charles becomes the Caribbean's first female prime minister. In her first year, she survives two coup attempts. Banana exports lead an economic recovery.

1995–2005 Multiparty elections and peaceful changes of government are signs that Dominica is among the most stable states in the Caribbean.

2008–2009 Dominica is the only Caribbean country to challenge Venezuela's sovereignty claim to a tiny outcrop called Aves Island, rejecting the contention that the island could sustain human habitation, a criterion under the United Nations Convention on the Law of the Sea. The claim would allow Venezuela* to extend its territorial waters and continental shelf claims over a large portion of the eastern Caribbean.

DOMINICAN REPUBLIC

OFFICIAL NAME

República Dominicana (Spanish); Dominican Republic (English)

POPULATION

9,944,900 (2009e)

INHABITANTS' NAME/NICKNAME

Dominican(s)

LANGUAGE/LANGUAGES

Spanish (official); French, English, others

RELIGION/RELIGIONS

Christian, 96 percent (mostly Roman Catholic, with smaller Protestant and Evangelical groups); other or no religion

NATIONAL FLAG

The flag has a centered white cross that extends to the edges, dividing the flag into four rectangles, blue over red on the hoist and red over blue on the fly. A small coat of arms is centered on the white cross. The blue stands for liberty, the red for the blood of the heroes who fought for independence, and the white for truth.

COAT OF ARMS/SEAL

The coat of arms is similar to the flag design and shows a Bible, a cross of gold, and six Dominican flags. There are branches of olive and palm around the shield, and above on a ribbon is the national motto. The blue stands for liberty and red for the fire and blood of the independence struggle. Below the shield is another ribbon bearing the name of the country in Spanish.

MOTTO

Dios, patria, libertad (Spanish); God, Homeland, Liberty (English)

CAPITAL CITY

Santo Domingo

TYPE OF GOVERNMENT

Presidential republic

NATIONAL EMBLEM

Columbus' lighthouse

NATIONAL COLORS

Red, blue, and white

NATIONAL ANTHEM

The anthem dates from the 19th century. The name refers to the name given the island of Hispaniola by the indigenous peoples.

Quisqueyanos Valientes (Spanish); Valiant Sons of Quisqueya (English)

Brave men of Quisqueya,
Let us sing with strong feeling
And let us show to the world
Our invincible, glorious banner.
Hail, O people who, strong and intrepid,
Launched into war and went to death!
Under a warlike menace of death,
You broke your chains of slavery.
No country deserves to be free
If it is an indolent and servile slave,
If the call does not grow loud within it,
Tempered by a virile heroism.
But the brave and indomitable Quisqueya
Will always hold its head high,
For if it were a thousand times enslaved,
It would a thousand times regain freedom.

PATRON SAINT

Saint Dominic de Guzman, Our Lady of Altagracia, Our Lady of Mercy

CURRENCY

Dominican peso

INTERNET IDENTIFIER

.do

VEHICLE IDENTIFICATION PLATES/STICKERS

DOM

PASSPORT

The passport cover has the word for passport in Spanish, *pasaporte,* the coat of arms, and the name of the country in Spanish.

AIRLINES

Air Dominicana; PAWA Dominicana

NATIONAL FLOWER

Caoba flower

NATIONAL TREE

Caoba (mahogany)

NATIONAL BIRD

Palm chat (official); ashy-faced owl, Hispaniola parrot (unofficial)

NATIONAL STONE

Amber

NATIONAL RESOURCES

Natural resources include nickel, bauxite, gold, silver, and arable land. Sandy beaches, historic cities, and a pleasant climate draw many tourists to the islands. The large Dominican population living in the United States* and Europe, mostly in Spain*, is a valuable asset and a source of foreign currency.

FOODS

La bandera, meaning "the flag," is considered the national dish. It consists of broiled chicken, white rice, and red beans. *Pastelitos,* empanadas, are also very popular. Other specialties include *santocho,* a stew of meat and vegetables; *habichuelas blancas y longaniza,* white beans with pork sausage; *rabo encendido,* a spicy oxtail soup; *locrio de camarones,* a dish of rice and shrimp; *moro de habichuelas,* rice and beans; *pescado con coco,* fish prepared in coconut milk; and *rés quisada,* a beef and vegetable stew.

SPORTS/SPORTS TEAMS

Baseball, as in nearby Cuba*, is the island nation's most popular sport. Association football (soccer) is also very popular. Dominican Republic national teams participate in many sports at an international level.

TEAM SPORTS

Badminton

Dominican Republic Badminton Team

Baseball

Dominican Republic Baseball Team; Dominican Republic Softball Team

Basketball

Dominican Republic Basketball Team; Dominican Republic Women's Basketball Team

Football

Dominican Republic Football Team, nickname Los Quisqueyanos; Dominican Republic Women's Football Team, nickname Las Quisqueyanas; Dominican Republic Rugby Union Team; Dominican Republic Under-19 Football Team; Dominican Republic Women's Under-19 Football Team

Handball

Dominican Republic Men's Beach Handball Team; Dominican Republic Women's Beach Handball Team

Hockey

Dominican Republic Field Hockey Team

Racing

Dominican Republic Speedway Team

Table Tennis

Dominican Republic Table Tennis Team

Tennis

Dominican Republic Davis Cup Team; Dominican Republic Fed Cup Team

Volleyball

Dominican Republic Men's Volleyball Team; Dominican Republic Women's Volleyball Team; Dominican Republic Men's Beach Volleyball Team; Dominican Republic Women's Beach Volleyball Team

Individual Sports

Dominican Republic Amateur Boxing Team; Dominican Republic Archery Team; Dominican Republic Athletics Team; Dominican Republic Canoeing Team; Dominican Republic Cycling Team; Dominican Republic Equestrian Team; Dominican Republic Fencing Team; Dominican Republic Gymnastics Team; Dominican Republic Judo Team; Dominican Republic Modern Pentathlon Team; Dominican Republic Sailing Team; Dominican Republic Shooting Team; Dominican Republic Swim Team; Dominican Republic Tae Kwon Do Team; Dominican Republic Triathlon Team; Dominican Republic Weight Lifting Team; Dominican Republic Wrestling Team

NATIONAL HEROES OR PERSONIFICATIONS

Juan Pablo Duarte, founder of a secret society called La Trinitaria that sought independence for the country; Francisco del Rosario Sánchez, a leader of the independence movement; General Gregorio Luperón, the leader of the restoration of independence in the 1860s

NATIONAL HOLIDAY/INDEPENDENCE DAY

Independence Day, February 27

FESTIVALS/FAIRS

Merengue Festival, October; Holy Week, the week before Easter; Carnival, February–March; Cultural Festival, June; Latin Music Festival, June

SIGNIFICANT EVENTS IN FORMATION OF NATIONAL IDENTITY

600 C.E.–1450 C.E.   The Tainos, an Arawakan-speaking people originally from the South American mainland, occupy the island around 600 C.E., displacing the earlier inhabitants. The island of Hispaniola is divided into five chiefdoms.

1492   On his first voyage to the New World, Christopher Columbus lands on the island, naming it La Española.

1496   Bartholomeo Columbus, Christopher's brother, builds the city of Nueva Isabella, later called Santo Domingo. It is the first permanent European settlement in the New World.

1500–1550   The Tainos valiantly resist the conquest of their island. The regional chiefs lead their warriors in fighting the Spanish, but infectious diseases to which they had no immunity, combined with mistreatment, slavery, starvation, and war, devastate the population.

16th century   The plantation economy created by the Spanish requires vast number of laborers. When the Tainos prove unfit for forced labor, African slaves are imported. Hispaniola becomes the center of Spanish conquest in the Caribbean and later on the American mainland. The conquest of the mainland empires of the Incas and the Aztecs, with their mountains of gold and riches, becomes the focus of Spanish colonial policy. Santo Domingo declines and is neglected. French buccaneers settle the western part of the island.

1697   Spain cedes the western part of Hispaniola to France*.

1795–1801   The French take control of the entire island during the French Revolution and its aftermath. Spain cedes its claims to France, but slaves in revolt in the French half capture Santo Domingo and take control of the entire island.

1802–1808   An army sent by Napoleon captures the slave leaders, but yellow fever and a renewed revolt end the French successes. The French half of the island is declared independent as the Republic of Haiti*. The French recover Spanish Santo Domingo.

1808   Following Napoleon's invasion of Spain, the people of Santo Domingo rebel against French rule. With the aid of Spain's ally, Britain, and the neighboring Haitians, Santo Domingo is returned to Spanish rule.

1821   After years of turbulence and several independence movements, Santo Domingo is declared independent as the state of Haití Español. Haitian troops invade to end the movement. The Haitians, as in their part of the island, abolish slavery.

1838–1944   Juan Pablo Duarte founds La Trinitaria, a movement dedicated to independence without any foreign interference. The Trinitarios declare Santo Domingo independent of Haiti.

1861–1863   Pedro Santana, a wealthy rancher and a hero of the fight against the Haitians, signs a pact that returns Santo Domingo to Spanish rule, the only Latin American to do so. Patriots revolt and succeed in expelling the Spanish, and independence is restored.

1863–1906 Decades of disorder, military coups, arbitrary rule, and the amassing of an enormous foreign debt ensue.

1906–1916 European countries seek to recoup loans. President Theodore Roosevelt of the United States* wards off the European powers and signs a 50-year treaty. The U.S. military occupies the republic to restore order.

1921–1924 U.S. forces are withdrawn. Subsequent governments allow democratic elections, and the country prospers.

1930–1961 Rafael Leonidas Trujillo takes control of the country, ruling as a dictator for more than three decades with the support of the United States and the Roman Catholic Church. Trujillo's rule is brutal and arbitrary. In 1937, he orders the massacre of between 17,000 and 35,000 Haitians living in the republic. Trujillo is assassinated in Santo Domingo.

1965–1978 U.S. Marines again land to restore order. They stay to supervise new elections won by Joaquín Balaguer, whose rule is a period of repression of civil liberties, presumably to prevent Cuban-style socialism from spreading to the island.

1978–2000 Several decades of relative freedom and basic human rights follow. Balaguer returns to office in fraudulent elections in 1986 and is re-elected in 1990 and 1994. He finally steps aside in 2000, leaving the Dominican Republic among the poorest countries in Latin America.

2000–2009 Peaceful elections and economic expansion finally end centuries of underdevelopment and chaotic politics. The relative prosperity of the country draws in Haitians seeking work. Many Dominicans cross the Mona Passage each year to find better work in Puerto Rico*.

GREENLAND

Official Name

Kalaallit Nunaat (Greenlandic); Grøland (Danish); Greenland (English)

Population

56,700 (2009e)

Inhabitants' Name/Nickname

Kalaallit(s); Greenlander(s)

Language/Languages

Greenlandic (official); Danish, English, others

Religion/Religions

Evangelical Lutheran; other or no religion

National Flag

The flag, known as *Erfalasorput,* or "our flag" in the Greenlandic language, features two equal horizontal stripes of white over red, with a large disk slightly to the hoist side of center divided red over white. The white represents Greenland's glaciers and ice cap, which cover over 80 percent of the islands, and the red represents the ocean. The disk stands for the rising sun over the ice pack.

Coat of Arms/Seal

The coat of arms is a blue shield bearing a silver polar bear. Adherents of independence use the same shield, but with a green background.

Capital City

Nuuk (Godthåb)

Type of Government

Parliamentary democracy and constitutional monarchy as part of the Kingdom of Denmark*

National Emblem

Greenland ice pack

National Colors

Red and white

NATIONAL ANTHEM

The anthem was adopted in 1979 and has official status alongside the anthem of Denmark.

Nuna asiilasooq (Greenlandic); The Land of Great Length (English)

Our country, which has become so old your
   head is all covered with white hair,
Always held us, your children, in your bosom
   and gave us the riches of your coasts.
As middle children in the family, we blos-
   somed here, Kalaallit
We want to call ourselves before your proud
   and honorable head.
With a burning desire to develop what you
   have to give, renewing,
Removing your obstacles to our desire to
   move forward, forward.
The way of matured societies is our zealous
   goal to attain;
The effect of speech and letters we long to
   behold.
Humbleness is not the course, Kalaallit, wake
   up and be proud!
A dignified life is our goal; courageously take
   a stand.

PATRON SAINT

Saint Nicholas, patron saint of seafarers

CURRENCY

Danish krone

INTERNET IDENTIFIER

.gl

VEHICLE IDENTIFICATION PLATES/ STICKERS

DK Denmark (official), KN Greenland (unofficial)

PASSPORT

Greenlanders are Danish citizens and travel on Danish passports.

AIRLINE

Air Greenland

NATIONAL FLOWER

Niviarsiaq (broad-leaf fireweed)

NATIONAL TREE

Grayleaf willow (unofficial)

NATIONAL ANIMAL

Polar bear

NATIONAL BIRD

Ptarmigan (unofficial)

NATIONAL RESOURCES

Natural resources include coal, iron ore, lead, zinc, molybdenum, diamonds, gold, platinum, niobium, tantalite, uranium, fish, seals, whales, hydropower, and possible oil and natural gas. The island is critically dependent on fishing and fish exports. Grants from the Danish government account for about half the yearly government revenues.

FOODS

The national dishes are *suaasat*, seal meat boiled with rice and onions, and *mattak*, whale skin with a thin layer of fat, which is cut into squares and eaten raw, much like the Japanese specialty sushi. Other specialties include *suaasat*, a hearty soup made of fish, seal, whale, or reindeer with rice and root vegetables; *ammassat*, dried capelin, a small fish of the salmon family; and cod served in various ways is a mainstay of the cuisine.

SPORTS/SPORTS TEAMS

Association football (soccer) is Greenland's national sport. Traditional sports, winter sports, and team sports, such as handball, are also very popular. Greenland national teams participate in a number of sports at the international level.

TEAM SPORTS

Badminton

Greenland Badminton Team

Football

Greenland Football Team, nickname Polar-Bamseme (the Polar Teddy Bears); Greenland Women's Football Team, nickname Polar-Bamseme (the Polar Teddy Bears)

Handball

Greenland Handball Team, nickname Team Grønland; Greenland Women's Handball Team, nickname Team Grønland

Table Tennis

Greenland Table Tennis Team

Volleyball

Greenland Men's Volleyball Team; Greenland Women's Volleyball Team

WINTER SPORTS

Greenland Biathlon Team

NATIONAL HEROES OR PERSONIFICATIONS

An Inuit (Eskimo) is the personification of Greenland. National heroes include Eric the Red, the Viking leader who established Greenland's original ties to Europe; and Esker Burn, governor of the island during World War II.

NATIONAL HOLIDAY/INDEPENDENCE DAY

National Day, June 21 (longest day of the year)

FESTIVALS/FAIRS

National Day, June; Return of the Sun, January; Christmas, December

SIGNIFICANT EVENTS IN FORMATION OF NATIONAL IDENTITY

200 C.E.–982 C.E. Early culture on the island disappears around the year 200 C.E. The island remains uninhabited for nearly eight centuries.

982 Settlers from Iceland* led by Eric the Red establish two colonies on the southern tip of the uninhabited island.

12th century–13th century The number of settlers grows to about 10,000 in the 12th century. The first contacts occur between the settlers and the vanguard of the Inuit migration. The colony comes under Norwegian rule.

14th century Sometime in the 14th century, the weather grows colder, and agriculture and livestock decline. The Black Death arrives from Europe, killing about half the colonists. The last message from Greenland arrives in Europe in 1410. The colonists disappear, and their fate still is not known.

1721 Settlers from Norway*, then part of the Danish realm, begin to resettle the island.

1815–1850 Denmark loses Norway to Sweden* but retains control of Greenland. The Danes mostly ignore the colony, while the indigenous Inuit suffer from European diseases and are often abused by colonial bureaucrats. U.S. naval officer Matthew Perry, explores northern Greenland and claims it for the United States*.

1917 The United States relinquishes its claim when it purchases the Virgin Islands* from Denmark.

1931 Norway occupies and claims part of uninhabited East Greenland. The claim is disputed by Denmark, and the international court confirms Danish sovereignty.

1940–1945 Germans occupy Denmark during the Second World War, severing its ties to Greenland. The governor of the island becomes acting head of state, giving the Greenlanders their first taste of self-government.

1953–1960 Greenland is made a Danish county eligible for the benefits of Denmark's generous welfare system. Modern medicine helps eradicate tuberculosis and other European diseases that had ravaged the population. Immigration from Denmark increases, as do ethnic mixing and intermarriage.

1960–1972 Greenlandic activists begin to denounce the Danish welfare system as creating a culture of dependency. The first small regionalist movement is formed to promote Greenlandic interests. Greenlanders vote against Denmark's plan to join the European Community.

1977–1979 The first openly nationalist political party forms on a platform of independence. In 1979, in a referendum on home rule, 70 percent of the Greenlanders vote in favor. Greenland, officially renamed Kalaallit Nunaat, becomes an autonomous state in association with Denmark.

1979–1982 Greenlanders denounce Denmark's retention of mineral rights in their country. Greenlanders vote to withdraw their autonomous state from the European Community, the first and, so far, only territory to do so.

1991–2000 Island politics polarize between proindependence and pro-Danish political parties. The island rejects a move to renew its membership in the European Community. The Greenland government allows oil exploration in an effort to diversify the economy.

2008–2009 A referendum on greater autonomy was approved on November 25, 2008, making Greenlandic the official language and allowing Greenland to assume responsibility of judicial affairs, policing, and natural resources. The referendum is seen as a step toward full independence in the near future.

GRENADA

OFFICIAL NAME
Grenada

POPULATION
106,500 (2009e)

INHABITANTS' NAME/NICKNAME
Grenadian(s)

LANGUAGE/LANGUAGES
English (official); Grenadian Creole, Antillean Creole French, others

RELIGION/RELIGIONS
Roman Catholic, 53 percent; Anglican, 14 percent; other or no religion

NATIONAL FLAG
The flag is divided diagonally into triangular quadrants, colored green at hoist and fly and yellow at top and bottom. A red border surrounds the flag, with six yellow, five-pointed stars, three at top and three at bottom, and a central red disk charged with a seventh yellow star. The stars represent the island's seven parishes, with the center star representing the parish of Saint George's, the island's capital. On the green triangle on the hoist side is a symbol representing a clove of nutmeg. The color combination is based on the pan-African colors and represents the origins of the majority of the Grenadians. The color red stands for courage and vitality, yellow for wisdom and warmth, and green for vegetation and agriculture.

COAT OF ARMS/SEAL
The coat of arms has a central shield divided into four parts by a yellow cross. In the center of the cross is a ship, identified as the Santa Maria, Christopher Columbus' flagship. A British lion on a red field fills the upper left and lower right quadrants, with a golden crescent out of which a lily grows in the upper right and lower left quadrants. Above the shield is a golden crown topped with a garland of bougainvillea. Within the garland are seven red roses, which stand for the island's seven parishes. An armadillo standing before a corn stalk and a Grenada dove standing before a banana plant, support the shield. The base below the shield shows grasslands and mountains and Grand Etang Lake. A banner displays the national motto.

MOTTO
Ever conscious of God, we aspire, build, and advance as one people

CAPITAL CITY
Saint George's

TYPE OF GOVERNMENT

Parliamentary democracy

NATIONAL EMBLEM

Nutmeg

NATIONAL COLORS

Red, yellow, and green

NATIONAL ANTHEM

The anthem was adopted at independence in 1974 and has remained despite changes of government.

Hail Grenada

Hail! Grenada, land of ours,
We pledge ourselves to thee,
Heads, hearts and hands in unity
To reach our destiny.
Ever conscious of God,
Being proud of our heritage,
May we with faith and courage
Aspire, build, advance
As one people, one family.
God bless our nation.

PATRON SAINT

Saint George

CURRENCY

East Caribbean dollar

INTERNET IDENTIFIER

.gd

VEHICLE IDENTIFICATION PLATES/STICKERS

WG

PASSPORT

The passport has the initials CC for Caribbean Community and the name of the country in English, the coat of arms, and the word *passport* in English.

NATIONAL FLOWER

Bougainvillea

NATIONAL TREE

Banana

NATIONAL ANIMAL

Armadillo

NATIONAL BIRD

Grenada dove

NATIONAL FISH

Jack crevalle (unofficial)

NATIONAL RESOURCES

Natural resources include timber, tropical fruit, and deepwater harbors. The island, known as the Spice Isle, produces several spices, including the most emblematic: nutmeg. Sandy beaches, underwater reefs, a pleasant climate, island culture, and proximity to North American markets support an important tourist industry. Ecotourism is growing due to Grenada's unspoiled coasts and rainforests.

FOODS

The national dish is oildown, a varied combination of salted pigtail, pig's feet, salt beef, chicken, breadfruit, carrots, and onion with dumplings cooked in coconut milk until the all of the coconut milk is absorbed leaving just a base of coconut oil at the bottom of the pot. Other specialties include coleslaw and fried plantains, crab and callaloo (a spinach-like vegetable), rice and peas; lightly fired snapper often served with callaloo; Grenadian caviar (the roe of white sea urchins), and Creole chicken, a traditional dish simmered in a garlic tomato sauce and seasoned with nutmeg. Eggplant casserole, yam pie, calypso rice, and pumpkin round are popular dishes.

SPORTS/SPORTS TEAMS

Association football (soccer) is Grenada's most popular sport. Cricket and rugby union are also very popular. Grenada national teams participate in many sports at the national level.

TEAM SPORTS

Badminton

Grenada Badminton Team

Basketball

Grenada Basketball Team; Grenada Women's Basketball Team

Cricket

West Indies Cricket Team, nickname the Windies (represents a number of English-speaking Caribbean countries)

Football

Grenada Football Team, nickname the Spice Boyz; Grenada Women's Football Team, nickname the Spice Girlz; Grenada Futsal Team; West Indies Rugby League Team, nickname The Wahoos (West Indies teams represent a number of English-speaking Caribbean countries)

Kabaddi

West Indies Kabaddi Team (West Indies teams represent a number of English-speaking Caribbean countries)

Netball

Grenada Netball Team

Table Tennis

Grenada Table Tennis Team

Tennis

Eastern Caribbean Davis Cup Team; Eastern Caribbean Fed Cup Team (Eastern Caribbean teams represent a number of English-speaking Caribbean countries)

Volleyball

Grenada Men's Volleyball Team

INDIVIDUAL SPORTS

Grenada Amateur Boxing Team; Grenada Athletics Team; Grenada Cycling Team; Grenada Judo Team; Grenada Sailing Team; Grenada Swim Team; Grenada Tae Kwon Do Team; Grenada Triathlon Team

NATIONAL HEROES OR PERSONIFICATIONS

Sir Eric Matthew Gairy, independence leader and the country's first premier; Maurice Bishop, the leader of the revolution of 1979 assassinated in 1983

NATIONAL HOLIDAY/INDEPENDENCE DAY

Independence Day, February 7

FESTIVALS/FAIRS

Jazz festival, May–June; La Source Grenada Sailing Festival, January; Carriacou Carnival, February; Carnival, August

SIGNIFICANT EVENTS IN FORMATION OF NATIONAL IDENTITY

1300 C.E.–1400 C.E. Warlike Caribs drive the indigenous Arawaks from the island.

1498 The recorded history of Grenada begins in 1498, when Christopher Columbus first sights the island and gives it the name Conception Island. Columbus later calls it Granada, after the city in Andalusia, Spain*.

1609 The Spanish attempt to colonize the island, but Carib attacks end the project.

1650 The Spanish ignore the island and its fierce Caribs. The English attempt to establish a settlement but are driven off. The French fight the Caribs and conquer the island. The French name the new colony La Grenade. Sugar plantations are established with imported African slaves as laborers. Grenada's natural harbor becomes an important way station on the slave routes between Africa and the Caribbean islands.

1763 The Treaty of Paris cedes the island to the United Kingdom*.

1830–1877 The emancipation of the slaves and the disintegration of the plantation system leave the former slaves to depend on a few local industries and their own smallholdings. Grenada becomes a British Crown Colony.

1950–1962 A trade union organization takes hold among the island workers, led by a firebrand ex-teacher named Eric Gairy. Grenada joins the short-lived West Indies Federation.

1974 Grenada is granted independence, with Gairy as its first leader.

1974–1983 The opposition, led by leftist idealists, is unhappy with Gairy's leadership. Maurice Bishop leads an armed revolution against the Gairy government. A leftist government begins distributing lands and goods to the people of the island. Cuba* sends doctors and teachers and military aid.

1983–1990 Bishop is deposed and arrested. He is eventually executed, along with other former cabinet members. A revolutionary government is formed. The United States*, with the aid of many Caribbean countries, invades the island. The revolutionary government is ousted

2000–2002 The events of the 1970s and 1980s are again in the people's consciousness, with the opening of a truth and reconciliation commission.

2004–2005 Hurricane Ivan is the first deadly storm to hit the island in 45 years. Over 90 percent of homes and businesses are damaged. A second hurricane hits northern Grenada.

2005–2008 Grenada recovers rapidly due to domestic labor and international help.

2007–2008 Grenada jointly hosts, along with other Caribbean states, the Cricket World Cup. China* pays for a new national stadium and sends 300 Chinese laborers to build and repair it. The men convicted of Maurice Bishop's murder in 1983 are released from prison.

2009 Grenada's people celebrate 35 years of independence amid a general economic slump.

GUADELOUPE

OFFICIAL NAME
Région Guadeloupe (French); Region of Guadeloupe (English)

POPULATION
411,600 (2009e)

INHABITANTS' NAME/NICKNAME
Guadeloupean(s)

LANGUAGE/LANGUAGES
French (official); Antillean Creole French, English, others

RELIGION/RELIGIONS
Roman Catholic, 91 percent; Protestant, 5 percent; other or no religion

NATIONAL FLAG
The official flag of Guadeloupe is the French tricolor. The unofficial local flag has a black field bearing a large yellow sun and green sugarcane with a broad blue stripe across the top charged with three golden fleurs-de-lis. The flag is a version of the unofficial coat of arms. The flags of various independence movements are mostly composed of the colors red, green, and white.

COAT OF ARMS/SEAL
The coat of arms is a black shield bearing a yellow sun and green sugarcane with a blue stripe across the top charged with three golden fleurs-de-lis. Both the coat of arms and the flag are sometimes shown with a red background.

CAPITAL CITY
Basse-Terre

TYPE OF GOVERNMENT
Multiparty democracy with limited autonomy within the French Republic

NATIONAL COLORS

Red, green, and white

NATIONAL ANTHEM

"La Marseillaise," the French anthem, is the official anthem of Guadeloupe. The French government forbids the use of local anthems.

PATRON SAINT

Saint Pierre

CURRENCY

Euro

INTERNET IDENTIFIER

.gp

VEHICLE IDENTIFICATION PLATES/STICKERS

F Frabce (official); GP Guadeloupe (unofficial)

PASSPORT

Guadeloupeans are French citizens and travel on French passports.

AIRLINE

Air Caraïbes (jointly with Martinique)

NATIONAL FLOWER

Red ginger (unofficial)

NATIONAL TREE

Nance (unofficial)

NATIONAL ANIMAL

Racoon (Guadeloupe raccoon) (unofficial)

NATIONAL BIRD

Guadeloupean wren (unofficial)

NATIONAL RESOURCES

Natural resources, other than timber and hydropower, are negligible. Sandy beaches, a pleasant climate, and island culture have made Guadeloupe a favored destination for tourists and cruise ships in the Caribbean. The economy of Guadeloupe depends on tourism, agriculture, light industry, and services. It also depends on France for large subsidies and imports.

FOODS

Local specialties include *accra,* cod fritters with shrimp; *chiquetaille de morue,* shredded and grilled cod served with vinaigrette sauce; *dombré,* flour balls cooked with dried vegetables; and *colombo,* a curry dish with lamb, chicken, or goat. Other specialties include *fricassee,* a curry and coconut chicken dish; *court-bouillon,* marinated fish prepared with onion and tomatoes; and *plantain au gratin,* fried plantains with white sauce.

SPORTS/SPORTS TEAMS

Association football (soccer) is the most popular sport. A French favorite, cycling, is also a favorite sport in Guadeloupe. Basketball is gaining popularity. Guadeloupe national teams participate in football, basketball, volleyball, and cycling at the international level.

TEAM SPORTS

Basketball

Guadeloupe Basketball Team; Guadeloupe Women's Basketball Team

Football

Guadeloupe Football Team, nickname Les Gars de Guadeloupe or Gwada Boys

Volleyball

Guadeloupe Men's Volleyball Team; Guadeloupe Women's Volleyball Team

INDIVIDUAL SPORTS

Guadeloupe Cycling Team

NATIONAL HEROES OR PERSONIFICATIONS

Louis Delgrès, the leader of a rebellion that resisted the reoccupation of the island and the reinstitution of slavery in the early 19th century; Saint-John Perse, the winner of the 1960 Nobel Prize for Literature; Maryse Condé, noted author and activist

NATIONAL HOLIDAY/INDEPENDENCE DAY

Bastille Day, July 14; Abolition of Slavery Day, May 27

FESTIVALS/FAIRS

Guadeloupe International Film Festival, January–February; Mardi Gras, February; Les Nuits Caraïbes Classical Music Festival, February–March; Festival de la Guadeloupe, July–August

SIGNIFICANT EVENTS IN FORMATION OF NATIONAL IDENTITY

300 B.C.E.–1400 C.E. Arawak peoples from the South American mainland settle the island. The agricultural Arawaks are eliminated or absorbed by the warlike Caribs, who give their name to the sea surrounding the islands they control.

1493–1626 Christopher Columbus, on his second voyage to the New World, names the island for an image of the Virgin Mary in Guadalupe, in southern Spain*. Not finding gold on the island, the Spanish ignore the island. Attempts to establish settlement fail in 1604 and 1626.

1635–1674 French explorers are sent to take control of the island, which they do by nearly wiping out the island's Carib population. Called Guadeloupe, the island is annexed to the French kingdom.

1674–1789 A plantation economy is created, with imported African slaves as labor. The smaller islands are settled by colonists from Brittany* and Normandy.

1789–1798 Revolution in France arrives in Guadeloupe. Slavery is abolished, and a guillotine eliminates the planter aristocracy, leaving the island with a large population of freed slaves, a small number of mixed-race residents, and a few poor Europeans.

1802 Louis Delgrès leads an uprising against the return of French rule. He and 300 followers choose to die rather than submit to the French army. Napoleon reinstates slavery.

1848–1854 Slavery is abolished in the French Empire. Indentured servants are imported from India*.

1870 A worldwide glut of sugar brings poverty to many Guadeloupeans dependent on the sugar industry.

1923 Bananas are first exported.

1946 Guadeloupe becomes a department of the French Republic. The reality for the Guadeloupeans remains the same: poverty, unemployment, and subsistence farming.

1955–1968 Guadeloupeans mobilize as neighboring British islands gain independence. Serious rioting and violence by proindependence groups rock the island.

1974–1981 High unemployment, overpopulation, and underdevelopment continue to plague the island. Guadeloupe's status is upgraded to that of a region of France. The French welfare system and generous subsidies give the islanders one of the highest standards of living in the Caribbean.

1984–1987 France rushes gendarme units to the island to quell serious violence instigated by groups seeking Guadeloupean independence. Nationalists form a provisional government of a future Republic of Guadeloupe.

1990–2008 Guadeloupe's political life is characterized by disillusionment and apathy. Elections attract barely more than 15 percent of eligible voters. Support for self-government is widespread, but the economic reality tempers support for outright independence.

2007 The formerly dependent territories of Saint Martin* and Saint Barthélemy* are detached from Guadeloupe to become separate territorial collectives with status equal to that of Guadeloupe.

2008–2009 The growing disparity between the local Guadeloupeans and the European administrators, whose inflated civil service salaries allow consumption of imported and luxury goods, continues. Strikes and demonstrations are held in favor of economic reform.

See also France

HAITI

OFFICIAL NAME

République d'Haïti (French); Repiblik d Ayiti (Haitian Creole); Republic of Haiti (English)

POPULATION

8,723,400 (2009e)

INHABITANTS' NAME/NICKNAME

Haitian(s)

LANGUAGE/LANGUAGES

French, Haitian Creole (official); Spanish, English, others

RELIGION/RELIGIONS

Roman Catholic, 80 percent; Baptist, 10 percent; Pentecostal, 4 percent; Seventh-day Adventist, 1 percent; other or no religion. An estimated half of the population practices voodoo.

NATIONAL FLAG

The flag is a horizontal bicolor of blue over red bearing the coat of arms in a small, centered white rectangle. The red represents the blood of the patriots who died for liberty, and the blue stands for the sea, the sky, and hope for the future. The white is for purity and reason.

COAT OF ARMS/SEAL

The coat of arms shows six draped flags behind a palm tree and cannons on a green lawn with a drum, a bugle, long guns, and ship anchors. Above the palm tree is a Phrygian cap as a symbol of freedom. The weapons symbolize the country's willingness to defend its freedom. The palm tree represents Haiti's independence. Also on the lawn is a banner that bears the country's national motto.

MOTTO

L'union fait la force (French); Union Makes Strength (English)

CAPITAL CITY

Port-au-Prince

TYPE OF GOVERNMENT

Republic

NATIONAL EMBLEM

Henri Christophe's citadel

NATIONAL COLORS

Blue and red

NATIONAL ANTHEM

The anthem was adopted on the occasion of Haiti's centennial in 1904, replacing another anthem adopted in 1893.

La Dessalinienne (French); The Dessalines Song (English)

For our country,
For our forefathers,
United let us march.
Let there be no traitors in our ranks!
Let us be masters of our soil.
United let us march
For our country,
For our forefathers.

For our forebears,
For our country,
Let us toil joyfully.
May the fields be fertile
And our souls take courage.
Let us toil joyfully
For our forebears,
For our country.

For our country
And for our forefathers,
Let us train our sons.
Free, strong, and prosperous,
We shall always be as brothers.
Let us train our sons
For our country
And for our forefathers.

For our forebears,
For our country,
O God of the valiant!
Take our rights and our life
Under your infinite protection,
O God of the valiant!
For our forebears,
For our country.

For the flag,
For our country,
To die is a fine thing!
Our past cries out to us:
Have a disciplined soul!
To die is a fine thing
For the flag,
For our country.

PATRON SAINT

Our Lady of Perpetual Help

CURRENCY

Haitian gourde

INTERNET IDENTIFIER

.ht

VEHICLE IDENTIFICATION PLATES/ STICKERS

RH

PASSPORT

The passport cover has the initials CC for Caribbean Community, in French and English, the name of the country in French and Haitian Creole, the coat of arms, and the word *passport* in French and Haitian Creole.

AIRLINE

Tortug' Air

NATIONAL FLOWER

Hibiscus (unofficial)

NATIONAL TREE

Breadfruit (unofficial)

NATIONAL BIRD

Foucon pè (Haitian hawk), tundra peregrine hawk (unofficial)

NATIONAL RESOURCES

Natural resources include bauxite, copper, calcium carbonate, gold, marble, and hydropower. Foreign aid makes up approximately 30 percent to 40 percent of the Haitian government's budget. Another important resource is the very large number of Haitians living in other countries and the remittances they send to families in Haiti. Sandy beaches, a pleasant climate, and a unique culture are the basis of a growing tourist industry.

FOODS

Du riz colée a pois, or *didi kolé ak pwa* (Haitian Creole), brown rice with red kidney or pinto beans glazed with a marinade and topped with red snapper, tomatoes, and onions; and *sancocho,* a hearty stew of goat or beef, potatoes, tomatoes, and spices, are considered the two most typical national dishes. Other specialties are *tassot de dinde,* a dish containing dried turkey; *diri et djondjon,* a rice dish with black mushrooms; and *grillot,* Haitian fried pork.

SPORTS/SPORTS TEAMS

Association football (soccer) and basketball are the two most popular sports in Haiti. Haiti national teams participate in many sports at an international level.

TEAM SPORTS

Basketball

Haiti Basketball Team; Haiti Women's Basketball Team

Football

Haiti Football Team, nickname Les Bicolores (the Bicolors); Haiti Women's Football Team, nickname Les Bicolores; Haiti Futsal Team; Haiti Women's Under-19 Football Team

Table Tennis

Haiti Table Tennis Team

Tennis

Haiti Davis Cup Team; Haiti Fed Cup Team

Volleyball

Haiti Men's Volleyball Team; Haiti Women's Volleyball Team

INDIVIDUAL SPORTS

Haiti Amateur Boxing Team; Haiti Archery Team; Haiti Athletics Team; Haiti Cycling Team; Haiti Equestrian Team; Haiti Judo Team; Haiti Karate Team; Haiti Tae Kwon Do Team; Haiti Weight Lifting Team; Haiti Wrestling Team

NATIONAL HEROES OR PERSONIFICATIONS

Anacaona, a Taino queen who resisted Spanish rule and was brutally executed; Jean-Jacques Dessalines, a leader of the Haitian Revolution and the first ruler of independent Haiti; Toussaint L'Ouverture, called the Black Napoleon, a leader of the Haitian Revolution; Henri Christophe, another leader of the Haitian Revolution and later king of Haiti in the north; Alexandre Pétion, the last of the four founding fathers of Haiti; Charlemagne Péralte, who led a rebellion against the U.S. occupation in 1919

NATIONAL HOLIDAY/INDEPENDENCE DAY

Independence Day, January 1

FESTIVALS/FAIRS

Carnival, February–March; Voodoo Festival, August; Jakmel Film Festival, July

SIGNIFICANT EVENTS IN FORMATION OF NATIONAL IDENTITY

600 C.E.–1450 C.E. The Tainos, an Arawakan-speaking people originally from South America, occupy the island around 600 C.E., displacing the earlier inhabitants. The Tainos call the island Ayti.

1492 Christopher Columbus, on his first voyage to the New World, encounters the island, naming it La Española.

1492–1520 Slavery, harsh treatment, and European diseases devastate the Taino population. In need of labor, the Spanish begin to import African slaves to search for the storied gold on the island.

1625–1697 The French begin to colonize the island. France* formally claims the western portion in 1664, which is ceded to France by Spain* by treaty in 1697. France names its new colony Saint-Domingue.

1700–1780 While the Spanish Santo Domingo languishes through official neglect, the French side of the island flourishes, becoming the richest colony in the New World. The colony is divided into Europeans, *gens de coleur* of mixed blood, and the vast majority of African slaves.

1790–1801 Inspired by the French Revolution, the *gens de coleur* press for greater freedom. They initiate a rebellion that spreads across the island. A slave army led by Toussaint L'Ouverture defeats the French sent against him. In 1801, L'Ouverture conquers Spanish Santo Domingo and abolishes slavery there.

1804 The country, renamed Haiti after the original Taino name, is declared independent, becoming the first independent black state and the second independent country in the Americas. Jean Jacques Dessalines becomes Haiti's first emperor.

1805–1826 The slave-holding countries isolate Haiti, and the Vatican withdraws its priests from the country. The French conquer the Spanish half of the island in 1808. The first meeting of the hemisphere's independent states is held, but Haiti is excluded.

1833 France refuses recognition of independent Haiti until it agrees to pay an indemnity of 150 million francs to compensate for French losses. The payment puts the new government heavily into debt and cripples economic expansion.

1915–1934 Fearful of growing German influence in Haiti, the United States* invades and occupies the country. The United States reforms the economy; builds schools, roads, and hospitals; and eradicates yellow fever and malaria. The occupation troops leave the island.

1957–1971 François Duvalier is elected president. Called Papa Doc, he rules as dictator from 1964 to 1971. His brutal administration is responsible for the deaths of some 30,000 Haitians. Mass emigration of the educated and professional groups deprives the country of much-needed skills. At his death, power passes to his son, Jean-Claude, known as Baby Doc.

1971–1986 Jean-Claude Duvalier systematically sacks the country and is finally overthrown.

1990–2004 Jean-Bertrand Aristide wins presidential elections but is overthrown in a coup that leaves several thousand dead. Subsequent chaos brings a very near invasion by the United States in 1994. Aristide returns to power, only to be ousted again in 2004.

2004–2009 United Nations peacekeeping troops intervene to restore order. An interim government is formed that gives way to democratic elections. About 8,000 U.N. peacekeepers remain as a stabilizing force. Haitians continue to leave in search of a better life, mostly to the United States or the French islands in the Caribbean.

JAMAICA

OFFICIAL NAME
Jamaica

POPULATION
2,805,600 (2009e)

INHABITANTS' NAME/NICKNAME
Jamaican(s)

LANGUAGE/LANGUAGES
English (official); Jamaican English (English patois), others

RELIGION/RELIGIONS
Seventh-day Adventist, 11 percent; Pentecostal, 10 percent; Baptist, 7 percent; New Testament Church of God, 6 percent; Church of God in Jamaica, 5 percent; Church of God Prophecy, 4 percent; Anglican, 3.5 percent; Roman Catholic, 2.5 percent; other Church of God denominations, 8 percent; other or no religion

NATIONAL FLAG
The flag consists of a gold Saint Andrew's cross that divides the field into green triangles at top and bottom and black triangles at each side. Gold represents sunlight and Jamaica's natural wealth; black represents the strength and creativity of the Jamaican people and also the historical struggles and hardship they have faced; and green stands for hope for the future and agricultural richness.

COAT OF ARMS/SEAL
The coat of arms consists of a central shield of white with a red cross, representing the country's historic ties to England. The red is charged with five pineapples, representing the country's agriculture. Above the shield is a heraldic royal helmet topped with a crocodile, representing Jamaica's indigenous animal life. The shield is supported by depictions of a male and female Taino, representing Jamaica's first inhabitants. Below is a banner in red and white inscribed with the country's national motto.

MOTTO
Out of many, one people

CAPITAL CITY

Kingston

TYPE OF GOVERNMENT

Parliamentary democracy

NATIONAL COLORS

Yellow, black, and green

NATIONAL ANTHEM

The anthem was adopted at independence in 1962 and was written and composed especially for the occasion.

Jamaica, Land We Love

Eternal Father, Bless our land
Guide us with thy mighty hand
Keep us free from evil powers
Be our light through countless hours
To our leaders, Great Defender,
Grant true wisdom from above
Justice, truth be ours forever
Jamaica, land we love
Jamaica, Jamaica, Jamaica, land we love.

Teach us true respect for all
Stir response to duty's call
Strengthen us the weak to cherish
Give us vision lest we perish
Knowledge send us, Heavenly Father,
Grant true wisdom from above
Justice, truth be ours forever
Jamaica, land we love
Jamaica, Jamaica, Jamaica, land we love

PATRON SAINT

Mary, on the feast of her Assumption

CURRENCY

Jamaican dollar

INTERNET IDENTIFIER

.jm

VEHICLE IDENTIFICATION PLATES/ STICKERS

JA

PASSPORT

The passport cover has the initials CC for Caribbean Community and the name of the country, the coat of arms, and the word *passport*, all in English.

AIRLINE

Air Jamaica

NATIONAL FLOWER

Guaiacum officinale (lignum vitae)

NATIONAL TREE

Blue mahoe

NATIONAL ANIMAL

Jamaican crocodile

NATIONAL BIRD

Doctor bird (red-billed streamertail)

NATIONAL FISH

Yellowtail snapper (unofficial)

NATIONAL FRUIT

Ackee

NATIONAL RESOURCES

Natural resources include bauxite, gypsum, limestone, sandy beaches, pleasant climate, and arable land. A flourishing tourist industry is based on the country's sandy beaches, Caribbean culture, and pleasant climate. Jamaicans living outside the country are an important source of remittances and investment.

FOODS

The national dish is ackee and codfish, salt cod and the cooked fruit of the ackee tree. Other specialties are rice and peas, white rice with kidney beans, coconut milk, scallions, and coconut oil; Jamaican pepperpot soup, a tasty mixture of salt pork, salt beef, okra, and Indian kale or callaloo; Jamaican chicken fricassee, chicken stew with carrots, scallions, yams, onions, tomatoes, and peppers prepared in coconut oil; roast suckling pig, a boned piglet stuffed with rice, peppers, diced yam, and thyme mixed with shredded coconut and cornmeal.

SPORTS/SPORTS TEAMS

Cricket and association football (soccer) are the most popular sports. Athletics and racing are also very popular. Jamaica national teams participate in many sports at an international level.

TEAM SPORTS

Badminton

Jamaica Badminton Team

Baseball

Jamaica Baseball Team; Jamaica Softball Team

Basketball

Jamaica Basketball Team; Jamaica Women's Basketball Team

Cricket

Jamaica Cricket Team; West Indies Cricket Team, nickname the Windies (West Indies teams represent a number of English-speaking Caribbean countries)

Football

Jamaica Football Team, nickname the Reggae Boyz; Jamaica Women's Football Team, nickname the Reggae Girlz; Jamaica Women's Under-19 Football Team; Jamaica Rugby Union Team; Jamaica Women's Rugby Union Team; Jamaica Rugby League Team; Jamaica Beach Soccer Team; West Indies Rugby League Team, nickname the Wahoos (West Indies teams represent a number of English-speaking Caribbean countries)

Hockey

Jamaica Field Hockey Team

Kabaddi

West Indies Kabaddi Team (West Indies teams represent a number of English-speaking Caribbean countries)

Netball

Jamaica Netball Team

Table Tennis

Jamaica Table Tennis Team

Tennis

Jamaica Davis Cup Team; Jamaica Fed Cup Team

Volleyball

Jamaica Men's Volleyball Team; Jamaica Women's Volleyball Team

INDIVIDUAL SPORTS

Jamaica Amateur Boxing Team; Jamaica Athletics Team; Jamaica Cycling Team; Jamaica Equestrian Team; Jamaica Gymnastics Team; Jamaica Judo Team; Jamaica Karate Team; Jamaica Rowing Team; Jamaica Sailing Team; Jamaica Shooting Team; Jamaica Swim Team; Jamaica Tae Kwon Do Team; Jamaica Triathlon Team; Jamaica Weight Lifting Team

NATIONAL HEROES OR PERSONIFICATIONS

Tacky, the leader of a slave revolt in 1760; Paul Bogle, the leader of the slave revolt of 1865; William Gordon, a Baptist minister accused of rebellion and hanged in 1865; Norman Manley, the chief minister who led Jamaica to independence; Alexander Bustamante, Jamaica's first prime minister; Marcus Garvey, Jamaican-born black civil-rights leader; Bob Marley, the musician who introduced Jamaican reggae music to the world

National Holiday/Independence Day

Independence Day, August 6

Festivals/Fairs

Festival of Foods, April; Song Festival, June–July; National Festival, July; Jonkunnu Festival, December

Significant Events in Formation of National Identity

4000 b.c.e.–1000 b.c.e. The Taino people, an Arawak group from South America, settle the island between 4000 and 1000 b.c.e. Several Taino chiefdoms control the island, and the population continues to grow.

1494–1655 Christopher Columbus visits the island, naming it Santiago. It is later the site of his family's private estate. European diseases, slavery, and harsh treatment devastate the Taino population. African slaves are imported to work the large plantations.

1655–1800 The English seize the island. The island is divided into numerous sugar plantations, mostly owned by absentee landlords and worked by slaves of African origin. Jamaica becomes one of the world's leading sugar producers. Jamaica has the largest number of slave revolts in the Caribbean. By 1800, blacks outnumber whites on the island by 20 to one.

1834–1865 Slavery is abolished in the British Empire. Chinese and Indian indentured servants are imported as agricultural workers. Over half a million emancipated slaves are denied land rights by the remaining whites on the island. Baptist preacher Paul Bogle leads the former slaves in a widespread revolt in 1865.

1866–1900 The island's white legislature renounces its powers, and Jamaica becomes a crown colony. Some self-government is returned to the island in the 1880s. The growth of a middle class and the rapid urbanization of former agricultural workers continue into the 20th century.

1930–1955 The Great Depression has a serious impact on the island's economy. Sugar workers and dockworkers rebel in 1938 but are suppressed by colonial forces. Jamaican emigration, which began in the late 19th century, continues, mostly to the United Kingdom*. Universal suffrage is introduced in 1944.

1958–1962 Jamaica joins the Federation of the West Indies, a loose federation of the British Caribbean islands, but leaves the federation to become an independent republic in 1962.

1962–1992 Political polarization between pro-British, later pro-American, and nationalist groups often leads to violence. Emigration, restricted by the United Kingdom, mostly goes to the United States* and Canada*.

2000–2009 Support is growing to replace the British monarch as Jamaica's head of state with an elected office for Jamaicans. The island's difficult economic situation continues to force Jamaicans to leave in search of a better life.

MARTINIQUE

Official Name

Région Martinique (French); Martinique Region (English)

Population

411,300 (2009e)

Inhabitants' Name/Nickname

Martiniquaise; Martinican(s)

Language/Languages

French (official); Antillean Creole (Créole Martiniquais), Spanish, English, others

Religion/Religions

Roman Catholic, 85 percent; Protestant, 11 percent; Muslim, Hindu, other or no religion

National Flag

The official flag of Martinique is the French tricolor. The unofficial flag is a blue field divided by a white cross with a serpent in each of the quadrants. The flag dates from the

18th century and is based on the French flag of that period. The snakes represent the fer-de-lance vipers native to Martinique.

COAT OF ARMS/SEAL

The official coat of arms is a dark blue and white, highly stylized representation of the island in the same colors as the unofficial flag. Around the logo is inscribed, "La collectivité au service du pays" and below is written Région Martinique. The unofficial coat of arms is a representation of the unofficial flag, a blue shield divided by a white cross with a white serpent in each quadrant.

CAPITAL CITY

Fort-de-France

TYPE OF GOVERNMENT

Overseas department of the French Republic

NATIONAL EMBLEM

Fer-de-lance viper, as depicted on the regional flag

NATIONAL COLORS

Blue and white

NATIONAL ANTHEM

The official anthem is "La Marseillaise," the French national anthem.

PATRON SAINT

Saint Martin

CURRENCY

Euro

INTERNET IDENTIFIER

.mq

VEHICLE IDENTIFICATION PLATES/ STICKERS

F France (official); MQ Martinique (unofficial)

PASSPORT

Martinicans are French citizens and travel on French passports.

AIRLINE

Air Caraïbes (with Guadeloupe*)

NATIONAL FLOWER

Anthurium (official); *oiseau du paradis* (bird of paradise) (unofficial)

NATIONAL ANIMAL

Fer-de-lance viper

NATIONAL BIRD

Colibri hummingbird (unofficial)

NATIONAL RESOURCES

Natural resources are negligible, other than sandy beaches, a pleasant climate, and a unique culture that supports a thriving tourist industry. Although some sugarcane is still produced, the majority of the economy is based on tourism, with many French citizens visiting for holiday and cruise ships docking on almost a daily basis. French financial subsidies form the largest part of the island's annual budget.

FOODS

Martinique has a hybrid cuisine, mixing elements of French, African, and Asian traditions. Island specialties include *colombo*, a spicy curry of chicken, meat, or fish with vegetables, spiced with a distinctive masala of Bengali or Tamil origins; *crabe à la joséphine*, a salad of minced crab and island fruits; *crabe farci*, spicy stuffed crab; *feroce*, avocado stuffed with spicy codfish; *migan*, a dish of breadfruit and salt cod; *court-bouillon*, marinated fish cooked with onion and tomato; and fricassee, a chicken dish with onion, grated coconut, and curry.

SPORTS/SPORTS TEAMS

Association football (soccer) is the most popular sport. Rugby union, basketball, and volleyball are also popular. Martinique national teams participate in many sports at an international level.

TEAM SPORTS

Basketball

Martinique Basketball Team; Martinique Women's Basketball Team

Football

Martinique Football Team; Martinique Rugby Union Team

Volleyball

Martinique Men's Volleyball Team; Martinique Women's Volleyball Team

INDIVIDUAL SPORTS

Martinique Cycling Team

NATIONAL HEROES OR PERSONIFICATIONS

Aimé Césaire, a famous poet and author and an outspoken defendant of Martinican identity in the mid-20th century; Édouard Glissant, writer and poet; Frantz Fanon, writer and anticolonial politician

NATIONAL HOLIDAY/INDEPENDENCE DAY

Bastille Day, July 14; Abolition of Slavery Day, May 22

FESTIVALS/FAIRS

Carnival, February–March

SIGNIFICANT EVENTS IN FORMATION OF NATIONAL IDENTITY

3000 B.C.E.–11th century C.E. Waves of seafaring Arawak peoples settle the islands from the South American mainland. They create large villages on Martinique and engage in agriculture. The more warlike Caribs conquer the island, killing the Arawak males and taking the females as slaves.

1502 C.E. Christopher Columbus lands in Martinique and claims it for Spain, but no colonization is undertaken because of attacks by the indigenous peoples and a lack of gold. European diseases ravage the population.

1635–1674 The French colonize the island. Forced labor and mistreatment further devastate the original inhabitants, who decline and disappear. Black African slaves are imported to work the plantations.

1789–1794 News of the French Revolution leads to severe conflicts and a serious slave rebellion. Monarchists attempt to declare independence but are overcome. Most are sent to a guillotine set up by revolutionaries.

1848–1869 Slavery is abolished, and many of the island's wealthy planters are ruined and leave the island. Most former slaves settle as subsistence farmers. Chinese and Indian laborers are imported to work on the sugar plantations.

1902 Mount Pelée erupts, killing the 25,000 to 35,000 people living in the island's capital, Saint-Pierre.

1940–1946 The island is under the control of the fascist Vichy French government during World War II but is later taken over by the Free French. At the war's end, the status of Martinique is changed from colony to that of an overseas department.

1950–1980 The Martinique independence movement wins the support of intellectuals, such as Aimé Césaire and Frantz Fanon. Proindependence rioting rocks the island in 1974 and again in 1980–81. In the late 1970s, the French government aids the island to become self-sufficient in preparation for independence. Two severe hurricanes in 1979 and 1980 force the transition to independence to be postponed.

1980–2000 Periodic demands for a referendum on independence are ignored by the French government and rejected by nationalists, who realize that the majority of the islanders would reject independence if it meant losing generous French subsidies and one of the highest standards of living in the Caribbean.

2000–2009 The island's economy, overly dependent on sugar production, French government subsidies, and tourism, is unable to create jobs for the young, who leave the island in search of work. As French citizens, over 250,000 Martinicans live in mainland France.

See also France

MEXICO

OFFICIAL NAME

Estados Unidos Mexicanos (Spanish); United Mexican States (English)

POPULATION

109,383,100 (2009e)

INHABITANTS' NAME/NICKNAME

Mexican(s)

LANGUAGE/LANGUAGES

Spanish (de facto); more than 60 regional indigenous languages (recognized as official in the areas where they are spoken); English, others

RELIGION/RELIGIONS

Roman Catholic, 77 percent; Protestant, 6.5 percent; other or no religion

NATIONAL FLAG

The flag is a vertical tricolor of green, white, and red, with the national coat of arms centered on the white stripe. The green stands for hope, the white stands for national unity, and the red stands for the blood of the country's national heroes. The national coat of arms was added to the flag to distinguish it from the national flag of Italy*.

COAT OF ARMS/SEAL

The coat of arms depicts a Mexican golden eagle perched upon a prickly pear cactus devouring a snake. The cactus is situated on a rock that rises from a lake. The depiction is derived from an Aztec legend that their gods told them to build a city where they saw an eagle with a snake in its talon; that city later became Mexico City. To the Aztecs, this would have strong religious connotations, but to the Europeans, it came to symbolize the triumph of good over evil.

CAPITAL CITY

Mexico City (Ciudad de México)

TYPE OF GOVERNMENT

Federal presidential republic

NATIONAL EMBLEM

Mexican golden eagle devouring a snake

NATIONAL COLORS

Green, white, and red

NATIONAL ANTHEM

The anthem was written and composed as part of a competition for a new national anthem in the 19th century, although the official adoption came only in 1942.

Mexicanos, Al Grito de Guerra (Spanish); Mexicans, to the War Cry (English)

Chorus

Mexicans, when the war cry is heard,
Have sword and bridle ready.
Let the Earth's foundations tremble
At the loud cannon's roar.

May the divine archangel crown your brow,
Oh fatherland, with an olive branch of peace,
For your eternal destiny has been written
In heaven by the finger of God.
But should a foreign enemy
Dare to profane your soil with his tread,
Know, beloved fatherland, that heaven gave
  you
A soldier in each of your sons.

Chorus

War, war without truce against who would
  attempt
to blemish the honor of the fatherland!

War, war! The patriotic banners
saturate in waves of blood.
War, war! On the mount, in the vale
The terrifying cannon thunder
and the echoes nobly resound
to the cries of union! liberty!

Chorus

Fatherland, before your children become
  unarmed
Beneath the yoke their necks in sway,
May your countryside be watered with blood,
On blood their feet trample.
And may your temples, palaces and towers
crumble in horrid crash,
and their ruins exist saying:
The fatherland was made of one thousand
  heroes here.

Chorus

Fatherland, oh fatherland, your sons vow
To give their last breath on your altars,
If the trumpet with its warlike sound
Calls them to valiant battle.
For you, the garlands of olive,
For them, a glorious memory.
For you, the victory laurels,
For them, an honored tomb.

PATRON SAINT

Our Lady of Guadalupe (La Morenita); Saint
Joseph; Saint Elias Nieves

CURRENCY

Mexican peso

INTERNET IDENTIFIER

.mx

VEHICLE IDENTIFICATION PLATES/ STICKERS

MEX

PASSPORT

The passport cover has the short name of the
country, Mexico; the coat of arms, including
the full name of the country, Estados Unidos
Mexicanos, above the eagle; and the Spanish
word for passport.

AIRLINES

Aeromexico; Mexicana

NATIONAL FLOWER

Dahlia

NATIONAL TREE

Árbol del Tule (Tule tree) (unofficial)

NATIONAL PLANT

Prickly pear cactus

NATIONAL ANIMAL

Mexican burro (unofficial)

NATIONAL BIRD

Golden eagle

NATIONAL RESOURCES

Natural resources include petroleum, silver,
copper, gold, lead, zinc, natural gas, timber,
and arable land. Mexico's booming tourist industry is based on the country's sandy
beaches, pleasant climate, ruins of ancient
civilizations, unique culture, and proximity
to large North American population centers.
Remittances from Mexicans living in the
United States* are a valuable resource for
foreign currency and investment.

FOODS

Mexican cuisine is made up of many regional cuisines each known for a type of
regional cooking. The most internationally recognized are *enchiladas,* meat or fish
rolled up in a flour or corn tortilla, covered
with a spicy sauce, and baked; *quesadillas,*
different types of cheese melted between
two tortillas and usually served with a spicy
sauce or sliced hot peppers; *tacos,* crisp tortillas filled with meat or fish and vegetables;
mole, which refers to several sauces based

on garlic and chilies; and *guacamole,* a dip or sauce of avocados, tomatoes, onions, and spices. *Chiles en nogada,* Mexico's national dish, is a dish of beef or pork with green chilies, white walnut sauce, and pomegranate seeds, reflecting the colors of the national flag.

SPORTS/SPORTS TEAMS

Association football (soccer) is the country's most popular sport. The traditional rodeo, called *charreria,* was declared the national sport in 1933.

TEAM SPORTS

Badminton

Mexico Badminton Team

Baseball

Mexico Baseball Team; Mexico Softball Team

Basketball

Mexico Basketball Team; Mexico Women's Basketball Team; Mexico Wheelchair Basketball Team; Mexico Women's Wheelchair Basketball Team

Cricket

Mexico Cricket Team

Football

Mexico Football Team, nickname Los Tricolores or El Tri (the Tricolors); Mexico Women's Football Team; nickname Los Tricolores or El Tri (the Tricolors); Mexico Under-17 Football Team, nickname Los Tricolores or El Tri (the Tricolors); Mexico Women's Under-19 Football Team; Mexico Rugby Union Team; Mexico Rugby Union Team (Sevens); Mexico Wheelchair Rugby Team; Mexico American Football Team; Mexico Beach Soccer Team; Mexico Futsal Team

Handball

Mexico Handball Team; Mexico Women's Handball Team

Hockey

Mexico Ice Hockey Team; Mexico Field Hockey Team

Kabaddi

Mexico Kabaddi Team

Polo

Mexico Polo Team

Racing

A1 Team Mexico; Mexico Speedway Team

Table Tennis

Mexico Table Tennis Team

Tennis

Mexico Davis Cup Team; Mexico Fed Cup Team

Volleyball

Mexico Men's Volleyball Team; Mexico Women's Volleyball Team; Mexico Fistball Team; Mexico Beach Volleyball Team; Mexico Women's Beach Volleyball Team

Water Polo

Mexico Men's Water Polo Team; Mexico Women's Water Polo Team

INDIVIDUAL SPORTS

Mexico Aikido Team; Mexico Amateur Boxing Team; Mexico Archery Team; Mexico Athletics Team; Mexico Canoeing Team; Mexico Cycling Team; Mexico Equestrian Team; Mexico Fencing Team; Mexico Gymnastics Team; Mexico Judo Team; Mexico Karate Team; Mexico Modern Pentathlon Team; Mexico Rowing Team; Mexico Sailing Team; Mexico Shooting Team; Mexico

Swim Team; Mexico Tae Kwon Do Team; Mexico Triathlon Team; Mexico Weight Lifting Team; Mexico Wrestling Team

Winter Sports

Mexico Bobsleigh and Tobogganing Team; Mexico Ice Hockey Team; Mexico Skating Team

National Heroes or Personifications

Miguel Gregorio Antonio Ignacio Hidalgo y Costilla Gallaga Mondarte Villaseñor, commonly referred to as Miguel Hidalgo, was a leader of the independence war with Spain* and has come to personify Mexico, with many stories and tales about his adventures; Adelita, dressed in traditional costume, is another personification of the Mexican people.

Other national heroes include Francisco González Bocanegra, the poet responsible for the lyrics of the anthem; Álvaro Obregón, leader of the 1914 revolution; Victoriano Huerta, a leader of the 1914 revolution; Benito Juárez, leader of the rebellion that overthrew French rule in Mexico in the 19th century; Guadalupe Victoria, a revolutionary soldier and a leader in the Mexican War of Independence; Venustiano Carranza, responsible for the 1917 constitution; and Porfirio Diaz, president from 1876 to 1911.

National Holiday/Independence Day

Independence Day, September 16; Cinco de Mayo, May 5

Festivals/Fairs

Semana Santa (Holy Week), February–March; Carnival, February–March; Mexico City International Contemporary Film Festival, February–March; Guadalajara International Film Festival, March; Xochimilco Festival de la Flor mas Bella, March; Mexico City Festival, April; Cinco de Mayo, May; International Music and Scene Festival, August–September; Mariachi Festival, August–September; Independence Day celebrations, September; Octoberfest (Guadalajara), October–November; International Book Fair, November–December; Festival of the Virgin of Guadalupe, December

Significant Events in Formation of National Identity

7000 B.C.E.–1500 C.E. The indigenous peoples domesticate corn, initiating an agricultural revolution that allows the formation of many complex civilizations. These civilizations revolve around cities with writing, monumental architecture, astronomical studies, mathematics, and military power, the most powerful being the Aztec Empire in central Mexico.

1517 A Spanish expedition from Cuba* explores the Yucatan Peninsula in southern Mexico. The local Maya civilization whets the appetite of the Spanish, who seek gold and treasures in the New World. Stories of the fabulous Aztec Empire begin to circulate.

1519–1750 Hernán Cortés leads an expedition that eventually defeats the Aztecs. Over two centuries are needed to complete the conquest of Mexico. European diseases, slavery, mistreatment, and wars devastate the indigenous populations. Rebellions and attacks continue to harass the Spanish colony of New Spain. The riches of the conquered civilizations are carried off. Christianity, often forced, becomes the predominant religion. Spain claims a huge area of the North American continent, but the northern part of Mexico, although explored by early Spanish treasure hunters, is not settled until the 18th century.

1807–1821 Dissatisfaction with Spanish rule becomes more widespread with the French overthrow of the Spanish monarchy in Europe. Miguel Hidalgo y Costilla, a Catholic priest of Spanish descent, declares Mexico's independence, setting off a long war of independence. Spain recognizes Mexican independence in 1821.

1821–1848 The first decades of independence are marked by strife between liberals and conservatives. Under the Mexican dictatorship, Texas declares its independence of Mexico, initiating the Mexican-American War. By the terms of the Treaty of Guadalupe Hidalgo, Mexico loses one third of its area to the United States.

1860s The French occupy Mexico and install the Hapsburg Archduke Ferdinand Maximilian of Austria as emperor. The empire is overthrown and the French depart. Benito Juárez restores the republic in 1867.

1876–1920 The presidency of Porfirio Diaz is known as *Porfiriato*, a period of peace and rising prosperity. The Diaz era ends in fraudulent elections and leads to the Mexican Revolution.

1926–1929 The Cristero War begins over the government's anti-Catholic and anticlerical measures. The war leaves over 90,000 dead.

1929–1970 The predecessor of the Partido Revolucionario Institucional (PRI) is formed as the ruling political party. Virtual one-party rule continues for decades, during which Mexico experiences impressive economic growth called the Mexican Miracle.

1970s–1980s Mexico's economic problems drive millions to seek work and security in the United States. A severe earthquake compounds a succession of economic crisis in 1985.

1994 Mexico joins the United States and Canada* in the North American Free Trade Agreement (NAFTA).

2000 The ruling political party, the PRI, is defeated in presidential elections, ending over 70 years of hegemony.

2006–2008 Inconclusive presidential elections cause a serious national crisis. Mexico becomes the 12th-largest economy in the world, but the uneven distribution of income and continuing insecurity hamper efforts to share prosperity across the vast nation.

2009 Drug-related violence, corrupt police, and smuggling make the states along the U.S. border among the most violent and insecure regions of the Americas.

MONTSERRAT

OFFICIAL NAME

Montserrat; British Overseas Territory of Montserrat

NICKNAME

Emerald Isle of the Caribbean

POPULATION

5,100 (2009e); the total population of Montserratians, including refugees in other parts of the Caribbean and in the United Kingdom*, is estimated at over 15,000.

INHABITANTS' NAME/NICKNAME

Montserratian(s)

LANGUAGE/LANGUAGES

English (official); local patois

RELIGION/RELIGIONS

Protestant, Roman Catholic, other or no religion

NATIONAL FLAG

The flag is a blue field with the British Union Jack on the upper hoist and the arms of Montserrat on the fly.

COAT OF ARMS/SEAL

The arms consist of shield of aquamarine over brown, with the depiction of a lady in green representing Erin, the personification of Ireland*. The lady is holding a golden harp, another symbol of Ireland, and supports a black cross, symbolizing Christianity. The Irish symbols are a tribute to the Irish ancestry of many Montserratians, descendants of Irish Catholics exiled to the island in the 17th century.

MOTTO

Each endeavoring, all achieving

CAPITAL CITY

Plymouth (official); following the 1997 volcanic eruption, many government offices were transferred to Brades, making it the de facto capital. A new capital is planned at Little Bay.

TYPE OF GOVERNMENT

British overseas territory

NATIONAL EMBLEM

Shamrock

NATIONAL COLORS

Green and red

NATIONAL ANTHEM

As a British overseas territory, the British anthem, "God Save the Queen," is the official anthem. A local instrumental anthem is also used.

PATRON SAINT

Saint Patrick (unofficial)

CURRENCY

Eastern Caribbean dollar

INTERNET IDENTIFIER

.ms

VEHICLE IDENTIFICATION PLATES/STICKERS

GB Great Britain (official); GBMS Great Britain Montserrat (unofficial)

PASSPORT

Montserratians are British citizens and travel on British passports.

NATIONAL FLOWER

Heliconia (lobster claw)

NATIONAL TREE

Calabash

NATIONAL ANIMAL

Galligasp (a species of lizard endemic to Montserrat) (unofficial)

NATIONAL BIRD

Montserrat oriole

NATIONAL FISH

Blue tang (unofficial)

NATIONAL FRUIT

Julie mango

NATIONAL RESOURCES

Natural resources include sandy beaches, volcanoes, a pleasant climate, and arable land. Severe volcanic activity, which began in July 1995, has devastated the small, open economy and the formerly important tourist industry. Remittances from the large number of Montserratians living outside the country, more than twice the number still living on the island, is an important source of revenue, as is British and foreign financial assistance.

FOODS

Goat water is the national dish, a goat stew often served in a hollowed loaf of crusty bread. Mountain chicken (frogs' legs) is also a national dish. Other specialties include peas and rice; Montserrat jerk shrimp, a spicy shrimp dish usually served with rice; buttered yucca; chicken with peanut sauce; carrot and coconut bread; and chicken and coconut stew.

SPORTS/SPORTS TEAMS

Cricket and association football (soccer) are the most popular sports. Montserrat national teams participate in many sports at an international level.

TEAM SPORTS

Basketball

Montserrat Basketball Team; Women's Basketball Team

Cricket

Montserrat Cricket Team; Montserrat Women's Cricket Team; Montserrat Under-13 Cricket Team; West Indies Cricket Team, nickname the Windies (West Indies teams represent a number of English-speaking Caribbean countries)

Football

Montserrat Football Team; Montserrat Women's Football Team; West Indies Rugby League Team, nickname the Wahoos (West Indies teams represent a number of English-speaking Caribbean countries)

Kabaddi

West Indies Kabaddi Team

Tennis

Eastern Caribbean Davis Cup; Eastern Caribbean Fed Cup Teams (Eastern Caribbean teams represent a number of English-speaking countries in the Caribbean)

Volleyball

Montserrat Men's Volleyball Team; Montserrat Women's Volleyball Team

INDIVIDUAL SPORTS

Montserrat Athletics Team

NATIONAL HEROES OR PERSONIFICATIONS

William Henry Bramble, chief minister of Montserrat from 1960 to 1970, known for modernizing the island

NATIONAL HOLIDAY/INDEPENDENCE DAY

Birthday of Queen Elizabeth, second Saturday in June; St. Patrick's Day, March 17; Emancipation Day, August 7

FESTIVALS/FAIRS

St. Patrick's Week, March; Annual Christmas Festival, December; Montserrat Festival, December–January

SIGNIFICANT EVENTS IN FORMATION OF NATIONAL IDENTITY

3000 B.C.E.–11th century C.E. Waves of seafaring Arawak peoples settle the islands from the South American mainland. They live in small villages and engage in agriculture. The more warlike Caribs conquer the island, killing the males and taking the females as slaves.

1493 Christopher Columbus claims the island for Spain* on his second voyage to the New World. He names the island Santa Maria de Montserrate, after the Virgin of Montserrat in Catalonia*, in northeastern Spain.

1632 The island comes under English rule and is settled by Irish Catholics exiled by Oliver Cromwell and by other Irish fleeing anti-Roman Catholic sentiment in Saint Kitts and Nevis*. French attempts to take the island in 1664–67 are repulsed. During the next two centuries, African slaves are imported to work plantations of sugar and Sea Island cotton.

1782–1783 Following the French Revolution and war with Britain, a French squadron takes control of Montserrat for a short period of time.

1830s The abolition of slavery ends the plantation economy. Most planters leave the island, while the freed slaves settle on smallholdings carved out of the former estates.

1958–1962 Montserrat joins the short-lived Federation of the West Indies.

1989 Hurricane Hugo causes widespread destruction.

1995 Chances Peak volcano erupts for the first time in 350 years, forcing thousands of Montserratians to flee their homes. Many move to the safe zone in the north of the island, while many others leave for neighboring islands, the United Kingdom, and the United States*.

1997 Soufriere Hills volcano erupts with devastating effects. Two-thirds of the island is left uninhabitable, and both the capital, Plymouth, and the international airport are abandoned. Many Montserratians flee the island.

2001–2003 Further eruptions continue to disrupt island life. The British government grants British citizenship to refugee Montserratians.

2004 The U.S. government revokes the "temporary protected status" granted to refugees from the island in 1995.

2005–2009 A new international airport opens to replace the airport destroyed in the eruptions. The southern two-thirds of the island are expected to remain uninhabitable for another decade. The majority of the estimated 15,000 Montserratians continue to live outside the country.

See also United Kingdom

NETHERLANDS ANTILLES

OFFICIAL NAME

Nederlandse Antillen (Dutch); Antia Hulandes (Papiamento); Netherlands Antilles (English)

POPULATION

183,600 (2009e) for all five islands; 19,500 (2009e) for the three remaining islands when Curaçao* and Saint Maarten* leave the federation

INHABITANTS' NAME/NICKNAME

Antillean(s)

LANGUAGE/LANGUAGES

Dutch, Papiamento, English (all official); Spanish, Dutch Creole, others

RELIGION/RELIGIONS

Roman Catholic, 14 percent; Anglican, 15 percent; other or no religion

NATIONAL FLAG

The flag has a white field with a horizontal blue stripe in the center, superimposed on a vertical red band, also centered. Five white, five-pointed stars are arrange in an oval pattern in the center of the blue stripe, representing the five main islands of Bonaire, Curaçao, Saba, Saint Eustatius, and Saint Maarten. After Curaçao and Saint Maarten separate from the Netherlands Antilles the five stars will probably be reduced to three.

COAT OF ARMS/SEAL

The coat of arms consists of a shield with a golden background charged with five blue stars and a bordered in red. The stars stand for the five islands of the Netherlands Antilles. Above the shield is a crown representing the Dutch monarchy and Dutch sovereignty. Under the shield is a gold banner inscribed with the national motto.

MOTTO

Libertate unanimous (Latin); Unified by Freedom (English)

CAPITAL CITY

Willemstad

TYPE OF GOVERNMENT

Parliamentary democracy and constitutional monarchy as part of the Kingdom of the Netherlands*

NATIONAL COLORS

White, red, and blue

NATIONAL ANTHEM

"Het Wilhelmus," the Dutch national anthem, is the official anthem. Each island also has its own anthem. The present unofficial anthem, called "Anthem Without a Title," may be changed or replaced when the federation is dissolved in 2010 or 2011.

Anthem without a Title

Our islands in the sea, like gems they seem to be,
Outstanding from a golden crown of blissful
    royalty.
Though their people and their colorful islands
    may seem to differ amply,
They yet uniquely blend to be just one family.

Bridge

So we, your people raise our voice in love and
    unity

Chorus

Dear Netherlands Antilles, so beautiful to me.
I'm proud to be a part of you, a patriot I shall
    be.
Yes, Netherlands Antilles, I pledge my loyalty,
To you always will be true; I say may God
    bless you.

So blessed with sunny skies and clear welcom-
    ing seas,
Each island like a link that forms this chain
    of unity.
May differ in our language, yet meet on com-
    mon ground,
When some say "Sweet Antilles," some say
    "Dushi Antia ta."

Yes, proud are we to be identified with you,
Dear Netherlands Antilles, to you we will be
    true.
So we declare and vow, with dignity and love,
Our nation we will always serve, may God
    keep us as one.

CURRENCY

Netherlands Antilles guilder

INTERNET IDENTIFIER

.an

VEHICLE IDENTIFICATION PLATES/ STICKERS

NA

PASSPORT

Antilleans are Dutch citizens and travel on
Dutch passports.

AIRLINE

Windward Islands Airways (Winair)

NATIONAL FLOWER

Poponax acacia (unofficial)

NATIONAL BIRD

Brown-throated parakeet; Bonaire flamingo
(both unofficial)

NATIONAL RESOURCES

Natural resources include phosphates in Cu-
racao; salt in Bonaire; tourism in Curaçao,
Saint Maarten, and Bonaire; petroleum refining in Curaçao; and petroleum transshipment facilities in Curaçao and Bonaire. The
Netherlands provides financial aid to support the economy.

FOODS

Iguana soup is a national specialty. Other
national dishes include *kabrito stoba,* a stew
of goat meat and vegetables; *pika siboyo,* a
sauce of onions marinated in vinegar mixed
with hot peppers; *pastechi,* pastries filled with
spicy meat, shrimp, or fish; *sopi di binja,* a
soup made of wine, prunes, and cinnamon;
and *cocade,* a candy made of coconut.

SPORTS/SPORTS TEAMS

Association football (soccer) and baseball are
the most popular sports. Netherlands Antilles national teams participate in many sports
at an international level.

TEAM SPORTS

Baseball

Netherlands Antilles Baseball Team; Netherlands Antilles Softball Team

Basketball

Bonaire Basketball Team; Saba Basketball
Team; Saint Eustatius Basketball Team;
Bonaire Women's Basketball Team; Saba

Women's Basketball Team; Saint Eustatius Women's Basketball Team

Football

Netherlands Antilles Football Team; Netherlands Antilles Futsal Team

Hockey

Netherlands Antilles Field Hockey Team

Korfball

Bonaire Korfball Team

Tennis

Netherlands Antilles Davis Cup Team

Table Tennis

Netherlands Antilles Table Tennis Team

Volleyball

Netherlands Antilles Men's Volleyball Team; Netherlands Antilles Women's Volleyball Team

INDIVIDUAL SPORTS

Netherlands Antilles Amateur Boxing Team; Netherlands Antilles Athletics Team; Netherlands Antilles Canoeing Team; Netherlands Antilles Cycling Team; Netherlands Antilles Equestrian Team; Netherlands Antilles Fencing Team; Netherlands Antilles Karate Team; Netherlands Antilles Sailing Team; Netherlands Antilles Shooting Team; Netherlands Antilles Swim Team; Netherlands Antilles Tae Kwon Do Team; Netherlands Antilles Triathlon Team; Netherlands Antilles Weight Lifting Team

WINTER SPORTS

Netherlands Antilles Luge Team

NATIONAL HEROES OR PERSONIFICATIONS

Queen Juliana of the Netherlands, who granted self-government to the Dutch Caribbean islands in 1954; Christopher Columbus, who encountered Curaçao and Bonaire in 1499; Emily de Jongh-Elhage, the first female prime minister of the Netherlands Antilles, since 2006; Frits Goedgedrag, the governor of the Netherlands Antilles and Bonaire's most famous son

NATIONAL HOLIDAY/INDEPENDENCE DAY

Antillean Day, October 21; Queen's Birthday (Queen Juliana) and accession to the throne of Queen Beatrix, April 30 (official)

FESTIVALS/FAIRS

Bonaire Carnival, January–February; Curaçao Jazz Festival, May; Bonaire International Sailing Regatta, October; Saint Maarten Carnival, April–May; Bonaire Jazz and Salsa Festival, May; Saint Maarten Summer Fest, July

SIGNIFICANT EVENTS IN FORMATION OF NATIONAL IDENTITY

1000 C.E. The Caquetios people, a branch of the Arawaks, settle the islands from the South American mainland.

1499 The island are claimed for Spain*, and colonization begins. Most of the indigenous peoples are enslaved and transported to Hispaniola to work on Spanish plantations. By 1530, the islands are mostly depopulated. Bonaire is turned into a large cattle plantation.

1633–1648 The Dutch take control of the islands. Curaçao becomes a center of the slave trade, while Bonaire is a plantation worked by Indians, African slaves, and convicts cultivating maize, dyewood, and salt in the island's salt ponds. On Saint Maarten, French and Dutch prisoners of war, released by the departing Spanish, amicably divide the island.

1781 The small island of Saint Eustatius, a center of the slave trade in the eastern Caribbean, has a prosperous capital at Oranjestad. The small city is sacked and burned by the British after it gives the first salute to the new flag of the United States* by a foreign power.

1828–1845 The islands are governed from Suriname* on the South American mainland until the five islands are joined in a separate colony of the Netherlands Antilles.

1863–1915 The emancipation of the slaves is a devastating blow to the islands' economies, which do not recover until the early 20th century. In 1915, the first oil refinery begins operation with oil from the fields of nearby Venezuela*.

1929–1940 Venezuelan rebels occupy the southern islands, claiming they are part of Venezuela's national territory. The rebels are driven out, but the incident begins a Dutch program to develop the islands to forestall radical political movements or claims by foreign governments.

1954 The Netherlands Antilles becomes an autonomous state as part of the Kingdom of the Netherlands.

1960s–1970s The tourist boom provides much-needed income, but racial tensions, separatist agitation, and economic problems provoke severe rioting and arson in Curaçao in 1969. The decolonization of the islands is pressed by the Netherlands government, which insists that the federation be maintained.

1986–1995 Aruba secedes from the federation and becomes a separate autonomous state within the Dutch kingdom. The remaining islands indicate that they prefer continued Dutch rule, rather than independence in a federation dominated by Curaçao.

2000–2005 Referendums on each of the islands show majority support for separation and independent status in Curaçao and Saint Maarten, while the smaller islands vote for closer ties to the Netherlands.

2008–2009 The separation of Curaçao and Saint Maarten, scheduled for December 15, 2008, is postponed, but the islands are already taking on many of the trappings and symbols of their new status. The three smaller islands, scheduled to become special municipalities within the Netherlands, prefer also to maintain the Netherlands Antilles federation, with its membership in many international organizations, such as the International Olympic Games, that would be more difficult for the tiny island states to join individually.

See also Curaçao; Netherlands; Saint Maarten

NEVIS

OFFICIAL NAME
Nevis

POPULATION
12,800 (2009e)

INHABITANTS' NAME/NICKNAME
Nevisian(s)

LANGUAGE/LANGUAGES
English (official); a Caribbean Creole called Nevisian, others

RELIGION/RELIGIONS
Christian (Anglican, other Protestant, Roman Catholic); other or no religion

NATIONAL FLAG
The flag has a golden field with the flag of the Federation of Saint Kitts and Nevis as a canton on the upper hoist and, centered on the fly, a green triangle with a blue base and a small white triangle at the top. The gold stands for sunshine. The triangle represents the conical shape of Nevis, with blue representing the sea, green representing the verdant slopes of the mountain, and white representing the clouds that usually shroud the peak.

COAT OF ARMS/SEAL
Nevis currently uses the coat of arms of Saint Kitts and Nevis, but with the shield and pelicans colored gray for the famous gray pelicans of Nevis. The coat of arms has a central shield or crest with a fleur-de-lis, a Carib's head, and a Tudor rose across the top representing the islands' French, Carib, and

English history. The center of the shield has a red chevron, two poinciana flowers, and a sailing ship. Above the shield are a heraldic helmet and two hands holding a torch. A pelican on each side supports the shield. Below is a banner inscribed with the country's motto.

The proposed coat of arms of independent Nevis has a central triangle represents the conical shape of Nevis, with the blue being the ocean, the green being the verdant slopes of the island, and the white being the clouds that usually wreathe Nevis Peak. The shield is supported by two Nevisian cranes.

CAPITAL CITY
Charlestown

TYPE OF GOVERNMENT
A state in the Federation of Saint Kitts and Nevis, a parliamentary democracy

NATIONAL EMBLEM
Nevis Peak

NATIONAL COLORS
Yellow and green

CURRENCY
East Caribbean dollar

INTERNET IDENTIFIER
.nk

VEHICLE IDENTIFICATION PLATES/ STICKERS
KAN Federation of Saint Kitts and Nevis (unofficial); NEV Nevis (unofficial)

PASSPORT
Nevisians are citizens of the Federation of Saint Kitts and Nevis and travel on that country's passports.

NATIONAL FLOWER
Caribbean daisy (unofficial)

NATIONAL BIRD
Nevis crane; Gray pelican (both unofficial)

NATIONAL RESOURCES
The island's natural resources are negligible, other than sandy beaches, island scenery, island culture, and a pleasant climate, which foster tourism. Remittances from Nevisians living outside the country are an important source of foreign currency and investment.

FOODS
Staples considered national foods are rice and beans and goat water, a stew of goat meat, vegetables and herbs. Other specialties include roti, thin pastry filled with curried potatoes, chickpeas, beef, goat, shrimp, or vegetables; *pelau,* a rice dish similar to Spanish paella; conch, usually served curried, soused, or in salads; and spiny lobsters and crabs.

SPORTS/SPORTS TEAMS
Cricket and association football (soccer) are the most popular sports. Nevis national teams participate in cricket and football at an international level.

TEAM SPORTS
Cricket
Nevis Cricket Team

Football
Nevis Football Team, nickname the Junior Sugar Boyz

NATIONAL HEROES OR PERSONIFICATIONS
Alexander Hamilton, one of the leaders of the American Revolution, who was born in Charlestown, the island's capital; Vance Amory, leader of the proindependence

Concerned Citizens Movement; Simeon Daniel, the first premier of Nevis in the 1980s

NATIONAL HOLIDAY/INDEPENDENCE DAY

Emancipation Day, August 4; Independence Day (Federation of Saint Kitts and Nevis), September 19; Pirates Festival, October-November

FESTIVALS/FAIRS

Nevis Culturama, July–August; Fruit Festival, June–July; Caribbean International Food Fait, August

SIGNIFICANT EVENTS IN FORMATION OF NATIONAL IDENTITY

600 B.C.E.–1500 C.E. Various seafaring peoples from the South American mainland settle on the island, calling the island Oualie, the land of beautiful waters.

1498 Christopher Columbus sights the island, calling it San Martin, a name that is later used for another island due to confusion over early nautical charts. The tall peak in the middle of the island is christened Nuestra Señora de las Nieves, Our Lady of the Snows, due to the clouds that obscure the mountain. The term *nieves* is later Anglicized as Nevis.

16th century Nevis is a popular stop for English and Dutch ships en route between Europe and the Americas. The Spanish, having deported most of the indigenous population as slaves, mostly ignore the island.

1620–1700 The English claim the island. Settlers from Saint Kitts arrive in 1628. The island becomes a center of the Leeward Islands slave trade. Plantation agriculture requires many slaves on Nevis. By the end of the 17th century, the population of Nevis consists of a small, rich planter class, a marginal population of poor whites, and a large population of slaves.

1776–1783 Food supplies fail to arrive due to the American Revolution. Over 300 slaves on the island starve to death.

1834 Slavery is abolished in the British Empire, and the slave owners of Nevis are compensated for the loss of their labor. Most former slaves settle on small plots as subsistence farmers.

1871–1956 Nevis forms part of the British colony of the Leeward Islands. In 1882, Nevis and nearby Saint Kitts are united in a single administrative unit, along with Anguilla* farther to the north.

1971 Anguilla secedes from the federation of the three islands. Nevisians, also unhappy with the domination of Saint Kitts, mobilize to follow Anguilla.

1977 Nevisians vote for secession in a referendum that shows overwhelming support for separate status, but the vote is ignored.

1983 The Federation of Saint Kitts and Nevis becomes independent.

1997–1998 The new Nevisian parliament votes for separation from Saint Kitts. A vote on independence fails because the yes vote is 61.74 percent, less than the two-thirds needed by law. Nevis has the unique constitutional arrangement of being part of the federal parliament while having a separate parliament and its own Nevis Island Administration headed by a premier.

2005 The island acquires its first resident judge.

2006–2009 Proindependence groups continue to work for the secession of Nevis from the federation. A new referendum is to be held, but the date has yet to be set.

See also Saint Kitts and Nevis

PUERTO RICO

OFFICIAL NAME

Estado Libre Asociado de Puerto Rico (Spanish); Commonwealth of Puerto Rico (English)

POPULATION

4,059,700 (2009e)

INHABITANTS' NAME/NICKNAME

Puerto Rican(s); Borincano(s)/Borincana(s)

LANGUAGE/LANGUAGES

Spanish, English (both official); others

RELIGION/RELIGIONS

Roman Catholic, 75 percent; Protestant, 19 percent; other or no religion

NATIONAL FLAG

The flag consists of five equal red and white horizontal stripes, with a blue triangle at the hoist charged with a single white five-pointed star. The original flag was modeled on that of Cuba* with the colors reversed, although the inspiration for both flags comes from the flag of the United States*. The flag came to symbolize the ideals of Puerto Rico.

COAT OF ARMS/SEAL

The coat of arms, first granted by the Spanish Crown in 1511, consists of a central shield with a green field, representing the island's vegetation. The lamb and the flag on the shield are those of Saint John the Baptist, while the book represents the Book of Revelation. The border has seven elements, representing Castile, León, Aragon, Sicily, the Kingdom of Jerusalem, and Ferdinand II of Aragon and Joanna I of Castile, who originally granted the arms. Below is a banner inscribed in Latin, *Joannes Est Nomen Eius*, meaning "John is his name," referring to Saint John the Baptist or San Juan Bautista, the original name given the island by the Spanish.

MOTTO

Joannes est nomen eius (Latin); *Juan es su nombre* (Spanish); His name is John (English)

CAPITAL CITY

San Juan

TYPE OF GOVERNMENT

Republic in association with the United States

NATIONAL EMBLEM

El Moro (shown on license plates)

NATIONAL COLORS

Blue, white, and red

NATIONAL ANTHEM

The name of the anthem refers to the pre-Columbian name of the island, Borinquen. It was adopted in 1952, but the lyrics were not made official until 1977.

La Borinqueña (Spanish); The Puerto Rican (English)

The land of Borinquen
where I have been born
is a flowery garden
of magical beauty.

A constantly clear sky
serves as its canopy
and placid lullabies are sung
by the waves at its [Borinquen's] feet.

When at her beaches Columbus arrived
full of awe he exclaimed,
"Oh!, oh!, oh!, this is the lovely land
that I seek"

Borinquen is the daughter,
the daughter of the sea and the sun.
Of the sea and the sun,
of the sea and the sun,
of the sea and the sun,
of the sea and the sun.

PATRON SAINT

Our Lady of Divine Providence; Saint John the Baptist

CURRENCY

U.S. dollar

INTERNET IDENTIFIER

.pr

Vehicle Identification Plates/Stickers

USA United States (official); PR Puerto Rico (unofficial)

Passport

Puerto Ricans are U.S. citizens and travel on United States passports.

National Flower

Flor de Maga (Puerto Rico hibiscus)

National Tree

Ceiba (kapok or silk-cotton tree)

National Animal

Coquí frog

National Bird

Reinita Mora (Puerto Rican spindalis)

National Fish

Chapin (unofficial)

National Resources

Natural resources include some copper and nickel, potential for onshore and offshore oil, and timber. The important tourist industry is based on the island's proximity to large North American population centers and its historic cities, varied scenery, sandy beaches, and pleasant climate. Puerto Rico has one of the most dynamic and diverse economies in the Caribbean region. The industrial sector far surpasses agriculture as the primary locus of economic activity and income. Remittances from Puerto Ricans living in the mainland United States are an important source of income and investment for the island.

Foods

The national dish is *arroz con gandules,* a Puerto Rican rice dish of vegetables, smoked ham, pork, spicy sausage, olives, and red peppers. Other national dishes are *mofongo,* a dish of fried green plantains or yucca seasoned with garlic, olive oil, and pork cracklings, then mashed and served with chicken broth; *empanadillas,* small pastries of meat, seafood, cheese, or fruit; *sancocho de patitas,* a stew of pork feet with potatoes, plantains, and garbanzos; *bacalaitos,* fritters of flour, seasonings, and codfish; and *arroz con habichuelas,* a dish of rice, kidney beans, ham, potatoes, and pumpkin.

Sports/Sports Teams

Baseball is the most popular sport. Boxing, basketball, association football (soccer) and volleyball are also popular. Puerto Rico participates in many sports at an international level.

Teams Sports

Badminton

Puerto Rico Badminton Team

Baseball

Puerto Rico Baseball Team; Puerto Rico Softball Team; Puerto Rico Women's Softball Team

Basketball

Puerto Rico Basketball Team; Puerto Rico Women's Basketball Team; Puerto Rico Wheelchair Basketball Team; Puerto Rico Women's Wheelchair Basketball Team; Puerto Rico Under-21 Basketball Team

Football

Puerto Rico Football Team, nickname Boricuas, Coquies, El Huricán Azul (the Blue Hurricane); Puerto Rico Women's Football Team, nickname Boricuas; Puerto Rico American Football Team; Puerto Rico Futsal Team

Handball

Puerto Rico Handball Team; Puerto Rico Women's Handball Team

Hockey
Puerto Rico Field Hockey Team

Racing
Puerto Rico Speedway Team

Table Tennis
Puerto Rico Table Tennis Team

Tennis
Puerto Rico Davis Cup Team; Puerto Rico Fed Cup Team

Volleyball
Puerto Rico Men's Volleyball Team; Puerto Rico Women's Volleyball Team

INDIVIDUAL SPORTS
Puerto Rico Amateur Boxing Team; Puerto Rico Archery Team; Puerto Rico Athletics Team; Puerto Rico Canoeing Team; Puerto Rico Cycling Team; Puerto Rico Equestrian Team; Puerto Rico Fencing Team; Puerto Rico Gymnastics Team; Puerto Rico Judo Team; Puerto Rico Karate Team; Puerto Rico Modern Pentathlon Team; Puerto Rico Rowing Team; Puerto Rico Sailing Team; Puerto Rico Shooting Team; Puerto Rico Swim Team; Puerto Rico Tae Kwon Do Team; Puerto Rico Triathlon Team; Puerto Rico Weight Lifting Team; Puerto Rico Wrestling Team

WINTER SPORTS
Puerto Rico Biathlon Team; Puerto Rico Luge Team; Puerto Rico Skating Team

NATIONAL HEROES OR PERSONIFICATIONS
Jibaro originally referred to the mountain peasants but now is the personification of the Puerto Rican identity.

National heroes include Lola Rodríguez de Tió, the poetess of the Puerto Rican revolution; Dr. Pedro Albizu Campos, a nationalist leader in the mid-20th century; Antonio de los Reyes Correa, a military leader who defeated a British invasion in the 18th century; and Ramón Betances, leader of the *Grito de Lares,* a revolt against Spanish rule in 1868.

NATIONAL HOLIDAY/INDEPENDENCE DAY
U.S. Independence Day, July 4; Constitution Day (Puerto Rico Day), July 25

FESTIVALS/FAIRS
Festival de la Calle de San Sebastian, January; International Folklore Festival, January; Carnival, February–March; Ponce Crafts Fair, March; Albonito Flower Festival, June–July; Festival Casals, June–July; Bacardi Artisan's Fair, December

SIGNIFICANT EVENTS IN FORMATION OF NATIONAL IDENTITY
7th century–11th century   The Taino culture develops on the island, replacing or absorbing earlier peoples.

1493   Christopher Columbus reaches the island on his second expedition to the New World. He names the island San Juan Bautista.

1508–1511   The first permanent Spanish settlement is founded by Juan Ponce de León. Diseases introduced by the Europeans ravage the indigenous people. Slavery and mistreatment also take a heavy toll. The Tainos rebel in 1511 but are defeated and forced to surrender or flee. African slaves begin to be imported to work the settlers' plantations.

1778   A royal decree allows foreign immigrants to settle on the island.

1797   Spain* joins the French war against the United Kingdom*. Puerto Rico becomes a military and naval base for attacks on British islands in the Caribbean.

1810–1821   The overthrow of the Spanish monarchy by Napoleon begins the revolt of the Spanish colonies. Spanish reinforcements and loyalists fleeing other colonies hold onto Puerto Rico and

Cuba. The slave trade is officially banned but continues.

1868–1890 A revolt breaks out in Lares led by Ramón Betances. The revolt is defeated, but by the 1870s, even the Creole elite begins to support the idea of Puerto Rican autonomy.

1898 At the outbreak of the Spanish-American War, the Spanish government finally grants autonomy. The island falls to American military control.

1948–1952 The island elects its first governor after 50 years of direct rule from Washington, D.C. A nationalist revolt is defeated. Puerto Rico becomes a commonwealth in free association with the United States.

1960s–1990s Rapid industrialization gives the island the highest standard of living in the Caribbean. Puerto Ricans vote in 1967, 1993, and 1998 on the island's future. Given the choice of continued commonwealth status, statehood, or independence, the majority opts for continuing the commonwealth.

2000–2009 The debate over Puerto Rico's future and its relationship with the United States continues to dominate island politics. The majority continue to favor sovereignty and self-government in an association of respect and dignity between the two nations and a common citizenship. Advocates of statehood have considerable support while the sentiment for independence is usually less than 10 percent in voting and political polls.

See also United States

QUEBEC

OFFICIAL NAME
Québec (French); Quebec (English)

POPULATION
7,745,200 (2009e)

INHABITANTS' NAME/NICKNAME
Québécois; Quebecker(s); Quebecer(s)

LANGUAGE/LANGUAGES
French (official); English, Italian, indigenous languages, others

RELIGION/RELIGIONS
Roman Catholic, 83 percent; Protestant, 5 percent; Eastern Orthodox, 1.5 percent; Muslim, Jewish, other or no religion

NATIONAL FLAG
The flag, called the *Fleurdelisé,* has a blue field charged with a broad, white, centered cross and a white fleur-de-lis on each of the four quadrants. The white cross is derived from the ancient royal flags of France* and the white fleurs-de-lis and blue field from a banner honoring the Virgin Mary that Quebecker troops carried in the 18th century.

COAT OF ARMS/SEAL
The coat of arms is a shield or crest divided into three horizontal fields. The top has three gold fleurs-de-lis on a blue background, symbolizing Quebec's ties to France; the middle has a gold lion on a red field, symbolizing the United Kingdom*; the bottom has three green maple leaves on a gold field, symbolizing Canada*. A Tudor crown surmounts the shield. Below is a silver banner inscribed with the national motto.

MOTTO
Je me souviens (French); I Remember (English)

CAPITAL CITY
Quebec City

TYPE OF GOVERNMENT
Provincial government with wide powers of autonomy

NATIONAL EMBLEM
Fleur-de-lis

NATIONAL COLORS

Blue and white

NATIONAL ANTHEM

The official anthem is the Canadian anthem, "O Canada." The Quebec anthem is an unofficial national anthem first performed in 1975.

Gens du Pays (French); People of My Country (English)

The time that we take, saying "I love you"
Is all that remains at the end of our days
The vows that we make
The flowers that we sow
The harvest is within our heart
Through the splendid gardens of time's
  changes.

Chorus

People of my country, your turn has come
To let love speak to you
People of my country, your turn has come
To let love speak to you

The time to love each other, and the day we
  say it,
Melt like the snow caressed by the spring.
Celebrate our joys, celebrate our laughter
Our eyes meeting in embrace
Tomorrow I was only 20.

Chorus

People of my country, your turn has come
To let love speak to you
People of my country, your turn has come
To let love speak to you

The stream of our days today comes to a
  pause
And forms into a pool where everyone can see
As if it were a mirror, the love that it reflects,
For those hearts to whom I wish
The time to live out all our hopes.

People of my country, your turn has come
To let love speak to you

PATRON SAINTS

Saint John the Baptist; Saint Anne

CURRENCY

Canadian dollar

INTERNET IDENTIFIER

.ca Canada (official); .qc (unofficial)

VEHICLE IDENTIFICATION PLATES/ STICKERS

CDN Canada (official); QC Quebec (unofficial)

PASSPORT

Quebeckers are Canadian citizens and travel on Canadian passports.

AIRLINE

Air Transat

NATIONAL FLOWER

Blue flag iris

NATIONAL TREE

Merisier (yellow birch)

NATIONAL ANIMAL

Beaver (unofficial)

NATIONAL BIRD

Harfang des neiges (snowy owl)

NATIONAL INSECT

White admiral butterfly

NATIONAL RESOURCES

Natural resources include copper, zinc, gold, silver, iron ore, titanium, tellurium, clay, limestone, granite, mica, building materials, hydropower, and arable land. Traditionally, agriculture, forestry, and livestock were the most important industries; while they are still important service industries, high-tech and aerospace industries are now the mainstays of the economy.

FOODS

Tourtiìres, meat pies of ground pork, veal, or beef, are considered the national dish. Other specialties include *soupe aux pois,* yellow pea soup, also considered a national dish; baked beans flavored with maple syrup; *cretons,* a spread of ground pork with onions and spices; *oreilles de crises,* deep-fried pork grills; *poitrine de poule au sirop d'érable,* chicken breast baked with maple syrup; *cipalle,* a layered meat pie; and *pain à la compote de pommes,* applesauce bread made with maple syrup.

SPORTS/SPORTS TEAMS

Ice hockey is Quebec's national and most popular sport. Association football and basketball are also popular. Quebec national teams participate in football, ice hockey, and wheelchair basketball at an international level.

TEAM SPORTS

Basketball

Quebec Wheelchair Basketball Team, nickname Les Bulldogs

Football

Quebec Football Team

Hockey

Quebec Ice Hockey Team, nickname Team Quebec; Quebec Women's Ice Hockey Team, nickname Team Quebec; Quebec Under-17 Ice Hockey Team, nickname Team Quebec

WINTER SPORTS

Quebec Ice Hockey Team, nickname Team Quebec; Quebec Women's Ice Hockey Team, nickname Team Quebec; Quebec Under-17 Ice Hockey Team, nickname Team Quebec

NATIONAL HEROES OR PERSONIFICATIONS

Big Joe Mufferaw, a figure akin to Paul Bunyan in the United States*. Samuel de Champlain, a French explorer known as the Father of New France; Hélène Desportes, the first child of French descent born in New France in 1620; Robert Nelson, the Anglo-Quebec leader of the 1838 uprising; Jean Lesage, the prime minister of Quebec who oversaw the modernization process known as the Quiet Revolution in the 1960s; René Lévesque, nationalist leader in the 1970s and 1980s; Mackenzie King, who served five terms as prime Minister of Canada, including during the difficult period of World War II.

NATIONAL HOLIDAY/INDEPENDENCE DAY

Quebec Day, June 24

FESTIVALS/FAIRS

Fête nationale du Québec (Quebec National Festival), June; Montreal International Arts Festival, July; Osheaga Music and Arts Festival, August; Wine and Cheese Fair, October–November; Quebec Winter Carnival, January–February; Quebec Summer Festival, July–August.

SIGNIFICANT EVENTS IN FORMATION OF NATIONAL IDENTITY

1000 B.C.E. Algonquin nomads and Iroquoian peoples, mostly living in towns with settled agriculture and a political hierarchy, control the southern region. Inuit peoples populate the far north.

1525 C.E.–1530 C.E. Basque fishermen and whalers from southern France and northern Spain* regularly visit the Saint Lawrence and Saguenay rivers region.

1534–1541 Jacques Cartier plants a cross on the Gaspé peninsula and claims the territory for France. The first settlement in North America is constructed.

1603–1625 Samuel de Champlain claims for France the land he calls Terre-Neuve (Newfoundland) and Acadie (Acadia). Catholic missionaries and Jesuits begin to convert the indigenous peoples. Settlers arrive from France to settle on small farms.

1630–1663 European diseases devastate the indigenous tribes. New France becomes a royal French province. The first *filles du roi* (king's daughters) arrive as spouses for the many unattached colonists.

1754–1763 The French and Indian War begins as a colonial rivalry between France and the United Kingdom. France cedes New France to British rule.

1780–1791 Over 50,000 British loyalists move north out of the new United States*, many to settle among the 90,000 French inhabitants.

1837–1838 A rebellion breaks out among French-speakers, led by Anglo-Quebecker Robert Nelson.

1848 French is permitted in the parliament and the courts. Many French-Canadians immigrate to the United States.

1867 The various British territories unite to form the confederation of Canada. In a local vote, 55 percent of Quebeckers vote for confederation and 45 percent vote against.

1930–1960 While English-speaking Canada urbanizes and modernizes, Quebec remains mostly rural, intensely Roman Catholic, and agricultural.

1960–1966 The Quiet Revolution changes Quebec into a modern, French-speaking North American state. Quebec nationalism begins to win support.

1970s Nationalist political parties come to power in Quebec. Radical nationalists use violence to publicize the cause of Quebec independence. French becomes the sole official language in Quebec.

1995 A referendum on separation from Canada results in 50.56 percent against and 49.44 in favor.

2000–2008 The nationalist government of Quebec publishes a plan for a sovereign Quebec state. Following the 2001 terrorist attacks on the United States, the economy flounders and secession becomes a lesser issue.

2009 Economic growth and greater confidence in Quebec as a viable state again win support for nationalists demanding another referendum on independence, although nationalists seeking greater autonomy within a Canadian federation are gaining support among Quebeckers who fear a complete separation from Canada.

See also Canada

SAINT BARTHELEMY

OFFICIAL NAME

Collectivité d'ourte-mer de Saint-Barthélemy (French); Collectivity of Saint Barthelemy (English)

NICKNAME

Saint Barts or Saint Barth

POPULATION

8,300 (2009e)

INHABITANTS' NAME/NICKNAME

Saint-Bartian(s)

LANGUAGE/LANGUAGES

French (official); Creole, English, others

RELIGION/RELIGIONS

Roman Catholic, Protestant, Jehovah's Witness, other or no religion

NATIONAL FLAG

The official flag is the French tricolor. The unofficial national flag is a white field charged with the traditional coat of arms of the territory. Although the flag is used extensively on the island, it has no official status.

COAT OF ARMS/SEAL

The coat of arms consists of a central crowned shield bearing three fleurs-de-lis on blue, symbolizing the island's historic ties to France*, a Maltese cross on red representing the rule of the Order of Malta from

1651 to 1665, and three crowns on blue representing Swedish rule from 1785 to 1878. Two white pelicans, representing the island's fauna, support the shield. Below the shield is a banner with the name Ouanalao, the name of the island before European colonization.

CAPITAL CITY

Gustavia

TYPE OF GOVERNMENT

Overseas collectivity of France

NATIONAL EMBLEM

St. Bart's pelican; Straw ladies (the women who create objects from straw for use at home or for sale to tourists, often wearing the island's traditional costume)

NATIONAL COLORS

Blue and red

NATIONAL ANTHEM

As a French territory, the official anthem is "La Marseillaise." The local anthem is used when a separate anthem is needed, such as for sporting events. The anthem is also very popular on the island.

> **Hymne à Saint-Barthélemy (France); Anthem of Saint Barthelemy (English)**
>
> Isle forgotten by the gods, unknown by the men,
> You were sleeping, languid, waiting for a given name,
> When the drum of the feet trampling your blond coves,
> Tore you out of your dream and opened you to the world.
>
> **Refrain**
>
> Ouanalao or Saint Barthélemy
> Isle of the Antilles and isle of France
> Don't give up your faith, don't give up your hope
> Your freedom remains our motto

Arawaks, Caraibes, Bretons and pirates
English, Flemish, French, Spanish and settlers
Canoes, caravelles, galiotes and galleons
Have written your history at the bottom of your bays.

> **Refrain**
>
> Ouanalao or Saint Barthélemy, etc.
>
> Your children, seamen they were, went from isle to isle
> To catch elsewhere the fortune you didn't give to them
> But from the kings' words, Swedish and then French
> They received as inheritance honor and dignity.
>
> **Refrain**
>
> Ouanalao or Saint Barthélemy, etc.
>
> Land of hope, of fire, of pain and of spirit
> Defying the ocean, the winds, the hurricanes
> Without complaint your daughters and sons they rebuild
> As their parents have always done before them.
>
> **Refrain**
>
> Ouanalao or Saint Barthélemy, etc…
>
> To your barren hills give your beautiful beaches
> To your years of drought, your hours of plenty
> To your exiled sons, their strength and their power
> To your moments of doubts, the word of the wise men.
>
> **Refrain**
>
> Ouanalao or Saint Barthélemy, etc…

PATRON SAINT

Saint Bartholomew

CURRENCY

Euro; the U.S. dollar is also widely used

INTERNET IDENTIFIER

.bl

VEHICLE IDENTIFICATION PLATES/ STICKERS

F France (official); BL Saint Barthelemy (unofficial)

PASSPORT

Saint-Bartians are French citizens and travel on French passports

AIRLINE

Saint Barth Commuter

NATIONAL ANIMAL

Saint Barts scorpion (unofficial)

NATIONAL BIRD

Saint Barts pelican

NATIONAL RESOURCES

The island has few natural resources, other than sandy beaches and a pleasant climate. The economy of Saint Barthelemy is based upon high-end tourism and duty-free luxury commerce, serving visitors primarily from North America. The luxury hotels and villas host over 70,000 visitors each year, with another 130,000 arriving by cruise ship. The island's relative isolation and high cost of living inhibits mass tourism. With limited freshwater resources, all food except seafood must be imported, as must all energy resources and most manufactured goods.

FOODS

Bouillabaisse creole, a stew of fresh seafood, is considered the island dish. Local specialties include *civeche de coco*, marinated fresh fish with coconut; *chiquetaille de morue*, shredded and grilled cod served with vinaigrette sauce; *dombré*, flour balls cooked with dried vegetables; and *colombo*, a curry dish with lamb, chicken, or goat meat.

SPORTS/SPORTS TEAMS

Association football (soccer) is the most popular sport. Saint Barthelemy participates as part of the Saint Martin national football team at an international level.

TEAM SPORTS

Football

Saint Barthelemy Football Team

NATIONAL HEROES OR PERSONIFICATIONS

Gustavia, dressed in Greek or Roman dress, is the personification of Saint Barthelemy.

NATIONAL HOLIDAY/INDEPENDENCE DAY

Saint Barthelemy Day, August 24; Bastille Day, July 14 (celebrated in France and all French territories)

FESTIVALS/FAIRS

Saint Barts Music Festival, January; Saint Barts Bucket Regatta, March; Saint Barts Film Festival, April

SIGNIFICANT EVENTS IN FORMATION OF NATIONAL IDENTITY

1493 C.E. Christopher Columbus encounters the uninhabited island on his second voyage to the New World. He names the island for his brother, Bartolomeo.

1648–1651 Settlers from nearby Saint Kitts colonize the island, but the colony fails and the island is sold to the Knights of Malta.

1656 Caribs raid the island, which is abandoned until 1673, when settlers from Normandy and Brittany* settle the island. French buccaneers use the island as a base to prey on Spanish shipping, bringing wealth in the form of plunder to the island.

1650–1784 The settlers maintain small farms or are tradesmen or shopkeepers. The dry climate and limited land do not lend themselves to plantation agriculture, so only a few slaves are imported, and the population remains largely European in origin. The island is sold to Sweden* in exchange for trading rights.

1784–1878 The Swedes name the capital Gustavia after their King Gustav III, open the port to trade, and declare the island's neutrality. The island prospers as a neutral supply center during the colonial wars. The slaves on the island are officially freed in 1847. Saint Barthelemy is sold back to France and becomes part of the territory of Guadeloupe*.

1878–2000 The island's free port status remains after the return of French rule and remains to the present. The island, along with France, becomes part of the European Union.

2003 The Saint-Bartians vote to separate from Guadeloupe and to establish a separate country as a territorial unit of France.

2004–2008 The island becomes a separate state within the French Republic. The prosperous island is a hideaway for celebrities seeking a Caribbean stay away from the islands of mass tourism.

2009 The island's emphasis on upmarket tourism as a getaway for wealthy travelers cushions its economy as other islands feel the pinch of the world economic slump.

See also France

SAINT KITTS AND NEVIS

OFFICIAL NAME
Federation of Saint Christopher and Nevis; Federation of Saint Kitts and Nevis (both versions are included in the country's constitution)

POPULATION
40,200 (2009e)

INHABITANTS' NAME/NICKNAME
Kittitian(s); Nevisian(s)

LANGUAGE/LANGUAGES
English (official); St. Kitts Creole

RELIGION/RELIGIONS
Anglican, 26 percent; Methodist, 25 percent; Pentecostal, 8 percent; Moravian, 8 percent; Roman Catholic, 7 percent; Hindu, 1.5 percent; other or no religion

NATIONAL FLAG
The flag has two right triangles, green at the hoist and red at the fly, divided by a broad black diagonal stripe outlined in gold and containing two white five-pointed stars. Green symbolizes the fertility of the islands; red stands for the struggles of the people from slavery through colonialism to independence; yellow symbolizes sunshine; black symbolizes the African heritage of the majority; and white represents hope and liberty.

COAT OF ARMS/SEAL
The coat of arms has a central shield or crest with a fleur-de-lis, a Carib's head, and a Tudor rose across the top representing the islands' French, Carib, and English history. The center of the shield has a red chevron, two poinciana flowers, and a sailing ship. Above the shield are a heraldic helmet and two hands holding a torch. A pelican on each side supports the shield. Below is a banner inscribed with the country's motto.

MOTTO
Country Above Self

CAPITAL CITY
Basseterre

TYPE OF GOVERNMENT
Parliamentary democracy and federal constitutional monarchy

NATIONAL EMBLEM
Red royal poinciana

NATIONAL COLORS
Red, black, and green

NATIONAL ANTHEM

The anthem was written and composed for adoption on independence in 1983.

O Land of Beauty

O Land of Beauty!
Our country where peace abounds,
Thy children stand free
On the strength of will and love.
With God in all our struggles,
Saint Kitts and Nevis be
A nation bound together,
With a common destiny.

As stalwarts we stand
For justice and liberty.
With wisdom and truth
We will serve and honor thee.
No sword nor spear can conquer
For God will sure defend.
His blessings shall forever
To posterity extend.

PATRON SAINT

Saint Christopher

CURRENCY

East Caribbean dollar

INTERNET IDENTIFIER

.kn

VEHICLE IDENTIFICATION PLATES/STICKERS

KAN (unofficial)

PASSPORT

The passport has the initials CC, for Caribbean Community, and the name of the country in English, the coat of arms and the word *passport*.

NATIONAL FLOWER

Red royal poinciana (flamboyant tree)

NATIONAL TREE

Coconut palm

NATIONAL ANIMAL

Velvet monkey

NATIONAL BIRD

Brown pelican

NATIONAL FISH

French angelfish (unofficial)

NATIONAL RESOURCES

National resources are negligible, other than arable land. Sandy beaches, a pleasant climate, island scenery, and a unique culture support a thriving tourist industry. Remittances from Kittians and Nevisians living outside the federation are an important source of foreign currency and investment.

FOODS

Goat water stew, the national dish, is made of goat, breadfruit, green pawpaw, and dumplings in a tomato-based broth. Other island specialties include roast suckling pig; *pelau,* also known as cook-up, a dish of pigeon peas and meat; conch curry; turtle stew; salt cod with vegetables, rice and pigeon peas; *conkies,* minced meat, vegetables, or cheese in cornmeal dough wrapped in banana leaves and boiled; and roti, thin pastry filled with curried potatoes, chickpeas, beef, goat, chicken, shrimp, or vegetables.

SPORTS/SPORTS TEAMS

Cricket and association football (soccer) are the most popular sports. Saint Kitts and Nevis national teams participate in many sports at an international level.

TEAM SPORTS

Basketball

Saint Kitts and Nevis Basketball Team; Saint Kitts and Nevis Women's Basketball Team

Cricket

West Indies Cricket Team, nickname the Windies (West Indies teams represent a number of English-speaking Caribbean countries)

Football

Saint Kitts and Nevis Football Team, nickname the Sugar Boyz; Saint Kitts and Nevis Women's Football Team, nickname the Sugar Girlz; West Indies Rugby League Team, nickname the Wahoos (West Indies teams represent a number of English-speaking Caribbean countries)

Kabaddi

West Indies Kabaddi Team (West Indies teams represent a number of English-speaking Caribbean countries)

Netball

Saint Kitts and Nevis Netball Team

Table Tennis

Saint Kitts and Nevis Table Tennis Team

Tennis

Saint Kitts and Nevis Davis Cup Team; Saint Kitts and Nevis Fed Cup Team; Eastern Caribbean Davis Cup; Eastern Caribbean Fed Cup teams (Eastern Caribbean teams represent a number of English-speaking Caribbean countries)

Volleyball

Saint Kitts and Nevis Men's Volleyball Team; Saint Kitts and Nevis Women's Volleyball Team

INDIVIDUAL SPORTS

Saint Kitts and Nevis Amateur Boxing; Saint Kitts and Nevis Athletics Team; Saint Kitts and Nevis Cycling Team; Saint Kitts and Nevis Tae Kwon Do Team; Saint Kitts and Nevis Wrestling Team

NATIONAL HEROES OR PERSONIFICATIONS

Thomas Warner, the founder of the first European settlement on the islands; Thomas Manchester, founder of the Workers League in 1932; Kennedy Simmonds, politician who led the country to independence; Robert Bradshaw, proindependence leader of the country in the years before independence

NATIONAL HOLIDAY/INDEPENDENCE DAY

Independence Day, September 19

FESTIVALS/FAIRS

Carnival, December–January; Saint Kitts Music Festival, June; Culturama (Nevis), July–August

SIGNIFICANT EVENTS IN FORMATION OF NATIONAL IDENTITY

100 B.C.E.–1300 C.E. Seafaring migrants from mainland South America settle the islands, followed by the Arawaks around 800 and the warlike Caribs or Kalinago people around 1300. The Kalinago either drove the earlier settlers off the island or killed the men and kept the women.

1493 Christopher Columbus sights the islands on his second voyage to the New World.

1625 Thomas Warner persuades the Kalinago chief to allow a European settlement, the first English colony in the Caribbean. The French establish a settlement on the other side of the island, which becomes the first French settlement in the Caribbean.

1626 The Kalinago chief becomes suspicious of the growing number of Europeans. He gathers allies from other islands and plans to wipe the European from the island. His plan is betrayed, and the English and French attack the gathered Caribs, killing over 2,000 in a massacre later called the Kalinago Genocide.

1628–1700 Nevis is colonized by settlers from Saint Kitts, which becomes the base for both English and French colonization in the Caribbean.

African slaves are imported to work the European plantations.

1783 France* relinquishes its claims to Saint Kitts in the Treaty of Versailles.

1800–1871 Saint Kitts and Nevis remain separate colonies with their own administrations until the British government unites the two islands and Anguilla* to form a British dependency. Relations between Saint Kitts, the seat of the dependency government, and the other islands are strained from the beginning.

1932 The Workers League, later the Labor Party, is founded to press for independence from the United Kingdom*.

1967 The three-island state becomes an internally self-governing member of the West Indies Associated States, with Robert Bradshaw as premier.

1970–1971 The Nevis Reformation Party is founded to campaign for separate independence. Anguilla separates from the state following a rebellion against domination by the Kittians.

1983 Saint Kitts and Nevis jointly attain independence with Kennedy Simmonds as prime minister.

1993–1995 Antigovernment demonstrations on Saint Kitts lead to the declaration of a state of emergency. Nevisians press for separate independence.

1997 The Nevis legislature authorizes a referendum on secession. The independence referendum just fails to achieve the two-thirds required for the island to secede.

2005 The government closes the last remnants of the centuries-old but loss-making sugar industry.

2006–2009 Nevisians continue to press for separation from Saint Kitts, which is seen as neglecting the smaller island. A second referendum on independence is to be held at a future date. The global economic slump slows economic development as the number of tourists dwindles.

See also Nevis

SAINT LUCIA

OFFICIAL NAME
Saint Lucia

POPULATION
169,400 (2009e)

INHABITANTS' NAME/NICKNAME
Saint Lucian(s); Lucian(s)

LANGUAGE/LANGUAGES
English (official); Saint Lucian Creole (Kreole or Kweyol), French

RELIGION/RELIGIONS
Roman Catholic, 67 percent; Seventh-day Adventist, 8 percent; Pentecostal, 6 percent; Rastafarian, 2 percent; Anglican, 2 percent; Evangelical, 2 percent; other or no religion

NATIONAL FLAG
The flag has a pale blue field with a gold isosceles triangle below a black arrowhead with a white border. The blue stands for the sky and the ocean that surround the island and for fidelity, gold stands for sunshine and prosperity, and the black and white symbolize racial equality and harmony. The triangles (gold on black) symbolize the Pitons, the island's two large peaks.

COAT OF ARMS/SEAL
The coat of arms has a central shield divided into quarters containing two Tudor roses, representing England, two fleurs-de-lis, representing France*, and a stool at the center, representing the African origins of most of the population. Above the shield are a heraldic helmet and a hand holding a torch, representing a beacon to light the path. Two Saint Lucia parrots support the shield, while a banner beneath is inscribed with the country's national motto.

MOTTO

The land, the people, the light

CAPITAL CITY

Castries

TYPE OF GOVERNMENT

Parliamentary democracy and constitutional monarchy as part of the British Commonwealth

NATIONAL EMBLEM

The Pitons, Saint Lucia's two large peaks that rise from the ocean

NATIONAL COLORS

Pale blue, yellow, and black

NATIONAL ANTHEM

The anthem was adopted by the self-governing state of Saint Lucia in 1967 and became the national anthem on independence in 1979.

> **Sons and Daughters of Saint Lucia**
>
> Sons and daughters of Saint Lucia,
> love the land that gave us birth,
> land of beaches, hills and valleys,
> fairest isle of all the earth.
> Wheresoever you may roam,
> love, oh, love your island home.
>
> Gone the times when nations battled
> for this Helen of the west,
> gone the days when strife and discord
> dimmed her children's toil and rest.
> Dawns at last a brighter day,
> stretches out a glad new way.
>
> May the good Lord bless our island,
> guard her sons from woe and harm!
> May our people live united,
> strong in soul and strong in arm!
> Justice, truth, and charity,
> our ideal for ever be!

PATRON SAINT

Saint Lucia

CURRENCY

East Caribbean dollar

INTERNET IDENTIFIER

.lc

VEHICLE IDENTIFICATION PLATES/ STICKERS

WL

PASSPORT

The passport cover has the initials CC, for Caribbean Community, and the name of the country in English, the coat of arms, and the word *passport*.

NATIONAL FLOWER

Rose; marguerite

NATIONAL TREE

Calabash

NATIONAL PLANT

Bamboo

NATIONAL ANIMAL

Leatherback turtle (unofficial)

NATIONAL BIRD

Saint Lucia parrot

NATIONAL RESOURCES

Natural resources include forests, sandy beaches, minerals (pumice), mineral springs, and geothermal potential. Offshore banking and tourism are the major industries. The government is trying to revitalize the sagging banana industry. Remittances from Saint Lucians living outside the country are an important source of foreign currency and investment.

FOODS

Salt fish and green figs, a salt cod preparation, is considered the national dish. Other island specialties include baked stuffed breadfruit, a dish of local breadfruit stuffed with minced meat, minced ham, onion, tomato, and garlic; creole fish stew, a stew of fresh bream or snapper and vegetables; green fig salad; coconut pie; *lambi* (conch), served in a variety of dishes; *langouste* (local lobster); and fried plantains.

SPORTS/SPORTS TEAMS

Cricket and association football (soccer) are the most popular sports. Saint Lucia national teams participate in many sports at an international level.

TEAM SPORTS

Badminton

Saint Lucia Badminton Team

Basketball

Saint Lucia Basketball Team

Cricket

West Indies Cricket Team, nickname the Windies (West Indies teams represent a number of English-speaking Caribbean countries)

Football

Saint Lucia Football Team; Saint Lucia Women's Football Team; Saint Lucia Rugby Union Team; West Indies Rugby League Team, nickname the Wahoos (West Indies teams represent a number of English-speaking Caribbean nations)

Kabaddi

West Indies Kabaddi Team (West Indies teams represent a number of English-speaking Caribbean countries)

Netball

Saint Lucia Netball Team

Table Tennis

Saint Lucia Table Tennis Team

Tennis

Saint Lucia Davis Cup Team; Eastern Caribbean Davis Cup; Eastern Caribbean Fed Cup Team (Eastern Caribbean teams represent a number of English-speaking Caribbean countries)

Volleyball

Saint Lucia Men's Volleyball Team

INDIVIDUAL SPORTS

Saint Lucia National Amateur Boxing Team; Saint Lucia National Athletics Team; Saint Lucia National Cycling Team; Saint Lucia National Judo Team; Saint Lucia National Sailing Team; Saint Lucia National Shooting Team; Saint Lucia National Swim Team; Saint Lucia National Tae Kwon Do Team

NATIONAL HEROES OR PERSONIFICATIONS

Derek Walcott, considered Saint Lucia's national poet, winner of the Nobel Prize for Literature in 1992; Allan Louisy, the country's first prime minister in 1979; Sir John Compton, the independence leader known as Father of the Nation

NATIONAL HOLIDAY/INDEPENDENCE DAY

Independence Day, February 22

FESTIVALS/FAIRS

Saint Lucia Carnival, mid-July; Saint Lucia Jazz Festival, May; Jounen Kweyol Entennasyonal (International Creole Festival), October; International Food Fair, November; Marguerite Festival, October; Fishermen's Festival, June; Rose Festival, August; National Day Festival, December

SIGNIFICANT EVENTS IN FORMATION OF NATIONAL IDENTITY

200 C.E.–400 C.E. Arawak seafarers from the South American mainland settle the island.

800 C.E.–1000 C.E. The more aggressive Caribs replace the Arawaks.

1501–1635 Christopher Columbus sights the island, which he calls Santa Lucia. Dutch, English and French settlers attempt to colonize the island but are driven off by Carib attacks.

1635–1660 The French officially claim the island. An English settlement is established in 1659 but is wiped out by Carib attacks. French settlers from Martinique* establish a settlement in 1651. A treaty with the Caribs in 1660 brings the new settlement peace.

18th century The island is used as a bargaining chip in a number of European treaties, changing hands between the United Kingdom* and France 14 times in all. Slaves are imported to work European sugar plantations.

1803–1814 The British occupy the island during the Napoleonic Wars. British possession is confirmed in 1814. Slavery is abolished in 1834. Most former slaves settle on small plots as subsistence farmers.

1871–1956 The island becomes part of the British Leeward Islands Federation.

1924–1951 The British government grants representative government with a local legislature. A new constitution provides for a majority of elected seats in the legislature in 1936. Universal adult suffrage is granted.

1964 The unprofitable sugar industry is closed.

1967–1979 The island is granted self-government as a British associated state and gains full independence in 1979.

1993–2002 A fall in the price of bananas leads to unrest and strikes. A tropical storm destroys about half the island's banana crop.

2004–2008 The volcanic twin peaks, the Pitons, are declared a UNESCO World Heritage site.

2009 The global economic crisis hurts the tourist industry, the island's main source of income.

SAINT MAARTEN

OFFICIAL NAME

Ellandgebled Sint Maarten (Dutch); Island Area of Saint Maarten;

Country Sint Maarten; Saint Maarten (English)

POPULATION

39,300 (2009e)

INHABITANTS' NAME/NICKNAME

Saint Martiner(s)

LANGUAGE/LANGUAGES

Dutch, English (both official); French, Papiamento, Spanish, others

RELIGION/RELIGIONS

Roman Catholic, 41 percent; Methodist, Seventh-day Adventist, Baptist, Anglican, Jewish, others

NATIONAL FLAG

The flag has two equal horizontal stripes of red over blue with a white triangle at the hoist containing the coat of arms. The flag's colors are those of the Netherlands tricolor, red, white, and blue, symbolizing Saint Maarten's historic ties to the Dutch kingdom.

COAT OF ARMS/SEAL

The colors are those of the flag of the Netherlands. The arms show the old Philipsburg courthouse, a bouquet of yellow sage, and a silhouette of the monument honoring Dutch-French friendship and the unity of both parts of the island. The orange border symbolizes loyalty to the ruling Dutch house of Orange-Nassau. The crest is formed by a yellow disc, which represents the sun, and a gray silhouette of a pelican in flight. A banner below the crest is inscribed with the official motto.

MOTTO

Semper pro grediens (Latin); Always Moving Forward (English)

CAPITAL CITY

Philipsburg

TYPE OF GOVERNMENT

Part of the Netherlands Antilles* until 2010 or 2011, when it will become an autonomous country associated with the Kingdom of the Netherlands*

NATIONAL EMBLEM

Old Philipsburg courthouse

NATIONAL COLORS

Blue and green

NATIONAL ANTHEM

The anthem was written on the French side of the island in 1958 and now serves as the anthem of both sides of the divided island.

O Sweet Saint Martin's Land (Shared with neighboring Saint Martin*)

Where over the world, say where,
You find an island there,
So lovely small with nations free
With people French and Dutch
Though talking English much,
As thee Saint Martin in the sea?

Chorus

O sweet Saint Martin's Land
So bright by beach and strand
With sailors on the sea and harbors free
Where the chains of mountains green
Variously in sunlight sheen

O I love thy paradise,
Nature-beauty fairly nice (twice)

How pretty between all green
Flamboyants beaming gleam
Of flowers red by sunlight set
Thy cows and sheep and goats
In meadows or on roads
Thy donkeys keen can't I forget

Saint Martin I love thy name
In which Columbus fame
And memories of old are those
For me a great delight
Thy Southern Cross the night
May God the Lord protect thy coast!

PATRON SAINT

Saint Martin of Tours

CURRENCY

Antillean guilder; U.S. dollar

INTERNET IDENTIFIER

.na (Netherlands Antilles)

VEHICLE IDENTIFICATION PLATES/STICKERS

NA Netherlands Antilles (official); SIM Saint (Sint) Maarten (unofficial)

PASSPORT

Saint Martiners are Dutch citizens and travel on Dutch passports.

NATIONAL FLOWER

Yellow sage

NATIONAL BIRD

Brown pelican

NATIONAL RESOURCES

National resources include fish and arable land. Tourism is the major industry, drawn to varied island scenery, a pleasant climate, and island culture. Cruise ships bring over 150,000 visitors to the island every year.

FOODS

Island specialty callaloo soup, made of kale, callaloo (a spinach-like vegetable), okra, and salt pork, is considered the national dish. Other dishes include crab backs, blue crab shells stuffed with a crab meat mixture; bakes, a type of cornmeal flatbread; Philipsburg pancakes, pancakes made of pumpkin; coconut sugar cake; and coconut turnovers. Guavaberry liqueur is considered the national drink.

SPORTS/SPORTS TEAMS

Association football (soccer) is the most popular sport. Tennis is also very popular. Saint

Maarten national teams participate in many sports at an international level.

TEAM SPORTS

Baseball

Saint Maarten Baseball Team; Saint Maarten Softball Team

Basketball

Saint Maarten Basketball Team; Saint Maarten Women's Basketball Team

Cricket

West Indies Cricket Team, nickname The Windies (West Indies teams represent a number of English-speaking Caribbean countries)

Football

Saint Maarten Football Team; Saint Maarten Women's Football Team; Saint Maarten Rugby Union Team; Saint Maarten Futsal Team

Hockey

Saint Maarten Field Hockey Team

Table Tennis

Saint Maarten Table Tennis Team

Tennis

Saint Maarten Davis Cup Team

Volleyball

Saint Maarten Men's Volleyball Team; Saint Maarten Women's Volleyball Team

INDIVIDUAL SPORTS

Saint Maarten Amateur Boxing Team; Saint Maarten Athletics Team; Saint Maarten Canoeing Team; Saint Maarten Equestrian Team; Saint Maarten Fencing Team; Saint Maarten Judo Team; Saint Maarten Sailing Team; Saint Maarten Shooting Team; Saint Maarten Swim Team; Saint Maarten Tae Kwon Do Team; Saint Maarten Triathlon Team; Saint Maarten Wrestling Team

NATIONAL HEROES OR PERSONIFICATIONS

One-Tété Lohkay, a slave woman who resisted oppression and came to embody the people of Saint Maarten; Emilio Johan Wilson, a local landowner who resisted overdevelopment on the island; Jan Claeszen Van Campen, the first Dutch governor, who fought Spanish, French, and English attacks

NATIONAL HOLIDAY/INDEPENDENCE DAY

Saint Maarten Day, November 11

FESTIVALS/FAIRS

Saint Maarten Carnival, April–May; Saint Maarten Summer Fest, July; Caribbean Comedy Festival, August–September; Saint Maarten Book Fair, June; Sualouiga Festival, August

SIGNIFICANT EVENTS IN FORMATION OF NATIONAL IDENTITY

800 C.E.–1000 C.E. Arawak seafarers settle the island from their home in the Orinoco river basin of the South American mainland. They call the island Sualouiga the land of salt, for its abundant salt pans.

1300 Warlike Caribs take control of the island, driving the Arawaks away or killing the men and taking the women as slaves.

1493 Christopher Columbus sights the island on his second voyage to the New World on the holy day of Saint Martin of Tours, whose name he applies to the island.

1620–1633 The Spanish ignore the island for greater conquests in Mexico* and South America. Dutch settlers began harvesting salt to transport to the Netherlands. An expedition from Puerto Rico* builds a fort to assert Spanish control.

1644–1648 A Dutch fleet under the command of Peter Stuyvesant unsuccessfully attempts to take control of the island. The Spanish abandon the island in 1648, leaving behind Dutch and French prisoners. The prisoners amicably divide the island into Dutch and French halves.

18th century The island changes hands many times among the Dutch, French, and English. The introduction of sugarcane requires the importation of African slaves to work the European plantations.

1816–1848 At the end of the Napoleonic Wars, the island is again divided into Dutch and French areas. Slavery is abolished in 1848, allowing freed slaves to settle on small plots as farmers and fishermen.

1919 Saint Maarten, Saba, and Saint Eustatius are joined as the Netherlands Windward Islands.

1936 The Dutch officially adopt Sint Maarten, the Dutch spelling, as the territory's official name. English speakers use Saint Maarten to differentiate between it and French Saint Martin.

2000 A referendum supports the island's separation from the Netherlands Antilles and the creation of a separate country. An agreement with the Netherlands on *status aparte* is signed in 2006.

2008–2009 On December 15, 2008, the islands of Saint Maarten and Curaçao* are scheduled to leave the Netherlands Antilles to become separate countries in association with the Kingdom of the Netherlands, but the date is postponed.

See also Netherlands; Netherlands Antilles

SAINT MARTIN

OFFICIAL NAME
Collectivité d'outre mer de Saint-Martin (French); Collectivity of Saint Martin (English)

POPULATION
33,600 (2009e)

INHABITANTS' NAME/NICKNAME
Martinois; Saint Martiner(s)

LANGUAGE/LANGUAGES
French (official); English, Dutch, Spanish, others

RELIGION/RELIGIONS
Roman Catholic, Jehovah's Witness, Protestant, Hindu, other or no religion

NATIONAL FLAG
The official flag of Saint Martin is the French tricolor. The unofficial flag began as the flag of the sovereignty movement. The flag has a blue field with a large white triangle, base to the top of the flag, with a white stripe connecting it to the bottom. At the point of the triangle are a small red triangle and a yellow semicircle. The blue stands for the sea that surrounds the island, the white stands for purity and the future, the red and yellow stand for the rising sun over a morning sea.

COAT OF ARMS/SEAL
The unofficial coat of arms has a narrow, ornate gold frame around a blue sea, a white sailing ship, green vegetation, and a palm tree. Below the frame are crossed drumsticks and a draped white banner.

CAPITAL CITY
Marigot

TYPE OF GOVERNMENT
Overseas collectivity of France*

NATIONAL COLORS
Blue, white, and red

NATIONAL ANTHEM
The French anthem, "La Marseillaise," is the official anthem. French priest Father Gerard

Kemps wrote the local anthem, used on both sides of the island, in 1958.

O Sweet Saint Martin's Land (shared with neighboring Saint Maarten*)

Where over the world, say where,
You find an island there,
So lovely small with nations free
With people French and Dutch
Though talking English much,
As thee Saint Martin in the sea?

Chorus

O sweet Saint Martin's Land
So bright by beach and strand
With sailors on the sea and harbors free
Where the chains of mountains green
Variously in sunlight sheen

O I love thy Paradise,
Nature-beauty fairly nice (twice)

How pretty between all green
Flamboyants beaming gleam
Of flowers red by sunlight set
Thy cows and sheep and goats
In meadows or on roads
Thy donkeys keen can't I forget

Saint Martin I love thy name
In which Columbus fame
And memories of old are those
For me a great delight
Thy Southern Cross the night
May God the Lord protect thy coast!

PATRON SAINT

Saint Martin of Tours

CURRENCY

Euro (official); U.S. dollar

INTERNET IDENTIFIER

.mf

VEHICLE IDENTIFICATION PLATES/STICKERS

F France (official); MF Saint Martin (unofficial)

PASSPORT

Saint Martiners are French citizens and travel on French passports

NATIONAL RESOURCES

The territory has no natural resources other than salt. Tourism, based on sandy beaches, a pleasant climate, underwater reefs, and French island culture, is the mainstay of the economy. Generous French government subsidies are an important source of income.

FOODS

Soupe callaloo, made of kale, callaloo, okra, and pork, is considered the national dish of the island. Other specialties include *bouillabaisse creole,* a stew of fresh seafood; *civeche de coco,* marinated fresh fish with coconut; *chiquetaille de morue,* shredded and grilled cod served with vinaigrette sauce; *dombré,* flour balls cooked with dried vegetables; *colombo,* a curry dish with lamb, chicken, or goat; and croissant, the French-style breakfast pastry.

SPORTS/SPORTS TEAMS

Association football (soccer) and cycling are the most popular sports. Saint Martin national teams participate in basketball, football, and cycling at an international level.

TEAM SPORTS

Basketball

Saint-Martin Basketball Team; Saint-Martin Women's Basketball Team

Football

Saint-Martin Football Team

INDIVIDUAL SPORTS

Saint-Martin Cycling Team

NATIONAL HEROES OR PERSONIFICATIONS

Father Gerard Kemps, author of the local anthem in 1958; Frantz Gumba, leader of the sovereignty movement; Victor Schoelcher, French abolitionist responsible for the end of slavery

NATIONAL HOLIDAY/INDEPENDENCE DAY

Schoelcher Day (Emancipation Day), July 12; Bastille Day, July 14 (France and all French territories)

FESTIVALS/FAIRS

Carnaval (Carnival), February; Black Heritage Week, May; Saint Martin Book Fair, June; Bastille Day celebrations, July; Schoelcher Day celebrations, July; Sualouiga Festival, August

SIGNIFICANT EVENTS IN FORMATION OF NATIONAL IDENTITY

800 C.E.–1000 C.E. Arawak seafarers settle the island from their home in the Orinoco river basin on the South American mainland. They call the island Sualouiga, the land of salt, for its abundant saltpans.

1300 Warlike Caribs take control of the island, driving the Arawaks away or killing the men and taking the women as slaves.

1493 Christopher Columbus sights the island on his second voyage to the New World on the holy day of Saint Martin of Tours, whose name he applies to the island.

1620–1633 The Spanish ignore the island for greater conquests in Mexico* and South America. French settlers begin cultivating tobacco. An expedition from Puerto Rico* builds a fort to assert Spanish control.

1648 The island is divided into French and Dutch zones.

18th century The island changes hands several times among the Dutch, French, and English. Slaves are imported to work the cotton, tobacco and sugar plantations.

1810–1816 France annexes the Dutch side, along with the Netherlands* during the Napoleonic Wars. The division of the island resumes fol-lowing Napoleon's final defeat and the liberation of the Netherlands.

1848 Slavery is abolished in the French colonies. The economy declines with the end of plantation agriculture.

1939 Saint Martin is declared a duty-free port, which stimulates the economy.

1946 Guadeloupe becomes an overseas depart-ment of France, with Saint Martin and Saint Bar-thelemy* as dependencies.

2003 The islanders vote in a referendum to se-cede from Guadeloupe* in order to form a sepa-rate country within the French Republic.

2007–2009 Saint Martin becomes a separate overseas collectivity with greater powers of local government. New initiatives stimulate the island economy, although tourism slumps due to the global economic slowdown.

See also France

SAINT PIERRE AND MIQUELON

OFFICIAL NAME

Collectivité territoriale de Saint-Pierre-et-Miquelon; Territorial Collectivity of Saint Pierre and Miquelon

POPULATION

6,400 (2009e)

INHABITANTS' NAME/NICKNAME

Pierrois; Pierrotin(s)

LANGUAGE/LANGUAGES

French (official); English

RELIGION/RELIGIONS

Roman Catholic, 98 percent; other or no religion

NATIONAL FLAG

The official flag is the French tricolor. The local flag of Saint Pierre and Miquelon is blue with a yellow ship, said to be the *Grande*

Hermine that brought Jacques Cartier to Saint Pierre on June 15, 1536. Three square fields placed along the hoist recall the origin of most inhabitants of the islands, descended from Basques, Bretons, and Normans.

COAT OF ARMS/SEAL

The coat of arms is similar to the flag, a crest with the ship below the three squares referring to the Basques, Bretons, and Normans. Above the shield is a line of five sailing ships, and behind are two black anchors. Beneath the shield is a white banner inscribed with the island motto.

MOTTO

A mare labor (Latin); From the sea, work (English)

CAPITAL CITY

Saint-Pierre

TYPE OF GOVERNMENT

Representative democracy as a French collectivity

NATIONAL EMBLEM

Pointe aux Canons Lighthouse

NATIONAL COLORS

Blue, white, and red

NATIONAL ANTHEM

The official anthem is the French national anthem, "La Marseillaise"

PATRON SAINT

Saint Peter

CURRENCY

Euro; Canadian dollar

INTERNET IDENTIFIER

.pm

VEHICLE IDENTIFICATION PLATES/STICKERS

F France (official); SPM (unofficial)

PASSPORT

Pierrotins are French citizens and travel on French passports.

AIRLINE

Air Saint-Pierre

NATIONAL BIRD

Sandhill crane; Northern gannet (both unofficial)

NATIONAL RESOURCES

Natural resources are limited to fish and deepwater ports. The islands were dependent upon the cod fishery for most of the past four centuries. However, overfishing on the Grand Banks has led Canada* to impose a long-term closure of this industry. In Saint Pierre and Miquelon, many efforts are being made, with the help of the French government, to diversify the local economy. Tourism, fish farming, crab fishing, and agriculture are being developed.

FOODS

The typical food of the islands is traditional French cuisine, with an emphasis on recipes utilizing fresh or salted cod. Fish and seafood chowders are very popular. *Tiaude,* a highly seasoned stew of cod, vegetables, and other local ingredients is considered the national dish. Other specialities include Basque fish and lamb dishes.

SPORTS/SPORTS TEAMS

Ice hockey and association football (soccer) are the popular sports. Saint Pierre and Miquelon national teams participate in football, ice hockey and basketball at an international level.

TEAM SPORTS

Basketball

Saint Pierre and Miquelon Basketball Team; Saint Pierre and Miquelon Women's Basketball Team

Football

Saint Pierre and Miquelon Football Team

Hockey

Saint Pierre and Miquelon Ice Hockey Team

NATIONAL HEROES OR PERSONIFICATIONS

Jacques Cartier, French explorer who found the uninhabited islands in 1536; Admiral Émile Muselier, military leader responsible for the overthrow of the pro-Vichy government in the islands during World War II

NATIONAL HOLIDAY/INDEPENDENCE DAY

Bastille Day, July 14 (France and all French territories); Assumption Day/National Day, August 15

FESTIVALS/FAIRS

Basque Festival, August; Summer Fête de la Musique (Music Festival), July; Snow Crab Festival, first weekend of September; Seafood Festival, August

SIGNIFICANT EVENTS IN FORMATION OF NATIONAL IDENTITY

16th century C.E. Basque fishermen find and utilize the islands as bases for fishing in the Grand Banks.

1536 French explorer Jacques Cartier visits the island, beginning the period of permanent European settlements.

1713–1763 British attacks drive the settlers from the island, which remains under British rule for 50 years.

1780–1815 French support for the American Revolution leads to another British invasion and deportation of the French colonists. Possession of the islands passes back and forth until they are confirmed as French territory in 1815.

1919–1933 The economy of the islands booms during the era of Prohibition in the United States*. The islands become centers of alcohol smuggling. The boom ends with the repeal of the Prohibition, and the islands sink into the Great Depression.

1940–1941 The island government comes under the fascist Vichy regime following the fall of France during the Second World War. Saint Pierre and Miquelon are liberated on December 24, 1941, by the Free French Naval Forces under Admiral Émile Muselier.

1992 A dispute with Canada over the maritime boundary is settled by the International Court of Arbitration. France is awarded only 18 percent of the territorial waters it requests.

2000–2009 At various times, proposals are published about joining Canada, primarily for access to the Canadian national waters for island fishermen, but most islanders oppose the idea. Tourism from the Canadian mainland increases as the economic slump curtails the exotic travel plans of many Canadians.

See also France

SAINT VINCENT AND THE GRENADINES

OFFICIAL NAME

Saint Vincent and the Grenadines

POPULATION

120,800 (2009e)

INHABITANTS' NAME/NICKNAME

Vincentian(s), Vincy(s)

LANGUAGE/LANGUAGES

English (official); Creole or Vincentian (Vincy) English, others

RELIGION/RELIGIONS

Anglican, 47 percent; Methodist, 28 percent; Roman Catholic, 13 percent; Hindu, Seventh-day Adventist, other or no religion

NATIONAL FLAG

The flag, known as "the gems," has three vertical stripes of blue, yellow, and green, the yellow stripe double the width of the other stripes. Three green lozenges, or diamonds, in the form of a V are centered on the yellow, symbolizing the islands' position as the gems of the Antilles. The blue represents the sky and the sea; the gold represents warmth, the bright spirit of the people and the golden sands of the Grenadines; and the green represents the lush vegetation and the enduring vitality of the people.

COAT OF ARMS/SEAL

The coat of arms consists of an ornate, gilded frame featuring two women in classical Roman dress, one standing and holding a palm branch, the other kneeling before the yellow altar between them. Above the shield is the depiction of a cotton plant, representing agriculture, and beneath is a banner inscribed with the national motto in Latin.

MOTTO

Pax et justitia (Latin); Peace and Justice (English)

CAPITAL CITY

Kingstown

TYPE OF GOVERNMENT

Parliamentary democracy and constitutional monarchy as part of the British Commonwealth

NATIONAL COLORS

Blue, yellow, and green

NATIONAL ANTHEM

The anthem was adopted in 1967, when the islands became self-governing, and was adopted as the national anthem at independence in 1979.

Saint Vincent, Land So Beautiful

Saint Vincent, land so beautiful,
With joyful hearts we pledge to thee.
Our loyalty and love and vow to keep you
 ever free.

Chorus

Whate'er the future brings.
Our faith will see us through.
May peace reign from shore to shore,
And God bless and keep us true.

Hairouna, our fair and blessed isle
Your mountains high, so clear and green
Are home to me, though I may stray
A haven calm serene

Our little sister islands are,
Those gems, the lovely Grenadines.
Upon their seas and golden sands,
The sunshine ever beams.

PATRON SAINT

Saint Vincent

CURRENCY

East Caribbean dollar

INTERNET IDENTIFIER

.vc

VEHICLE IDENTIFICATION PLATES/STICKERS

WV

PASSPORT

The passport cover has the initials CC, for Caribbean Community, and name of the country in English, the coat of arms, and the word *passport*.

AIRLINE

SVG Air

NATIONAL FLOWER

Soufriere flower (spachea perforata)

NATIONAL TREE

Breadfruit; *Soufriere* tree (both unofficial)

NATIONAL PLANT
Cotton

NATIONAL BIRD
Saint Vincent parrot

NATIONAL FISH
Bigeye scad

NATIONAL RESOURCES
Natural resources are limited to hydropower and arable land. Tourism is the leading industry, supported by sandy beaches, a pleasant climate, island culture, and proximity to large North American population centers. Remittances from Vincentians living outside the country are an important source of foreign currency and investment.

FOODS
The national dish of Saint Vincent and the Grenadines is roast breadfruit and jack fish, a dish of breadfruit, salt fish, onion, tomato, and cucumber. Other island specialties include callaloo soup, made of kale, a leafy vegetable called callaloo, and pork; *lambi souse,* conch prepared with onion, cucumber, limes, celery, and hot pepper; curried goat; cornmeal dumplings; green pigeon peas soup; stuffed cucumbers; and stuffed sweet potatoes.

SPORTS/SPORTS TEAMS
Cricket is the most popular sport, followed by association football (soccer) and rugby. Saint Vincent and the Grenadines national teams participate in many sports at an international level.

TEAM SPORTS

Basketball
Saint Vincent and the Grenadines Basketball Team; Saint Vincent and the Grenadines Women's Basketball Team

Cricket
West Indies Cricket Team, nickname the Windies (West Indies teams represent a number of English-speaking countries in the Caribbean)

Football
Saint Vincent and the Grenadines Football Team, nickname Vincy Heat; Saint Vincent and the Grenadines Women's Football Team, nickname Vincy Heat; Saint Vincent and the Grenadines Rugby Union Team, nickname Amazona Guildingi; Saint Vincent and the Grenadines Futsal Team; West Indies Rugby League Team, nickname the Wahoos (West Indies teams represent a number of English-speaking countries in the Caribbean)

Kabaddi
West Indies Kabaddi Team (West Indies teams represent a number of English-speaking countries in the Caribbean)

Netball
Saint Vincent and the Grenadines Netball Team

Table Tennis
Saint Vincent and the Grenadines Table Tennis Team

Tennis
Saint Vincent and the Grenadines Davis Cup Team; Eastern Caribbean Davis Cup Team; Eastern Caribbean Fed Cup Team (Eastern Caribbean teams represent a number of English-speaking countries in the Caribbean)

Volleyball
Saint Vincent and the Grenadines Men's Volleyball Team; Saint Vincent and the Grenadines Women's Volleyball Team

INDIVIDUAL SPORTS

Saint Vincent and the Grenadines Amateur Boxing Team; Saint Vincent and the Grenadines Athletics Team; Saint Vincent and the Grenadines Canoeing Team; Saint Vincent and the Grenadines Cycling Team; Saint Vincent and the Grenadines Judo Team; Saint Vincent and the Grenadines Swim Team; Saint Vincent and the Grenadines Tae Kwon Do Team; Saint Vincent and the Grenadines Weight Lifting Team; Saint Vincent and the Grenadines Wrestling Team

NATIONAL HEROES OR PERSONIFICATIONS

Joseph Chatoyer, leader of the black Carib resistance to British rule in the late 18th century; James Mitchell, independence leader who won four general elections; Dr. Ralph Gonsalves, prime minister since 2001; Chatoyer, a Carib chief who led a rebellion against the British in the late 18th century

NATIONAL HOLIDAY/INDEPENDENCE DAY

Independence Day, October 27

FESTIVALS/FAIRS

Carnival, varied dates; Blues and Rhythms Festival, March; Gospel Festival, April; Maroon Festival, May; Emancipation Day celebrations, August; Breadfruit Festival, August; Independence Day celebrations, October; Theater Arts Festival, November; Nine Mornings Festival, December

SIGNIFICANT EVENTS IN FORMATION OF NATIONAL IDENTITY

1000 C.E. Seafaring Arawaks from the South American mainland settle the island as farmers and fishermen.

1300 Warlike Caribs conquer the island, absorbing or killing the Arawak population.

1498 Christopher Columbus sights the main island on Saint Vincent's Day.

1500–1700 Resistance by the Caribs prevents colonization. The island is granted to Britain's Lord Carlisle. Escaped slaves from other islands seek refuge with the Caribs of Saint Vincent. Many marry Caribs, leading to a growing population of black Caribs, called Garifuna.

1719–1763 The French take control of the island, establishing plantations and importing African slaves. The island is ceded to the United Kingdom* in 1763.

1795–1796 The black Caribs, led by Joseph Chatoyer, fight British rule until the rebellion is crushed and over 5,000 people are deported.

1834 Slavery is abolished, allowing the former slaves to settle on small plots. Most Europeans leave the islands.

1877–1951 The colony becomes a crown colony. La Soufrière volcano erupts in 1902, killing over 2,000 people. A legislative council is created in 1925. Universal suffrage is granted.

1967–1979 Saint Vincent and the Grenadines are united in an autonomous state, which becomes fully independent in 1979, the last of the Windward Islands to gain independence. La Soufrière again erupts, forcing the evacuation of thousands of inhabitants.

1980–1999 Severe hurricanes in 1980, 1987, and 1999 damage the banana and coconut plantations.

2003 The country joins the Non-Aligned Movement of developing nations. The government passes new laws to tighten the financial sector, which is accused of abetting money laundering.

2003–2008 Discontent grows in the Grenadines over perceived neglect by the government.

2009 Mustique, Palm Island, and Union Island, haunts of the rich and famous, continue to attract visitors, despite a general downturn in Caribbean tourism.

TRINIDAD AND TOBAGO

OFFICIAL NAME

Republic of Trinidad and Tobago

POPULATION

1,340,300 (2009e)

INHABITANTS' NAME/NICKNAME

Trinidadian(s); Trini(s); Tobagonian(s); Trinbagonian(s)

LANGUAGE/LANGUAGES

English (official); Spanish (special status); Creole, Urdu, Chinese, others

RELIGION/RELIGIONS

Roman Catholic, 26 percent; Hindu, 22 percent; Anglican, 8 percent; Baptist, 7 percent; Pentecostal, 6.5 percent; Muslim, 5 percent; Seventh-day Adventists, 4 percent; other or no religion

NATIONAL FLAG

The flag is a red field crossed by a black stripe outlined in white from the upper hoist to the lower fly. Red symbolizes the people's generosity and the sunlight, white is for equality and the sea, and black stands for tenacity and the vocation of unity.

COAT OF ARMS/SEAL

The coat of arms has a central crest or shield of red and black divided by a narrow inverted white V. On the red are three gold ships, representing the *Santa Maria, Niña,* and *Pinta,* of Christopher Columbus; on the black are two golden hummingbirds. Above the shield are a heraldic helmet, a ship's wheel, and a palm tree. A scarlet ibis and a cocrico, the national birds of Trinidad and Tobago, support the shield. Below is a banner inscribed with the national motto.

MOTTO

Together we aspire, together we achieve

CAPITAL CITY

Port of Spain

TYPE OF GOVERNMENT

Parliamentary republic

NATIONAL COLORS

Red and black

NATIONAL ANTHEM

The anthem was originally adopted by the short-lived West Indies Federation in 1958 and was retained when Trinidad and Tobago gained independence in 1962.

Forged from the Love of Liberty

Forged from the love of liberty
In the fires of hope and prayer
With boundless faith in our destiny
We solemnly declare

Side by side we stand
Islands of the blue Caribbean Sea
This our native land
We pledge our lives to thee

Here every creed and race finds an equal place
And may God bless our nation
Here every creed and race finds an equal place
And may God bless our nation.

PATRON SAINT

The Immaculate Conception of Mary

CURRENCY

Trinidad and Tobago dollar

INTERNET IDENTIFIER

.tt

VEHICLE IDENTIFICATION PLATES/ STICKERS

TT

PASSPORT

The passport cover has the large initials CC, in small letters Caribbean Community, the coat of arms, the name of the country, and the word *passport.*

AIRLINE

Caribbean Airlines

NATIONAL FLOWER

Chaconia

NATIONAL TREE

Palm tree

NATIONAL ANIMAL

Blue morpho (emperor butterfly)

NATIONAL BIRD

Scarlet ibis; cocrico; hummingbird

NATIONAL FISH

Cascadura (unofficial)

NATIONAL RESOURCES

Natural resources include petroleum, natural gas, and asphalt. Tourism is an important resource, based on sandy beaches, a pleasant climate, underwater reefs, and island culture. The economy is dependent on petroleum and petrochemicals.

FOODS

Doubles, a sandwich of two fried flatbreads called *bara,* filled with curried chickpeas, called *channa,* and a variety of spicy chutneys or pepper sauce, is considered the national dish. Chicken curry served with roti, a crepe-like bread, is also considered a national dish. Other specialties include callaloo, a soup of dasheen leaves, okra, crab, coconut milk and spices; *pelau,* a rice dish; skewered chicken; macaroni pie; and pepperpot, a spicy meat dish flavored with cinnamon.

SPORTS/SPORTS TEAMS

Cricket and association football (soccer) are the most popular sports. Trinidad and Tobago national teams participate in many sports at an international level.

TEAM SPORTS

Badminton

Trinidad and Tobago Badminton Team

Baseball

Trinidad and Tobago Baseball Team

Cricket

Trinidad and Tobago Cricket Team; Trinidad and Tobago Women's Cricket Team; West Indies Cricket Team, nickname the Windies (West Indies teams represent a number of English-speaking Caribbean countries)

Football

Trinidad and Tobago Football Team, nickname the Soca Warriors; Trinidad and Tobago Women's Football Team; Trinidad and Tobago Under-19 Football Team; Trinidad Women's Under-19 Football Team; Trinidad and Tobago Rugby Union Team; Trinidad and Tobago Women's Rugby Union Team; Trinidad and Tobago Futsal Team; West Indies Rugby League Team, nickname the Wahoos (West Indies teams represent a number of English-speaking Caribbean countries)

Hockey

Trinidad and Tobago Field Hockey Team

Kabaddi

West Indies Kabaddi Team (West Indies teams represent a number of English-speaking Caribbean countries)

Netball

Trinidad and Tobago Netball Team

Table Tennis

Trinidad and Tobago Table Tennis Team

Tennis

Trinidad and Tobago Davis Cup Team; Trinidad and Tobago Fed Cup Team

Volleyball

Trinidad and Tobago Men's Volleyball Team; Trinidad and Tobago Women's Volleyball Team

INDIVIDUAL SPORTS

Trinidad and Tobago Amateur Boxing Team; Trinidad and Tobago Archery Team; Trinidad and Tobago Athletics Team; Trinidad and Tobago Canoeing Team; Trinidad and Tobago Cycling Team; Trinidad and Tobago Equestrian Team; Trinidad and Tobago Gymnastics Team; Trinidad and Tobago Judo Team; Trinidad and Tobago Karate Team; Trinidad and Tobago Sailing Team; Trinidad and Tobago Shooting Team; Trinidad and Tobago Swim Team; Trinidad and Tobago Tae Kwon Do Team; Trinidad and Tobago Triathlon Team; Trinidad and Tobago Weight Lifting Team

NATIONAL HEROES OR PERSONIFICATIONS

Tubal Uriah Butler, labor leader and politician in the 1940s and 1950s; Adrian Cola Rienzi, a politician in the 1930s and 1940s; Audrey Jeffers, a female leader of the independence movement; Arthur Andrew Cipriani, World War I military hero and leader of the self-government movement; Eric Williams, leader of the independence movement and the country's first prime minister

NATIONAL HOLIDAY/INDEPENDENCE DAY

Independence Day, August 31

FESTIVALS/FAIRS

Carnival, February–March; Divali (Festival of Light), variable dates; Emancipation Day celebrations, August; Eid al-Fitr, variable dates; Hosay Festival, variable dates; Independence Day celebrations, August; Phagwa (Spring Festival), March; Santa Rosa Festival, April; We Beat Festival, June

SIGNIFICANT EVENTS IN FORMATION OF NATIONAL IDENTITY

250 B.C.E. Settlers from the South American mainland settle the islands, absorbing or displacing the earlier inhabitants, some of the earliest in the Caribbean.

1498 Christopher Columbus visits Trinidad, naming the island for the three peaks in its southeast corner, and calling Tobago after a local type of tobacco pipe due to its cigarlike shape.

1532 A Spanish colony is established under a local governor. Spanish slavers decimate the native tribal peoples and many are transported to Margarita Island or the mainland of South America.

1592–1700 The first lasting settlement is made at San José de Oruña (modern St. Joseph). Thousands of African slaves are imported to work the Spanish plantations. The Amerindian peoples are mostly eliminated or assimilated.

1781 The French capture Tobago from the Spanish. Tobago becomes a sugar-producing French colony.

1797–1802 A British naval squadron captures Trinidad from Spain* during the wars that follow the French Revolution in Europe. Spain cedes the island to the United Kingdom*.

1814–1834 France* cedes Tobago to the British. Slavery in the islands is abolished. Indentured workers are brought in from India* to work the plantations.

1889 Trinidad and Tobago are joined in a single colony.

1945 Universal suffrage begins, giving all nationalities resident in the islands the same right to vote.

1958–1962 The islands join the British-sponsored West Indies Federation. Britain grants self-government with Eric Williams as the first prime minister in 1959. Trinidad and Tobago leave the federation and become a separate state.

1970–1972 Violent protests by the island's black population lead to a mutiny and a state of emergency before order is restored.

1990 An abortive coup by Islamic radicals disrupts the island.

2001–2002 An unprecedented tie in national elections between the major black and Indian political parties paralyzes the government. The tie is resolved when the leader of the mainly black party is named head of government even though the Indian party won the largest number of votes.

2007–2009 Plans are made to close the centuries-old sugar industry. Soaring crime becomes a national issue, with street protests and demands for greater security. Tourism slumps due to the global economic crisis.

TURKS AND CAICOS ISLANDS

OFFICIAL NAME
Turks and Caicos Islands

POPULATION
30,600 (2009e)

INHABITANTS' NAME/NICKNAME
Turks and Caicos Islander(s); Belonger(s)

LANGUAGE/LANGUAGES
English (official); Turks and Caicos Islands Creole, others

RELIGION/RELIGIONS
Baptist, 40 percent; Anglican, 18 percent; Methodist, 16 percent; Church of God, 12 percent; other or no religion

NATIONAL FLAG
The flag is a blue field with the British Union Jack as a canton on the upper hoist and the central shield from the coat of arms centered on the fly.

COAT OF ARMS/SEAL
The coat of arms is a gold shield charged with a queen conch shell, a spiny lobster, and a Turk's head cactus, representing the abundance of the Caribbean Sea and the cactus that gave the Turks islands their name.

The shield is supported by two pink flamingos, and above are a silver helmet, a white pelican, and two sisal plants, representing the historic connection to the rope industry.

CAPITAL CITY
Cockburn Town

TYPE OF GOVERNMENT
Parliamentary democracy as a British Overseas Territory

NATIONAL EMBLEM
Queen conch shell

NATIONAL COLORS
White and blue

NATIONAL ANTHEM
As a British territory, the official anthem is "God Save the Queen," but the local anthem is often used at official ceremonies and international events.

This Land of Ours

Oh, we salute this land of ours
Our country we declare
This promised land
With its beauties grand
Though small, it is our own

Chorus

Turks and Caicos, Turks and Caicos
Our country firm and free
Our allegiance, Turks and Caicos
We pledge and we affirm.

From the east, west, north and south
Our banks and oceans meet
Surrounding sands and hills of glee
Our pristine beauties see

Chorus

Our people forged and blend
With multiplicity
Of race and kind and creed and tongue
United by our goals

Chorus
We stand with courage brave
To maintain this land of ours
With islands scattered here and there
With trust in God we stand.

CURRENCY
U.S. dollar

INTERNET IDENTIFIER
.tc

VEHICLE IDENTIFICATION PLATES/STICKERS
GB Great Britain (official); TC Turks and Caicos Islands (unofficial)

PASSPORT
Turks and Caicos Islanders are British citizens and travel on British passports.

AIRLINE
Air Turks & Caicos

NATIONAL FLOWER
Turk's head cactus flower

NATIONAL TREE
Turk's head cactus

NATIONAL PLANT
Sisal

NATIONAL ANIMAL
Spiny lobster

NATIONAL BIRD
Flamingo; pelican

NATIONAL FISH
Queen conch; blue marlin (unofficial)

NATIONAL RESOURCES
Natural resources include spiny lobster and conch. The economy of the Turks and Caicos Islands is based on tourism, fishing, and offshore financial services. Tourism is a major resource, supported by sandy beaches, a pleasant climate, underwater reefs, island culture, and proximity to large North American population centers.

FOODS
Peas 'n rice, a dish of rice and pigeon peas, often served with fresh fish or meat, is considered the national dish. Other island specialties include hominy, cooked with peas or dried conch; whelk soup, made from the small whelks, or mussels, that grow in the islands; conch chowder, made with dried or fresh conch and various vegetables; spiny lobster; lobster curry; and *conkies,* a desert of sweet potatoes and spices.

SPORTS/SPORTS TEAMS
Cricket and association football (soccer) are the most popular sports. Turks and Caicos Islands national teams participate in many sports at an international level.

TEAM SPORTS
Baseball
Turks and Caicos Islands Softball Team

Basketball
Turks and Caicos Islands Basketball Team; Turks and Caicos Islands Women's Basketball Team

Cricket
Turks and Caicos Islands Cricket Team

Football
Turks and Caicos Islands Football Team; Turks and Caicos Islands Women's Football Team; Turks and Caicos Islands Futsal Team

INDIVIDUAL SPORTS

Turks and Caicos Islands Athletics Team; Turks and Caicos Islands Judo Team; Turks and Caicos Swim Team; Turks and Caicos Islands Triathlon Team; Turks and Caicos Islands Weight Lifting Team

NATIONAL HEROES OR PERSONIFICATIONS

National heroes include James Alexander George Smith McCartney, the territory's first chief minister, who died in 1980 in a plane crash. The international airport bears his name.

NATIONAL HOLIDAY/INDEPENDENCE DAY

Constitution Day, August 30

FESTIVALS/FAIRS

Turks and Caicos Music and Cultural Festival, July–August; Conch Festival, November

SIGNIFICANT EVENTS IN FORMATION OF NATIONAL IDENTITY

600 B.C.E.–1200 C.E. Arawaks from the South American mainland settle the islands. Later, Caribs occupy the islands.

1512 Spanish explorer Juan Ponce de Leon sights the islands, which he claims for Spain*.

16th century–17th century The islands change hands among the European powers, but no settlements are established. The islands become a popular hideout for pirates. Around 1680, salt collectors from Bermuda* settle on Grand Turk.

1765–1790 The islands are under French control until 1783, when they pass to the United Kingdom*. Many loyalists flee to the islands during the American Revolution.

1848–1873 The Turks and Caicos islands are joined under a joint colonial government. The islands become part of Jamaica* colony.

1917 The Canadian prime minister suggests that the islands become part of Canada, but the British government rejects this.

1959–1962 The islands are again separated from Jamaica and become a crown colony.

1982 Negotiations for independence reach an agreement, but a change of the territorial government leads to a policy reversal.

2006–2008 A new constitution is adopted. Commercial conch farms are established. A severe storm, in September 2008, does considerable damage to the islands.

2009 A corruption scandal forces the premier to resign.

See also United Kingdom

UNITED STATES

OFFICIAL NAME

United States of America

POPULATION

305,617,900 (2009e)

INHABITANTS' NAME/NICKNAME

American(s); Yankee(s); Yank(s)

LANGUAGE/LANGUAGES

No language is official at the federal level. English is the de facto official language and is the official language of 28 states. Other languages spoken include Spanish, French, German, indigenous languages, Chinese, Japanese, Filipino, and many others.

RELIGION/RELIGIONS

Protestant, 51 percent; Roman Catholic, 24 percent; Mormon, 1.7 percent; Jewish, 1.7 percent; Buddhist, Muslim, other or no religion

NATIONAL FLAG

The flag consists of 13 equal horizontal stripes of red and white, with a blue canton on the upper hoist charged with 50 small, white, five-pointed stars. The 13 stripes represent the 13 original colonies. The 50 stars represent the 50 states. Nicknames for the flag include the Stars and Stripes, Old Glory, the Red, White, and Blue, and the Star-Spangled Banner.

COAT OF ARMS/SEAL

The emblem, called the Great Seal of the United States, is a circle charged with the coat of arms, a bald eagle with outstretched wings holding a bundle of 13 arrows in its left talon, representing the original 13 states, and an olive branch in its right talon, representing a strong desire for peace. In its beak, the eagle clutches a banner with the Latin motto *E pluribus unum* (out of many, one). Over its head is a "glory" with 13 white stars on a blue field.

MOTTO

In God we trust (on currency)

E pluribus unum (Latin); Out of many, one (English) (on national seal)

CAPITAL CITY

Washington, District of Columbia (D.C.)

TYPE OF GOVERNMENT

Federal presidential republic

NATIONAL EMBLEM

American eagle; Statue of Liberty

NATIONAL COLORS

Red, white, and blue

NATIONAL ANTHEM

The anthem was adopted from a poem written during a battle in the War of 1812. It was set to the music of a popular song and became very popular. It was adopted as the official anthem in 1931. Only the first stanza is sung on most occasions.

The Star-Spangled Banner

O! Say, can you see, by the dawn's early light,

What so proudly we hailed at the twilight's last gleaming?
Whose broad stripes and bright stars through the perilous fight,
O'er the ramparts we watched were so gallantly streaming?
And the rockets' red glare, the bombs bursting in air,
Gave proof through the night that our flag was still there.
Oh, say, does that star-spangled banner yet wave
O'er the land of the free and the home of the brave?

On the shore, dimly seen through the mists of the deep,
Where the foe's haughty host in dread silence reposes,
What is that which the breeze, o'er the towering steep,
As it fitfully blows, half conceals, half discloses?
Now it catches the gleam of the morning's first beam,
In full glory reflected now shines in the stream,
'Tis the star-spangled banner! Oh, long may it wave
O'er the land of the free and the home of the brave!

And where is that band who so vauntingly swore
That the havoc of war and the battle's confusion,
A home and a country should leave us no more!
Their blood has washed out their foul footsteps' pollution.
No refuge could save the hireling and slave
From the terror of flight, or the gloom of the grave:
And the star-spangled banner in triumph doth wave
O'er the land of the free and the home of the brave.

O! Thus be it ever, when freemen shall stand

Between their loved home and the war's
desolation!
Blest with victory and peace, may the heav'n-
rescued land
Praise the Power that hath made and preserved us a nation.
Then conquer we must, when our cause it is
just,
And this be our motto: "In God is our trust."
And the star-spangled banner in triumph shall
wave
O'er the land of the free and the home of the
brave!

NATIONAL MARCH

"The Stars and Stripes Forever"

PATRON SAINT

Immaculate Conception of Mary

CURRENCY

U.S. dollar

INTERNET IDENTIFIER

.us

VEHICLE IDENTIFICATION PLATES/ STICKERS

USA

PASSPORT

The passport cover has the word *passport,* in large letters, at the top; the National Emblem; the name of the country; and the standard biometric symbol.

AIRLINE

American Airlines; United Airlines; Delta Airlines; Continental Airlines; US Air

NATIONAL FLOWER

Rose

NATIONAL TREE

Oak

NATIONAL ANIMAL

Buffalo (American bison) (unofficial)

NATIONAL BIRD

Bald eagle

NATIONAL FISH

Atlantic halibut (unofficial)

NATIONAL RESOURCES

Natural resources include coal, copper, lead, molybdenum, phosphates, uranium, bauxite, gold, iron, mercury, nickel, potash, silver, tungsten, zinc, petroleum, natural gas, and timber. The United States is richly endowed with natural resources, a well-educated population, and the world's largest national economy.

FOODS

Food in the United States is an amalgam of regional cuisines and the continuing influences introduced by immigrants. The hamburger, a patty of ground meat served on a special roll accompanied by lettuce, tomato, onion, and sauce, is considered the national dish. Other national specialties include apple pie, a pastry shell filled with sliced apples mixed with sugar and cinnamon and then baked; stuffed turkey, the centerpiece of the annual Thanksgiving meal; pumpkin pie, a sweetened squash mixture baked in a pastry shell; hot dogs, sausages served on a special roll with mustard; doughnuts, sweet deep-fried pastries; and macaroni and cheese, a pasta and cheese dish. Spaghetti and meatballs, of Italian origin, has become part of the national cuisine as has pizza, another Italian import. Regional cuisines remain very popular, often based on local produce and dishes introduced by immigrants to the different regions.

SPORTS/SPORTS TEAMS

The most popular sports are American football, basketball, baseball, and ice hockey. Association football, called soccer, is becoming more popular. United States national teams participate in many sports at an international level.

Team Sports

Badminton

United States Badminton Team

Baseball

United States Women's Softball Team; United States Baseball Team

Basketball

United States Basketball Team; United States Women's Basketball Team; United States Wheelchair Basketball Team; United States Women's Wheelchair Basketball Team; United States Under-21 Basketball Team; United States Under-19 Basketball Team

Bowls

United States Bowls Team

Cricket

United States Cricket Team; United States Women's Cricket Team

Football

United States Soccer (Football) Team, nickname the Red, White, and Blue or the Yanks; United States Women's Soccer Team, nickname the Yanks or the Red, White, and Blue; United States Men's Under-23 Football Team; United States Men's Under-20 Football Team; United States Under-17 Men's Football Team; United States Women's Under-19 Football Team; United States Rugby Union Team, nickname the Eagles; United States Women's Rugby Union Team, nickname the Women Eagles; United States Rugby League Team, nickname Tomahawks; United States American Football Team; United States Australian-Rules Football Team, nickname The Revolution; United States Women's Australian-Rules Football Team, nickname Freedom; United States Beach Soccer Team; United States Rugby Union Team (Sevens), nickname USA Sevens; United States Women's Rugby Union Team (Sevens), nickname USA Sevens or USA 7s; United States Under-21 Women's Soccer Team; United States Wheelchair Rugby Team; United States Futsal Team; United States Touch Football Team; United States Women's Touch Football Team

Handball

United States Handball Team; United States Women's Handball Team; United States Beach Handball Team; United States Women's Beach Handball Team

Hockey

United States Field Hockey Team; United States Women's Field Hockey Team; United States Men's Ice Hockey Team; United States Women's Ice Hockey Team; United States Junior Ice Hockey Team

Kabaddi

United States Kabaddi Team

Korfball

United States Korfball Team

Lacrosse

United States Men's Lacrosse Team; United States Women's Lacrosse Team; United States Men's Under-19 Lacrosse Team; United States Women's Under-19 Lacrosse Team

Netball

United States Netball Team

Polo

United States Polo Team

Racing

A1 Team USA; United States Speedway Team

Table Tennis

United States Table Tennis Team

Tennis

United States Davis Cup Team; United States Fed Cup Team

Volleyball

United States Men's Volleyball Team; United States Women's Volleyball Team; United States Fistball Team; United States Men's Beach Volleyball Team; United States Women's Beach Volleyball Team

Water Polo

United States Water Polo Team; United States Women's Water Polo Team

INDIVIDUAL SPORTS

United States Aikido Team; United States Amateur Boxing Team; United States Archery Team; United States Athletics (Track and Field) Team; United States Canoeing Team; United States Men's Cycling Team; United States Equestrian Team; United States Fencing Team; United States Gymnastics Team; United States Judo Team; United States Karate Team; United States Modern Pentathlon Team; United States Rowing Team; United States Sailing Team; United States Shooting Team; United States Swim Team; United States Tae Kwon Do Team; United States Triathlon Team; United States Weight Lifting Team; United States Wrestling Team

WINTER SPORTS

United States Alpine Ski Team; United States Bandy Team; United States Biathlon Team; United States Bobsleigh and Tobogganing Team; United States Curling Team; United States Luge Team; United States Skating Team

NATIONAL HEROES OR PERSONIFICATIONS

Uncle Sam is the personification of the United States, along with Lady Liberty (from the Statue of Liberty). Columbia was the first popular personification and the origin for the name of the District of Columbia, the national capital.

National heroes include George Washington, leader of the American Revolution and first president, known as the father of his country; Thomas Jefferson, author of the Declaration of Independence, independence leader, and third president; John Adams, independence leader and second president; Abraham Lincoln, leader during the Civil War; and Franklin Roosevelt, president during the Great Depression and the Second World War; John Kennedy, the president during the height of the Cold War, assassinated in 1963; Barack Obama, the first black president, elected in 2008.

NATIONAL HOLIDAY/INDEPENDENCE DAY

Independence Day, July 4

FESTIVALS/FAIRS

Fourth of July celebrations, July; National Cherry Blossom Festival (Washington, D.C.), March; National Buffalo Wing Festival (Buffalo, N.Y.), September; National Storytelling Festival (Jonesborough, TN), October; Newport Jazz Festival (Newport, RI), August; New Orleans Jazz and Heritage Festival (New Orleans, LA), April–May

SIGNIFICANT EVENTS IN FORMATION OF NATIONAL IDENTITY

Prehistory Peoples from northern Asia cross an ancient land bridge from Siberia to populate the Americas.

1492–1565 Christopher Columbus, sailing for Spain*, encounters the North American continent beginning with the islands of the Bahamas*. Later explorer Juan Ponce de Leon visits mainland Florida in 1513. The Spanish establish Saint Augustine, the first permanent European settlement, in 1565.

1607 The first English settlement, Jamestown, is founded in Virginia. Puritans fleeing religious persecution in England found Plymouth Colony, in Massachusetts.

17th century–18th century The first settlements grow into 13 colonies along the east coast of the continent. Hundreds of thousands of Africans are imported to work cotton and tobacco plantations. European diseases ravage the indigenous peoples. Indigenous resistance to colonization is ruthlessly put down.

1763 The British take control of French territory up to the Mississippi River as a result of the French and Indian War.

1774 The colonists form the First Continental Congress as tensions increase and British troops are deployed against groups protesting unjust taxes.

1775 The American Revolution spreads through the colonies. General George Washington leads the colonial army against the British.

1776–1781 The 13 colonies declare independence and form a loose confederation. Thousands of British loyalists leave the colonies, mostly to Canada*.

1787–1789 The leaders of the new nation draw up a constitution for the United States of America, which goes into effect in 1788. George Washington becomes the first president.

1803 France* sells the Louisiana territories, stretching from the Gulf of Mexico to Canada, to the United States.

19th century Resistance by indigenous peoples is crushed as immigration from Europe assumes mass proportions. Settlers continue to move westward. The number of new states joining the union continues to grow.

1846–1848 Vast tracts of territory come into U.S. possession at the end of the Mexican-American War, including California, on the coast of the Pacific Ocean.

1854–1861 Opponents of slavery, called abolitionists, establish the Republican Party. The party's candidate, Abraham Lincoln, wins the 1860 presidential election. Eleven southern states secede and form the Confederate States of America, initiating the American Civil War.

1865 The defeat of the Confederacy results in the abolition of slavery. Lincoln is assassinated.

1876 Sioux warriors defeat the U.S. military at Little Big Horn, the most important victory of the indigenous peoples in a series of wars for territory in the west.

1917–1918 The United States enters World War I in Europe.

1920–1924 Women receive the right to vote in federal elections. The indigenous peoples are finally granted citizenship.

1929–1939 The stock market crash in 1929 ushers in the Great Depression, bringing hardship and economic problems that last for most of the 1930s. President Franklin Delano Roosevelt's New Deal attempts to soften the effects of the Depression. Roosevelt is elected to an unprecedented four terms, leading to the adoption of the 22nd Amendment to the Constitution, which limits presidential terms to two four-year terms.

1941–1945 A bombing attack by the Japanese on the U.S. military base in Pearl Harbor, Hawaii, prompts the nation's entry into World War II, which is fought in Europe and the Pacific. The United States emerges as the world's first superpower.

1947 The Cold War, the armed standoff between the West and the Soviet bloc, begins.

1950s–1970s The nation takes on the self-appointed role of the leader of the Free World. Wars in Asia result in inconclusive results. The civil rights movement in the 1960s, supported by blacks and many white liberals, spreads across the nation and is often emulated by other groups, including women, Native Americans, gays and lesbians, Asians, and others.

1979 In Iran*, radical students, beginning an era of radical Islamic expansion and threats, seize the U.S. embassy.

1980–1991 Government spending on military equipment forces the Soviet Union into an arms race that eventually bankrupts that government, which leads to the collapse of the Soviet system of alliances. U.S. forces lead the liberation of Kuwait* following an invasion by Iraq*.

2000 In a controversial and close election, George W. Bush becomes president.

2001 Islamic terrorists attack New York and Washington, D.C. The government mobilizes to fight the newest threat to global security.

2003–2008 The United States, with some allied nations, invades Afghanistan* and Iraq*, beginning long and costly wars that bog down the unplanned occupation of hostile countries. Thousands of American soldiers are killed while the stability promised at the onset of the invasions continues to elude the occupiers.

2009 A new administration, under President Barack Obama, begins its term by reversing many of the more radical impositions of the former Bush administration. The notorious military prison at Guantanamo Bay in Cuba* is scheduled to be closed, a plan for a military withdrawal from Iraq is formulated, and national health care is again under discussion.

See also Guam; Northern Marianas; Puerto Rico; Virgin Islands

VIRGIN ISLANDS

OFFICIAL NAME
United States Virgin Islands

POPULATION
108,600 (2009e)

INHABITANTS' NAME/NICKNAME
Virgin Islander(s); Thomian(s) in Saint Thomas; Cruzan(s) or Crucian(s) in Saint Croix

LANGUAGE/LANGUAGES
English (official); Spanish, Virgin Islands English, others

RELIGION/RELIGIONS
Baptist, 42 percent; Roman Catholic, 34 percent; Anglican, 17 percent; other or no religion

NATIONAL FLAG
The flag is a white field charged with a simplified version of the Great Seal of the United States between the letters *V* and *I* for Virgin Islands, in turquoise blue. A yellow eagle holds a green laurel branch in one talon and three blue arrows in the other, representing the three major islands: Saint Thomas, Saint John, and Saint Croix. The color yellow represents various characteristics of the islands and their flowers, green is for the hills, white represents clouds, and blue represents water.

COAT OF ARMS/SEAL
The seal of the U.S. Virgin Islands is a blue circle, representing the sea, with the three islands in green. A bananaquit, the official bird, is perched on a branch of yellow cedar, the official tree and flower, in the center. Around the disk is a broad border of yellow inscribed with *Government of the United States Virgin Islands.*

MOTTO
United in pride and hope

CAPITAL CITY
Charlotte Amalie

TYPE OF GOVERNMENT
Representative democracy as a U.S. external territory

NATIONAL EMBLEM
The three-island design is seen everywhere in the islands.

NATIONAL COLORS
Blue and yellow

NATIONAL ANTHEM

The anthem was composed in 1919 and adopted as the official anthem in 1963.

Virgin Islands March

All hail our Virgin Islands.
Em'ralds of the sea,
Where beaches bright with coral sand
And trade winds bless our native land.
All hail our Virgin Islands,
Bathed in waters blue,
We give our loyalty,
Full to thee,
And pledge allegiance forever true.

To thee our Virgin Islands,
Loving voices raise
A song in praise of brotherhood,
Where right makes might to fight for good.
To thee our Virgin Islands,
Haven of the free,
We sing our love to thee,
Joyously,
Our own fair islands of liberty.

March on, O Virgin Islands,
In the joyful throng,
Uphold the right and right the wrong
Where only peace and love belong.
March on, O Virgin Islands,
Democratic land.
Together hand in hand,
Take your stand,
Forever soldiers in freedom's band.

God bless our Virgin Islands,
Humbly now we pray,
Where all mankind can join today
In friendly warmth of work and play.
God bless our Virgin Islands,
Beautiful and tall.
Beneath a sunny sky,
Hilltops high
Hold out a welcome for one and all.

PATRON SAINT

Saint John; Saint Thomas; Holy Cross

CURRENCY

U.S. dollar

INTERNET IDENTIFIER

.vi

VEHICLE IDENTIFICATION PLATES/ STICKERS

USA United States (official); VI Virgin Islands (unofficial)

PASSPORT

Virgin Islanders are U.S. citizens and travel on U.S. passports

AIRLINE

Seaborne Airlines

NATIONAL FLOWER

Yellow cedar

NATIONAL TREE

Yellow cedar

NATIONAL BIRD

Bananaquit (also known as yellow breast in the islands)

NATIONAL FISH

Blue marlin (unofficial)

NATIONAL RESOURCES

Natural resources are negligible. Tourism, based on a pleasant year-round climate, sandy beaches, island culture, and proximity to large North American population centers, is the largest resource and accounts for about 80 percent of the economy. Poor soil quality and little available farmland limits agriculture.

FOODS

Funji, a thick cornmeal mush often served with okra and salt cod, is the national dish. Other specialties include callaloo, a soup of meat and okra and the leaves of the callaloo bush; red conch chowder, a seafood stew of conch, vegetables, and spices; *pate-patty*, a meat of salt cod patty usually fried; roti, a very thin dough wrapped around curried vegetables and meat, served with rice and beans (introduced from other Caribbean islands where immigrants from India* settled); johnnycake, a local pastry; mango chicken; and key lime pie.

SPORTS/SPORTS TEAMS

Baseball and basketball are the most popular sports. United States Virgin Islands national teams participate in many sports at an international level.

TEAM SPORTS

Baseball

United States Virgin Islands Baseball Team; United States Virgin Islands Softball Team

Basketball

United States Virgin Islands Basketball Team; United States Virgin Islands Women's Basketball Team

Cricket

West Indies Men's Cricket Team, nickname the Windies; West Indies Women's Cricket Team, nickname the Windies (West Indies teams represent a number of English-speaking Caribbean countries)

Curling

United States Virgin Islands Curling Team

Football

United States Virgin Islands Soccer (Football) Team, nickname the Dashing Eagle; United States Virgin Islands Women's Football Team, nickname the Dashing Eagle; United States Virgin Islands American Football Team; West Indies Rugby League Team, nickname the Wahoos (West Indies teams represent a number of English-speaking Caribbean countries)

Hockey

United States Virgin Islands Field Hockey Team

Kabaddi

West Indies Kabaddi Team (West Indies teams represent a number of English-speaking Caribbean countries)

Tennis

United States Virgin Islands Davis Cup Team

Volleyball

United States Virgin Islands Men's Volleyball Team; United States Virgin Islands Women's Volleyball Team

INDIVIDUAL SPORTS

United States Virgin Islands Amateur Boxing Team; United States Virgin Islands Athletics Team; United States Virgin Islands Cycling Team; United States Virgin Islands Equestrian Team; United States Virgin Islands Fencing Team; United States Virgin Islands Judo Team; United States Virgin Islands Sailing Team; United States Virgin Islands Shooting Team; United States Virgin Islands Swim Team; United States Virgin Islands Tae Kwon Do Team; United States Virgin Islands Weight Lifting Team; United States Virgin Islands Wrestling Team

WINTER SPORTS

United States Virgin Islands Biathlon Team; United States Virgin Islands Curling Team; United States Virgin Islands Luge Team

NATIONAL HEROES OR PERSONIFICATIONS

Valmy Thomas, the first Virgin Islander to play Major League Baseball; Eulalie Rivera, a noted educator and defender of island culture; Moses Gottlieb, a leader of the slave rebellion on Saint Croix in 1848;

Ralph M. Paliewonsky, governor of the territory from 1961 to 1969, who oversaw the modernizing of the islands; Paul Emanuel Joseph, a civil rights leader in the 1940s and 1950s

NATIONAL HOLIDAY/INDEPENDENCE DAY
Transfer Day, March 27

SIGNIFICANT EVENTS IN FORMATION
OF NATIONAL IDENTITY

1000 B.C.E. The islands are inhabited by the Ciboney, Caribs, and Arawaks. The tribal peoples live by farming, hunting, and fishing.

1493 Christopher Columbus lands on the island he names for the holy cross (Santa Cruz), later called Saint Croix. A conflict in which a Spaniard and a Carib are killed is the first recorded battle between Europeans and indigenous peoples in the New World.

1400–1600 The Spanish ignore the islands, which become the haunts of pirates preying on Spanish shipping. European diseases and mistreatment devastate the indigenous population.

1672–1694 The Danish West India Company settles colonists on Saint Thomas and Saint John to produce tropical products, especially sugar. African slaves are imported to work the plantations. Dutch and English settlers colonize Saint Croix, which came under French rule in 1650.

1733–1848 Saint Croix is sold to the Danes. The islands become royal Danish colonies in 1754. Slave rebellions, especially serious in 1733 on Saint John and in 1848 on Saint Croix, are a reaction to harsh Danish slave laws. Slavery is abolished in the islands.

1867–1902 The Danish propose to sell the islands of Saint John and Saint Thomas to the United States*. A second draft treaty to sell the islands is narrowly defeated in the Danish parliament.

1916–1917 The islands remain a drain on the Danish treasury, so in 1917, they are finally sold to the United States.

1927 The islanders are granted U.S. citizenship.

1940s–1950s The islands become a popular tourist destination.

1960s A progressive governor leads the modernization of the islands, with advances in education, infrastructure, and communications.

1989 Hurricane Hugo devastates the islands.

2008–2009 The Virgin Islanders remain under the U.S. flag, but as an unincorporated territory, their islands pay no taxes to the U.S. Treasury; however, they do pay local taxes. The territory has a nonvoting delegate to the U.S. House of Representatives. Most Virgin Islanders are content with the political situation of their islands although very small independence and statehood organizations exist.

See also United States

6

Sub-Saharan Africa

The symbols adopted by the nations of sub-Saharan Africa often derive from the symbols and colors of Ethiopia*, the only African nation to maintain its independence during the centuries of European colonization. Ethiopia's national colors of green, yellow, and red are now considered pan-African colors and are repeated in the national flags, colors, uniforms, and symbols of a number of African nations. Other African countries modified the colors and symbols of the former colonial powers or drew on ancient traditions for their symbols. Religion has also played a part in the formation of national symbols in many countries, particularly the symbols and green color of Islam. Many national flags and coats of arms are modified versions of those adopted by liberation movements, pre-independence political organizations, or traditional tribal states. Some nations adopted symbols and flags of several distinct colors to represent their diverse national populations.

Ambazania, Cabinda, Casamance, Katanga, Mthwakazi, Somaliland, Southern Sudan, and Zanzibar are included in this section, although they are not independent nations. A sizable percentage of the populations of each of these territories is seeking to create their own national states with their own recognized national symbols. Saint Helena, Reunion, and Mayotte are included as distinct territories still under European authority.

AMBAZANIA

OFFICIAL NAME

Formerly known as the Southern Cameroons, the territory now forms part of the Republic of Cameroon. The proposed name for an independent republic is the Republic of Ambazania, which was declared independent in 2006 but is not yet recognized as an independent nation. Another pro-independence group uses the name Federal Republic of Southern Cameroons.

POPULATION

6,012,500 (2009e)

INHABITANTS' NAME/NICKNAME

Southern Cameroonian(s); Ambazanian(s)

LANGUAGE/LANGUAGES

English, French (both official); various indigenous languages, others

RELIGION/RELIGIONS

Christian, Muslim, indigenous beliefs, other or no religion

NATIONAL FLAG

The flag has nine stripes of sky blue and white, with a blue canton charged with a circle of 10 stars and a dove. The color blue represents the sky and the sea, and the white stands for purity and hope for the future. The stars represent the 10 major clans or tribes in the territory. The dove represents peace.

COAT OF ARMS/SEAL

The seal is a pale blue circle bearing a map of Ambazania in dark blue outlined in white; the circle is surrounded by a wide, dark blue border bearing the name Republic of Ambazania at the top, 14 small white stars (seven on each side), and the national motto on the bottom.

MOTTO

Beacon of Prosperity

CAPITAL CITY

Bamenda

TYPE OF GOVERNMENT

Representative democracy as a government-in-exile

NATIONAL COLORS

Sky blue and white

NATIONAL ANTHEM

The anthem is titled "Freedom Land." No further information or lyrics are available.

CURRENCY

CFA franc (Cameroon*)

VEHICLE IDENTIFICATION PLATES/STICKERS

COM Cameroon (official); SCS Southern Cameroons (Ambazania) (unofficial)

PASSPORT

Ambazanians are Cameroon* citizens and travel on Cameroon passports.

NATIONAL TREE

Banana

NATIONAL BIRD

Mourning dove

NATIONAL RESOURCES

Natural resources include timber, petroleum, natural gas, arable land, fisheries, hydropower, and deepwater ports.

FOODS

National specialties include fried fish in peanut sauce; banana and pineapple salad; beef Cameroon, a dish of cubed beef, onions, pineapple, and coconut water; chicken in cumin sauce; beef and greens in peanut sauce; *dongo-dongo*, a stew of salted or smoked fish, onions, chilies, and spices; okra and greens; and *gali akpono*, a dessert of cornmeal, sugar, and eggs.

SPORTS/SPORTS TEAMS

Association football (soccer) is the most popular sport. The Ambazania national team participates in football at an international level under the name Southern Cameroons.

TEAM SPORTS

Football

Ambazania Football Team

NATIONAL HEROES OR PERSONIFICATIONS

Emmanuel Mbela Lifate Endeley, political leader of the struggle for separate Southern Cameroons autonomy in the 1950s; John Ngu Foncha, last premier of the British Cameroons and a leader of the Southern Cameroons National Council

NATIONAL HOLIDAY/ INDEPENDENCE DAY

Independence Day, October 1 (unofficial)

FESTIVALS/FAIRS

Ambazanian Culture Festival, May

SIGNIFICANT EVENTS IN FORMATION OF NATIONAL IDENTITY

Fourth century C.E.–sixth century C.E. Bantu peoples settle the region, displacing the earlier Pygmy inhabitants.

500 C.E.–1500 C.E. The Bantu peoples create a series of small kingdoms and chiefdoms,

1472–1750 Portuguese sailors visit the coast. Noting an abundance of prawns in the Wouri

River, they name the territory Rio do Camerões, "river of prawns." Over the following centuries, Europeans establish trading posts and Christian missionaries push inland.

1884–1914 The German Empire lays claim the region as the colony of Kamerun. The Germans push steadily into the interior to pacify resistance. Many improvement projects begin, based on a brutal system of forced labor.

1918–1919 The defeat of the German Empire in World War I leaves Cameroon under the authority of the League of Nations as a mandate territory, which is split into British Cameroons and French Cameroon.

1920–1946 The British rule their portion from the neighboring colony of Nigeria*. Many Nigerians settle in British Cameroons, angering local people but bringing an end to forced labor. At the end of World War II, the mandates are converted into United Nations trusteeships in 1946.

1950–1960 French Cameroon is the scene of a vicious guerilla war and instability in the 1950s. In British Cameroons, peaceful and economically secure, the people complain of being the "colony of a colony" and demand an end to rule from Nigeria. Nationalist movements in both regions demand independence, but in the British region, it is felt that the territory is too small for separate independence, and a debate opens as to joining Nigeria or Cameroon.

1960–1961 French Cameroon is granted independence under President Ahmadou Ahidjo. On October 1, 1961, following a referendum on their future, the people of the British Cameroons vote for union with ethnically related Cameroon, except for some small northern districts that vote for union with Nigeria. The two territories are joined in the Federal Republic of Cameroon, which gives the former British territory widespread cultural, linguistic, and economic autonomy.

1966–1972 In 1972, the federal system of government is abolished in favor of a unitary republic. The name of the country is changed from Federal Republic of Cameroon to United Republic of Cameroon. The two yellow stars on the flag are removed and are replaced by the single "star

of unity." The people of Southern Cameroons feel further marginalized.

1981 Cameroon nearly goes to war with neighboring Nigeria over the disputed region of the Bakassi Peninsula in former British Cameroons.

1990 The reintroduction of multiparty politics allows Anglophone groups in the former British portion to legally form political parties, many calling for the secession of their homeland as the Republic of the Southern Cameroons or the Republic of Ambazania.

1994 Cameroon President Paul Biya clashes with neighboring Nigeria over possession of the disputed Bakassi Peninsula. Formerly part of the Calabar Kingdom in modern Nigeria, the region remained under Nigerian control when the British Cameroons voted for union with Cameroon in 1972, although the border was never delineated. Ambazanian nationalists claim the peninsula as part of the national territory of the Southern Cameroons. A delegation sent by the Southern Cameroons National Council presents the region's case for secession to the United Nations, but the motion is blocked by Cameroon and other African nations.

1999 Armed members of the nationalist groups take over the primary radio station to broadcast a proclamation of independence on December 30, which is not supported by all nationalist groups.

2001 Several people are killed and many injured when pro-independence rallies are broken up by Cameroonian police.

2006 The Bakassi dispute is submitted to the International Court of Justice, which rules in favor of Cameroon on August 14. The nationalists respond by declaring the independence of the Republic of Ambazania, to include the territory of Bakassi.

2007–2008 In August 2008, Nigeria formally cedes its claims to the Bakassi Peninsula, a 100,000-square-kilometer territory thought to be rich in oil, to Cameroon sovereignty. Ambazanian leaders reiterate their claim to the region as part of the former German, then British colonial territory of Southern Cameroons.

2009 In March, the headquarters of the Southern Cameroons National Council are raided, its offices looted, and all present arbitrarily arrested and detained.

See also Southern Cameroons

ANGOLA

OFFICIAL NAME

República de Angola (Portuguese); Republic of Angola (English)

POPULATION

16,437,800 (2009e)

INHABITANTS' NAME/NICKNAME

Angolan(s)

LANGUAGE/LANGUAGES

Portuguese (official); Kongo, Chokwe, South Mundu, Mundu (recognized regional languages); others

RELIGION/RELIGIONS

Roman Catholic, 41 percent; Protestant, 17 percent; indigenous beliefs, other or no religion

NATIONAL FLAG

The flag is a horizontal bicolor of red over black bearing a cogwheel, a machete, and a star. Red stands for socialism and black for Africa. Proposals for a new flag representing the new Angola have been studied.

COAT OF ARMS/SEAL

The coat of arms shows a segment of a cogwheel, sheaves of maize, coffee, and cotton around a blue field with a golden star above a crossed machete and hoe over an open book.

MOTTO

Virtus unita fortior (Latin); Unity Provides Strength (English)

CAPITAL CITY

Luanda

TYPE OF GOVERNMENT

Nominally a multiparty democracy, but free elections have never been held

NATIONAL COLORS

Red, black, and yellow

NATIONAL ANTHEM

Angola is studying possible changes to its national symbols. The anthem contains references to dates and events important to the ruling party that have become obsolete with the advent of multiparty politics.

Angola Avante! (Portuguese); Forward, Angola! (English)

O Fatherland, we shall never forget
The heroes of the fourth of February.
O Fatherland, we salute your sons
Who died for our independence.
We honor the past and our history
As by our work we build the new man.
  (*Repeat previous two lines*)

Chorus

Forward, Angola!
Revolution through the power of the people!
A united country, freedom,
One people, one nation! (*Repeat chorus*)

Let us raise our liberated voices
To the glory of the peoples of Africa.
We shall march, Angolan fighters,
In solidarity with oppressed peoples.
We shall fight proudly for peace
Along with the progressive forces of the
  world.

PATRON SAINT

Immaculate Heart of Mary

CURRENCY

Angolan kwanza

INTERNET IDENTIFIER

.ao

VEHICLE IDENTIFICATION PLATES/STICKERS

ANG

PASSPORT

The passport cover has the name of the republic in Portuguese, the coat of arms, and the word *passport* in Portuguese.

AIRLINE

Linhas Aéreas de Angola (TAAG Air Angola)

NATIONAL FLOWER

Begonia poculifera (unofficial)

NATIONAL TREE

Mangrove (unofficial)

NATIONAL ANIMAL

Giant sable antelope

NATIONAL RESOURCES

Natural resources include petroleum, diamonds, iron ore, phosphates, copper, feldspar, gold, bauxite, and uranium. Petroleum has become the primary income earner for the Angolan state, although much of Angola's reserves are located in the disputed region of Cabinda*.

FOODS

Muamba de galinha, chicken prepared in a red palm oil sauce, is the national dish. Other national dishes include *calulu,* a thick porridge served with either meat or fish; *funge,* a dish resembling polenta made of pounded cassava; *farofa,* a pudding made of yams; *mufete of kakusso,* tilapia in sauce; *cafréal de galinha,* a chicken dish with ginger, cloves, coriander, cinnamon, garlic, and chilies; and *kizaka,* a stew made of fish and peanuts.

SPORTS/SPORTS TEAMS

Association football (soccer) and basketball are both very popular in Angola. Angola national teams participate in many sports at an international level.

TEAM SPORTS

Basketball

Angola Basketball Team; Angola Women's Basketball Team

Football

Angola Football Team, nickname Palancas Negras (the Black Antelopes); Angola Under-23 Football Team, nickname Palanquinhas (the Young Antelopes); Angola Under-20 Football Team, nickname Palanquinhas (the Young Antelopes); Angola Under-17 Football Team, nickname Palanquinhas (the Young Antelopes); Angola Futsal Team

Handball

Angola Handball Team; Angola Women's Handball Team

Table Tennis

Angola Table Tennis Team

Tennis

Angola Davis Cup Team

Volleyball

Angola Men's Beach Volleyball Team; Angola Men's Volleyball Team; Angola Women's Volleyball Team

INDIVIDUAL SPORTS

Angola Amateur Boxing Team; Angola Athletics Team; Angola Canoeing Team; Angola Cycling Team; Angola Gymnastics Team; Angola Rowing Team; Angola Sailing Team; Angola Shooting Team; Angola Swim Team; Angola Tae Kwon Do Team; Angola Weight Lifting Team

National Heroes or Personifications

Agostinho Neto, leader of the independence movement and first president of Angola; José Eduardo dos Santos, nationalist leader and second president; Jonas Malheiro Savimbi, nationalist leader and leader of the anticommunist rebel movement until 2002

National Holiday/Independence Day

Independence Day, November 11

Festivals/Fairs

Carnival is the largest yearly festival.

Significant Events in Formation of National Identity

Sixth century C.E.–ninth century C.E. Bantu peoples, part of the great Bantu migrations, arrive in present Angola. The migrations continue over centuries, with each group taking on ethnic characteristics that mostly persist to the present.

13th century The largest and most important of the several Bantu kingdoms, the Kingdom of Congo, or Kongo, develops in the 13th century and is a major power in the region. Kongo's wealth comes from agriculture, minerals, and from slaves.

1482 A Portuguese expedition visits the region. Other expeditions follow, and close economic and diplomatic relations are established between Kongo and Portugal.

1575 The Portuguese colony of Angola is founded with the arrival of 100 families of colonists and 400 soldiers.

17th century–19th century Slaves from Angola become essential to the development of the Portuguese colony of Brazil*. Slavery was always present in the region, but the insatiable demands of the Portuguese disrupt a wide region of southwestern Africa as slave raids extend ever farther into the interior.

1764–1844 From 1764, there is a gradual change from a slave-based society to one based on production for domestic use. The slave trade is abolished in 1836, and Angola's ports open to foreign shipping in 1844.

1884–1885 The Berlin Conference of colonial powers formalizes European claims in Africa. Cabinda, divided from Angola by Belgian territory, is added to the colony despite its geographical separation.

20th century Portugal* becomes a republic and extends many of the reforms taking place in Europe to its overseas colonies. The practices of land expropriation and forced labor are outlawed. Changes in the administration allow some Angolans access to education and advancement.

1933 The establishment of a dictatorship in Portugal in 1933 again changes the status of Angola from a colony to a province of Portugal.

1951–1961 The appearance of nationalist movements in the 1950s quickly disrupts the region. Demands for civil rights lead to demands for outright independence. An armed uprising begins a conflict known as the Colonial War in 1961.

1974 A revolution in Portugal is followed by democratic reforms, including freedom for Portugal's colonial empire. A mass exodus of the civilian Portuguese population adds to the chaos. After many years of conflict, unprepared Angola is granted independence on November 11, 1975, with a government made up of the three largest independence movements based on the three largest ethnic groups.

1975–2002 The Angolan coalition quickly breaks down, and civil war spreads across the country. Many of the combatants are children pressed into service by the various military factions. As many as 1.5 million people die in the violence between 1975 and 2002, when the war ends with the death of the opposition UNITA leader Jonas Savimbi.

2002–2009 Angola's economy, following the end of the civil war, becomes one of the fastest growing in the world. Driven by oil exports, which reach 1.4 million barrels in 2007, Angola undergoes a rapid transformation, although it still faces huge social and economic problems as a result of almost continual war since 1961. The

Madeira

Malawi

Malaysia

Maldives

Mali

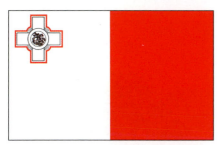

Malta

Marshall Islands

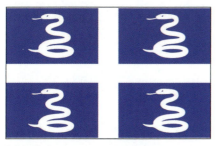

Martinique

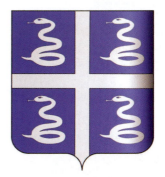

Mauritania

Mauritius

Mayotte

Mexico

Micronesia

Moldova

Monaco

Mongolia

Montenegro

Montserrat

Morocco

Mozambique

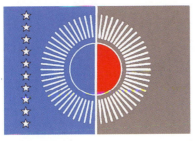

Mthwakazi

No Coat of Arms Available

Myanmar

Nagaland

Namibia

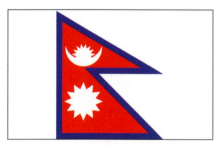

Nauru

Nepal

Netherlands

Netherlands Antilles

Nevis

New Caledonia

New Zealand

Nicaragua

Niger

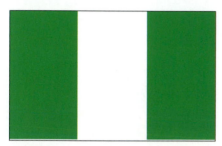

Nigeria

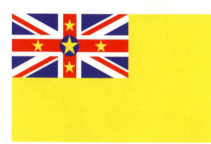

Niue

Norfolk Island

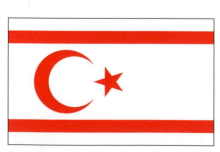

Northern Cyprus

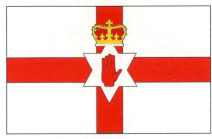

Northern Ireland

Northern Mariana Islands

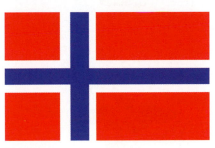

Norway

Oman

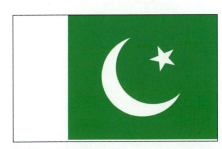

Pakistan

Palau

Palestine

Panama

Papua New Guinea

Paraguay

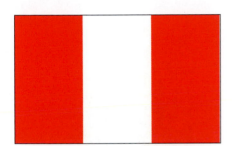

Peru

Philippines

Pitcairn

Poland

Portugal

Puerto Rico

Qatar

Quebec

Reunion

Romania

Russia

Rwanda

Sahrawi

Saint Barthelemy

Saint Helena

Saint Kitts and Nevis

Saint Lucia

Saint Maarten

Saint Martin

Saint Pierre and Miquelon

Saint Vincent and the Grenadines

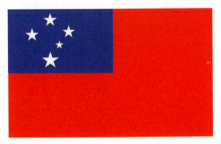

Samoa

San Marino

Santa Cruz

Sâo Tomé and Príncipe

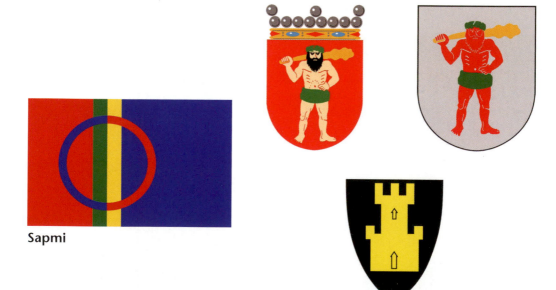

Sapmi

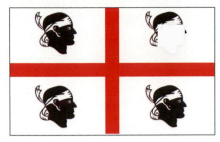

Sardinia

Saudi Arabia

Scania

Scotland

Senegal

Serbia

Seychelles

Sierra Leone

Singapore

Slovakia

Slovenia

Solomon Islands

Somalia

Somaliland

No Coat of Arms Available

South Africa

South Africa

Southern Sudan

No Coat of Arms Available

South Ossetia

Spain

Sri Lanka

Sudan

Suriname

Swaziland

Sweden

Switzerland

Syria

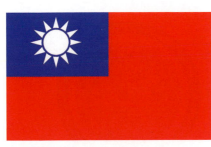

Taiwan

Tajikistan

Tamil Eelam

Tanzania

Tatarstan

Thailand

Tibet

Togo

Tokelau

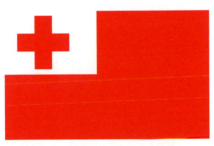

Tonga

Transnistria

Trinidad and Tobago

Tunisia

Turkey

Turkmenistan

Turks and Caicos Islands

Tuva

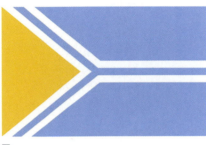

Tuvalu

Uganda

Ukraine

United Arab Emirates

United Kingdom

United States

Uruguay

Uzbekistan

Vanuatu

Vatican City

Venezuela

Vietnam

Virgin Islands

Wales

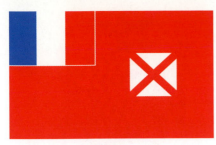 

Wallis and Futuna

Wallonia

West Papua

Yemen

Zambia

Zanzibar

Zimbabwe

Zulia

oil-producing region, Cabinda, continues to be destabilized by the activities of a number of nationalist organizations seeking to detach the territory from Angola.

BENIN

OFFICIAL NAME
République du Bénin (French); Republic of Benin (English)

POPULATION
10,098,500 (2009e)

INHABITANTS' NAME/NICKNAME
Beninese

LANGUAGE/LANGUAGES
French (official); Fon, Yoruba, other regional languages

RELIGION/RELIGIONS
Roman Catholic, 45 percent; Muslim, 24.5 percent; Vodoun, 17 percent; Celestial, 5 percent; Methodist, 3.5 percent; other or no religion

NATIONAL FLAG
The flag is a yellow over red bicolor on the fly with a broad vertical green stripe at the hoist. The colors are the traditional pan-African colors. Green symbolizes hope and a new spring, yellow stands for wealth and the future, and red symbolizes courage and the courage of the ancestors.

COAT OF ARMS/SEAL
At the top of the emblem are two horns filled with corn and sand, symbolizing prosperity. The central crest or shield is quartered, depicting the local Somba fortress, the medal of the Order of the Star of Benin, a palm tree, and a sailing ship. Two leopards support the shield. Below the shield is a white banner inscribed with the national motto in French.

MOTTO
Fraternité, justice, travail (French); Fellowship, Justice, Labor (English)

CAPITAL CITY
Porto Novo; Cotonou is the seat of government

TYPE OF GOVERNMENT
Multiparty democracy

NATIONAL EMBLEM
Somba *tata* (Somba fort-houses)

NATIONAL COLORS
Yellow, red, and green

NATIONAL ANTHEM
The anthem was adopted by the newly independent Republic of Dahomey in 1960 and was retained when the name of the country was changed to Benin. The chorus is usually sung on its own without accompaniment.

L'Aube Nouvelle (French); The Dawn of a New Day (English)

Formerly, at her call, our ancestors
Knew how to engage in mighty battles
With strength, courage, ardor, and full of joy,
    but at the price of blood.
Builders of the present, you, too, join forces
Each day for the task stronger in unity.
Build without ceasing for posterity.

Chorus

Children of Benin, arise!
The resounding cry of freedom
Is heard at the first light of dawn,
Children of Benin, arise!

When all around there blows a wind of anger
    and hate:
Citizen of Benin be proud, and with calm spirit
Trusting in the future, behold your flag!
In the green you read hope of spring;
The red signifies the courage of your
    ancestors;
The yellow foretells the greatest treasures.

Chorus

Beloved Benin, your sunny mountains, palm
  trees, and green pastures
Show everywhere your brightness;
Your soil offers everyone the richest fruits.
Benin, from henceforth your sons are united
With one brotherly spirit sharing the hope of
  seeing you
Enjoy abundance and happiness forever.

CURRENCY

CFA franc

INTERNET IDENTIFIER

.bj

VEHICLE IDENTIFICATION PLATES/STICKERS

DY

PASSPORT

The passport cover has the name of the country in French, the coat of arms, and the word *passport* in French.

AIRLINE

Benin Golf Air

NATIONAL TREE

Palm

NATIONAL ANIMAL

Leopard

NATIONAL RESOURCES

Small offshore oil deposits, limestone, marble, and timber are the major natural resources. Benin plans to attract more foreign investment, place more emphasis on tourism, facilitate the development of new food processing systems and agricultural products, and encourage new information and communication technology. The privatization policy should continue in telecommunications, water, electricity, and agriculture, in spite of initial government reluctance.

FOODS

Kuli-kuli, deep-fried peanut sticks, are considered the national dish. Other national specialties include *riz au gras* (fat rice), a rice dish with chicken or meat, cloves, chilies, tomatoes, and tomato purée; *akassa,* a thick cornmeal porridge; *crabe Béninoise,* a dish of hard-boiled eggs, onions, crab meat, chilies, and tomatoes; *moyo de poulet fume,* smoked chicken; and *riz jollof,* a dish of rice and black-eyed peas with vegetables and chilies.

SPORTS/SPORTS TEAMS

Association football (soccer) is the most popular sport in Benin. Traditional sports, such as wrestling and canoeing, are also very popular. Benin national teams participate in many sports at an international level.

TEAM SPORTS

Football

Benin Football Team, nickname Les Écureuils (the Squirrels); Benin Women's Football Team, nickname Les Écureuils (the Squirrels); Benin Under-20 Football Team; Benin Rugby Union Team

Table Tennis

Benin Table Tennis Team

Tennis

Benin Davis Cup Team

Volleyball

Benin Men's Volleyball Team; Benin Women's Volleyball Team

INDIVIDUAL SPORTS

Benin Amateur Boxing Team; Benin Archery Team; Benin Athletics Team; Benin Cycling Team; Benin Judo Team; Benin Karate Team; Benin Swim Team; Benin Tae Kwon Do Team; Benin Weight Lifting Team

National Heroes or Personifications

Sourou Apithy, Hubert Maga, and Justin Ahomadegbé are considered the nation's heroes. Each of them representing a different area and ethnicity of the country, they agreed to form a presidential council after violence marred the postindependence period in Benin. They were overthrown in 1972, and a Marxist dictatorship was established. Wegbaja, the third king of Dahomey in the mid-17th century, is revered for expanding the kingdom and developing an advanced bureaucracy and a political culture that remains to the present; She-Dong-Hong-Beh, the leader of the famed Amazons, the king of Dahomey's female army in the 18th century.

National Holiday/Independence Day

National Day, August 1

Festivals/Fairs

National Arts and Cultural Festival, November; Vodoun Festival, February

Significant Events in Formation of National Identity

1650 C.E. The Dahomey kingdom, the predecessor of modern Benin, is established. Wegbaja declares himself king of the new state.

17th century Wegbaja and his successors create a highly centralized kingdom with a kingship cult often involving sacrificial offerings of captives taken in war.

17th century–18th century European contacts increase after the first voyages of discovery in the 16th century. Slavery becomes the mainstay of the economy, leading to the region becoming known as the Slave Coast.

1708–1732 Under King Agadja, the Dahomey kingdom expands to the coast, coming into direct contact with European slave traders.

1725–1800 War between Dahomey and Oyo to the east, Dahomey's main rival in the slave trade, ends with Dahomey becoming a vassal state of Oyo in about 1730.

1890 The French lay claim to Dahomey, setting off the First Franco-Dahomean War. Territories around Dahomey fell to French rule, but Dahomey remains a potent force and quickly rearms with modern weapons in anticipation of a second conflict with France*.

1892–1894 The Second Franco-Dahomean War ends with the French conquest of the kingdom.

1899 In 1899, Dahomey is integrated into the French West Africa colony. Dahomey maintains its traditions under French rule.

1957–1960 The decolonization of Africa, beginning in the late 1950s, gives rise to nationalist movements. In 1958, France grants autonomy to the Republic of Dahomey, Full independence is achieved in 1960.

1960–1972 Ethnic conflicts and instability plague the new republic, including several coups and regime changes. Three main political figures, Sourou Apithy, Hubert Maga, and Justin Ahomadegbé, each representing a different area and ethnic group, agree to form a presidential council after violence mars the 1970 elections.

1972–1989 Two years later, in 1972, a coup led by Mathieu Kérékou overthrows the council, and a Marxist state was proclaimed. In 1975, the name of the country is changed to the People's Republic of Benin. In the late 1980s, Kérékou abandons Marxism as unworkable. He decides to reestablish a parliamentary political system with a capitalist economy.

1991–2001 In 1991, Kérékou is defeated in presidential elections and becomes the first black African president to peacefully step down following an election.

2006 The 2006 elections are considered remarkably free and fair. The success of the multiparty elections in Benin wins high praise from the international community.

2008 In February, U.S. President George W. Bush and First Lady Laura Bush visit Benin, the first head of state of a major power to visit the tiny republic. The visit singles out Benin as a successful democracy, even though the country remains one of the poorest in Africa.

2009 The north-south divide, a legacy of arbitrary colonial boundaries, continues to disrupt the country, as political parties and other institutions normally split along the ethnic divide.

BOTSWANA

OFFICIAL NAME

Lefatshe la Botswana (Setswana); Republic of Botswana (English)

POPULATION

1,914,800 (2009e)

INHABITANTS' NAME/NICKNAME

Botswanan(s)

LANGUAGE/LANGUAGES

Setswana (national); English (official); Kalanga, Sekgalagadi, others

RELIGION/RELIGIONS

Protestant, 51 percent; Roman Catholic, 7 percent; Badimo, 6 percent; indigenous religions, Hindu, Muslim, other or no religion

NATIONAL FLAG

The flag is a pale blue field bearing a horizontal black stripe centered and outlined in white. The blue symbolizes water, specifically rain, which comes from the national motto. The white and black stand for racial harmony.

COAT OF ARMS/SEAL

The shape of the shield is rather strange, as it is a shape used in East Africa and not by the Tswana tribes. The cogwheels symbolize mining and industry in the country. The waves symbolize the (few) rivers in the country and the importance of water. The bull's head symbolizes the importance of cattle herding for the economy of the country. The supporters are two zebras (*Equus zebra*), which are common among the wildlife in Botswana. The supporters hold an elephant's tusk, as a symbol for the former ivory trade, and an ear of sorghum, the main local crop.

MOTTO

Pula (Setswana); Rain, or Let there be rain (English)

CAPITAL CITY

Gaborone

TYPE OF GOVERNMENT

Parliamentary republic

NATIONAL EMBLEM

Zebra

NATIONAL COLORS

Pale blue, black, and white

NATIONAL ANTHEM

The national anthem was adopted at independence in 1966.

Fatshe leno la rona (Setswana); Blessed Be This Noble Land (English)

Blessed be this noble land,
Gift to us from God's strong hand,
Heritage our fathers left to us.
May it always be at peace.

Chorus

Awake, awake, O men, awake!
And women close beside them stand,
Together we'll work and serve
This land, this happy land!
Word of beauty and of fame,
The name Botswana to us came.
Through our unity and harmony,
We'll remain at peace as one.

PATRON SAINT

Mary, on the Feast of her Assumption, is the patron saint of southern Africa.

CURRENCY
Botswanan pula

INTERNET IDENTIFIER
.bw

VEHICLE IDENTIFICATION PLATES/STICKERS
RB

PASSPORT
The passport cover has the name of the country in Setswana and English, the coat of arms, and the word *passport* in Setswana and English.

AIRLINE
Air Botswana

NATIONAL FLOWER
Mowana flower (unofficial)

NATIONAL TREE
Mowana (baobab) (unofficial)

NATIONAL ANIMAL
Burchell's zebra

NATIONAL BIRD
Lilac-breasted roller

NATIONAL FISH
Tiger fish (unofficial)

NATIONAL RESOURCES
Natural resources include diamonds, copper, nickel, salt, soda ash, potash, coal, iron ore, and silver. Botswana has had one of the fastest growth rates in per capita income in the world and has transformed itself from one of the poorest countries in the world to a middle-income country with a per capita GDP of $11,200 in 2006. Diamonds remain the most important export. Tourism is also becoming popular because of the country's ethnic cultures, herds of wild animals, and scenery.

FOODS
Seswaai, a soft salted pounded meat similar to a soft jerky, is considered the national dish. Other national dishes include *bogobe,* a cornmeal porridge, often accompanied by a meat stew, cabbage, spinach, wild greens, or beans; chicken and groundnut stew; chicken and lamb pies, pastries with meat and vegetables; *diphaphta,* a type of fried muffin; *phane,* a stew of *mopane* worms, onions, bell peppers, tomatoes, curry, and chilies; *potjie,* a vegetable stew; and rice balls.

SPORTS/SPORTS TEAMS
The most popular sport is association football (soccer), while other popular sports include cricket, tennis, rugby union, softball, athletics, and volleyball. Botswana national teams participate in many sports at an international level.

TEAM SPORTS

Badminton
Botswana Badminton Team

Baseball
Botswana Softball Team

Basketball
Botswana Basketball Team; Botswana Women's Basketball Team

Cricket
Botswana Cricket Team

Football
Botswana Football Team, nickname the Zebras; Botswana Women's Football Team nickname, the Zebras; Botswana Under-20 Football Team, nickname the Young Zebras; Botswana Rugby Union Team, nickname

the Vultures; Botswana Rugby Union Team (Sevens), nickname Botswana Sevens or Botswana 7s

Hockey

Botswana Field Hockey Team

Netball

Botswana Netball Team

Table Tennis

Botswana Table Tennis Team

Tennis

Botswana Fed Cup Team; Botswana Davis Cup Team

Volleyball

Botswana Men's Volleyball Team; Botswana Women's Volleyball Team

INDIVIDUAL SPORTS

Botswana Amateur Boxing Team; Botswana Athletics Team; Botswana Chess Team; Botswana Equestrian Team; Botswana Fencing Team; Botswana Judo Team; Botswana Swim Team

NATIONAL HEROES OR PERSONIFICATIONS

Unity Dow, a noted lawyer, women's rights activist, and first female High Court judge in Botswana; Seretse Khama, a leader of the independence movement and first president of independent Botswana

NATIONAL HOLIDAY/ INDEPENDENCE DAY

Independence Day/Botswana Day, September 30

FESTIVALS/FAIRS

Eisteddfod, an annual festival of school choirs and traditional dance groups; Maitisong Festival, April

SIGNIFICANT EVENTS IN FORMATION OF NATIONAL IDENTITY

1000 B.C.E.–600 C.E. The earliest inhabitants are the San, sometimes called Bushmen. A Bantu people, the ancestors of the Tswana, settle the region as part of the great Bantu migrations.

19th century Encroachments by Zulus and Ndebeles, and later the expansion of the Boers into the region, disrupt tribal life. After appeals by the leaders for assistance, the British Government declares "Bechuanaland" under its protection in 1895.

1910–1961 When the Union of South Africa is formed in 1910 out of the main British colonies in southern Africa, the Bechuanaland Protectorate, Basutoland (now Lesotho*), and Swaziland* are not included. The election of the National Party government in 1948, which institutes apartheid, and South Africa's withdrawal from the Commonwealth in 1961 end any prospect of incorporation of the territories into South Africa. Proclamations in 1934 regularize tribal rule and powers. A European-African advisory council is formed in 1951, and the 1961 constitution establishes a consultative legislative council.

1964 In June 1964, Britain accepts official proposals for democratic self-government in Botswana. The seat of government is moved from Mafikeng in South Africa to newly established Gaborone in 1965. Seretse Khama, a leader of the independence movement, is elected as the first president of independent Botswana.

1981–2001 Botswana's economic outlook continues to improve, based on diamond exports but also on new industries and agriculture. The advent of AIDS threatens to destroy the country's future. In 2001, Botswana has the highest rate of HIV infection in the world. By 2004, the government's ambitious national campaign sharply reduces new cases and provides medication for any citizen who needs it, but the country remains on the edge of catastrophe due to the large number of people infected before the campaign.

2008 After serving 10 years as deputy president, Ian Khama, the son of the country's first president, is inaugurated as head of state.

2009 Botswana's democratic government and diversified economy allow the country to prosper in spite of the world economic slump. The large numbers of refugees from Zimbabwe in the country are a drain on finances and a source of insecurity.

BURKINA FASO

OFFICIAL NAME
Burkina Faso

POPULATION
14,397,300 (2009e)

INHABITANTS' NAME/NICKNAME
Burkinabè; Burkinabe (English)

LANGUAGE/LANGUAGES
French (official); local languages

RELIGION/RELIGIONS
Muslim, 50 percent; indigenous beliefs, 20–40 percent; Roman Catholic, 10 percent; Protestant, other or no religion

NATIONAL FLAG
The flag is a red over green bicolor bearing a centered, five-pointed yellow star. The colors are the popular Pan-African colors adopted from the Ethiopian flag. The red represents the country's revolutionary struggle, the green represents hope and abundance, and the yellow star represents the country' mineral wealth.

COAT OF ARMS/SEAL
The coat of arms has a central shield based on the national flag in front of two crossed lances, which symbolize of the Burkinabe determination to protect their country. Above the shield is a silver banner with the name of the country, and below is another banner with the national motto, an open book, and millet stalks. The supports are two white stallions, symbolizing the nobility of the Burkinabe people.

MOTTO
Unité, progrès, justice (French); Unity, Progress, Justice (English)

CAPITAL CITY
Ouagadougou

TYPE OF GOVERNMENT
Semipresidential republic

NATIONAL EMBLEM
White stallion

NATIONAL COLORS
Green and red

NATIONAL ANTHEM
The anthem, also called "Une Seule Nuit (One Single Night)," was adopted when the country changed its name from Upper Volta to Burkina Faso in 1984.

Le Ditanye (French); Anthem of Victory (English)

Against the humiliating bondage of a thou-
  sand years
Rapacity came from afar to subjugate them
  for a hundred years.
Against the cynical malice in the shape
Of neocolonialism and its petty local servants.
Many gave in and certain others resisted.
But the frustrations, the successes, the sweat,
  the blood
Have fortified our courageous people and fer-
  tilized its heroic struggle.

Chorus

And one single night has drawn together
The history of an entire people,
And one single night has launched its trium-
  phal march.
Toward the horizon of good fortune.
One single night has brought together our
  people

With all the peoples of the world,
In the acquisition of liberty and progress.
Motherland or death, we shall conquer.

Nourished in the lively source of the
Revolution,
The volunteers for liberty and peace
With their nocturnal and beneficial energies of
the fourth of August
Had not only hand arms, but also and above
all
The flame in their hearts lawfully to free
Faso forever from the fetters of those who
Here and there were polluting the sacred soul
of independence and sovereignty.

Chorus

And seated henceforth in rediscovered dignity,
Love and honor partnered with humanity,
The people of Burkina sing a victory hymn
To the glory of the work of liberation and
emancipation.
Down with exploitation of man by man!
Forward for the good of every man
By all men of today and tomorrow, by every
man here and always!

Chorus

Popular revolution our nourishing sap.
Undying motherhood of progress in the face
of man.
Eternal hearth of agreed democracy,
Where at last national identity has the right of
freedom.
Where injustice has lost its place forever,
And where from the hands of builders of a
glorious world
Everywhere the harvests of patriotic vows
ripen and suns of boundless joy shine.

PATRON SAINT

The Immaculate Conception is the patron of
the Archdiocese of Ouagadougou

CURRENCY

CFA franc

INTERNET IDENTIFIER

.bf

VEHICLE IDENTIFICATION PLATES/STICKERS

BF

PASSPORT

The passport cover has the flag of the country,
in color, at the top; the name of the country; the coat of arms, in color; and the word
passport in French.

AIRLINE

Air Burkina

NATIONAL FLOWER

Hibiscus sabdariffa (unofficial)

NATIONAL ANIMAL

White stallion (shown on the coat of arms)

NATIONAL RESOURCES

Natural resources include manganese,
limestone, marble, small deposits of gold,
phosphates, pumice, salt, and arable land.
Burkina Faso is one of the world's poorest
countries, leading to emigration of many
Burkinabe, especially to neighboring Cote
d'Ivoire*. Remittances from these emigrants
are one of the major sources of hard cash
in the country. A large part of the economic
activity of the country is funded by international aid.

FOODS

Riz gras, a rice dish with meat or chicken
with vegetables, is considered the national
dish. The main staple food is *tô,* a kind of
paste prepared with millet or corn flour.
It is eaten lukewarm and accompanied by
a sauce. Other specialties include *maan
nezim nzedo,* a fish and vegetable stew;
manyu caf, a dish of couscous, meat, peanut butter, onion, tomatoes, cabbage, and
eggplant; and *banji* (palm wine), made of
fermented palm sap, is considered the national drink.

SPORTS/SPORTS TEAMS

Association football (soccer) is the country's most popular sport. Burkina Faso national teams participate in many sports at an international level.

TEAM SPORTS

Baseball

Burkina Faso Baseball Team; Burkina Faso Softball Team

Basketball

Burkina Faso Basketball Team; Burkina Faso Women's Basketball Team

Football

Burkina Faso Football Team, nickname Les Etalons (the Stallions); Burkina Faso Women's Football Team; Burkina Faso Under-20 Football Team

Table Tennis

Burkina Faso Table Tennis Team

Tennis

Burkina Faso Davis Cup Team

Volleyball

Burkina Faso Volleyball Team

INDIVIDUAL SPORTS

Burkina Faso Amateur Boxing Team; Burkina Faso Athletics Team; Burkina Faso Canoeing Team; Burkina Faso Cycling Team; Burkina Faso Fencing Team; Burkina Faso Judo Team; Burkina Faso Rowing Team; Burkina Faso Swim Team; Burkina Faso Tae Kwon Do Team; Burkina Faso Weight Lifting Team

NATIONAL HEROES OR PERSONIFICATIONS

Norbert Zongo, a journalist murdered in December 1998; Thomas Sankara, a popular hero of the 1975 frontier war with Mali who took power in 1983 and instituted many reforms, including changing the name of the country, before his death in 1987 in yet another coup d'état.

NATIONAL HOLIDAY/INDEPENDENCE DAY

Republic Day, December 11

FESTIVALS/FAIRS

Pan-African Film and Television Festival (FESPACO), February–March; National Culture Week, biannually in December; Panafrican Film and Television Festival, biannually February-March.

SIGNIFICANT EVENTS IN FORMATION OF NATIONAL IDENTITY

1000 B.C.E.–600 C.E. Settled farmers replace the hunter-gatherer societies that first populated the region.

15th century–16th century Burkina Faso is a very important economic region for the Songhai Empire.

1885–1898 After a decade of intense rivalry between the British and French colonial forces, the Mossi kingdom of Ouagadougou is defeated by the French and becomes a protectorate. By 1898, the majority of the territory of modern Burkina Faso is under French rule.

1904 The territories are integrated into French West Africa with its capital at Bamako, now in Mali*.

1915–1916 During the First World War, a serious rebellion erupts as French troops are withdrawn to Europe.

1919–1932 The region, called Haute Volta, becomes a separate territory. The colony fails, and in 1932, the territory is divided among neighboring colonies, the largest share going to Cote d'Ivoire.

1946–1958 The decision to dismantle Haute Volta is reversed at the end of the Second World War, and the colony is recreated. Haute Volta achieves self-government in 1958.

1960 Haute Volta, know in English as Upper Volta, is granted full independence in 1960.

Instability and ethnic conflicts lead to a series of coups.

1983–1987 A countercoup in 1983 brings the charismatic Thomas Sankara to the leadership of the country, His reforms are popular, although many are wary of close ties to radical states such as Cuba* and Libya*. Sankara is killed in yet another coup in 1987. He is revered as a national hero.

1987–1991 Blaise Compaoré, who came to power in 1987, introduces a semipresidential government with a parliament in 1991.

2008–2009 Burkina Faso has one of the lowest per capita incomes in the world at just $1,200. The country ranks as the 28th poorest in world rankings. Agriculture still accounts for 32 percent of its exports and occupies 80 percent of the country's population. In August 2009, the worst flooding in the nation's history leaves over 150,000 homeless.

BURUNDI

Official Name
Republika y'u Burundi (Kirundi); Republique du Burundi (French); Republic of Burundi (English)

Population
8,733,400 (2009e)

Inhabitants' Name/Nickname
Burundian(s)

Language/Languages
Kirundi, French (both official); Swahili (along Lake Tanganyika and in the Bujumbura area), others

Religion/Religions
Roman Catholic, 62 percent; Animist, 22 percent; Muslim, 8–10 percent; Protestant, 5 percent; indigenous beliefs, other or no religion

National Flag
The flag is divided by a white diagonal cross into red panels (top and bottom) and green panels (hoist and fly) with a white disk superimposed at the center, bearing three red, six-pointed stars outlined in green arranged in a triangular design, with one star above and two stars below. The three stars stand for the three major ethnic groups, the Hutu, the Tutsi, and the Twa. They also represent the three elements of the national motto.

Coat of Arms/Seal
The coat of arms of Burundi, adopted in 1966, consists of a shield surrounded by three spears. Below the shield is the motto of the nation, and on the red shield is the yellow and black head of a lion. Behind the shield are three crossed traditional African spears.

Motto
Unité, travail, progrès (French); Unity, Work, Progress (English)

Capital City
Bujumbura

Type of Government
Republic

National Emblem
Leopard's head

National Colors
Red and green

National Anthem
The anthem, adopted at independence in 1962, has two official versions, in Kirundi and in French.

> **Burundi bwacu (Kirundi); Our Beloved Burundi (English)**
>
> Beloved Burundi, gentle country,
> Take your place in the concert of nations,
> Acceding to independence with honorable
>   intentions.
> Wounded and bruised, you have remained
>   master of yourself.

When the hour came, you arose,
Lifting yourself proudly into the ranks of free
    peoples.
Receive, then, the congratulations of the
    nations
And the homage of your sons.
May your name ring out through the
    universe.

Beloved Burundi, sacred heritage from our
    forefathers,
Recognized as worthy of self-government,
With your courage you also have a sense of
    honor.
Sing the glory of liberty conquered again.

Beloved Burundi, worthy of our most tender
    love,
We vow to your noble service our hands and
    hearts and lives.
May God, who gave you to us, keep you for
    us to venerate,
Under the shield of unity,
In peace, joy, and prosperity.

PATRON SAINT

Regina Mundi, Mary, Queen of the World,
is the patron of the archdioceses of Bujumbura.

CURRENCY

Burundi franc

INTERNET IDENTIFIER

.bi

VEHICLE IDENTIFICATION PLATES/STICKERS

BU

PASSPORT

The passport cover has the name of the
country in Kirundi and French, the coat of
arms, and the word for passport in Kirundi
and French.

NATIONAL ANIMAL

Cattle (unofficial). The Tutsi are historically
a herding people. Cows, therefore, hold a
great deal of symbolic power in the culture.
A typical Kirundi greeting, *Amashyo,* translates as "May you have many cattle."

NATIONAL BIRD

Wagtail (official); *hirondelle* (swallow)
(unofficial)

NATIONAL RESOURCES

Natural resources include nickel, uranium,
rare earth oxides, peat, cobalt, copper, platinum, vanadium, niobium, tantalum, gold,
tin, tungsten, kaolin, and limestone. Other
assets include arable land and potential hydropower. One of the poorest countries in
the world, over 90 percent of the population is engaged in agriculture. International
aid is one of the major sources of hard
currency.

FOODS

Fufu, a thick cornmeal porridge, served with
meat, vegetables, or sauces, is considered the
national dish. Typical dishes include *boko
boko harees,* a dish of chicken and bulgur
wheat; *ibiharage,* Burundian fried beans;
maharggwe, a dish of potatoes, beans, tomatoes, cabbage or spinach, onions, and
spices; *soupe aux lentilles et legumes,* a soup
of sweet potato, carrots, onion, cabbage, lentils, and beans; and *matura* and *mahu,* a dish
of beef, onions, garlic, and chilies.

SPORTS/SPORTS TEAMS

Athletics, basketball, and association football (soccer) are the most popular sports.
Burundi national teams participate in many
sports at an international level.

TEAM SPORTS

Badminton

Burundi Badminton Team

Basketball

Burundi Basketball Team; Burundi Women's
Basketball Team

Football

Burundi Football Team, nickname Les Hirondelles (the Swallows) or Itamba; Burundi Women's Football Team, nickname Les Hirondelles (the Swallows); Burundi Rugby Union Team; Burundi Women's Rugby Union Team (Sevens), nickname Burundi Women's Sevens or 7s

Table Tennis

Burundi Table Tennis Team

Volleyball

Burundi Men's Volleyball Team; Burundi Women's Volleyball Team

INDIVIDUAL SPORTS

Burundi Amateur Boxing Team; Burundi Athletics Team; Burundi Canoeing Team; Burundi Cycling Team; Burundi Judo Team; Burundi Swim Team

NATIONAL HEROES OR PERSONIFICATIONS

Prince Louis Rwagasore, a leader of the pro-independence movement in the 1950s, assassinated in 1961, possibly by an agent working for Belgian interests; Ntara Rugamba, the 19th century king who expanded the country's borders by conquest; Melchior Ndadaye, the country's first democratically elected president, in 1993, and the first ethnic Hutu to hold the office; King Mwezi Gisabo, one of the greatest kings of Burundian history.

NATIONAL HOLIDAY/INDEPENDENCE DAY

Independence Day, July 1

FESTIVALS/FAIRS

Independence Day Festival, July; Victory of Uprona Festival, September

SIGNIFICANT EVENTS IN FORMATION OF NATIONAL IDENTITY

1000 B.C.E.–600 C.E.   The earliest people to settle the region are the Pygmy Twa. The Bantu Hutu people, from the mountainous regions of central Africa, take control of the region, forcing the Twa into the heavily forested areas.

3000 B.C.E.–1580 C.E.   The Hutu settle as farmers under a loose system of kingship. Around 1580, a tall, Nilo-Hamitic people, the Tutsi, move into the region with their herds of longhorn cattle.

1580–1750   The Tutsi establish a feudal system within the local Hutu chiefdoms. All Tutsis are considered nobles, while the Hutus are relegated to minding cattle herds, farming, or serving the Tutsi nobility.

1852–1903   King Mwezi IV takes the throne during a time of turmoil. In order to defeat his rivals to the throne, he makes an alliance with the Germans. As a result of the alliance, the Germans declare Burundi a protectorate in 1903.

1918–1924   At the end of World War I, defeated Germany* turns over its central African colonies to Belgium* with Burundi officially becoming part of the Belgian Empire in 1924. The Tutsi dynasty of Burundi is allowed to continue under Belgian guidance.

1946–1959   After World War II, Burundi becomes a United Nations Trust Territory. The Burundi king, in 1959, requests that Belgium separate Burundi from Rwanda* and dissolve the trust territory of Ruanda-Urundi.

1959–1962   Ethnic violence between Hutus and Tutsis in Rwanda enflames tensions in Burundi. Burundi is separated from Rwanda and granted independence. During Burundi's transition to independence, Hutu forces take control.

1962–1966   Thousands of Tutsi flee into Burundi to escape violence in Rwanda. Tutsi soldiers in Burundi kill many Hutus in retaliation for the violence in the neighboring state. The Burundi Civil War results in about 12,000 Tutsi deaths. The monarchy is overthrown in 1966, and a military government takes power.

1972   Fighting spreads across the country, with the Tutsi military fighting Hutu militias and eventually taking retaliation against Hutu civilians. An estimated 250,000 people, mostly Hutus but also many moderate Tutsis, die in the Burundi genocide.

1970s–1980s Under a series of dictatorships, all from the Tutsi minority, ethnic conflict between Tutsis and Hutus continues, leaving thousands dead and wounded.

1990s Reforms in the national army and the government bring a fragile peace that soon turns to renewed coups and violence.

2000 The leading political parties, representing Hutus and Tutsis, sign a peace deal, but the violence continues.

2008–2009 In Burundi, both Hutu and Tutsi civilians have been targets of mass killings and acts of genocide organized by the state and by armed militia groups. The present government is made up of both Hutu and Tutsi, supported by an integrated military. The restoration of a multiethnic, multiparty democracy brings renewed expectations of an end to Burundi's long and bloody ethnic conflict. An estimated 450,000 refugees begin to return to the country.

CABINDA

OFFICIAL NAME

Provincia de Cabinda (Portuguese); Province of Cabinda (English)

Separatist republic: Kilansi Kia Kabinda (Ibinda); República de Cabinda (Portuguese); Republic of Cabinda (English)

POPULATION

398,700 (2009e); An estimated 200,000 Cabindans are refugees living in the neighboring Democratic Republic of Congo* and Republic of Congo*.

INHABITANTS' NAME/NICKNAME

Cabindan(s); Cabindese

LANGUAGE/LANGUAGES

Portuguese, French (both official); Ibinda, Kikongo, other regional languages

Separatist republic: Ibinda, Portuguese (both official)

RELIGION/RELIGIONS

Roman Catholic, 73 percent; Protestant, 2 percent; indigenous beliefs, other or no religion

NATIONAL FLAG

The flag used by the Front for the Liberation of Cabinda (FLEC) is a horizontal tricolor of red, yellow, and pale blue, bearing a centered yellow circle outlined in red around a green triangle, with a centered white, five-pointed star. The flag of the FLEC government-in-exile has blue, yellow, and black horizontal stripes, with the Simulambuco monument centered.

COAT OF ARMS/SEAL

The arms of the Republic of Cabinda are a circle bearing ancient Kongo symbols of man, sun, and moon flanked by two leopards and carved ivory above palm fronds and backed by traditional weapons, a traditional drum, and a headdress. Another nationalist faction uses the yellow circle and white star from the national flag with a banner reading *República de Cabinda* below and green arrows above.

CAPITAL CITY

Cabinda City

TYPE OF GOVERNMENT

Provincial government as a province of Angola*; a government-in-exile (Kinshasa, Congo Democratic Republic/Paris, France) claims Cabinda as a sovereign nation.

NATIONAL EMBLEM

Front for the Liberation of Cabinda (FLEC): a yellow circle with a green triangle, surmounted by a white, five-pointed star; government-in-exile: the monument to the 1885 Simulambuco Treaty on a yellow shield

NATIONAL COLORS

Blue and black

NATIONAL ANTHEM

The official anthem of Cabinda is the Angolan national anthem. The anthem of the nationalists who seek independence is called "Immortal Homeland" in English, but no English translation is available.

N'Kinga Tsi (Ibinda); Patria Imortal (Portuguese); Immortal Homeland (English)

Cabinda Tsi luzitu beni i fwang' a ko
Matondo ma nene beni ma ke mu bana baku
N'vingu n'zingu u nungwang' a ko
Befu boso wa tu n'tchinzin kanga

Mu nana Kumi N'gondi Mweka
Lumbu tchi luzitu lu Bwala
Tu n'vumunna mangolo
Ma n'kuna mona
Wa i dula i phanga

N'doko Bwala
Tu baka lu kuku
Lu tsi i luzitu beni
i ba kulu bitu

Tu kanana, tu budana tu n'liyata va tchimweka
mu n'zingu mu ku ituma
Ku natanaga n'tela mu tchi limbu
Mbwetila mweka i tu nata
Ku lu nungu lu mana

Muna tsi i luzitu beni
Muna Bwala
Twala zimbakana ko
Bi fwila muna n'vita

PATRON SAINT

Saint George

CURRENCY

Angolan kwanza (official); Republic of Cabinda ibinda (separatist republic)

VEHICLE IDENTIFICATION PLATES/STICKERS

ANG Angola (official); RC Republic of Cabinda (unofficial)

PASSPORT

Cabindans are Angolan citizens and travel on Angolan passports. The unrecognized Republic of Cabinda issues passports that have the name of the country in Portuguese and English, the coat of arms, and the word *passport* in Portuguese and English.

NATIONAL ANIMAL

Leopard (unofficial)

NATIONAL RESOURCES

Natural resources include hardwoods, coffee, cacao, rubber, palm oil products, and petroleum, the province's most important export. Petroleum production began in 1968 and now accounts for most of Angola's total output. Cabinda produces over 700,000 barrels of crude oil per day.

FOODS

Funje, a porridge made of cassava flour, served with sauces, vegetables, or meat, is considered the national dish. Cassava leaves (*saka saka*), pounded and cooked, are also considered a national dish. White beans, eaten with rice, *fufu,* a thick porridge made of cassava leaves, or *chikwange,* a cassava loaf prepared in banana leaves, are also considered a national dish in all areas inhabited by ethnic Kongo people. Other specialties include *frango grelhado piri piri,* a spicy grilled chicken; *arroz verde,* a rice dish with greens; *kizaka,* a stew of meat, vegetables, and peanut butter; and *cocada amerela,* a coconut pudding with yellow herbs.

SPORTS/SPORTS TEAMS

Association football (soccer) is the most popular sport in Cabinda. The Cabinda national team participates in football at an international level.

TEAM SPORTS

Football

Cabinda Football Team, nickname the Leopards

NATIONAL HEROES OR PERSONIFICATIONS

Luis Ranque Franque, the president of the FLEC and one of the original leaders of the Cabinda independence movement; Henriques Tiago N'Zita, head of the provisional government of the Federal Republic of Cabinda; Jorge Casimiro Congo, Roman Catholic priest currently imprisoned for denouncing Angolan atrocities in Cabinda

NATIONAL HOLIDAY/INDEPENDENCE DAY

Separatist republic: Independence Day, August 1

SIGNIFICANT EVENTS IN FORMATION OF NATIONAL IDENTITY

14th century C.E.–15th century C.E. Bantu peoples create three separate kingdoms on the north bank of the lower Zaire (Congo) River—Loango, Ngoyo, and Kakongo—as vassal states of the powerful Kongo kingdom.

1535–1575 The Portuguese establish a slave trading station at Cabinda.

17th century The kingdoms, visited by European explorers and traders in the 1620s, expand and consolidate their power. Europeans and their local allies trade in copper, ivory, and, most importantly, slaves.

18th century By 1710, the Kongo state disintegrates under the impact of colonial rule and the accompanying slave trade. The three kingdoms become important commercial centers,

1883–1885 Portuguese soldiers occupy the region north of the Congo River. In 1883, the three European powers demarcate and formalize the partition of the old Kongo kingdom. Cabinda is separated from Portuguese West Africa (Angola) by 25 miles (40 kilometers) of territory belonging to the Belgian Congo. The Portuguese authorities sign several treaties with the three local kings, including the Treaty of Simulambuco, which establish the region as a Portuguese protectorate called the Portuguese Congo.

1886–1933 Administered as a separate colony, Portuguese Congo is the poorest and most ne-

glected of the Portuguese colonies. The 1933 Portuguese Constitution lists Portuguese Congo as a separate colony, distinct from Portuguese West Africa to the south.

1954–1961 Oil exploration begins in Portuguese Congo, which, for financial reasons, is administratively joined to Angola and renamed Cabinda in 1956. Agitation for a resumption of the former separate status causes serious outbursts in the colony and gradually evolves into a nationalist, anticolonial mass movement.

1961–1967 The Cabindans rebuff overtures from Angola's rival national movements, insisting on separation from Angola and an independent Cabinda. In 1964, the Organization of African Unity (OAU) publishes a list of territories still to be decolonized, listing Angola as number 35 and Cabinda as number 39.

1966–1978 Oil is discovered in Cabinda. Despite a growing separatist war, production begins in 1968 and expands dramatically over the next decade.

1974 The government of Portugal*, drained by long and costly colonial wars, is overthrown in a leftist coup in Lisbon. Cabindan leaders petition for separate independence, but Angola's three major nationalist groups all lay claim to Cabinda and its oil wealth. Troops of the Marxist faction, reportedly financed by Chevron Oil, invade and take control of Cabinda.

1975 The new Marxist Angolan government declares it is ready to negotiate a settlement for Cabinda but rejects demands for Cabinda's right to self-determination. On August 1, 1975, Cabindan leaders, in spite of military occupation, declare the enclave independent as the Republic of Cabinda.

1976 Troops are dispatched to end Cabinda's secession and to secure its oil reserves.

1984 The reorganized Cabindan nationalists take up arms against Angolan government installations and foreign oil workers. The nationalist cause is undermined by factional rivalries.

1991 Five Cabindan factions meet in Lisbon in an effort to end divisions and to coordinate the fight for independence.

2000 By 2000, the Cabindans have paid a high price for their dream of independence with over 70,000 dead and up to 300,000 people displaced. Many Portuguese politicians criticize the injustice of the 1975 Alvor Agreement, which left Cabinda to the mercy of Angola's warring factions, and question the legality of Cabinda's inclusion in Angola.

2006 A number of Cabindan factions begin cease-fire negotiations. The government-in-exile in Paris rejects the negotiations and declares that the only acceptable solution is total independence.

2007 The Angolan economy flourishes following the end of the civil war but is highly dependent on Cabindan oil. In October 2007, the Angolan parliament approves "special status" for Cabinda. Cabinda's oil makes Angola the second biggest oil producer in sub-Saharan Africa.

2009 The territory remains under military occupation, leading to continued atrocities. Cabindan leaders continue to contend that the 1885 Treaty of Simulambuco has never been abrogated and remains in force, so that Cabinda is legally still a Portuguese territory and not an integral part of Angola.

See also Angola

CAMEROON

OFFICIAL NAME
République du Cameroun (French); Republic of Cameroon (English)

POPULATION
19,204,500 (2009e)

INHABITANTS' NAME/NICKNAME
Cameroonian(s)

LANGUAGE/LANGUAGES
French, English (both official); Camfranglais (French/English Creole), 24 major African languages, others

RELIGION/RELIGIONS
Indigenous beliefs, 30–40 percent; Christian, 40 percent; Muslim, 20 percent; other or no religion

NATIONAL FLAG
The flag is a vertical tricolor of green, red, and yellow bearing a five-pointed yellow star centered on the red stripe. The center red stripe stands for unity, and the star is referred to as the Star of Unity. The yellow represents the sun and also the savannas in the northern part of the country, while the green symbolizes the forests in the southern provinces.

COAT OF ARMS/SEAL
The coat of arms, called the National Emblem, consists of a shield with the colors of the national flag, a map of the country behind a scale, and above, the Star of Unity. Below the shield is a banner with the name of the country in French (large letters) and English (small letters). Behind the shield are two crossed fasces, representing strength through unity, and above the shield is the national motto in French (large letters) and English (small letters).

MOTTO
Paix—travail—patrie (French); Peace—Work—Fatherland (English)

CAPITAL CITY
Yaoundé

TYPE OF GOVERNMENT
Unitary republic

NATIONAL EMBLEM
Star of Unity

NATIONAL COLORS
Green, red, and yellow

NATIONAL ANTHEM
The anthem was written in 1928 and served as an unofficial anthem from 1948. It became the official anthem when Cameroon became an autonomous state in 1957. There are two official versions, one in French and one in English.

Ô Cameroun, Berceau de nos Ancêtres (French); O Cameroon, Cradle of our Forefathers (English)

O Cameroon, thou Cradle of our Fathers,
Holy Shrine where in our midst they now
  repose,
Their tears and blood and sweat thy soil did
  water,
On thy hills and valleys once their tillage rose.
Dear Fatherland, thy worth no tongue can tell!
How can we ever pay thy due?
Thy welfare we will win in toil and love and
  peace,
Will be to thy name ever true!

Chorus

Land of Promise, land of Glory!
Thou, of life and joy, our only store!
Thine be honor, thine devotion,
And deep endearment, for evermore.

From Shari, from where the Mungo meanders
From along the banks of lowly Boumba
  Stream,
Muster thy sons in union close around thee,
Mighty as the Buea Mountain be their team;
Instill in them the love of gentle ways,
Regret for errors of the past;
Foster, for Mother Africa, a loyalty
That true shall remain to the last.

CURRENCY

CFA franc

INTERNET IDENTIFIER

.cm

VEHICLE IDENTIFICATION PLATES/STICKERS

CAM

PASSPORT

The passport cover has the name of the country in French and English, the coat of arms, and the word *passport* in French and English.

AIRLINE

Elysian Airlines

NATIONAL FLOWER

Gloriosa lily (unofficial)

NATIONAL ANIMAL

Lion (unofficial)

NATIONAL BIRD

Black-shouldered kite (unofficial)

NATIONAL FISH

Pink shrimp (unofficial)

NATIONAL RESOURCES

Natural resources include petroleum, bauxite, iron ore, hydropower, and timber. Fishing is a major industry, including the traditional gathering of prawns. Forest products, such as essences, oils, nuts, fruits, and resins, are an important resource for many people living near the country's rain forests. The forests are now being logged so extensively that many are in danger of disappearing. The petroleum reserves are nearly depleted, with the government looking to the forests for revenue.

FOODS

Kondre, a porridge made of plantains and served with sauce or meat, is the most popular food and is considered the national dish. Other national specialties include *suya,* a dish of beef or lamb, sweet peppers, onions, and spices; *folon,* chicken with greens and onions in peanut sauce; *mbongo tjobi,* fish with a black sauce of herbs and spices; *safou a la sauce tomate,* prunes in a sauce of tomatoes, peanuts, and chilies; *zom,* a stew of beef, onion, spinach, tomatoes, and peanut butter; and *mbanga,* a soup made of palm nuts.

SPORTS/SPORTS TEAMS

Traditional sports, such as canoe racing and wrestling, remain very popular, but the most popular sport is association football (soccer). Cameroon national teams participate in many sports at an international level.

TEAM SPORTS

Badminton

Cameroon Badminton Team

Baseball

Cameroon Baseball Team; Cameroon Softball Team

Basketball

Cameroon Basketball Team; Cameroon Women's Basketball Team; Cameroon Wheelchair Basketball Team

Cricket

Cameroon Cricket Team

Football

Cameroon Football Team, nickname Lions Indomptables (Indomitable Lions); Cameroon Women's Football Team, nickname Lions Indomptables (Indomitable Lionesses); Cameroon Under-23 Football Team, nickname Lions Espoir (the Lion Hopefuls); Cameroon Under-20 Football Team, nickname Lions Junior (the Junior Lions); Cameroon Under-17 Football Team, nickname Lionceaux (the Lion Cubs); Cameroon Women's Under-19 Football Team; Cameroon Rugby Union Team; Cameroon Beach Soccer Team; Cameroon Futsal Team; Cameroon Rugby Union Team (Sevens), nickname Cameroon Sevens or Cameroon 7s

Handball

Cameroon Handball Team; Cameroon Women's Handball Team

Hockey

Cameroon Field Hockey Team

Table Tennis

Cameroon Table Tennis Team

Tennis

Cameroon Davis Cup Team

Volleyball

Cameroon Men's Volleyball Team; Cameroon Women's Volleyball Team

INDIVIDUAL SPORTS

Cameroon Amateur Boxing Team; Cameroon Athletics Team; Cameroon Canoeing Team; Cameroon Cycling Team; Cameroon Equestrian Team; Cameroon Gymnastics Team; Cameroon Judo Team; Cameroon Modern Pentathlon Team; Cameroon Rowing Team; Cameroon Swim Team; Cameroon Tae Kwon Do Team; Cameroon Weight Lifting Team; Cameroon Wrestling Team

NATIONAL HEROES OR PERSONIFICATIONS

Paul Biya, second president of Cameroon who initiated many reforms that aided the country; Marc Vivien Foé, a famous football player who collapsed and died during a game in France in 2003; Adama bi Ardo Hassana (Modibbo Adama) is revered in northern Cameroon as a scholar and military leader who created a Fulani Muslim empire in the late 18th and early 19th centuries.

NATIONAL HOLIDAY/INDEPENDENCE DAY

Republic Day or National Day, May 20

FESTIVALS/FAIRS

Taste of Cameroon, October; Cameroon National Festival, May; Ngondo Festival, December; Nyem-Nyem Festival, January; Medumba Festival, July

SIGNIFICANT EVENTS IN FORMATION OF NATIONAL IDENTITY

1000 B.C.E.–500 C.E.   The Pygmy groups are the first inhabitants of the region. Later, Bantu peoples from the region spread across central and southern Africa in the great Bantu migrations. The Sao culture emerges around Lake Chad.

500 C.E.–1500 C.E.   The Bantu peoples create a series of small kingdoms and chiefdoms across the western part of present Cameroon.

1472–1750 Portuguese sailors visit the coast. Noting an abundance of prawns in the Wouri River, they name the territory Rio do Camerões, "river of prawns." Over the following centuries, European interests found trading posts and Christian missionaries push inland.

1809–1847 The Fulani people, devout Muslims from south of the Sahara, begin a jihad or holy war against non-Muslims. A Fulani commander, Modibbo Adama, creates a powerful Muslim state near Lake Chad as a vassal state of the Fulani Empire.

1884–1914 The German Empire lays claim the region as the colony of Kamerun. German rule is marked by brutality and forced labor.

1918–1919 The defeat of the German Empire in World War I leaves Cameroon under the authority of the League of Nations as a mandate territory, which is split into British Cameroons and French Cameroon in 1919.

1920–1946 The French integrate their Cameroon territory into the French system with large investments and continued forced labor. The British rule their portion from the neighboring colony of Nigeria*. At the end of World War II, the mandates are converted into United Nations trusteeships in 1946.

1950–1960 French Cameroon is the scene of a vicious guerilla war and instability in the 1950s. In British Cameroons, peaceful and economically secure, the people complain of being the "colony of a colony" and demand an end to rule from Nigeria. Nationalist movements in both regions demand independence, but in the British region, it is felt that the territory is too small for separate independence, and a debate opens as to joining Nigeria or French Cameroon.

1960–1961 French Cameroon is granted independence under President Ahmadou Ahidjo. Following a referendum on their future, the people of British Cameroons vote for union with ethnically-related Cameroon in the Federal Republic of Cameroon, which gives the former British territory widespread cultural, linguistic, and economic autonomy.

1966–1972 The government abolishes the federal system in favor of a unitary republic. The two yellow stars on the flag are removed and are replaced by the single Star of Unity.

1981 Cameroon nearly goes to war with neighboring Nigeria over the disputed region of the Bakassi Peninsula.

1984 A failed coup ends the democratization program. An economic crisis made worse by drought, falling oil prices, and years of corruption, mismanagement, and cronyism continues from the mid-1980s to the late 1990s.

1990 The reintroduction of multiparty politics allows Anglophone groups to legally form in the former British portion, many calling for the secession of their homeland as the Republic of the Southern Cameroons or the Republic of Ambazania*.

1994 President Paul Biya clashes with neighboring Nigeria over possession of the disputed Bakassi Peninsula, which remained under Nigerian control when the rest of Southern Cameroons united with Cameroon in 1961. Cameroon submits the Bakassi dispute to the International Court of Justice.

2006–2009 International Court of Justice rules in favor of Cameroon. In August 2008, Nigeria formally cedes its claims to the Bakassi Peninsula, a 100,000-square-kilometer territory thought to be rich in oil, to Cameroon sovereignty. The region, part of the former British Cameroons, is claimed by the nationalists of Ambazania as part of their national territory, further complicating the politics of the region.

CAPE VERDE

OFFICIAL NAME
República de Cabo Verde (Portuguese); Republic of Cape Verde (English)

POPULATION
499,600 (2009e)

INHABITANTS' NAME/NICKNAME
Cape Verdean(s)

Language/Languages

Portuguese (official); Cape Verde Creole (Cape Verdean Portuguese), others

Religion/Religions

Roman Catholic, 90 percent; Protestant (mostly Church of the Nazarene), indigenous beliefs, other or no religion

National Flag

The flag has a blue field with three narrow stripes below the center, white, red, and white, with a circle of 10 gold stars on the hoist side near the center. The 10 stars represent the main islands of the archipelago. The blue stands for the sky and the ocean. The bands of white and red represent the road toward the construction of the nation, and the colors stand for peace (white) and effort (red).

Coat of Arms/Seal

The national emblem contains a blue and white circle with the name of the country in Portuguese in a circle above a torch against a blue triangle, symbols of freedom and national unity. The circle is ringed by 10 small gold stars that represent the islands of Cape Verde. At the top of the shield is a plumb bob, a symbol of righteousness. Below the shield are three gold chain links and two sprigs of olive, symbolizing freedom and peace.

Motto

Unidade, luta, progresso (Portuguese); Unity, Work, Progress (English)

Capital City

Praia

Type of Government

Republic

National Emblem

White torch on a blue triangle (from the national coat of arms)

National Colors

Blue and white

National Anthem

From independence in 1975 until 1996, Cape Verde shared the same anthem as Guinea-Bissau* to reflect a proposed merger of the two former Portuguese colonies. When the merger was abandoned, Cape Verde changed its flag and anthem to national symbols unique to its country.

Cântico da Liberdade (Portuguese); Song of Freedom (English)

Chorus

Sing, brother
Sing, my brother
For freedom is a hymn
And man a certainty

With dignity, bury the seed
In the dust of the naked island
In life is precipice
Hope is as big as the sea
Which embraces us
Unwavering sentinel of the seas and winds
Between the stars and the Atlantic Ocean
Sing the chant of freedom

Chorus

Sing, brother
Sing, my brother
For freedom is a hymn
And man a certainty

Patron Saint

Our Lady of the Assumption

Currency

Cape Verde escudo

Internet Identifier

.cv

Vehicle Identification Plates/Stickers

CV

PASSPORT

The passport cover has the name of the country in Portuguese, the coat of arms, and the word *passaporte*, Portuguese for passport.

AIRLINE

Cabo Verde Airlines TACV

NATIONAL FLOWER

Cardeal (unofficial)

NATIONAL ANIMAL

Gray nurse shark (unofficial)

NATIONAL BIRD

Cagarra (Cape Verde shearwater) (unofficial)

NATIONAL RESOURCES

Natural resources include salt, basalt rock, limestone, kaolin, fish, clay, and gypsum. A booming tourist industry depends on sandy beaches, a pleasant climate, the unique culture, and proximity to Europe.

FOODS

Cachupa, a stew made with beans, hominy, and meat or fish, is considered the national dish. Other specialties include *pastel com diablo dentro* (pastry with the devil inside), a mix of fresh tuna, onions, and tomatoes in a pastry made of potatoes and corn flour; *jagacinda,* rice and beans; *canja de gahlinha,* chicken and vegetables stew; *polvo a modo ze de lino,* octopus stew; and *aguardiente,* sugarcane rum, considered the national drink.

SPORTS/SPORTS TEAMS

Association football (soccer) is the most popular sport in the islands. Basketball and volleyball, particularly beach volleyball, are also very popular. Cape Verde national teams participate in many sports at an international level.

TEAM SPORTS

Basketball

Cape Verde Basketball Team; Cape Verde Women's Basketball Team

Football

Cape Verde Football Team, nickname Tubarões Azuis (Blue Sharks) or Crioulos (Creoles); Cape Verde Beach Soccer Team

Volleyball

Cape Verde Men's Beach Volleyball Team; Cape Verde Women's Beach Volleyball Team

INDIVIDUAL SPORTS

Cape Verde Amateur Boxing Team; Cape Verde Athletics Team; Cape Verde Cycling Team; Cape Verde Judo Team; Cape Verde Tae Kwon Do Team

NATIONAL HEROES OR PERSONIFICATIONS

Aristides Pereira, the country's first president, from 1975 until 1991; Cesária Évora, the best-known singer of the *morna,* a specifically Cape Verdean music style, who is well known internationally

NATIONAL HOLIDAY/INDEPENDENCE DAY

Independence Day, July 5

FESTIVALS/FAIRS

Carnival, February–March

SIGNIFICANT EVENTS IN FORMATION OF NATIONAL IDENTITY

1456–1462 Portuguese sailors visit the uninhabited archipelago. The sailors, impressed by the rich vegetation of the island, name the archipelago Cape Verde (Green Cape). The first European settlement is established in 1462 at Ribeira Grande, the first European settlement in the tropics.

1492–1496 The Inquisition begins in Portugal*. In 1496, thousands of Portuguese Jews are rounded up and exiled to the new Portuguese colonies of São Tome, Príncipe, and Cape Verde.

1550–1770 The islands' situation on the new transatlantic trade routes brings prosperity but also the unwanted attention of pirates.

18th century–19th century The islands are hit by a severe drought, the first of many that have plagued the islands since, with an average interval of five years. Overgrazing and deforestation worsen the situation. Three major droughts in the 18th and 19th centuries result in over 100,000 deaths by starvation.

1810–1940 The decline of the lucrative slave trade is another blow to the islands' fragile economy. Cape Verdeans begin immigrating to the New England region of the United States*, a popular destination because of the many whaling ships that visit the islands from Massachusetts and Rhode Island. The advent of steam ships revives the economy, as the harbor at Mindelo becomes a major coaling and refitting station for ships bound for the Americas. The British use Cape Verde as a storage depot for ships sailing to the Americas or southern Africa.

1941–1960 During World War II, the economy again collapses as shipping is drastically reduced. The British abandon Cape Verde as a way station, another blow to the fragile economy.

1965–1975 The Cape Verdeans, being lighter-skinned than the inhabitants of other Portuguese colonies, fare marginally better under Portuguese rule. By the time of independence, in 1975, a quarter of the population can read, a very high number for a Portuguese territory.

1976–1980 Cape Verde gives up the idea of a merger with newly independent Guinea-Bissau on the African mainland. New symbols are adopted to reflect the culture and aspirations of the Cape Verdeans.

2000–2005 An improving economy and a government of democratic institutions greatly benefit the islands. The Portuguese government urges the European Union (EU) to begin membership negotiations with Cape Verde.

2007 The United Nations upgrades Cape Verde from the category of Least Developed Countries, making Cape Verde only the second country to be so honored.

2008–2009 Portugal's government is committed to closer relations with Cape Verde, which helps the island nation's desires for closer ties to the EU. Cape Verde has a "special partnership" agreement with the EU and may apply for full membership in the future.

CASAMANCE

OFFICIAL NAME
Ziguinchor Region (Lower Casamance) and Kolda Region (Upper Casamance); Cassamoukou (Diola); Casamance (English)

POPULATION
1,404,600 (2009e)

INHABITANTS' NAME/NICKNAME
Casamançais; Casamancer(s)

LANGUAGE/LANGUAGES
French (official); Diola, Portuguese Creole, others

RELIGION/RELIGIONS
Roman Catholic, Muslim, other or no religion

NATIONAL FLAG
The flag of the Democratic Forces Movement of Casamance has vertical stripes of white, green, and red with a white, five-pointed star centered on the green. The white stripe strands for peace, justice, freedom, and unity; the green represents the forest and agriculture; and the red stands for the blood spilled. The centered white star represents the people of Casamance.

COAT OF ARMS/SEAL
The coat of arms is a crest showing (from bottom) the brown earth, blue water, green

vegetation, and pale blue sky behind a tall palm tree. Two smaller crests, at either side of the upper part of the palm tree, show traditional regional symbols below a narrow black stripe with one small white star. Above the crest is written *Casamance Libre* and around the crest is a green wreath bearing the national motto in French.

MOTTO

Unité, liberte, justice (French); Unity, Liberty, Justice (English)

CAPITAL CITY

Ziguinchor

TYPE OF GOVERNMENT

Divided and governed as two administrative regions of the Republic of Senegal*. The MFDC (Mouvement des Forces Democratiques de Casamance/Democratic Forces Movement of Casamance) is an active separatist movement seeking an independent Casamance republic.

NATIONAL EMBLEM

A leaping leopard

NATIONAL COLORS

White, green, and red

NATIONAL ANTHEM

The song is the anthem of the MFDC and the proposed anthem for an independent Casamance. No English translation is available.

Hymne National de la Casamance (French); Casamance National Anthem (English)

O Casamance, mon beau pays
Lieu de mon enfance
Du bonheur, des chansons et des rires.
Ta souvenance
Laisse à ma dolence
Un peu d'espérance.

Hélas! sur cette terre
Où je suis exilé,

Mon âme est solitaire
Et mon coeur désolé:
J'attends chaque jour
Le moment du retour.

Finis chants d'allégresse,
Finis les clairs matins,
Voici que ma jeunesse
Au fond des yeux s'éteint:
Puisque je n'ai plus d'espoir
De te revoir.

PATRON SAINT

Saint Anthony of Padua

CURRENCY

CFA franc

VEHICLE IDENTIFICATION PLATES/ STICKERS

SN Senegal (official); CAS (unofficial)

NATIONAL TREE

Palm (shown on the coat of arms)

NATIONAL ANIMAL

Cheetah

NATIONAL BIRD

Flamingo (unofficial)

NATIONAL RESOURCES

Natural resources include arable land, fish, and phosphates. Sandy beaches, a pleasant climate, beautiful scenery, and a unique culture are the attractions that have drawn some tourists. The tourist trade could become a major industry in the region when peace is assured.

FOODS

Yassa, a dish of chicken or fish marinated in lemon juice, pepper, and onions and then baked and served accompanied by plain white rice, is considered the national dish. Other specialties include *macarra com citi*, a chicken dish with peanuts and palm oil; *bolinhos de mancarra,* fried balls of cassava, peanuts, and fish; *nyeleng,* a stew of meat with peanuts and vegetables; and *ceebu jen,* a dish of fish and rice.

SPORTS/SPORTS TEAMS

Association football (soccer) is the most popular sport in the region. The Casamance national team participates in football at an international level.

TEAM SPORTS

Football

Casamance Football Team

NATIONAL HEROES OR PERSONIFICATIONS

Victor Dialla, the first African to receive a degree in literature in France* in 1930 and one of the founders of the MFDC; Aline Sitoé Diatta, the queen of the Diola, exiled by the French to Timbukto in 1943, where she died just a year later; Assane Seck, a leader of the modern separatist movement; Father Augustin Diamacoune Senghor, a nationalist leader who died in 2007

NATIONAL HOLIDAY/INDEPENDENCE DAY

Casamance Day, December 26

FESTIVALS/FAIRS

The King's Festival, June; Abéné Festival, December

SIGNIFICANT EVENTS IN FORMATION OF NATIONAL IDENTITY

2000 B.C.E.–1472 C.E. Diola kings rule Casamance, a region of small villages and lush rice fields in the Casamance River Valley. Isolated from the north, the Diola do not develop the strong caste systems prevalent among the other peoples of Senegal.

1472–1850 Portuguese seamen establish trade relations with the Diola king and local chiefs and construct a permanent settlement at the mouth of the Casamance River in 1645. The Casamance region remains a loose appendage of the Portuguese colony of Guinea, just to the south, for several centuries. The slave trade grows with an important Portuguese slave market at Ziguinchor.

1850–1870 Casamance is incorporated into the French Empire, as recognized by other European powers in 1870. The European claims divide the historic Diola nation.

1886–1920s The Portuguese government, under French pressure, officially sells Casamance to France. French troops take control of Ziguinchor, the Diola capital. Many people in the region adopt Christianity. In 1903, the French authorities begin taking control of other areas. In 1920 Casamance is added to French Senegal as a district. Diola resistance continues into the 1920s.

1914–1948 A young soldier, Victor Dialla, later becomes the first African to receive a degree in literature from a French university. He and three others found the MFDC as a cultural group in 1947. Dialla is murdered in 1948, possibly by French agents. The British allow direct access to Casamance through their colony of Gambia* in 1947.

1950s Religious and cultural differences feed unrest and resistance to domination by the Wolofs, Senegal's largest tribal group. Nationalist groups form to press for greater self-government and a separate administration within French West Africa.

1960 Senegal gains independence from France. According to historians, Senegal's first president makes a promise to Casamance leaders before independence that the province would be allowed a vote on independence after 20 years.

1961–1980 The Casamance political parties and cultural groups are banned as secessionist and go underground. By the mid-1970s, the fertile Casamance produces half of Senegal's vegetables and fruits but receives little but neglect and indifference from the Senegalese government. When the Senegalese government refuses to honor the promise of a vote on independence made in 1960, street demonstrations in Ziguinchor turn violent.

1981–1983 Senegal and Gambia form a short-lived confederation, allowing Casamance to trade through the Gambian capital, Banjul, rather than through Dakar, the much more distant capital of Senegal. The leaders of the Casamance movement are jailed. Severe rioting prompts the Senegalese government to abolish the province of Casamance, which is replaced with the new regions of Ziguinchor and Kolda.

1989–1990 The discovery of oil in the Casamance region gives the nationalists hope for a viable economy to sustain an independent Casamance state. Mass demonstrations in favor of immediate independence rock the region and fighting spreads.

1990–1994 A cease-fire signed in May 1991 breaks down within seven months. Government troops, given wide powers to combat the insurrection, retaliate against suspected supporters of the nationalists with great brutality. By mid-1994, over 30,000 people have been driven from their homes, most to refugee camps in Gambia and Guinea-Bissau*. Splits appear within the nationalist movement between pro-independence and proautonomy factions.

1995–1999 Government forces launch a full-scale invasion of Casamance.

1999–2000 A new cease-fire is signed in 2001. Further splits within the Casamance movement make a united front very difficult.

2004 One of the nationalist factions signs a cease-fire and a peace accord with the Senegalese government. Other factions denounce the accord and reiterate their support for nothing less than full independence.

2006 Separatist violence again erupts in the region over the Senegalese government's failure to live up to the terms of the 2004 peace accord.

2007 The Senegal government wishes to keep Casamance as an internal problem, but nationalists demand that representatives of Gambia and Guinea-Bissau, both with thousands of Casamance refuges, be included in any future talks, which would make Casamance a regional issue.

2008 Casamance civilians grow increasingly desperate to return to their homes from camps in Gambia and Guinea-Bissau. The peace process is at a stalemate. In June, displaced families march in Ziguinchor alongside community and religious and local officials to demand that the Senegalese government do more to reinvigorate the peace process.

2009 Separatist activity continues, although a move to revive the tourist industry in the region meets with some success.

See also Senegal

CENTRAL AFRICAN REPUBLIC

OFFICIAL NAME

République Centrafricaine (French); Ködörösêse tî Bêafrîka (Sango); Central African Republic (English)

POPULATION

4,305,600 (2009e)

INHABITANTS' NAME/NICKNAME

Central African(s)

LANGUAGE/LANGUAGES

Sango, French (both official); Banda, Gbaya, Arabic, others

RELIGION/RELIGIONS

Indigenous beliefs, 35 percent; Roman Catholic, 25 percent; Protestant, 22 percent; Muslim, 15 percent; other or no religion

NATIONAL FLAG

Four horizontal stripes of blue, white, green, and yellow divided by a centered vertical red stripe and bearing a gold, five-pointed star on the upper hoist. The flag is based on the colors of the French flag and the pan-African colors. Red represents the blood spilled to bring about independence and the blood the people would spill to protect the nation. Blue represents the sky and freedom, white stands for peace and dignity, green represent hope and faith, and yellow stands for tolerance.

COAT OF ARMS/SEAL

The coat of arms of the Central African Republic consists of a shield in the center, with two flags on its edges and a sun rising over the shield. The shield is divided in four quarters, with an elephant and a baobab tree that represent nature and the backbone of the country. The gold star on a map of Africa symbolizes the position of the Central African Republic. The hand was the symbol of the dominant party in 1963, when the arms were adopted. Below the shield are a medal and a banner with the national motto in French.

MOTTO

Unité, dignité, travail (French); Unity, Dignity, Work (English)

CAPITAL CITY

Bangui

TYPE OF GOVERNMENT

Republic

NATIONAL EMBLEM

Elephant

NATIONAL COLORS

Blue, white, yellow, and green

NATIONAL ANTHEM

The first president of the autonomous territory of Oubangui-Chari, Barthélemy Boganda, who believed that the African territories must retain close ties to the former colonial power, France*, wrote the words of the anthem.

> **Le Renaissance (French); The Renaissance (English)**
>
> Oh! Central Africa, cradle of the Bantu!

Take up again your right to respect, to life!
Long subjugated, long scorned by all,
But, from today, breaking tyranny's hold.

Through work, order, and dignity
You reconquer your rights, your unity,
And to take this new step
The voices of our ancestors call us.

Chorus

To work! In order and dignity,
in the respect for rights and in unity,
Breaking poverty and tyranny,
Holding high the flag of the fatherland.

PATRON SAINT

Saint Therese of Lisieux

CURRENCY

CFA franc

INTERNET IDENTIFIER

.cf

VEHICLE IDENTIFICATION PLATES/STICKERS

RCA

PASSPORT

The passport cover has the name of the country in French and Sango, the coat of arms, and the word *passport,* also in French and Sango.

NATIONAL TREE

Baobab

NATIONAL ANIMAL

Elephant

NATIONAL RESOURCES

Natural resources include diamonds, uranium, timber, gold, oil, and hydropower. The economy is dominated by the sale of food crops, such as cassava, maize, peanuts, sorghum, millet, plantains, and sesame. The cultivation of cotton is also an important resource. International aid, particularly from France, is essential to the country.

FOODS

Gonzo, a thick porridge made of cassava or sorghum, served with vegetables, meat, or fish, is considered the national dish. Other specialties include *makara,* a fried flatbread; *shichinga,* goat meat cooked on skewers over charcoal; *kanda ti nyma,* a dish of minced beef, onions, chilies, garlic, sliced okra, peanut butter, and eggs; and *boullie,* a rice dish with peanut butter and lemon juice, a favorite of the Fulani people.

SPORTS/SPORTS TEAMS

Association football (soccer) is by far the most popular sport. Athletics and martial arts sports, such as judo and tae kwon do, are also popular. Central Africa national teams participate in many sports at an international level.

TEAM SPORTS

Badminton

Central African Republic Badminton Team

Basketball

Central African Republic Basketball Team; Central African Republic Women's Basketball Team

Football

Central African Republic Football Team, nickname Low-Ubangi Fawns; Central African Republic Women's Football Team, nickname Low-Ubangi Fawns

Table Tennis

Central African Republic Table Tennis Team

Volleyball

Central African Republic Men's Volleyball Team

INDIVIDUAL SPORTS

Central African Republic Amateur Boxing Team; Central African Republic Athletics Team; Central African Republic Judo Team; Central African Republic Tae Kwon Do Team; Central African Republic Weight Lifting Team

NATIONAL HEROES OR PERSONIFICATIONS

Barthélemy Boganda, leading nationalist politician before independence, who was killed in a mysterious plane crash in 1959, just before independence; David Dacko, first president of the country and the man responsible for the end of the Bokassa dictatorship

NATIONAL HOLIDAY/INDEPENDENCE DAY

Republic Day, December 1

FESTIVALS/FAIRS

Bangui International Human Rights Film Festival, May; Festival of Smoke and Mirrors/Boganda Day, January

SIGNIFICANT EVENTS IN FORMATION OF NATIONAL IDENTITY

1000 B.C.E.–100 C.E. Adamawa-Eastern tribes spread eastward from Cameroon* to settle most of the present Central African Republic. About the same time, a much smaller number of Bantu people settle in the territory, and some Sudanic-speaking people settle along the Oubangui River.

7th century C.E.–18th century C.E. Overlapping empires claim the territory. Later, various sultanates claim the same region, using the Oubangui River region as a slave reserve. Slaves are traded north across the Sahara and to West Africa for export by Europeans to the New World.

1800–1910 The tribal peoples live beyond the expanding Islamic frontier until the early 1800s, when Muslim traders begin to penetrate the region. Between 1860 and 1910, Muslim slave traders capture and sell much of the population of the present eastern Central African Republic, which remains underinhabited to the present.

1875–1894 French explorers travel from the coast up the Oubangui in an effort to expand France's claims to territory in Central Africa. In 1889, the French establish a post at Bangui. Oubangui-Chari becomes a French territory.

1910–1940 For the next three decades, the region is the scene of small-scale revolts against French rule and the development of plantation agriculture under 17 private companies, often using forced labor and brutality.

1940–1946 The territory rallies to the Free French after the fall of France at the beginning of the Second World War. After the war, a series of reforms are applied in 1946 and the inhabitants are granted French citizenship and permitted to form local legislative assemblies.

1946–1959 Barthélemy Boganda, a Catholic priest and an outspoken supporter of African emancipation, leads pro-independence movement. In 1958, the country is declared an autonomous republic, with Boganda as head of state. He serves until his mysterious death in March 1959. Full independence is granted in August 1960.

1966–1976 Colonel Jean-Bedel Bokassa assumes power in a coup. He quickly abolishes the constitution, dissolves the legislature, and places all power in his own hands. In 1976, Bokassa declares the country a monarchy, with himself as Emperor Bokassa I. His regime is characterized by corruption, violence, and mass abuse of human rights.

1979–2000 Following rioting and the murder of between 50 and 200 schoolchildren, Bokassa is overthrown. The following 20 years are characterized by coups, mutinies, rebellions, and ethnic confrontations.

2002–2003 A coup once again overthrows the government. General Francois Bozize becomes head of state and makes significant progress in restoring order in the country. In 2005, the country holds national elections, which Bozize wins. He becomes president, promoting national reconciliation, strengthening the economy, and improving the dismal human-rights situation.

2008 A countrywide strike brings the Central African Republic to a standstill. Fighting between rebel groups and government troops in the north of the country leaves hundreds dead and displaces nearly 300,000 people.

2009 The republic remains one of the world's least developed. The global economic slump further damages the fragile economy.

CHAD

OFFICIAL NAME

Jumhūriyyat Tshād (transliteration from Arabic); République du Tchad (French); Republic of Chad (English)

POPULATION

10,132,800 (2009e)

INHABITANTS' NAME/NICKNAME

Chadian(s)

LANGUAGE/LANGUAGES

Arabic, French (both official); Sara (spoken across the southern region), other indigenous languages

RELIGION/RELIGIONS

Muslim, 54 percent; Roman Catholic, 21 percent; Protestant, 14 percent; Animist, 10 percent; other or no religion

NATIONAL FLAG

The flag of Chad is a horizontal tricolor of blue, yellow, and red. The flag's colors combine the colors of the flag of France* with some traditional pan-African colors. Blue represents the sky, hope, and water; yellow represents the sun and the desert; and red stands for progress, unity, and sacrifice and also the blood shed for independence.

COAT OF ARMS/SEAL

The coat of arms consists of a central shield with wavy blue lines, with a sun rising over it. The shield is supported by a goat and a lion. Below the shield is a scroll with the national motto in French. The wavy lines on the shield are representative of Lake Chad, and the sun rising over it represents a new beginning. The goat on the left represents the northern part of the nation, while the southern part is represented by the lion. Hanging from the bottom of the shield is the medal for the National Order of Chad.

MOTTO
Unité, travail, progrès (French); Unity, Work, Progress (English)

CAPITAL CITY
N'Djamena

TYPE OF GOVERNMENT
Republic

NATIONAL EMBLEM
Lake Chad

NATIONAL COLORS
Blue, yellow, and red

NATIONAL ANTHEM
The anthem was composed by a student group and adopted at independence in 1960.

La Tchadienne (French); The Song of Chad (English)

People of Chad, arise and take up the task!
You have conquered the soil and won your rights;
Your freedom will be born of your courage.
Lift up your eyes, the future is yours.
O, my country, may God protect you,
May your neighbors admire your children.
Joyful, peaceful, advance as you sing,
Faithful to your fathers who are watching you.

PATRON SAINT
The archdiocese of N'Djamena, which covers all of Chad, is dedicated to Notre Dame.

CURRENCY
CFA franc

INTERNET IDENTIFIER
.td

VEHICLE IDENTIFICATION PLATES/ STICKERS
TCH (unofficial)

PASSPORT
The passport has the name of the country in French and Arabic, the coat of arms, and the word *passport* in French and Arabic.

AIRLINE
Toumaï Air Chad

NATIONAL ANIMAL
Lion, *aoudad* (goat) (unofficial)

NATIONAL RESOURCES
Natural resources include petroleum, uranium, natron, kaolin, fish from Lake Chad, gold, limestone, sand and gravel, and salt. Oil reserves in southern Chad are estimated at 1 billion barrels.

FOODS
Balls of millet, known as *aiysh* in the Arabic-speaking north and *biya* in the south, served with various sauces of vegetables, meat, or fish, are considered the national dish. Other specialties include *beignets soufflés*, a type of fried pastry; *capitaine pili-pili*, perch prepared with a spicy sauce; *courgette aux arachides*, squash prepared with peanuts and chilies; *iyan*, pounded yams; and *flan de citron*, a sweet dessert of citrus custard.

SPORTS/SPORTS TEAMS
Association football (soccer) is the country's most popular sport. Other popular sports include basketball, boxing, martial arts, and

fishing in Lake Chad. Chad national teams participate in many sports at an international level.

TEAM SPORTS

Basketball

Chad Basketball Team; Chad Women's Basketball Team

Football

Chad Football Team, nickname Sao; Chad Women's Football Team, nickname Sao; Chad Rugby Union Team

Volleyball

Chad Men's Volleyball Team

INDIVIDUAL SPORTS

Chad Amateur Boxing Team; Chad Archery Team; Chad Athletics Team; Chad Tae Kwon Do Team; Chad Judo Team; Chad Weight Lifting Team

NATIONAL HEROES OR PERSONIFICATIONS

Idris Alooma, *mai* (king) of Kanem-Bornu in the 17th century, known for his military skills and Muslim piety; François Tombalbaye, also known as Ngarta Tombalbaye, a teacher and trade union activist who led Chad to independence; Félix Malloum, chief of state from 1975 to 1979; Idriss Déby, the present ruler

NATIONAL HOLIDAY/INDEPENDENCE DAY

Independence Day, August 11

FESTIVALS/FAIRS

Festival of Freedom and Democracy, December; National Day, April

SIGNIFICANT EVENTS IN FORMATION OF NATIONAL IDENTITY

1000 B.C.E.–1000 C.E. Bantu people spread eastward from present Cameroon* to settle the region. The early Sao civilization comes under the Kanem-Bornu Empire, the first and longest-lasting of the kingdoms that develop at the end of the first millennium C.E.

9th century–11th century Traders and Arab invaders bring Islam to the region. At the end of the 11th century, the king of Kanem adopts the new religion. The power of Kanem is based on control of the trans-Saharan trade routes.

17th century Kanem-Bornu reaches the height of its power and expansion, ruling vast territories. Muslims are forbidden to take other Muslims as slaves—one of the reasons for the rapid spread of Islam in the sub-Saharan region.

1891–1900 A French expedition visits the region. The forces of Rabeh Zobier, called the Napoleon of Africa, overrun the empire of Kanem-Bornu. Rabeh's empire extends into areas claimed by European colonizers, and a multinational European force defeats him in 1900.

1910–1920 French troops extend colonial control, although clashes continue. The northern region is occupied in 1914. Chad joins the Federation of French Equatorial Africa in 1910.

1929–1945 The French never attempt to unify the two parts of the territory, the Arabic north and the Bantu south, viewing the region as a source of labor and raw cotton. Large-scale cotton production is introduced in 1929. Only the south is effectively under French control, with the French presence in the north and east only nominal.

1946–1975 After World War II, France grants Chad the status of overseas territory. On August 11 1960, Chad is granted independence, with François Tombalbaye as its first president. Tombalbaye's autocratic rule exacerbates interethnic tensions. Muslims in the north rebel against rule by the southerners they once took as slaves. Tombalbaye is overthrown and killed in 1975.

1979 Muslim rebels capture the capital and all authority in the country collapses. Armed factions, mostly from the north, contend for power.

1979–1990 Fighting between factions leads to continued instability and coups. In 1990, Idriss

Déby takes power in a coup. He attempts to reconcile rebel groups and reintroduces multiparty politics.

2003 Oil exploitation begins, bringing hope for economic stability and prosperity. Instead, a new civil war breaks out.

2006–2008 Rebel forces attempt to take the capital, N'Djamena, but fail due to French military assistance. Ethnic violence continues to undermine the country's unity and stability, as does the lack of democracy.

2009 The large number of refugees from the Darfur region of Sudan* continues to destabilize the eastern provinces, already beset by local rebel groups and bandit gangs.

COMOROS

OFFICIAL NAME

Udzima wa Komori (Comorian); Union des Comores (French); Al- Ittiḥād Al-Qumuriyy (transliteration from Arabic); Union of the Comoros (English)

POPULATION

734,800 (2009e)

INHABITANTS' NAME/NICKNAME

Comorian(s)

LANGUAGE/LANGUAGES

Comorian (Shikomoro), French, Arabic (all official); others

RELIGION/RELIGIONS

Sunni Muslim, 97 percent; Roman Catholic, 2 percent; other or no religion

NATIONAL FLAG

The flag has four horizontal stripes of yellow, white, red, and blue, with a green triangle at the hoist bearing a white crescent moon and four small, white, five-pointed stars. The four stripes represent the four islands: yellow for Mohéli, white for Mayotte* (claimed by Comoros but constituting a French territory), red for Anjouan, and blue for Grande Comore. The four stars also represent the four islands, while the crescent moon represents Islam, the country's major religion.

COAT OF ARMS/SEAL

The coat of arms of Comoros has the crescent found on the national flag at the center; within this crescent are the four stars found on the flag. A sun with rays extended sits right above the crescent. Around the focal point, the name of the nation is written in both French and Arabic. The border is composed of two olive branches, with the national motto at the bottom in French.

MOTTO

Unité—justice—progrès (French); Unity—Justice—Progress (English)

CAPITAL CITY

Moroni

TYPE OF GOVERNMENT

Federal republic

NATIONAL EMBLEM

Crescent moon and four stars

NATIONAL COLORS

Green and white

NATIONAL ANTHEM

The anthem was adopted at independence in 1978 and refers to the union of the four islands of the archipelago, including French Mayotte.

Udzima wa ya Masiwa (Comorian); The Union of the Great Islands (English)

The flag is flying,
Announcing complete independence;
The nation rises up
Because of the faith we have
In this, our Comoros.

Let us always have devotion
To love our great islands.
We Comorians are of one blood,
We Comorians are of one faith.

On these islands we were born,
These islands brought us up.
May God always help us;
Let us always have the firm resolve
To love our fatherland,
Love our religion and the world.

The flag is flying.
From the sixth of July
The nation rises up;
Our islands are lined up.
Mahori and Anjouan, Mohéli and Comore,
Let us always have devotion
To love our great islands.

CURRENCY
Comorian franc

INTERNET IDENTIFIER
.km

VEHICLE IDENTIFICATION PLATES/ STICKERS
COM

PASSPORT
The passport cover has the name of the country in the three official languages, the coat of arms, and the word *passport*, also in the three official languages.

NATIONAL FLOWER
Vanilla (unofficial)

NATIONAL TREE
Ylang-ylang (unofficial)

NATIONAL FISH
Coelacanth (unofficial)

NATIONAL RESOURCES
Natural resources are negligible, but tourism, based on the archipelago's sandy beaches, pleasant climate, underwater reefs, and unique culture, could become a major asset. The islands have abundant arable land, and agriculture remains a traditional occupation.

FOODS
National dishes include *poulet de Comores,* a chicken dish with coconut milk, onions, sweet potatoes, carrots, and spices; *pilao,* a rice dish with chicken or fish; *ladu,* a type of bread made of rice; *le me tsolola,* a dish of fish, meat, onions, bananas, tomatoes, and coconut milk; *poulet à l'indienne,* a chicken dish with onions, garlic, tomatoes, chilies, and spices; *poulet au coco,* chicken with onions, clover, curry, and coconut milk; and *langouste a la vanille,* lobster cooked in vanilla sauce, a famous Comorian dish.

SPORTS/SPORTS TEAMS
Association football (soccer) is the most popular game in the islands. Traditional sports, such as athletics and swimming, are also popular. Comoros national teams participate in many sports at an international level.

TEAM SPORTS
Basketball
Comoros Basketball Team; Comoros Women's Basketball Team

Football
Comoros Football Team, nickname Les Coelecantes; Comoros Women's Football Team, nickname Les Coelecantes

Table Tennis
Comoros Table Tennis Team

Volleyball
Comoros Men's Volleyball Team

INDIVIDUAL SPORTS
Comoros Amateur Boxing Team; Comoros Athletics Team; Comoros Cycling Team;

Comoros Judo Team; Comoros Swim Team; Comoros Weight Lifting Team

NATIONAL HEROES OR PERSONIFICATIONS

Sultan Said Ali bin Said Omar, who unified the seven states of Grande Comore into one sultanate in 1886; Ahmad 'Abdallah, president in the 1970s and 1980s

NATIONAL HOLIDAY/INDEPENDENCE DAY

Independence Day, July 6

FESTIVALS/FAIRS

Eid al-Adha, the Festival of Sacrifice, January; Muharram (Islamic New Year), February

SIGNIFICANT EVENTS IN FORMATION OF NATIONAL IDENTITY

Sixth century C.E.–1500 C.E. Polynesians, Melanesians, Malays, and Austronesians arriving by boat settle the islands. Later waves of diverse settlers arrive from the coast of Africa, the Persian Gulf, Indonesia*, and Madagascar*. Swahili settlers reach the islands as part of the great Bantu migrations. The most influential of the many groups are the Shirazi clans, who arrive from the Persian Gulf area. They stay to introduce Islam, build mosques, create a dynasty, and introduce many arts, including new forms of architecture.

1503–1505 Portuguese explorers visit the islands.

1529 French explorers visit the islands, but, like the Portuguese, they do not claim the islands.

16th century–19th century The islands' former unity fragments into many small statelets, usually ruled by a sultan. At one time, there are 12 statelets ruled by sultans on the island of Grande Comore alone.

1830–1887 The French turn their attention to the islands. In 1841, France* annexes Mahori called Mayotte by the French. The other islands are added to the protectorate of Mayotte between 1852 and 1886. The Protectorate of the Comoros is proclaimed in 1887.

1908–1914 The Comoros are made a dependent territory of the French colony of Madagascar.

French settlers, French-owned companies, and Arab merchants establish a plantation economy for export crops. France officially annexes the other islands, which are added with Mayotte as the colony of Mayotte and Dependencies.

1947–1961 The Comoros are granted separate status from Madagascar as an overseas territory of France. The islands gain internal autonomy in 1961.

1973–1975 An agreement is reached for Comoros to become independent in 1978. On July 6, 1975, the Comorian parliament passes a resolution of unilateral independence, with the deputies from Mayotte abstaining.

1974–1976 In two referendums, the people of Mayotte vote against independence from France. Mayotte, with its large Christian population, remains under French administration. The Comoros government gains control of the three other islands, Grande Comore, Anjouan, and Mohéli.

1976–1996 A number of coups, the intervention of mercenary groups working for France and South Africa*, and general instability continue to plague the islands.

1997–2001 The islands of Anjouan and Mohéli declare their independence. Internal conflicts and military intervention, including aid from other African nations, end the secession attempts.

2007–2008 After a disputed election on Anjouan, held in defiance of the federal government, Anjouan is again declared independent of the Comoros. In March 2008, a military assault, backed by African Union troops from Sudan*, Tanzania*, and Senegal*, with logistical support from Libya* and France, brings the secessionist island back into the federation.

2009 The country is a potentially prosperous tourist destination but the effort to consolidate political stability amid tensions between the semiautonomous islands and the central government continues to spur instability and economic problems. In May 2009, with about half the eligible voters participating, 93.8 percent voted in a referendum to greatly reduce the unwieldy bureaucracy, which absorbs much of the country's annual budget.

CONGO, DEMOCRATIC REPUBLIC

OFFICIAL NAME

République Démocratique du Congo (French); Democratic Republic of the Congo (English)

POPULATION

65,783,400 (2009e)

INHABITANTS' NAME/NICKNAME

Congolese

LANGUAGE/LANGUAGES

French (official); Lingala, Kingwana (Swahili), Kikongo, Tshiluba, others

RELIGION/RELIGIONS

Roman Catholic, 41 percent; Protestant, 32 percent; Kimbanguist, 10 percent; Muslim, 10 percent; indigenous beliefs, other or no religion

NATIONAL FLAG

The flag is a pale blue field bearing a diagonal red stripe outlined in yellow from the lower hoist to the upper fly, with a yellow, five-pointed star on the upper hoist. The red stands for the blood spilled to win independence, yellow for prosperity, blue for hope, and the star for unity.

COAT OF ARMS/SEAL

The coat of arms of the Democratic Republic of the Congo has changed several times since 1997. The present coat of arms was introduced in 2006 and depicts a leopard head, surrounded by an elephant tusk to the left and a spear to the right. Below are the three words that make up the national motto.

MOTTO

Justice—paix—travail (French); Justice—Peace—Work (English)

CAPITAL CITY

Kinshasa

TYPE OF GOVERNMENT

Semipresidential republic

NATIONAL EMBLEM

Leopard's head

NATIONAL COLORS

Blue and yellow

NATIONAL ANTHEM

The anthem was adopted at independence in 1960 and remained until 1972, when the name of the country was changed to Zaire and all national symbols were also changed. Following a coup in 1997, the original symbols, including the anthem, were restored.

Debout Congolais (French); Arise, Congolese (English)

Chorus

Arise, Congolese, united by fate,
United in the struggle for independence,
Let us hold up our heads, so long bowed,
And now, for good, let us keep moving boldly ahead, in peace.
Oh, ardent people, by hard work we shall build,
In peace, a country more beautiful than before.

Verse

Countrymen, sing the sacred hymn of your solidarity,
Proudly salute the golden emblem of your sovereignty, Congo.

Chorus

Blessed gift (Congo) of our forefathers (Congo),
Oh (Congo) beloved country (Congo),
We shall people your soil and ensure your greatness.
(30th June) Oh gentle sun (30th June) of 30th June,

(Sacred day) Be witness (sacred day) of the
   immortal oath of freedom
That we pass on to our children for ever.

Note: The words in parentheses are to be
sung by a choir; the rest are to be sung by
soloists.

PATRON SAINT

Immaculate Conception of Mary; Our Lady,
Queen of Nations

CURRENCY

Congolese franc

INTERNET IDENTIFIER

.cd

VEHICLE IDENTIFICATION PLATES/STICKERS

CGO

PASSPORT

The passport cover has the name of the country in French and English, the coat of arms,
and the word *passport* in both French and
English.

AIRLINE

Hewa Bora Airways

NATIONAL ANIMAL

Leopard (on the coat of arms) (unofficial)

NATIONAL RESOURCES

Natural resources include cobalt, copper, niobium, tantalum, petroleum, industrial and
gem diamonds, gold, silver, zinc, manganese,
tin, uranium, coal, hydropower, and timber.
Congo has significant deposits of tantalum,
a rare mineral that is used in the fabrication
of electronic components for computers and
mobile phones

FOODS

Maombé, meaning "eight" in the Lingala
language and referring to the eight ingredients, is a dish of pounded palm nuts, chicken,
fish, peanuts, rice, cassava leaves, bananas,
and hot pepper sauce. It is considered the national dish. *Fufu,* made of cassava flour and
served with various types of meat or fish and
sauces, is also very popular. Other specialties
include *akara,* bean fritters; *muamba ususu,*
chicken and vegetable soup; *liboké de viande,*
cubed meat with peanuts cooked in banana
leaves; and *mboto à l'oseille,* fish prepared
with sorrel.

SPORTS/SPORTS TEAMS

Association football (soccer) is the country's most popular sport. Traditional sports,
such as martial arts sports, including boxing and judo, are also very popular. Democratic Republic of Congo national teams
participate in many sports at an international level.

TEAM SPORTS

Basketball

Democratic Republic of Congo Basketball
Team; Democratic Republic of Congo Wom-
en's Basketball Team

Football

Democratic Republic of Congo Football
Team, nickname Simbas (the Leopards);
Democratic Republic of Congo Women's
Football Team, nickname Simbas (the Leop-
ards); Democratic Republic of Congo Wom-
en's Under-19 Football Team; Democratic
Republic of Congo Futsal Team

Handball

Democratic Republic of Congo Handball
Team; Democratic Republic of Congo Wom-
en's Handball Team

Table Tennis

Democratic Republic of Congo Table Tennis
Team

Volleyball

Democratic Republic of Congo Men's Volleyball Team; Democratic Republic of Congo Women's Volleyball Team

INDIVIDUAL SPORTS

Democratic Republic of Congo Amateur Boxing Team; Democratic Republic of Congo Athletics Team; Democratic Republic of Congo Equestrian Team; Democratic Republic of Congo Fencing Team; Democratic Republic of Congo Judo Team; Democratic Republic of Congo Tae Kwon Do Team; Democratic Republic of Congo Weight Lifting Team; Democratic Republic of Congo Wrestling Team

NATIONAL HEROES OR PERSONIFICATIONS

Simon Kimbangu, a religious and political leader who led a rebellion against Belgian rule in the 1920s; Joseph Kasavubu, the first president of independent Congo; Patrice Lumumba, a leader of the independence movement in 1960 and the first prime minister, who was later deposed, imprisoned, and assassinated under controversial circumstances

NATIONAL HOLIDAY/INDEPENDENCE DAY

Independence Day, June 30

FESTIVALS/FAIRS

Festival of African Languages (Festila), September

SIGNIFICANT EVENTS IN FORMATION OF NATIONAL IDENTITY

2500 B.C.E.–2300 B.C.E. Villages appear based on settled agriculture. The original inhabitants, Pygmy peoples, the ancestors of the Twa, are pushed into less accessible regions.

Seventh century C.E.–eighth century C.E. The Bantus spread across the region, eliminating or absorbing the area's earlier inhabitants. Settling into small groups, the Bantus quickly separate into distinct cultural groups and tribes.

1482–1520 Portuguese explorer Diego Cao explores the coast at the outlet to the sea of the Congo River. Most of the region is part of the vast Kingdom of Kongo. The Kongo people welcome the Europeans and allow the Portuguese to establish trading posts. By 1500, the king of Kongo and most of his court have adopted Christianity. The kingdom exchanges ambassadors with Portugal* and the Vatican*, and in 1520, the pope consecrates history's first black bishop, a member of the Kongo royal family.

1550–1665 The Portuguese turn their attention to the slave trade, which is disastrous for Kongo and its peaceful citizens. Raids on surrounding peoples for slaves to sell to the voracious Europeans disrupt a vast area of the Congo River Basin.

1665–1878 Portuguese adventurers, believing stories of vast treasures of gold, invade the already declining kingdom, which quickly disintegrates into a number of small warring states.

1878–1884 King Leopold of Belgium* engages explorer Henry M. Stanley to establish Belgian claims in the basin of the Congo River. The French, alarmed by Stanley's mission, establish a protectorate over the territory north of the river in 1882. Portugal continues to recognize Kongo until 1884.

1885–1917 The Berlin Conference partitions the territory of the Kingdom of Kongo between France*, Portugal, and Belgium. The Belgian Congo becomes famous for its riches, particularly diamonds, but also for brutality, forced labor, and other atrocities.

1921 A Kongo prophet, Simon Kimbangu, creates a religious-political movement against Belgian rule. His movement lays the ground for the later nationalist movement.

1947 Nationalists call for the reunification of the Kongo nation.

1958–1959 ABAKO leaders send the Belgian authorities a detailed proposal for a separate republic for the Kongo people of the colony, including the mostly Kongo capital, Leopoldville, later renamed Kinshasa. Other ethnic groups in the colony also demand separate independence, particularly the mineral-rich region of Katanga in the southeast.

1960–1965 The Belgian authorities begin to lose control and hastily grant independence under Joseph Kasavubu. The country quickly disintegrates as several provinces proclaim independence. Civil war breaks out and continues until the United Nations intervenes to end the secessions and to restore order in the country.

1965–1990 Mobutu Sese Seko takes control of the country and continues as president for 32 years. Vast sums earned from diamonds, agriculture, and timber disappear. The country, one of the best endowed in Africa, is destitute, corrupt, backward, and undeveloped. Mobutu changes the country's name to Zaire and replaces all national symbols. The Mobutu dictatorship wins the support of the United States* and other Western countries for its anticommunist rhetoric.

1990–1994 The end of the Cold War undermines support for Mobutu's vicious regime. Massive economic problems and unrest push Mobutu to end the ban on other political parties. Mobutu falls ill and seeks medical treatment. During one of his visits to Europe, ethnic Tutsis capture much of eastern Zaire.

1996–1997 Angered at Mobutu's support of the genocidal Hutu government in Rwanda*, ethnic Tutsis and their allies in eastern Zaire march west to overthrow Mobutu. Too frail to organize a defense, his government collapses, and he is overthrown. The country is renamed the Democratic Republic of Congo.

1997–2006 Civil war engulfs eastern Congo, with neighboring countries contributing troops or materials. A new constitution establishes more democratic conventions. A peace conference brings an end to most fighting in the country. In July 2006, the country holds its first free, multiparty elections in more than 40 years.

2008 Cease-fires are signed with most of the antigovernment groups operating in the east of the country. Although the country has vast potential in natural resources and mineral wealth, it is one of the world's poorest, the result of decades of mismanagement, corruption, and war.

2009 In spite of the presence of UN peacekeeping troops in the region, the eastern provinces of the country remain in a perpetual state of war, ethnic conflicts, and interference by the military forces of neighboring countries. An estimated 45,000 Congolese die every month in the ongoing armed conflicts in the country.

CONGO, REPUBLIC

OFFICIAL NAME

République du Congo (French); Republika ya Kongo (Kituba); Republiki ya Kongó (Lingala); Republic of the Congo (English)

POPULATION

4,215,600 (2009e)

INHABITANTS' NAME/NICKNAME

Congolese

LANGUAGE/LANGUAGES

French (official); Kituba/Kikongo, Lingala (official in regions where they predominate); Swahili, others

RELIGION/RELIGIONS

Christian, mostly Roman Catholic, 50 percent; indigenous beliefs, 40–50 percent; Muslim, 2 percent; other or no religion

NATIONAL FLAG

The flag is a tricolor divided diagonally from the lower hoist to the upper fly in green, yellow, and red, with the yellow stripe narrower than the other portions. The colors are the traditional pan-African colors originally based on the flag of Ethiopia*.

COAT OF ARMS/SEAL

The coat of arms has a shield with a red lion rampant holding a torch on a yellow field with a green wavy stripe in the middle. A golden crown sits above the shield. Two large African elephants support the shield.

A banner with the national motto is draped from a bar supporting the elephants.

Motto

Unité, travail, progrès (French); Unity, Work, Progress (English)

Capital City

Brazzaville

Type of Government

Presidential republic

National Emblem

Red rampant lion on a yellow shield with a green wavy line (from the coat of arms)

National Colors

Red and yellow

National Anthem

The anthem was originally adopted at independence in 1959 and was used until 1969. It was reinstated as the official anthem in 1991.

> **La Congolaise (French); Song of the Congo (English)**
>
> On this day the sun rises
> And our Congo stands resplendent.
> A long night is ended,
> a great happiness has come.
> Let us all, with wild joyfulness, sing
> The song of freedom.
>
> **Chorus**
>
> Arise, Congolese, proud every man,
> Proclaim the unity of our nation.
> Let us forget what divides us
> And become more united than ever.
> Let us live our motto:
> Unity, work, progress.
> Let us live our motto:
> Unity, work, progress.
>
> From the forest to the bush,
> From the bush to the ocean,
> One people, one soul,

> One heart, ardent and proud.
> Let us all fight, every one of us,
> For our black country.
>
> **Chorus**
>
> And if we have to die,
> What does it really matter? Our children
> Everywhere will be able to say how
> Triumph comes through battle,
> And in the smallest village
> Sing beneath our three colors.

Patron Saint

Saint Anthony of Padua

Currency

CFA franc

Vehicle Identification Plates/Stickers

RCB

Passport

The passport cover has the name of the country in French, a seated figure of a woman holding a slate with the words of the national motto, and below the French word for passport, *passeport*. A thin gold line frames the words and picture.

Airline

Trans Air Congo

National Animal

Elephant, lion (unofficial)

National Bird

Royal tern (unofficial)

National Resources

Natural resources include petroleum, timber, potash, lead, zinc, uranium, copper, phosphates, gold, magnesium, natural gas, and hydropower. Petroleum production has replaced forestry as the mainstay of the country's economy. Diamonds are also important to the country. Most agriculture is village based.

FOODS

Yassa, chicken prepared with lemon, is the national dish. *Fufu,* made of pounded cassava or cassava flour shaped into balls that are served with various sauces containing meat, fish, or vegetables and hot peppers, is eaten across West Africa. Other typical dishes include *mwamba,* a dish of chicken, onions, chilies, and tomatoes; *poulet nyembwe,* chicken prepared with onion, tomato, okra, garlic, and palm oil; *liboké,* meat or chicken cooked with peanuts in banana leaves; and *akara,* fritters of pounded beans or chickpeas

SPORTS/SPORTS TEAMS

Association football (soccer) is the most popular sport in the country. Athletics, swimming, and table tennis are other sports with a significant following. Republic of Congo national teams participate in many sports at an international level.

TEAM SPORTS

Badminton

Republic of Congo Badminton Team

Basketball

Republic of Congo Basketball Team; Republic of Congo Women's Basketball Team

Football

Congo Football Team, nickname Diable Rouge (the Red Devils); Congo Women's Football Team, nickname Diable Rouge (the Red Devils); Congo Under-20 Football Team, nickname Diable Junior (the Young Devils); Republic of Congo Rugby Union team

Table Tennis

Republic of Congo Table Tennis Team

Volleyball

Republic of Congo Men's Volleyball Team; Republic of Congo Women's Volleyball Team

INDIVIDUAL SPORTS

Republic of Congo Amateur Boxing Team; Republic of Congo Athletics Team; Republic of Congo Cycling Team; Republic of Congo Fencing Team; Republic of Congo Judo Team; Republic of Congo Karate Team; Republic of Congo Swim Team; Republic of Congo Tae Kwon Do Team; Republic of Congo Weight Lifting Team; Republic of Congo Wrestling Team

NATIONAL HEROES OR PERSONIFICATIONS

André Matsoua, known as the father of modern Congolese nationalism; Abbé Fulbert Youlou, first president of independent Congo

NATIONAL HOLIDAY/INDEPENDENCE DAY

Independence Day, August 15

FESTIVALS/FAIRS

Pan-African Music Festival, July; Pointe Noire Music Festival, July

SIGNIFICANT EVENTS IN FORMATION OF NATIONAL IDENTITY

1000 B.C.E. The region's original inhabitants are related to the Pygmy peoples of central Africa. They are replaced or absorbed by the Bantu peoples, part of the great Bantu migrations.

Seventh century C.E.–eighth century C.E. The Bantus spread across the basin of the Congo River displacing or absorbing the area's earlier inhabitants. Settling into small groups, they quickly separate into distinct cultural groups and tribes.

1482–1520 Portuguese explorer Diego Cao explores the coast and makes contact with local peoples, subjects of the vast Kingdom of Kongo. The Kongo people welcome the Europeans and allow the Portuguese to establish trading posts. By 1500, the king of Kongo, the Manikongo, and most of his court have adopted Christianity.

1550–1665 The slave trade proves disastrous for Kongo and its citizens. Ever more raids on surrounding peoples for slaves to sell to the voracious Europeans disrupt a vast area of central Africa.

1665–1878 Portuguese adventurers invade the already disrupted kingdom, which quickly disintegrates into a number of small warring states. The kingdom of Téké takes control of territory that includes present Brazzaville. The French and Belgians officially outlaw slavery, but the practice continues.

1878–1882 King Leopold of Belgium* engages explorer Henry M. Stanley to establish Belgian claims in the basin of the Congo River. The French, alarmed by Stanley's explorations, begin to take a larger interest in the region.

1885–1917 The Berlin Conference partitions the territory of the Kingdom of Kongo between France*, Portugal*, and Belgium. French explorer Pierre Savorgnan de Brazza arrives in the Kingdom of Téké in 1880, where he signs a treaty with the king establishing French control over the territory.

1921–1934 The construction of a railroad from Brazzaville to Pointe Noire on the coast is said to have cost the lives of 23,000 Congolese and a few hundred Europeans. Any resistance to French colonial authority in the French Congo is brutally put down.

1957–1960 Oil is discovered near Pointe Noire on the coast. French Congo is granted independence.

1960–1968 Under its first president, a Roman Catholic priest, Abbé Fulbert Youlou, the country lurches from crisis to crisis. Revolts and antigovernment demonstrations proliferate. Youlou is overthrown, and eventually, a military government takes power. The People's Republic of Congo is proclaimed as Africa's first communist state.

1991–1992 In 1992, the country undergoes a transition to democracy.

1997–1999 A civil war erupts and draws in neighboring countries. Fighting causes widespread destruction in Brazzaville and other areas. Government agreements with most rebel groups end the violence.

2002 Flawed but fair elections usher in a new government and a new constitution.

2007–2009 An amnesty for past crimes allows many former leaders and their followers to return to the country. A slow social and economic recovery that began in 2000 continues, although the world economic slump slows the recovery.

CÔTE D'IVOIRE

OFFICIAL NAME

République de Côte d'Ivoire (French); Republic of Côte d'Ivoire, sometimes called Ivory Coast (English)

POPULATION

20,319,800 (2009e)

INHABITANTS' NAME/NICKNAME

Ivorian(s)

LANGUAGE/LANGUAGES

French (official); Dioula, many regional languages, others

RELIGION/RELIGIONS

Muslim, 39 percent; Christian, 31 percent; Animist, 12 percent; other or no religion

NATIONAL FLAG

The flag is a vertical tricolor of three equal stripes of orange, white, and green. The orange stands for the land, the savannah of the north of the country and its fertility; the white represents peace; and the green stands for hope and also for the forest lands in the south of the country.

COAT OF ARMS/SEAL

The coat of arms consists of a central shield bearing the likeness of a white elephant on a green background. The elephant is symbolically important to the nation, as it is the largest animal found in Côte d'Ivoire, as well as the source of the ivory for which the nation is named. A rising sun above the shield is a traditional symbol of a new beginning. Below the shield is a banner containing the name of the nation. The coat of arms follows the same color pattern as the national flag

MOTTO
Union, discipline, travail (French); Unity, Discipline, Labor (English)

CAPITAL CITY
Yamoussoukro; Abidjan (administrative center)

TYPE OF GOVERNMENT
Republic

NATIONAL EMBLEM
Elephant

NATIONAL COLORS
Orange, white, and green

NATIONAL ANTHEM
The anthem was adopted before the name of the country was changed from Ivory Coast to Cote d'Ivoire and the capital was moved from Abidjan to Yamoussoukro in the 1980s.

L'Abidjanaise (French); Song of Abidjan (English)

We salute you, O land of hope,
Country of hospitality;
Thy gallant legions
Have restored thy dignity.

Beloved Ivory Coast, thy sons,
Proud builders of thy greatness,
All mustered together for thy glory,
In joy will construct thee.

Proud citizens of the Ivory Coast, the country
  calls us.

If we have brought back liberty peacefully,
It will be our duty to be an example
Of the hope promised to humanity,
Forging ahead, united in new faith
The fatherland of true brotherhood.

PATRON SAINT
Our Lady of Peace

CURRENCY
CFA franc

INTERNET IDENTIFIER
.ci

VEHICLE IDENTIFICATION PLATES/ STICKERS
CI

PASSPORT
The passport cover has the name of the country in French, the coat of arms, and the French word for passport, *passeport.*

AIRLINE
Air Ivoire

NATIONAL TREE
Palm (unofficial)

NATIONAL ANIMAL
Elephant (shown on the coat of arms) (unofficial)

NATIONAL RESOURCES
Natural resources include petroleum, natural gas, diamonds, manganese, iron ore, cobalt, bauxite, copper, gold, nickel, tantalum, silica sand, clay, cocoa beans, coffee, palm oil, and hydropower. Close ties to France* since independence, the diversification of agriculture, and encouragement of foreign investment have made the country one of the most prosperous in sub-Saharan Africa, but corruption, civil war, and falling prices for

the principal crops, coffee and cocoa, have ended the economic miracle.

FOODS

Maquis, a dish of chicken and fish with onions and tomatoes, is considered the national dish. *Fufu,* dough made of boiled cassava and plantains and served with meat, fish, or various sauces, is the most popular food across much of West Africa. Other specialties include *kedjenou,* a stew of seasoned meat and vegetables served with rice; *poulet aux N'Gatietro,* chicken cooked with peanuts, onion, tomatoes, and chilies; and *ajoma,* a stew of meat cooked with palm oil.

SPORTS/SPORTS TEAMS

Association football (soccer) is the most popular sport in the Cote d'Ivoire. Basketball is also a popular spectator sport and is gaining support among younger players. Cote d'Ivoire national teams participate in many sports at an international level.

TEAM SPORTS

Baseball

Cote d'Ivoire Baseball Team; Cote d'Ivoire Softball Team

Basketball

Cote d'Ivoire Basketball Team; Cote d'Ivoire Women's Basketball Team

Football

Cote d'Ivoire Football Team, nickname Les Éléphants (the Elephants); Cote d'Ivoire Women's Football Team, nickname Les Éléphants (the Elephants); Cote d'Ivoire Under-23 Football Team, nickname Ivoire Olympique (the Olympic Team); Cote d'Ivoire Under-20 Football Team, nickname Les Elephanteaux Juniors (the Young Elephants); Cote d'Ivoire Under-17 Football Team, nickname Les Elephanteaux Cadets; Cote d'Ivoire Rugby Union Team, nickname

Les Éléphants (the Elephants); Cote d'Ivoire Beach Soccer Team; Cote d'Ivoire Rugby League Team; Cote d'Ivoire Rugby Union Team (Sevens), nickname Cote d'Ivoire Sevens or Cote d'Ivoire 7s

Handball

Cote d'Ivoire Handball Team; Cote d'Ivoire Women's Handball Team

Racing

Cote d'Ivoire Speedway Team

Table Tennis

Cote d'Ivoire Table Tennis Team

Tennis

Cote d'Ivoire Davis Cup Team

Volleyball

Cote d'Ivoire Volleyball Team; Cote d'Ivoire Women's Volleyball Team

INDIVIDUAL SPORTS

Cote d'Ivoire Amateur Boxing Team; Cote d'Ivoire Archery Team; Cote d'Ivoire Athletics Team; Cote d'Ivoire Canoeing Team; Cote d'Ivoire Cycling Team; Cote d'Ivoire Judo Team; Cote d'Ivoire Rowing Team; Cote d'Ivoire Swim Team; Cote d'Ivoire Tae Kwon Do Team; Cote d'Ivoire Weight Lifting Team

NATIONAL HEROES OR PERSONIFICATIONS

Queen Abia Pokou, the 18th century queen of the Baule who led them to the region from present Ghana*; Félix Houphouët-Boigny, who led the country to independence and served as president until his death in 1993; Dandi Lou Hélène Amanan, a peace advocate and activist nominated for the Nobel Peace Prize in 2005; Bernard Binlin Dadié, a poet, novelist, and politician

NATIONAL HOLIDAY/INDEPENDENCE DAY

Independence Day, August 7

FESTIVALS/FAIRS

Mask Festival (Fêtes des Masques), November; Bouaké Carnival, March

SIGNIFICANT EVENTS IN FORMATION OF NATIONAL IDENTITY

2000 B.C.E–600 C.E. Bantu tribes, part of the great Bantu migrations, settle the region from the east. Little is known of the early cultures, as artifacts disappear in the humid climate.

1460 Portuguese sailors visit the coast, the first Europeans to see the region.

1637 French missionaries land at Assinie. Early contacts are limited to a few missionaries, due to the inhospitable coastline and fear of the indigenous peoples.

16th century–18th century Two related Akan tribes invade the region: the Agnis, who settle in the southeast and along the coast, and the Baules, who settle the central region.

1843–1844 The French sign treaties with local kings in the southeast, placing their kingdoms under French protection.

1860–1895 The region, called the Ivory Coast, is joined with Gabon* in a French colony. In 1883, the region is subordinated to the Guinea colony. The Ivory Coast is added to French West Africa.

1895–1915 Traders, missionaries, explorers, and military men gradually extend French control inland from the coast. Total pacification is finally accomplished.

1946 After the Second World War, the colony becomes an overseas territory of France. French citizenship is granted, the right to organize politically is recognized, and various forms of forced labor are abolished.

1960–1993 Dissatisfied with limited independence, the country becomes fully independent but retains close ties to France. Large agricultural projects of coffee and cocoa are retained and enlarged. Félix Houphouët-Boigny, hailed as the father of independence, becomes the first president and remains in office until 1993, overseeing an economic expansion and widespread prosperity but restricting democratic rights.

1993 The president's death ushers in a period of instability. The government is overthrown in a military coup in 1999, leading to increasing ethnic and religious violence and rioting.

2002 A rebellion in the north and west leads to civil war, atrocities, and widespread destruction. The war divides the mainly Muslim north from the mostly Christian south.

2003–2006 A reconciliation process under international auspices begins. Foreign troops intervene in the fighting and remain as peacekeepers. Thousands of foreigners, mainly French, are evacuated. Attempts to broker a peace by African leaders fail repeatedly.

2007 After weeks of negotiations, a peace agreement is signed. A reconciliation government is formed with leaders from both sides. Disarmament and integration of the opposing armed forces begins.

2008–2009 The people of Cote d'Ivoire show their frustration by blaming politicians and leaders on both sides of the civil war. The country's standard of living, once one of the highest in West Africa, has dropped dramatically, corruption remains widespread, and forced labor is again a social problem in many areas.

DJIBOUTI

OFFICIAL NAME

Jumhūriyyat Jībūtī /Jamhuuriyadda Jabuuti (transliteration from Arabic); République de Djibouti (French); Republic of Djibouti (English)

POPULATION

527,900 (2009e)

INHABITANTS' NAME/NICKNAME

Djiboutian(s)

LANGUAGE/LANGUAGES

Arabic, French (both official); Somali, Afar, others

RELIGION/RELIGIONS

Muslim, 94 percent (official); Christian, 6 percent; other or no religion

NATIONAL FLAG

The flag has two equal stripes of pale blue over green, with a white isosceles triangle on the hoist bearing a red five-pointed star. The star represents the five historical Somali regions and also stands for unity. The green symbolizes the earth, the blue represents the sky, and the white stands for peace.

COAT OF ARMS/SEAL

The coat of arms is bordered on the sides with laurel branches. Within this perimeter is a vertical spear, in front of which is a traditional shield. Underneath the shield, two hands rise away from the spear and each holding a large knife. These two hands symbolize the two ethnic groups of the nation: the Afar and the Somali group Issa.

CAPITAL CITY

Djibouti

TYPE OF GOVERNMENT

Parliamentary democracy

NATIONAL COLORS

Pale blue, green, and white

NATIONAL ANTHEM

The anthem, called simply "Djibouti" or "National Anthem of Djibouti," was adopted at independence in 1977.

Djibouti, or National Anthem of Djibouti

Arise with strength, for we have raised our flag,
The flag that has cost us dear
With extremes of thirst and pain.

Our flag, whose colors are the everlasting green of the earth,

The blue of the sky, and white, the color of peace;
And in the center, the red star of blood.

O flag of ours, what a glorious sight!

CURRENCY

Djibouti franc

INTERNET IDENTIFIER

.dj

VEHICLE IDENTIFICATION PLATES/STICKERS

DJ

PASSPORT

The passport cover has the name of the country in Arabic and French, the coat of arms, and the word *passport* in Arabic and French.

AIRLINE

Daallo Airlines

NATIONAL ANIMAL

Gazelle (unofficial)

NATIONAL RESOURCES

Natural resources include geothermal capacity, gold, clay, granite, limestone, marble, salt, diatomite, gypsum, pumice, and petroleum. The port of Djibouti, with its strategic position on the Red Sea, is one of the country's most important resources.

FOODS

Skoudehkaris, a rice dish of lamb, tomatoes, onion, and spices, also called Djibouti rice, is considered the national dish. *Ingera,* traditional Djiboutian bread, is considered the national staple. Other typical dishes include *fah-fah,* a soup of goat, potatoes, cabbage, leeks, tomatoes, garlic, onions, and chilies; *yetakelt w'et,* a spicy vegetable stew; and *harira*, a dish of meat, lentils, tomatoes, and spices.

SPORTS/SPORTS TEAMS

Association football (soccer) is the country's most popular sport. Djibouti national teams participate in many sports at an international level.

TEAM SPORTS

Basketball

Djibouti Basketball Team; Djibouti Women's Basketball Team

Football

Djibouti Football Team, nickname Riverains de la Mer Rouge (Red Sea Coasters); Djibouti Under-20 Football Team, nickname the Young Red Sea Coasters; Djibouti Women's Football Team, nickname Riverains de la Mer Rouge (Red Sea Coasters)

Table Tennis

Djibouti Table Tennis Team

Tennis

Djibouti Davis Cup Team

Volleyball

Djibouti Men's Volleyball Team

INDIVIDUAL SPORTS

Djibouti Athletics Team; Djibouti Judo Team; Djibouti Modern Pentathlon Team

NATIONAL HEROES OR PERSONIFICATIONS

Hassan Gouled Aptidon, the country's first president; Ahmed Dini Ahmed, an Afar politician and leader; Ismael Omar Guelleh, the president since 1999; Abdourahman Waberi, Djibouti's most famous author, with works translated into more than 10 languages.

NATIONAL HOLIDAY/INDEPENDENCE DAY

Independence Day, June 27

FESTIVALS/FAIRS

Labor Day (Fete du Travail), May 1; Independence Day Festival, June 27

SIGNIFICANT EVENTS IN FORMATION OF NATIONAL IDENTITY

2000 B.C.E.–799 C.E. Nomadic tribes trade hides and skins for perfumes and spices at small ports on the Red Sea. The forbidding landscape discourages most invaders, although at times the region is under the nominal rule of Ethiopia*.

700 C.E.–900 C.E. Seafaring Arabs convert the coastal tribes to Islam. Carried by caravans and raiders, the new religion spreads to the tribes of the isolated interior.

1839–1862 A French expedition into the Horn of Africa marks the beginning of French interest. France* signs treaties with local rulers and purchases the anchorage of Obock.

1884–1897 French Somaliland is declared a protectorate. The French administration is moved from Obock to Djibouti, with its important port. France and Ethiopia agree to the boundaries of the protectorate.

1940–1945 After the fall of France in World War II, French Somaliland comes under fascist rule from Vichy France. The British maintain a 101-day blockade until the colony is surrendered. The colony is returned to France at the end of the war.

1957–1958 Political reforms in the French Empire give French Somaliland considerable self-government. The colony votes to join the French Community as an overseas territory.

1966–1967 A visit by French President Charles de Gaulle is marked by large demonstrations of ethnic Somalis demanding independence and union with neighboring Somalia*. The Afars, favored by the French administration, reject the Somali demands. A referendum on the territory's future results in 60 percent support for continued association with France. The name of the territory is changed to the French Territory of the Afars and Issas.

1976–1977 Citizenship laws that favored the Afar minority are changed to reflect the desires of the majority Somalis. A vote on independence leads to the establishment of the Republic of Djibouti under Hassan Gouled Aptidon.

1981   Djibouti is made a one-party state.

1991   Civil war breaks out between the Somali-dominated government and a predominately Afar rebel group.

2001   A peace accord ends the decade-long civil war. The accord provides for an ethnic Somali president and an Afar prime minister.

2002   A new Family Law is adopted that enhances the protection of women and children, replacing traditional Islamic Sharia law.

2006   More than 50 percent of girls attend school, a high percentage for the region.

2008–2009   The thousands of ethnic Somali refugees in the country present an economic and logistical problem.

EQUATORIAL GUINEA

OFFICIAL NAME
République de Guinea Équatoriale (French), República de Guinea Ecuatorial (Spanish); Republic of Equatorial Guinea (English)

POPULATION
1,137,300 (2009e)

INHABITANTS' NAME/NICKNAME
Equatorial Guinean(s); Equatoguinean(s)

LANGUAGE/LANGUAGES
French, Spanish (both official); Fang, Bubi, others

RELIGION/RELIGIONS
Roman Catholic, 87 percent; Protestant, indigenous beliefs, others

NATIONAL FLAG
The flag is a horizontal tricolor of green, white, and red, with a blue triangle at the hoist and the coat of arms centered on the white stripe. Green symbolizes the country's natural resources and the jungles; blue symbolizes the sea, which connects the mainland Rio Muni with the islands; white symbolizes peace; and red stands for independence.

COAT OF ARMS/SEAL
The coat of arms has a silver shield, which contains a silk cotton tree (God tree). Underneath the shield, the national motto of Equatorial Guinea is shown. Over the shield are six yellow, six-pointed stars. The silk-cotton tree represents the country's ties to Spain, the former colonial power, as the first treaty between Spain and a local chief was signed beneath a silk-cotton tree.

MOTTO
Unidad, paz, justicia (Spanish); Unity, Peace, Justice (English)

CAPITAL CITY
Malabo

TYPE OF GOVERNMENT
Republic

NATIONAL EMBLEM
Silk-cotton tree

NATIONAL COLORS
Red, white, green, and blue

NATIONAL ANTHEM
The anthem was adopted at independence from Spain in 1968 and has remained despite several upheavals and changes of government.

> **Caminemos Pisando La Senda (Spanish); Let Us Walk the Path (English)**
>
> Let us walk the path
> Of our immense happiness,
> In brotherhood, without separation,
> Let us sing, "Liberty!"

After two centuries of being subjected
To colonial domination,
In fraternal union, without discrimination,
Let us sing, "Liberty!"

Let us cry, "Long live free Guinea,"
And let us always remain united.
Let us cry, "Long live free Guinea,"
And let us always defend our liberty.

Let us cry, "Long live free Guinea,"
And let us always conserve national
  independence
And let us conserve, and let us conserve,
National independence.

PATRON SAINT
Our Lady of the Immaculate Conception

CURRENCY
CFA franc

INTERNET IDENTIFIER
.gq

VEHICLE IDENTIFICATION PLATES/ STICKERS
GQ (unofficial)

PASSPORT
The passport cover has the name of the country in Spanish and French, the coat of arms, and the word *passport* in Spanish and French.

AIRLINE
Ecuato Guineana (EGA Ecuato Guineana de Aviación)

NATIONAL FLOWER
Silk-cotton blossom

NATIONAL TREE
Silk-cotton tree

NATIONAL RESOURCES
Natural resources include petroleum, natural gas, timber, gold, bauxite, diamonds, tanta-lum, sand and gravel, and clay. The discovery of oil reserves in 1996 has contributed to a dramatic increase in revenues. By 2004, Equatorial Guinea had become the third-largest oil producer in Sub-Saharan Africa. The large number of Equatorial Guineans living outside the country is an important source of foreign currency through family remittances.

FOODS
Pollo del Congo, a chicken dish with crushed pumpkin seeds and served with rice, is considered the national dish. Other specialties include *maiz con judias,* a dish of corn and beans, also considered a national dish; *paella de cordonices,* a rice dish with guinea fowl; *peacaso al fuego,* grilled fresh fish; *espinacas,* spinach cooked with peanut butter; and *sopa de pimientos,* a soup of meat, onions, and peppers.

SPORTS/SPORTS TEAMS
Association football (soccer) is the country's most popular sport. Equatorial Guinea has been chosen to co-host, along with Gabon*, the 2012 African Cup of Nations. Equatorial Guinea national teams participate in many sports at an international level

TEAM SPORTS
Badminton
Equatorial Guinea Badminton Team

Football
Equatorial Guinea Football Team, nickname Nzalang Nacional; Equatorial Guinea Women's Football Team, nickname Nzalang Nacional; Equatorial Guinea Women's Under-19 Football Team; Equatorial Guinea Under-20 Football Team

Table Tennis
Equatorial Guinea Table Tennis Team

Volleyball

Equatorial Guinea Men's Volleyball Team

INDIVIDUAL SPORTS

Equatorial Guinea Amateur Boxing Team; Equatorial Guinea Athletics Team; Equatorial Guinea Canoeing Team; Equatorial Guinea Swim Team; Equatorial Guinea Tae Kwon Do Team

NATIONAL HEROES OR PERSONIFICATIONS

Eric Moussambani, famous swimmer nicknamed "Eric the Eel" who won an Olympic medal at the 2000 Olympics

NATIONAL HOLIDAY/INDEPENDENCE DAY

Independence Day, October 12

FESTIVALS/FAIRS

Independence Day celebrations, October; President's Birthday, June

SIGNIFICANT EVENTS IN FORMATION OF NATIONAL IDENTITY

1000 B.C.E. The first inhabitants of the region are believed to be Labelabes, a Pygmy people. Later migrations from Central Africa populate the region with various Bantu peoples.

1472 C.E.–1474 C.E. Portuguese explorer Frenão do Pó, seeking a route to India*, arrives at Bioko Island, which he calls *Formosa*, meaning "beautiful." The island is soon called Fernando Pó after its first European visitor. Portugal* colonizes the islands of Fernando Pó and Annobón.

1778–1810 The Treaty of El Pardo, between Portugal and Spain*, cedes the islands and commercial rights on the African mainland between the rivers Niger and Ogoue to Spain in exchange for territory in the New World. The territory is governed as part of the viceroyalty of Río de la Plata, situated in Buenos Aires, Argentina. Argentina's independence brings the territory under direct Spanish rule.

1827 The British establish a base on Bioko to combat the slave trade.

1844 The territory is reorganized and becomes known as the Spanish Territories of the Gulf of Equatorial Guinea.

1885 The mainland territory, Rio Muni, becomes a protectorate. The Spanish develop large cacao plantations and import workers from Nigeria* to Bioko as paid labor.

1926 The mainland, Rio Muni, and the island territories are joined in the colony of Spanish Guinea.

1959 The colony becomes a Spanish province with the same status as the provinces of Spain. Legislative elections are held, with voters given a choice of several political parties, while voters in Spain, under the dictatorship of Francisco Franco, are given no choice.

1963 The province is granted limited autonomy under a joint legislative assembly representing the two provinces, Rio Muni and the islands. The province has one of the highest per capita incomes in sub-Saharan Africa.

1968–1972 Equatorial Guinea becomes an independent republic. Francisco Macias Nguema is elected president. Macias creates a one-party state, abrogates key clauses of the constitution, and proclaims himself president for life. Mass executions, the violent suppression of a separatist movement on Bioko, and military suppression leave thousands dead, while many flee to other countries.

1972–1979 The Macias regime is characterized by pilferage, corruption, brutality, and neglect. The country's infrastructure falls into ruin. Nigerian cocoa workers, some 60,000 people, are evacuated from Bioko in 1976. All schools are ordered closed in 1975, and the churches are closed in 1978. All citizens are ordered to change their names to authentic African names. Macias' nephew, Teodoro Obiang Nguema Mbasogo, the warden of a notorious government prison, leads a successful coup. The country's population is only a third of what it was at independence.

1982–2002 Obiang ends military rule, and a new constitution is adopted. Oil reserves are discovered in 1996. Obiang is reelected with 97 percent of the vote in an election noted for irregularities.

2006–2009 Equatorial Guinea is the third largest oil producer in sub-Saharan Africa, but the population remains among the poorest in Africa. Macias Nguema, the longest-serving leader in Africa south of the Sahara, oversees an oil-rich country with one of Africa's poorest populations and levels of corruption, lack of public services, and official poverty among Africa's worst, while an American firm trains the growing national army, the only government institution to receive adequate financing.

ERITREA

OFFICIAL NAME

Hagere Ertra (Tiginya); Dawiat Iritriya (transliteration from Arabic); State of Eritrea (English)

POPULATION

4,461,200 (2009e)

INHABITANTS' NAME/NICKNAME

Eritrean(s)

LANGUAGE/LANGUAGES

Tiginya, Arabic, English (working languages/de facto official); Afar, Kunama, Tigre, others

RELIGION/RELIGIONS

Eritrean Orthodox, about 50 percent; Muslim, about 50 percent; Roman Catholic, Protestant, other or no religion

NATIONAL FLAG

The flag is dominated by a red triangle extending from the hoist to the fly with complementary green and blue triangles above and below, respectively. In the red triangle is a yellow wreath symbol with 14 leaves on each side. Green stands for the fertility of the country and for agriculture; blue for the ocean; and red for the blood lost in the fight for freedom. The use of triangles is also symbolic, because the red triangle diminishes, symbolizing the end of bloodshed for the independence of the country.

COAT OF ARMS/SEAL

The coat of arms consists of a dromedary in natural colors standing on sand surrounded by an olive wreath. On the bottom is a band with the name of the nation in the three de facto official languages—English in the middle, Tigrinya on the left, and Arabic on the right.

CAPITAL CITY

Asmara

TYPE OF GOVERNMENT

Transitional republic

NATIONAL EMBLEM

Dromedary

NATIONAL COLORS

Green, red, and blue

NATIONAL ANTHEM

The anthem is based on the separatist anthem during the 30-year war with Ethiopia. It was adopted at independence in 1993 with only a few changes to the lyrics.

Ertra, Ertra, Ertra (Tiginya); Eritrea, Eritrea, Eritrea (English)

Eritrea, Eritrea, Eritrea,
Her enemy decimated,
and her sacrifices vindicated by liberation.
Steadfast in her goal,
symbolizing endurance,
Eritrea, the pride of her oppressed people,
proved that the truth prevails.
Eritrea, Eritrea,
holds her rightful place in the world.
Dedication that led to liberation,
Will build up and make her green,
We shall honor her with progress,
a word for her to embellish.
Eritrea, Eritrea, holds her rightful place in the world.

PATRON SAINT

Saint Isaac (Yeshaq)

CURRENCY
Eritrean nakfa

INTERNET IDENTIFIER
.er

VEHICLE IDENTIFICATION PLATES/STICKERS
ER

PASSPORT
The passport cover has the name of the country in Tiginya, Arabic, and English; the coat of arms; and the word *passport* in the three languages.

AIRLINE
Eritrean Airlines

NATIONAL TREE
Olive (unofficial)

NATIONAL ANIMAL
Dromedary

NATIONAL RESOURCES
Natural resources include potash, gold, zinc, copper, salt, and potential oil and natural gas. Fish from the Red Sea are important to the economy. The port of Massawa, one of the most important in the region, is a major asset and is being developed.

FOODS
Zigini, a stew of lamb and vegetables, is considered the national dish. *Tsebhis,* stews of beef, chicken, mutton, or vegetables served with *injera* or *taita,* flatbreads made from teff, wheat, or sorghum, are also considered national dishes. *Hilbet,* pasta made from lentils or fava beans, a legacy of the Italian colonial era, is also popular. Other national dishes include *alitcha birsen,* a dish of lentils, tomatoes, garlic, and chilies; *be'geh zigni,* a lamb stew; *d'nish zigni,* a spicy stew of potatoes, tomatoes, and onions; *doro zigni,* chicken stew; and *kulu'wa,* a dish of beef, onion, tomatoes, cloves, and spices.

SPORTS/SPORTS TEAMS
Association football (soccer) is the most popular sport. Cycling and bicycle racing, a legacy of the Italian occupation, are also very popular. Volleyball is becoming increasingly popular. Eritrea national teams participate in many sports at an international level

TEAM SPORTS
Badminton
Eritrea Badminton Team

Basketball
Eritrea Basketball Team; Eritrea Women's Basketball Team; Eritrea Wheelchair Basketball Team

Football
Eritrea Football Team, nickname the Red Sea Boys; Eritrea Women's Football Team, nickname the Red Sea Girls

Volleyball
Eritrea Men's Volleyball Team; Eritrea Women's Volleyball Team

INDIVIDUAL SPORTS
Eritrea Athletics Team; Eritrea Cycling Team

NATIONAL HEROES OR PERSONIFICATIONS
Isaias Afewerki, leader of the independence movement and Eritrea's first president; The Eritrean Martyrs, the many who died to bring independence to Eritrea.

NATIONAL HOLIDAY/INDEPENDENCE DAY
Liberation Day, May 24; Martyr's Day, June 20

FESTIVALS/FAIRS
National Festival of Eritrea, August

SIGNIFICANT EVENTS IN FORMATION OF NATIONAL IDENTITY

3500 B.C.E. Cultures related to those of the Nile Valley flourish along the Red Sea.

Eighth century B.C.E.–fifth century B.C.E. A kingdom known as D'mt is established in Eritrea and northern Ethiopia*. The kingdom expands to become an important regional state.

Fourth century B.C.E. Aksum becomes the major power in much of Eritrea and the Ethiopian Highlands.

Fourth century C.E. The kingdom adopts Christianity, becoming the second official Christian state (after Armenia) and the first country to feature a Christian cross on coinage.

7th century–10th century The advent of Islam across the Red Sea and the Arab invasion lead to a decline, and the empire breaks into smaller rival states. Islam is introduced into northern Eritrea.

1557 Invading Ottoman Turks occupy the coast, leaving the interior to the tribal peoples. The Ottomans move south, absorbing several small sultanates. Ottoman rules lasts for over 300 years in one form or another.

1813–1882 Egyptians, also nominally under Ottoman rule, take control of the region. Direct Ottoman rule is restored over most of Eritrea. Egypt* again assumes control from 1865 to 1882. An Italian colonial company purchases the port of Asseb in 1869.

1882–1888 Italy* takes direct control of Asseb and wrests Massawa from the Egyptians. Italian expansion into the interior begins. Italy proclaims the protectorate of Asseb, including Asseb, Massawa, and parts of the hinterland.

1890 The territory is unified as the Italian colony of Eritrea.

1936 Eritrea and parts of Ethiopia conquered by Italy become Italian East Africa.

1941–1951 During the Second World War, British troops take control of the Italian territories on the Horn of Africa. The British remain after the war as administrators under a United Nations mandate.

1952 Eritrea and Ethiopia form a federation under the sovereignty of the Ethiopian monarch. Eritrea is granted autonomy, but separatist organizations begin actions to separate from Ethiopia.

1962–1985 The Ethiopian government revokes Eritrea's autonomy and incorporates the country into Ethiopia as a province. Heavy fighting follows the overthrow of the Ethiopian monarchy and the establishment of a Marxist state.

1990–1993 The nationalist groups fighting for independence control virtually all of Eritrea. Independence is declared.

1993 Isaias Afewerki, a leader of the war for independence, becomes the country's first president. The reconstruction of the war-shattered country begins.

1998 Hostilities between Eritrea and Ethiopia are renewed. A vicious border war breaks out.

1998–2006 The Afewerki government becomes increasingly authoritarian, closing down opposition political parties and the press and arresting outspoken critics.

2006–2009 Increased tensions between Eritrea and Ethiopia again threaten war, but the 2002 peace accords and border demarcation remain in effect and are extended every six months. Elections continue to be postponed.

ETHIOPIA

OFFICIAL NAME

ye- Ītyōp̣p̣yā Fēdēralāwī; Dīmōkrāsīyāwī Rīpeblīk (transliteration from Amharic); Federal Democratic Republic of Ethiopia (English)

POPULATION

79,646,800 (2009e)

INHABITANTS' NAME/NICKNAME

Ethiopian(s)

LANGUAGE/LANGUAGES

Amharic (official); Oromigna, Tigrigna, Samoligna, others

RELIGION/RELIGIONS

Ethiopian Orthodox, 51 percent; Muslim, 33 percent; Protestant, 10 percent; indigenous beliefs, other or no religion

NATIONAL FLAG

The flag is a horizontal tricolor of green, yellow, and red with a centered pale blue disk bearing a gold pentagram (star) with five golden rays. Blue represents peace, the star stands for the diversity and unity of Ethiopia, and the rays symbolize the sun and prosperity. The green symbolizes the land and hope for the future, yellow represents peace and love, and red symbolizes strength.

COAT OF ARMS/SEAL

The coat of arms is a pale blue disk that contains a golden pentagram radiating rays of light. The pentagram originates from the seal of King Solomon, from whom the former Ethiopian royal family claimed descent. Today, the pentagram stands for the diversity of the nationalities in Ethiopia and the unity of the country.

CAPITAL CITY

Addis Ababa

TYPE OF GOVERNMENT

Federal republic

NATIONAL EMBLEM

King Solomon's pentagram; the famed obelisk at Aksum

NATIONAL COLORS

Green, yellow, and red

NATIONAL ANTHEM

Ethiopia has had three official national anthems, the first under the monarchy from 1930 to 1975 and the second under the one-party state from 1975 to 1992, the year the present anthem was adopted.

> **Wodefit Gesgeshi, Widd Innat Ityopp'ya (transliteration from Amharic); March Forward, Dear Mother Ethiopia (English)**
>
> Respect for citizenship is strong in our Ethiopia;
> National pride is seen, shining from one side to another.
> For peace, for justice, for the freedom of peoples,
> In equality and in love we stand united.
> Firm of foundation, we do not dismiss humanness;
> We are people who live through work.
> Wonderful is the stage of tradition, mistress of a proud heritage,
> Natural grace, mother of a valorous people.
> We shall protect you—we have a duty;
> Our Ethiopia, live! And let us be proud of you!

PATRON SAINT

Saint Frumentius; Saint George

CURRENCY

Ethiopian birr

INTERNET IDENTIFIER

.et

VEHICLE IDENTIFICATION PLATES/STICKERS

ETH

PASSPORT

The passport cover has the name of the country in Amharic and English, the coat of arms, and the word *passport* in Amharic and English.

AIRLINE

Ethiopian Airlines

NATIONAL FLOWER

Calla lily

NATIONAL ANIMAL

Ethiopian wolf (unofficial); lion (historical)

NATIONAL RESOURCES

Natural resources include potash, salt, copper, platinum, natural gas (unexploited), small reserves of gold, and hydropower. Ethiopia has abundant arable land but suffers periodic droughts that hinder agriculture; also, Ethiopians are not allowed to own land but only to rent or lease it. The Ethiopian Diaspora is a valuable source of foreign currency and investment.

FOODS

Doro wat, a stew of chicken, beef, lamb, a variety of vegetables, and spices, is considered the national dish. *Injera,* a tangy flatbread, is also considered a specialty. Other national specialties include *abish,* a dish of beef, onions, eggs, and goat cheese; *siga wat,* a beef stew; *tibs wat,* a dish of beef, onions, and spices; *yemiser w'at,* a spicy lentil and tomato stew; *yeshimbra asa,* fish prepared with onions, chickpea flour, and spices; *shero wat,* a dish of dried green peas; and *atklit,* a vegetarian dish of potatoes, onions, carrots, cabbage, and spices.

SPORTS/SPORTS TEAMS

Athletics, particularly middle-distance and long-distance races, are very popular. Association football (soccer) is the most popular spectator sport. Ethiopia national teams participate in many sports at an international level.

TEAM SPORTS

Badminton

Ethiopia Badminton Team

Basketball

Ethiopia Basketball Team; Ethiopia Women's Basketball Team

Football

Ethiopia Football Team, nickname the Walya Antelopes or the Walyas; Ethiopia Women's Football Team, nickname the Walya Antelopes or the Walyas

Handball

Ethiopia Handball Team

Kabaddi

Ethiopia Kabaddi Team

Table Tennis

Ethiopia Table Tennis Team

Tennis

Ethiopia Davis Cup Team; Ethiopia Fed Cup Team

Volleyball

Ethiopia Men's Volleyball Team

INDIVIDUAL SPORTS

Ethiopia Amateur Boxing Team; Ethiopia Athletics Team; Ethiopia Cycling Team; Ethiopia Canoeing Team; Ethiopia Equestrian Team; Ethiopia Gymnastics Team; Ethiopia Judo Team; Ethiopia Swim Team; Ethiopia Tae Kwon Do Team; Ethiopia Weight Lifting Team

NATIONAL HEROES OR PERSONIFICATIONS

Menelik I, believed to be the son of King Solomon and Makeda, the Queen of Sheba, who, according to tradition, brought the Ark of the Covenant to Ethiopia; Emperor Tewodros II, who reunited Ethiopia in 1855; Haile Selassie, the last emperor of Ethiopia who was overthrown in 1974 and died under mysterious circumstances in 1975.

NATIONAL HOLIDAY/ INDEPENDENCE DAY

National Day, May 28

FESTIVALS/FAIRS

Enkutatash, Ethiopian New Year, September; Timket (Eiphany), January 19; Meskal (Finding of the True Cross), March

SIGNIFICANT EVENTS IN FORMATION OF NATIONAL IDENTITY

Eighth century B.C.E.–fifth century B.C.E. A kingdom known as D'mt is established in Ethiopia and northern Eritrea*.

First century B.C.E. The Aksumite kingdom arises, the predecessor of the later Ethiopian kingdom.

316 C.E. Groups of Middle Eastern Christians, including Frumentius, the nation's patron saint, embark on a journey of exploration along the coast. Frumentius is credited with introducing Christianity to Ethiopia. Christianity is proclaimed the official state religion, making Ethiopia the second official Christian state, after Armenia*.

1428–1508 Surrounded by hostile Muslim peoples, the Empire of Ethiopia attempts to make diplomatic contact with Christian Europe. The first continuous relations with a European country are established with Portugal*.

1541–1543 Portugal sends soldiers and arms to aid the Ethiopians engaged in war with the Muslims.

1632 Ethiopian Orthodox Christianity is declared the state religion.

1755–1855 Ethiopia isolates itself from the world using diplomacy or war to maintain a Christian kingdom in an area that is majority Muslim.

1880s Sahie Selassie, the king of the small state of Showa, begins to expand his kingdom to the south and east. His expansion results in the borders of modern Ethiopia.

1896 The Ethiopians defeat an invading army sent from Italy* and remain an independent state, the Empire of Ethiopia or Abyssinia.

1916–1930 Ethiopia begins to modernize under the imperial regent and later emperor, Haile Selassie.

1936–1941 The Second Italo-Abyssinian War ends with Ethiopian defeat. Ethiopia becomes part of Italian East Africa until it is liberated by British troops during the Second World War.

1942–1952 Emperor Haile Selassie returns to the throne and again attempts to modernize the country. He outlaws slavery and orchestrates the federation with former Italian Eritrea.

1974 A long and costly war against Eritrean and other disaffected minorities, the worldwide oil crisis, drought, and food shortages result in a coup that overthrows the monarchy.

1975–1992 Coups, uprisings, and droughts characterize the first years of the republic. A new government declares a communist state and begins the red terror, with forced deportations, mass executions, suppression of ethnic minorities, and the persecution of the former ruling Amhara people.

1980s–1990s Droughts and famines leave over 1 million people dead. A coalition of ethnic national groups defeats the communists and takes control of the government in 1991. A long border war begins with neighboring Eritrea.

1993–2000 Eritrea separates from Ethiopia as an independent country. Ethiopia is made a federation of autonomous ethnic states. Ethiopia's first free elections are held. The border war ends, but tensions remain.

2000–2009 Government harassment and intimidation prompt the major opposition parties to withdraw from local elections. Sporadic rebellions continue among the country's many ethnic groups, particularly outside the core Semitic areas of Amhara and Tigre.

GABON

OFFICIAL NAME

République Gabonaise (French); Gabonese Republic (English)

POPULATION

1,726,700 (2009e)

INHABITANTS' NAME/NICKNAME

Gabonese

LANGUAGE/LANGUAGES

French (official); Fang, Myene, Nzebi, Bapounou/Eschira/Bandjabi, others

RELIGION/RELIGIONS

Roman Catholic, 50–75 percent; Muslim, animist, other or no religion

NATIONAL FLAG

The flag is a horizontal tricolor of green, yellow, and blue. The color green represents the forests and the country's natural resources, gold represents the equator and the equatorial sun, and blue stands for the water that comes from the sea and the sky.

COAT OF ARMS/SEAL

The coat of arms consists of a central shield supported by black panthers, which symbolize the vigilance and courage of the president who protects the country. The shield is charged with three golden disks, called bezants, that symbolize the mineral wealth of Gabon. Below the bezants is a sailing ship that represents Gabon moving forward to a brighter future. The *okoumé* tree at the top symbolizes the timber trade.

The coat of arms is unusual in having two ribbons with mottos in two different languages. The ribbon below the shield has the motto in French. The second ribbon is placed beneath the branches of the *okoumé* tree and has the motto in Latin.

MOTTO(S)

Union, travail, justice (French); Union, Work, Justice (English)

Uniti progrediemur (Latin); Let us go forward together (English)

CAPITAL CITY

Libreville

TYPE OF GOVERNMENT

Republic

NATIONAL EMBLEM

Black panther

NATIONAL COLORS

Green, yellow, and blue

NATIONAL ANTHEM

La Concorde (French); The Concord (English)

Chorus

United in concord and brotherhood,
Awake, Gabon, dawn is at hand.
Stir up the spirit that thrills and inspires us!
At last we rise up to attain happiness.

Dazzling and proud, the sublime day dawns,
Dispelling for ever injustice and shame.
May it still advance and calm our fears,
May it promote virtue and banish warfare.

Chorus

Yes, may the happy days of which our ancestors dreamed
Come for us at last, rejoicing our hearts,
And banish the sorcerers, those perfidious deceivers
Who sowed poison and spread fear.

Chorus

So that, in the eyes of the world and of friendly nations,
The immortal Gabon may maintain her good repute,
Let us forget our quarrels, let us build together
The new structure of which we all have dreamed.

Chorus

From the shores of the ocean to the heart of the forest,
Let us remain vigilant, without weakness and without hatred!
Around this flag which leads us to honor,
Let us salute the fatherland and ever sing!

PATRON SAINT
Saint Mary

CURRENCY
CFA franc

INTERNET IDENTIFIER
.ga

VEHICLE IDENTIFICATION PLATES/ STICKERS
G

PASSPORT
The passport cover has the name of the country in French, the coat of arms, and the word for passport in French.

AIRLINES
Gabon Airlines; Arrinat Airlines

NATIONAL TREE
Okoumé (torchwood)

NATIONAL ANIMAL
Black panther

NATIONAL RESOURCES
Natural resources include petroleum, natural gas, diamonds, niobium, manganese, uranium, gold, timber, iron ore, and hydropower. Offshore oil production gives the Gabonese per capita incomes of four times the average for sub-Saharan Africa.

FOODS
Poulet nyembwe, chicken cooked with onions, tomatoes, okra, chilies, and *nyembwe* (palm butter), is considered the national dish. *Injera,* round flatbread, is a Gabonese staple. *Fufu,* rice or cassava paste shaped into balls and served with various sauces, including meats or fish, is also considered a national dish. Another characteristic dish is *boeuf ogbono,* beef prepared with a sauce of wild mango seeds, palm oil, tomatoes, and dried shrimp.

SPORTS/SPORTS TEAMS
Association football (soccer) is the country's most popular sport. Basketball is also very popular. Gabon national teams participate in many sports at international level.

TEAM SPORTS

Basketball
Gabon Basketball Team; Gabon Wheelchair Basketball Team; Women's Basketball Team

Football
Gabon Football Team, nickname Azingo Nationale or Les Panthères (the Panthers); Gabon Women's Football Team, nickname Azingo Nationale

Table Tennis
Gabon National Table Tennis Team

Tennis
Gabon Davis Cup Team

Volleyball
Gabon Men's National Volleyball Team

INDIVIDUAL SPORTS
Gabon National Amateur Boxing Team; Gabon National Athletics Team; Gabon National Cycling Team; Gabon National Judo Team; Gabon National Tae Kwon Do Team; Gabon National Weight Lifting Team

NATIONAL HEROES OR PERSONIFICATIONS
Léon M'ba, leader of the independence movement and the first president of the country; Omar Bongo Ondimba, the president since 1967, who has been reelected several times by a substantial majority

NATIONAL HOLIDAY/INDEPENDENCE DAY
Independence Day, August 17

FESTIVALS/FAIRS
Festival of Cultures, May

SIGNIFICANT EVENTS IN FORMATION
OF NATIONAL IDENTITY

300 C.E.–1300 C.E. Bantu tribes arrive in Gabon from several directions, fleeing enemies or seeking new land. The original Pygmy peoples are displaced or absorbed.

15th century Portuguese traders visit the coast, calling the region after the Portuguese word *gabao,* the name of a hooded coat that resembles the estuary of the Komo River.

16th–18th century The coastal ports become centers of the African slave trade. Portuguese, Dutch, French, English, and other traders buy or capture slaves in the region.

1839–1842 French explorers sign treaties with several coastal chiefs and then declare a protectorate over the coast and the interior. American missionaries establish a mission at the present site of Libreville.

1849 The French liberate a shipload of slaves and land them at the American mission, which the freed slaves rename Libreville, French for "free town."

1862–1903 French explorers penetrate the dense jungles of the interior. French administration of the colony begins.

1910 Gabon becomes part of French Equatorial Africa, a federation of French colonies.

1950–1959 France* allows limited self-government. The dominant position of the largest tribe, the Fang, leads to unrest.

1959–61 Gabon is granted independence. Léon M'Ba becomes prime minister, and in 1961, he is elected president.

1967 Omar Bongo becomes president on the death of M'ba and establishes a one-party state.

1990 Economic problems and demands for political liberalization provoke violent demonstrations and student strikes. Opposition figures mount two coup d'etat attempts. Elections for a national assembly are held, the first in almost 30 years.

1993–1994 President Bongo is reelected by a narrow margin in an election disputed by the opposition. Serious civil disturbances lead to an agreement and finally to the creation of a government of national unity, including key opposition figures.

2001–2002 Legislative elections are boycotted by the opposition and are criticized internationally.

2005 President Bongo is reelected for a sixth term.

2005–2009 Gabon and Equatorial Guinea* are involved in a serious dispute over some small islands and their oil-rich waters.

GAMBIA

OFFICIAL NAME
Republic of the Gambia

POPULATION
1,548,900 (2009e)

INHABITANTS' NAME/NICKNAME
Gambian(s)

LANGUAGE/LANGUAGES
English (official); Mandinka, Wolof, Fula, others

RELIGION/RELIGIONS
Muslim, 90 percent; Christian, 9 percent; indigenous beliefs, other or no religion

NATIONAL FLAG
The flag is a horizontal tricolor of red, blue, and green, the stripes separated by narrow white stripes. Red symbolizes the sun and the savanna, blue represents the Gambia River

that flows through the country, and green stands for the country's land and forests. The two narrow white stripes represent peace.

COAT OF ARMS/SEAL

The coat of arms contains a central shield supported by two lions holding an axe and a hoe. The shield depicts another hoe and axe, crossed. Above the shield is set a heraldic knight's helmet with an oil palm above. A banner at the bottom carries the national motto. The two lions represent the colonial history of Gambia as part of the British Empire. The crossed axe and hoe represent the importance of agriculture to the country. They are also considered to represent the two major ethnic groups of the Gambia: the Mandinka and the Fulani. The palm tree, found above the heraldic crest, is a vital national tree.

MOTTO

Progress, Peace, Prosperity

CAPITAL CITY

Banjul

TYPE OF GOVERNMENT

Republic

NATIONAL EMBLEM

River Gambia

NATIONAL COLORS

Red, blue, and green

NATIONAL ANTHEM

The anthem is based on a traditional Mandinka song. It was adopted as the national anthem at independence in 1965.

For the Gambia Our Homeland

For the Gambia, our homeland
We strive and work and pray,
That all may live in unity,
Freedom and peace each day.

Let justice guide our actions
Toward the common good,
And join our diverse peoples
To prove man's brotherhood.

We pledge our firm allegiance,
Our promise we renew;
Keep us, great God of nations,
To the Gambia ever true.

PATRON SAINT

Saint Mary (Sang Marie)

CURRENCY

Gambian dalasi

INTERNET IDENTIFIER

.gm

VEHICLE IDENTIFICATION PLATES/STICKERS

WAG

PASSPORT

The passport cover has the name of the country in English, the coat of arms, and the word *passport.*

AIRLINE

Gambia International Airlines GIA

NATIONAL FLOWER

Rattle box (unofficial)

NATIONAL TREE

Oil palm

NATIONAL ANIMAL

Lion

NATIONAL BIRD

Abyssinian roller (unofficial)

NATIONAL FISH

African bonytongue (unofficial)

NATIONAL RESOURCES

Natural resources include fish, titanium, tin, zircon, silica sand, clay, and petroleum. Oil exploration promises future prosperity. The region's English-speaking population, pleasant climate, culture, sandy beaches, and other attractions are the basis of a growing tourist industry.

FOODS

Domoda, a stew of groundnuts, meat, chilies, and squash or eggplant, is considered the national dish. Gambian specialties include *benacin,* rice cooked with fish or meat, vegetables, and tomatoes, *superkanja,* a stew of fish or meat, okra, palm oil, onions, and peppers; *yassa,* chicken cooked with fresh limes, black pepper, chilies, and onions; *chakery,* a sauce of yogurt, sour cream, milk, crushed pineapple, nutmeg, and vanilla served with couscous; pepper soup, a highly spiced soup of chicken, tomatoes, black pepper, and red pepper; and *benachin,* a stew of chicken, beef, onions, tomatoes, peppers, cabbage, eggplant, and rice

SPORTS/SPORTS TEAMS

Association football (soccer) is the most popular sport in the country. Traditional sports, such as wrestling, remain very popular. Gambian national teams participate in many sports at the international level.

TEAM SPORTS

Baseball

Gambia Softball Team

Basketball

Gambia Basketball Team; Gambia Women's Basketball Team

Cricket

Gambia Cricket Team

Football

Gambia Football Team, nickname the Scorpions; Gambia Women's Football Team, nickname the Scorpions; Gambia Under-20 Football Team

Table Tennis

Gambia Table Tennis Team

Volleyball

Gambia Men's Volleyball Team; Gambia Women's Volleyball Team

INDIVIDUAL SPORTS

Gambia Athletics Team; Gambia Amateur Boxing Team; Gambia Judo Team; Gambia Tae Kwon Do Team; Gambia Weight Lifting Team

NATIONAL HEROES OR PERSONIFICATIONS

Sir Dawda Kairaba Jawara, the head of state from 1970 until he was overthrown in 1994, was reelected five times and is revered as the father of Gambian prosperity; Yahya Jammeh, the current president of Gambia, elected three times since 1999 and the self-proclaimed hero of Gambia

NATIONAL HOLIDAY/ INDEPENDENCE DAY

Independence Day, February 18

FESTIVALS/FAIRS

Sang Marie Festival, August; Koriteh, variable dates; Tabaski, variable dates

SIGNIFICANT EVENTS IN FORMATION OF NATIONAL IDENTITY

470 B.C.E. The first mention of the region is in the account of Hanno the Carthaginian of his expedition through West Africa.

Fifth century C.E.–eighth century Most of Senegal* and Gambia form part of the Empire of Ghana*.

Ninth century–10th century Arabic traders raid the region for slaves, gold, and ivory to send north on their trans-Saharan caravan routes.

15th century The region forms part of the Empire of Mali*. The Portuguese begin visiting the mouth of the Gambia River. The Europeans soon take over the old caravan trade on their maritime routes.

1588–1818 The Portuguese sell exclusive trade rights on the Gambia River to English merchants. Queen Elizabeth I confirms the territorial grant. The slave trade becomes the primary activity of European traders.

17th century–18th century England and France* struggle for centuries for control of the lucrative regions of the Senegal and Gambia rivers. The Treaty of Paris, in 1783, gives Great Britain possession of the Gambia.

1807 Slavery is outlawed in the British Empire, and British naval squadrons try unsuccessfully to end the slave trade on the Gambia River. They establish a post at Bathurst (now Banjul) in 1816.

1888–1906 The Gambia becomes a separate British colony. Granted a legislative council in 1901, the region moves progressively toward an autonomous government. In 1906, an ordinance abolishes domestic slavery.

1945–1963 After World War II, the local government is given additional rights. Full internal autonomy is achieved.

1965 The Gambia is granted independence within the Commonwealth.

1970 Gambia becomes a republic, with Sir Dawda Kairaba Jawara as head of state.

1981 A coup is staged against the Jawara government, disrupting a period of peace and economic growth. The violence leaves several hundred dead. Jawara appeals to neighboring Senegal. Senegalese troops arrive to defeat the rebels.

1982–1989 Following the attempted coup, Gambia and Senegal sign a treaty creating the Senegambia Confederation. Although plans are made to combine the economies and armed forces of the two countries, the Gambians, feeling dominated by the more numerous Senegalese, decide to withdraw in 1989.

1994–2006 The Jawara government is deposed in a military coup. Political activity is banned, but a transition to democracy begins in 1996. The leader of the coup, Yahya A.J.J. Jammeh, wins elections in 2001 and 2006.

2007–2009 The government works to stem the flow of refugees, cross-border raids, arms smuggling, and activities by separatists fighting the Senegalese government in the neighboring region of Casamance*. The president, Al-Haji Yahya Jammeh, in May 2009, announces his own herbs and banana cure for AIDS, threatens to behead gays, and continues to imprison and torture dozens of journalists and political opponents.

GHANA

OFFICIAL NAME
Republic of Ghana

POPULATION
23,428,800 (2009e)

INHABITANTS' NAME/NICKNAME
Ghanaian(s)

LANGUAGE/LANGUAGES
English (official); Asante, Ewe, Fante, Brong, Dagoma, Dangme, Dagarte, Akyem, Ga, others

RELIGION/RELIGIONS
Pentecostal/Charismatic, 24 percent; other Protestant, 18 percent; Muslim, 16 percent; Roman Catholic, 15 percent; indigenous beliefs, other or no religion

NATIONAL FLAG
The flag is a horizontal tricolor of red, yellow, and green, bearing a centered five-pointed star in black. Red symbolizes the blood shed in the struggle for freedom, yel-

low represents mineral wealth, and green stands for the country's extensive forests. The black star stands for African freedom, pride, and power and a commitment to pan-African unity.

COAT OF ARMS/SEAL

The coat of arms features a centered shield divided into four by a green cross with a golden outline and with a centered golden lion of the United Kingdom*; this symbolizes the close relationship between Ghana and the Commonwealth. The first quadrant on the upper left shows a ceremonial sword called an *okyeame*. In the upper right quadrant are a castle and the sea, representing the presidential palace in Accra and the sea of the Gulf of Guinea, which themselves symbolize the national government. The third quadrant shows a cacao tree, symbolizing Ghana's agricultural wealth. The fourth quadrant shows a gold mine, which stands for the rich natural resources of the country. Above the shield are beads in the colors of the national flag and a single black star with a golden border, symbolizing the freedom of Africa. The shield is supported by two golden eagles. Below the shield is a banner with the country's national motto.

MOTTO

Freedom and Justice

CAPITAL CITY

Accra

TYPE OF GOVERNMENT

Constitutional presidential republic

NATIONAL EMBLEM

Black star of African liberation

NATIONAL COLORS

White and red

NATIONAL ANTHEM

The lyrics of the anthem were written at independence in 1957. They were changed upon declaration of the republic in 1960 and again in 1966, when the government was overthrown.

God Bless Our Homeland Ghana

God bless our homeland Ghana
And make our nation great and strong,
Bold to defend forever
The cause of Freedom and of Right;
Fill our hearts with true humility,
Make us cherish fearless honesty,
And help us to resist oppressors' rule
With all our will and might for evermore.

Hail to thy name, O Ghana,
To thee we make our solemn vow:
Steadfast to build together
A nation strong in Unity;
With our gifts of mind and strength of arm,
Whether night or day, in the midst of storm,
In ev'ry need, whate'er the call may be,
To serve thee, Ghana, now and evermore.

Raise high the flag of Ghana
And one with Africa advance;
Black star of hope and honor
To all who thirst for liberty;
Where the banner of Ghana freely flies,
May the way to freedom truly lie;
Arise, arise, O sons of Ghanaland,
And under God march on for evermore!

CURRENCY

Ghanaian cedi

INTERNET IDENTIFIER

.gh

VEHICLE IDENTIFICATION PLATES/STICKERS

GH

PASSPORT

The passport cover has the name of the country in English, the coat of arms, and the word *passport* in English.

AIRLINE
Ghana International Airlines

NATIONAL FLOWER
Bougainvillea (unofficial)

NATIONAL TREE
Cacao

NATIONAL ANIMAL
African golden cat (unofficial)

NATIONAL BIRD
Fish eagle

NATIONAL FISH
Sardine (unofficial)

NATIONAL RESOURCES
Natural resources include gold, timber, industrial diamonds, bauxite, manganese, fish, rubber, hydropower, petroleum, silver, salt, limestone, and arable land. Tourism, based on the country's sandy beaches, fascinating cultures, historical monuments, and pleasant climate, has become one of Ghana's largest foreign income earners, and the Ghanaian Government has placed great emphasis upon further tourism support and development.

FOODS
Waakye, rice and beans, and *fufu,* pounded cassava and plantain or yam and plantain shaped into a ball and served with soups or sauces with meat or fish, are considered the national dishes. Okra soup or stew is also very popular, as is *kontomirem,* mashed taro (cocoyam) leaves mixed with tuna and pumpkin seeds and dressed with palm oil. Other specialties include *fante mbire flowee,* a soup of beef and mushrooms; *agushi,* squash soup; and Jollof rice, a rice dish eaten across West Africa.

SPORTS/SPORTS TEAMS
Association football (soccer) is Ghana's most popular sport. Cricket and rugby union are also very popular. Ghana national teams participate in many sports at an international level.

TEAM SPORTS
Badminton
Ghana Badminton Team

Baseball
Ghana Baseball Team; Ghana Softball Team

Basketball
Ghana Basketball Team; Ghana Women's Basketball Team

Cricket
Ghana Cricket Team

Football
Ghana Football Team, nickname the Black Stars; Ghana Women's Football Team, nickname the Black Queens; Ghana Under-23 Football Team, nickname the Black Meteors; Ghana Under-20 Football Team, nickname the Black Satellites; Ghana Under-17 Football Team, nickname the Black Starlets; Ghana Women's Under-19 Football Team; Ghana Rugby Union Team; Ghana Futsal Team

Hockey
Ghana Field Hockey Team

Netball
Ghana Netball Team

Table Tennis
Ghana Table Tennis Team

Tennis
Ghana Davis Cup Team

Volleyball

Ghana Men's Volleyball Team

INDIVIDUAL SPORTS

Ghana Amateur Boxing Team; Ghana Athletics Team; Ghana Canoeing Team; Ghana Judo Team; Ghana Swim Team; Ghana Tae Kwon Do Team; Ghana Triathlon Team; Ghana Weight Lifting Team

WINTER SPORTS

Ghana Alpine Ski Team

NATIONAL HEROES OR PERSONIFICATIONS

Kwame Nkrumah, the first president of independent Ghana and the leader of the African decolonization movement; Osei Tutu, the founder of the Ashanti Empire in the early 18th century; Opoku Ware, the ruler of the Ashanti Empire at its height in the mid-18th century; Flight Lieutenant Jerry Rawlings, leader during Ghana's economic expansion in the 1980s and 1990s

NATIONAL HOLIDAY/INDEPENDENCE DAY

Independence Day, March 6

FESTIVALS/FAIRS

Homowo Festival (Harvest Festival), November; Damba Festival, July–August; Bakatue (Fish Festival), July; Adae (Festival of Purification of the Sacred Stools), every 40 days

SIGNIFICANT EVENTS IN FORMATION OF NATIONAL IDENTITY

4th century C.E.–13th century C.E. Oral traditions tell of migrations from the ancient kingdom of Ghana, far to the north, to present Ghana.

13th century C.E. Various Akan-speaking groups migrate into the forest belt north of the coast, establishing small states. The consolidation of the region becomes the Ashanti Empire, one of the most sophisticated and powerful states in precolonial Africa.

15th century Portuguese sailors visit the coast and find so much gold that they call the region La Mina, "the mine." This is later changed to the Gold Coast by English explorers.

1481–1700 The Portuguese construct Elmina Castle, which becomes a center of trade in gold, ivory, and slaves. Dutch, English, Danes, and Swedes all build fortified trading settlements along the coast, giving it the tightest concentration of military architecture outside Europe.

1700 The Europeans maintain alliances with indigenous states while warring with others. Europeans sell arms and help both sides during the Ashanti-Fante wars between the two largest ethnic groups in the region.

1850–1902 Following the abolition of the slave trade, most of the Europeans leave the region, except the Dutch and the British. The Dutch abandon the region in 1874, and the British proclaim the Gold Coast Protectorate on the coast. The Ashanti fight four colonial wars against British encroachment on their kingdom but are finally defeated and incorporated in the Gold Coast in 1896–1902.

1946–1957 After the Second World War, regional decolonization begins. Formed from the former British Gold Coast, the Ashanti kingdom, and British Togoland, Ghana becomes an independent republic under Kwame Nkrumah. Ghana is the first black African country to win independence.

1966–1981 Nkrumah is overthrown in a coup. A series of subsequent coups ends with Flight Lieutenant Jerry Rawlings taking power and banning all political parties.

1992 Multiparty democracy is restored.

2000 Ghana's first democratic change of power follows elections in 2000.

2007 Ghana celebrates its 50th anniversary as an independent state.

2008–2009 Ghana struggles to accommodate thousands of nationals returning from turbulent Cote d'Ivoire*. Nearly 40,000 refugees from Liberia* are also a drain on resources.

GUINEA

OFFICIAL NAME
République de Guinée (French); Republic of Guinea (English)

POPULATION
10,234,700 (2009e)

INHABITANTS' NAME/NICKNAME
Guinean(s)

LANGUAGE/LANGUAGES
French (official); Peuhl, Malinke, Soussou, others

RELIGION/RELIGIONS
Muslim, 85 percent; Christian, 8 percent; indigenous beliefs, other or no religion

NATIONAL FLAG
The flag is a horizontal tricolor of red, yellow, and green. The red represents the blood and sacrifice of the people, the yellow represents the sun and the riches of the earth, and green stands for the country's vegetation.

COAT OF ARMS/SEAL
The coat of arms had a central shield divided vertically red and green. Above is a dove with an olive branch in its beak. The olive branch covers the shield behind a rifle and sword crossed. Below is a banner with the country's motto.

MOTTO
Travail, justice, solidarité (French); Work, Justice, Solidarity (English)

CAPITAL CITY
Conakry

TYPE OF GOVERNMENT
Republic

NATIONAL EMBLEM
The *nimba*, a wooden headdress

NATIONAL COLORS
Red, yellow, and green

NATIONAL ANTHEM
The anthem was adopted at independence in 1958. It may be based on a traditional folk song.

> **Liberté (French); Liberty (English)**
> People of Africa!
> The historic past!
> Sing the hymn of a Guinea proud and young
> Illustrious epic of our brothers
> Who died on the field of honor while liberating Africa!
> The people of Guinea, preaching unity,
> Call to Africa.
> Liberty! The voice of a people
> Who call all her brothers to find their way again.
> Liberty! The voice of a people
> Who call all her brothers of a great Africa.
> Let us build African unity in a newly found independence!

PATRON SAINT
Saint Mary; Immaculate Heart of Mary

CURRENCY
Guinean franc

INTERNET IDENTIFIER
.gn

VEHICLE IDENTIFICATION PLATES/STICKERS
RG

PASSPORT
The passport cover has the name of the country in French, the coat of arms, and the word *passport* in French.

NATIONAL ANIMAL

Elephant

NATIONAL RESOURCES

Natural resources include bauxite, iron ore, diamonds, gold, uranium, hydropower, fish, and salt. The country is richly endowed with minerals and has considerable potential in agriculture and fishing. The possibility of petroleum in Guinea's territorial waters holds the promise of future prosperity.

FOODS

Poulet yassa, a chicken dish prepared with lemon juice, is the national dish. *Riz Jolof,* a rice dish with chicken or fish; *poulet Conakry,* chicken stuffed with groundnuts; and *brochettes,* marinated meat and vegetables served on a skewer, are also considered national dishes. Other specialties include *bouille,* small rolls made of cornmeal, and *poulet de Guinée,* fried chicken with onions, tomatoes, okra, bell peppers, and peanut butter.

SPORTS/SPORTS TEAMS

Association football (soccer) is the most popular sport. Cycling, introduced by French soldiers, is also very popular in Guinea. Guinea national teams participate in many sports at an international level.

TEAM SPORTS

Baseball

Guinea Softball Team

Basketball

Guinea Basketball Team; Guinea Women's Basketball Team

Football

Guinea Football Team, nickname Syli Nationale or the Elephants; Guinea Football Team nickname Syli Nationale or the Elephants

Table Tennis

Guinea Table Tennis Team

Volleyball

Guinea Men's Volleyball Team

INDIVIDUAL SPORTS

Guinea Amateur Boxing Team; Guinea Athletics Team; Guinea Cycling Team; Guinea Fencing Team; Guinea Judo Team; Guinea Swim Team; Guinea Tae Kwon Do Team

NATIONAL HEROES OR PERSONIFICATIONS

Alfa Yaya Maudo of Labé, a 19th-century Fula leader arrested and deported for resisting French rule; Samori Turé, another leader of the resistance to French rule in the late 19th century; Ahmed Sékou Touré, the leader of the independence movement and president of the republic from 1958 to 1984

NATIONAL HOLIDAY/ INDEPENDENCE DAY

Independence Day, October 2

FESTIVALS/FAIRS

Festival de Guinée (Guinea Festival), April; Independence Day, October

SIGNIFICANT EVENTS IN FORMATION OF NATIONAL IDENTITY

900 C.E.–13th century The region forms part of the Empire of Ghana*, followed by the kingdom of the Soussou people in the 12th and 13th centuries.

1235–1591 Guinea becomes part of the Empire of Mali* and prospers on trade and slavery. Later, the Songhai Empire rules the region until 1591, when the region fragments into a number of small kingdoms.

18th century A Muslim state is founded, bringing some stability to the peoples of the region. The Muslim Fulani people occupy the highland region known as Fuuta Jalloo.

15th century–19th century Portuguese sailors explore the coast and trade begins, particularly in slaves. The European presence is restricted to the slave ports along the coast. French expeditions begin the colonization of the region in the mid-19th century. Conakry is founded as a French settlement in 1890.

1895–1898 The territory claimed by France* is incorporated into French West Africa. The French defeat the armies of Samori Turé, ensuring French domination of the coast and the interior.

1958 Guinea is the first French colony to opt for independence. Sékou Touré becomes head of state, instituting a dictatorial regime with little regard for the country's people.

1984 Touré dies in office, but little changes other than economic policies.

2005–2009 Political instability, corruption, frequent ministerial changes, and economic mismanagement lead to numerous strikes and mass demonstrations. Over 100 are killed in violent clashes. A new prime minister, supported by the trade unions and civic leaders, is chosen, and the strikes are called off. Tens of thousands of refugees from neighboring countries strain the resources of the government.

GUINEA-BISSAU

OFFICIAL NAME

República da Guiné-Bissau (Portuguese); Republic of Guinea-Bissau (English)

POPULATION

1.404,500 (2009e)

INHABITANTS' NAME/NICKNAME

Guinean(s)

LANGUAGE/LANGUAGES

Portuguese (official); Crioulo, indigenous languages, others

RELIGION/RELIGIONS

Indigenous beliefs, 45 percent; Muslim, 45 percent; Christian (mostly Roman Catholic), 8 percent; other or no religion

NATIONAL FLAG

The flag has two horizontal stripes of yellow over green with a broad vertical red stripe at the hoist bearing a five-pointed black star. The colors are the pan-African colors first used by Ethiopia. Red stands for the blood shed during the struggle for independence, yellow represents the sun, green represents hope, and black stands for the unity of Africa.

COAT OF ARMS/SEAL

The coat of arms consists of a red disk between two palm fronds bearing a five-pointed black star above a conch shell and the country's motto. The star, often referred to as the black star of Africa, represents freedom and African unity. The conch shell symbolizes the republic's position on the coast of Africa.

MOTTO

Unidade, luta, progresso (Portuguese); Unity, Struggle, Progress (English)

CAPITAL CITY

Bissau

TYPE OF GOVERNMENT

Republic

NATIONAL COLORS

Red, green, and yellow

NATIONAL ANTHEM

The anthem was written and composed in the 1960s during the struggle for independence. It was adopted as the national anthem in 1974.

> **Esta é a Nossa Pátria Bem Amada (Portuguese); This Is Our Beloved Country (English)**
>
> Sun, sweat, verdure and sea,
> Centuries of pain and hope;
> This is the land of our ancestors.
> Fruit of our hands,
> Of the flower of our blood:
> This is our beloved country.

Chorus

Long live our glorious country!
The banner of our struggle
Has fluttered in the skies.
Forward, against the foreign yoke!
We are going to build
Peace and progress
In our immortal country!
Peace and progress
In our immortal country!

Branches of the same trunk,
Eyes in the same light;
This is the force of our unity!
The sea and the land,
The dawn and the sun are singing
That our struggle has borne fruit!

Chorus

PATRON SAINT

Our Lady of Grace

CURRENCY

CFA franc

INTERNET IDENTIFIER

.gw

VEHICLE IDENTIFICATION PLATES/ STICKERS

RGB

PASSPORT

The passport cover has the name of the country in Portuguese, the coat of arms, and the word *passport* in Portuguese.

NATIONAL TREE

King palm

NATIONAL RESOURCES

Natural resources include fish, timber, phosphates, bauxite, clay, granite, limestone, and unexploited deposits of petroleum. Remittances from citizens living outside the country, many of whom fled the civil war in the 1990s, are an important resource and a source of foreign currency.

FOODS

Arroz Jollof, a rice dish with chicken or fish, is considered the national dish. Other specialties include *macarra con citi,* a chicken dish prepared with peanuts and palm oil; *bolinhos de mancarra con peixe,* a type of fried dough with peanuts and fish; and *cana de cajeu,* cashew rum, which, along with palm wine, is considered a national drink.

SPORTS/SPORTS TEAMS

Association football (soccer) is the country's most popular sport. Traditional sports, such as wrestling and athletics, are also popular. Guinea-Bissau national teams participate in many sports at an international level.

TEAM SPORTS

Baseball

Guinea-Bissau Softball Team

Basketball

Guinea-Bissau Basketball Team; Guinea-Bissau Women's Basketball Team

Football

Guinea-Bissau Football Team; Guinea-Bissau Women's Football Team

Table Tennis

Guinea-Bissau Men's Table Tennis Team; Guinea-Bissau Women's Table Tennis Team

Volleyball

Guinea-Bissau Men's Volleyball Team; Guinea-Bissau Men's Beach Volleyball Team; Guinea-Bissau Women's Beach Volleyball Team

INDIVIDUAL SPORTS

Guinea-Bissau Athletics Team; Guinea-Bissau Canoeing Team; Guinea-Bissau Judo Team;

Guinea-Bissau Karate Team; Guinea-Bissau Swim Team; Guinea-Bissau Tae Kwon Do Team; Guinea-Bissau Weight Lifting Team

NATIONAL HEROES OR PERSONIFICATIONS

Domingos Ramos, who was killed leading the first organized guerrilla battalion against Portuguese forces; Amílcar Cabral, leader of the nationalist movement assassinated just before independence.

NATIONAL HOLIDAY/INDEPENDENCE DAY

Independence Day, September 24

FESTIVALS/FAIRS

Guinea-Bissau Festival (Carnival), February–March; Korité, August–September

SIGNIFICANT EVENTS IN FORMATION OF NATIONAL IDENTITY

600 C.E.–1300 C.E. Bantu peoples, part of the great Bantu migrations, settle the region. The Mandinka tribe arrives in the region around 1200.

14th century–15th century The region is controlled by the Empire of Mali* and is ruled by a provincial king loyal to the high king of Mali.

1446 Portuguese ships visit the coast. The region is claimed as Portuguese territory.

1537 The Kingdom of Kaabu (Gabu) is created by the Mandinka people, with other ethnic groups as subjects, as the Mali Empire disintegrates.

17th century–18th century The Portuguese presence is restricted to the slave ports of Bissau and Cacheu. Kaabu comes under attack by Muslim Fulas.

1850–1900 Portuguese explorers visit the interior of the region. The Kaabu kingdom comes under Fula control in 1867. Portugal loses the region of Casamance* to the French.

1900–1940 Portuguese conquest and consolidation of the colony's borders is accomplished by using Muslims to subdue the region's animist tribes. The interior is finally brought under control after more than 30 years of fighting.

1941 The capital of the colony is transferred from Bolama Island to Bissau on the mainland.

1952 Portuguese Guinea becomes an overseas province of Portugal.

1956 An armed rebellion breaks out.

1973 Portuguese agents assassinate Amílcar Cabral, the leader of the independence movement just months before independence is declared. Thousands of soldiers who fought in the Portuguese forces, often innocent conscripts, are massacred in several regions.

1984–1998 A revolutionary council rules the country until 1984. The first multiparty elections are held in 1994. An army uprising and an attempted coup initiate the Guinea-Bissau Civil War.

2000 National elections are again held, but a coup ousts the new president in 2003. A military mutiny disrupts the capital in 2004, but elections are again held in 2005.

2007–2009 The major political parties agree to support a government of consensus in the interests of the country's stability. South American drug cartels increasingly use the country as a transit point for drugs en route to Europe.

KATANGA

OFFICIAL NAME

Region du Katanga (French); Region of Katanga (English). The province/region of Katanga was divided into four new provinces in February 2009.

POPULATION

5,526,400 (2009e)

INHABITANTS' NAME/NICKNAME

Katangan(s)

LANGUAGE/LANGUAGES

Swahili, Chilunda, Tshiluba, French, others

RELIGION/RELIGIONS

Roman Catholic, Protestant, indigenous beliefs, other or no religion

NATIONAL FLAG

The unofficial flag, the flag of the former province and the republic in the 1960s, is a diagonal bicolor of red over white divided by a green stripe lower hoist to upper fly, charged with three red crosses (croisettes) on the white triangle. The red represents the people's power and sovereignty, green represents hope, white stands for peace, and the crosses represent prosperity.

COAT OF ARMS/SEAL

The coat of arms is a shield or crest showing the same symbolism and colors as the flag, a diagonal red over white divided by a green stripe lower left to upper right and bearing three red crosses on the white. The crosses represent a historic form of smelted copper, money used in Katanga.

CAPITAL CITY

Lubumbashi

TYPE OF GOVERNMENT

A provincial government under the administration of a government appointed by the central government of the Democratic Republic of Congo until February 2009, when the province was divided into four new provinces.

NATIONAL COLORS

Red, white, and green

NATIONAL ANTHEM

The official anthem is that of the Democratic Republic of Congo. The unofficial anthem, the official anthem of the former independent State of Katanga, is banned. No lyrics are available in English.

La Katangaise (French); The Katanga Anthem (English)

Allons, allons, marchons,
Katangais valeureux
le soleil s'est levé

sur le sol des aïeux
vieille terre ancestrale
du ciel aux profondeurs
tu revis opulente
a l'appel du honheur
enfants du Katanga
enfants du Katanga
défendez le jusqu'à la mort
rendez la fier rendez le fort
aven vos bras et votre sang
avec vos dents

PATRON SAINT

The Most Pure Heart of Mary

CURRENCY

Congolese franc

INTERNET IDENTIFIER

.cd Democratic Republic of Congo

VEHICLE IDENTIFICATION PLATES/STICKERS

CGO Democratic Republic of Congo (official); KAT Katanga (unofficial) (mostly used by Katangans living in Europe and North America)

PASSPORT

Katangans are Congolese citizens and travel on Congolese passports.

NATIONAL RESOURCES

Natural resources include cobalt, copper, tin, radium, uranium, diamonds, timber, building materials, and arable land. The region, formerly one of the richest and most advanced in Africa, in 2009 is impoverished and ravaged by continuing violence.

FOODS

Kosa kosa", giant freshwater shrimp (crayfish) from Lake Tanganyika cooked in a spicy chili sauce, is considered the national dish; *Maombe Katangaise,* a dish made of eight ingredients, including cassava, chicken, root vegetables, palm hearts, and palm oil, is a very popular traditional dish. *Fufu,* dumplings made of cassava flour, often served with vegetables or meat, is also considered a traditional dish. Other regional specialties include *chikwanga,* made of cassava and meat and served in banana leaves; *sombe,* a dish of boiled, mashed, and fried cassava leaves; *ndakala,* a dish made of small dried fish, often served with *fufu*

Sports/Sports Teams

Association football (Soccer) and Basketball are both very popular in Katanga. The Mazembe Lubambashi Football Club is unofficially considered the national team of Katanga.

Team Sports

Football

Tout Puissant Mazembe Lubumbashi Football Club

National Heroes or Personifications

Moise Tsombe, the leader of the secessionist State of Katanga, 1960–1963; Godefroid Munongo, the descendant of the ancient kings of Katanga and a cultural leader of the Lunda people

National Holiday/Independence Day

Independence Day, July 11 (unofficial)

Significant Events in Formation of National Identity

Sixth century C.E.–Ninth century C.E. Bantu peoples, part of the great Bantu migrations, move into the present Katanga. The migrations continue over centuries with each group taking on ethnic characteristics that mostly persist to the present.

16th century A number of linguistically and culturally related tribes are joined in the extensive Lunda kingdom.

18th century The Lunda empire expands into surrounding tribal territories, particularly into the Luba homeland to the north, setting off a series of bloody wars.

1650–1800 The Lundas, through vassal states on the coast, establish contact with Portuguese outposts. Soon the Lunda chiefs are trading ivory and slaves for firearms, cloth, and iron implements. Although their expansion is blocked by the powerful Luba tribe to the north, the Lunda empire controls vast territories in present Congo, Zambia, and Angola and draws its wealth from copper, mostly mined by Swahili Muslims from Africa's east coast.

1800–1891 The Lunda empire is divided into often-warring sections and soon splits into several rival states. In the 1850s, M'siri, a local chief, begins to expand his small kingdom by conquering neighboring tribes, including a chiefdomship known as Katanga, whose name he takes for his expanding state. M'siri is assassinated by a European and his kingdom disintegrates, allowing Europeans to gain control of the vast wealth of Katanga.

1898–1910 Belgian troops occupy Katanga, which is added to the Belgian Congo colony. The region is split between the colonial territories of Belgium* and Portugal*. The Belgians organize the Katanga Company to exploit the regions mineral wealth, often using forced labor drawn from local populations.

1940–1955 Katanga is industrialized and flourishes as one of Africa's wealthiest and most advanced regions. Many Katangans migrate to the expanding cities to find work in the burgeoning industries. The residents of Katanga, both African and European, enjoy Africa's highest standard of living.

1957 Belgium lifts a long-standing ban on political activity in its African territories. Katangans organize several political parties, including a widely supported organization that demands separation of Katanga from the Congo territory. Nationalists begin to demand a separate independent Katanga state.

1960 The vast Belgian Congo territory, unprepared and politically divided, is granted independence on June 30, 1960. Supported by the large European community and protected by a Belgian-officered and -supplied army, Katanga leader Moise Tsombe declares Katanga independent of the Congo on July 11. The new state, which produces 60 percent of the Congo's revenues, remains calm and continues to function as the Congo dissolves in civil war and violence.

1961–1963 Amid the chaos a Congolese military officer, Mobutu Sese Seko, assumes power in the Congo, winning Western backing for his anticommunist rhetoric and promises of lucrative mineral concessions. With Western military aid and advice he begins to holds most of the Congo together, except for Katanga and another breakaway republic, South Kasai. Appealing to the United Nations (UN), Mobutu wins support for a UN-sanctioned invasion of Katanga, which quickly collapses into bloodshed, violence, and looting. Many flee the region, including the majority of the European population. The Katanga secession is brought to an end and the state is integrated into the Congo republic ruled by Western-backed Mobutu dictatorship.

1964–1965 Moise Tsombe is recalled form exile and named prime minister of Congo in an effort to reconcile the rebellious Katangans. Mobutu takes complete control of the country and ends all pretence of democracy but maintains the backing of the West as an outspoken anticommunist.

1968–1978 Katangan exiles in neighboring Angola* organize to resurrect the independence of Katanga. The name of the region is officially changed from Katanga to Shaba in 1972 as part of the integration of Katanga into the vast and unstable Congo republic. Katangan exile groups invade the region in 1977 and again in 1978 but are unable to gain control of Katanga against the Western-equipped Congolese army.

1980–1990 The Mobutu government, propped up by the United States* and other Western governments, plunders the Congo, stashing vast sums of Katanga's mineral wealth in banks in Europe. The Katangans, once among Africa's most affluent, are now among the continent's poorest.

1992–1993 The forbidden name, Katanga, is restored during spreading unrest in the region. The province of Katanga uses the flag and symbols of the former Katanga republic. The provincial governor declares the political and economic autonomy of Katanga in 1993 but the movement is suppressed.

1996–1997 A local rebellion in northern Katanga grows to take control of much of eastern Congo and to finally drive Mobutu from power in the Congo. Some 300 Katangan military and cultural leaders are jailed for demanding the autonomy promised during the anti-Mobutu campaign.

2000–2009 Civil war and numerous local and tribal wars spread across the Congo, drawing in the armies of several neighboring countries. Katanga, part of the territory held by rebel groups, is the scene of widespread violence, death, and looting. Nostalgia for the tranquility and prosperity of the early 1960s continues to motivate Katangan demands for autonomy and to give nationalists reason to plan for eventual Katangan independence away from the huge and hugely chaotic Congo. For younger Katangans the period before and during the brief period of independence is looked on as a golden age ended by the greedy West and its puppet dictator, Mobutu.

KENYA

OFFICIAL NAME

Jamhuri ya Kenya (Swahili); Republic of Kenya (English)

POPULATION

37,955,600 (2009e)

INHABITANTS' NAME/NICKNAME

Kenyan(s)

LANGUAGE/LANGUAGES

Swahili (Kiswahili), English (both official); Kikuyu, Luhya, Luo, Kalenjin, Kamba, Kisii, Meru, others

RELIGION/RELIGIONS

Protestant, 45 percent; Roman Catholic, 33 percent; Muslim, 10 percent; traditional beliefs, 10 percent; Hindu, Jain, Baha'i, other or no religion

NATIONAL FLAG

The flag is a horizontal tricolor of black, red, and green, the stripes separated by narrow white lines. In the center is a traditional Maasai shield before two crossed spears. The color black symbolizes the black majority, the red stands for the blood shed during the struggle for independence, the green is for natural wealth, and the white is for unity and peace. The shield and spears symbolize the country's willingness to defend its freedom.

COAT OF ARMS/SEAL

The coat of arms has a central shield striped with the national colors of black, red, and green and a centered rooster holding an axe. The shield is supported by two golden lions holding spears standing on a depiction of Mount Kenya and agricultural produce. Below is a red banner with the national motto in white. The symbolism of the colors is the same as in the national flag. The rooster denotes a new and prosperous life. The lions symbolize Kenya's abundant wildlife.

MOTTO

Harambee (Swahili); Let us all pull together (English)

CAPITAL CITY

Nairobi

TYPE OF GOVERNMENT

Parliamentary republic

NATIONAL EMBLEM

Mount Kenya, which gave the country its name

NATIONAL COLORS

Red and black

NATIONAL ANTHEM

The anthem is based on a traditional folk song, often sung by mothers to their children. It was adopted at independence in 1963.

Ee Mungu Nguvu Yetu (Swahili); O God of All Creation (English)

O God of all creation,
Bless this our land and nation.
Justice be our shield and defender,
May we dwell in unity,
Peace and liberty.
Plenty be found within our borders.

Let one and all arise
With hearts both strong and true.
Service be our earnest endeavor,
And our homeland of Kenya,
Heritage of splendor,
Firm may we stand to defend.

Let all with one accord
In common bond united,
Build this our nation together,
And the glory of Kenya,
The fruit of our labor
Fill every heart with thanksgiving.

PATRON SAINT

Mary, Queen of Africa

CURRENCY

Kenyan shilling

INTERNET IDENTIFIER

.ke

VEHICLE IDENTIFICATION PLATES/ STICKERS

EAK

PASSPORT

The passport cover has the name of the country in Swahili and English, the coat of arms, and the word *passport* in Swahili and English.

AIRLINE

Kenya Airways

NATIONAL ANIMAL

African lion (shown on the coat of arms)

NATIONAL BIRD

Rooster (shown on the coat of arms)

NATIONAL FISH

Broadbill swordfish (unofficial)

NATIONAL RESOURCES

Natural resources include limestone, soda ash, salt, gemstones, fluorspar, zinc, diatomite, gypsum, wildlife, and hydropower. The thriving tourist industry in built on Kenya's abundant wildlife, sandy beaches, pleasant climate, and varied scenery. The possibility of petroleum reserves is being explored near the border with Sudan* and along the coast.

FOODS

National dishes include *ugali,* cornmeal balls served with vegetables or meat; *kachumbari,* a mixture of chopped tomatoes, onions, and chili peppers used as a sauce or condiment; *nyma choma,* roasted meat; and *mandazi,* a doughnutlike fried pastry. Other specialties include *mtuza wa samaki,* baked curried fish; *kuku na nazi,* chicken cooked in coconut milk; Kenya beef stew; *nyama na irio,* beef cooked with corn; *nyma choma,* meats roasted over charcoal; *maharagwe,* spicy red beans in coconut milk; and *m'baazi,* beans or black-eyed peas prepared with chilies, onion, and bell peppers.

SPORTS/SPORTS TEAMS

Cricket, association football (soccer), rugby union, and boxing are the most popular sports. Kenya national teams participate in many sports at an international level.

TEAM SPORTS

Badminton

Kenya Badminton Team

Baseball

Kenya Baseball Team; Kenya Softball Team

Basketball

Kenya Basketball Team; Kenya Women's Basketball Team; Kenya Wheelchair Basketball Team

Cricket

Kenya Cricket Team; Kenya Women's Cricket Team

Football

Kenya Football Team, nickname the Harambee Stars; Kenya Women's Football Team, nickname Nyayo Stars; Kenya Under-23 Football Team, nickname the Junior Harambee Stars; Kenya Under-20 Football Team, nickname the Junior Harambee Stars; Kenya Under-17 Football Team, nickname the Junior Harambee Stars; Kenya Rugby Union Team; Kenya Women's Rugby Union Team; Kenya Rugby Union Team (Sevens), nickname Kenya Sevens or Kenya 7s

Handball

Kenya National Handball Team

Hockey

Kenya National Field Hockey Team

Netball

Kenya Netball Team

Table Tennis

Kenya Table Tennis Team

Tennis

Kenya Davis Cup Team; Kenya Fed Cup Team

Volleyball

Kenya Men's Volleyball Team; Kenya Women's Volleyball Team

INDIVIDUAL SPORTS

Kenya Amateur Boxing Team; Kenya Archery Team; Kenya Athletics Team; Kenya Canoeing Team; Kenya Cycling Team; Kenya Equestrian Team; Kenya Judo Team; Kenya Modern Pentathlon Team; Kenya Rowing Team; Kenya Sailing Team; Kenya Shooting Team; Kenya Swim Team; Kenya Tae Kwon Do Team; Kenya Triathlon Team; Kenya Weight Lifting Team; Kenya Wrestling Team

NATIONAL HEROES OR PERSONIFICATIONS

Dedan Kimathi, a leader of the Mau Mau rebellion against British rule who was captured and executed in 1957; Jomo Kenyatta, the leader of the independence movement and Kenya's first president

NATIONAL HOLIDAY/INDEPENDENCE DAY

Independence Day, December 12

FESTIVALS/FAIRS

Lamu Dugong Festival, May; Mombasa Carnival, November; Cultural Music Festival, October; Kijani Festival, February–March

SIGNIFICANT EVENTS IN FORMATION OF NATIONAL IDENTITY

2000 B.C.E. Cushitic-speaking nomads from northern Africa move into the region.

First century C.E.–eighth century C.E. Arab traders settle at trading posts along the coast. Arab and Persian coastal colonies are founded, mostly for trade in ivory and slaves. At the same time, Nilotic and Bantu people continue moving into the region from the west. Swahili, a Bantu language with loanwords from Arabic, Persian, and other Middle Eastern and South Asian languages, develops as a lingua franca for trade between the different groups.

1498–1505 The Portuguese conquer the coastal cities and create a colonial administration, giving Portugal* control of the spice trade and the sea-lanes between India* and Europe.

17th century–18th century English, Dutch, and Arabs from Oman* establish bases on the coast. The Omani Arabs expel the last of the Portuguese forces in 1730. The coastal cities are ruled from the new Omani capital at Zanzibar*, further south along the coast of East Africa.

1834–1890 The British pressure the Omanis to end the slave trade. German and British forces seize key coastal ports and sign treaties with influential local rulers. Germany* cedes its ports on the coast to Britain in 1890.

1895–1905 The British build the Kenya-Uganda railway through the region to unite the different parts of British East Africa. The railway is resisted by several tribes that are pacified or pushed aside. The authorities import laborers from British India as railway workers.

1905–1952 Europeans settle the central highlands, which become known as the White Highlands. The Europeans, to protect their own interests, place restrictions on indigenous agriculture and land claims, driving many into the growing cities.

1952–1959 The Mau Mau rebellion begins with attacks on European farms and installations. The rebellion spreads across Kenya. The capture and execution of Dedan Kimathi in 1957 signals the defeat of the Mau Mau movement.

1963–1978 Kenya becomes independent of British rule under the leadership of Jomo Kenyatta. Kenya becomes a single-party state.

1988–2002 Undemocratic practices lead to demands for constitutional reform. Democratic multiparty elections are held in 1992 and 1997. In 2002, the opposition party wins the elections, marking the first time power is peacefully transferred from one political party to another.

2007 A close presidential election, with both candidates declaring victory, sets off demonstrations and rioting that turn to ethnic violence in many parts of the country. Over 1,000 are killed, and 600,000 flee the violence or are displaced.

2008 An agreement to form a coalition government ends the violence. Reforms are enacted in an effort to end ethnic rivalries and enmities.

2009 The Kenya Anti-Corruption Commission accuses a number of present and former government officials of taking illegal allowances and other corrupt practices.

LESOTHO

OFFICIAL NAME
Muso oa Lesotho (Sesotho); Kingdom of Lesotho (English)

POPULATION
2,021,700 (2009e)

INHABITANTS' NAME/NICKNAME
Mosotho (singular), Basotho (plural)

LANGUAGE/LANGUAGES
Sesotho (Southern Sotho), English (both official); Zulu, Xhosa, others

RELIGION/RELIGIONS
Christian, 80 percent; indigenous beliefs, other or no religion

NATIONAL FLAG
The flag is a horizontal tricolor of blue, white, and green bearing a black *mokorotlo* (a Basotho hat) centered. The blue represents rain, the white represents peace, and the green stands for prosperity. The black Basotho hat represents the indigenous people of the country.

COAT OF ARMS/SEAL
The coat of arms has a central Basotho shield with a depiction of a crocodile, representing the dynasty of the Sotho. Behind the shield are two crossed 19th century weapons. Two Basotho horses support the shield. Below is

yellow banner on green grass inscribed with the national motto.

MOTTO
Khotso, pula, nala (Sesotho); Peace, Rain, Prosperity (English)

CAPITAL CITY
Maseru

TYPE OF GOVERNMENT
Parliamentary constitutional monarchy

NATIONAL EMBLEM
Basotho hat; crocodile

NATIONAL COLORS
Blue, white, and green

NATIONAL ANTHEM
The anthem was originally published in a Swiss songbook of about 1823 and appeared in a songbook in a local high school in 1869. With different lyrics, it was adopted as the national anthem at independence in 1966.

Lesotho Fatse la bo Ntat'a Rona (Sesotho); Lesotho, Land of Our Fathers (English)

Lesotho, land of our fathers,
You are the most beautiful country of all.
You give us birth,
In you we are reared
And you are dear to us.

Lord, we ask you to protect Lesotho.
Keep us free from conflict and tribulations.
Oh, land of mine,
Land of our fathers,
May you have peace.

CURRENCY
Lesotho loti (maloti)

INTERNET IDENTIFIER
.ls

VEHICLE IDENTIFICATION PLATES/
STICKERS
LS

PASSPORT
The passport cover has the name of the
country in Sesotho and English, the coat of
arms, and the word *passport* in Sesotho and
English.

NATIONAL FLOWER
Spiral aloe

NATIONAL ANIMAL
Basotho pony

NATIONAL FISH
Smallmouth yellowfish (unofficial)

NATIONAL RESOURCES
Natural resources include water, agricultural
and grazing land, diamonds, sand, clay, and
building stone.

FOODS
Pap-pap, cornmeal porridge, is the staple of
the Basotho and is considered the national
dish. Other specialties include *chakalaka,*
a vegetable dish of bell peppers, tomatoes,
onions, chilies, and carrots; spinach and tan-
gerine soup; *stoofschotel,* a dish of onion,
cabbage, potatoes, and curry introduced by
the Afrikaners; beef stew made with squash;
and grilled chicken with chilies.

SPORTS/SPORTS TEAMS
Association football (soccer) is the country's
most popular sport. Lesotho national teams
participate in many sports at an international
level.

TEAM SPORTS
Badminton
Lesotho Badminton Team

Baseball
Lesotho Baseball Team; Lesotho Softball
Team

Basketball
Lesotho Basketball Team; Lesotho Women's
Basketball Team

Cricket
Lesotho Cricket Team

Football
Lesotho Football Team, nickname Likuena
(the Crocodiles); Lesotho Women's Football Team, nickname Mehalalitoe (the Lil-
ies); Lesotho Women's Under-19 Football
Team, nickname the Beautiful Flowers; Lesotho Under-23 Football Team, nickname
the Young Crocodiles; Lesotho Under-20
Football Team, nickname Makoanyane XI;
Lesotho Under-17 Football Team, nickname
Bahlabani (the Warriors)

Handball
Lesotho Handball Team

Table Tennis
Lesotho Table Tennis Team

Tennis
Lesotho Fed Cup Team; Lesotho Davis Cup
Team

Volleyball
Lesotho Men's Volleyball Team

INDIVIDUAL SPORTS
Lesotho Amateur Boxing Team; Lesotho
Athletics Team; Lesotho Gymnastics Team;
Lesotho Swim Team; Lesotho Tae Kwon Do
Team; Lesotho Wrestling Team

NATIONAL HEROES OR PERSONIFICATIONS
Moshoeshoe I, the first king of the Sotho
in 1822; Moshoeshoe II, the Sotho king

stripped of his powers and exiled in 1990; Chief Leabua Jonathan, independence leader and first prime minister of independent Lesotho; King Letsie III, who became king in 1996 and is revered as the head of the nation; Queen 'Masenate Mohato Seeiso, who has taken an active part in cultural and political events and promotes women's rights.

NATIONAL HOLIDAY/INDEPENDENCE DAY

Independence Day, October 4; Independence Day celebrations, October; Family Festival, July; Moshoeshoe's Day, March; National Sports Festival, October

FESTIVALS/FAIRS

Morija Arts and Cultural Festival, October

SIGNIFICANT EVENTS IN FORMATION OF NATIONAL IDENTITY

15th century C.E. Bantu migrants arrive in the region, mostly settling into small autonomous villages speaking a common dialect called seSotho.

18th century The Zulus to the east began to increase in population and power. A militaristic king organizes the Zulus into the most powerful state in southern Africa.

1800–1843 The Zulus, beset by drought, famine, and civil war, begin to expand in a great movement called the Mfecane, "the crushing" or "the scattering." The Zulus' superior weapons and tactics allow them to conquer neighboring peoples, who then conquer more distant peoples in a great ripple effect. A Sotho chief, Moshoeshoe, gathers the mountain clans together in an alliance against the advancing Zulus in 1818. The territory controlled by Moshoeshoe becomes a kingdom in 1822. Europeans begin to visit the region, mostly Christian missionaries setting up mission stations. In 1843, the Basotho kingdom negotiates an alliance with the British Cape Colony.

1856–1868 Land-hungry Europeans take Sotho territory, later known as the Lost Territory, setting off a series of wars with the Boers and the British. A war with the Boers in 1865 devastates the region. Moshoeshoe appeals to the British for protection.

1871–1884 The Basutoland Protectorate is annexed to the British Cape Colony. A Sotho rebellion grows into the Gun War of 1880–81. Basutoland is returned to crown control in 1884.

1910 The formation of the Union of South Africa includes plans to incorporate Basotho into the new formation, which is resisted by the Sotho. The imposition of apartheid in South Africa* halts the incorporation plan.

1955–1966 Internal self-government with an elected legislature begins as the last step before independence, which is granted in 1966.

1980s Sotho sympathies and active aid for antiapartheid groups result in the closure of the borders with South Africa and internal chaos that ends in a military coup in 1986.

1990–1993 King Moshoeshoe II is stripped of his executive and legislative powers and exiled by the military leaders. A new constitution leaves the king banned from political activities. A military mutiny overthrows the government but is halted by the intervention of neighboring states.

2000–2009 Stability returns to Lesotho with democratic reforms and elections. A severe drought threatens crops and livelihoods in 2007–2008. The king's role becomes mainly symbolic, with no executive or legislative powers.

LIBERIA

OFFICIAL NAME
Republic of Liberia

POPULATION
3,490,200 (2009e)

INHABITANTS' NAME/NICKNAME
Liberian(s)

LANGUAGE/LANGUAGES
English (official); Liberian English (Creole), indigenous languages

RELIGION/RELIGIONS

Christian, 40 percent; Muslim, 20 percent; indigenous beliefs, other or no religion

NATIONAL FLAG

The flag has 11 red and white stripes with a blue square bearing a single white, five-pointed star on the upper hoist. The flag closely resembles the flag of the United States*, denoting the origins of the country. The 11 stripes symbolize the 11 signatories of the Liberian Declaration of Independence. Red stands for courage and white for moral excellence. The blue represents the African continent, and the white star stands for the freedom given the ex-slave colonists and Liberia's long history as the Lone Star, the only independent state in Africa during the colonial period other than Ethiopia*.

COAT OF ARMS/SEAL

The coat of arms consists of a central shield or crest with a depiction of a 19th century ship arriving in Liberia, symbolizing the ships that brought the original freed slaves from the United States. A plow and shovel represent the dignity of labor and hard work to make the nation prosper. A rising sun in the background represents the birth of the new nation. The palm tree, venerated as the nation's most important source of food, represents prosperity. A white dove represents the breath of peace. Above the shield is a white banner inscribed with the national motto. Another banner below the shield is inscribed with the name of the country.

MOTTO

The love of liberty brought us here

CAPITAL CITY

Monrovia

TYPE OF GOVERNMENT

Republic

NATIONAL COLORS

Red, white, and blue

NATIONAL ANTHEM

The anthem was adopted by the independent Republic of Liberia in 1847. The present music was written and adopted in 1860.

All Hail, Liberia, Hail!

All hail, Liberia, hail!
All hail, Liberia, hail!
This glorious land of liberty
Shall long be ours.
Though new her name,
Green be her fame,
And mighty be her powers,
And mighty be her powers,
In joy and gladness
With our hearts united,
We'll shout the freedom
Of a race benighted,
Long live Liberia, happy land!
A home of glorious liberty,
By God's command!
A home of glorious liberty,
By God's command!

All hail, Liberia, hail!
All hail, Liberia, hail!
In union, strong success is sure
We cannot fail!
With God above
Our rights to prove
We will o'er all prevail,
We will o'er all prevail,
With heart and hand
Our country's cause defending
We'll meet the foe
With valor unpretending.
Long live Liberia, happy land!
A home of glorious liberty,
By God's command!
A home of glorious liberty,
By God's command!

PATRON SAINT

Many, Queen of Africa (patron saint of all of Africa)

CURRENCY
Liberian dollar; U.S. dollar

INTERNET IDENTIFIER
.lr

VEHICLE IDENTIFICATION PLATES/ STICKERS
LB (unofficial)

PASSPORT
The passport cover has the name of the country in English, the coat of arms, and the word *passport* in English.

NATIONAL FLOWER
Pepper flower

NATIONAL TREE
Palm tree

NATIONAL ANIMAL
Kuhni (Liberian mongoose) (unofficial)

NATIONAL RESOURCES
Natural resources include iron ore, timber, diamonds, gold, and hydropower. The large numbers of Liberians living outside the country since the civil war are a source of remittances and foreign investment. Liberia has one the world's largest national registries of ships, with the Liberian flag a well-known flag of convenience.

FOODS
Rice is the staple food of Liberia, often served with meats and vegetables, such as cassava, peppers, sweet potatoes, tomatoes, ginger, and palm oil. Rice bread is also a national staple. *Dumboy,* boiled and pounded cassava served with meat or vegetables, and *fufu* or *foofoo,* pounded or mashed cassava shaped into balls and served with various sauces or meats, are also considered national dishes.

Other specialties include beef and cassava leaf soup; bonnie pepper soup; cassava flour bread; and collards and cabbage.

SPORTS/SPORTS TEAMS
Association football (soccer) is the most popular sport in the country. Liberia national teams participate in many sports at an international level.

TEAM SPORTS
Baseball
Liberia Baseball Team

Basketball
Liberia Basketball Team; Liberia Women's Basketball Team

Football
Liberia Football Team, nickname the Lone Stars; Liberia Women's Football Team, nickname the Lone Stars; Liberia Softball Team

Handball
Liberia Men's Handball Team

Table Tennis
Liberia Table Tennis Team

Volleyball
Liberia Men's Volleyball Team

INDIVIDUAL SPORTS
Liberia Amateur Boxing Team; Liberia Athletics Team; Liberia Canoeing Team; Liberia Swim Team; Liberia Tae Kwon Do Team; Liberia Judo Team; Liberia Wrestling Team

NATIONAL HEROES OR PERSONIFICATIONS
Joseph Jenkins Roberts, the first president of Liberia; Stephen Allen Benson, Liberia's second president, responsible for obtaining diplomatic recognition from the United States and many European states; William

Tubman, president from 1944 to 1971; Ellen Johnson-Sirleaf, Africa's first female president in 2006

NATIONAL HOLIDAY/INDEPENDENCE DAY

Independence Day, July 26

FESTIVALS/FAIRS

Independence Day celebrations, July; Pioneer's Festival, January; Matilda Newport Festival, December

SIGNIFICANT EVENTS IN FORMATION OF NATIONAL IDENTITY

12th century C.E.–16th century C.E. Bantu peoples migrate to the region from the north and east.

1461–1800 The Bantu peoples of the region are visited by Portuguese and other European expeditions. The region is known as the Costa de Pimenta, "pepper coast," later translated as the Grain Coast, due to the abundance of the grains of melegueta pepper.

1821–1822 The American Colonization Society establishes a coastal settlement as a place to send freed slaves. Other African Americans, free men, also chose to emigrate to the new settlement. The first settlers are joined by later arrivals from the United States and by Congos, slaves taken from captured slave ships after slavery is abolished by the European powers. These groups merge to form the Americo-Liberians.

1822–1835 Indigenous peoples attack the colonists, who suffer from diseases and the harsh climate. A lack of food and medicine and poor housing conditions are finally overcome as agriculture begins to spread. Between 1822 and 1835, five more settlements are founded and the Americo-Liberians take more responsibility for their own government.

1846–1847 The American Colonization Society is bankrupted by the cost of the colonization. Society officials direct the Americo-Liberian leaders to declare independence. The first president, Joseph Jenkins Roberts, as leader of over 3,000 Americo-Liberian colonists, declares the independence of the Republic of Liberia.

1847–1857 The Americo-Liberian elite forms the True Whig Party, the only political party allowed, and rules the 95 percent of the population made up of indigenous peoples as subjects.

1857–1930 A number of serious uprisings by indigenous tribes threaten the Americo-Liberian hold on the republic, but they are repulsed, often with American help. The League of Nations accuses the Liberians of systematically engaging in the sale of contract laborers taken from among the indigenous peoples. The scandal brings down the Liberian government.

1926 The Liberian government gives a concession to the American rubber company Firestone, which creates the world's largest rubber plantation.

1940–1980 Thousands of indigenous Liberians migrate from the interior to the coast in search of work. Foreign investments create plantations that absorb the workforce, but the benefits never reach beyond the Americo-Liberian elite.

1980–1989 A military coup led by soldiers from indigenous peoples overthrows the Americo-Liberian government. Civil war spreads across the country, involving support or interference by many other nations. The country is devastated in more than a decade of indiscriminate violence and corruption.

2003 A transitional government takes power as the war ends. Foreign peacekeeping troops insure a measure of stability.

2005 Ellen Johnson-Shirleaf is elected to the presidency, the first female elected as a head of state in Africa.

2008–2009 The country is still chaotic, with local outbreaks of violence, but it has remained relatively stable since 2005. The 18,000 peacekeepers begin to leave the country.

MADAGASCAR

OFFICIAL NAME

Repoblikan'l Madagasikara (Malagasy); République de Madagascar (French); Republic of Madagascar (English)

POPULATION
20,053,400 (2009e)

INHABITANTS' NAME/NICKNAME
Malagasy(s)

LANGUAGE/LANGUAGES
Malagasy, French, English (all official since April 27, 2007); others

RELIGION/RELIGIONS
Traditional religions, 52 percent; Christian, 41 percent; Muslim, 7–10 percent; other or no religion

NATIONAL FLAG
The flag has three stripes: equal horizontal stripes of red over green, with a vertical white stripe, equal in width to the others, at the hoist. The red and white represent the country's past, the Merina Kingdom, which traditionally used red and white flags. Green was added to represent the coastal peoples.

COAT OF ARMS/SEAL
The coat of arms is a circle with a centered white disk, representing the sun, charged with an outline map of Madagascar in red above the head of a zebu, the country's national animal. Above the sun symbol are 15 red and green rays and the name of the country in Malagasy. Below the zebu's head is a white insert inscribed with the country's motto in Malagasy.

MOTTO
Tanindrazana, fahafahana, fandrosoana (Malagasy); *Patrie, liberté, progrès* (French); Fatherland, Liberty, Progress (English)

CAPITAL CITY
Antananarivo

TYPE OF GOVERNMENT
Republic

NATIONAL EMBLEM
Zebu

NATIONAL COLORS
Red, white, and green

NATIONAL ANTHEM
The anthem was written, composed and adopted by the autonomous state of Madagascar within the French Union in 1959, and was retained when the country achieved full independence in 1960.

Ry Tanindrazanay malala ô (Malagasy); Oh, Our Beloved Fatherland (English)

Oh, our beloved fatherland
Oh good Madagascar.
Our love for you will always stay,
For you, for you forever.

Protect for you, O God creator,
This island of our ancestors
So that it may live in peace and joy
Hey! We are truly blessed.

Oh, our beloved fatherland!
We wish to serve you with
The body and heart, spirit that is ours,
You are precious and truly deserving

Oh, our beloved fatherland!
We wish that you will be blessed,
So that the creator of the universe
Will be the foundation of your laws.

PATRON SAINT
Saint Vincent de Paul

CURRENCY
Malagasy ariary

INTERNET IDENTIFIER
.mg

VEHICLE IDENTIFICATION PLATES/STICKERS
RM

PASSPORT

The passport cover has the name of the country in Malagasy, French, and English, the coat of arms, and the word *passport* in the same three languages.

AIRLINE

Air Madagascar

NATIONAL FLOWER

Traveler's tree flower

NATIONAL TREE

Traveler's tree

NATIONAL ANIMAL

Zebu

NATIONAL RESOURCES

Natural resources include graphite, chromite, coal, bauxite, salt, quartz, tar sands, semiprecious stones, mica, fish, and hydropower. Agriculture and fishing are the major resources, although, since the 1990s, the economy has been diversified. The Malagasy population living outside the country is a valuable source of foreign currency and investment.

FOODS

Malagasy food is based on a large serving of rice accompanied by various sauces, meat, fish, or vegetables, and seasonings. National dishes include *ro,* a mixture of herbs and greens with rice; *ravitoto,* a dish of meat and greens; *ramazava,* beer and pork browned in oil and served with cooked greens; *vary amid 'anana,* rice, greens or herbs, and meat or shrimp, cooked together; *kitoza,* long slices of smoked or cured meat; *akoho sy voanio,* chicken cooked in coconut milk and served with rice; *lasopy,* vegetable soup; *lasary voatabia,* a salad of tomatoes and spring onions; and *foza sy hena-kisoa,* a dish of crab, pork, and rice

SPORTS/SPORTS TEAMS

Association football (soccer) is the most popular sport. Rugby and basketball are also very popular. Madagascar national teams participate in many sports at an international level.

TEAM SPORTS

Badminton

Madagascar Badminton Team

Basketball

Madagascar Basketball Team; Madagascar Woman's Basketball Team

Football

Madagascar Football Team, nickname Barea (the Scorpions); Madagascar Women's Football Team, nickname Barea (the Scorpions); Madagascar Under-23 Football Team, nickname Scorpion Kely; Madagascar Under-20 Football Team, nickname Zandry Kely; Madagascar Women's Under-19 Football Team; Madagascar Rugby Union Team (Sevens), nickname Madagascar Sevens or Madagascar 7s

Table Tennis

Madagascar Table Tennis Team

Tennis

Madagascar Davis Cup Team; Madagascar Fed Cup Team

Volleyball

Madagascar Men's Volleyball Team

INDIVIDUAL SPORTS

Madagascar Amateur Boxing Team; Madagascar Athletics Team; Madagascar Cycling Team; Madagascar Equestrian Team; Madagascar Judo Team; Madagascar Rowing Team; Madagascar Swim Team; Madagascar Tae Kwon Do Team; Madagascar Weight Lifting Team; Madagascar Wrestling Team

NATIONAL HEROES OR PERSONIFICATIONS

Andrianampoinimerina, a Merina military and political leader who united most of Madagascar in the late 18th century; Radama I, who united all of Madagascar in the early 19th century; Radama II, who ruled briefly between 1861 and1863 but ended a long period of repression and opened the Merina kingdom to the world until his murder by a faction opposed to modernization; Queen Ranavalona III, the last ruler of the Imerina kingdom, deposed and exiled by the French; Philibert Tsiranana, the first president of independent Madagascar

NATIONAL HOLIDAY/INDEPENDENCE DAY

Independence Day, June 26

FESTIVALS/FAIRS

Donia Music Festival, May–June; Famadihana, variable dates; Gasyfara Music Festival, November–December; Sambatra, March

SIGNIFICANT EVENTS IN FORMATION OF NATIONAL IDENTITY

200 C.E.–500 C.E. Seafaring settlers from Southeast Asia, probably present Indonesia*, arrive in Madagascar in large outrigger sailing canoes to settle the east coast and move into the highlands. Bantu migrations from East Africa settle the west coast soon after the Asian colonization.

7th century–12th century Muslim Arabs establish trading posts along the northwest coast. Other Arab groups and slave traders from Zanzibar* settle the west coast. Chiefdoms established by the Asian settlers develop as small states, some extending over large areas and controlling trade with the Arabs.

1500 A Portuguese explorer and trader, Diogo Dias, is blown off course and becomes the first European to visit Madagascar.

1646–1674 English and French expeditions attempt to establish colonies but are defeated by hostile indigenous peoples, fevers, and the climate.

1680–1725 Madagascar becomes a stronghold of pirates preying on shipping along the East African coast and in the Indian Ocean. The coastal tribes engage in the lucrative slave trade with the Europeans.

1815–1824 Andrianampoinimerina, a chief of the isolated highland kingdom of Imerina, begins to expand his kingdom. His son, Radama I, aided by the British during the Napoleonic Wars, continues the conquest until nearly all of Madagascar is under Merina rule. The slave trade is outlawed, and Protestant missionaries are allowed into the kingdom.

1895–1897 A French military expedition defeats the Merinas and takes control of Madagascar. The last queen, Ranavalona III, is deposed and exiled to French Algeria*. The British accept French rule in Madagascar in exchange for British control of Zanzibar.

1947 After the Second World War, a nationalist uprising spreads across the island. The Malagasy war claims between 80 and 90 thousand lives in a year of heavy fighting.

1956–1960 Political reforms allow the Malagasy to organize political parties. The Malagasy Republic is proclaimed in 1958 as part of the French Union and achieves full independence in 1960.

1972 Widespread protests over government policies lead to military rule and close ties to the Soviet Union, followed by political upheaval, assassinations, and coups. A socialist government nationalizes the economy and cuts all ties to France*.

1980–1996 Devastated by the communist experiment, a new Malagasy government creates a market economy and renews ties to France. Instability and political upheavals continue to disrupt the island.

2000–2008 Opposition political parties boycott elections. Inconclusive presidential elections in 2001 lead to bloody clashes between rival groups. Marc Ravalomanana becomes president in 2006 and institutes political and economic reforms. Madagascar reiterates claims to small islands still administered by France.

2009 President Ravalomanana resigns as political chaos spreads and part of the national army mutinies. Some 70 percent of Madagascar's people continue to live on less than $1 a day, leading to growing resentment. The opposition leader, Andry Rajoelina, promises new elections within two years.

MALAWI

OFFICIAL NAME
Dziko la Malawi (Republic of Malawi)

POPULATION
13,935,300 (2009e)

INHABITANTS' NAME/NICKNAME
Malawian(s)

LANGUAGE/LANGUAGES
English (official); Chichewa (national); Chinyanja, Chiyao, Chitumbuka, Chisena, Chilomwe, Chitonga, others

RELIGION/RELIGIONS
Christian, 80 percent; Muslim, 13 percent; other or no religion

NATIONAL FLAG
The flag is a horizontal tricolor of black, red, and green with a red rising sun on the top black stripe. The rising sun represents the dawn of hope and freedom for the continent of Africa. The black represents the people of the continent, the red symbolizes the martyrs of African freedom, and the green represents nature.

COAT OF ARMS/SEAL
The coat of arms has a central shield divided horizontally into three parts. The upper part contains wavy blue and white lines representing Lake Malawi, the second is a red field with a gold lion representing Malawi's past as a British territory, and the bottom is a black field with a gold rising run. A lion and a leopard support the shield. Above the shield are another rising sun and the national bird, the fish eagle. Below the shield is a banner inscribed with the national motto in English.

MOTTO
Unity and Freedom

CAPITAL CITY
Lilongwe

TYPE OF GOVERNMENT
Parliamentary democracy

NATIONAL EMBLEM
Lake Malawi

NATIONAL COLORS
Red and black

NATIONAL ANTHEM
The anthem was written and composed as part of a competition just before it was adopted at independence in 1964.

> **Mulungu dalitsa Malawi (Chichewa); O God Bless Our Land of Malawi (English)**
> O God bless our land of Malawi,
> Keep it a land of peace.
> Put down each and every enemy,
> Hunger, disease, envy.
> Join together all our hearts as one,
> That we be free from fear.
> Bless our leader,
> each and every one,
> And Mother Malawi.
>
> Our own Malawi, this land so fair,
> Fertile and brave and free.
> With its lakes, refreshing mountain air,
> How greatly blest are we.
> Hills and valleys, soil so rich and rare
> Give us a bounty free.
> Wood and forest, plains so broad and fair,
> All-beauteous Malawi.

Freedom ever, let us all unite
To build up Malawi.
With our love, our zeal and loyalty,
Bringing our best to her.
In time of war, or in time of peace,
One purpose and one goal.
Men and women serving selflessly
In building Malawi.

CURRENCY
Malawian kwacha

VEHICLE IDENTIFICATION PLATES/STICKERS
MW

PASSPORT
The passport cover has the name of the country in Chichewa and English, the coat of arms, and the word *passport* in Chichewa and English.

AIRLINE
Air Malawi

NATIONAL FLOWER
Aerangis orchid (unofficial)

NATIONAL TREE
Baobab (unofficial)

NATIONAL ANIMAL
African lion; African leopard

NATIONAL BIRD
Fish eagle

NATIONAL FISH
Regal fish (unofficial)

NATIONAL RESOURCES
Natural resources include limestone, arable land, hydropower, and unexploited deposits of uranium, coal, and bauxite. Agriculture is the major industry, particularly the export crops of coffee, tea, and tobacco. Tourism is growing as travelers discover Malawi's natural beauty, uncrowded game parks, and comparatively low prices.

FOODS
Chambo, tilapia fish prepared in several ways; *nsima,* the staple food, a thick porridge made from cassava or corn; *ndiwo,* a mixture of greens, onions, and tomatoes, usually served with rice; *mkhwani,* pumpkin leaves, tomatoes, and ground peanuts; and *mandasi,* a fried pastry similar to a doughnut, are considered national dishes. Other specialties include *zitumbuwa,* banana fritters; *nthochi,* banana bread; *futali,* mashed pumpkin, squash, yam, or cassava mixed with peanut flour and fried; and *mbatata,* sweet potato biscuits

SPORTS/SPORTS TEAMS
Association football (soccer) is the most popular sport. Netball is also very popular, especially among schoolgirls. Malawi national teams participate in many sports at an international level.

TEAM SPORTS

Badminton
Malawi Badminton Team

Basketball
Malawi Basketball Team; Malawi Women's Basketball Team

Cricket
Malawi Cricket Team

Football
Malawi Football Team, nickname the Flames; Malawi Women's Football Team, nickname the Flames; Malawi Under-20 Football Team, nickname The Young Flames

Hockey
Malawi Field Hockey Team

Korfball

Malawi Korfball Team

Netball

Malawi Netball Team

Table Tennis

Malawi Table Tennis Team

Volleyball

Malawi Men's Volleyball Team

INDIVIDUAL SPORTS

Malawi Amateur Boxing Team; Malawi Athletics Team; Malawi Cycling Team; Malawi Equestrian Team; Malawi Swim Team; Malawi Tae Kwon Do Team; Malawi Weight Lifting Team

NATIONAL HEROES OR PERSONIFICATIONS

Zwangendaba, a powerful chief in the 19th century; Dr. Hastings Kamuzu Banda, who led the country to independence in 1964; Bakili Muluzi, president of Malawi from 1994 to 2004.

NATIONAL HOLIDAY/INDEPENDENCE DAY

Independence Day, July 6

FESTIVALS/FAIRS

Malawi Lake of Stars Festival, October; Republic Day celebrations, July; Kamuzu Festival, May

SIGNIFICANT EVENTS IN FORMATION OF NATIONAL IDENTITY

15th century C.E.   The ancestors of the Chewa tribe migrate to the region around Lake Malawi. The original inhabitants, a Pygmy people, were killed or driven out. The newcomers create the Maravi Empire that expands to include parts of Malawi, Mozambique*, and Zambia*.

16th century–18th century   The Portuguese visited the coastal region of the empire, carrying with them maize, or corn, seeds that later become a staple crop. The local people trade in ivory, iron, and slaves with Portuguese and Arab traders.

19th century   A tribal migration from present South Africa* conquers the Maravi Empire. The newcomers raid the local tribal settlements for food and slaves. Another migration from northern Mozambique colonizes the region and raids the established tribes for slaves. Arab traders who establish trading posts around Lake Malawi introduce Islam.

1859–1883   European explorer David Livingston reaches the shores of Lake Malawi. Christian missions are set up in an attempt to end the slave trade, which continues until 1878. The region becomes part of the British Central African Protectorate.

1907–1944   The territory is called Nyasaland. A small number of British- or American-educated leaders forms the first cultural and political organizations. The Nyasaland African Congress is formed.

1958–1964   Dr. Hastings Banda returns to Nyasaland after a long absence to assume the leadership of the national movement. Nyasaland, rechristened Malawi after the early Maravi Empire, becomes an independent republic, with Hastings Banda as its first president.

1970–1993   Hastings Banda declares one-party rule and becomes president for life. Banda's controversial and authoritarian rule ends in 1993. Multiparty democracy is introduced.

1995–2009   Tribal animosities disappear as Malawi advances. Corruption remains a major problem. The first political transition of power from one political party to another takes place in 2004. Tourism, particularly ecotourism, becomes an important part of the economy.

MALI

OFFICIAL NAME

Répblic du Mali (French); Republic of Mali (English)

POPULATION

12,134,600 (2009e)

INHABITANTS' NAME/NICKNAME

Malian(s)

LANGUAGE/LANGUAGES

French (official); Bambara, Malian French, Arabic, others

RELIGION/RELIGIONS

Sunni Muslim, 60 percent; Christian, 1 percent; traditional beliefs, other or no religion

NATIONAL FLAG

The flag is a vertical tricolor of the traditional pan-African colors of green, gold, and red. The colors symbolize unity with other African nations. Green represents forests and agriculture, gold represents the land and mineral wealth, and red represents the blood spilled in pursuit of liberty.

COAT OF ARMS/SEAL

The coat of arms is a circle with depictions of a rising sun at the bottom, bows and arrows, the Great Mosque of Djenné at the center, and the legendary vulture of Malian folklore at the top. Around the circle is a green border inscribed with the name of the country in French above and the national motto, also in French, below.

NATIONAL MOTTO

Un peuple, un but, une foi (French); One people, one goal, one faith (English)

CAPITAL CITY

Bamako

TYPE OF GOVERNMENT

Semipresidential republic

NATIONAL EMBLEM

Great Mosque of Djenné

NATIONAL COLORS

Green, gold, and red

NATIONAL ANTHEM

The anthem is based on an ancient Malian folk song, possibly dating from the Malian Empire in the 13th century. The lyrics, in French, were added when the anthem was officially adopted.

Pour L'Afrique et pour toi, Mali (French); For Africa and for You, Mali (English)

For Africa and for you, Mali,
Our banner shall be liberty.
For Africa and for you, Mali,
Our fight shall be for unity.
Oh, Mali of today,
Oh, Mali of tomorrow,
The fields are flowering with hope
And hearts are thrilling with confidence.

CURRENCY

CFA franc

INTERNET IDENTIFIER

.ml

VEHICLE IDENTIFICATION PLATES/STICKERS

RMM

PASSPORT

The passport cover has the name of the country in French, the coat of arms, and the French word for passport, *passeport*.

AIRLINE

Air Mali

NATIONAL BIRD

Lappet-faced vulture

NATIONAL RESOURCES

Natural resources include gold, phosphates, kaolin, salt, limestone, uranium, gypsum, granite, and hydropower. Deposits of bauxite, iron ore, manganese, tin, and copper are known but not exploited. The remittances sent home by Malians working in other countries are a valuable source of foreign currency.

FOODS

National dishes include *la captaine sangha,* a type of Nile perch served with a spicy chili sauce, whole fried bananas, and rice; *fufu,* a porridge made of millet, corn, or rice served with a variety of accompaniments made with peanuts, okra, baobab leaves, or sweet potato leaves; *poulet kedjennou,* chicken stewed with vegetables; *diabadji,* meat in onion sauce; *nadoulou,* meat with baobab leaves in peanut sauce; *saga saga,* meat with a sauce made of sweet potato leaves; *tigadeguena,* chicken in peanut sauce; and *maasa,* sweet millet fritters.

SPORTS/SPORTS TEAMS

Association football (soccer) is the country's most popular game, followed by basketball and rugby union. Mali national teams participate in many sports at an international level.

TEAM SPORTS

Baseball

Mali Baseball Team

Basketball

Mali Basketball Team; Mali Women's Basketball Team

Cricket

Mali Cricket Team

Football

Mali Football Team, known as Les Aigles (the Eagles); Mali Women's Football Team, nickname Les Aigles (the Eagles); Mali Rugby Union Team

Tennis

Mali Davis Cup Team

Volleyball

Mali Men's Volleyball Team

INDIVIDUAL SPORTS

Mali Amateur Boxing Team; Mali Athletics Team; Mali Fencing Team; Mali Judo Team; Mali Karate Team: Mali Swim Team; Mali Tae Kwon Do Team; Mali Weight Lifting Team; Mali Wrestling Team

NATIONAL HEROES OR PERSONIFICATIONS

Makhara Makhang Konate, also known as Sundiata Keita, founder of the medieval Mali Empire; Amadou Toumani Touré, military leader who took control of the autocratic government and appointed a civilian government to oversee the transition to democracy in the 1990s; Amadou Hampâté Bâ, a novelist and ethnologist; Tierno Bokar, a Muslim spiritual teacher famous for his message of religious tolerance and universal love in the early 20th century; Mansa Musa, the 14th-century ruler of the Mali Empire responsible for the introduction of Islam

NATIONAL HOLIDAY/INDEPENDENCE DAY

Independence Day, September 22

FESTIVALS/FAIRS

Crepissage de la grande mosquee de Djenné (Grand Mosque Festival), April; Nugu Mô, (Festival of Masks), May–June; Diarwara (Festival of Puppets), November; Takoubelt (Music and Handicrafts Festival), November

SIGNIFICANT EVENTS IN FORMATION OF NATIONAL IDENTITY

100 C.E.–750 C.E. Bantu peoples settle the Sahel region as part of the great Bantu migrations. Small kingdoms merge into the first of the great empires, the Empire of Ghana.

1078–1600 The empire falls to invading Muslim Berbers from North Africa. The Mali Empire expands from 1230 to eventually control part of the Atlantic coast. Its influence extends across a wide area of West Africa. Timbuktu and Djenné become centers of the trans-Saharan trade and of Islamic learning.

1390–1591 The Songhai Empire gains its independence from Mali and takes much territory from the declining Mali Empire. An invasion of troops from Morocco* destroys Songhai's power and marks the end of the region's role as a trading crossroads.

1591–1892 The end of the empires allows small kingdoms to succeed each other as regional powers before the French colonize the Sahel in 1892.

1892–1958 Known as French Sudan, the region is subdued by 1905 and becomes part of the Federation of French West Africa. French Sudan, renamed the Sudanese Republic, becomes an autonomous state of the French Union.

1959–1960 The Sudanese Republic and Senegal* are joined in the Mali Federation, which becomes fully independent in 1960, but Senegal soon withdraws, and the Sudanese Republic becomes the Republic of Mali.

1974–1980 A one-party state is created under a military government. The economy suffers excesses, corruption and a disastrous drought in the Sahel region. Several coup attempts and widespread student demonstrations are met with suppression.

1980s The political and economic upheavals stabilize, and elections are held. A long war between the nomadic Tuaregs in the north and the military continues to impede progress.

1990s Dictatorship is brought to an end by a military coup led by Amadou Touré, who hands over power to a civilian government. A transition to multiparty democracy and an improving economy help to end the Tuareg insurrection.

2000–2009 The first successful transfer of political power following national elections takes place in 2002, when Amadou Touré is elected president. Touré is reelected in 2007, a sign that Mali's political life is maturing and stable. Tuareg rebels in the north and east of the country again become active.

MAURITIUS

OFFICIAL NAME
Republic of Mauritius (English)

POPULATION
1,266,800 (2009e)

INHABITANTS' NAME/NICKNAME
Mauritian(s)

LANGUAGE/LANGUAGES
English (official); French, Mauritian Creole, Malagasy, Portuguese (recognized regional languages); Bhojpuri, others

RELIGION/RELIGIONS
Hindu, 48 percent; Roman Catholic, 24 percent; Muslim, 17 percent; Buddhist, Protestant, Sikh, other or no religion

NATIONAL FLAG
The flag consists of four equal horizontal stripes of red, blue, yellow, and green. The red represents the struggle for independence; the blue represents the Indian Ocean that surrounds Mauritius; the yellow represents the new light of independence shining over the country; and the green represents Mauritius' lush vegetation.

COAT OF ARMS/SEAL
The coat of arms has a centered shield or crest divided into quarters. The first quadrant depicts a ship, representing colonization. The second quadrant depicts palm trees, representing the country's tropical vegetation. The third quadrant depicts a key, representing the island's place as the key to the Indian Ocean. The fourth quadrant depicts a star, representing the island's status as the star of the Indian Ocean. A dodo and a sambur deer and poles of sugarcane support the shield. Below the shield is a banner inscribed with the country's motto in Latin.

Motto

Stella clavisque maris indici (Latin); Star and key of the Indian Ocean (English)

Capital City

Port Louis

Type of Government

Parliamentary republic

National Emblem

Dodo

National Colors

Red and white

National Anthem

The anthem, adopted at independence in 1968, describes the island landscape, the qualities of the people, and the national virtues.

> **Motherland**
>
> Glo-o-ory to thee,
> Motherland, O motherland of mine,
> Sweet is thy beauty,
> Sweet is thy fragrance,
> around thee we gather,
> as one people,
> as one nation,
> In peace, justice and liberty,
> Beloved country, may God bless thee,
> for ever and ever.

Patron Saint

Saint Maurice

Currency

Mauritian rupee

Internet Identifier

.mu

Vehicle Identification Plates/ Stickers

MS

Passport

The passport cover has the name of the country in English and French, the coat of arms, and the word *passport* in English and French.

Airline

Air Mauritius

National Flower

Boucle d'Oreille (Earring flower)

National Tree

Earring tree

National Plant

Sugar cane

National Animal

Sambur deer

National Bird

Dodo (extinct)

National Resources

Natural resources include arable land and fish. Since 1968, Mauritius has developed from an economy based on agriculture into a prosperous economy based on agriculture, manufacturing, services, and tourism. The country's sandy beaches, pleasant climate, and unique culture support a thriving tourist industry.

Foods

Cari poulet, chicken curry, is considered the national dish. Other specialties include *dholl puri,* a type of bread made with lentils; *mine-frit,* fried Chinese noodles served with fish, meat, or vegetables; *niouk nein,* Chinese-style dumplings; *biryani,* meat mixed with spiced rice and potatoes; *mari bon,* beef biryani served with spiced rice; *rougaille,* salt fish served with tomato sauce, *achards* (pickles) and rice; and *civet d lièvre,* hare or rabbit in red wine sauce.

SPORTS/SPORTS TEAMS

Association football (soccer) is the most popular sport, followed by basketball, cricket and kabaddi, particularly among the Indo-Mauritians. Mauritian national teams participate in many sports at an international level.

TEAM SPORTS

Badminton

Mauritius Badminton Team

Basketball

Mauritius Basketball Team; Mauritius Women's Basketball Team; Mauritius Wheelchair Basketball Team

Football

Mauritius Football Team, nickname Club M or Les Dodos; Mauritius Women's Football Team, nickname Club M or Les Dodos; Mauritius Under-20 Football Team; Mauritius Rugby Union Team

Kabaddi

Mauritius Kabaddi Team

Table Tennis

Mauritius Table Tennis Team

Tennis

Mauritius Davis Cup Team; Mauritius Fed Cup Team

Volleyball

Mauritius Men's Volleyball Team; Mauritius Women's Volleyball Team

INDIVIDUAL SPORTS

Mauritius Amateur Boxing Team; Mauritius Athletics Team; Mauritius Cycling Team; Mauritius Equestrian Team; Mauritius Judo Team; Mauritius Sailing Team; Mauritius Swim Team; Mauritius Tae Kwon Do Team; Mauritius Triathlon Team; Mauritius Weight Lifting Team; Mauritius Wrestling Team

NATIONAL HEROES OR PERSONIFICATIONS

Dookhee Gungah, a pioneer of free education in Mauritius; Seewoosagur Ramgoolam, a leader of the independence movement and the first prime minister of independent Mauritius; Maurice Cure, founder of the Mauritius Labor Party to safeguard the interests of the laborers in the 1930s

NATIONAL HOLIDAY/INDEPENDENCE DAY

Independence Day, March 12

FESTIVALS/FAIRS

Cavadee, January–February; Maha Shivratree, February–March; Divali, October–November; Eid al-Fitr, October–November; Chinese Spring Festival, January–February

SIGNIFICANT EVENTS IN FORMATION OF NATIONAL IDENTITY

1511 C.E.–1513 C.E. A Portuguese ship visits the uninhabited island. The sailors name the flightless, seemingly stupid birds found on the island the *doudo,* meaning "fool" or "crazy." Another Portuguese sailor, Don Pedro Mascarenhas, gave his name, Mascarene, to the group of islands made up of Mauritius, Rodrigues, and Réunion.

1598–1710 A Dutch expedition visits the island, which is named for Prince Maurits (*Mauritius,* in Latin) of the Dutch House of Nassau. The Dutch harvest the precious bark of the ebony trees that cover the island. The first permanent Dutch settlement is founded in 1638. After several attempts, the Dutch finally leave the island after introducing sugarcane, domestic animals, and the sambur deer brought from the Dutch East Indies.

1715–1810 The French claim the island and found a new settlement in 1721. The island, renamed Isle de France, remains under the control of the French East India Company until 1767 and then comes under the rule of governors sent from France.

1810–1814 A British force overpowers the French defenders and takes control of the island during the Napoleonic Wars. The island is permanently ceded to the United Kingdom* under the original name, Mauritius, in 1814. The British promise to respect the language, customs, and laws of the local population.

1825–1886 A Council of Government is created as a local appointed legislature. The abolition of slavery in 1835 is compensated by payments to the slave owners. The planters import large numbers of indentured laborers from India to work the sugarcane plantations. The legislature is enlarged with the addition of elected members.

1920s–1930s Conflicts arise between the Indian community and the wealthy Franco-Mauritians who control the plantations, banks, and most businesses. The Mauritius Labor Party is established in 1936 to safeguard the rights of the laborers.

1947–1948 The Labor Party wins the first elections for a newly created legislature. The election marks the first time the Franco-Mauritian upper class is ousted from power. In 1948, the franchise is extended to all literate adults.

1968 Communal strife spreads across the island until British troops intervene. Mauritius becomes an independent country under a government dominated by the largest segment of the population, the Indo-Mauritians.

1992–2009 Mauritius becomes a republic but remains in the Commonwealth. The stable politics and diversification of the economy gives the Mauritians one of the highest standards of living in the region. The inhabitants of Rodrigues, the large island dependency of Mauritius, demand greater representation in national institutions.

MAYOTTE

Official Name

Collectivité Départementale de Mayotte (French); Departmental Collectivity of Mayotte (English); Mahoré or Shimaore (Swahili dialect spoken on the islands)

Population

191,600 (2009e)

Inhabitants' Name/Nickname

Mahori(s); Mahoran(s); Mayottais

Language/Languages

French (official); Shimaore (Mahoran), Shindzwani, Kibushi, Shingazidza, Shimwali, Arabic, others

Religion/Religions

Sunni Muslim, 96 percent; Roman Catholic, 3 percent; other or no religion

National Flag

The French tricolor is the official flag. The unofficial local flag is a white field with the unofficial coat of arms centered, often with the name Mayotte in red letters across the top.

Coat of Arms/Seal

The coat of arms, also unofficial, shows a centered crest of blue over red with a white crescent moon on the blue, points to the top, and two yellow ylang-ylang flowers on the red. The crest is supported by two white sea horses. Below is a banner with the motto in the local Shimaore language.

Motto

Ra hachiri (Shimaore); *Nous sommes vigilants* (French); We are vigilant (English)

Capital City

Mamoudzou

Type of Government

Overseas departmental collectivity of France*

National Emblem

Sea horse

NATIONAL COLORS
White and green

NATIONAL ANTHEM
The French anthem, "La Marseillaise" (official)

CURRENCY
Euro

INTERNET IDENTIFIER
.yt

VEHICLE IDENTIFICATION PLATES/ STICKERS
F France (official); MAH Mahoré/Mayotte (unofficial)

PASSPORT
Mahorans are French citizens and travel on French passports.

NATIONAL FLOWER
Ylang-ylang flower

NATIONAL TREE
Ylang-ylang tree (unofficial)

NATIONAL ANIMAL
Sea horse

NATIONAL RESOURCES
Natural resources are negligible. Tourism, based on the island's sandy beaches, pleasant climate, and unique culture, is becoming an important industry. Remittances from Mahorans living in France are a source of foreign currency, but the mainstay of the island economy remains generous French subsidies that give Mayotte per capita incomes nine times higher than those of the neighboring islands in the archipelago.

FOODS
Mataba, a dish made of cassava cooked with garlic, meat or fish, and coconut milk, is considered the national dish. Other specialties include *muhogo ya nadzi na nyama,* a meat and cassava dish; *mbawa ya tomati,* chicken wings with tomatoes; *pilaou,* a rice dish with chicken, cloves, tomatoes, and spices; *pilaou ya nyama,* a rice dish with diced beef, onions, tomatoes, palm oil, and spices; *poulet au coco,* chicken cooked in coconut milk; and *poulet à l'indienne,* a chicken curry dish.

SPORTS/SPORTS TEAMS
Association football (soccer) and basketball are the most popular sports. Mayotte national teams participate in basketball, football, and rugby union at an international level.

TEAM SPORTS
Basketball
Mayotte Basketball Team; Mayotte Women's Basketball Team

Football
Mayotte Football Team; Mayotte Rugby Union Team

NATIONAL HEROES OR PERSONIFICATIONS
Andriantsuli, the last sultan of Mahoré (Mayotte); Marcel Henry, leader of the anti-Comoros movement in the 1960s and 1970s

NATIONAL HOLIDAY/INDEPENDENCE DAY
Bastille Day, July 14 (France and all French territories); Slavery Abolition Day, April 27

FESTIVALS/FAIRS
Mayotte Festival, November; Mayotte Blues Festival, February; Slavery Abolition Day/National Festival, April

SIGNIFICANT EVENTS IN FORMATION OF NATIONAL IDENTITY
1000 B.C.E. The Comoro islands, including Mayotte, are settled from the African mainland. Malay seafarers from Southeast Asia colonize the islands.

Eighth century C.E.–**ninth century** C.E.   The island becomes a center of the East African dhow trade. Arab traders settle in the islands, introducing the Muslim religion. The island becomes part of the Sultanate of Oman*. Shirazi Persians come to the island.

1500–1503   The Shirazi people establish a separate sultanate. Portuguese sailors record the sighting of the island.

16th century–19th century   The mixing of the various ethnic groups produces a distinct island nationality. Unlike on the other islands in the Comoro archipelago, Islam remains a minority religion.

1832–1843   Andriantsuli, from Madagascar*, conquers the island. Following attacks from neighboring island sultanates, Andriantsuli grants the French a military base in 1840 and finally cedes the sultanate to French rule. Mayotte becomes the center of French activity in the Comoros*. Christian missionaries convert many to Christianity and introduce education.

1886–1940   The other islands of the Comoro group come under French rule, but Mayotte remains a separate colony. The powerful Roman Catholic minority rejects French moves to integrate Mayotte and the Comoros.

1941–1945   Military installations provide work to islanders during the Second World War. The bases increase the island's military importance.

1947   Mayotte is joined with the other islands to form the French Overseas Territory of the Comoro Islands.

1966–1974   The islanders organize to fight inclusion in an independent Comoro state. Their refusal delays the independence of the Comoros for many years.

1974–1985   Mayotte is the only one of the four islands that votes to retain its ties to France in referendums organized in 1974 and again in 1979. The Comoros declares independence in 1975, beginning a long series of conflicts with France* over control of Mayotte. After independence, the Comoros experience a brutal reign of terror, entrenching the Mahorans refusal to join the country, even though the United Nations backs the Comoro claim. In 1984, the Mahorans vote overwhelmingly to remain under French rule. The French vow to remain as long as that is the wish of the majority.

1992–1993   Continued attempts by the Comoro government to gain control of prosperous Mayotte lead nationalist to state that the island would seek separate independence should the French withdraw. Anti-Comoro sentiment becomes violent, with attacks on Comoran immigrants.

1997–1998   The two smaller islands of the Comoro group, Anjouan and Moheli, attempt to throw off rule by the largest island, Grande Comore. They appeal for a return to French control, which the French reject.

2007–2009   French laws become applicable to Mayotte for the first time. The United Nations continues to annually pass a resolution demanding that France relinquish Mayotte to the Comoros. A referendum in mid-2009 shows that the majority of the Mahoris prefer continued ties to France rather than incorporation into the Comoros or separate independence. Mayotte is scheduled to become an overseas department of the French Republic in 2011.

See also France

MOZAMBIQUE

OFFICIAL NAME

República de Moçambique (Portuguese); Republic of Mozambique (English)

POPULATION

21,745,600 (2009e)

INHABITANTS' NAME/NICKNAME

Mozambican(s)

LANGUAGE/LANGUAGES

Portuguese (official); Makhuwa, Tsonga, Lomwe, Sena, English, others

RELIGION/RELIGIONS

Roman Catholic, 24 percent; Muslim, 18 percent; Zionist Christian, 18 percent; other or no religion

NATIONAL FLAG

The flag has three equal horizontal stripes of green, black, and yellow divided by white fimbriations. At the hoist is a red triangle charged with a yellow, five-pointed star with a white book centered and a black hoe and a black AK-47. Green represents the riches of the land, white represents peace, black represents the African continent, yellow symbolizes the country's minerals, and red represents the struggle for independence. The yellow star is the star of Marxism. A new, less partisan flag is under consideration.

COAT OF ARMS/SEAL

The coat of arms is in the form of a circle, with the center depicting a large gear wheel containing a red sun over a map of Mozambique in green, blue and white waves, an AK-47 crossed with a hoe, and an open book. The gear is surrounded by sheaves of corn and sugarcane tied by a red banner inscribed with the name of the country in Portuguese. Above the gear is a red star. The gear wheel represents labor and industry, the book represents education, the hoe is for the peasantry and agricultural production, and the AK-47 represents defense and vigilance. The red banner and the red star stand for socialism.

CAPITAL CITY

Maputo

TYPE OF GOVERNMENT

Multiparty republic

NATIONAL COLORS

Red and black

NATIONAL ANTHEM

The anthem was written and composed to reflect the country's new multiparty political system. It was adopted as the national anthem in 2002.

Pátria Amada (Portuguese); Beloved Fatherland (English)

In the memory of Africa and the World
Beautiful fatherland for which we dared to fight
Mozambique, your name is Freedom
The Sun of June forever will shine

Chorus

Mozambique, our Glorious Land
Rock by rock constructing the new day
Millions of arms in one only force
O loved fatherland, we go to be successful.

Joined people from Rovuma to Maputo
It harvests the fruits of the combat for the peace
The dream grows waving in the flag
It goes cultivating in the certainty of tomorrow.

Chorus

Flowers sprouting of the soil of your sweat
For mounts, the rivers, the sea
We swear for you, O Mozambique
No tyrant will ever enslave you

CURRENCY

Mozambican metical

INTERNET IDENTIFIER

.mz

VEHICLE IDENTIFICATION PLATES/STICKERS

MOC

PASSPORT

The passport cover has the name of the country in Portuguese, the coat of arms, and the word *passport* in Portuguese.

AIRLINE

Linhas Aéreas de Moçambique LAM

NATIONAL FLOWER

Mountain sugarbush (unofficial)

NATIONAL TREE

Mpingo (African blackwood) (unofficial)

NATIONAL ANIMAL

Mamba (unofficial)

NATIONAL FISH

Black tiger shrimp (unofficial)

NATIONAL RESOURCES

Natural resources include coal, titanium, natural gas, hydropower, tantalum, and graphite. Economic reforms have stimulated economic growth since 2002. Tourism, particularly from South Africa* and Europe, is becoming an important industry. Remittances from Mozambicans living outside the country are an important source of foreign currency.

FOODS

National dishes include *xima,* a porridge made of corn or cassava; *fringe,* chicken cooked over charcoal; *galinha piri piri,* chicken with hot pepper sauce; *galinha Zambezi,* a chicken dish; *matata,* a clam and peanut stew; *sopa de feijao verde,* green bean soup; *pãzinho,* Portuguese-style bread rolls; *salada pera de abacate,* a salad of tomatoes and avocado; *malasadas,* fried pastries similar to doughnuts; *bolo polana,* a dish of potatoes and cashews; *peri peri kari,* a spicy prawn curry; and *feijoada moçambicana,* a bean and meat stew.

SPORTS/SPORTS TEAMS

Association football (soccer) is the most popular game. Basketball is also becoming very popular. Mozambique national teams participate in many sports at an international level.

TEAM SPORTS

Badminton

Mozambique Badminton Team

Basketball

Mozambique Basketball Team; Mozambique Women's Basketball Team

Cricket

Mozambique Cricket Team

Football

Mozambique Football Team, nickname the Mambas; Mozambique Women's Football Team, nickname the Mambas; Mozambique Under-20 Football Team; Mozambique Women's Under-19 Football Team; Mozambique Beach Soccer Team; Mozambique Futsal Team

Volleyball

Mozambique Men's Volleyball Team; Mozambique Women's Volleyball Team; Mozambique Men's Beach Volleyball Team; Mozambique Women's Beach Volleyball Team

INDIVIDUAL SPORTS

Mozambique Amateur Boxing Team; Mozambique Athletics Team; Mozambique Canoeing Team; Mozambique Judo Team; Mozambique Rowing Team; Mozambique Swim Team; Mozambique Tae Kwon Do Team

NATIONAL HEROES OR PERSONIFICATIONS

Jose Craveirinha, a revered poet who inspired the struggle for independence; Eduardo Mondlane, the assassinated founder of Frelimo, the nationalist movement in the 1960s; Mateus Sansão Muthemba, leader of the independence movement assassinated in 1968; Josina Machal, a freedom fighter who died fighting the Portuguese in 1970; Marcelino dos Santos, leader of the independence movement; Samora Machel, first president of independent Mozambique

NATIONAL HOLIDAY/INDEPENDENCE DAY

Independence Day, June 25

FESTIVALS/FAIRS

Avante Mozambique!, August–September; Festival of Documentary Films, September; Mozambique Festival, August; Independence Day celebrations, June

SIGNIFICANT EVENTS IN FORMATION OF NATIONAL IDENTITY

First century C.E.–fourth century C.E. Waves of Bantu-speaking peoples migrate to the region, displacing the earlier inhabitants.

1000–1500 Numerous small kingdoms establish trade with Arab, Persian, and Asian traders, who establish trading posts on the coast. The Arab influence in the ports is strong, and Swahili is the lingua franca of trade.

1498–1600 Portuguese mariner Vasco da Gama explorers the coast. He returns in 1500 to conquer the region, attacking any port or kingdom unwilling to surrender. The Portuguese take control of the trade routes.

1600s The Portuguese colonists begin to penetrate the interior. Settlement from Portugal* is encouraged. After losing Mombasa and East Africa to the Arabs, the Portuguese concentrate on the subjugation of Mozambique.

1752–1869 Portugal proclaims the colony of Portuguese East Africa. The slave trade becomes a major part of economic activity. An estimated 1 million slaves are shipped from Mozambique before slavery is abolished in 1869.

1878–1885 Much of the north is leased to large private companies that use *chibalo*, or forced labor, to work mines and plantations and to construct roads and railroads. The scramble for Africa begins, with European countries claiming all available territories.

1891–1900 Portugal and the United Kingdom* agree on the present borders of Mozambique.

1926–1959 A new fascist government in Portugal tightens control over the colonies. Forced labor becomes more widespread. Schools and hospitals are restricted to the growing Portuguese settler population. Few improvements are made for the general population.

1960–1964 Government troops kill more than 500 people at a peaceful demonstration, the Mueda Massacre. The event marks the beginning of the struggle for independence. Fighting breaks out in 1964.

1974–1975 The overthrow of Portugal's fascist government brings an end to the colonial war. Mozambique becomes independent under a Marxist government. Over 400,000 Portuguese settlers return to Europe.

1981–1988 Civil war, droughts, and floods plague the country as the Marxist economy collapses. The government turns to the West for help. A new, more moderate government dismantles much of the Marxist society.

1992–1995 The civil war comes to an end under United Nations auspices. The first free, multiparty elections are held. More than 1.7 million refugees return to the country.

2001–2002 Severe flooding disrupts the country. Estimates reach as many as 1 million deaths from war and natural disasters between 1977 and 2002.

2002–2009 The economy slowly recovers, but expensive showpiece projects are emphasized that provide little for the general population.

MTHWAKAZI

OFFICIAL NAME

Mthwakazi (refers to the provinces of Matabeleland North, Matabeleland South, Bulawayo, and Midlands of Zimbabwe)

Proposed name: United Mthwakazi Republic

POPULATION
2,990,300 (2009e)

INHABITANTS' NAME/NICKNAME
Mthwakazian(s)

LANGUAGE/LANGUAGES
Sindebele, English (proposed official languages); Shona, others

RELIGION/RELIGIONS
Roman Catholic, Anglican, Methodist, Presbyterian, Baptist, Dutch Reformed, traditional beliefs, others

NATIONAL FLAG
The flag of the proposed state is a vertical bicolor of blue and gray charged with a multirayed sun divided blue (hoist) and red (fly) and a vertical line of 10 white, five-pointed stars on the blue near the hoist. The blue color represents the sky and the people's hopes and dreams for the future; gray represents the land and the rain clouds that bring the nourishing rain; the sun symbolizes the Mthwakazi people and goodwill toward the world; and the stars symbolize determination in the face of adversity. The red symbolizes the blood spilled by patriots and is a tribute to those who fell and were killed in the Gukurahundi.

COAT OF ARMS/SEAL
The coat of arms is a traditional Mthwakazi shield with a spear and an axe above two drums and crossed pipes. The shield represents the resilience and determination of the Mthwakazi people. The spear symbolizes history and the defense of the homeland. The *ukaleba,* the Mthwakazi axe, is an expression of determination to cut issues out of contention. The drums are a historical means of communication. The pipes, called *igudu* or *indombonda,* are traditional symbols of responsibility, sonority, and meditation.

MOTTO
Si ye, pambili (Sindebele); Let us go forward (English)

CAPITAL CITY
Bulawayo

TYPE OF GOVERNMENT
Mthwakazi is divided into four provincial governments within Zimbabwe. Nationalists propose a federal republic of five autonomous states.

NATIONAL EMBLEM
Eagle in full flight

NATIONAL COLORS
Blue and gray

CURRENCY
Zimbabwe* kwacha

VEHICLE IDENTIFICATION PLATES/STICKERS
ZW Zimbabwe (official); UMR United Mthwakazi Republic (unofficial)

PASSPORT
Mthwakazians are Zimbabwe citizens and travel on Zimbabwe passports.

NATIONAL ANIMAL
Elephant; *imbila* (rock rabbit)

NATIONAL BIRD
Eagle

NATIONAL RESOURCES
Natural resources include arable land, hydropower, methane gas, limestone, timber, gold, and platinum. Although agriculture

remains the main economic activity, the region is short on water and must import the staple food, maize, with access often manipulated by the government. Remittances from Mthwakazians living in South Africa* are a source of foreign currency and investment.

FOODS

National dishes include *isitshwala,* a staple made of corn and served with chicken, meat, beans, or vegetables; *dovi,* a stew of chicken, vegetables, and peanut butter; cornmeal cakes; greens prepared with tomatoes, onions, and peanut butter; fish and prawns with spinach and coconut; curried spinach with peanut butter; *sadza,* a cornmeal porridge; chicken stew with *sadza* dumplings; *nhopi,* cornmeal cooked with mashed pumpkin; and *nyma ye huku,* chicken stew with peanuts.

SPORTS/SPORTS TEAMS

Cricket is the most popular sport, along with association football (soccer). As yet, no national teams have been formed.

TEAM SPORTS

Football

The Football Club Highlanders of Bulawayo is considered the national team.

NATIONAL HEROES OR PERSONIFICATIONS

Mzilikazi Khumalo (King Mzilikazi), the leader who led the Mthwakazi from South Africa to conquer their present homeland; Lobengula, king of the Mthwakazi in the late 19th century; Joshua Nkomo, Mthwakazi leader in the fight for independence; Kirth Dube, Mthwakazi pro-independence activist; Mthandazo Ndema Ngwenya, a nationalist and activist killed under mysterious circumstances; Lookout Masuku, leader of the pro-independence movement

NATIONAL HOLIDAY/INDEPENDENCE DAY

Mzilikazi Day, September 9

FESTIVALS/FAIRS

King Mzilikazi Commutation, September; King Lobengula Festival, December

SIGNIFICANT EVENTS IN FORMATION OF NATIONAL IDENTITY

18th century C.E. Small groups of Zulu peoples begin moving north into present Zimbabwe.

1820–1827 Mzilikazi, a Zulu leader under the Zulu king, Shaka, gathers a large following of loyal soldiers. Violence and chaos accompany the expansion of the Zulus. Mzilikazi leads a large group of refugees over the Drakensburg Mountains. The marchers destroy or absorb conquered tribes.

1837 Threatened by the resurgent Zulus and the Boer wagon trains moving north, the majority of Mzilikazi's people cross the Limpopo River into present Zimbabwe to conquer the pastoral Shona tribe.

1880–1891 Lobengula, the King of the Ndebele, as the group is known to the British, signs a treaty with the British that is used to take control of the kingdom, then covering all of Zimbabwe. The British declare a protectorate over the territory they call Matabeleland.

1893–1894 European gold hunters provoke an armed conflict, leading to the defeat of the Mthwakazi warriors and their Shona serfs. The kingdom collapses and land is parceled out to European settlers.

1923 The separate British Matabeleland is dissolved and is joined to Mashonaland to form the British colony of Southern Rhodesia.

1957–1965 Joshua Nkomo forms the first nationalist organization in Matabeleland. After initial union with the Shona nationalists, Nkomo forms a separate Mthwakazi political party in 1963. Rhodesia issues a unilateral declaration of independence under a white minority government, and fighting breaks out between the Rhodesian military and the nationalist groups.

1980–1982 A negotiated settlement to the long war turns white-ruled Rhodesia into black-majority Zimbabwe under a government dominated by the majority Shona tribe. Fighting breaks out between the Shona military and Mthwakazian groups demanding autonomy. Nkomo and other Mthwakazian ministers are dismissed from the Zimbabwe government.

1982–1987 Mthwakazi moves toward secession as chaos spreads. An elite Shona battalion, the North Korean–trained Fifth Brigade, unleashes a reign of terror in the region that leaves between 10 thousand and 20 thousand dead.

1991 Mthwakazi leaders rejoin the Zimbabwe government as part of a new multiparty political system.

1994 The Zimbabwe government, run by Robert Mugabe, becomes increasingly brutal and incompetent. Chronic food shortages, political violence, and corruption leave the Mthwakazi poorer than before independence. Mthwakazians are targeted as being antigovernment. Tens of thousands flee poverty and violence to live and work illegally in neighboring South Africa.

1999 Joshua Nkomo, the unofficial Father of Zimbabwe, dies, and with him the long-standing political association of Mthwakazians and Shonas. Rampant inflation, continued violence, and growing poverty continue to disrupt the country.

2000–2007 The Mthwakazians support opposition candidates against the Mugabe government, but intimidation and violence make free elections impossible. Nationalists form the Mthwakazi Foundation as a provisional government of a proposed separatist state in central and western Zimbabwe. Zimbabwe's inflation rate hits 66,000 percent.

2008 Morgan Tsvangirai, the Shona leader of the opposition in Zimbabwe, concludes a pact with Mugabe for a government of national unity. The disillusioned Mthwakazians call the decision a sellout to Mugabe's dictatorship. South African tribal gangs attack the shantytowns where the refugees from Zimbabwe are concentrated, leaving hundreds dead and injured.

2009 Mthwakazian leaders send a formal protest to the government as Mugabe spends over $250,000 on a lavish birthday party while his country suffers extreme poverty, starvation, a cholera epidemic, and political oppression. A meeting of the SADC (Southern African Development Community) fails to curb the excesses of the Mugabe government or to force Mugabe to honor the terms of the power-sharing agreement of 2008. The people of Mthwakazi, along with the more favored Shona people in the north of Zimbabwe, slip further into poverty, newspapers remain closed, and corruption is rampant.

See also Zimbabwe

NAMIBIA

OFFICIAL NAME
Republic of Namibia

POPULATION
2,129,400 (2009e)

INHABITANTS' NAME/NICKNAME
Namibian(s)

LANGUAGE/LANGUAGES
English (official); Afrikaans, German, Oshiwambo (recognized regional languages); Herero, Nama, others

RELIGION/RELIGIONS
Christian, 80 percent to 90 percent (Lutheran 50% at least); indigenous beliefs, 10 percent to 20 percent; Muslim, 3 percent; other or no religion

NATIONAL FLAG
The flag comprises diagonal stripes of blue, red, and green separated by white fimbriations. On the blue stripe at the upper hoist is a gold sun with 12 rays. The blue represents the sky, the Atlantic Ocean, the rain, and the country's precious water resources. The white represents peace and unity. The red is for the country's most important resource, the people, and their heroism and determination to build a future of equal opportunity

for all. The green stands for vegetation and agricultural resources. The gold sun represents life and energy.

COAT OF ARMS/SEAL

The coat of arms consists of a central shield bearing the colors and symbols of the national flag. Above the shield is perched an African fish eagle. Supporting the shield are two oryx antelopes, representing courage, elegance, and pride. Below the shield is a desert flower, *Welwitschia mirabilis,* a symbol of survival and good fortune. Below is a banner inscribed with the national motto.

MOTTO

Unity, Liberty, Justice

CAPITAL CITY

Windhoek

TYPE OF GOVERNMENT

Parliamentary republic

NATIONAL EMBLEM

African fish eagle

NATIONAL COLORS

Red and white

NATIONAL ANTHEM

The anthem was adopted and performed a year after Namibian independence in 1990.

Namibia, Land of the Brave

Namibia, land of the brave
Freedom fight we have won
Glory to their bravery
Whose blood waters our freedom
We give our love and loyalty
Together in unity
Contrasting beautiful Namibia
Namibia our country
Beloved land of savannas,
Hold high the banner of liberty

Chorus

Namibia our Country,
Namibia Motherland,
We love thee.

CURRENCY

Namibian dollar

INTERNET IDENTIFIER

.na

VEHICLE IDENTIFICATION PLATES/ STICKERS

NAM

PASSPORT

The passport cover has the name of the country in English, the coat of arms, and the word passport in English.

AIRLINE

Air Namibia

NATIONAL FLOWER

Welwitschia

NATIONAL TREE

Acacia (unofficial)

NATIONAL ANIMAL

Oryx antelope

NATIONAL BIRD

African Fish Eagle

NATIONAL FISH

Horse mackerel (unofficial)

NATIONAL RESOURCES

Natural resources include diamonds, copper, uranium, gold, silver, lead, tin, lithium, cadmium, tungsten, zinc, salt, hydropower, and fish. Exploration has begun to confirm possible deposits of oil, coal, and iron ore. Mining and minerals are the most important industry. Tourism, particularly ecotourism, is an important resource, based on the country's different climate zones, nature parks, the great eastern desert, and the variety of animal life.

FOODS

National dishes include *bitong,* air-dried meats; *rauchfleisch,* smoked meats; *potjiekos,* one-pot bush stew; *braal,* barbecued meat with vegetables, dried fruits, and herbs; *landjäger,* smoked beef and pork sausage; *oshifima,* a thick porridge made of millet; *evanda,* wild spinach, dried and pressed into cakes; bushmeat skewers with peanut satay; Namibian lamb, cooked over charcoal with herbs and anchovies; and veldt bread, a sweet bread with cinnamon, cloves, and allspice.

SPORTS/SPORTS TEAMS

Association football (soccer), cricket, and rugby union are the most popular sports. Namibia national teams participate in many sports at an international level.

TEAM SPORTS

Badminton
Namibia Badminton Team

Baseball
Namibia Baseball Team; Namibia Softball Team

Basketball
Namibia Basketball Team; Namibia Women's basketball team

Cricket
Namibia Cricket Team

Football
Namibia Football Team, nickname the Brave Warriors; Namibia Women's Football Team, nickname the Brave Gladiators; Na-mibia Under-20 Football Team, nickname the Young Warriors; Namibia Rugby Union Team; Namibia Rugby Union Team (Sevens), nickname Namibia Sevens or Namibia 7s

Hockey
Namibia Ice Hockey Team; Namibia Field Hockey Team

Netball
Namibia Netball Team

Racing
Namibia Speedway Team

Tennis
Namibia Davis Cup Team; Namibia Fed Cup Team

Table Tennis
Namibia Table Tennis Team

Volleyball
Namibia Fistball Team; Namibia Men's Volleyball Team; Namibia Women's Volleyball Team

INDIVIDUAL SPORTS

Namibia Amateur Boxing Team; Namibia Archery Team; Namibia Athletics Team; Namibia Canoeing Team; Namibia Cycling Team; Namibia Equestrian Team; Namibia Fencing Team; Namibia Gymnastics Team; Namibia Judo Team; Namibia Modern Pentathlon Team; Namibia Sailing Team; Namibia Shooting Team; Namibia Swim Team; Namibia Triathlon Team; Namibia Weight Lifting Team

WINTER SPORTS

Namibia Ice Hockey Team

NATIONAL HEROES OR PERSONIFICATIONS

Hendrik Witbooi, the leader of the Nama revolt in 1904–08; Samuel Maharero, the leader of the Herero revolt in 1904; Mandume Ya Ndemufayo, the last king of the Kwanyama, who died resisting South African troops in 1917; Sam Nujoma, leader of the independence movement and first president of independent Namibia

NATIONAL HOLIDAY/INDEPENDENCE DAY
Independence Day, March 21

FESTIVALS/FAIRS
Oktoberfest, October; National Dance Festival, November–December; Maharero Day celebrations, August; Windhoek Karneval, April–May; Kuste Karneval (Coast Carnival), August–September

SIGNIFICANT EVENTS IN FORMATION OF NATIONAL IDENTITY

5th century B.C.E.–14th century C.E. The San people, later known as Bushmen, are the first inhabitants of the region. The Damara and Nama, who live by herding, move into the central pasturelands.

14th century Bantu peoples migrating from the north occupy the fertile regions in the north.

1485–1797 Portuguese mariner Diogo Cão explores the region known as the Skeleton Coast. Other European expeditions follow, but the Namib Desert constitutes a formidable barrier to exploration of the interior. The Dutch take control of Walvis Bay, the only deepwater port on the coast, which is ceded to the United Kingdom* along with Cape Colony.

1805 British missionaries begin working in the region.

1878–1884 The British annex Walvis Bay to the Cape Colony. In 1884, the German government claims the region, outside of Walvis Bay, calling the new colony German South West Africa.

1904–1908 German colonists establish farms and towns. The Herero and Nama peoples rebel against German rule, but the arrival of thousands of German troops defeats the rebels. The Herero are driven into the waterless desert, where most die of thirst while German troops guard every water source, with orders to shoot any Herero on sight. Over 80 percent of the Herero, about 65,000 people, and 50 percent of the Nama, about 10,000 people, die between the wars and the German punishments.

1915–1946 During the First World War, South Africa* occupies the German colony, which becomes a League of Nations mandate under South African administration after the war and becomes a United Nations trust territory after the Second World War. South Africa extends its apartheid laws to South-West Africa.

1966–1990 The United Nations revokes the trusteeship, but South Africa refuses to relinquish the territory. Nationalist guerrillas begin attacks on the territory from the newly independent countries on its borders. South Africa finally agrees to return the territory to United Nations control, which begins the transition to independence in 1990 after almost 25 years of war.

1990–1994 The former Marxist guerrillas moderate their policies, and a democratic system is created. The coastal enclave of Walvis Bay is transferred to Namibia from South Africa.

2004–2009 The German government officially apologizes for the Herero Genocide of the early 20th century. The expropriation of white-owned farms for distribution to landless citizens begins.

NIGER

OFFICIAL NAME
République de Niger (French); Republic of Niger (English)

POPULATION
13,804,900 (2009e)

INHABITANTS' NAME/NICKNAME
Nigerien(s)

LANGUAGE/LANGUAGES
French (official); Hausa, Derma, Tamara, Paul, Bari, Ted, others

RELIGION/RELIGIONS

Muslim, 80 percent; Christian, 1 percent; indigenous beliefs, other or no religion

NATIONAL FLAG

The flag is a horizontal tricolor of orange, white, and green bearing a centered orange disk on the white. Unofficially, the orange stands for the Sahara Desert and the Sahel, the white represents purity and the River Niger, and the green represents hope and the fertile regions of southern Niger. The central disk represents the sun and independence.

COAT OF ARMS/SEAL

The coat of arms has four national flags draped behind a central green shield with gold depictions of the sun, a vertical spear, and two crossed Tuareg swords, three pearl millet heads, and the front view of a zebu's (humped cattle) head. Below the shield is a banner with the name of the country in French. The sun represents the unity of the country, the spear and crossed swords represent the Tuareg north, and the millet represents the agricultural south.

MOTTO

Fraternité, travail, progrès (French); Fraternity, Work, Progress (English)

CAPITAL CITY

Niamey

TYPE OF GOVERNMENT

Parliamentary democracy

NATIONAL COLORS

Orange, white, and green

NATIONAL ANTHEM

The anthem was adopted at independence in 1961.

La Nigérienne (French); The Nigerien (English)

Throughout great powerful Niger
Which makes nature more beautiful,
Let us be proud and grateful
Of our new freedom!
Let us avoid vain quarrels
In order to spare ourselves bloodshed,
and may the glorious voices
Of our race be free of domination!
Let us rise in a single leap
As high as the dazzling sky,
Where stands guard its eternal soul
Which will make the country greater!

Chorus

Arise! Niger! Arise!
May our fruitful labors
Rejuvenate the heart of this old continent!
And may the song be heard
In the four corners of the Earth
As the cry of a fair and valiant people!
Arise! Niger! Arise!
On the ground and on the wave,
To the sound of the drums
In their growing rhythms
Let us always remain united,
And may each one respond
To this noble future
Which tells us, "Go forward!"

CURRENCY

CFA franc

INTERNET IDENTIFIER

.ne

VEHICLE IDENTIFICATION PLATES/STICKERS

RN

PASSPORT

The passport cover has the name of the country, the coat of arms, and the French word for passport, *passeport*.

NATIONAL ANIMAL

Zebu (official); Roan antelope (unofficial)

NATIONAL RESOURCES

Natural resources include uranium, coal, iron ore, tin, phosphates, gold, molybdenum, gypsum, salt, and petroleum. The economy of Niger centers on subsistence crops, livestock, and some of the world's largest uranium deposits. Tourism is becoming an important industry, particularly visits to the ancient cities in the north of the country. Remittances from Nigerians living outside the country are a major source of foreign currency and investment.

FOODS

Foura, ground millet or rice, slightly fermented and shaped into balls, served with vegetables or meat, and *riz Jollof,* a rice dish of tomatoes, onions, spices, and chilies, are considered the national dishes. Other specialties include *funkaso,* a type of pancake served with honey or spicy condiments; *apon ogbono,* a dish of chicken, smoked fish, tomatoes, sweet peppers, onions, and spices; and *kuka,* a soup of *kuka* (baobab) leaves, tomatoes, dried fish, palm oil, and spices.

SPORTS/SPORTS TEAMS

Association football (soccer) is the most popular sport. Traditional sports, such as horse racing, camel racing, and wrestling, remain very popular. Niger national teams participate in many sports at an international level.

TEAM SPORTS

Basketball

Niger Basketball Team; Niger Women's Basketball Team

Football

Niger Football Team, nickname Mena; Niger Women's Football Team, nickname Mena; Niger Rugby Union Team

Table Tennis

Niger Table Tennis Team

Volleyball

Niger Men's Volleyball Team

INDIVIDUAL SPORTS

Niger Amateur Boxing Team; Niger Athletics Team; Niger Cycling Team; Niger Rowing Team; Niger Swim Team; Niger Tae Kwon Do Team; Niger Wrestling Team

NATIONAL HEROES OR PERSONIFICATIONS

Sarraounia Mangou, a local queen who led the resistance to the Tuareg invasion and the later French invasion in the late 19th century; Alfa Saibou, a leader of the early 20th century rebellion against French rule; Fihroun, a Tuareg leader of the anti-French war who died fighting in 1916; Hamani Diori, independence leader and first president of independent Niger

NATIONAL HOLIDAY/INDEPENDENCE DAY

Republic Day, December 18

FESTIVALS/FAIRS

Festival sur le Niger (Festival on the Niger), February; Independence Day celebrations, August; Cure Salee, August–September; Gerwool Festival, September

SIGNIFICANT EVENTS IN FORMATION OF NATIONAL IDENTITY

2000 B.C.E. The Sahara dries into desert. Settlements and trade routes remain in the north, but the majority of the population settles in the fertile south.

500 B.C.E.–1880 C.E. The region is an important crossroads controlled by several successive empires and a number of smaller kingdoms. British, German, and French explorers visit the region. The French claim the region and begin the pacification of the various states and tribes.

1890–1922 The French occupy the region. Resistance continues, particularly among the Tuaregs in the north. Niger is added to French West Africa.

1958 Niger becomes an autonomous state within the French Community and gains full independence in 1960 under Hamani Diori.

1968–1989 Devastating droughts in the northern Sahel region kill livestock and disrupt crop production. Unrest leads to a military coup and the installation of a military government. A new constitution creates a civilian government.

1990–1993 The ban on political parties is lifted. The Tuaregs in the north, marginalized and excluded from government, begin a long war for Tuareg rights or even independence. Multiparty elections are held.

1995 A cease-fire in the north brings relative peace.

2001 The government bans hunting in an effort to save its remaining wildlife, which includes lions, giraffes, and hippopotamuses.

2005 A planned ceremony to free over 7,000 slaves is canceled after the government claims that slavery does not exist in the country. Drought and locust infestations lead to malnutrition and hardship.

2007–2009 The Tuareg rebellion resumes due to government neglect of the terms of the earlier cease-fires. The spreading insecurity devastates Niger's once-promising tourist industry and deters investment in mining and oil production.

NIGERIA

OFFICIAL NAME
Federal Republic of Nigeria

POPULATION
149,388,500 (2009e)

INHABITANTS' NAME/NICKNAME
Nigerian(s)

LANGUAGE/LANGUAGES
English (official); Hausa, Igbo, Yoruba (recognized regional languages); many other indigenous languages

RELIGION/RELIGIONS
Muslim, 44 percent; Nigerian Christian, 15 percent; Anglican, 13 percent; Roman Catholic, 8 percent; other Protestant, traditional beliefs, other or no religion

NATIONAL FLAG
The flag has three equal vertical stripes of green, white, and green. The green represents the forests and abundant natural wealth of Nigeria. The white stands for peace between the many peoples of Nigeria.

COAT OF ARMS/SEAL
The coat of arms has a central black shield divided by a white Y-shape. These represent the two main rivers flowing through Nigeria and also the three major regions of the country. The black represents Nigeria's good earth, while the two white horses supporting the shield represent dignity. The eagle above the shield represents strength, while the green and white bands on the top of the shield represent the rich agricultural land of the country. The yellow flowers at the base are *Costus spectabilis,* Nigeria's national flower.

MOTTO
Unity and faith, peace and progress

CAPITAL CITY
Abuja

TYPE OF GOVERNMENT
Presidential federal republic

NATIONAL COLORS
Green and white

NATIONAL ANTHEM
The anthem was adopted at independence in 1960. The lyrics are an amalgamation of the five winning entrants to a national contest, set to music by the director of the Nigerian Police Band.

Arise, Oh Compatriots, Nigeria's Call Obey

Arise, Oh compatriots,
Nigeria's call obey
To serve our Fatherland
With love and strength and faith.
The labor of our heroes past
Shall never be in vain,
To serve with heart and might
One nation bound in freedom, peace,
  and unity.

Oh God of creation,
Direct our noble cause;
Guide our Leaders right:
Help our Youth the truth to know,
In love and honesty to grow,
And living just and true,
Great lofty heights attain,
To build a nation where peace and justice
  reign.

PATRON SAINT

Mary, Queen of Nigeria; Saint Patrick

CURRENCY

Nigerian naira

INTERNET IDENTIFIER

.ng

VEHICLE IDENTIFICATION PLATES/STICKERS

WAN

PASSPORT

The passport cover has the name of the country, the coat of arms, and the word *passport.*

AIRLINES

Virgin Nigeria; Arik Air; Bellview Airlines

NATIONAL FLOWER

Aluka (Costus spectabilis)

NATIONAL TREE

Albizia (unofficial)

NATIONAL ANIMAL

Horse

NATIONAL BIRD

Niger delta eagle

NATIONAL FISH

Nile perch (unofficial)

NATIONAL RESOURCES

Natural resources include natural gas, petroleum, tin, iron ore, coal, limestone, niobium, lead, zinc, and arable land. Nigeria has abundant natural resources, particularly oil and natural gas, but has long been hobbled by political instability, corruption, inadequate infrastructure, and mismanagement. Nigerian officials are undertaking some reforms under a new, reform-minded administration. Remittances from Nigerians living outside the country are an important source of foreign currency and investment.

FOODS

Nigeria is a large country with many regional cuisines. Groundnut stew, made of groundnuts, tomatoes, and onions, with any variety of chicken, meat, or fish, vegetables, and assorted herbs, is considered the national dish. Other well-known dishes include plantain and pepper soup; *suya,* skewered liver and meat cooked over charcoal; *egussi* soup, a stew of meat, dried fish, and melon seeds from eastern Nigeria; *kilishi,* spiced dried meat; *fufu,* a thick dough of yams or cassava rolled into balls and served with vegetables, sauces, or meat from northern Nigeria; *moimoi,* a dish of black-eyed peas, onions, and spices cooked in a *moimoi* leaf; and *ogbono* soup, a soup of *ogbono* seeds, leaf vegetables, seasonings and meat.

SPORTS/SPORTS TEAMS

Association football (soccer) is considered the national sport. Basketball, athletics, and boxing are also popular. Nigeria national teams participate in many sports at an international level.

TEAM SPORTS

Badminton
Nigeria Badminton Team

Baseball
Nigeria Baseball Team; Nigeria Softball Team

Basketball
Nigeria Basketball Team; Nigeria Women's Basketball Team

Cricket
Nigeria Cricket Team

Football
Nigeria Football Team, nickname the Super Eagles; Nigeria Women's Football Team, nickname the Super Falcons; Nigeria Under-23 Football Team, nickname the Green Eagles; Nigeria Under-20 Football Team, nickname the Flying Eagles; Nigeria Women's Under-19 Football Team, nickname the Falconets; Nigeria Under-17 Football Team, nickname the Junior Eagles or the Golden Eaglets; Nigeria Rugby Union Team; Nigeria Beach Soccer Team; Nigeria Futsal Team

Handball
Nigeria Handball Team

Hockey
Nigeria Field Hockey Team

Kabaddi
Nigeria Kabaddi Team

Netball
Nigeria Netball Team

Table Tennis
Nigeria Table Tennis Team

Tennis
Nigeria Davis Cup Team

Volleyball
Nigeria Men's Volleyball Team; Nigeria Women's Volleyball Team

INDIVIDUAL SPORTS

Nigeria Amateur Boxing Team; Nigeria Archery Team; Nigeria Athletics Team; Nigeria Canoeing Team; Nigeria Cycling Team; Nigeria Gymnastics Team: Nigeria Judo Team; Nigeria Modern Pentathlon Team; Nigeria Rowing Team; Nigeria Shooting Team; Nigeria Swim Team; Nigeria Tae Kwon Do Team; Nigeria Triathlon Team; Nigeria Weight Lifting Team; Nigeria Wrestling Team

NATIONAL HEROES OR PERSONIFICATIONS

Yakubu Dan-Yumma Gowan, head of the federal military government from 1966 to 1975 during the Biafra secession war; Patrick Chukwuma Kaduna Nzeogwu, military leader who died in the Biafran War; Alhaji Sir Ahmadu Bello, premier of Northern Nigeria who attempted to unify the tribes of Nigeria until his assassination in 1966; Ken Saro-Wiwa, a writer and campaigner against the excesses of the oil industry who was executed in 1995; Abubakar Tafawa Belawa, the first president of independent Nigeria

NATIONAL HOLIDAY/INDEPENDENCE DAY

Independence Day, October 1

FESTIVALS/FAIRS

Abuja Carnival, November; Katsina Dubar Festival, July; Sharo/Shadi Festival, variable dates; Eyo Festival, variable dates; the Sango Festival, June; Benin Festival, October; Ibo Celebration of Onitsha Ivories, July;

Argungu Fishing Festival, August; New Yam Festival, July

SIGNIFICANT EVENTS IN FORMATION OF NATIONAL IDENTITY

800 B.C.E. The advanced Nok civilization emerges in the Jos plateau region.

11th century C.E. Numerous states, kingdoms, and empires form across the region, including the Hausa kingdoms and the Borno state in the north and the Oyo and Benin kingdoms in the south.

1472 The first Europeans, Portuguese explorers, visit the coast.

16th century–18th century Europeans establish trading posts along the coast, mostly to engage in the lucrative slave trade. States along the coast in alliance with the Europeans raid far into the interior for slaves to sell to the Europeans. Islamic states in the north also engage in the slave trade, capturing non-Muslims to send on trans-Saharan caravans to Arab markets in North Africa.

1809 The northern kingdoms and emirates are unified under the rule of the Sokoto Caliphate.

1830s–1886 Civil wars disrupt the many urban city-states in the southwestern Yoruba territory.

1850s The British establish military posts around Lagos in Yorubaland.

1861–1914 Predominately Muslim Northern Nigeria is amalgamated with Christian and pagan Southern Nigeria to form the colony of Nigeria with three regions, Northern, Eastern, and Western Nigeria.

1950–1963 The first conference is held of delegates from both north and south to discuss Nigeria's future. Nigeria gains full independence as a federation of the three regions. The country severs all remaining ties to the United Kingdom* and becomes a republic.

1966–1967 A coup by southerners overthrows the government, followed by a countercoup by northern officers. Violence and chaos erupt, including massacres of Ibos living in Northern Nigeria that triggers the flight of over a million Ibos

back to the Eastern Region, which secedes as the Republic of Biafra, setting off a bloody civil war.

1970 Biafra surrenders and is reintegrated into Nigeria.

1975–1990 Military governments, coups, mismanagement, and corruption plague the country. Distrust among the major tribes continues to destabilize the government.

1990–2000 Serious disturbances break out in the oil-producing Niger River delta over massive pollution and the abject poverty of the region's people. Ken Saro-Wiwa, a poet and campaigner against the oil industry, is arrested, hastily tried, and executed.

2000 The adoption of Sharia, Islamic law, by several northern Muslim states over the opposition of Christians results in hundreds of deaths in clashes between Christians and Muslims.

2002 Ethnic violence in Lagos between Hausa Muslims from northern Nigeria and Yorubas from Lagos and the southwest leaves hundreds dead. Thousands flee the city to escape the violence before the military intervenes. Violence again breaks out in the north over plans to host the Miss World beauty pageant. The event is relocated to the United Kingdom.

2006 Rebels in the oil-rich Niger delta attack pipelines and other oil facilities and kidnap oil workers to publicize demands for more local control over the oil wealth of their homeland. Shell Oil is heavily criticized for its part in the pollution and corruption that plague the region.

2006–2009 Nigeria continues to be plagued by local nationalist feeling and the lack of a unified Nigerian sentiment among the diverse population. Oil production is cut by about half by militants' attacks on pipelines in the Niger delta, contributing to continued high oil prices worldwide.

REUNION

OFFICIAL NAME

Région Réunion (French); Reunion Region (English)

POPULATION

824,600 (2009e)

INHABITANTS' NAME/NICKNAME

Réunionnais; Reunionese

LANGUAGE/LANGUAGES

French (official); Réunion Creole, Chinese languages, Urdu, Hindustani, others

RELIGION/RELIGIONS

Roman Catholic, 86 percent; Pentecostal, 3 percent; Hindu, Muslim, Buddhist, other or no religion

NATIONAL FLAG

The French tricolor is the official flag. The flag proposed by the Association Réunionnaise de Vexillologie (Reunion Vexillological Association) is a medium blue field bearing a red triangle at the bottom with five yellow rays emanating from its point to the edges of the field. The red represents the Piton de la Fournaise volcano and strength, the blue stands for the sky and sweetness, and the yellow signifies the sun and cleanliness. The official flag of the region is a white field with a stylized representation of the volcano and the name of the region.

COAT OF ARMS/SEAL

The coat of arms has a central quartered crest. The first quadrant has a white mountain on a green background; the second upper quadrant shows a ship, the Saint-Alexis, which landed on the island in 1638; the third quarter has three yellow fleurs-de-lis on a blue background, representing royal France*; the fourth quadrant has bees on a red background, representing republican France. A small shield in the center has the French tricolor and RF for République Française. Above and on the sides is a green vanilla liana twined through a yellow banner with the island's unofficial motto in Latin.

MOTTO

Florebo quocumque ferar (Latin); I shall flower wherever I am planted (English) (unofficial)

CAPITAL CITY

Saint-Denis

TYPE OF GOVERNMENT

Overseas Department of France

NATIONAL EMBLEM

Piton de la Fournaise

NATIONAL COLORS

Blue, red, and white

NATIONAL ANTHEM

The official anthem is the "La Marseillaise," the French national anthem. The local anthem originated as a popular Creole song in the 19th century and is now taught in local schools. No English translation is available.

P'tit fleur fanée (Réunion Creole)

Vi souviens mon Nénène adorée
Le p'tit bouquet, vou la donne à moin
Na longtemps que li l'est fané,
Vi souviens, com' ça l'est loin.
P'tit' fleur fanée
P'tit' fleur aimée
Di à moin toujours
Kouk cek l'amour?
Mi marché dans la forêt,
Y faisait bon, y faisait frais,
Dan' z'herbes n'avait la rosée,
Dan le ciel zoiseaux y chantait.
P'tit' fleur fanée . . .
Depuis ça, le temps la passé,
Y reste plus qu'un doux souvenir,
Quand mi pense, mon coeur l'est brisé,
Tout ici ba, com' ça y doit finir.
P'tit' fleur fanée . . .

PATRON SAINT

Saint Denis

CURRENCY
Euro

INTERNET IDENTIFIER
.re

VEHICLE IDENTIFICATION PLATES/ STICKERS
F France (official); RE Reunion (unofficial)

PASSPORT
Reunionese are French citizens and travel on French passports.

AIRLINE
Air Austral

NATIONAL FLOWER
Vanilla liana

NATIONAL ANIMAL
Panther chameleon (unofficial)

NATIONAL BIRD
Wandering albatross (unofficial)

NATIONAL RESOURCES
Natural resources include fish, arable land, and hydropower. Varied scenery, sandy beaches, a pleasant climate, and a unique culture support the important tourist industry. French financial subsidies and remittances from Reunionese living outside the country are important sources of revenue and investment. Traditionally, sugarcane is the major crop.

FOODS
Zambrocal, a rice and seafood dish, is considered the national dish. Other island specialties include *tambor en papillotte,* drum fish cooked in parchment with vegetables, lemon, tomatoes, and herbs; *rougail,* codfish prepared with tomatoes, onions, cloves, and chilies; *trute flambé avec sauce vanille,* fresh trout with cloves, soy sauce, cream, and vanilla; *massalé,* a dish of diced swordfish, tomatoes, onions, garlic, spices, and chilies; *brochetted de porc,* marinated skewered pork cooked over charcoal; *les lentilles,* lentils cooked with onion and spices; *riz mais,* rice mixed with cornmeal; and *cari,* curries brought by Indian immigrants.

SPORTS/SPORTS TEAMS
Rugby union and association football (soccer) are the most popular sports. Basketball is also very popular. Reunion national teams participate in football, rugby union, and basketball at an international level.

TEAM SPORTS

Basketball
Reunion Basketball Team; Reunion Women's Basketball Team

Football
Reunion Football Team; Reunion Rugby Union Team; Ligue Réunionaise de Football (Football Association of Réunion)

NATIONAL HEROES OR PERSONIFICATIONS
Henri Hubert-Delisle, the first native of the island to be appointed governor in the mid-19th century; Edmond Albius, a slave who found a method for pollinating vanilla, making it one of the island's most important exports; Roland Garros, a First World War hero and namesake of the international airport; Dr. Camille Sudre, the Creole leader of the island's independence movement

NATIONAL HOLIDAY/INDEPENDENCE DAY
Bastille Day, July 14 (France and all French territories); Abolition of Slavery (Reunion Day), December 20

FESTIVALS/FAIRS
Mango Festival, January; Coffee Festival, June; Guava Festival, June; La Fête Kaf, December

SIGNIFICANT EVENTS IN FORMATION OF NATIONAL IDENTITY

1507 C.E. Tristan da Cunha, sailing for Portugal*, sights the island, which he names Santa Appolinia. The island soon appears on Portuguese charts.

1530–1642 Ships sailing around the Horn of Africa between Europe and India* use the deepwater harbor for shelter and provisions. The French ship *Saint Louis* arrives at the island, which is claimed for France.

1649 The French governor of Madagascar* takes possession of the island, giving it the name of the French dynasty, Bourbon. French settlement of the island begins with slaves from Madagascar and the African mainland brought in to work the newly established plantations.

1735–1746 The last dodo on the island dies. The French Indies Company goes bankrupt, and the island is sold to the French Crown.

1793 The name of the island is changed to La Réunion.

1810–1814 The British occupy the island of some 70,000 inhabitants during the Napoleonic Wars.

1848 Slavery is abolished on the island. To replace the freed slaves, indentured laborers are imported from India and China*.

1870 The opening of the Suez Canal ends the need for the port, as the trade route is moved to the north. The island's prosperity, built on the port, vanilla, and sugarcane, declines rapidly.

1929 The first airplane lands on the island, initiating the end of the island's geographic isolation.

1946 Reunion becomes a department of the French Republic. The Reunionese become French citizens.

1952 On March 15, the town of Cilaos, at the center of the island, receives 869.9 centimeters (73.6 inches) of rainfall, the greatest 24-hour precipitation total ever recorded in the world.

1974 The island becomes an administrative region of France.

1982–1993 Reunion's status as an administrative region is finalized. The island is officially recognized as a region of the European Union.

2001 Due to Reunion's location in a time zone to the east of Europe, the island becomes the first territory where the euro is legal tender.

1991 French attempts to shut down a pro-independence radio station lead to serious Creole rioting.

2002–2009 A lack of opportunities is offset by emigration of about 5,000 Reunionese every year. There remains considerable support for demands of greater autonomy. The independence movement suffers from the knowledge that a full separation from France would mean the end of generous French and European Union financial subsidies.

See also France

RWANDA

OFFICIAL NAME

Repubulika y'u Rwanda (Kinyarwanda); République du Rwanda (French); Republic of Rwanda (English)

POPULATION

10,211,300 (2009e)

INHABITANTS' NAME/NICKNAME

Rwandan(s)

LANGUAGE/LANGUAGES

Kinyarwanda, French, English (all official); Kiswahili (Swahili), others

RELIGION/RELIGIONS

Roman Catholic, 56 percent; Protestant, 26 percent; Adventist, 11 percent; Muslim, 5 percent; indigenous beliefs, other or no religion

NATIONAL FLAG

The flag has three horizontal stripes of blue, yellow, and green, the blue twice the width of the other stripes. The blue stripe is charged with a gold sun with 24 rays on the upper fly. The blue band represents happiness and peace, the yellow symbolizes economic development, and the green symbolizes the hope of prosperity. The sun represents enlightenment.

COAT OF ARMS/SEAL

The coat of arms is a green circle tied with a square knot at the bottom surrounding a blue cogwheel with a traditional Rwandan basket, a sorghum flower, and a branch of coffee, side views of shields, a gold sun, and a banner inscribed with the name of the country in Kinyarwanda. The coat of arms symbolizes the unity of the country, work, patriotism, and hope for the future. Below the knot is another banner inscribed with the national motto.

MOTTO

Ubumwe, umurimo, gukunda igihugu (Kinyarwanda); Unity, Work, Patriotism (English)

CAPITAL CITY

Kigali

TYPE OF GOVERNMENT

Republic

NATIONAL EMBLEM

Mountain gorillas

NATIONAL COLORS

Blue, yellow, and green

NATIONAL ANTHEM

The anthem was adopted in 2001, along with other new national symbols, as a break with Rwanda's dark and bloody past.

Rwanda Nziza (Kinyarwanda); Our Beautiful Country (English)

Rwanda, our beautiful and dear country
Adorned of hills, lakes, and volcanoes

Our Motherland, would be always filled with happiness
We are all your children: Abanyarwanda
Let us sing your praises and proclaim your beauty
You, maternal bosom of us all
Will be admired forever, prosperous and forever praised.

Our nvaluable heritage that God protects
You give us priceless goods
Our common culture identifies us
Our single language unifies us
May our intelligence, our conscience and our forces
Fill you with varied riches
For an unceasing development.

Our valorous ancestors
Gave themselves bodies and souls
As far as making you a big nation
You overcame the colonial-imperialistic yoke
That has devastated Africa entirely
And has your joy of your sovereign independence
That we will constantly defend.

Maintain this cape, beloved Rwanda,
Standing, we commit for you
So that peace reigns countrywide
That you are free of all hindrance
That your determination brings progress
That you have excellent relations with all countries
And that finally your pride is worth your esteem.

CURRENCY

Rwandan franc

INTERNET IDENTIFIER

.rw

VEHICLE IDENTIFICATION PLATES/ STICKERS

RWA

PASSPORT

The passport cover has the name of the country in Kinyarwanda, French, and English; the coat of arms; and the word *passport* in the three official languages of the country.

AIRLINE
Rwandair Express

NATIONAL FLOWER
Sorghum flower

NATIONAL TREE
Acacia (unofficial)

NATIONAL PLANT
Coffee

NATIONAL ANIMAL
Lion (unofficial)

NATIONAL BIRD
Wattled crane (unofficial)

NATIONAL INSECT
Wasp (unofficial)

NATIONAL RESOURCES
Natural resources include gold, cassiterite (tin ore), wolframite (tungsten ore), methane, hydropower, and arable land. Rwanda is still a rural country, with about 90 percent of the population engaged in subsistence agriculture. It is landlocked with few natural resources and minimal industry. Tourism is a growing sector, notably ecotourism in the Nyungwe Forest and Lake Kivu regions and Virunga Park, with its world-famous and unique mountain gorillas. Remittances from Rwandans living outside the country are a valuable source of foreign currency and investment.

FOODS
Isombe, a dish of cassava leaves, onions, eggplant, spinach, bell peppers, and peanut butter, often served with dried fish, is considered a national dish, as is *foufou,* a starchy ball of pounded cassava served with beans and meat. Other specialties include *bugli,* manioc root ground into flour and cooked with water to make porridge; banana beer; *brochettes,* skewered goat meat cooked over charcoal; *matoke,* cooked plantain; *ubugali,* cassava porridge; *kachumbari,* a relish made of tomatoes, onions, chilies, lime juice, and coriander; and french fries, introduced by the Belgians, which are served with most meals.

SPORTS/SPORTS TEAMS
Association football (soccer) is the most popular sport. Traditional sports, such as wrestling and athletics, also remain very popular. Rwanda national teams participate in many sports at an international level

TEAM SPORTS

Basketball
Rwanda Basketball Team; Rwanda Women's Basketball Team

Cricket
Rwanda Cricket Team

Football
Rwanda Football Team, nickname Amavubi (the Wasps); Rwanda Women's Football Team, nickname Amavubi (the Wasps); Rwanda Rugby Union Team; Rwanda Woman's Rugby Union Team

Table Tennis
Rwanda Table Tennis Team

Tennis
Rwanda Davis Cup Team

Volleyball
Rwanda Men's Volleyball Team; Rwanda Women's Volleyball Team

INDIVIDUAL SPORTS
Rwanda Athletics Team; Rwanda Amateur Boxing Team; Rwanda Cycling Team; Rwanda Swim Team

NATIONAL HEROES OR PERSONIFICATIONS

Abanyarwanda personifies the country or motherland of Rwanda.

National heroes include King Charles Rudahigwa Mutara III, who resisted Belgian conquest of his kingdom; Fred Rwigema, a Tutsi leader who opposed the Hutu extremists and was killed in 1990; and Grégoire Kayibanda, who led Rwanda's struggle for independence from Belgium*

NATIONAL HOLIDAY/INDEPENDENCE DAY

Independence Day, July 1

FESTIVALS/FAIRS

Umuganura (Harvest Festival), August; Independence Day celebrations, July; Rwanda Film Festival, March

SIGNIFICANT EVENTS IN FORMATION OF NATIONAL IDENTITY

1100 C.E.–1200 C.E. The Pygmy Twa people, who live by hunting and gathering, inhabit the region. The Hutu migrate to the region as part of the great Bantu migrations. The Twa are pushed into the less-accessible forest zones as the Hutu settle into farming villages.

14th century–16th century The tall Tutsi people, nomadic herders from the north, move into the region. They subdue the Hutus, who become a population of serfs responsible for looking after the Tutsi herds and the farms that provide for the population.

18th century The Rwanda kingdom is a highly structured state with social classes based on occupation criteria: the Tutsi cattle-owning nobility, the Hutu working class, and the Twa hunters. All three classes pay tribute to the king for protection and various favors.

1858–1885 The first European visits the region. Germany* lays claim to the kingdom, but little changes in Rwanda.

1895–1910 King Mwami's death leads to a period of unrest. German soldiers and missionaries enter Rwanda from Tanganyika. Rwanda becomes part of the German territory of Ruanda-Urundi, which also includes the neighboring Tutsi kingdom of Burundi*.

1916 During World War I, Belgian troops occupy the region from the neighboring Belgian Congo. After the war, Belgium is granted a League of Nations mandate.

1946 Ruanda-Urundi becomes a United Nations trust territory governed by Belgium.

1957–1959 Hutu activists demand changes in Rwanda's power structure to give them a voice commensurate to their status as the largest segment of the population. Skirmishes break out between Hutu and Tutsi groups. The death of a Hutu politician leads to violence against Tutsis. Thousands are killed, and many others, including the king and his court, flee to Uganda*.

1960–1961 The Belgians hold municipal elections, which are won by the Hutu majority, threatening the centuries-old power structure. Rwandans vote to abolish the monarchy and establish an independent republic. Many Tutsis leave the country.

1990 Rebel Tutsi invade Rwanda from Uganda. Ethnic violence becomes a civil war.

1993–1994 The president of Rwanda is killed in a mysterious plane crash. Tutsi rebels again invade Rwanda. Extremist Hutu militias and elements of the Rwandan military begin the systematic massacre of Tutsis and moderate Hutus. France* withdraws its peacekeeping troops. Within months, around 800,000 people are slaughtered. Many of the militant Hutus, along with over two million Hutu refugees, flee into the Democratic Republic of Congo* as international forces finally intervene.

1994–1996 The Hutu groups responsible for the genocide take control of the refugee camps in Congo and attack local Tutsi populations.

1995 A United Nations tribunal begins charging and sentencing a number of people responsible for the atrocities.

2000 A new, moderate government begins the reconciliation. A new flag and national anthem are adopted, breaking ties to the past.

2005 The main Hutu rebel group, including many responsible for atrocities, ends its campaign against the government.

2007 An official inquiry begins into the plane crash that sparked the 1994 genocide.

2008–2009 Rwanda accuses France of having played an active role in the 1994 genocide. The trials of those accused of taking part in the atrocities continue, although some 60,000 suspects have been freed over the years to alleviate overcrowding in Rwanda's prisons.

SAINT HELENA

OFFICIAL NAME
Saint Helena

POPULATION
5,600 (2009e)

INHABITANTS' NAME/NICKNAME
Saint Helenian(s); Saint(s)

LANGUAGE/LANGUAGES
English

RELIGION/RELIGIONS
Anglican, Baptist, Seventh-day Adventist, Roman Catholic, other or no religion

NATIONAL FLAG
The flag is a defaced Blue Ensign with the coat of arms of Saint Helena on the fly. The coat of arms features a three-masted sailing ship and a rocky coastline.

COAT OF ARMS/SEAL
The coat of arms has a central crest or shield divided with a depiction of a plover, called a wirebird locally, on a gold background on the upper third. The bottom portion depicts a three-masted sailing ship with the mountainous coastline taken from the colonial seal. Above the shield are a heraldic helmet and a representation of Saint Helena of Constantinople holding a flower and a cross. Below the shield is a banner inscribed with the island motto.

MOTTO
Loyal and Unshakeable

CAPITAL CITY
Jamestown

TYPE OF GOVERNMENT
Legislative democracy as a British Overseas Territory

NATIONAL COLORS
Red and white

NATIONAL ANTHEM
The official anthem is the British national anthem, "God Save the Queen." The island also has an unofficial local anthem.

> **My Saint Helena Island**
> My heart is drifting southward
> To my home down in the sea
> Near the isle of Saint Helena
> Where my loved ones wait for me
> Too long ago I left them
> For those things I'm going home
> To my Saint Helena island
> That's where I'll never roam

PATRON SAINT
Saint Helen

CURRENCY
Saint Helenian pound

INTERNET IDENTIFIER
.sh

VEHICLE IDENTIFICATION PLATES/STICKERS
GBS

Passport

Saint Helenians are British citizens and travel on British passports.

National Flower

Tungi (cactus pear) (unofficial)

National Plant

Saint Helena ebony (unofficial)

National Bird

Wirebird (Saint Helena plover)

National Fish

Albacore tuna (unofficial)

National Resources

Natural resources are limited to fish and lobster and what is said to be the most expensive coffee in the world. The island depends largely on financial assistance from the United Kingdom*. The local population earns income from fishing, raising livestock, and sale of handicrafts. Remittances from Saint Helenians living away from the island are an important source of income and investment.

Foods

Fish chowder, a stew of local seafood, tomatoes, onions, and herbs, is considered the national dish. Other island specialties include fish and chips, steak and kidney pie, shepherd's pie, and roast goat.

Sports/Sports Teams

Cricket, association football (soccer), and basketball are the most popular sports. Saint Helena national teams participate in several sports at an international level.

Team Sports

Badminton

Saint Helena Badminton Team

Basketball

Saint Helena Basketball Team; Saint Helena Women's Basketball Team

Cricket

Saint Helena Cricket Team

Football

Saint Helena Football Team; Saint Helena Futsal Team

National Heroes or Personifications

Adam Dennison, the first rebel to stand up to the English East India Company in 1684; Thomas Cavendish, an English sea captain who visited the island in 1588 and wrote glowing reports of its beauty

National Holiday/Independence Day

Birthday of Queen Elizabeth II, second Saturday of June; Saint Helena Day, May 21

Festivals/Fairs

Saint Helena Island Festival, August; Saint Helena Festival of Running, July–August

Significant Events in Formation of National Identity

1502 A Portuguese ship returning to Europe from India* encounters the uninhabited island.

1588 Sea captain Thomas Cavendish, although not the first Englishman to visit the island, carries news of its beauty and strategic location back to England.

1600–1630 The islands are used as staging points for attacks on Spanish and Portuguese ships moving between Europe and Asia.

1633 The Dutch claim the island, which is used by ships as a safe anchorage between Europe and the East.

1657–1659 Due to the island's importance as a staging post on the route to India, the English East India Company claims and takes possession of the island, which becomes the company's first overseas settlement. The Dutch capture the island but are later driven out, confirming English rule. Settlers begin to arrive on the island.

1792 New laws regulate the possession of slaves on the island. Further importation of slaves is forbidden.

1806 The Saint Helena Telegraph System is installed, the first outside Europe.

1815–1821 Napoleon Bonaparte, following his defeat at Waterloo, is interned on the island. The increased military presence doubles the island population. Napoleon dies on the island in 1821.

1830–1870 The island becomes the center of the South Atlantic whaling industry, with as many as a thousand ships visiting the port every year.

1832–1840 The East India Company abolishes slavery on the island, freeing 614 slaves and compensating the owners. The administration of the island is transferred from the company to the British government. Many islanders leave the island for South Africa*.

1890 Chief Dinizulu, son of Cetawayo, of the defeated Zulu kingdom, is exiled on the island with his family for nine years. He becomes a Christian before returning to his homeland.

1899 Submarine telegraph cables connect the island to South Africa and Europe.

1951 The flourishing flax industry gives the island its one and only year of exports exceeding imports.

1969 The first elections under a new constitution are held for a 12-member legislature.

1989–1994 Transportation links to Ascension Island and the Falkland Islands* are planned but eventually abandoned, leaving the island with fewer links to the rest of the world than it had two centuries before.

2000–2009 The British Government announces plans to construct an airport on the island to bolster the island economy and to reduce dependence on ships to supply the island.

See also United Kingdom

SÃO TOMÉ AND PRÍNCIPE

OFFICIAL NAME

República Democrática de São Tomé e Príncipe (Portuguese); Democratic Republic of São Tomé and Príncipe (English)

POPULATION

158,200 (2009e)

INHABITANTS' NAME/NICKNAME

Santomean(s); São Tomean(s)

LANGUAGE/LANGUAGES

Portuguese (official); Forro, Angolar, Principense (recognized regional languages); Creole, others

RELIGION/RELIGIONS

Roman Catholic, 70 percent; Evangelical, 3.5 percent; New Apostolic, 2 percent; Seventh-day Adventist, 2 percent; other or no religion

NATIONAL FLAG

The flag has three horizontal stripes of green, yellow, and green. The yellow, twice the width of the green stripes, is charged with two black, five-pointed stars. A red triangle is based at the hoist, symbolizing the hard-fought struggle for independence. The two stars represent the country's two main islands, and the colors are the pan-African colors.

COAT OF ARMS/SEAL

The coat of arms has a central frame with a palm tree on a yellow background below a blue, five-pointed star. The frame is supported by an African gray parrot and a black kite holding a banner above the frame inscribed with the country's name in Portuguese and another banner below the frame inscribed with the country's motto in Portuguese.

MOTTO

Unidad, disciplina, trabalho (Portuguese); Unity, Discipline, Work (English)

CAPITAL CITY

São Tomé

TYPE OF GOVERNMENT

Semipresidential republic

NATIONAL COLORS

Green, yellow, and red

NATIONAL ANTHEM

The anthem was written during the struggle for independence and was adopted at independence in 1975.

Independência total (Portuguese); Total Independence (English)

Chorus

Total independence,
Glorious song of the people,
Total independence,
Sacred hymn of combat.

Dynamism
In the national struggle,
Eternal oath
To the sovereign country of São Tomé and
  Príncipe.

Warriors in the war without weapons,
Live flame in the soul of the people,
Congregating the sons of the islands
Around the immortal motherland.

Total independence, total and complete,
Building, in progress and peace,
With the heroic hands of the people,
The happiest nation on earth.

Chorus

Working, struggling, struggling and
  conquering,
We go ahead with giant steps
In the crusade of the African peoples,
Raising the national flag.

Voice of the people, present, present and
  united,
Strong beat in the heart of hope
To be a hero in the hour of peril,
A hero of the nation's resurgence.

Chorus

Dynamism
In the national struggle,
Eternal oath
To the sovereign country of São Tomé and
  Príncipe.

PATRON SAINT

Saint Thomas

CURRENCY

Santomean dobra

INTERNET IDENTIFIER

.st

VEHICLE IDENTIFICATION PLATES/ STICKERS

STP

PASSPORT

The passport cover has the name of the country in Portuguese, the coat of arms, and the Portuguese word for passport, *passaporte*.

NATIONAL FLOWER

Cocoa flower (unofficial)

NATIONAL TREE

Coconut palm

NATIONAL BIRDS

African gray parrot; black kite

NATIONAL RESOURCES

Natural resources include fish and hydropower. Tourism, based on the country's sandy beaches, pleasant climate, unique culture, and proximity to Europe, is becoming very important. The small, poor island economy has become increasingly dependent on cocoa since independence in 1975. Cocoa production has substantially declined in recent years because of drought and mismanagement. Foreign aid and debt rescheduling have become important resources. Remittances from citizens living outside the country are another source of foreign currency and investment.

FOODS

Catchupa, a dish of beans, hominy, and dried or fresh meat, is considered the national dish. Other specialties include *buzios,* large land snails; *pastel del diablo,* a pastry of potatoes and corn flour filled with fresh fish, onions, and tomatoes; *calulu,* fresh grouper steaks cooked with tomatoes, okra, eggplant, onions, and spices; *canjica,* a sweet made of green maize, sugar, eggs, and cinnamon; and *malamba,* a type of rum made of sugarcane, which is considered the national drink.

SPORTS/SPORTS TEAMS

Association football (soccer) is the most popular sport, along with volleyball. São Tomé and Príncipe national teams participate in many sports at an international level.

TEAM SPORTS

Basketball

São Tomé and Príncipe Basketball Team; São Tomé and Príncipe Women's Basketball Team

Football

São Tomé and Príncipe Football Team; São Tomé and Príncipe Women's Football Team

Volleyball

São Tomé and Príncipe Men's Volleyball Team

INDIVIDUAL SPORTS

São Tomé and Príncipe Athletics Team; São Tomé and Príncipe Canoeing Team: São Tomé and Príncipe Tae Kwon Do Team; São Tomé and Príncipe Wrestling Team

NATIONAL HEROES OR PERSONIFICATIONS

Manuel Pinto da Costa, the first president of independent São Tomé and Príncipe; Miguel Torovoada, former prime minister responsible for economic advances

NATIONAL HOLIDAY/INDEPENDENCE DAY

Independence Day, July 12

SIGNIFICANT EVENTS IN FORMATION OF NATIONAL IDENTITY

1469–1472 The uninhabited islands are visited by Portuguese expeditions and claimed for Portugal*. They are settled as land grants from the Portuguese crown.

1522–1573 Sugar plantations worked by slaves brought from the African mainland make the islands Portugal's main source of sugar. The land grants are revoked, and the islands come under direct control. The islands become important staging points for the African slave trade.

19th century Cocoa and coffee are introduced as cash crops on *rocas,* plantations owned by the government or absentee owners. São Tomé develops as one of the world's major cocoa producers.

1876–1900 The *rocas* system leads to widespread abuses of the workers. Slavery is finally outlawed, but forced labor continues. International criticism surrounds the practice of forced labor around the turn of the new century.

1950–1953 Sporadic uprisings by abused laborers culminate in widespread rioting in which several hundred Africans are killed, the Batepa Massacre.

1960 Nationalists organize to press for autonomy or independence from Portugal.

1974 A military coup in Portugal begins the liberation of the African colonies. The new leftist government in Lisbon recognizes the islands' right to independence. Unrest forces some 4,000 Europeans to leave.

1975 The country becomes independent under a leftist government that establishes strong ties to communist countries. Sugar, coffee, and cocoa plantations are nationalized.

1980s Socialist experiments ravage the economy, which rapidly deteriorates. A new government declares neutrality and seeks Western aid.

1990 A new constitution allows multiparty democracy.

1997–2000 Unrest spreads over poor economic conditions. By 2000, the country's debt is five times its annual revenues. Petroleum exploration returns positive tests.

2002–2009 The government announces plans for a United States* naval base in the country to protect the island's oil interests. Oil companies bid for exploration rights in territorial waters, bringing in millions of dollars in revenue.

SENEGAL

OFFICIAL NAME
République du Sénégal (French); Republic of Senegal (English)

POPULATION
11,859,000 (2009e)

INHABITANTS' NAME/NICKNAME
Senegalese

LANGUAGE/LANGUAGES
French (official); Wolof (recognized regional language); Pulaar, Jola, Mandinka, others

RELIGION/RELIGIONS
Muslim, 94 percent; Roman Catholic, 5 percent; indigenous beliefs, other or no religion

NATIONAL FLAG
The flag has three equal vertical stripes of green, yellow, and red, with a green, five-pointed star centered on the yellow. The flag represents unity and hope. For Muslims, the color green is the color of the Prophet's flag, while for Christians, it is the color of hope, and for animists, it is a symbol of fecundity. Gold or yellow is the symbol of wealth and represents the product of work. Red represents the color of blood; therefore, it represents life and sacrifice for the nation.

COAT OF ARMS/SEAL
The coat of arms has a central crest or shield divided vertically, with a gold rampant lion on the left side and a baobab tree on a gold background on the right. Above the shield is a five-pointed green star. Around the shield is a white wreath bearing a white banner entwined and inscribed with the national motto in French.

MOTTO
Un peuple, un but, un foi (French); One people, one goal, one faith (English)

CAPITAL CITY
Dakar

TYPE OF GOVERNMENT
Semipresidential republic

NATIONAL EMBLEM
The baobab tree, known as a *pencha*, the traditional meeting place where discussions and political rallies take place

NATIONAL COLORS
Green and white

NATIONAL ANTHEM
The anthem was composed so that it can be played on traditional instruments. Senegal's first president, Leopold Senghor, wrote the words.

Pincez tous vos koras, frappez les balafons (French); Everyone Pluck Your Koras, Strike the Balafons (English)

The lion has roared.
The tamer of the savannah

Has leapt forward
And scattered the gloom.
Sunlight on our terrors, sunlight on our
   hopes.
Stand up, brothers, here is Africa assembled.

Chorus

Fibers of my green heart,
Shoulder to shoulder, my more than brothers,
O Senegalese, arise!
Join sea and springs, join steppe and forest!
Hail mother Africa, hail mother Africa.

Senegal, you the son of the lion's froth,
Sprung from the night to the gallop of horses,
Give us, oh! give us the honor of our
   ancestors,
Splendid as ebony and strong as muscle,
We say it clearly—the sword has no flaw.

Chorus

Senegal, we take on your great work:
To shelter the chicks from the falcons,
To make, from east to west, north to south,
Arisen, one single people, a people without
   seams,
But a people turned to all the winds of the
   earth.

Chorus

Senegal, like you, like all our heroes,
We will be hard without hatred, with open
   arms.
The sword in peacetime we will store in the
   scabbard,
As work and words will be our weapon.
The Bantu is a brother, and so are the Arab
   and the White.

Chorus

But if the enemy burns our borders
We will be raised with weapons in our hands:
One people defying all sorrows with its faith,
Young and old, men and women.
Death, yes! We say death, but not shame.

CURRENCY

CFA franc

INTERNET IDENTIFIER

.sn

VEHICLE IDENTIFICATION PLATES/STICKERS

SN

PASSPORT

The passport cover has the name of the country in French, the coat of arms, and the French word for passport.

NATIONAL TREE

Baobab

NATIONAL ANIMAL

Lion

NATIONAL RESOURCES

Natural resources include fish, phosphates, and iron ore. Tourism is increasingly important, based on the country's sandy beaches, pleasant climate, interesting scenery, and unique cultures. Tourism has been hurt in recent years by the ongoing secessionist violence in Casamance*. High unemployment forces many to leave for Europe in search of work. Remittances from Senegalese living outside the country are an important source of foreign currency and investment.

FOODS

Ceebu jen, marinated fish cooked with tomato paste and vegetables and served with rice, is the national dish. Other national specialties include *poulet au yassa,* chicken cooked with pimento and onions; *maffe,* chicken or mutton cooked in peanut sauce; *dem à la Saint-Louis,* stuffed mullet; *accras,* a type of fried doughnut or fritter; *bassi-salté,* seasoned meat cooked with tomato paste and vegetables and served with *cere,* a local couscous; *thiou,* a fish stew with vegetables; *sombi,* a slightly sweet rice soup; *nyeleng,* a beef and peanut stew; and *kima,* chopped beef fried with chilies.

SPORTS/SPORTS TEAMS

Association football (soccer) and rugby are the most popular sports. Senegal national teams participate in many sports at an international level.

TEAM SPORTS

Baseball

Senegal Softball Team

Basketball

Senegal Basketball Team; Senegal Women's Basketball Team

Football

Senegal Football Team, nickname Les Lions de la Teranga (the Lions of Teranga); Senegal Women's Football Team, nickname Les Lions de la Teranga (the Lionesses of Teranga); Senegal Rugby Union Team; Senegal Beach Soccer Team; Senegal Rugby Union Team (Sevens), nickname Senegal Sevens or Senegal 7s

Hockey

Senegal Field Hockey Team

Table Tennis

Senegal Table Tennis Team

Tennis

Senegal Davis Cup Team; Senegal Fed Cup Team

Volleyball

Senegal Men's Volleyball Team; Senegal Women's Volleyball Team

INDIVIDUAL SPORTS

Senegal Amateur Boxing Team; Senegal Athletics Team; Senegal Canoeing Team; Senegal Cycling Team; Senegal Equestrian Team; Senegal Fencing Team; Senegal Gymnastics Team; Senegal Judo Team; Senegal Karate Team; Senegal Modern Pentathlon Team; Senegal Rowing Team; Senegal Sailing Team; Senegal Shooting Team; Senegal Swim Team; Senegal Tae Kwon Do Team; Senegal Weight Lifting Team; Senegal Wrestling Team

WINTER SPORTS

Senegal Alpine Ski Team

NATIONAL HEROES OR PERSONIFICATIONS

Ahmadou Bamba, a leader of the independence movement exiled to Gabon* for many years; Lat Dior, a warrior who led the resistance to French efforts to build a railway in the Sahara; Bamba, a religious and cultural leader who led a peaceful campaign against French colonization; Blaise Diagne, the first elected African deputy to the French National Assembly in 1914; Leopold Senghor, the scholarly poet and politician who led Senegal to independence and becomes the country's first president

NATIONAL HOLIDAY/INDEPENDENCE DAY

Independence Day, April 4

FESTIVALS/FAIRS

Independence celebrations, April; Tamkharit, variable dates; Tabaski, December; Festa 2H, June; Abene Festival, December–January; Kartong Festival, March

SIGNIFICANT EVENTS IN FORMATION OF NATIONAL IDENTITY

800 C.E.–11th century Tribal people inhabit the Senegal River valley. Slavery becomes part of life in the region with raids on rival tribes for slaves to sell to the Arabs. Islam becomes the major religion.

13th century–14th century The region forms part of the Mandingo empires.

14th century–16th century The indigenous Wolof people create the Jolof or Wolof Empire. The empire splits into four competing kingdoms.

1444–1550 Portuguese explorers turn the island of Gorée into a cemetery for sailors. Gorée becomes a center of the profitable slave trade. Other European nations soon follow.

1638–1677 France* establishes a settlement at Saint Louis on the Senegal River. The French take control of Gorée and the slave trade.

1840 The French governor declares all of Senegal a French possession, abolishes all forms of slavery, and grants French citizenship to those born in Senegal, allowing the Senegalese to elect and send a representative to the National Assembly in Paris.

1902 The French, having taken possession of and pacified most of West Africa not already occupied by another European power, make Dakar the administrative center of French West Africa.

1946–1958 A national assembly is established, and Senegal becomes an autonomous republic within the French Community.

1960 Senegal and Mali* gain joint independence as the Mali Federation. Senegal soon leaves the federation for separate independence under Leopold Senghor.

1982–1989 Senegal and Gambia* form a short-lived union. Separatists in southern Casamance organize to fight for independence from Senegal. The Senegambian Confederation is dissolved.

2006–2009 The army launches an offensive against the rebels in Casamance. Spain* agrees to jointly patrol the coast to curb the growing exodus of illegal migrants heading to Spain's Canary Islands. The Spanish authorities launch a campaign on Senegal television to discourage illegal migration.

SEYCHELLES

OFFICIAL NAME
République des Seychelles (French); Repiblik Sesel (Seychellois); Republic of Seychelles (English)

POPULATION
86,200 (2009e)

INHABITANTS' NAME/NICKNAME
Seychellois

LANGUAGE/LANGUAGES
French, Seychellois, English, Seychellois Creole (all official); others

RELIGION/RELIGIONS
Roman Catholic, 90 percent; Anglican, 7 percent; Seventh-day Adventist, 1.5 percent; Hindu, 2 percent; Muslim, 1 percent; other or no religion

NATIONAL FLAG
The flag consists of wedges or rays in a fan from the lower left corner. The colors are yellow, red, white, and green, with a blue wedge at the upper hoist. The oblique bands symbolize a dynamic new country moving into the future and the multicolored nature of the population. The color blue represents the sky and the sea that surrounds the Seychelles. Yellow is for the sun which gives light and life, red symbolizes the people and their determination to work for the future in unity and love, while the white band represents social justice and harmony. The green depicts the land and natural environment.

COAT OF ARMS/SEAL
The coat of arms has a central crest or shield showing a turtle below a coconut palm on green land. Behind the tree is a blue sea with two islands and a boat. The shield is crowned by a heraldic silver helmet, above which a tropical bird is flies before blue and white waves. Two white swordfish support the shield. Beneath the shield is a banner inscribed with the country's national motto in Latin.

MOTTO
Finis coronat opus (Latin); The end crowns the work (English)

CAPITAL CITY
Victoria

TYPE OF GOVERNMENT
Parliamentary republic

NATIONAL COLORS
Red and blue

NATIONAL ANTHEM

The anthem was replaced, along with other national symbols, in 1996 to reflect the country's new democratic multiparty political system.

Koste Seselwa (Seychellois); Join Together All Seychellois (English)

Seychelles, our only fatherland
Where we live in harmony
Happiness, love and peace
We give thanks to God.
Preserve the beauty of our country
The riches of our oceans
A precious heritage
For the happiness of our children.
Live forever in unity
Raise our flag
Together for all eternity
Join together, all Seychellois.

PATRON SAINT

The Immaculate Conception

CURRENCY

Seychellois rupee

INTERNET IDENTIFIER

.sc

VEHICLE IDENTIFICATION PLATES/ STICKERS

SY

PASSPORT

The passport cover has the name of the country in French, Seychellois, and English; the coat of arms; and the word *passport* in the three languages.

AIRLINE

Air Seychelles

NATIONAL TREE

Coco-de-mer palm

NATIONAL ANIMAL

Giant tortoise

NATIONAL BIRD

Seychelles black parrot

NATIONAL FISH

Swordfish; Seychelles blenny (unofficial)

NATIONAL RESOURCES

Natural resources include fish, copra, and cinnamon trees. Tourism is the major resource, based on the islands' pleasant climate, varied scenery, unique culture, and sandy beaches. Remittances from Seychellois living outside the country are an important source of foreign currency and investment.

FOODS

Chauve-souris, fruit bat, served in a variety of recipes, is considered the national dish. Other specialties include *salade de palmiste,* a salad made from palm hearts; *daube,* a sweet mixture of breadfruit, yams, cassava, and bananas; *bouillon brède,* a soup of greens cooked in bouillon; *chatini requin,* a chutney made of papaya and golden apple; *ladob,* a mixture of bananas, yams, and coconut; grilled octopus with a sauce of crushed chilies, ginger and garlic; *chatini de bringelle,* eggplant chutney; and *daube ourite,* octopus stew.

SPORTS/SPORTS TEAMS

Association football (soccer) and volleyball are the most popular sports. Seychelles national teams participate in many sports at an international level.

TEAM SPORTS

Badminton

Seychelles Badminton Team

Basketball

Seychelles Basketball Team; Seychelles Women's Basketball Team

Cricket

Seychelles Cricket Team

Football

Seychelles Football Team, nickname the Pirates; Seychelles Women's Football Team, nickname the Pirates; Seychelles Under-20 Football Team, nickname the Young Pirates

Hockey

Seychelles Field Hockey Team

Netball

Seychelles Netball Team

Table Tennis

Seychelles Table Tennis Team

Volleyball

Seychelles Men's Volleyball Team; Seychelles Women's Volleyball Team

INDIVIDUAL SPORTS

Seychelles Amateur Boxing Team; Seychelles Athletics Team; Seychelles Canoeing Team; Seychelles Cycling Team; Seychelles Gymnastics Team; Seychelles Judo Team; Seychelles Sailing Team; Seychelles Swim Team

NATIONAL HEROES OR PERSONIFICATIONS

France-Albert René, known as "the Boss," the country's president from 1977 to 2004; James Mancham, leader of the independence movement

NATIONAL HOLIDAY/INDEPENDENCE DAY

Constitution Day (National Day), June 18

FESTIVALS/FAIRS

Festival Kreole, October; Beau Vallon Regatta, August–September; Subios, November

SIGNIFICANT EVENTS IN FORMATION OF NATIONAL IDENTITY

1502 C.E. Portuguese explorer Vasco da Gama sails through the inhabited islands.

1609 The first recorded visit by an English East India vessel is in 1609. The islands become a transshipment point for trade between East Africa and Asia and, at times, the haunts of pirates.

1756 The French take possession of the islands, naming them for Jean Moreau de Séchelles, the French minister of finance. French planters import slaves from the African mainland.

1794–1814 France* and the United Kingdom* contest control during the Napoleonic Wars. In 1814, the islands become a British possession, although the French settlers are allowed to remain. The islands attract settlers from Europe, Africa, and India*, leading to a very mixed population.

1835 Slavery is abolished in the islands by the British authorities.

1903 The Seychelles is separated from the administration of Mauritius* to become a separate crown colony.

1976–1977 The islands gain independence within the Commonwealth. A coup ousts the country's first president, James Mancham, replacing him with France Albert René.

1979–1991 René oversees the creation of a socialist one-party state, which lasts until 1991, when the Soviet Union and other socialist governments collapse.

1993 An amended constitution allows the creation of political parties and national elections. President René is reelected several times.

2006–2009 The island recovers from the socialist experiment of the 1980s, mostly due to a boom in tourism. About 4,000 foreigners work in the islands, many from the United States*.

SIERRA LEONE

OFFICIAL NAME

Republic of Sierra Leone

POPULATION

5,229,600 (2009e)

INHABITANTS' NAME/NICKNAME

Sierra Leonean(s); Sierra Leonian(s)

LANGUAGE/LANGUAGES

English (official); Mende, Temne, Krio, others

RELIGION/RELIGIONS

Muslim, 60 percent; Christian, 10 percent; indigenous beliefs, other or no religion

NATIONAL FLAG

The flag is a horizontal tricolor of green, white, and blue. The green represents agriculture, mountains and natural resources, the white stands for unity and justice, and the blue represents hope that the natural harbor at Freetown will make a contribution to world peace.

COAT OF ARMS/SEAL

The coat of arms has a central shield with a depiction of a lion beneath a zigzag border, representing the Lion Mountains, for which the country was named. The upper portion of the shield is white with three torches that represent peace, progress, and education. At the base are wavy bars depicting the sea. Two golden lions on green vegetation and two tall coconut palm trees support the shield. Below the shield is the national motto on a white banner.

MOTTO

Unity, Freedom, Justice

CAPITAL CITY

Freetown

TYPE OF GOVERNMENT

Constitutional republic

NATIONAL EMBLEM

Lion

NATIONAL COLORS

Green, white, and blue

NATIONAL ANTHEM

The anthem was written and composed for adoption at independence in 1961.

High We Exalt Thee, Realm of the Free

High we exalt thee, realm of the free;
Great is the love we have for thee;
Firmly united ever we stand,
Singing thy praise, O native land.
We raise up our hearts and our voices on high,
The hills and the valleys re-echo our cry;
Blessing and peace be ever thine own,
Land that we love, our Sierra Leone.

One with a faith that wisdom inspires,
One with a zeal that never tires;
Ever we seek to honor thy name,
Ours is the labor, thine the fame.
We pray that no harm on thy children
    may fall,
That blessing and peace may descend on us
    all;
So may we serve thee ever alone,
Land that we love, our Sierra Leone.

Knowledge and truth our forefathers spread,
Mighty the nations whom they led;
Mighty they made thee, so too may we
Show forth the good that is ever in thee.
We pledge our devotion, our strength and our
    might,
Thy cause to defend and to stand for thy
    right;
All that we have be ever thine own,
Land that we love, our Sierra Leone.

CURRENCY

Sierra Leonean leone

INTERNET IDENTIFIER

.sl

VEHICLE IDENTIFICATION PLATES/ STICKERS

WAL

PASSPORT

The passport cover has the name of the country in English, the coat of arms, and the word *passport*.

AIRLINE

Sierra National Airlines

NATIONAL TREE

Coconut palm

NATIONAL PLANT

Rice

NATIONAL ANIMAL

Lion (shown on coat of arms)

NATIONAL FISH

African butterfly (unofficial)

NATIONAL RESOURCES

Natural resources include diamonds, titanium ore, bauxite, iron ore, gold, and chromite. During the civil war, diamonds were fought over and often illegally exported, giving them the name "blood diamonds." Remittances from Sierra Leoneans living outside the country are a source of foreign currency and investment.

FOODS

Rice is the staple food and is eaten every day. In the local languages, there are more than 20 words to describe rice in its different forms. National dishes include meat stew, made with beef or pork with onions, eggplant, and tomatoes; *egusi,* a soup of meat, smoked fish, tomatoes, and onions; groundnut stew, a stew of meat, groundnuts, tomatoes, peanut butter, onions, and green peppers; and *plasas,* a dish of spinach, smoked fish, onions, and peanut butter.

SPORTS/SPORTS TEAMS

Association football (soccer) and basketball are the most popular sports. Sierra Leone national teams participate in many sports at the international level.

TEAM SPORTS

Baseball

Sierra Leone Softball Team

Basketball

Sierra Leone Basketball Team; Sierra Leona Women's Basketball Team

Cricket

Sierra Leone Cricket Team

Football

Sierra Leone Football Team, nickname the Leone Stars; Sierra Leone Women's Football Team, nickname the Sierra Queens; Sierra Leone Under-23 Football Team, nickname the Shooting Stars; Sierra Leone Under-17 Football Team, nickname the Sierra Stars

Table Tennis

Sierra Leone Table Tennis Team

Volleyball

Sierra Leone Men's Volleyball Team

INDIVIDUAL SPORTS

Sierra Leone Amateur Boxing Team; Sierra Leone Athletics Team; Sierra Leone Cycling Team; Sierra Leone Fencing Team; Sierra Leone Judo Team; Sierra Leona Swim Team; Sierra Leone Weight Lifting Team; Sierra Leone Wrestling Team

NATIONAL HEROES OR PERSONIFICATIONS

Milton Margai, independence leader and first prime minister; Siaka Stevens, prime minister responsible for restoring order following several coups in the mid-1960s; Ella Koblo Gulama, a paramount chief who led the campaign for women's rights; Dr. Soccoh Kabia, honored for extending basic medical care to much of the country

NATIONAL HOLIDAY/INDEPENDENCE DAY

Independence Day, April 27

FESTIVALS/FAIRS

Lantern Festival, variable dates; Freetown Film Festival, March; Sierra Leone Music

Festival, December; Independence Day celebrations, April.

SIGNIFICANT EVENTS IN FORMATION OF NATIONAL IDENTITY

600 C.E.–1000 C.E. The region is populated in successive waves of migrants. Agricultural communities dominate the coastal regions, while the heavily forested interior is the home of less sedentary tribal groups.

1462–1562 Portuguese explorer Pedro da Cintra maps the hills surrounding a large natural harbor, calling them *Sierra de Leão* or Lion Mountains, which gives the region its name. The Portuguese establish a slave port and are soon followed by Dutch and French traders. The English join the slave trade in the region in 1562.

1787–1792 Colonization of the region by freed slaves is financed by British antislavery organizations. Thousands arrive, in spite of resistance by indigenous peoples.

1800–1900 The growing population of freed slaves becomes known as Creole or Krio people. The language of the freed slaves, an 18th-century African American English, quickly spreads across the region as a lingua franca for trade and Christian teaching. The indigenous tribes mount several rebellions against British rule and Krio domination.

1900–1950 Freetown is the center of British administration of Sierra Leone, the Gold Coast, and Gambia* and becomes the educational center of West Africa.

1951–1961 A new constitution provides the framework for future independence. Limited self-government is granted in 1953, and full independence is granted in 1961.

1967–1978 A succession of coups by military officers disrupts the country. Siaka Stevens becomes prime minister and restores order. Tribal rivalries become political rivalries. The country becomes a one-party state.

1990–1991 A multiparty political system is reinstated. Civil war breaks out, mostly due to government mismanagement of the country's diamond resources. The war is marked by atrocities on both sides and by interference by the leaders of the civil war in neighboring Liberia*. Abductions, rape, brutal amputations and house burnings become common occurrences.

1992–1998 Coups and countercoups again disrupt the government. A force of African peacekeepers, led by Nigeria*, takes control of the country. Fighting resumes with attacks on the peacekeepers.

2000–2002 A British force is sent to restore order. By 2001, over 50,000 have died in the fighting. The war finally ends.

2004 A United Nations court begins trials of senior leaders from both sides accused of human-rights abuses and atrocities.

2007–2009 Presidential and parliamentary elections are held and a new government installed. The country ranks lowest in the world in human development and among the lowest in levels of poverty.

SOMALIA

OFFICIAL NAME

Jamhuuriyadda Soomaaliya (Somali); Jumhū riyyat aṣ-Ṣūmālý (transliteration from Arabic); Somali Republic (English)

POPULATION

9,582,300 (2009e)

INHABITANTS' NAME/NICKNAME

Somali(s)

LANGUAGE/LANGUAGES

Somali (official); Arabic, Italian, English (recognized as secondary languages); others

RELIGION/RELIGIONS

Sunni Muslim, 95 percent; other or no religion

NATIONAL FLAG

The flag, known as the ocean star flag, has a pale blue field charged with a centered white, five-pointed star. Originally designed to resemble the flag of the United Nations, which helped Somalia win independence from Italy*, it was also planned as a pan-Somali flag, with the five points of the star representing the five branches of the Somali nation: Issas of Djibouti*, Somalis of Ethiopia*, Issaks of Somaliland*, Somalis of former Italian Somaliland, and Somalis of northeastern Kenya*.

COAT OF ARMS/SEAL

The coat of arms has a central shield bordered in gold bearing the blue of the national flag and the white, five-pointed star. Two leopards support the shield above crossed spears and palm fronds and a gold or white banner draped over the spears.

CAPITAL CITY

Mogadishu

TYPE OF GOVERNMENT

Transitional semipresidential republic

NATIONAL EMBLEM

Leopard

NATIONAL COLORS

Blue and white

NATIONAL ANTHEM

The anthem was adopted in 2000 in an effort to break with the country's violent past. It is based on a popular folk song.

Soomaallyeey toosoo (Somali); Somalis, Wake Up (English)

Chorus

Somalis, wake up,
Wake up and join hands
And whoever is most in need of support
Support them forever.

Chorus

I cry and shed tears
For the widespread calamity
That afflicts my whole country

Chorus

Our people have become destitute
They live in misery and hardship
The situation they are in
Prompts me to avoid all sustenance

Chorus

We are all Muslims
We share one land
We share one look
We share one language
The whole world knows that

Chorus

We shed blood in our land
Running away in shame
Leaving behind the young and the old

CURRENCY

Somali shilling

INTERNET IDENTIFIER

.so

VEHICLE IDENTIFICATION PLATES/STICKERS

SO

PASSPORT

The passport cover has the name of the country in Somali, the coat of arms, and the word *passport* in Somali.

AIRLINE

Jubba Airways

NATIONAL ANIMAL

Leopard; camel

NATIONAL RESOURCES

Natural resources include uranium and largely unexploited reserves of iron ore, tin, gypsum, bauxite, copper, salt, natural gas and likely oil reserves, The country is without a central government and is mostly controlled by regional warlords. Remittances from Somalis living outside the country are a major source of foreign currency.

FOODS

Maraq, a thick soup of vegetables, meat, and beans, served with flatbread called *laxoox,* is considered the national dish. Other specialties include *paasto forno,* a baked pasta dish borrowed from the Italians; *muufo,* patties made of oats or corn; *sabayad,* a crisp, thin cracker bread; *kalaandal,* a dish of rice-stuffed chicken; *malale,* fish baked with garlic, spices, and chilies; *basbousa,* a cake of semolina with a baked sugar glaze; and *sambusa,* a small pastry filled with minced beef, leeks, and spices.

SPORTS/SPORTS TEAMS

Association football (soccer) is the most popular sport. Somalia national teams participate in many sports at an international level.

TEAM SPORTS

Badminton

Somalia Badminton Team

Baseball

Somalia Softball Team

Basketball

Somalia Basketball Team; Somalia Basketball Team

Football

Somalia Football Team, nickname the Ocean Stars; Somalia Women's Football Team, nickname the Ocean Stars; Somalia Futsal Team

Table Tennis

Somalia Table Tennis Team

Volleyball

Somalia Men's Volleyball Team

INDIVIDUAL SPORTS

Somalia Amateur Boxing Team; Somalia Archery Team; Somalia Athletics Team; Somalia Canoeing Team; Somalia Fencing Team; Somalia Judo Team; Somalia Rowing Team; Somalia Swim Team; Somalia Tae Kwon Do Team; Somalia Weight Lifting Team; Somalia Wrestling Team

NATIONAL HEROES OR PERSONIFICATIONS

Hawo Tako, a young woman killed for her defiance of the Italians in the 1950s; Mohamed Ahmad ibn Ibrihim al-Ghazi, leader of the medieval sultanate defeated by the Ethiopians and Portuguese

NATIONAL HOLIDAY/INDEPENDENCE DAY

Foundation of the Somali Republic, July 1

FESTIVALS/FAIRS

Independence Day celebrations, July; Somali Youth Festival, May; Eid al-Fitr, variable dates

SIGNIFICANT EVENTS IN FORMATION OF NATIONAL IDENTITY

First century C.E. Port towns trade with Greek and Roman sailors.

Fifth century Arab tribal people establish the Sultanate of Adal on the coast of the Gulf of Aden. The sultanate grows prosperous on the dhow trade.

Eighth century Islam, brought by Arab traders to the port towns, spreads across the region, partly due to the Muslim prohibition against enslaving other Muslims.

1520–1543 Adal, led by Ahmad ibn Ibrihim al-Ghazi, conquers most of Ethiopia before the Portuguese come to the aid of their fellow Christians.

17th century Adal collapses into a number of small states.

1860–1875 France* acquires a foothold on the Somali coast at Djibouti. Egyptian troops, nominally part of the Ottoman Empire, occupy port towns and part of the interior.

1887–1889 The British take control of the northern region and proclaim a protectorate. The Italians take central Somalia.

1925 Jubaland, east of the Juba River, is detached from British Kenya to become part of Italian Somaliland.

1935–1936 The fascist government of Italy, determined to build a colonial empire, attacks and conquers Ethiopia. The Italians detach the Somali-speaking western districts of Ethiopia, which are combined to form a province of Italian East Africa.

1940–1950 When war begins in Europe, the Italians occupy British Somaliland, but the British counterattack and take control of Italian Somaliland. At the end of the war, the two Somalilands are made United Nations trust territories under British and Italian administration.

1960 British Somaliland becomes an independent state, and five days later, Italian Somaliland gains its independence. The two territories merge to form the Republic of Somalia.

1969–1974 A military coup brings Humahham Siad Barre to power. He declares Somalia a socialist state and joins the Arab League.

1974–1975 A severe drought causes widespread starvation. Barre uses nationalist rhetoric to deflect criticism.

1977–1978 The Somalis invade the Somali-inhabited Ogaden region of Ethiopia and advance until newly communist Ethiopia is aided by Soviet and Cuban troops.

1981 Clan conflicts become more serious as the government expels ministers from rival clans.

1991 Barre is ousted in a coup as clan warfare kills thousands. The former British Somaliland declares unilateral independence and severs all ties to the Somali government.

1993–1994 A U.S. mission to restore order turns to disaster as helicopters are downed by Somali rebels amid a battle in which hundreds of Somalis die and American troops are killed before the military withdraws.

1998–2000 Other regions declare autonomy under the rule of local warlords. The government virtually disappears, except for continued meetings outside the country.

2004–2006 Starvation again becomes serious as drought and crop failures continue. Severe fighting breaks out in Mogadishu. Islamic militias take control of Mogadishu and parts of the south. The airport and ports are opened for the first time in a decade. Ethiopian troops aid a transitional government to defeat the Islamists.

2007 African peacekeeping troops arrive in Mogadishu amid some of the heaviest fighting in over 15 years between insurgents and government forces.

2008 Over 350,000 people have fled the violence by the end of 2008, while those that stay face hunger, violence, and chaos. Attempts to form a coalition government with representatives of the various tribal groups and regional clans continue to fail, as the country remains divided, chaotic, and virtually without a functioning government, except in the secessionist north.

2009 Heavy fighting erupts for control of Mogadishu between Islamic forces and government troops, setting off an exodus of over 200,000 people, many crossing into Kenya*. Fighting swells in July, at times involving units of a peacekeeping mission sent by the African Union. Violence also occurs between the fighters of the various Islamic factions.

See also Somaliland

SOMALILAND

OFFICIAL NAME

Jamhuuriyadda Soomaaliland Jumhūrīyat (Somali); Arḍ Aṣ-ṣūmāl (transliteration from Arabic); Republic of Somaliland (English)

POPULATION

3,500,000 (2009e)

INHABITANTS' NAME/NICKNAME

Somalilander(s); Somali(s); Northern Somali(s)

LANGUAGE/LANGUAGES

Somali, Arabic, English (all official); Amharic, others

RELIGION/RELIGIONS

Sunni Muslim, 97 percent; Christian, other or no religion

NATIONAL FLAG

The flag is a horizontal tricolor of green, white, and red charged with a centered black, five-pointed star on the white stripe and the *shahadah* in Arabic script on the green stripe. The green represents Islam and symbolizes prosperity, the white represents peace and unity, and the red represents the blood spilled in the struggle for Somaliland independence. The *shahadah* is a copy of that on the flag of Saudi Arabia and means "There is no god but God (Allah), and Muhammad is his messenger." The black star is considered to symbolize the dream of a greater Somalia, symbolized by the flag of the Somalis.

COAT OF ARMS/SEAL

The coat of arms is a gold circle with a balanced scale symbolizing justice between the Somali people; a coffee-colored eagle holds the scale as a sign of democracy. Below are two hands shaking, representing the equality and freedom of the people of Somaliland. A wreath of olive branches, symbolizing peace, surrounds the symbols. The gold color represents the bright, beautiful culture and people. The Arabic calligraphy above the scales is the *bismillah,* which translates into English as "In the name of Allah, most gracious, most merciful," symbolizing Islam's role as the official religion practiced in Somaliland.

MOTTO

Justice, peace, freedom, democracy and success for all. Also in use is the *shahadah,* from the Arabic on the flag: "There is no god but God (Allah), and Muhammad is his messenger."

CAPITAL CITY

Hargeisa

TYPE OF GOVERNMENT

Representative democracy

NATIONAL EMBLEM

Kudu antelope

NATIONAL COLORS

White and green

NATIONAL ANTHEM

The anthem was adopted in 1991, following the secession of Somaliland from Somalia. No English translation is available.

Heesta Calanka Somaliland (Somali); Somaliland National Anthem (English)

Samo ku waar, samo ku waar, saamo ku waar
Sarreeye calanka sudhan bilay dhulkiisaa,
Samo ku waariyoo iyo bogaadin sugan
Hanbalyo suuban kugu salaannee saamo ku waar
Geesiyaashii naftooda u sadqeeyay qarannimada Somaliland
Xuskooda dhowrsan kugu salaannee samo ku waar
Guulside xanbaarsan soo noqoshadiisa
kalsooniduu mutaystayee dastuurka ku salaannee
Midnimo walaalnimo goobanimo islaanimo kugu salaanee samow samidiyo samo ku waar samo ku waar saamo ku waar

CURRENCY

Somaliland shilling

INTERNET IDENTIFIER

.som (unofficial)

VEHICLE IDENTIFICATION PLATES/STICKERS

SO Somalia (official); SOM (unofficial)

PASSPORT

The passport cover has the name of the country in Somali, Arabic, and English; the coat of arms; and the word *passport* in the three languages.

NATIONAL ANIMAL
Kudu (Somaliland antelope)

NATIONAL BIRD
Eagle

NATIONAL REPTILE
Chameleon (unofficial)

NATIONAL INSECT
Dung beetle (unofficial)

NATIONAL RESOURCES
Natural resources include gypsum, lime, mica, quartz, lignite coal, lead, gold, sulfur, natural gas, and likely oil reserves. The backbone of the economy is livestock, which is mostly exported to the Middle East. Many families now survive on remittances from relatives who fled to Europe and North America during the civil war.

FOODS
Maraq, a thick soup of vegetables, meat, and beans of Yemeni origin, served with flatbread called *laxoox,* is considered the national dish. Other specialties include *muufo,* patties made of oats or corn; *sabayad,* a crisp, thin cracker bread; *kalaandal,* a dish of rice-stuffed chicken; *malale,* fish baked with garlic, spices, and chilies; *basbousa,* a cake of semolina with a baked sugar glaze; *sambusa,* a small pastry filled with minced beef, leeks, and spices; *muufo baraawe,* Somali bread; *xalwa,* a dessert made with cardamom; and *shaax xawaash,* a tea made of cardamom and cinnamon that is considered the national drink.

SPORTS/SPORTS TEAMS
Association football (soccer) is the most popular sport. Somaliland national teams participate in football and basketball at an international level.

Basketball
Somaliland Basketball Team; Somaliland Women's Basketball Team

Football
Somaliland Football Team

NATIONAL HEROES OR PERSONIFICATIONS
Mohamed Abdullah Hassan, the leader of the resistance to British rule from 1886 to 1921; Mohamed Ibrahim Egal, the first prime minister of independent Somaliland in 1960, who stepped down in the cause of Somali unity but later led the movement to separate Somaliland from Somalia and served as the first president. He established an island of peace and stability in Somaliland but failed to win international recognition for the country.

NATIONAL HOLIDAY/INDEPENDENCE DAY
Independence Day, June 26; Restoration of Somaliland Sovereignty, May 18

FESTIVALS/FAIRS
Somali Week Festival, September

SIGNIFICANT EVENTS IN FORMATION OF NATIONAL IDENTITY
First century C.E.   Port towns trade with Greek and Roman sailors in the Red Sea.

Seventh century   The Warsangeli Sultanate is established on the coast of the Gulf of Aden. The sultanate grows prosperous on the dhow trade with India* and East Africa.

Eighth century   Islam, brought by Arab traders to the port towns, spreads across the region.

1520–1543   Led by Ahmad ibn Ibrihim al-Ghazi, the Somalis conquer most of Ethiopia* before the Portuguese came to the aid of their fellow Christians.

1860–1875   France* acquires a foothold on the Somali coast at Djibouti*. Egyptian troops, nominally part of the Ottoman Empire, occupy port towns and part of the interior.

1887–1889 The British take control of the northern region and proclaim a protectorate. The Italians conquer central Somalia.

1940–1941 The Italian forces invade and occupy British Somaliland during the Second World War. A British counterattack drives the Italians from the region. The British move south to occupy Italian Somaliland.

1946–1950 The two Somaliland territories are made United Nations trust territories under British and Italian administration.

1960 British Somaliland is granted independence under Mohamed Ibrahim Egal. The new country is invited to join the Commonwealth but defers to the ideal of Somali unity. Five days after independence, Italian Somaliland also becomes independent. Egal steps down to allow the merger of the two territories in the Somali Republic*.

1969 A military coup brings Mohammed Siad Barre to power. Egal and other northern leaders are jailed.

1981–1988 The northern Somali clans rebel against the Barre dictatorship. A civil war erupts that eventually takes 40,000 lives and drives hundreds of thousands to flee.

1991–1993 Barre is ousted in Mogadishu. Somalia splinters into dozens of local fiefs controlled by warlords. The northern portion of the country, former British Somaliland, declares unilateral independence under Mohamed Ibrahim Egal.

1997 Unlike chaotic and violent Somalia, Somaliland institutes a democratic system with regular elections and popular participation. Although not diplomatically recognized, the state maintains unofficial contacts with many countries.

2002 Mohammad Ibrahim Egal dies in office.

2002–2009 A territorial dispute involving the neighboring autonomous state of Puntland leads to skirmishing along the eastern border. The Somaliland government repeatedly appeals to world leaders for official recognition. The region is the only part of Somalia with a functioning, elected government.

See also Somalia

SOUTH AFRICA

OFFICIAL NAME
Republic of South Africa

POPULATION
47,346,800 (2009e)

INHABITANTS' NAME/NICKNAME
South African(s)

LANGUAGE/LANGUAGES
South Africa has 11 official languages: English, Afrikaans, Ndebele, Northern Sotho, Sotho, Swati, Tsonga, Tswana, Venda, Xhosa, and Zulu. Another nine languages are recognized as regional or national languages: Fanagalo, Khoe, Lobedu, Nama, Northern Ndebele, Phuthi, San, sign language, and Tamil. Also spoken are Portuguese, Hindi, Arabic, and other languages.

RELIGION/RELIGIONS
Christian, 79 percent; Muslim, 1.5 percent; Hindu, 1.3 percent; other or no religion

NATIONAL FLAG
The flag has horizontal stripes of red (on the top) and blue (on the bottom) of equal width, separated by a central green stripe that divides into a horizontal Y shape, the arms of which end at the corners of the hoist side. The Y embraces a black isosceles triangle separated from the green by narrow yellow stripes; the red and blue stripes are separated from the green stripe and its arms by narrow white stripes. The South African flag is the only national flag in the world that has six colors without a seal or brocade.

COAT OF ARMS/SEAL
The coat of arms consists of a circular design in green with the country's motto at the bottom that extends into pairs of elephant tusks. Within are ears of wheat and a golden shield

with a Koisan rock art design of two human beings greeting each other from the famous Linton stone. Above the shield are a crossed Zulu knobkerrie and a spear, a protea (the national flower), a secretary bird, and a rising sun.

MOTTO

ke e: /xarra //ke (|Xam—Koisan); Unity in Diversity (literally, "Diverse people unite") (English)

CAPITAL CITY

Pretoria (executive); Bloemfontein (judicial); Cape Town (legislative)

TYPE OF GOVERNMENT

Parliamentary republic

NATIONAL EMBLEM

Springbok; Table Mountain

NATIONAL COLORS

Yellow and green

NATIONAL ANTHEM

The anthem, adopted in 1994, is an amalgamation of the anthem of apartheid South Africa and the "people's anthem" favored by the majority of the population.

National Anthem of South Africa

God, we ask you to protect our nation
Intervene and end all conflicts
Protect us, protect our nation
Nation of South Africa, South Africa

From the blue of our heavens,
From the depths of our sea,
Over everlasting mountains,
Where the echoing crags resound,

Sounds the call to come together,
And united we shall stand,
Let us live and strive for freedom,
In South Africa, our land.

PATRON SAINT

Our Lady of the Assumption

CURRENCY

South African rand

INTERNET IDENTIFIER

.za

VEHICLE IDENTIFICATION PLATES/ STICKERS

ZA

PASSPORT

The passport cover has the name of the country in English, the coat of arms, the name of the country in French, and the word *passport* in English and French.

AIRLINE

South African Airways

NATIONAL FLOWER

King (giant) protea

NATIONAL TREE

Yellowwood

NATIONAL ANIMAL

Springbok

NATIONAL BIRD

Blue crane

NATIONAL FISH

Galjoen

NATIONAL RESOURCES

Natural resources include gold, chromium, antimony, coal, iron ore, manganese, nickel, phosphates, tin, uranium, gem diamonds, platinum, copper, vanadium, salt, and natural gas. The important tourist industry is based on varied and spectacular scenery, unique cultures, sandy beaches, a pleasant climate, and wild animals. The country's well-educated population, abundance of natural resources, and well-developed infrastructure give South Africa the largest and most advanced economy in Africa.

FOODS

Bobotie, a meat loaf of minced beef, curry, and spices, is the national dish. Other national specialties include *Cape kedgeree,* a dish of cooked, flaked fish, rice, and hard-boiled eggs; *gebraaide hoender,* spiced roast chicken; curried beef stew; *gestowe soetpatats,* slow-cooked sweet potatoes; *hoender pastei,* Boer chicken pie; *Kerrie-aartappels en uie,* a dish of curried potatoes and onions; *koeksisters,* a deep-fried pastry; springbok *potjekos,* springbok or venison prepared with onions, carrots, bacon, red wine, and spices; and *gesmoorde vis,* salt cod and potatoes in tomato sauce.

SPORTS/SPORTS TEAMS

Association football (soccer) and rugby are the most popular sports. South Africa participates in many sports at an international level.

TEAM SPORTS

Badminton

South Africa Badminton Team

Baseball

South Africa Baseball Team; South Africa Softball Team

Basketball

South Africa Basketball Team; South Africa Women's Basketball Team; South Africa Wheelchair Basketball Team; South Africa Women's Wheelchair Basketball Team

Bowls

South Africa Bowls Team

Cricket

South Africa Cricket Team, nickname the Springboks; South Africa Women's Cricket Team, nickname the Proteas

Football

South Africa Football Team, nickname Bafana Bafana (the Boys, the Boys); South Africa Women's Football Team, nickname Banyana Banyana (the Girls, the Girls); South Africa Women's Under-19 Football Team, nickname Basetsane; South Africa Under-23 Football Team, nickname Amaglug-glug; South Africa Under-20 Football Team, nickname Amajita; South Africa Under-17 Football Team, nickname the Tornadoes; South Africa Women's Under-19 Football Team; South Africa Rugby Union Team, nickname the Springboks (Springbokke, Amabokoboko, Bokke); South Africa Women's Rugby Union Team nickname the Springboks (Springbokke, Amabokoboko); South Africa Rugby League Team, nickname the Rhinos; South Africa Rugby Union Team (Sevens), nickname South Africa Sevens or the Emerging Springboks or Emerging Boks; South Africa Amateur Rugby Union Team, nickname the Springboks (Springbokke, Amabokoboko); South African Australian-Rules Football Team, nickname the Buffaloes; South Africa Wheelchair Rugby Team; South Africa Beach Soccer Team; South Africa Futsal Team; South Africa Touch Football Team; South Africa Women's Touch Football Team

Hockey

South Africa Ice Hockey Team; South Africa Junior Ice Hockey Team; South Africa Women's Ice Hockey Team; South Africa Field Hockey Team

Korfball

South Africa Korfball Team

Netball

South Africa Netball Team, nickname the Proteas

Polo

South Africa Polo Team

Racing

A1 Team South Africa; South African Speedway Team

Table Tennis

South Africa Table Tennis Team

Tennis

South Africa Davis Cup Team; South Africa Fed Cup Team

Volleyball

South Africa Men's Beach Volleyball Team; South Africa Women's Beach Volleyball Team; South Africa Men's Volleyball Team; South Africa Women Volleyball Team

Water Polo

South Africa Water Polo Team

INDIVIDUAL SPORTS

South Africa Amateur Boxing Team; South Africa Archery Team; South Africa Athletics Team; South Africa Cycling Team; South Africa Equestrian Team; South Africa Fencing Team; South African Gymnastics Team; South Africa Judo Team; South Africa Karate Team: South Africa Modern Pentathlon Team; South Africa Rowing Team; South Africa Sailing Team; South Africa Shooting Team; South Africa Swim Team; South Africa Tae Kwon Do Team; South Africa Triathlon Team; South Africa Weight Lifting Team; South Africa Wrestling Team

WINTER SPORTS

South Africa Ice Hockey Team; South Africa Junior Ice Hockey Team; South Africa Women's Ice Hockey Team; South Africa Skating Team

NATIONAL HEROES OR PERSONIFICATIONS

Khabazela, a clan name of the Mkhize, is often used to personify South Africans. Van der Merwe, the average Afrikaaner man, is often used to personify the Afrikaaner population.

Rolihlala Nelson Mandela, leader of the antiapartheid movement and first president of democratic South Africa in 1994; Steve Bantu Biko, leader of the Black Consciousness Movement, murdered by South African police in 1977; Archbishop Desmond Tutu, outspoken critic of apartheid and other evils; Chaka, the historical leader of the Zulu nation; Chief Gatsha Butulezi, the Zulu national leader; Robert Mangaliso Sobukwe, an antiapartheid leader; Joe Slovo, a white South African leader against apartheid

NATIONAL HOLIDAY/INDEPENDENCE DAY

Freedom Day, April 27

FESTIVALS/FAIRS

Cape Town Jazz Festival, March; National Arts Festival, June; Knysna Oyster Festival, July; Ellisras Bushveld Festival, July; Joy of Jazz, August; Arts Alive Festival, September; Woodstock, September; Awesome Africa Music Festival, September; Macufe, October

SIGNIFICANT EVENTS IN FORMATION OF NATIONAL IDENTITY

Fourth century C.E.–fifth century C.E. Bantu peoples, part of the great Bantu migrations, settle the region, displacing the earlier KhoiSan nomads.

1487 Portuguese explorers reach the cape at the southern tip of the African continent, naming it Cape of Good Hope because it would lead to the riches of India*.

1652–1750 The Dutch establish a way station on the route to the East at the site of present Cape

Town. Slaves, called Malays, are brought from the Dutch East Indies. Dutch settlers from Europe expand the colony over most of present South Africa, meeting the southward-migrating Bantu at Fish River.

1795 The British take control of South Africa during the Napoleonic Wars in Europe. The Cape Colony is annexed in 1806, and British colonization begins.

1833 The British ban the slave trade in the colonies. Disgruntled Boers take their slaves and trek north out of British territory to create several independent Boer republics.

1867–1881 The discovery of diamonds and then gold, in 1884, in the Boer republics brings an influx of immigrants, leading to tensions and eventually to the First Boer War between the British and the Boers, who successfully defend their republics against British encroachments.

1899–1902 Continued conflict results in the Second Boer War, which ends with British control of the Boer republics but is marked by the brutal incarceration of Boer women and children in concentration camps where several thousand die of disease and neglect.

1919 The Boer republics of Orange Free State and Transvaal are joined to the British Cape and Natal colonies to form the Union of South Africa.

1948 The National party, supported by the Boers and many English speakers, wins elections. The new government, dominated by the National Party, institutes the separation of the races, called apartheid in the Afrikaans language of the Boers.

1961–1990 A whites-only referendum votes to convert South Africa into a republic and to leave the British Commonwealth. The apartheid system is criticized internationally, and economic, sport, and other sanctions are applied.

1990–1994 Pressure to end apartheid leads to a negotiated transfer of power to a multiracial government in 1994. The largest African political party, the African National Congress (ANC), wins the most votes in free elections.

1994–2000 Although under a new government, millions of South Africans continue to live in poverty outside the major urban areas.

2007–2008 Government policies lead to the largest public strike since apartheid. A wave of violence crosses the country as people blame illegal immigrants for continuing poverty. Thousands flee to their home countries following attacks on immigrants by armed mobs.

2009 A new political party, with a membership mainly of dissident ANC defectors, chooses a Methodist bishop as its presidential candidate. Many South Africans of all races are disenchanted with rule by the African National Congress.

Southern Cameroons. *See* Ambazania

SOUTHERN SUDAN

OFFICIAL NAME
Dawla Junub el Sudan (transliteration from Arabic); Autonomous State of Southern Sudan (English)

POPULATION
7,800,000 (2009e)

INHABITANTS' NAME/NICKNAME
Southern Sudanese

LANGUAGE/LANGUAGES
English, Arabic (Juba Arabic) (both official); over 400 dialects are spoken

RELIGION/RELIGIONS
Christian, indigenous beliefs, Muslim, other or no religion

NATIONAL FLAG
The flag is a horizontal tricolor of black, red, and green, the colors divided by narrow white stripes. At the hoist is a blue isosceles triangle charged with a five-pointed yellow star. Black represents the people of Southern Sudan, red represents the blood shed in the

struggle for freedom, and the green represents the land. The blue is for the sky and water, and the star represents the Star of Bethlehem, symbolizing the Christian religion of the majority of the population.

COAT OF ARMS/SEAL

The interim coat of arms is the official coat of arms of Sudan* surrounded by a broad white circle with *Government of Southern Sudan* above the arms and *GOSS*, the initials of the government, below. A new coat of arms is to be adopted following the proposed referendum on independence in 2011.

CAPITAL CITY

Juba

TYPE OF GOVERNMENT

Autonomous parliamentary regional government as part of Sudan

NATIONAL COLORS

Black, red, and green

NATIONAL ANTHEM

A Southern Sudan national anthem is provided for in the terms of the 2005 autonomy agreement, but no anthem has been designated.

NATIONAL ANIMAL

Rhinoceros (unofficial)

CURRENCY

Sudanese pound

INTERNET IDENTIFIER

.ssd (unofficial)

VEHICLE IDENTIFICATION PLATES/ STICKERS

SUD Sudan (unofficial); SS Southern Sudan (unofficial)

PASSPORT

Southern Sudanese are Sudanese citizens and travel on Sudanese passports.

AIRLINE

Southern Sudan Airlines

NATIONAL RESOURCES

Natural resources include chrome, copper, manganese, asbestos, gypsum, mica, limestone, and possibly commercial reserves of petroleum and natural gas. Although the country is rich in natural resources, decades of conflict have made development impossible. Most Southern Sudanese live as subsistence farmers. Remittances by Southern Sudanese living outside the region are a major source of foreign currency and investment.

FOODS

Chickenat, a dish of chicken with peanut sauce, is considered the national dish. Other specialties include green peppers and spinach; fried sweet potatoes; peanut soup; smoked fish stew; and sweet potato and pea soup.

SPORTS/SPORTS TEAMS

Association football (soccer) is the most popular sport. Traditional sports, such as wrestling and athletics, also remain popular. The Southern Sudan national team participates in football at an international level.

TEAM SPORTS

Football

South Sudan Football Team

NATIONAL HEROES OR PERSONIFICATIONS

John Garang, leader of the largest pro-independence movement in the 1970s through 1990s; Ali Abdel Latif, leader of an uprising against British and Arab domination in 1924; Salva Kiir, leader of the autonomous state since 2005; Buth Diu, founder of the first Southern Sudanese political party in 1951

NATIONAL HOLIDAY/INDEPENDENCE DAY

Southern Sudan Day, July 9

SIGNIFICANT EVENTS IN FORMATION OF NATIONAL IDENTITY

2800 B.C.E. Egyptian slavers raid the tribes of the region, which they call Land of the Slaves.

9h century C.E.–10th century C.E. Bantu tribes, part of the great Bantu migrations, settle the region, displacing the earlier populations. The tribes remain divided, engaging in intertribal wars and cattle raids. Protected by formidable natural barriers, they have little contact with the outside world, and their cultures adapt to the annual migrations of their cattle herds, the local measure of wealth.

1840s Muslims from the north, searching for slaves and ivory, begin to penetrate the region. Slave traders depopulate whole districts as slaves are sent north in long caravans. European explorers begin to visit the region.

1874–1899 The British intervene to end the slave trade. Conflicting colonial claims to the region bring the United Kingdom* and France* to the brink of war in 1897. British claims to the region are recognized.

1900–1928 The southern districts are governed separately from Arab northern Sudan by traditional leaders. The last tribal resistance ends.

1940–1946 The British eliminate all Arab and Muslim influence in the south. Following agitation by the Arab north, the policy is reversed.

1950 Southern leaders reject possible Arab rule in an independent Sudan and form nationalist groups to press for separate administration under continued British rule. Southern resistance delays Sudanese independence for several years.

1955–1972 Southern soldiers mutiny, setting off a civil war between the Arab north and the African south that continues intermittently for decades, while in the north, military coups and growing Islamic influence harden attitudes. The national flag is replaced with a more explicitly Islamic flag.

1972 A peace agreement makes the south self-governing. Oil is discovered at Bentiu in Southern Sudan.

1983 The civil war resumes. John Garang leads the movement for independence. The Sudanese government declares the introduction of Islamic Sharia law.

2002 The government and the southern rebels sign a cease-fire and negotiate the Machakos Protocol, which gives Southern Sudan full autonomy with the right to a referendum on independence.

2005 John Garang is killed in a plane crash.

2008–2009 Fighting breaks out along the border between north and south over the disputed territory of Abyei. A referendum on the independence of Southern Sudan is tentatively scheduled for January 2011, when the Nuba Mountain region and the Blue Nile region also will vote on whether to stay with Sudan or join the new republic to the south.

See also Sudan

SWAZILAND

OFFICIAL NAME

Umbuso weSwatini (SiSwati); Kingdom of Swaziland (English)

NICKNAME

The Switzerland of Africa

POPULATION

1,188,300 (2009e)

INHABITANTS' NAME/NICKNAME

Swazi(s)

LANGUAGE/LANGUAGES

English, SiSwati (both official); others

RELIGION/RELIGIONS

Christian, 82 percent; indigenous beliefs, Muslim, other or no religion

NATIONAL FLAG

The flag has horizontal stripes of blue (double width), yellow, red (quadruple width), yellow, and blue (double width). Centered on the red are a horizontal black and white Swazi shield and two spears. The red symbolizes past battles, the blue is for peace and stability, and the yellow stands for Swaziland's resources. The black and white shield symbolizes the peaceful coexistence of blacks and whites in the country and, with the spears, symbolizes protection from the country's enemies.

COAT OF ARMS/SEAL

The coat of arms has a central blue crest charged with the Swazi shield of the national flag in the vertical position, symbolizing protection. Above the shield is the king's *lidlabe,* a crown of feathers. A lion, representing the king, and an elephant, representing the queen-mother, support the shield. On a banner below the shield is the national motto in SiSwati.

MOTTO

Siyinqaba (SiSwati); We are the fortress (English)

CAPITAL CITY

Mbabane (administrative); Lombaba (royal and legislative)

TYPE OF GOVERNMENT

Constitutional monarchy

NATIONAL COLORS

Blue and yellow

NATIONAL ANTHEM

The anthem was adopted at independence in 1968. It is a compromise between traditional Swazi and western-style music.

Nkulunkulu Mnikati wetibusiso temaSwati (SiSwati); O Lord Our God, Bestower of the Blessings of the Swazi (English)

O Lord our God, bestower of the blessings of the Swazi;

We give thee thanks for all our good fortune,
We offer thanks and praise for our king
And for our fair land, its hills and rivers.

Thy blessings be on all rulers of our country,
Thine alone is our Lord,
We pray thee to grant us wisdom without deceit or malice.
Establish and fortify us, Lord Eternal.

PATRON SAINT

Our Lady of the Assumption (patron saint of southern Africa)

CURRENCY

Swazi lilangeni

INTERNET IDENTIFIER

.sz

VEHICLE IDENTIFICATION PLATES/ STICKERS

SD

PASSPORT

The passport cover has the name of the country in English and French, the coat of arms, and the word *passport* in English and French.

AIRLINE

Swaziland Airlink

NATIONAL FLOWER

Crocosmia (unofficial)

NATIONAL ANIMALS

Lion; elephant

NATIONAL BIRD

Loury (widowbird)

NATIONAL FISH

Orange River mudfish (unofficial)

NATIONAL RESOURCES

Natural resources include asbestos, coal, clay, cassiterite, hydropower, forests, small gold and diamond deposits, quarry stone, and talc.

In this small, landlocked economy, subsistence agriculture occupies approximately 70 percent of the population. Swaziland is heavily dependent on South Africa*, from which it receives most of its imports and to which it sends over half its exports. South Africa also provides the bulk of the growing number of tourists that visit the kingdom to view traditional tribal life and ceremonies, game preserves, and varied scenery.

FOODS

Samp, a dish of hominy, sugar beans, onion, tomato, carrots, green beans, potatoes, cabbage, and squash, is considered a national dish. Other national dishes include impala Swazi-style, a leg of impala cooked with cloves, olives, bacon, potatoes, carrots, onions, and prunes; Swazi cornbread; karoo roast ostrich steak; banana and corn casserole; fried sweet potatoes; *biltong,* a dried meat similar to jerky; and green pea soup.

SPORTS/SPORTS TEAMS

Association football (soccer) and rugby are the most popular sports. Swaziland national teams participate in many sports at an international level.

TEAM SPORTS

Badminton

Swaziland Badminton Team

Basketball

Swaziland Basketball Team; Swaziland Women's Basketball Team

Cricket

Swaziland Cricket Team

Football

Swaziland Football Team, nickname Shiangu Semnikati (the King's Shield); Swaziland Women's Football Team, nickname Sitsebe; Swaziland Under-20 Football Team; Swaziland Rugby Union Team; Swaziland Rugby Union Team (Sevens), nickname Swaziland Sevens or Swaziland 7s

Netball

Swaziland Netball Team

Volleyball

Swaziland Men's Volleyball Team

INDIVIDUAL SPORTS

Swaziland Amateur Boxing Team; Swaziland Athletics Team; Swaziland Equestrian Team; Swaziland Modern Pentathlon Team; Swaziland Rowing Team; Swaziland Swim Team; Swaziland Tae Kwon Do Team; Swaziland Weight Lifting Team

NATIONAL HEROES OR PERSONIFICATIONS

King Sobhuza I, the leader who established the Swazi kingdom in the 19th century; Mswati II, the mid-19th century king known as the greatest of the Swazi fighting kings, who gave his name to the country; Tsandzile Ndwandwe, wife of Mzwazi II and regent of the kingdom from 1868 to 1875; King Mswati III, the present king

NATIONAL HOLIDAY/INDEPENDENCE DAY

Independence Day, September 6

FESTIVALS/FAIRS

Ncwala (Harvest Festival), December–January; Umhlanga, August–September; Somhlolo, September

SIGNIFICANT EVENTS IN FORMATION OF NATIONAL IDENTITY

600 C.E.–1000 C.E. Bantu tribes, part of the great Bantu migrations, settle the region, displacing the earlier Khoisan hunter groups.

15th century According to tradition, the followers of the royal Diamini dynasty migrate south to the area of modern Maputo in Mozambique*.

1750–1820s Following tribal conflicts, the people again move south into northern Zululand in about 1750. Unable to withstand the expanding Zulus, they move the center of their kingdom northward in the 1810s and 1820s under King Sobhuza I. Incorporating the area's small kingdoms and tribal groups into the nation, the kingdom becomes a regional power.

1840s–1865 Under King Mzwati II, the kingdom expands to the north and west and stabilizes the southern frontier with Zululand. Mzwati requests aid from the British in South Africa in combating Zulu raids into his kingdom. White Boer farmers settle in the kingdom.

1894–1899 The Boers of the Transvaal Republic establish nominal control over the kingdom but withdraw at the beginning of the Anglo-Boer War.

1902–1903 British forces enter the kingdom. Swaziland is made a British protectorate and in 1907 becomes a British High Commission territory under indirect rule by the Swazi king.

1921 King Sobhuza II succeeds to the throne, ensuring tradition and continuity.

1962–1964 Africa's decolonization process spurs nationalism in the kingdom. Swaziland's first constitution comes into force.

1968 Swaziland becomes an independent kingdom.

1973–1978 The king suspends the constitution and bans political parties. The parliamentary system is abolished and replaced by traditional tribal government.

1995–2000 Strikes, student demonstrations, and growing unrest force the king, Africa's last absolute monarch, to accept the limitations of a constitution and a parliamentary system.

2004–2008 Swaziland has the world's highest rate of HIV infection. Premature death due to AIDS decimates the population, leaving thousands of orphans. In 2005, the king signs the new constitution agreed to eight years before. Prodemocracy activism increases. Opposition groups announce a boycott of the 2008 elections as part of a campaign for multiparty elections.

2009 The global economic slump hurts the already ailing Swazi economy, which suffers from a lack of skilled workers. Growth is hampered by the effects of HIV and AIDS, the prevalence of which remains the highest in the world.

TANZANIA

OFFICIAL NAME
Jamhuri ya Muungano wa Tanzania (Swahili); United Republic of Tanzania

POPULATION
37,503,500 (2008e)

INHABITANTS' NAME/NICKNAME
Tanzanian(s)

LANGUAGE/LANGUAGES
Swahili (de facto official); English, Kiunjuja (Zanzibar Swahili), indigenous languages, others

RELIGION/RELIGIONS
Muslim, 35 percent; Christian, 30 percent; indigenous beliefs, other or no religion

NATIONAL FLAG
The flag is divided diagonally by a wide black stripe outlined in gold from the lower hoist to the upper fly. The upper hoist triangle is green and the lower fly is sky blue. The green represents the country's natural vegetation, gold represents the rich mineral deposits, black represents the native Swahili peoples, and blue represents the numerous lakes and rivers and the Indian Ocean.

COAT OF ARMS/SEAL
The coat of arms has a central warrior's shield divided into four quadrants, beginning with a gold quadrant and a torch at the top; the flag of Tanzania; a red field with a crossed hoe and axe; and white and blue wavy lines. A single spear is placed in front

of the shield. The gold represents mineral wealth; the torch symbolizes represents freedom; the red symbolizes the rich, fertile soil; and the wavy lines represent the sea, lakes and the Indian Ocean. Two human figures, a man and a woman, and two ivory tusks support the shield, which rests on earth representing Mount Kilimanjaro with cotton and clove plants, representing the country's major exports. A banner is inscribed with the national motto in Swahili.

MOTTO

Uhuru na umoja (Swahili); Freedom and Unity (English)

CAPITAL CITY

Dodoma

TYPE OF GOVERNMENT

Republic

NATIONAL EMBLEM

Mount Kilimanjaro

NATIONAL COLORS

Blue, yellow, and black

NATIONAL ANTHEM

The anthem is a popular African anthem first adopted by Tanganyika in 1961 and retained following the union with Zanzibar* in 1964.

Mungu ibariki Afrika (Swahili); God Bless Africa (English)

God bless Africa.
Bless its rulers.
Let wisdom, unity, and
Peace be the shield of
Africa and its people.

Chorus

Bless Africa,
Bless Africa,
Bless the children of Africa.

God bless Tanzania.
Grant eternal freedom and unity
To its sons and daughters.
God bless Tanzania and its people.

Chorus

Bless Tanzania,
Bless Tanzania,
Bless the children of Tanzania.

PATRON SAINT

Immaculate Conception of Mary

CURRENCY

Tanzanian shilling

INTERNET IDENTIFIER

.tz

VEHICLE IDENTIFICATION PLATES/ STICKERS

EAT

PASSPORT

The passport cover has the word *passport* in large letters, the coat of arms, and the name Tanzania, in English, also in large letters.

AIRLINE

Air Tanzania

NATIONAL FLOWER

Tanganyika orchid (unofficial)

NATIONAL ANIMAL

Lake Tanganyika cichlid (unofficial)

NATIONAL BIRD

Blue swallow (unofficial)

NATIONAL FISH

Vundu (unofficial)

NATIONAL RESOURCES

Natural resources include hydropower, tin, phosphates, iron ore, coal, diamonds, gemstones, gold, natural gas, and nickel. Agriculture is the basis of the economy. Tourism, based on varied scenery, sandy beaches, a pleasant climate, unique cultures, and wild game, is an important resource.

Foods

Baked chicken in groundnut sauce, a dish of chicken, onion, green pepper, tomatoes, chilies, spices, groundnuts, and coconut milk, is considered the national dish. Other specialties include *mchicha,* a dish of spinach, coconut, and peanuts; *mchuzi wa samaki,* fish curry; sweet potato soup; breadfruit with tomato and peppers; *supu ya ndizi,* plantain soup; Swahili-style roast beef; coconut bean soup; Tanzanian meat stew; and *dagaa,* dried fish with tomatoes.

Sports/Sports Teams

Association football (soccer), athletics, and boxing are the most popular sports. Tanzania national teams participate in many sports at an international level.

Team Sports

Badminton
Tanzania Badminton Team

Basketball
Tanzania Basketball Team; Tanzania Women's Basketball Team

Football
Tanzania Football Team, nickname the Taifa Stars or the Kilimanjaro Stars; Tanzania Women's Football Team, nickname the Taifa Stars; Tanzania Rugby Union Team, nickname Twigas (the Giraffes)

Hockey
Tanzania Field Hockey Team

Netball
Tanzania Netball Team

Table Tennis
Tanzania Table Tennis Team

Volleyball
Tanzania Men's Volleyball Team

Individual Sports

Tanzania Amateur Boxing Team; Tanzania Athletics Team; Tanzania Swim Team; Tanzania Tae Kwon Do Team; Tanzania Weight Lifting Team; Tanzania Wrestling Team

National Heroes or Personifications

Julius Nyerere, the first president and the man who led the country to independence; Edward Sokoine, prime minister in the 1970s and 1980s, responsible for reforming the economy and the political system

National Holiday/Independence Day

Union Day, April 26

Festivals/Fairs

Saba Saba, July; Nane Nane, August; Independence Day celebrations, December; Eid al-Adha (Festival of Sacrifice), varied dates; Maulid, various dates; Eid al-Fitr, various dates.

Significant Events in Formation of National Identity

600 C.E.–1200 C.E. The Bantu peoples settle the region as part of the great Bantu migrations. The Bantus mostly absorb the earlier inhabitants. Nilotic pastoralists with their herds begin arriving sporadically from the north.

800s–1200s Traders from the Persian Gulf and western India* establish trading posts on the mainland and the islands. Kilwa becomes the major trading center on the mainland. The mixture of Arabs, Persians, and Africans develops into the Swahili culture.

1498–1509 Vasco da Gama, the leader of a Portuguese expedition, sails up the coast. Drawn by the wealth described by da Gama, the Portuguese seize the coastal settlements.

1699 Zanzibar is conquered by the Arabs of Oman* and becomes the center of a maritime empire.

1858 European explorers visit Lake Tanganyika and Lake Victoria, beginning the exploration of the interior by Europeans.

1867–1873 The British stage a military campaign against the slave trade in Zanzibar. The Sultan of Zanzibar is forced to close his slave market by the British.

1884–1890 A German expedition explores mainland Tanganyika, which is declared a German protectorate in 1885. The British take control of the islands Zanzibar and Pemba.

1916–1919 British and South African troops occupy German East Africa during the First World War. Tanganyika becomes a League of Nations mandate under British administration.

1929 The first nationalist organization forms in Tanganyika.

1946 After the Second World War, Tanganyika becomes a United Nations Trust Territory under British administration.

1958–1962 Tanganyika is granted international self-government and two years later achieves full independence with Julius Nyerere as its first president. Nyerere introduces his own form of African socialism.

1963–1964 Zanzibar becomes an independent sultanate, which is soon overthrown in bloody revolution that installs a leftist government. Thousands of non-Africans flee the islands. Tanganyika and Zanzibar merge to form a united republic.

1978–1979 Tensions with neighboring Uganda* lead to a Tanzanian invasion and the overthrow of the Ugandan dictator Idi Amin.

1985–1992 A new government eases the extremes of Nyerere's socialist experimentation. The constitution is amended to allow multiparty democracy.

1999 Julius Nyerere, the father of the nation, dies.

2000–2001 Opposition to the union with Tanganyika gains support in Zanzibar. Separatist incidents lead to violence on the islands.

2005 Violence again breaks out in Zanzibar. Demands for autonomy are reiterated by the island's nationalist organizations.

2008–2009 The government is disrupted by the dismissals of two ministers and various others accused of corruption. Corruption scandals continue to undermine confidence in the government's ability to combat the growing economic crisis.

See also Zanzibar

TOGO

OFFICIAL NAME
République Togolaise (French); Togolese Republic (English)

POPULATION
5,487,900 (2009e)

INHABITANTS' NAME/NICKNAME
Togolese

LANGUAGE/LANGUAGES
French (official); Ewe, Mina, Kabyé, Dagoma, others

RELIGION/RELIGIONS
Christian, 29 percent; Muslim, 20 percent; indigenous beliefs, other or no religion

NATIONAL FLAG
The flag has five equal horizontal bands of green (including at top and bottom) alternating with yellow. There is a white, five-pointed star on a red square at the upper hoist. The red symbolizes the blood shed by the sons of the nation to protect its integrity and sovereignty against all aggressors; green stands for hope and nature; yellow stands for

the precious value of national unity, a common destiny, and mineral riches; and white symbolizes peace, wisdom, dignity, and light. The star symbolizes life.

Coat of Arms/Seal

The coat of arms has a central gold disk with the initials *RT* for République Togolaise. On each side is a red lion holding a bow and arrow, symbolizing the bravery of the people. Above the disk are two Togolese flags and a gold banner inscribed with the national motto in French.

Motto

Travail, liberté, patrie (French); Work, Liberty, Homeland (English)

Capital City

Lomé

Type of Government

Republic

National Colors

Yellow, green, and red

National Anthem

The anthem was originally adopted at independence in 1960, replaced in 1979 when a one-party system was adopted, and readopted in 1991 with the return to democracy.

> **Salut à toi, pays de nos aïeus (French); Hail to You, Land of Our Forefathers (English)**
>
> Hail to you, land of our forefathers,
> You who made them strong, peaceful and happy,
> Men who for posterity cultivated virtue and bravery.
> Even if tyrants shall come, thy heart yearns towards freedom.
> Togo arise! Let us struggle without faltering.
> Victory or death, but dignity.
> God almighty, You alone have made Togo prosper.
> People of Togo arise! Let us build the nation.

> To serve you in unity is the most burning desire of our hearts.
> Let us shout aloud our motto
> That nothing can tarnish.
> We the only builders of your happiness and of your future,
> Everywhere let us break chains and treachery,
> And we swear to you forever faith, love, service, untiring zeal,
> To make you yet, beloved Togo, a golden example for humanity.

Currency

CFA franc

Internet Identifier

.tg

Vehicle Identification Plates/ Stickers

TG (unofficial)

Passport

The passport cover has the name of the country in French, the coat of arms, and the word *passport* in French.

National Animal

African lion

National Bird

Sparrow hawk

National Resources

Natural resources include phosphates, limestone, marble, and arable land. Agriculture is the main activity, both commercial and subsistence. Tourism, although a minor resource, could be more important in the future. The country has interesting and varied scenery, sandy beaches, unique cultures, and proximity to European population centers. Remittances from Togolese living outside the country are an important source of foreign currency and investment.

FOODS

Fufu, mashed yam served with groundnut sauce, goat meat, or palm oil, is considered the national dish. Other national specialties include *riz sauce arachide,* a rice dish with peanut sauce; *akume avec sauce ademe,* small balls of dough made of maize and cassava served with vegetables, greens, and smoked fish; *huitres azi dessi,* fried oysters with chili, smoked prawns, and peanut sauce; *soupe archida,* groundnut soup; and *tchakpallo,* a drink made of fermented millet, considered the national drink.

SPORTS/SPORTS TEAMS

Association football (soccer) is the most popular sport. Togo national teams participate in many sports at an international level.

TEAM SPORTS

Badminton

Togo Badminton Team

Baseball

Togo Baseball Team

Basketball

Togo Basketball Team; Togo Women's Basketball Team

Football

Togo Football Team, nickname Les Eperviers (the Sparrow Hawks); Togo Women's Football Team, nickname Les Eperviers (the Sparrow Hawks); Togo Rugby Union Team

Table Tennis

Togo Table Tennis Team

Tennis

Togo Davis Cup Team

Volleyball

Togo Men's Volleyball Team

INDIVIDUAL SPORTS

Togo Amateur Boxing Team; Togo Athletics Team; Togo Cycling Team; Togo Judo Team; Togo Rowing Team; Togo Swim Team; Togo Tae Kwon Do Team; Togo Weight Lifting Team

NATIONAL HEROES OR PERSONIFICATIONS

Tavio Amorin, a politician shot dead by security forces in 1992; Sylvanus Olympio, first president of independent Togo, who was assassinated; Nicholas Grunitzky, second president of Togo, overthrown in 1967

NATIONAL HOLIDAY/INDEPENDENCE DAY

Independence Day, April 27

FESTIVALS/FAIRS

Evala Festival, July; Akpema Festival, August; Dzawuwu-Zaor (Harvest Festival), August; Agbogbo-Za, September; Independence Day celebrations, April

SIGNIFICANT EVENTS IN FORMATION OF NATIONAL IDENTITY

600 C.E.–800 C.E. Bantu tribes migrate to the region, settling in small tribal or clan groups.

15th century–17th century The Ewe people and others settle in the region, which is already occupied by several tribes. Portuguese explorers sail down the coast, giving the people their first contact with Europeans. Slave ports established by European traders flourish.

18th century The Danes take control of the region and the local slave trade.

1884–1914 The Germans establish a protectorate over the region they call Togoland. Under German rule, forced labor is widespread in the development of commercial plantations. When the First World War breaks out, British and French forces take control.

1922 The League of Nations splits the former German colony into a western part under British administration and an eastern zone under French administration.

1956–1963 The British merge Western Togoland into the Gold Coast, which gains independence. In 1960, French Togoland becomes an independent state under the name of Togo. Sylvanus Olympio is elected president but is assassinated in 1963.

1967 Gnassingbe Eyadema seizes power. A one-party state is declared, and all political parties are forcibly dissolved.

1970s–1990 Agitation spreads among the Ewe people, split between Ghana and Togo, for reunification. Eyadema is reelected every seven years as the sole candidate.

1991–1993 Prodemocracy demonstrations force Eyadema to allow some liberalization and free elections. A new constitution is approved, but Eyadema dissolves the government. Rioting breaks out and thousands flee to Ghana.

2005 Eyadema dies and is succeeded by his son, who is elected in a fraudulent election. Rioting and clashes with security forces leave 400–500 dead.

2006–2008 An agreement leads to government incorporating both the ruling political party and the opposition. Free elections are held, the first in Togo's history. The European Union and others restore ties and aid.

2009 The ethnic division between the northern Muslim peoples and the southern, mostly Christian peoples undermines political stability, despite a successful election in 2007.

UGANDA

OFFICIAL NAME

Jamhuri ya Uganda (Swahili); Republic of Uganda (English)

POPULATION

30,958,300 (2009e)

INHABITANTS' NAME/NICKNAME

Ugandan(s)

LANGUAGE/LANGUAGES

English, Swahili (both official); Arabic, indigenous languages, others

RELIGION/RELIGIONS

Roman Catholic, 42 percent; Anglican, 35 percent; Muslim, 13 percent; Pentecostal, 5 percent; Seventh-day Adventist, 1.5 percent; other or no religion

NATIONAL FLAG

The flag consists of six equal horizontal stripes of black, yellow, red, black, yellow, and red, with a centered white disk charged with the national symbol, a crested crane, facing the hoist. Black represents the African peoples; yellow represents African sunshine; and red, the color or blood, represents African brotherhood connected by blood.

COAT OF ARMS/SEAL

The coat of arms has a central African shield and spears on a green mound, representing the willingness of the Ugandans to defend their country. Three images on the shield represent the waves of Lake Victoria at the top, a centered yellow sun for the many days of brilliant sunshine in the country, and a traditional drum, a symbol of calling the people together, at the bottom. A crested crane and a Ugandan *kob,* a type of antelope, representing the country's abundant wildlife, support the shield. The green mound represents the fertile land around a representation of the River Nile with the two major crops, coffee and cotton, and a banner inscribed with the national motto in English.

MOTTO

For God and my country

CAPITAL CITY

Kampala

TYPE OF GOVERNMENT

Presidential democracy

NATIONAL EMBLEM

Crested crane

NATIONAL COLORS

Black, yellow, and red

NATIONAL ANTHEM

The anthem was adopted at independence in 1962 as a result of a national contest.

O Uganda, Land of Beauty

O Uganda! May God uphold thee,
We lay our future in thy hand.
United, free,
For liberty
Together we'll always stand.

O Uganda! The land of freedom.
Our love and labor we give,
And with neighbors all
At our country's call
In peace and friendship we'll live.

Oh Uganda! The land that feeds us
By sun and fertile soil grown.
For our own dear land,
We'll always stand,
The pearl of Africa's crown.

PATRON SAINT

Mary, Queen of Africa

CURRENCY

Ugandan shilling

INTERNET IDENTIFIER

.ug

VEHICLE IDENTIFICATION PLATES/STICKERS

EAU

PASSPORT

The passport cover has the short name of the country, Uganda; the coat of arms; and the word *passport.*

AIRLINE

Air Uganda

NATIONAL ANIMAL

Ugandan *kob*

NATIONAL BIRD

Crested crane

NATIONAL FISH

Tilapia (unofficial)

NATIONAL RESOURCES

Natural resources include copper, cobalt, hydropower, limestone, salt, and arable land. Uganda has substantial natural resources, including fertile soils, regular rainfall, and sizable mineral deposits. Agriculture is the most important sector of the economy, and coffee accounts for the bulk of export revenues. The growing tourism industry is based on varied scenery, wildlife, and unique cultures.

FOODS

Matoke, a dish made of steamed and mashed green plantains, onions, bell peppers, cloves, chilies, and smoked fish, is considered the national dish. Other national specialties include *amandazi,* a small, doughnutlike fried pastry; *amashaza mu gitoke,* a dish of dried peas, plantains, onions, tomatoes, chilies, and palm oil; *olouwombo,* a stew of chicken or meat, peanut butter, onions, tomatoes, mushrooms, smoked fish, and plantains; and *chickenat,* chicken prepared with peanut sauce. The national drink is *waragi,* a banana gin.

SPORTS/SPORTS TEAMS

Cricket and rugby union are the most popular sports. Uganda national teams participate in many sports at an international level.

TEAM SPORTS

Badminton

Uganda Badminton Team

Baseball

Uganda Baseball Team

Basketball

Uganda Basketball Team; Uganda Women's Basketball Team

Cricket

Uganda Cricket Team

Football

Uganda Football Team, nickname the Cranes; Uganda Women's Football Team, nickname the She-Kobs; Uganda Under-23 Football Team, nickname the Kobs; Uganda Under-20 Football Team, nickname the Hippos; Uganda Rugby Union Team, nickname the Rugby Cranes; Uganda Women's Rugby Union Team, nickname the Rugby Cranes; Uganda Rugby Union Team (Sevens), nickname Uganda Sevens or Uganda 7s or the Cranes; Uganda Women's Rugby Union Team (Sevens), nickname Uganda Sevens or Uganda 7s or the Lady Cranes

Hockey

Uganda Field Hockey Team

Netball

Uganda Netball Team

Table Tennis

Uganda Table Tennis Team

Tennis

Uganda Davis Cup Team

Volleyball

Uganda Men's Volleyball Team; Uganda Women's Volleyball Team

INDIVIDUAL SPORTS

Uganda Amateur Boxing Team; Uganda Archery Team; Uganda Athletics Team; Uganda Canoeing Team; Tanzania Uganda Cycling Team; Uganda Judo Team; Uganda Rowing Team; Uganda Shooting Team; Uganda Swim Team; Uganda Tae Kwon Do Team; Uganda Weight Lifting Team; Uganda Wrestling Team

NATIONAL HEROES OR PERSONIFICATIONS

Ignatius Musazi, the independence leader called the father of political parties; Yusuf Kironde Lule, the leader of the movement that ousted Idi Amin in 1979; Mukama Kabarega of Bunyoro, who led his people against the British until his capture and exile in 1899

NATIONAL HOLIDAY/INDEPENDENCE DAY

Independence Day, October 9

FESTIVALS/FAIRS

Amakula International Film Festival, May; Theater Arts Festival, August; Independence Day celebrations, October; Victory Festival, January

SIGNIFICANT EVENTS IN FORMATION OF NATIONAL IDENTITY

1000 B.C.E. Cushitic peoples from the north migrate to the region, displacing the earlier San-like people.

600 C.E.–1000 C.E. Bantu peoples migrate into the highlands of East Africa.

1000–1500 A number of highly centralized kingdoms form in the south under cattle-herding aristocracies, the most powerful being Bunyoro and Buganda.

1800–1879 The rivalry between Bunyoro and Buganda leads to a series of wars. In 1860, British explorers enter the region during a critical power struggle between the two kingdoms. The first Christian missionaries arrive.

1890–1920 The United Kingdom* and Germany* divide East Africa, with Uganda forming part of the British sphere of influence. The Kingdom of Buganda becomes a British protectorate in 1894, Bunyoro is added in 1896, and other areas to the north are joined to the territory called Uganda up to 1920.

1953–1955   A crisis disrupts the colony as Buganda, ruled indirectly through the king, seeks to separate from Uganda as a separate territory.

1962   Uganda becomes an independent state, with Buganda given wide powers of autonomy.

1966   Buganda's autonomy is ended by the government.

1971   Idi Amin, a northern Muslim, becomes the ruler in a military coup. The influential Asian community, around 60,000 people, is expelled.

1976–1979   Amin declares himself president for life. Critics of the government flee or disappear. Tens of thousands are killed in mass executions and other violence as the Amin government institutes a reign of terror.

1979   Tanzanian troops and anti-Amin forces invade from Tanzania*, forcing Amin to flee. A succession of unstable governments follows.

1986   A rebel army takes Kampala and installs Yoweri Museveni as president.

1993–1996   Museveni restores the traditional kings, including the king of Buganda, but only as ceremonial positions. The country recovers from the excesses and mismanagement of previous regimes. Museveni becomes Uganda's first elected president.

2000–2001   Ugandans vote to accept Museveni's "no-party" political system. The East African Community is created between Uganda, Tanzania, and Kenya,

2005–2008   Voters approve a return to multiparty politics. Continuing violence in the north of the country has displaced over 1 million people. A permanent cease-fire is signed with the largest rebel group in the north.

2009   Uganda's ability to combat the effects of the global economic slump is hampered by continuing involvement in eastern Congo and the high number of people with HIV and AIDS.

ZAMBIA

OFFICIAL NAME
Republic of Zambia

POPULATION
12,448,500 (2009e)

INHABITANTS' NAME/NICKNAME
Zambian(s)

LANGUAGE/LANGUAGES
English (official); Chibemba, Chichewa, Lunda, Tonga, Silozi, Nkoya, Luvale, Tumbuka, Kaonde (recognized regional languages); 70 other indigenous languages, others

RELIGION/RELIGIONS
Christian, 50–75 percent; Muslim, 25–49 percent; indigenous beliefs, other or no religion

NATIONAL FLAG
The flag has a green field with three equal vertical stripes of red, black, and gold on the fly below the depiction of a golden eagle. Green represents the country's natural resources, red represents the blood spilled in the struggle for independence, black symbolizes the majority of the country's people, and gold represents mineral wealth. The eagle of liberty symbolizes the people's ability to rise above the nation's problems.

COAT OF ARMS/SEAL
The coat of arms has a central crest or shield with a black background crossed by six vertical wavy white lines, representing Victoria Falls. Above the shield are a crossed pickaxe and hoe and the golden eagle, representing mining, agriculture, and liberty. The shield is supported by two human figures on green, a male and a female, representing the country's people. Below is a white banner inscribed with the country's national motto.

MOTTO

One Zambia, one nation

CAPITAL CITY

Lusaka

TYPE OF GOVERNMENT

Republic

NATIONAL EMBLEM

The most notable landmark is Victoria Falls, known locally as Mosi-oa-Tunya, which means "the smoke that thunders"

NATIONAL COLORS

Green and white

NATIONAL ANTHEM

At independence in 1964, Zambia adopted the melody from "God Bless Africa" with new lyrics written to reflect Zambian themes.

Lumbanyeni Zambia (Chibemba); Stand and Sing of Zambia, Proud and Free (English)

Stand and sing of Zambia, proud and free,
Land of work and joy in unity,
Victors in the struggle for the right,
We have won freedom's fight.
All one, strong and free.

Africa is our own motherland,
Fashion'd with and blessed by God's good
  hand,
Let us all her people join as one,
Brothers under the sun.
All one, strong and free.

One land and one nation is our cry,
Dignity and peace 'neath Zambia's sky,
Like our noble eagle in its flight,
Zambia, praise to thee.
All one, strong and free.

Chorus

Praise be to God.
Praise be, praise be, praise be,
Bless our great nation,

Zambia, Zambia, Zambia.
Free men we stand
Under the flag of our land.
Zambia, praise to thee!
All one, strong and free.

CURRENCY

Zambian kwacha

INTERNET IDENTIFIER

.zm

VEHICLE IDENTIFICATION PLATES/ STICKERS

Z

PASSPORT

The passport cover has the name of the country in English, the coat of arms, and the word *passport*.

AIRLINE

Zambian Airways (flights temporarily suspended in January 2009)

NATIONAL FLOWER

Victoria orchid (unofficial)

NATIONAL TREE

Mofu mahogany (unofficial)

NATIONAL PLANT

Maize

NATIONAL ANIMAL

Zebra

NATIONAL FISH

Newbwe (unofficial)

NATIONAL RESOURCES

Natural resources include copper, cobalt, zinc, lead, coal, emeralds, gold, silver, uranium, and hydropower, Economic activity has traditionally involved the copper mining industry; however, the government has recently diversified into other fields. Tourism is an important resource, supported by such attractions as game parks, unique cultures, Victoria Falls, and varied scenery.

FOODS

Nshima, a thick paste or porridge made from pounded cassava, yams, plantains, or maize, served with shredded meat and various sauces, is considered the national dish. Other national specialties include *golabjamoun,* sweet potato cakes; *ifisashi,* a dish of peanuts, tomatoes, onions, greens, cabbage, and meat; *kapenta,* a dish of dried fish, tomatoes, and onions, served with rice; *binch akara,* fried bean fritters; *tongabezi,* a chicken curry dish; curried gazelle; fish with greens and peanut sauce; and fish *piri piri,* fish served with a spicy sauce.

SPORTS/SPORTS TEAMS

Association football (soccer) and rugby are the most popular sports. Zambia national teams participate in many sports at an international level.

TEAM SPORTS

Badminton

Zambia Badminton Team

Baseball

Zambia Baseball Team; Zambia Softball Team

Basketball

Zambia Basketball Team; Zambia Women's Basketball Team

Cricket

Zambia Cricket Team

Football

Zambia Football Team, nickname Chipolopolo (the Copper Bullets); Zambia Women's Football Team, nickname Chipolopolo Queens (the Copper Bullet Queens); Zambia Under-23 Football Team, nickname Young Chipolopolo; Zambia Under-20 Football Team, nickname Young Chipolopolo; Zambia Rugby Union Team; Zambia Women's Rugby Union Team; Zambia Futsal Team; Zambia Rugby Union Team (Sevens), nickname Zambia Sevens or Zambia 7s

Racing

Zambia Speedway Team

Table Tennis

Zambia Table Tennis Team

Tennis

Zambia Davis Cup Team

Volleyball

Zambia Men's Volleyball Team

INDIVIDUAL SPORTS

Zambia Amateur Boxing Team; Zambia Archery Team; Zambia Athletics Team; Zambia Canoeing Team; Zambia Cycling Team; Zambia Equestrian Team; Zambia Gymnastics Team; Zambia Judo Team; Zambia Rowing Team; Zambia Swim Team; Zambia Tae Kwon Do Team; Zambia Weight Lifting Team

NATIONAL HEROES OR PERSONIFICATIONS

Kenneth Kaunda, Zambia's first president from 1964 to 1991; Nalumino Mundia, former prime minister and noted politician

NATIONAL HOLIDAY/INDEPENDENCE DAY

Independence Day, October 24

FESTIVALS/FAIRS

Kwanga Festival, October; Livingstone Festival, August; Nc'wala Festival (Harvest Festival), February; Lwiinde Ceremony, February; Zambia Agricultural Fair, July; Kuomboka

Festival, March–April; Kulumba Festival, August; Likumbi Lya Mize, August

SIGNIFICANT EVENTS IN FORMATION OF NATIONAL IDENTITY

300 C.E. Migrating tribal peoples displace the original Khoisan peoples.

12th century Major migrations of Bantu peoples, part of the great Bantu migrations, settle the region. The Shona people create the empire of Mwene Mutapa, which includes southern Zambia.

17th century–19th century Other Bantu and Ngoni tribes settle in different districts of the region. Each group creates a village hierarchy as the ultimate authority. European explorers begin to pass through the region. Portugal* claims the Barotse kingdom.

1855–1873 Explorer David Livingstone encounters the great falls, which he names for Britain's Queen Victoria. Highly publicized accounts of his explorations spur interest in central Africa following his death in 1873.

1889–1930 Copper is discovered, which encourages an influx of Europeans.

1891 The Portuguese cede Barotseland to the British, which is combined with other territories in the territory called Rhodesia.

1953 The British create the Federation of Rhodesia and Nyasaland, comprising Northern Rhodesia, Southern Rhodesia (now Zimbabwe*), and Nyasaland (now Malawi*).

1960 Kenneth Kaunda forms a political party to press for independence and the dissolution of the federation dominated by white-ruled Southern Rhodesia.

1963 The federation is dissolved, and, in 1964, Northern Rhodesia becomes independent as Zambia with Kenneth Kaunda as its first president.

1968–1975 Zambia becomes a one-party state. Key industries are nationalized along with private land in a failed agricultural scheme.

1976 Zambia aids rebels fighting for majority rule in neighboring Rhodesia.

1991 Multiparty democracy is again embraced following the end of Kenneth Kaunda's presidency.

1997 A military faction attempts a coup against the elected government.

2001–2009 Poor harvests, floods, and drought necessitate appeals for help in feeding over 2–3 million people in the affected regions. The global economic slump weakens the Zambian economy, particularly in the heavily populated Copper Belt region.

ZANZIBAR

OFFICIAL NAME

Serikali Mapinduzi ya Zanzibar (Kiungja); Revolutionary Government of Zanzibar (English)

POPULATION

1,151,600 (2009e)

INHABITANTS' NAME/NICKNAME

Zanzibari(s)

LANGUAGE/LANGUAGES

Kiungja (Zanzibar Swahili), English, Swahili (all official); Arabic, others

RELIGION/RELIGIONS

Muslim, 90 percent; Hindu, Christian, other or no religion

NATIONAL FLAG

The flag is a horizontal tricolor of sky blue, black, and green. The blue represents the Indian Ocean that surrounds the islands, the black represents the African majority of the population, and the green represents the natural vegetation and the clove trees. The official flag of the region has the flag of Tanzania* as a canton on the upper hoist.

COAT OF ARMS/SEAL

The coat of arms has a central vertical oval showing the two major islands against a pale blue sky, a palm tree, the sea, and a clove tree. An axe and a sword support the oval. Above the oval is a banner inscribed with the initials of the government, *SMZ,* and below is a larger banner inscribed with the full name of the Zanzibar government.

CAPITAL CITY

Stone Town (unofficial)

TYPE OF GOVERNMENT

Autonomous parliamentary state in association with Tanzania

NATIONAL EMBLEM

Cloves

NATIONAL COLORS

Blue, black, and green

NATIONAL ANTHEM

Zanzibar has adopted a new anthem, reportedly called the "National March." No lyrics are available as yet.

CURRENCY

Tanzanian shilling

VEHICLE IDENTIFICATION PLATES/ STICKERS

EAZ

PASSPORT

Zanzibaris are Tanzanian citizens and travel on Tanzanian passports.

NATIONAL FLOWER

Clove flower

NATIONAL TREE

Clove

NATIONAL ANIMAL

Zanzibar leopard (unofficial)

NATIONAL RESOURCES

Natural resources include spring water, phosphates, soda ash and salt. Pemba Island was once the world's leading clove producer, although when the national government decided to privatize the clove market, the island went into an economic slump. Zanzibar exports spices, seaweed, and fine raffia. It also has large fishing and dugout canoe production industries. Tourism is a major foreign currency earner, based sandy beaches, a pleasant climate, historic monuments, and a unique culture.

FOODS

M'chuzi wa nyama, a beef curry with garlic, cloves, chili powder, and lemon juice, is the national dish, often served with *wali,* the staple rice. Other national specialties include chapati, a fried wheat-flour flatbread; *supu ya kuku,* a chicken soup with cabbage and onions; *supu ya pemba,* a goat soup with curry and lime juice; *samaki wa kusonga,* fish croquettes; *m'chuzi wa samaki,* fish curry with spices; *maandazi,* Swahili doughnuts; and *n'dizi na kasted,* a dessert of bananas and coconut cream.

SPORTS/SPORTS TEAMS

Association football (soccer) is the most popular sport. Zanzibar national teams participate in several sports at an international level.

TEAM SPORTS

Basketball

Zanzibar Basketball Team; Zanzibar Women's Basketball Team

Football

Zanzibar Football Team; Zanzibar Women's Football Team

Hockey

Zambia Field Hockey Team

INDIVIDUAL SPORTS

Zanzibar Judo Team; Zanzibar Weight Lifting Team

NATIONAL HEROES OR PERSONIFICATIONS

Sayyid Majid bin Said Al-Busaid, the founder of the Zanzibari sultanate; Abeid Karume, the leader of the Zanzibari revolution and the first president of Zanzibar; Hassan bin Ali Sultan, the leader of the Shirazi migrants of the 10th century; Khalifah bin Said, the sultan during the mid-19th century

NATIONAL HOLIDAY/INDEPENDENCE DAY

Union Day, April 26; Zanzibar Revolution Day, January 12

FESTIVALS/FAIRS

Zanzibar International Culture Festival, July; Zanzibar International Film Festival, July; Swahili Music and Cultural Festival, February; Zanzibar Cultural Festival, July

SIGNIFICANT EVENTS IN FORMATION OF NATIONAL IDENTITY

First century C.E. Seafaring peoples from around the Indian Ocean settle the island, long a local trade center. Trade links with the East African coast and the Arabian Peninsula are established.

Eighth century Arab traders introduce Islam, which becomes the majority religion in the islands. Intermarriage is common between Arabs and islanders.

10th century Shirazi migrants settle Zanzibar from Persia, taking their name for the Persian city of Shiraz. From Zanzibar, they create a commercial empire that controls much of the coast of East Africa, mostly dealing in ivory, cloves and spices, and slaves.

13th century After centuries of mixing among the Africans, Arabs, and Shirazis, the islanders form a sultanate with a class structure based on tone of skin.

1498–1506 Portuguese explorer Vasco da Gama visits the island and returns to Portugal* with stories of vast wealth and opulence. A Portuguese expedition takes control of Zanzibar and its coastal possessions.

1699–1832 The Portuguese are defeated and driven out by Arabs from Oman* in the Arabian Peninsula. The Omanis make Zanzibar the capital of their maritime empire. Zanzibar becomes a center of the clove and spice trades.

1873 Under British pressure, the sultan closes the slave markets.

1886 The British establish a protectorate over the Sultanate of Zanzibar. The mainland territories are sold or ceded to Germany* or the United Kingdom*.

1896 History's shortest war breaks out. A British admiral anchors his fleet off Zanzibar so his men can watch a local cricket match. The fleet so angers the sultan that he declares war and sends his only warship against the British fleet. The ship is promptly sunk and the sultan's palace shelled. The sultan sues for peace, ending the Cricket War, which lasted exactly 37 minutes and 23 seconds.

1900–1926 Considering Zanzibar an Arab country, the British maintain the existing social order, which excludes Africans and mixed-race Shirazis from participation in the local government. An Arab-dominated legislature is created.

1950s Political parties form along racial lines, the governing party supported by the Arab and Asian minority and the opposition supported by the African and Shirazi majority.

1963–1964 The sultanate declares independence in December 1963 amid rising racial violence. A communist-inspired coup overthrows the sultanate, and a people's republic is declared. Thousands of Arabs and Asians flee or are killed in the ensuing violence.

1964 Without consulting the Zanzibaris, a treaty is signed between the revolutionary government and mainland Tanganyika, and the two merge as the United Republic of Tanzania.

1979 Growing unrest in the islands leads to a grant of autonomy.

1990 Cultural differences between the Zanzibaris and the mainlanders continue to cause friction. A coalition of cultural and ethnic organizations demands a referendum on Zanzibari independence.

1992 The Tanzanian government approves multiparty politics, allowing the creation of political parties that represent the islands.

1995–1999 Elections and suspicions of vote rigging lead to severe violence with many deaths. Rioting and violence continue as grievances are aired.

2001–2005 Several people are killed during a police raid on Zanzibar's major political party. Political rallies calling for elections are banned. Mainland troops occupy the island to ensure calm. Political violence again breaks out in 2005.

2005–2009 Zanzibar political leaders plead for calm and a return of the important tourist industry. Demands for a referendum on independence continue to be voiced, but political violence diminishes.

See also Tanzania

ZIMBABWE

OFFICIAL NAME
Republic of Zimbabwe

POPULATION
13,352,700 (2009e)

INHABITANTS' NAME/NICKNAME
Zimbabwean(s)

LANGUAGE/LANGUAGES
English (official); Shona, Sindebele, others

RELIGION/RELIGIONS
Christian, 62 percent; indigenous beliefs, 24 percent; Muslim, 1 percent; other or no religion

NATIONAL FLAG
The flag has seven equal stripes of green, yellow, red, black, red, yellow, and green with a white triangle, edged in black, at the hoist, charged with a soapstone bird superimposed on a red five-pointed star. Green represents agricultural and the rural areas; yellow represents the mineral wealth of the country; red stands for the blood shed during the war of liberation; black represents the heritage and ethnicity of the indigenous peoples; and white stands for peace. The soapstone bird represents a statuette found in the ruins of Great Zimbabwe, and the red star symbolizes the revolutionary struggle for liberation and peace.

COAT OF ARMS/SEAL
The coat of arms has a central crest or shield with a green background, the top third featuring 14 wavy white and blue lines representing Victoria Falls. At the bottom of the shield is a representation of Great Zimbabwe. Placed behind the shield are an agricultural hoe and an AK-47. Above the shield are the star and soapstone figure from the national flag. Two kudus standing on golden earth support the shield. A banner at the bottom is inscribed with the national motto.

MOTTO
Unity, Freedom, Work

CAPITAL CITY
Harare

TYPE OF GOVERNMENT
Presidential republic

NATIONAL EMBLEM
Zimbabwe Bird, the carved soapstone bird found in the ruins of Great Zimbabwe

NATIONAL COLORS
Yellow and green

NATIONAL ANTHEM
The anthem was chosen in a contest for a new anthem in 1994. There are official versions in Shona, Sindebele, and English.

Simudzai Mureza wedu WeZimbabwe (Shona); Kalibusiswe Illizwe leZimbabwe (Sindebele); Blessed Be the Land of Zimbabwe (English)

Oh, lift high the banner, the flag of Zimbabwe
The symbol of freedom proclaiming victory;
We praise the sacrifice of our heroes,
And vow to keep our land from foes;
And may the Almighty protect and bless our
    land.

Oh, lovely Zimbabwe, so wondrously
    adorned
With mountains, and rivers cascading, flow-
    ing free;
May rain abound, and fertile fields;
May we be fed, our labor blessed;
And may the Almighty protect and bless our
    land.

Oh God, we beseech Thee to bless our native
    land;
The land of our fathers bestowed upon us all;
From Zambezi to Limpopo
May leaders be exemplary;
And may the Almighty protect and bless our
    land.

CURRENCY
Zimbabwe dollar

INTERNET IDENTIFIER
.zw

VEHICLE IDENTIFICATION PLATES/ STICKERS
ZW

PASSPORT
The passport cover has the name of the country in Shona, Sindebele, and English; the coat of arms; and the word *passport* in the three languages.

AIRLINE
Air Zimbabwe

NATIONAL FLOWER
Flame lily

NATIONAL TREE
Baobab (unofficial)

NATIONAL ANIMAL
Kudu

NATIONAL BIRD
Fish eagle

NATIONAL FISH
Tilapia (unofficial)

NATIONAL RESOURCES
Natural resources include coal, chromium ore, asbestos, gold, nickel, copper, iron ore, vanadium, lithium, tin, and platinum group metals. The economy, formerly one of the most dynamic in Africa, has deteriorated due to mismanagement and government policies. Tourism has also declined dramatically, due to political unrest and rising violence.

FOODS
Bota, a thick porridge made of cornmeal, often served with meat and vegetables, is considered the national dish. Other specialties include *sadza,* similar to *bota* but thicker, closer in consistency to corn bread; chicken stew with *sadza* dumplings; *nhopi,* a dish of cornmeal, pumpkin, and peanut butter served with cooked greens; *dovi,* a stew of chicken, onion, bell peppers, tomatoes, peanut butter, and spinach; *nyma ye huku,* a chicken stew with tomatoes, chilies, and onions; and *malva,* a pudding of apricot preserves, eggs, flour, sugar, and vinegar.

SPORTS/SPORTS TEAMS
Association football (soccer), rugby union, and cricket are the most popular sports. Zimbabwe national teams participate in many sports at an international level.

TEAM SPORTS

Badminton

Zimbabwe Badminton Team

Baseball

Zimbabwe Baseball Team; Zimbabwe Softball Team

Basketball

Zimbabwe Basketball Team; Zimbabwe Women's Basketball Team; Zimbabwe Wheelchair Basketball Team

Cricket

Zimbabwe Cricket Team

Football

Zimbabwe Football Team, nickname the Warriors; Zimbabwe Under-23 Football Team, nickname the Young Warriors; Zimbabwe Under-17 Football Team, nickname the Young Warriors; Zimbabwe Rugby Union Team, nickname the Sables; Zimbabwe Woman's Rugby Union Team, nickname the Sables; Zimbabwe Rugby Union Team (Sevens), nickname Zimbabwe Sevens or Zimbabwe 7s

Hockey

Zimbabwe Field Hockey Team

Korfball

Zimbabwe Korfball Team

Netball

Zimbabwe Netball Team

Racing

Zimbabwe Speedway Team

Table Tennis

Zimbabwe Table Tennis Team

Tennis

Zimbabwe Davis Cup Team; Zimbabwe Fed Cup Team

Volleyball

Zimbabwe Men's Volleyball Team

INDIVIDUAL SPORTS

Zimbabwe Amateur Boxing Team; Zimbabwe Archery Team; Zimbabwe Athletics Team; Zimbabwe Cycling Team; Zimbabwe Equestrian Team; Zimbabwe Gymnastics Team: Zimbabwe Modern Pentathlon Team; Zimbabwe Rowing Team; Zimbabwe Sailing Team; Zimbabwe Shooting Team; Zimbabwe Swim Team; Zimbabwe Tae Kwon Do Team; Zimbabwe Triathlon Team; Zimbabwe Weight Lifting Team; Zimbabwe Wrestling Team

NATIONAL HEROES OR PERSONIFICATIONS

Bishop Able Muzorewa, a churchman who became the first black prime minister in 1979; Morgan Tsvangirai, the leader of the opposition to the Mugabe government until he joined a coalition government of national unity in 2008 as prime minister of Zimbabwe.

NATIONAL HOLIDAY/INDEPENDENCE DAY

Independence Day, April 18

FESTIVALS/FAIRS

Zimbabwe International Film Festival, August–September; Rushing Arts Festival, September; Harare International Arts Festival, April

SIGNIFICANT EVENTS IN FORMATION OF NATIONAL IDENTITY

300 C.E. Bantu-speaking migrants settle the most productive regions, displacing the original Khoisan people.

10th century–11th century Bantu migrants, part of the great Bantu migrations, occupy the region, absorbing the earlier Bantu migrants and killing most of the Khoisan, Trade is established with Muslim merchants on the East African coast.

13th century–17th century The Momomotapa civilization is created with its capital at Zimbabwe, now the ruins called Great Zimbabwe. The culturally and militarily advanced state creates an empire engaged in trade and slave trafficking until its decline in the 1600s.

1837–1838 The Ndebele conquer the Shona from the south. They establish a warrior state, Mthwakazi*, that forces the Shona to move north and to pay tribute.

1888–1895 King Lobengula of Mthwakazi grants a mining concession to Cecil Rhodes of South Africa*. Rhodes promotes the colonization of the territory called Matabeleland and its tributary, Mashonaland. Pioneer trains bring settlers to the region, resulting in an Ndebele uprising led by Lobengula, which is crushed. The conquered territories are named Rhodesia.

1922–1930 The white minority receives self-government with full control over the African majority. Land restrictions force many blacks into wage labor on white properties.

1940–1953 Opposition to colonial rule and white domination spurs the growth of nationalist organizations. A federation is formed from Southern Rhodesia (Zimbabwe), Northern Rhodesia (Zambia*), and Nyasaland (Malawi*).

1963 The federation is dissolved as Zambia and Malawi achieve independence under black majority governments. Britain refuses independence for Southern Rhodesia under a white minority government.

1965 Ian Smith, the white leader, unilaterally declares Rhodesia independent. Guerilla war against the white minority government begins, with two major organizations representing Shonas and Ndebeles.

1978–1980 Negotiations finally lead to elections and the installation of a black majority government under Robert Mugabe with participation by the Ndebele leader, Joshua Nkomo. Mostly due to the efficient production of white farmers, the new country begins as one of the most prosperous in Africa.

1981–1982 Splits between the Ndebele and Shona lead to the deployment of the North Korean-trained Fifth Brigade in the Ndebele region in a terror campaign that leaves over 10,000 dead and decapitates most of the Ndebele leadership.

1987 The two major political parties merge, which brings as end to the violence in the south.

1990–2000 The Mugabe government becomes increasingly authoritarian. White farmers are dispossessed and their farms parceled out to Mugabe supporters. A severe economic crisis leads to riots and strikes.

2002–2005 Mugabe wins another term as president in openly fraudulent elections. Party militias attack opposition leaders and Ndebele nationalists, demanding a referendum on the independence of Mthwakazi. International sanctions are applies as violence spreads.

2005–2007 A government-planned "cleanup" of urban areas razes shantytowns, leaving an estimated 700,000 people homeless, mostly opposition supporters. Inflation reaches 1,000 percent, and international food aid is necessary in a country that once fed itself and exported great quantities.

2008 The opposition candidate wins the first round of a presidential vote but later pulls out, following threats and attacks on his supporters. Mugabe is elected to another term. A 100 billion-dollar banknote is introduced in response to the official inflation rate of 2 million percent. Mugabe and opposition leader Morgan Tsvangirai sign a power-sharing agreement that allows Mugabe to remain as president while Tsvangirai becomes prime minister.

2009 Despite the fractured opposition and growing separatist sentiment in the southern half of the country, the Zimbabwean public is increasingly desperate, as food shortages, a cholera epidemic, and violence against anyone criticizing the government continue to take a large toll. President Mugabe, in the midst of the country's worst crisis since independence, throws a lavish birthday party costing over $250,000. At a meeting in September of the Southern Africa Development Community (SADC) the member states again failed to agree on ways to curb the excesses of the Mugabe government or to force him to honor the power-sharing agreement of 2008.

International Organizations

AFRICAN UNION

Flag

The flag has three equal horizontal stripes of green, white, and green, the stripes separated by thin gold stripes. The flag is charged with the official emblem centered on the white.

Emblem/Seal

The emblem is a circle depicting a gold map of Africa on a white background within concentric green and gold circles surrounded by palm fronds, symbolizing peace. Below is a white rectangle with seven interlocking red circles. The green symbolizes African hopes and the aspiration to unity, the gold stands for African wealth and a bright future, the white represents the purity of Africa's desire to have genuine friends around the world, and the red stands for African solidarity and the blood shed for the liberation of Africa.

Headquarters

Addis Ababa, Ethiopia; Midrand, South Africa

Official Languages

Arabic, English, French, Spanish, Portuguese, Swahili

Anthem

"Let Us All Unite and Celebrate Together"

Membership

Algeria, Angola, Benin, Botswana, Burkina Faso, Burundi, Cameroon, Cape Verde, Central African Republic, Chad, Comoros, Democratic Republic of Congo, Cote d'Ivoire, Djibouti, Egypt, Equatorial Guinea, Gabon, Gambia, Ghana, Guinea, Guinea-Bissau, Eritrea, Ethiopia, Kenya, Lesotho, Liberia, Libya, Madagascar, Malawi, Mali, Mauritania, Mauritius, Morocco, Mozambique, Namibia, Niger, Nigeria, Rwanda, Sahrawi (Western Sahara), São Tomé and Príncipe, Senegal, Seychelles, Sierra Leone, Somalia, South Africa, Sudan, Swaziland, Tanzania, Togo, Tunisia, Uganda, Zambia, Zimbabwe

AMNESTY INTERNATIONAL

Emblem/Seal

A candle with flame surrounded by a string of barbed wire, all in black and white.

Headquarters

London

Membership

Over 2 million members and supporters

ANDEAN COMMUNITY
COMUNIDAD ANDINA

Flag

The flag is a white field charged with a rising sun in the style of traditional Andean textiles.

Headquarters

Lima, Peru

Official Language

Spanish

Membership

Bolivia, Colombia, Ecuador, Peru

ARAB LEAGUE (LEAGUE OF ARAB STATES) (ENGLISH) JĀMA'AT AD-DUWAL AL-'ARABIYYA (TRANSLITERATION FROM ARABIC)

Flag

The flag is a green field charged with the official seal centered.

Emblem/Seal

The seal has a central circle showing a white crescent moon and the name of the organization in the Arabic script surrounded by a chain of 20 links, representing the 20 original member states. Around the circle is a white wreath joined at the top and tied at the bottom.

Headquarters

Cairo, Egypt

Official Language

Arabic

Membership

Algeria, Bahrain, Comoros, Djibouti, Egypt, Iraq, Jordan, Kuwait, Lebanon, Libya, Mauritania, Morocco, Oman, Palestine, Qatar, Sudan, Saudi Arabia, Syria, Tunisia, United Arab Emirates, Yemen

ARAB MAGHREB UNION ITTIHAD AL-MAGHRIB AL-ARABY

Flag

The flag is a horizontal bicolor of red over green divided by a thin white stripe. Centered are a gold crescent moon, points to the top, and five white stars in an arc, representing the member states.

Emblem/Seal

The emblem is a central yellow disk bearing a blue map of the Maghreb, the five member states, within a larger white circle.

Headquarters

Rabat, Morocco

Official Language

Arabic

Membership

Algeria, Libya, Mauritania, Morocco, Tunisia

ASIA-PACIFIC ECONOMIC COOPERATION (APEC)

Emblem/Seal

The emblem is a stylized globe of blue with the continents shown in green behind the initials of the organization, APEC.

Headquarters

Singapore, Singapore

Membership

Australia, Brunei Darussalam, Canada, Chile, People's Republic of China, Hong Kong, Indonesia, Japan, Republic of Korea, Malaysia, Mexico, New Zealand, Papua New Guinea, Peru, Philippines, Russian Federation, Singapore, Taiwan (Chinese Taipei), Thailand, United States, Vietnam

ASSOCIATION OF SOUTHEAST ASIAN NATIONS (ASEAN)

Flag

The flag has a blue field with a central red disk edged in white charged with a bundle of 10 rice stalks, representing the organization's 10 member states.

Emblem/Seal

The emblem is that shown in the center of the organization's flag, a red disk edged in white charged with a bundle of 10 rice stalks, representing the organization's 10 member states.

Motto

One vision, one identity, one community

Anthem
"The ASEAN Way"

Headquarters
Jakarta, Indonesia

Working Language
English

Membership
Brunei Darussalam, Cambodia, Indonesia, Laos, Malaysia, Myanmar, Philippines, Singapore, Thailand, Vietnam

Caribbean Community (CARICOM)

Flag
The flag is a horizontal bicolor of sky blue over blue with a centered gold disk bearing the initials CC for Caribbean Community. The colors represent the sky and the sea.

Headquarters
Georgetown, Guyana

Official Language
English; Dutch, French, and Haitian Creole are used unofficially.

Membership
Antigua and Barbuda, Bahamas, Barbados, Belize, Dominica, Grenada, Guyana, Haiti, Jamaica, Montserrat, Saint Kitts and Nevis, Saint Lucia, Saint Vincent and the Grenadines, Suriname, Trinidad and Tobago; associate members: Anguilla, Bermuda, British Virgin Islands, Cayman Islands, Turks and Caicos Islands

Common Market for Eastern and Southern Africa (COMESA)

Flag
The flag has a blue field charged with a yellow map of Africa showing the member countries in red, within a black circle inscribed with COMESA above and below the map.

Headquarters
Lusaka, Zambia

Official Languages
English, French, Portuguese

Membership
Burundi, Comoros, Democratic Republic of the Congo, Djibouti, Egypt, Eritrea, Ethiopia, Kenya, Libya, Madagascar, Malawi, Mauritius, Rwanda, Seychelles, Sudan, Swaziland, Uganda, Zambia, Zimbabwe

Commonwealth of Independent States (CIS)

Sodruzhestvo Nezavisimykh Gosudarstv (SNG)

Flag
The flag has a sky blue field with a small yellow disk, representing grain, heart, the sun, and the idea of light. Around the disk is a white arcade representing cooperation, collective unity, and the warmth of the sun for humanity.

Emblem/Seal
The emblem is a blue disk outlined in white depicting the same logo as that centered on the flag.

Headquarters
Minsk, Belarus

Working Language
Russian

Membership
Armenia, Azerbaijan, Belarus, Kazakhstan, Kyrgyzstan, Moldova, Russia, Tajikistan, Turkmenistan (associate member), Ukraine (participating member), Uzbekistan

Commonwealth of Nations

Flag
The flag is a blue field with a centered globe, representing the global nature of the

organization and the breadth of its membership. The globe is surrounded by 61 radiating spears or rays forming a C for Commonwealth. The 61 spears stand for the member states of the Commonwealth and their dependencies.

Headquarters
London, United Kingdom

Official Language
English

Membership
Antigua and Barbuda, Australia, Bahamas, Bangladesh, Barbados, Belize, Botswana, Brunei, Cameroon, Canada, Cyprus, Dominica, Fiji (suspended), Gambia, Ghana, Grenada, Guyana, India, Jamaica, Kenya, Kiribati, Lesotho, Malawi, Malaysia, Maldives, Malta, Mauritius, Mozambique, Namibia, Nauru, New Zealand, Nigeria, Pakistan, Papua New Guinea, Saint Kitts and Nevis, Saint Lucia, Saint Vincent and the Grenadines, Samoa, Seychelles, Sierra Leone, Singapore, Solomon Islands, South Africa, Sri Lanka, Swaziland, Tanzania, Tonga, Trinidad and Tobago, Tuvalu, Uganda, United Kingdom, Vanuatu, Zambia

COMMUNITY OF PORTUGUESE-SPEAKING COUNTRIES
COMUNIDADE DOS PAÍSES DE LÍNGUA PORTUGUESA (CPLP)

Flag
The flag is a white field edged in blue with a central blue circle divided into eight around a small blue central disk. The divisions represent the original eight member states. Below the emblem are the initials of the organization in Portuguese.

Headquarters
Lisbon, Portugal

Official Language
Portuguese

Membership
Angola, Brazil, Cape Verde, East Timor, Equatorial Guinea, Guinea-Bissau, Mauritius, Mozambique, São Tomé and Príncipe, Senegal

COOPERATION COUNCIL FOR THE ARAB STATES OF THE GULF (CCASG)
GULF COOPERATION COUNCIL (GCC)

Flag
The flag is a green field charged with the organization's emblem centered.

Emblem/Seal
The emblem consists of two concentric circles. The wide brown outer circle features the *bismillah* ("In the name of God, most gracious, most merciful") and the name of the organization in tan Arabic script. The inner circle contains an embossed hexagon on white representing the council's member countries. The inside of the hexagon is a map of the Arabian Peninsula in yellow with blue water showing the member countries in tan.

Official Language
Arabic

Membership
Bahrain, Kuwait, Oman, Qatar, Saudi Arabia, United Arab Emirates

COUNCIL OF ARAB ECONOMIC UNITY (CAEU)
GREATER ARAB FREE TRADE AREA (GAFTA)

Flag
The flag is a white field charged with a wreath of olive leaves enclosing two clasped hands

and the name of the organization in Arabic, all in green.

Official Language
Arabic

Headquarters
Cairo, Egypt

Membership
Algeria, Bahrain, Egypt, Iraq, Jordan, Kuwait, Lebanon, Libya, Morocco, Oman, Palestinian Authority, Qatar, Saudi Arabia, Sudan, Syria, Tunisia, United Arab Emirates, Yemen; candidates: Comoros, Djibouti, Mauritania, Somalia

COUNCIL OF EUROPE
CONSEIL DE L'EUROPE

Flag
The flag is a blue field charged with a circle of 12 gold, five-pointed stars.

Emblem/Seal
The emblem is a rectangular blue field bearing the 12 gold, five-pointed stars behind a pale yellow stylized *e,* centered.

Anthem
"Ode to Joy"

Headquarters
Strasbourg, France

Membership
Albania, Andorra, Armenia, Austria, Azerbaijan, Belgium, Bosnia and Herzegovina, Bulgaria, Croatia, Cyprus, Czech Republic, Denmark, Estonia, Finland, France, Georgia, Germany, Greece, Hungary, Iceland, Ireland, Italy, Latvia, Liechtenstein, Lithuania, Luxembourg, Macedonia, Malta, Moldova, Monaco, Montenegro, Netherlands, Norway, Poland, Portugal, Romania, Russia, San Marino, Serbia, Slovakia, Slovenia, Spain, Sweden, Switzerland, Turkey, Ukraine, United Kingdom

ECONOMIC COMMUNITY OF WEST AFRICAN STATES (ECOWAS)
LA COMMUNAUTÉ ECONOMIQUE DES ETATS DE L'AFRIQUE DE L'OUEST (CEDEAO)

Flag
The flag is a white field with the emblem of the organization centered.

Emblem/Seal
The emblem is a white circle with a gold map of Africa with the member states in green. The central circle is surrounded by a brown circle broken at the top by a full sun containing a cocoa bean. Around the whole is a green circle with the initials of the organization in French at the top and in English at the bottom.

Headquarters
Abuja, Nigeria

Official Languages
French, English, Portuguese

Membership
Benin, Burkina Faso, Cape Verde, Côte d'Ivoire, Gambia, Ghana, Guinea, Guinea-Bissau, Liberia, Mali, Niger, Nigeria, Senegal, Sierra Leone, Togo

ECONOMIC COOPERATION ORGANIZATION (ECO)

Flag
The flag is a white field charged with an *e* within a *c* within a circle or *o,* representing the organization's initials in English. The circle grows out of olive leaves. The logo is all blue on white.

Headquarters
Tehran, Iran

Membership

Afghanistan, Azerbaijan, Iran, Kazakhstan, Kyrgyzstan, Pakistan, Tajikistan, Turkey, Turkmenistan, Uzbekistan

EUROPEAN FREE TRADE ASSOCIATION (EFTA)

Emblem/Seal

The emblem is the flags of the four member nations in a semicircle above the initials of the organization.

Headquarters

Geneva, Switzerland

Official Languages

German, French, Icelandic, Norwegian

Membership

Iceland, Liechtenstein, Norway, Switzerland

EUROPEAN UNION (EU)

Flag

The flag is a blue field charged with a circle of 15 gold stars, representing the original member states.

Emblem/Seal

Fifteen gold, five-pointed stars on a blue background

Motto

United in Diversity

Anthem

"Ode to Joy"

Headquarters

Brussels, Belgium; some functions in Strasbourg, France, and Luxembourg City, Luxembourg

Official Languages

Bulgarian, Czech, Danish, Dutch, English, Estonian, Finnish, French, German, Greek, Hungarian, Irish, Italian, Latvian, Lithuanian, Maltese, Polish, Portuguese, Romanian, Slovak, Slovenian, Spanish, Swedish

Membership

Austria, Belgium, Bulgaria, Cyprus, Czech Republic, Denmark, Estonia, Finland, France, Germany, Greece, Hungary, Ireland, Italy, Latvia, Lithuania, Luxembourg, Malta, Netherlands, Poland, Portugal, Romania, Slovakia, Slovenia, Spain, Sweden, United Kingdom

FRANCOPHONIE (ORGANISATION INTERNATIONALE DE LA FRANCOPHONIE)

Flag

The flag is a white field bearing a circle of five colors, representing the five continents where French-speaking communities are located.

Motto

Égalitié, complémentarité, solidarité

Headquarters

Paris, France

Official Language

French

Membership

Albania, Andorra, Belgium, French Community of Belgium (Wallonia and the French population of the Brussels–Capital Region), Benin, Bulgaria, Burkina Faso, Burundi, Cambodia, Cameroon, Canada (New Brunswick, Quebec), Cape Verde, Central African Republic, Chad, Comoros, Democratic Republic of Congo, Republic of Congo, Côte d'Ivoire, Djibouti, Dominica, Egypt, Equatorial Guinea, France, Gabon, Greece, Guinea, Guinea-Bissau, Haiti, Laos, Lebanon, Luxembourg, Macedonia, Madagascar, Mali, Mauritania, Mauritius, Moldova, Monaco, Morocco, Niger, Romania, Rwanda, Saint Lucia, São Tomé and Príncipe, Senegal, Seychelles, Switzerland, Togo, Tunisia, Vanuatu, Vietnam; associate members: Armenia, Cyprus, Ghana

GREENPEACE

Emblem/Seal

The emblem is a stylized green version of the organization's name.

Headquarters

Amsterdam

Membership

Around 3 million members and supporters

INTERNATIONAL FEDERATION OF RED CROSS AND RED CRESCENT SOCIETIES

Flag

The flag is a white field charged with a large red cross on the hoist and a large red crescent on the fly.

Headquarters

Geneva, Switzerland

INTERNATIONAL OLYMPIC COMMITTEE (IOC)

COMITÉ INTERNATIONAL OLYMPIQUE (CIO)

Flag

The flag is a white field charged with the intertwined Olympic rings of red, green, black, yellow, and blue, representing the five continents.

Emblem/Seal

The five intertwined rings of red, green, black, yellow, and blue on a white field

Headquarters

Lausanne, Switzerland

Official Languages

English, French

Anthem

"The Olympic Hymn"

Motto

Citius, altius, fortius (Latin); Swifter, Higher, Stronger (English)

Membership

Over 200 national Olympic committees

MÉDECINS SANS FRONTIÈRES/DOCTORS WITHOUT FRONTIERS

Emblem/Seal

A red and white human figure with four red lines and the name of the organization in black.

Headquarters

Geneva, Switzerland

NORTH AMERICAN FREE TRADE AGREEMENT (NAFTA)

Emblem/Seal

The emblem is an amalgam of the three flags of the United States, Mexico, and Canada in the form of a waving flag.

Headquarters

Mexico City, Mexico; Ottawa, Canada; Washington, D.C.

Official Languages

English, French, Spanish

Membership

Canada, Mexico, United States

NORTH ATLANTIC TREATY ORGANIZATION (NATO)

Flag

The flag is a blue field charged with a centered white compass rose with white lines stretching to the north, south, east, and west.

Emblem/Seal

A white compass rose on a blue background

Headquarters

Brussels, Belgium

Official Languages

English, French

Membership

Belgium, Bulgaria, Canada, Czech Republic, Denmark, Estonia, France, Germany, Greece, Hungary, Iceland, Italy, Latvia, Lithuania, Luxembourg, Netherlands, Norway, Poland, Portugal, Romania, Slovakia, Slovenia, Spain, Turkey, United Kingdom, United States

ORGANIZATION OF AMERICAN STATES (OAS)

Flag

The flag is a blue field charged with the emblem of the organization centered.

Emblem/Seal

The emblem of the organization is a white circle bearing a representation of the flags of the member states within a brown border inscribed with the name of the organization in English.

Headquarters

Washington, D.C.

Official Languages

English, French, Portuguese, Spanish

Membership

Argentina, Bahamas, Barbados, Belize, Bolivia, Brazil, Canada, Chile, Colombia, Costa Rica, Cuba (readmitted in 2009 but must first comply with treaties signed by the membership since 1962), Dominica, Dominican Republic, Ecuador, El Salvador, Grenada, Guatemala, Guyana, Haiti, Honduras (suspended in 2009), Jamaica, Mexico, Nicaragua, Panama, Paraguay, Peru, Saint Kitts and Nevis, Saint Lucia, Saint Vincent and the Grenadines, Suriname, Trinidad and Tobago, United States, Uruguay, Venezuela

ORGANIZATION OF BLACK SEA ECONOMIC COOPERATION (BSEC)

Flag

The flag has a blue field with the name of the organization in white across the top, a white oval with the initials *BSEC* centered, and three wavy white lines at the bottom representing the Black Sea.

Emblem/Seal

A blue oval with the initials of the organization in white

Headquarters

Istanbul, Turkey

Membership

Albania, Armenia, Azerbaijan, Bulgaria, Georgia, Greece, Moldova, Romania, Russia, Serbia, Turkey, Ukraine

ORGANISATION OF EASTERN CARIBBEAN STATES (OESC)

Flag

The flag has a pale green field with a centered symbolic sun, an inner ring representing the eastern Caribbean, and an outer ring representing the world at large.

Emblem/Seal

A stylized yellow sun around two green clasped hands on a field of green

Headquarters

Castries, Saint Lucia

Membership

Antigua and Barbuda, Dominica, Grenada, Montserrat, Saint Kitts and Nevis, Saint

Lucia, Saint Vincent and the Grenadines; associate members: Anguilla, British Virgin Islands

ORGANIZATION OF IBERO-AMERICAN STATES

Emblem/Seal

A disk divided vertically green and pale blue over the initials of the group in Spanish, *OEI*

Headquarters

Madrid, Spain

Official Languages

Portuguese, Spanish

Membership

Andorra, Argentina, Bolivia, Brazil, Chile, Colombia, Costa Rica, Cuba, Dominican Republic, Ecuador, El Salvador, Equatorial Guinea, Guatemala, Honduras, Mexico, Nicaragua, Panama, Paraguay, Peru, Portugal, Puerto Rico, Spain, Uruguay, Venezuela

ORGANIZATION FOR ECONOMIC COOPERATION AND DEVELOPMENT (OECD)

Emblem/Seal

The emblem of the organization comprises a large aquamarine disk, representing the Earth, on the fly, and two black or gray arrows pointing toward the hoist, representing advancing in unity, above the initials of the organization, all on a white background.

Headquarters

Paris, France

Membership

Australia, Austria, Belgium, Canada, Czech Republic, Denmark, Finland, France, Germany, Greece, Hungary, Iceland, Ireland, Italy, Japan, Republic of Korea, Luxembourg, Mexico, Netherlands, New Zealand, Norway, Poland, Portugal, Slovakia, Spain, Sweden, Switzerland, Turkey, United Kingdom, United States

ORGANIZATION OF THE ISLAMIC CONFERENCE

Flag

The flag is a green field with a large, centered white disk bearing a red crescent moon and the name of the organization in black Arabic script.

Headquarters

Jeddah, Saudi Arabia

Official Languages

Arabic, English, French

Membership

Afghanistan, Algeria, Bahrain, Bangladesh, Benin, Brunei, Burkina Faso, Cameroon, Chad, Comoros, Côte d'Ivoire, Djibouti, Egypt, Gabon, Gambia, Guinea, Guinea-Bissau, Guyana, Indonesia, Iran, Iraq, Jordan, Kazakhstan, Kuwait, Kyrgyzstan, Lebanon, Libya, Malaysia, Maldives, Mali, Mauritania, Morocco, Mozambique, Niger, Nigeria, Oman, Pakistan, Palestine, Qatar, Saudi Arabia, Senegal, Sierra Leone, Somalia, Sudan, Suriname, Syria, Tajikistan, Togo, Tunisia, Turkey, Turkmenistan, Uganda, United Arab Emirates, Uzbekistan, Yemen

PACIFIC ISLANDS FORUM

Emblem/Seal

The emblem of the organization is a blue disk representing the Pacific Ocean featuring two wavy yellow lines at the bottom and the Southern Cross constellation at the top, with a smaller white disk overlapping the blue at the left charged with a single palm tree.

Headquarters

Suva, Fiji

Membership

Australia, Cook Islands, Micronesia, Fiji, Kiribati, Marshall Islands, Nauru, New Zealand, Niue, Palau, Papua New Guinea, Samoa, Solomon Islands, Tonga, Tuvalu, Vanuatu; associate members: French Polynesia, New Caledonia

SHANGHAI COOPERATION ORGANIZATION (SCO)

Flag

The flag is a white field bearing an aqua disk containing a blue stylized globe with the member countries outlined, surrounded by a green wreath and the name of the organization in Russian and Chinese.

Headquarters

Beijing, China

Working Languages

Chinese, Russian

Membership

China, Kazakhstan, Kyrgyzstan, Russia, Tajikistan, Uzbekistan

SOUTH ASIAN ASSOCIATION FOR REGIONAL COOPERATION (SAARC)

Flag

The flag is a white field bearing the organization's emblem, two stylized peacocks, and initials in gold.

Headquarters

Katmandu, Nepal

Membership

Afghanistan, Bangladesh, Bhutan, India, Maldives, Nepal, Pakistan, Sri Lanka

SOUTHERN AFRICAN DEVELOPMENT COMMUNITY (SADC)

Flag

The flag has a blue field charged with a centered green disk bearing the yellow initials of the organization intertwined.

Emblem/Seal

The emblem features the intertwined initials of the organization in blue on a white disk bordered in blue, with the name of the organization written in white on the blue ring.

Headquarters

Gaborone, Botswana

Working Languages

Afrikaans, English, French, Portuguese

Membership

Angola, Botswana, Democratic Republic of Congo, Lesotho, Madagascar, Malawi, Mauritius, Mozambique, Namibia, South Africa, Swaziland, Tanzania, Zambia, Zimbabwe

SOUTHERN COMMON MARKET (MERCOSUR/MERCOSUL)

Flag

The flag has a white field charged with four blue stars forming the Southern Cross constellation above a curving green line representing the earth. The flag is often shown with either *MERCOSUR*, the Spanish abbreviation, or MERCOSUL, the Portuguese abbreviation (in Brazil).

Headquarters

Montevideo, Uruguay

Official Languages

Guarani, Portuguese, Spanish

Motto

Our north is the south

Membership

Argentina, Brazil, Paraguay, Uruguay, Venezuela (applicant)

UNION OF SOUTH AMERICAN NATIONS

SOUTH AMERICAN UNION (UNASUR)

TRATADO CONSTITUTIVE DE LA UNIÓN DE NACIONES SURAMERICANAS

Flag

The flag is a red field charged with a centered gold map of South America within a gold circle.

Emblem/Seal

An outline map of South America in gold on a red disk outlined in gold

Headquarters

Quito, Ecuador; Cochabamba, Bolivia

Official Languages

Dutch, English, Portuguese, Spanish

Membership

Argentina, Bolivia, Brazil, Chile, Colombia, Ecuador, Guyana, Paraguay, Peru, Suriname, Uruguay, Venezuela

UNITED NATIONS (UN)

Flag

The flag has a sky blue field bearing a representation of a map of the world within a wreath of olive branches, both in white. The map represents the people of the world, and the olive wreath symbolizes peace.

Headquarters

New York City, United States

Official Languages

Arabic, Chinese, English, French, Russian, Spanish

Membership

All internationally recognized independent states, with the exception of Vatican City and Palestine, which have observer status, and Sahrawi, which is in dispute between the republican government and Morocco

Selected Bibliography

BOOKS

Biedermann, Hans. *Dictionary of Symbolism: Cultural Icons and the Meaning behind Them*. Plume, 1994.

Briggs, Geoffrey. *National Heraldry of the World*. Dent, 1973.

Ciriot, J. E. *A Dictionary of Symbols*. Dover Publications, 2002.

Crampton, William. *Webster's Concise Encyclopedia of Flags and Coats of Arms*. Crescent, 1988.

Daly-Weir, Catherine. *Coat of Arms*. Grosset & Dunlap, 2000.

De Kleer, V.S. *A Visual Guide to the Flags of the World*. Chatham Publishing, 2007.

DK Publishing. *Complete Flags of the World*. DK Publishing, 2008.

Firefly Books. *Guide to Flags of the World*. Firefly Books, 2003.

Fox-Davies, A. C. *Complete Guide to Heraldry*. Sterling, 2007.

Geisler, Michael E., ed. *National Symbols, Fractured Identities: Contesting the National Narrative*. Middlebury, 2005.

Slater, Stephen. *The World Encyclopedia of Flags and Heraldry*. Lorenz Books, 2008.

Smith, Whitney. *Flag Lore of All Nations*. Milbrook Press, 2003.

Tresidder, Jack. *The Complete Dictionary of Symbols*. Chronicle Books, 2005.

Von Volborth, Carl-Alexander. *Heraldry of the World*. Blandford Press, 1980.

Znamierowski, Alfred. *The World Encyclopedia of Flags*. Lorenz Books, 2005.

INTERNET

Flags of the World (FOTW), http://www.crwflags.com/fotw/flags
A very large, noncommercial site on flags, coats of arms, and other national symbols

Heraldry of the World, http://www.ngw.nl
The largest Internet heraldry site with the coats of arms of all nations

National Birds, www.camacdonald.com/birding/CountryIndex.htm
A large collection of national birds with photos and illustrations

National Flowers by Country, www.nzflower.co.nz/national-flowers-country.php
A New Zealand site with plentiful information on national flowers

National Football Teams, www.national-football-teams.com
A very good, noncommercial site on the world of football (soccer)

Wikipedia, http://www.wikipedia.org
A free and constantly updated encyclopedia with articles on individual countries, flags, coats of arms, national flora and fauna, and so on

World Flag Database, http://www.flags.net/fullindex.htm
A large collection of flags and coats of arms

Index

About the Author

James Minahan has written a number of reference books dealing with national symbols and issues of national identity and statehood. His books include *Nations without States* (Greenwood, 1996), *Miniature Empires* (Greenwood, 1998), *One Europe, Many Nations* (Greenwood, 2000), *Encyclopedia of the Stateless Nations* (Greenwood, 2002), and *The Former Soviet Union's Diverse Peoples* (ABC-CLIO, 2004).